Care Planning in Mental Health

Dedication

For Charlotte (12.11.03–12.06.07):

'Whose courage and strength is our inspiration for writing this book'

Angela, Mike (Daddy) and Steve.

Care Planning in Mental Health

Promoting Recovery

Edited by Angela Hall, Mike Wren
and Stephan Kirby

 **Blackwell**
Publishing

© 2008 by Blackwell Publishing Ltd

Blackwell Publishing editorial offices:
Blackwell Publishing Ltd, 9600 Garsington Road, Oxford OX4 2DQ, UK
Tel: +44 (0)1865 776868
Blackwell Publishing Inc., 350 Main Street, Malden, MA 02148-5020, USA
Tel: +1 781 388 8250
Blackwell Publishing Asia Pty Ltd, 550 Swanston Street, Carlton, Victoria 3053, Australia
Tel: +61 (0)3 8359 1011

First published 2008 by Blackwell Publishing Ltd

ISBN: 978-1-4051-5285-3

Library of Congress Cataloging-in-Publication Data

Care planning in mental health : promoting recovery / edited by Angela Hall, Mike Wren,
and Stephan Kirby.
      p. ; cm.
Includes bibliographical references and index.
ISBN-13: 978-1-4051-5285-3 (pbk. : alk. paper)
ISBN-10: 1-4051-5285-0 (pbk. : alk. paper)   1. Psychiatric nursing—Planning.
I. Hall, Angela, 1962–   II. Wren, Mike, 1967–   III. Kirby, Stephan D.
[DNLM: 1. Mental Health Services—Great Britain.   2. Mental Disorders—rehabilitation—
Great Britain.   3. Patient Care Planning—Great Britain.   WM 30 C2715 2008]
                                RC440.C29 2008
                                616.89'0231—dc22
                                2007024266

A catalogue record for this title is available from the British Library

Set in 10/12.5pt Palatino
by Graphicraft Limited, Hong Kong
Printed and bound in Singapore
by Utopia Press Pte Ltd

For further information on Blackwell Publishing, visit our website:
www.blackwellpublishing.com

Contents

Contributors

Karen Bibbings RGN, RMN, Dip Health Visiting, Dip CAMH, BSc (Hons)
I commenced general nurse training in 1980 and worked for several years in a general medical ward setting. My interest in mental health issues developed over this period and in 1987 I studied as a Registered Mental Nurse and joined the team delivering services to adults experiencing acute episodes of mental illness. During this time my daughters Kate and Ruth arrived and I was visited by my Health Visitor. We discussed her role and my interest in community nursing and public health models of working developed and in 1992, I completed my Health Visitor training and worked for a number of years as a Health Visitor in Redcar and Stockton-on-Tees. In 1995 I studied for the ENB 603 or as it was then the Diploma in Child and Adolescent Mental Health and in doing so forged links with local child and adolescent mental health services (CAMHS). Along the way I have completed a BSc (Hons) Degree in Community Nursing. More recently I have worked within the local Sure Start programmes taking the lead on delivering services with a mental health focus and in the last eighteen months have taken up post within CAMHS as a Primary Mental Health Worker, working at present within the Stockton-on-Tees team.

Sarah Bonney BSc, Dip Nurs, RMN
Sarah has been a mental health nurse for 15 years and is currently a Nurse Specialist with the Lincolnshire eating disorders team. The focus of her research has been recovery in mental health as part of the Thorn degree. She is particularly interested in the use of a recovery approach in her day-to-day work.

Mary Bragg RMN, BSc (Hons)
Mary is a Lecturer Practitioner in the Section of Mental Health Nursing in the Health Service and Population Research Department at the Institute of Psychiatry, King's College London. She is the Course Leader for an Enhanced Skills for Inpatient Mental Health Professionals Course. Her research activities include team training in acute inpatient care and social inclusion for people with schizophrenia. She is also a Clinical Charge Nurse on a women's acute mental health unit in the South London and Maudsley Foundation NHS Trust.

Richard Brittle RNLD, Cert Ed (F/HE), M Ed.
I started the then Registered Nurse Mental Handicap training in 1977 at Balderton Hospital, Newark. I qualified in 1980 and was staff nurse on a forensic assessment and treatment unit caring for people with mild learning disabilities and dual needs. After 13 months, and in order to pad out my CV, I became Deputy Manager at a children's unit. However within 7 months I realised that a comprehensive CV was not as important as career satisfaction and so moved back to forensic services in August 1982, in rehabilitation of special hospital offenders. In April 1984 a vacancy as a Community Charge Nurse arose and I was fortunate to become a Community Learning Disability Nurse with Newark Community Learning Disability Team and my most fulfilling time in practice followed. Probably on the back of my community experience I blagged my way into nurse education in December 1985 and currently I am Common Foundation Programme (CFP) Lead in the Mansfield Centre of the University of Nottingham and Module Convenor for the Community Learning Disability Nursing component of the learning disability branch programme.

Jim Campbell MA, Dip (Therapeutic Massage), RN (Mental Health)
Jim has worked in various different health settings for over 15 years, including the NHS, Social Work Department and Voluntary Sector. As a mental health nurse, researcher and trainer Jim currently works as Research & Development Officer at AskClyde, an emerging social firm that provides employment, training and volunteering opportunities for people who see themselves recovering from mental ill health. With a growing expertise in mental health recovery he has worked in the Psychological Recovery Research Programme, University of Teesside and was awarded a prestigious Florence Nightingale Foundation Scholarship to undertake a scoping study tour looking at recovery-orientated practices, research and education in New Zealand and Australia.

Dennis Cross TD, BA (Hons), B Ed (Hons), MA, RMN, RGN, RNT
Dennis is employed as a Principal Lecturer at the University of Teesside and is presently undertaking a full-time consultancy role in mental health education at the Institute of Technology, Tralee in Eire. He is closely involved in a partnership between education and practice to enable the development of local mental health services in County Kerry. Recent educational developments to support modernisation of services include a Higher Diploma in Psychosocial Interventions in Mental Health and an MSc in Nursing (Mental Health) for qualified staff.

Dr David Duffy BA (Hons), MSc, PhD, RMN
David is a Nurse Consultant, specialising in suicide and self-harm, employed by Bolton Salford and Trafford Mental Health NHS Trust. David has wide experience in the mental health field and has researched and published extensively, with both a Master's and a Doctoral thesis on the subject of suicidality. From 2001–2002 he was lead coordinator of the National Suicide Prevention

Strategy for England. David is a member of the steering committee of the National Confidential Inquiry into Suicide and Homicide by People with Mental Illness. He was the lead author of *Preventing Suicide: A Toolkit for Mental Health Services* and with Dr Tony Ryan is editor of *New Approaches to Suicide Prevention: A Manual For Practitioners* (Jessica Kingsley, 2004).

Mike Firn RMN, BA (Hons), Dip (PSI)
Mike is a Mental Health Nurse who qualified in 1986. He has twelve years experience using the Assertive Outreach Model in the UK, and has set up and managed services comprising Assertive Outreach, Home Treatment and Early Intervention across five London Boroughs. He joined the London Development Centre (NIMHE/CSIP) in July 2005 as Service Improvement Lead. Mike is Chair of the National Forum for Assertive Outreach – a practitioner's good practice network delivering regional and national meetings. He has co-authored, with Prof. Tom Burns, the book *Assertive Outreach in Mental Health: A Manual For Practitioners*, published by Oxford University Press in 2002 and has published numerous journal articles.

Molly Halford (pseudonym)
Molly Halford trained and worked as a secondary school teacher. As a result of a number of health-related problems, including the acute psychotic illness of one of her children, she took early retirement. She subsequently joined Rethink (formerly the National Schizophrenia Association) and is currently active at a local and national level with this organisation. This chapter has been written with her husband and co-carer, whom she thanks for his continuing love and support.

Angela Hall BSc (Hons), MA, RMN, RGN, RNT, PGCE, Cert Coun, App Dip (co-editor)
Angela has worked as a Mental Health Practitioner for over 25 years and for the past 15 years as a Senior Lecturer in Mental Health within the School of Health and Social Care at Teesside University. She is Programme Leader for the BSc (Hons) Social Work/Mental Health Nursing framework at pre-registration level, the first of its kind to be established in the UK. Having qualified in both mental and general nursing she practised as a Community Mental Health Nurse firstly within Primary Care and more recently as part of a Community Mental Health Team. She became a nurse educator in 1992 and her MA study was gained in Humanistic Counselling and her current interests are in Inter-professional Working and Education, Recovery and Psychosocial Interventions for People with a Serious Mental Illness.

Mark Hopps RMN, PgD (PSI)
Mark currently works as a Senior Care Coordinator with the Early Interventions in Psychosis team in Bishop Auckland.

Stephan D. Kirby MSc, PgC (L&T), Dip MDO, RMN, PhD Candidate (co-editor)
Steve is a husband, father, son and occasional user of mental health services
(as well as a Registered Mental Nurse, a Senior Lecturer and Buddhist Practitioner). Currently he is a Senior Lecturer (Forensic Mental Health) in the School
of Health and Social Care at the University of Teesside. He has nearly three
decades of experience working with the mentally ill, the largest part being
within Forensic Mental Health Services. The research for his MSc Thesis looked
at Cognitive Distortions in Child Sexual Offenders. Currently he is studying
for his PhD, which is exploring the experiences of 'Life in a Segregation Unit'.
He has researched and published extensively on a range of mental health and
forensic matters, and was a co-editor of *Mental Health Nursing: Competencies
For Practice*, published by Palgrave in 2004 as well as being former Chair of the
National Forensic Nurses Research & Development Group.

Victoria Lumley RMN, Dip Nurs, Dip (PSI)
Victoria's career in mental health began over ten years ago when she worked
as a community care assistant in a rehabilitation setting. Being intrigued by
the nature of mental health difficulties she was inspired to undertake mental
health nurse training at the University of York. Once qualified she gained
diverse clinical experience working on a busy acute admission ward where
her client-centred approach to supporting individuals experiencing mental
health difficulties resulted in her enthusiasm to look towards delivering more
effective therapeutic interventions. Over the last decade she has observed the
adverse effects of the medical model of care that appears to dominate mental
health and prevent the opportunity of social inclusion and recovery. Victoria
is an ardent advocate of psychosocial approaches to promote mental well-
being and is focused on normalising the experience of psychosis, providing
cognitive therapy and opportunities to maximise social inclusion by empowering individuals to explore opportunities to return to work and continue
'their life' despite the presence of psychotic phenomena. Alongside studying
towards an MSc in Psychosocial Interventions Victoria has successfully researched, developed and implemented a Carers Training Programme aimed
at supporting and educating carers to endorse mental/physical well being and
journey of recovery. She is presently working as a Care Coordinator in a rural
Home Treatment Team with the ambition of developing local community
services to meet the individual needs of service users and families to promote
recovery and maintain wellness.

Graham Lyons
Graham currently works as the Manager of the Crisis Resolution Team in
Middlesbrough and has worked for Middlesbrough Integrated Mental Health
Services for 12 years. He continues to practise as an Approved Social Worker
and shares operational responsibility for the Approved Social Work Rota in
Middlesbrough.

Joan Murphy RMN, RGN, RM, BSc (Nursing), MSc (Advancing Health and Social Studies)
Joan is a lecturer in the Department of Nursing and Health Care Studies in the Institute of Technology, Tralee in Southern Ireland. Her clinical background is predominantly in acute mental health care. She currently teaches on the BSc in Mental Health and to a lesser extent in General Nursing. She is also involved at a postgraduate level with a Higher Diploma in Psychosocial Interventions in Mental Health and offers supervision to a number of students on this course. She is a registered instructor in the delivery of the Non-violent Crisis Intervention Training Programme. Her particular area of interest and the subject of recent research has been the involvement of service users in their care in particular in relation to achieving concordance with prescribed medication regimes.

Alan Pringle RGN, RMN, BSc (Hons), PhD Candidate
Alan is a lecturer in mental health nursing at the University of Nottingham. Alan's background is in general nursing and mental health nursing. After managing areas in acute psychiatry and day care he worked for 11 years as a teacher/practitioner between Millbrook mental health unit in Mansfield and the University of Nottingham before taking up a full time lecturer post with the University in 2003. His recent publications have included papers and book chapters on sexual health promotion, Post Traumatic Stress Disorder, dementia, user involvement in mental health care and Integrated Care Pathways. Alan has published on football and mental health and his PhD study looks at the effect watching Mansfield Town has on the mental health of the club's supporters! He currently supervises the 'It's a Goal!' project, which places Community Psychiatric Nurses in the football stadiums of Macclesfield Town and Manchester United.

Debbie Robson RMN, MSc, BSc (Hons), PhD Candidate
Debbie has been a Mental Health Nurse for over 20 years. She works in the Section of Mental Health Nursing in the Health Service and Population Research Department at the Institute of Psychiatry, King's College London. She is the Course Leader for a 10-day Medication Management course for Mental Health Workers. Her research work involves intervention and training trials in medication management and qualitative studies about patients' experiences of antipsychotic medication. She is currently studying for a PhD, undertaking a programme of research in smoking cessation for people with schizophrenia.

Julie Smith (pseudonym)
Following teacher training at Westminster College, Oxford, Julie taught mainstream Primary children for ten years. When her children were young she helped run a playgroup. Subsequently she taught children with Special Needs for nearly twenty years. Having now retired she works with two CPNs, delivering Training Programmes for carers of people who suffer from psychosis.

Edward Smith (pseudonym)
Edward became ill at the same time as graduating from Oxford Brookes with a degree in computer science. For many years he has voluntarily helped in the community, teaching people how to use computers. He helps with the desktop publishing of newsletters and on the IT for presentations.

Theo Stickley MA, RMN, Dip Nurs, Dip Couns
Theo is a Lecturer in mental health at the University of Nottingham. His research interests are mental health and the arts and any project working in collaboration with people who use mental health services. Theo trained and worked as a mental health nurse as well as a counsellor in Primary Care.

Dr Joy Trotter PhD, CQSW
Joy is Reader in Social Work at the University of Teesside and her research focuses on equality issues in higher education, domestic violence, child sexual abuse and on young people and sexuality issues. Her publications include: *'No-one's Listening': Mothers, Fathers and Child Sexual Abuse* [Whiting & Birch]; *Child Sexual Assault: Feminist Perspectives* [Palgrave] (with Pat Cox & Sheila Kershaw); and *Confronting Prejudice: Lesbian and Gay Issues in Social Work Education* [Arena] (with Janette Logan, Sheila Kershaw, Kate Karban, Sue Mills & Margo Sinclair). She has also published more recently in academic and professional journals, including *Youth & Policy, Practice, Socio-Analysis, Qualitative Social Work, Community Care* and *Protecting Children Update*.

Jenny Weinstein BA (Hons), B Phil Social Work, MSc Interprofessional Practice in Health and Social Care, PgCert (HE)
Jenny is Principal Lecturer in Mental Health Studies at London South Bank University where she manages a new mental health degree that she developed leading to a joint qualification in mental health nursing and social work. A Social Worker by background, Jenny spent many years working in the statutory sector as a practitioner, manager and trainer before joining the Central Council for Education and Training in Social Work (CCETSW) in 1989. There Jenny led on practice learning in the Diploma in Social Work and interprofessional learning, pioneering service user involvement in education and training. In 1998, Jenny moved to Jewish Care as Assistant Director Strategy and Quality before joining LSBU in 2004. Jenny has published widely on interprofessional learning and working – her most recent book being *Collaboration in Social Work Practice* edited with Whittington and Leiba and published by Jessica Kingsley in 2003. She has a particular interest in diversity issues, cultural competence and service user involvement.

Mike Wren BA (Ed), CSS, Cert Ed, FAETC, Dip PT, RSW (co-editor)
Has worked in a variety of Social Work positions spanning a career of more than 19 years including at a senior management level in relation to adults with a learning disability and older people services. Mike's career has predominantly

involved working with children, young people and adults with learning disabilities and mental health problems within educational, community based
services and teams with a particular interest in three specific areas of learning
disabilities and mental health practice developments: transitions into adult-
hood; development, maintenance and review of supported living schemes;
and the development of adult placement schemes to strengthen community
based provisions to enable people to live within their own community. Mike
joined the University of Teesside in July 2004 taking up the position of Course
Coordinator for the BSc (Hons) Social Work/Learning Disabilities and Social
Work/Mental Health Nursing Programmes and Senior Lecturer (Social Work)
to further utilise his social work, teaching, academic and management qualifi-
cations/experience with a particular interest in the development and enhancement of integrated collaborative working arrangements for people with a
learning disability and people with mental health problems. Mike is particularly passionate about encouraging closer collaborative models of integrated
practice across the domains of learning disability and mental health practices,
including shared learning opportunities that actively promote competent, safe,
effective and efficient practitioners who have a clear understanding of, respect
for and ability to deliver holistic, person-centred, social-v-medical model perspectives to the design of future models of integrated Learning Disability and
Mental Health practices and provisions operating predominantly within community based settings.

Introduction

Angela Hall, Michael Wren and Stephan D. Kirby

In this text the authors hope to outline some of the common issues when care planning for people experiencing mental illness. By emphasising the importance of taking a recovery based approach to helping people affected by a mental illness, the authors argue that effective care planning needs to be individualised yet collaborative, carried out in partnership with the individual and their family in order to meet their many needs.

As this book is aimed at predominantly mental health and social care practitioners it is intended to serve as a guide for mental health practitioners (MHPs) to explore and understand the theoretical foundations at each stage of the care planning process. This book offers examples of good practice in care planning for mental health recovery as well as providing a sound knowledge base and guidance for both the experienced and novice practitioners to assist in developing competent and recovery focused care planning.

It is intended (and indeed hoped) that this text will become an essential reference for practitioners, policy makers, researchers, carers, student nurses and social workers. Having said that, we also hope that the reader will be able to draw from this text a number of fundamental tenets that the editors and contributors see as crucial to the practice of care planning in mental health. Issues ranging from the value of a recovery orientated approach, through the understanding of a biopsychosocial model, to the application of a specialist body of evidence based knowledge. We hope that this text will highlight for the reader the importance of a positive approach to care planning, one which is of a collaborative nature, and that draws on multiple theoretical and practice perspectives as well as statutory and non-statutory personnel. Not forgetting the simple yet essential fact that team working and multi-agency collaboration with service users and carers is central to the success of the care planning process.

Section 1: Understanding Care Planning, initially provides the reader with an overview of the legislation, policies and professional issues that can influence the care planning process. This includes a review of the evolution of care coordination and its development from case management. This section also includes reference and discussion relating to relevant and associated ethical and legal frameworks in addition to multi-agency collaboration within a society that is increasingly risk and litigation aware.

Chapter 1: The Context and Nature of Care Planning in Mental Health
Angela Hall and Mike Wren

In this opening chapter Angela and Mike address the historical changes that have influenced the role and context of care planning in mental health. The introduction of individualised care and the nursing process as a framework for organising mental health care in nursing are explored. The adoption of case management, as an effective framework for mental health care planning, by both nursing and social work is described in terms of the care programme approach and care management respectively. Service users as consumers of mental health care are central to its development, the shaping of both mental health and social care services, as well as the introduction of a more seamless approach – essentially care coordination.

Chapter 2: The Ethical and Legal Implications of Care Planning in Mental Health
Graham Lyons

In this chapter, Graham outlines the key legislative and ethical issues impacting on the care planning process. The role and purpose of common law and its application to the planning and provision of care is discussed, in addition to the specific nature of the (still) proposed new Mental Health legislation in facilitating mental health care. Associated legislation (e.g. The Carers and Care in the Community Acts) are covered to help develop an insight into the context in which mental health care planning takes place.

Chapter 3: Therapeutic Risk and Care Planning in Mental Health
David Duffy

David examines the current risk culture within society, risk that is reflected and very evident within mental health care and therefore care planning. A number of modern day inquiries into mental health care are explored, with a view to demonstrating their influence on the development and application of policy. Within this chapter it is emphasised that risk assessment and risk management should be an integral part of the care planning process and should, therefore, be considered within the overall context of care. This allows for more positive, carefully reasoned risk-taking initiatives to be undertaken as part of the care planning process.

Chapter 4: Care Planning across Professional and Organisational Boundaries
Alan Pringle and Richard Brittle

This chapter focuses on the differences and common features of the professions as they contribute to mental health care planning. Alan and Richard explore the acquisition of the ten shared essential capabilities in relation to practitioners developing the necessary skills and competence in multidisciplinary care planning. The organisational and professional differences that minimise effective team working are also highlighted as well as the features of effective teams. It is argued that an integrated team approach to care planning in mental health improves the experiences for service users and carers.

Chapter 5: Safeguarding Children when Care Planning in Mental Health
Karen Bibbings

In this chapter, Karen focuses on the role of MHPs in the safeguarding of the children they come into contact with. All health practitioners need to be aware of their contribution and responsibilities in safeguarding children. This chapter does not focus on the child with mental health problems, rather, it is from the perspective of the impact of the adult's mental health on the child. It promotes an approach that acknowledges that the service user (adult) is central to care but also reinforces the message that other family members (particularly children) are affected by mental illness.

Section 2: Personal Experiences of Care Planning, gives the reader an insight into what it is like to be on the receiving end of current mental health services and the recipient(s) of care planning in the 20th and 21st centuries. As the reader will quickly ascertain, life does not (and did not) run smooth for the user of mental health services and their carer. Whilst these chapters are not awash with theoretical references, the accounts are personal and therefore written straight from the heart, making them all the more meaningful, important and valuable to any mental health text promoting a recovery paradigm.

Chapter 6: Care Planning and the Carer
Molly Halford

Molly describes her life as a carer. Little did she know at the outset that this was going to become a full time career and that help actually *was* available for her and her family. Now she helps new, first time carers, advising them and ensuring that they do not go through the same, lonely, ordeal that she had to endure. This chapter highlights and challenges the concept of the carer and the issues relating to their involvement in the care planning.

Chapter 7: Experiencing the Process
Edward Smith, Julie Smith, Mark Hopps and Victoria Lumley

This chapter gives a unique insight into the care planning process from four individual perspectives, that of the service user, Edward (Eddie), the carer Julie, and Mark and Victoria as the care providers. It explores in narrative form some of the key issues and experiences involved in mental health care planning.

Section 3: Promoting Recovery, examines the concept of recovery as being inherent to the care planning process. This collection of chapters will discuss issues relating to the performance of assessment, planning, implementation and evaluation. Case examples from practice are offered to illustrate key issues within care planning.

Chapter 8: Recovery as a Framework for Care Planning
Jim Campbell, Theo Stickley and Sarah Bonney

The concept of recovery provides an essentially person focused approach to care planning and acknowledges that the person's journey back to a satisfying life is very individual. It is not focused on symptoms or practitioner interventions rather the person's own subjective interpretation of a meaningful and valued state of life. A number of models for recovery are explored within this chapter and Jim, Theo and Sarah offer a very useful explanation of the social construction of recovery, the benefits of which are central to the care planning process.

Chapter 9: Engagement within the Care Planning Process
Mike Firn

In this chapter Mike examines how practitioners can relate to and engage with service users and their carers within the care planning process. Strategies to foster effective engagement as well as barriers that prevent engagement are identified. Mike also explores creative ways of encouraging engagement with those service users who are difficult to engage.

Chapter 10: Assessment
Angela Hall and Joy Trotter

Assessment is the first and crucial stage in the care planning process and Angela and Joy provide practitioners with some practical guidance on how to conduct a comprehensive biopsychosocial assessment. It provides a systematic approach to assessment including different methods of collecting information and examples of specific assessment tools as well as drawing on clinical examples.

Chapter 11: Promoting Inclusivity in Care Planning
Jenny Weinstein

Social inclusion is an integral part of the care planning process. It exposes a process that involves collaboratively the service user, carer and other members of the multidisciplinary team. In this chapter, Jenny talks about the practical stages and processes involved in the production of a socially inclusive care plan. The concept of social inclusion and its merits are discussed in relation to care planning and the possibilities for inclusion at a micro and macro level are examined.

Chapter 12: Physical Health and Serious Mental Illness: Promoting Good Health
Debbie Robson and Mary Bragg

Debbie and Mary examine and redirect the readers' focus to the issue of general health issues of people experiencing a severe mental illness. It is recognised that the physical health of people with serious mental illness is often neglected. A number of specific health related issues are discussed and the dilemmas in promoting health as part of the care planning process are highlighted.

Chapter 13: Integrated Care Pathways For Mental Health
Dennis Cross and Joan Murphy

This chapter examines the diverse range of interventions that are available to help alleviate a service user's distress. Dennis and Joan demonstrate that there is an increasing evidence base for mental health practice to aid practitioners in selecting and implementing the most effective interventions. Drawing on examples from Ireland Dennis and Joan discuss the main biopsychosocial interventions used in mental health and identify complementary and alternative interventions.

Chapter 14: Evaluation
Joan Murphy and Dennis Cross

Within this chapter Joan and Dennis highlight the often-neglected process of evaluation. Again drawing on examples from Irish mental health services,

Joan and Dennis outline and explore the concept and practical utilisation of evaluation, particularly in light of today's outcome focused culture. Methods for measuring service user outcomes and the efficacy of care are also identified and their validity and reliability are discussed.

Chapter 15: Reflections on the Future
Angela Hall, Mike Wren and Stephan D. Kirby

In this final chapter the themes and threads throughout this text are drawn together. We are reminded that we (service users and carers alike) are all people and as such we must put the person first in all our endeavours to plan care, the process must be made to fit the person and not the person fit the process. In closing, the editors leave the reader with some thoughts to consider in terms of the future direction of not only care planning but also mental health care in general, focusing this upon the concepts of recovery and hope – the underpinning tenets of this entire text. We are reminded that we learn how to prepare for the future by exploring the past.

Section 1

Understanding Care Planning

Chapter 1

The Context and Nature of Care Planning in Mental Health

Angela Hall and Mike Wren

'Mental Health is a significant area of social work (and nursing) practice, which will bring you face to face with people who may be vulnerable and confused. As a social worker [or nurse] you need to work together with other professionals in a way that is person-centred and upholds human rights. This is far from straight forward, with tension and conflict possible at virtually every stage of your work' (Golightley 2006:11).

Introduction

The quote above summarises the challenges for today's mental health practitioners in their approach to caring for some of society's most vulnerable but at the same time possibly most creative and resourceful individuals. Mental health practice often requires a delicate balance between caring for an individual and controlling the impact of the illness on the person and on others in society. This task has become increasingly onerous over the past decade, challenging mental health practitioners to respond to both service users and policy/legislative priorities whilst managing the care-v-control dilemma.

This chapter will consider the significant historical and legislative changes that have influenced the role and context of care planning in mental health. It will outline the introduction of individualised care and the nursing process as a framework for organising current mental health care as well as the emergence of case management as an effective foundation for developing mental health care planning adopted by mental health practitioners in the form of care management (Department of Health, 1994) and the care programme approach (CPA) (Department of Health, 1991a) respectively.

It acknowledges that while *recovery* is a relatively new concept, the involvement of service users, as consumers of mental health care is central to care planning and service delivery via care coordination. The chapter will include a brief critical analysis of associated mental health policies and government agenda in relation to competing dilemmas associated with care-v-control issues.

Organisation of care

The core tenets for organising current mental health care services across the domains of mental health social work and nursing practice, for the purposes of this chapter, can be sequentially traced back to the early 1900s, an era which marked the enactment of the Nurses Registration Act, 1919 (The United Kingdom Centre For the History Of Nursing and Midwifery, 2006) and advocated registered nurses be personally accountable for their own work. This was complemented by the subsequent appointment of the first social worker to the Tavistock Centre in London in 1920. This heralded the beginning of mental health social work and the earliest mental health practitioner developments that (arguably) set the scene for establishing a care planning process that continued to represent the appropriate delivery of a skilful balance between protecting the individual, other people and society. The tailoring of *individual packages of care* is designed to ensure that the person with mental health problems can maintain their recovery of independent functioning within available local community support networks and resources.

For many people with mental health problems this (initially) encompassed the long-stay (total institution) hospital that had been the focus of prolonged debate. Influenced by political and legislative frameworks there was a gradual shift from medically dominated dependency to the eventual closure of these long stay hospitals and the promotion of social and medical inter-dependency with the growth of community care. This was first enunciated within the context of the 1959 Mental Health Act (Department of Health, 1959), which was *'laying the foundations for community care policy that remains at the heart of treatment and maintenance systems today'* (Davies 1994:26).

This shift in discourse continues to contribute to contemporary care planning arrangements that actively promote the process of recovery by building on the strengths of the individual, their families and a range of other essential networks that consist of both formal and informal support systems. Hence they are actively seeking to collaborate, as envisaged within both the Mental Health Act (Department of Health, 1983) and subsequent enactment of the NHS and Community Care Act (Department of Health, 1990).

In terms of the journey toward promoting recovery of independent functioning the earliest notions can be indirectly related to the inception of those far reaching post-war health and social welfare reforms, first emphasised within the philosophy of the Beveridge Report (1942). The resultant social policy developments led to the creation of the National Health Service (NHS) in 1948. The subsequent enactments of the Mental Health Act (Department of Health, 1959, 1983) and the NHS and Community Care Act (1990) gradually led to the development of a more seamless approach to care planning, with significant changes in the design, delivery and direction of the care management and care programme approaches gaining greater momentum between 1994 and 1999. Society's view, however, continued to reflect the recurring theme of *control* as it translated into practice, alongside the search for a cure, prevention based approaches and alternative service provisions that seek (wherever possible) to minimise episodes of hospital admission or re-admission.

There have been significant historical transitions that have continued to influence the development of contemporary mental health policy, strategic thinking and care planning processes:

- **19th Century**: people with mental health problems were viewed as a societal nuisance with afflicted people being locked away in asylums and private mad houses. Removing such people from society strengthened the legislative emphasis upon local authorities' power to intervene. This was based, fundamentally, upon control, containment and segregation permeating into state controlled structures until the early part of the 20th Century.
- **20th Century**: the perception of nuisance was gradually shifting to the view that people with mental health problems were experiencing episodes of illness. A view that was further acknowledged by the noticeable advancements being made in terms of care and treatment, in particular the use of psychotropic drugs. A more humane approach to treatment, and a gradual smouldering of enthusiasm, was being ignited within a collaborative, recovery focused, care planning approach developing throughout the latter part of the 20th and (now with even greater prominence than ever) into the 21st Century through the plethora of models of care and treatment.
- **21st Century**: saw the advent of a plethora of models of care and treatment that viewed people with mental health problems as key resources to the alleviation of their mental health problems. These are reliant upon working in partnership, adopting a person-centred, seamless and proactive approach to the provision of both care and treatment, the purpose of which is enabling service users and their carers to cope with mental health problems with a sense of renewed hope. Also to begin the process of building a lifestyle that has meaning, value and provides opportunities for promoting the recovery of independent functioning within and beyond, the limits of their mental health problem. This is done through the provision of the impetus for mental health professionals and societal perspectives to complement this concept of collaboration between individuals, groups, voluntary services and statutory agencies collectively engaging with both curative and preventative practices. Collaborative working processes and experiences have been influenced further by the incremental implementation of competing legislative frameworks, where aspects of control remain at the core of the curative, as well as preventative mental health care approaches.

A social policy of *collective responsibility* co-existed between the state, its citizens and the statute book that was embodied in what is often referred to as the social contract for Beveridge's citizen, and was extended practically to the whole population, providing a model for the later National Health Service (Quinney, 2006). This social contract linked into Beveridge's *Five Giants* of:

- Idleness (unemployment)
- Want (poverty)
- Ignorance (education)
- Squalor (poor housing)
- Disease (ill health; physical and mental)

These all provide a further historical perspective to contrast with current comprehensive care planning processes that reflect those significant life factors of:

- **Employment**: without stigma of mental illness, paid work; maximisation of entitlements, moving from dependence to independence
- **Education**: meaningful activity building confidence and skills
- **Housing**: appropriate accommodation providing protection and shelter
- **Health and mental well being**: promoting recovery, actively encouraging compliance with medication, appropriate diet, exercise, relaxation and interests that could complement the development of
- **Meaningful relationships**: utilising family member support as well as other informal and formal networks of support, with the intention of striving (wherever possible) to avoid compulsory admission or re-admission to hospital.

One of the initial aims of the creation of National Health Service (NHS) in 1948, which is equally applicable to the provision of mental health care today, was that mental hospitals (asylums) should be amalgamated into the centralised control of the NHS. The 1959 Mental Health Act provided both a significant societal and political change. Hastened by a legislative thrust it brought about an emphasis on the importance and value of the informal, rather than formal (compulsory) admission to hospital thus encouraging the shift toward a more individualised approach to the assessment and care planning arrangements. Biesteck (1961) refers to this as the *'Casework Relationship'* striving *'to ensure that psychiatric patients were treated in the same way as other patients, setting them free, as a consequence, from their straightjacket of the past'* (Hoggett 1990:26). Some literature (Butler & Pritchard, 1983; Bulmer, 1987; Byrne & Padfield, 1990; Hoggett, 1990) equally suggests that the original 1959 Mental Health Act and the shift toward an individualised casework approach, actually heralded the arrival and realisation of community care for people with mental health problems *'both as a theoretical idea and as public policy'* (Davies 1994:22).

From a social work perspective this more humane approach was strengthened by the establishment of a set of casework principles that were to become as fundamental to the development of the casework relationship, as they would be to the implementation of treatment plans. Mental welfare officers (MWOs) came under the remit of Health Authorities and were perceived as assistants to the powerful and influential body of psychiatrists and the relatively new provision of large-scale psychiatric services that were being developed. This said, this era represented a period of rapid growth in terms of service provision that remained largely uncoordinated, fragmented and segmented into narrow specialist roles that prevailed for several decades.

Biesteck's (1961) principles for the case work relationship equally developed against this backdrop of fragmented service provision, yet continued to advocate: choice, the client's right to self determination, controlled emotional involvement, confidentiality and a non-judgemental attitude. This translates into current practice as providing the basis of underpinning knowledge, skills and values that are deemed as essential ingredients for the successful development of casework which is '*modelled on medicine (with) the casework tasks of data collection, analysis and planned intervention (being replicated in relation to) the study, diagnosis and treatment*' (Coulshed & Orme, 1998:17).

Meanwhile the introduction of the nursing process within the large institutional settings had provided a positive move within a custodial environment to a more individual needs led approach. The nursing process itself evolved in the USA with strong influences from nursing authors who began to concentrate on the process of nursing and the central role of patients (Peplau, 1952; Henderson, 1966). The expansion of nursing knowledge as an attempt to gain professional recognition and the need for insurance companies to audit clinical activity are both said to have influenced its development (Wright & Giddey, 1993).

The nursing process arrived in the UK during the early 1970s and by 1977 was included within the nursing curriculum (General Nursing Council, 1977). There was initially, and continues to be, some opposition from mental health nurses regarding the efficacy of this approach and the amount of associated documentation required, leading many to consider it a paper exercise. However this may be more to do with how the nursing process was introduced within the UK rather than the actual process itself. The emphasis was placed on the documentation of care rather than on the nurse/patient relationship and the involvement of the client as an active contributor in the problem-solving approach. This key aspect of the nursing process was neglected and the nurse was given the responsibility for carrying out the care planning process.

The nursing process is a four-stage model, which promotes individualised care for the client. The adoption of this was a positive move away from the task allocation delivery of care often practiced within the hospital (total institutional) setting. Within mental health institutions task allocation was based on a dominant medical model of care that had resulted in dehumanising activities and procedures for patients (Martin, 1984). Patients would be showered together, toileted together with no attention to individual needs, dignity or respect; clothes, toiletries and even underwear and false teeth would be shared. At this time there was widespread institutional abuse and neglect of vulnerable people, which to a large extent changed with the introduction of the nursing process. Each person had to have as a minimum: their own belongings, their own clothes, their own toiletries and their own locker for their own possessions. The nursing process brought about the institutional recognition of patients as individual human beings with specific wants, needs and preferences, people were being given choices, *'would you like sugar in your tea'*?

Kratz (1979) was seen as one of the first in the UK to provide a book on the nursing process. It detailed each stage of the nursing process and described the nurse's role within it.

The stages of the nursing process are well known today as:

- Assessment
- Planning
- Implementation
- Evaluation.

Assessment was the first step in the process and was aimed at determining the patient's need for nursing care or the identification of problems that could be alleviated by nursing care. *Planning* is the second step and involves setting goals that will alleviate the problems already identified in step 1, this stage should result in a written care plan. The third step is the *Implementation* stage and involves the delivery of a range of nursing interventions that are focused on meeting the patient's needs and reducing their problems. The fourth step is the *Evaluation* of nursing interventions, to determine the efficacy of the care delivered. The whole process is considered to be cyclical in that it would return to the assessment stage and begin all over again (Kratz, 1979). The nursing process is a framework to help nurses organise and implement care that is individualised to a specific person's needs and is based on sound theoretical evidence (empirical). Each of the stages continues to exist in contemporary mental health and social care but now occurs most commonly under the heading of care coordination.

Care coordination (Department of Health, 1999a) is the current framework for planning care for people involved with adult mental health services. It is the amalgamation of the previous care programme approach (used in healthcare) and care management (used in social care) to form a single point of access and care delivery for people experiencing a mental illness. It is a multidisciplinary approach to care planning that provides a more streamlined and seamless service devoted to service users.

> *'Conventionally and stereotypically medical practice has remained the dominant partner, with advances in medication reinforcing the idea that an individual's mental disorder can be managed and the key process is diagnosis, followed by treatment monitoring and evaluation. In this process however, the danger is that the treated are subservient to those in charge of treatment'* (Golightley 2006:8).

This process represents an overlap between social work (currently the dominant partner when working alongside a nearest relative, with regard to compulsory detention) and nursing (currently the dominant partner following initial admission to hospital). Each demonstrates that dominant professional practices meander between aspects of care, control, co-operation, conflict and maintaining professional practice based on a *common interest of collaboration* that seeks to always preserve the *'patient's best interests (and balance) the power of professionals to override the wishes of the patient, or sometimes the patient's family which is the power to deprive a person of his or her basic liberties'* (Brayne & Martin 1999:330).

Detaining the person (legally), in the pursuit of securing the most appropriate care and treatment for them, highlights probably the most controversial aspect of the intricately complicated care-v-control balances that are reconciled on a regular basis by mental health practitioners. This signifies the first competing dilemma associated with care-v-control issues becoming evident in practice, that is, the impact upon the casework relationship between the individual caseworker, other colleagues, society, the person with mental health problems when they become a danger to themselves and others, requiring their compulsory admission to hospital.

The theme of prevention and a recovery focused approach to service developments was equally woven further into the fabric of future changes to social work practice, explicitly articulated by the publication of the Barclay Report (National Institute for Social Work, 1982), which identified a similar need for social workers to become involved with informal caring resources; to *'work in partnership'* with them, noting that, *'Social Workers are advised to turn their attention to individuals and families within the context of all networks of which they are a part'*. Barclay went on to encourage social workers to develop their networks among those who share similar interests and concerns. Some observers noted that by the early 1980s, *'local authority Social Workers were having a minimal involvement with people with a mental illness, unless a crisis arose which forced them to arrange admission to hospital of their adult clients'* (Davies 1994:26).

Goldberg and Huxley (1980) took the debate a step further by vehemently criticising the structure of social work in mental health prior to 1982. By suggesting that it was becoming stagnant and with the emergence of community psychiatric nurses (CPNs) as a professional group from 1982, they alluded to the fact that it was being observed that social workers might be reduced to a welfare rights role and policy of crisis intervention as *'Social Workers after Seebohm (Social Services, 1968) were becoming confused about their role in mental health and lacking in professional confidence'* (Davies 1994:27).

Barclay's recasting of some specialist roles within smaller patch based social work teams widened the role of social work and strengthened the previous focus upon community orientated social work underpinned by psychosocial practices that aligned to humanistic approaches. Maslow's Hierarchy of Needs (Maslow, 1954) focused upon meeting psychological, emotional, spiritual and physiological needs while Biesteck's (1961) casework relationship continued to promote a theme of value based perspectives, striving to safeguard, uphold and encourage individual rights, choice and personal strengths that also involved generating the resources of self and community self help networks. Hopefully a more preventative focus to intervention (one that is stimulated by informal networking) is set to become an integral feature of future care planning processes, thus demonstrating that *'Social Work, until the 1980s, contained a focus on individuals (casework), as well as on groups and communities (group work and community work) even if only a few workers combined both approaches in their everyday practice'* (Ramon 2005:online). Indeed, both these approaches are equally evident in the style of informal networking that was taken up by the subsequent enactment of Mental Health Act (1983) and was extensively reflected throughout the central philosophy of the Griffiths Report (HMSO, 1988). This report strongly asserted the promotion of community care for people with a mental health problem. This further reinforced the view that such informal networking was not confined to service users, patients, carers or advocacy groups, but was extended to colleagues in related professions working across inter-professional boundaries. Such collaborations were responsible, through statute, for the design and delivery of appropriately funded care packages aimed at strengthening the concept of involvement as a practical reality via the needs assessment, care planning and review stages.

Community care and care management

Community care we would argue has always existed. However as a policy, it was given a renewed sense of vigour by the implementation of the 1983 Mental Health Act and the NHS and Community Care Act (1990) with the principal aims of enabling people with mental health problems to live within their own communities, with the support of a range of holistic and preventative services emphasising independence rather than dependence – independence that builds upon a history of very gradual, cautious, hostile and financially constraining response to the initial implementation of community care policy that prevailed throughout the early 1980s and late 1990s. The core formal networks namely, health and social services, were required to forge links with each other as interdependent partners. They were charged with confronting the stigma, oppression and inequalities of mental health from a strengths based perspective and, in the interests of forging an appropriate therapeutic relationship, actively working alongside other formal and informal networks of support, so as to connect with the lives of those in greatest need. The creation of support systems that promote the recovery of independent functioning (and are a direct consequence of working in partnership with service users, patients, carers and community resources) have a direct impact upon future care planning arrangements and were captured within the Mental Health Act (Department of Health, 1983). This was clearly advocating that mental health care services of the future should be delivered to ensure that:

- every person with a mental health problem should have their rights safeguarded

- compulsory admission, when necessary, should be carried out according to clear regulations
- compulsory care should be given in the least restrictive conditions possible
- the professionals concerned should be adequately trained and their competence assessed
- the quality of care and treatment should not fall below an accepted minimum standard.

The Code of Practice (Department of Health, 1993) to the 1983 Mental Health Act requires individuals to be fully involved (as far as practicably possible) in the formulation and delivery of their care and treatment. It stressed the need to bring them into decision making forums and discussions including (during the assessment, care planning and review phases) the patient and their family, friends as well as any other relevant people.

These specific facets of the Mental Health Act (Department of Health, 1983) emphasised that greater interagency co-operation (in relation to multi-agency care planning approaches) be adopted. This is in response to individual need, risks to the public and supervision of certain discharged patients in the community via the setting up of supervision registers (Department of Health, 1994 and 1995) and the Mental Health (Patients in the Community) Act (Department of Health, 1995). This reflected also a change in emphasis for nursing as it shifted more towards the community from 1982 and was evidenced by the growth in community psychiatric nurses (CPNs) and their deployment alongside social workers and other professionals into community mental health teams (CMHTs) and more recently named community home treatment teams (CHTTs). Their initial purpose was to manage the process of discharging people with long-term mental health problems from hospitals into the community, the basis for continuing to make community care a reality for all people with mental health problems. However, the Audit Commission Report, *Making a Reality of Community Care* (1986), suggested that community care was being implemented far too slowly and unevenly, providing the evidential basis for developing the future role, responsibilities and framework of care management.

Care management

By 1988 the Griffiths Report had spelt out a robust framework for providing a significant prelude to the establishment of care management (Department of Health, 1994) and the care programme approach (Department of Health, 1991a) respectively – signifying a further substantial change of policy, practice and philosophy of care. Proposing an ambitious programme of collaboration between central and local Government, health and social services, statutory, private and voluntary sectors in a mixed economy of care.

It was recommended here that Local Authority social service departments should be required to assess the community care needs in their area and then enable provision of the necessary services using a mixture of informal and formal professional support systems. Griffiths also emphasised the need to plan for the ultimate closure of all long stay mental hospitals, while asserting that no person should be discharged without a clear package of care.

The NHS and Community Care Act (1990) provided the influential legislation that was to shape both the provision and delivery of future community care services for adults with mental health problems for the next decade and beyond. The Act outlined main functions for the authority lead role in care management and indeed the subsequent implementation of the care programme approach (Department of Health, 1991a).

Both approaches were introduced as the cornerstone of community care policy implementation with assessment, care planning and service provision, providing the foundations for creating a more seamless approach to care delivery. This reaffirmed the concept that service users and their carers are placed at the centre of all activity, upholding their rights, choices and control over the services they received on a needs led basis. This was based on the following principles:

- Residential care (hospital admission or readmission) should generally be avoided and that people are better served by offering individual packages of care to enable them to continue to live in the community.
- People with needs should be offered a range of services and service providers that are underpinned by the value of empowerment and self-determination which were made so explicit in the (previously discussed) case work relationship arrangements. This led to specific requirements which emphasised collaboration between agencies and colleagues particularly in respect of holistic care planning arrangements and leading to the specific requirements (but *not* a duty, as with children) for agencies to work together cooperatively as enshrined within Sections 46, 47, and 49 of the NHS and Community Care Act (1990):
    - Section 46: requires that each Social Services Authority *must* publish a strategic plan for community services in their area
    - Section 47(1) and (2): require local authorities to assess individuals' needs if they appear to need community care services and
    - Section 49: articulates arrangements for the transferring of staff between health authorities and local authorities.

It acknowledged that when the new statutory arrangements for community care came fully into force in April 1993, local authority social services departments had lead responsibility at a local level for developing new patterns of services. Confusion and clarity collided in the interpretation of the role of care manager and the key worker role from the inception of the care programme approach (CPA) (Department of Health, 1991a).

For just as it was suggested earlier that community care has always existed, Renshaw (in Coulshed & Orme, 1998) acknowledged that:

'care management has always been with us inasmuch as it relates to Social Work (or nursing) as a problem solving process which relies on a mixture of administrative efficiency alongside what the North Americans call 'clinical' skills, that is Social Work (or nursing) practice and human relationship skills'.

When working together for the benefit of service users and their carers, all mental health practitioners experience these care management roles in action. This observation applies equally to the contrast with the role of CPNs too, as social work appeared to adopt care management arrangements, as the process by which those in need of community care services in their area should be helped. While CPNs appeared to adopt (in parallel) the arrangements outlined within the CPA for implementing a comparable, yet divergent, framework as the basis for effective mental health care planning in the community. Confusion was further compounded by this two system approach being implemented with very similar principles and guidance at different times, with differing terminology and being rolled out with an inconsistent pace of delivery throughout the country.

For care planning purposes it was still unclear, for years into the implementation of the CPA how this process linked to other statutory and local authority arrangements namely care management itself, which was led by social services and Section 117 (after care) of the Mental Health Act (1983) which clearly requires co-operation between health and social services in the production of care plans for those discharged patients previously compulsorily detained in hospital under Section 3 of the Mental Health Act (1983).

Orme and Glastonbury (1993) expanded upon this when they stated that *'care management requires the knowledge, values and skills provided by professional education and training for Social Work'* (Coulshed & Orme 1998:18) and we would equally add, incorporating the ethics and professional education and training of other mental health practitioners too. All qualified mental health professionals are eligible to undertake the care management/CPA role including psychologists, occupational therapists and psychiatrists it just happens that it was more likely to fall to the social worker or CPN.

We do concur, however, that this provided some clarity on the road toward the evolution of a more seamless care coordination and service delivery process. Yet the consistent confusion that remains is why the practicalities of these parallel systems were not integrated from their inception, particularly when related to mental health care planning processes that are devised within a legislative spirit and the requirement for health and social services to cooperate.

Further clarity between the parallel delivery of the care management and CPA processes were clearly circulated within the social services inspectorate care management and assessment guidance action checklist (Department of Health, 1991b) that outlined the stages of care management that were equally comparable with the newly emergent CPA and framework:

- Assessing need
- Care planning
- Implementing the care plan
- Reviewing of the process, with each providing the standard format for practitioners to replicate in practice. Strengthening a political drive to further integrate the care programme approach, care management and instigating seamless care into practice.

Care programme approach and care coordination processes

The care programme approach (Department of Health, 1991a) was hailed as an attempt by Government to provide some sense of structure to the coordination of the particularly complex and fragmented range of services that were being delivered to meet the specific needs of people with a range of mental health problems outside of a hospital setting.

This process was subsequently reviewed by the publication of *Building Bridges* (Department of Health, 1996) as a direct result of the Clunis Inquiry (Ritchie *et al.*, 1994) into the tragic death of Jonathan Zito. The criticisms from this highly influential inquiry highlighted a catalogue of missed opportunities for agencies to work together. This cited, particularly, aspects of poor coordination and communication between all key agencies involved in the care and treatment of Christopher Clunis (Ritchie *et al.*, 1994). This occurred despite the implementation of CPA some years earlier which had been designed to strengthen rather than weaken coordination and communication between those agencies responsible for the care and treatment of people with a mental health problem living outside of hospital settings. However the Department of Health (1994) publication of the *Implementing Care for People: Care Management* further reaffirmed this view of strengthening the coordination and communication processes by stating that:

> 'care planning includes the implementation of the care plan or "package of care", but this can only be achieved if services have been commissioned and the voluntary and independent sector stimulated to ensure that the range of needs identified have appropriate services in place to meet them. Finally, monitoring and review should include the ongoing assessment as well as methods of quality assurance that are designed to ensure that services are being provided in an appropriate manner, and to the required standard'.

From its initial inception the CPA process was aimed at those people considered at risk of falling through the net, including those discharged on Section 117 of the Mental Health Act (1983).

Clarity was further provided within the four key elements of the CPA including:

- assessment of health and social care needs
- a care plan being produced
- appointment of a key worker
- arrangements for regular reviews.

Since the introduction of these parallel systems of care planning and delivery, it has been recognised that, in order to ensure the most effective and efficient delivery of a seamless approach to care planning, one that is aimed at promoting the recovery of the individual, the integration of both these systems together into a single framework within mental health care services at both local and national levels is required. Integration of both these processes is designed to improve clarity of communication, consistency and continuity of responses, thereby minimising the catalogue of coordination failures and ensuring future service users, their carers and nearest relatives are not restricted by barriers created by collective arrangements made across organisational and professional boundaries. In response to this parallel delivery of separate care planning systems, came an equally parallel response from the Government, in the form of guidance (Department of Health, 1999a) which clearly emphasised that CPA and care management were one and the same for all those of working age in contact with specialist mental health and social care services.

Formalising the role of care coordinator from the previous key worker role re-emphasised that care coordination does *not* replace sound professional judgements and practice which remains central to achieving safe, effective and efficient recovery focused and achievable outcomes for people via their individual care planning process. Care coordinators can be any qualified member of the multidisciplinary team who:

- are competent in delivering mental health care
- have an understanding of the impact of mental illness
- have some knowledge of community services
- understand the role of other agencies
- have care coordination skills and an ability to access resources across both health and social care agencies.

Key changes to the CPA were also spelt out by this guidance that included the establishment of rigorous standards and specifying how the integration of care management with CPA will actually lead to the future delivery of a whole system approach being achieved – an approach that was formally described within the context of the current Government modernisation agenda outlined within the National Service Framework (NSF) for Mental Health (Department of Health, 1999b).

This National Service Framework for Mental Health represents a

'coherent set of national standards and objectives for Social Care focused on a particular service user group (people with mental health problems). It sets out the

vision, organisational arrangements and specific minimum standards that should be achieved including specific targets and statements of quality expected, timescales and indicators set to measure progress' (Hafford-Letchfield, 2006).

thus acknowledging and indeed reinforcing the fact that a recovery focused approach to care planning continues to rely upon the components of success or failure within the care planning meeting that builds upon the relationship between the person with mental health problems, their care coordinator (the new title introduced to replace the previously designated key worker) and carer or any known family members involved.

Each aspect of this modernisation agenda illustrates the most influential changes to contemporary as well as the future of care planning processes: processes that are specifically designed to promote recovery and are underpinned by a set of clear directives provided within the NSF (Department of Health, 1999b) Standards 1, 4 and 6. These key aspects of modernising mental health care services demonstrate the Government's aim to ensure that health and social care services are delivered in a way that people who use them (and their carers) value them, use them more and seek help earlier. This identifies that the features of a truly integrated system of CPA and care management process must include:

- one single operational policy
- joint training for health and social care staff
- one lead officer for care coordination across health and social care
- common and agreed risk assessment and risk management processes
- a shared information system across health and social care
- a single complaints process
- agreement on allocation of resources and, where possible devolved budgets
- a joint serious incident process
- one point access for coordinated health and social care assessments.
  (Department of Health in Brown, 2006)

The effectiveness of a care planning process that consistently promotes the recovery of independent functioning, cannot be determined in terms of targets and statistics alone. Indeed the NSF acknowledges this and suggests that a clear link also needs to be forged with evidence based practice and research by directing that:

'local audit should move away from a focus simply on numbers and more towards assessing the quality of CPA implementation, including the quality of care plans, the attainment of treatment goals and, in particular for those with multiple needs, the effectiveness of interagency working. The views of service users are an effective indicator of the quality of services and must be included in any audit of service delivery too' (Department of Health in Brown, 2006).

Whatever the debate about the actual effectiveness of the care coordination process and adopting the promotion of a recovery focused approach to care planning, there are some key factors that would enhance the actual implementation of this process and approach further by consistently establishing from the outset:

- What is the range of people this process and approach can directly apply to?
- How can they correspond and connect to other systems and approaches in place?
- The need to establish what the service user themselves and their wider family are entitled to
- Clarify what it is they should expect from the practitioners, processes, approaches and services available to them in their local community.

Only then, can we begin to create, sustain and maintain a care planning approach that is tailored around the recovery of independent functioning for a person with mental health problems. Particularly when the recurring presence of competing dilemmas associated with care-v-control issues are collectively brought into this consultative exchange between service users, carers and mental health social work and nursing colleagues.

Competing dilemmas associated with care-v-control issues

The recurring competing dilemmas associated with care-v-control issues we have referred to, throughout this chapter, fully acknowledge the observation that such conflict and competing dilemmas can emerge, for example the balances between rights over resources, roles and responsibilities and the potential for recall-v-recovery emerging into everyday practice.

Rights over resources

The involvement of the approved social worker (ASW) in the decision-making process of compulsory admission is always going to prove complex, despite the protective legislation which surrounds its implementation, although the Mental Health Act (1983) strengthened the rights of the detained person and the NHS and Community Care Act (1990) emphasised individual choice and a cost effective approach to service delivery.

Both Acts consistently *'deflected attention away from the fundamental issue of resources'* (Butler & Pritchard 1983:144), illustrating that the historical legacy of community based provision and alternatives to hospital admission have not been adequately funded. This is opposed to the vast resources available to the *'large institutions for the mentally ill (that) were designated as hospitals under the new NHS. Whilst Local Authorities had some responsibilities, there was minimal expenditure on any prevention and aftercare of patients'* (Hafford-Letchfield 2006:11).

This legacy of rights over resources prevails between the delivery of health and social care provision with the former being free at the point of delivery and the latter recouping costs through means testing, where people over the age of 18 years can (subject to a financial assessment) be charged for the provision of social care services. This is set against a local, yet different, eligibility criterion that does not align with a comparable responsibility placed upon the Health Authority (except with regard to) the Coughlan Judgement (Department of Health, 1999c) and its impact upon the subsequent delivery of continuing health care provision.

This has contributed to the growth of creative and innovative recovery focused practice aimed at minimising dependence and increasing independence for those who are traditionally hard to engage or disengaging users of services. These include assertive outreach teams, the expansion of community mental health teams, crisis resolution teams and 24 hour crisis help lines.

The development of community based preventative and recovery focused services (within the continuum of a mixed economy of care and treatment for people with mental health problems) exposes community based providers to logistical service delivery demand pressures, with a very real prospect of demand outstretching supply emerging. This could lead to the potential erosion of alternative provision being available within local communities, as they compete within and against each other for the same human market place. Specific care-v-control issues arising here relate directly to the emergent Government agenda related to the ability to pay for those who need care from a budget for services and packages of care that is often under increased scrutiny, constraint and pressures.

Despite the first 30% of the community care budgets (previously the mental illness specific grant) being devolved to Local Authority budgets, pressure continues for mental health community care based services with the control aspect relating directly to the health service maintaining its historical and indeed current, financial status quo of universality where service provision is *always* delivered *free of charge* at the point of delivery.

Roles and responsibility

'. . . good service requires both control and freedom. The presence of both enables control to criticise excessive freedom, and the availability of freedom to criticise excessive control' (Payne 2002:223).

This is probably the most powerful dilemma facing mental health practitioners, in particular ASWs, as they balance their professional responsibilities and judgements (to protect the person and society) against their legal intervention and jurisdiction (roles) to initiate the compulsory admission of a person to hospital instantly curtailing that person's freedom and instigating a perceived level of excessive control having previously elicited views from the person with mental health problems, their carers and the seeking of a medical opinion.

Policy and Government agenda, now more than ever, requires a collaboratively creative approach to harmonise conflicts, harness the creativity of practitioners, service users and carers and strive to reconcile very real issues. Fundamentally, to ensure that mental health legislation and policy makes a real and lasting difference to people with mental health problems, their carers, mental health practitioners and a range of mental health care providers, engagement with a collaborative process is crucial. Through this it is hoped to achieve that intricate and accountable balance that exists between promoting recovery of independent functioning, with the ever present reality of state control – the ultimate detention of a person with mental health problems and their compulsory recall back to a hospital setting when deemed in law to be serving the best interests and safety for that person, other people and society generally.

A compelling aspect of care-v-control that is effectively captured in the dilemma is illustrated quite succinctly by Horner (2006) in terms of achieving a balance between recovery-v-recall to hospital.

Recovery-v-recall

The concept of recovery has evolved in the last decade, particularly in the USA, New Zealand and the UK (Anthony, 1991) and is now allegedly at the core of mental health practice (Department of Health, 2006). In terms of the journey toward promoting recovery of independent functioning; earliest origins can be directly related to the inception of those far reaching post-war health and social welfare reforms, first emphasised within the philosophy of the Beveridge Report (1942) and the resultant social policy developments that led to the creation of the National Health Service in 1948. The subsequent enactments of the Mental Health Act (1959, 1983) and the NHS and Community Care Act (1990) gradually led to the development of a more seamless approach to care coordination evolving, with significant changes in the design, delivery and direction of the care management and care programme approaches gaining greater momentum from 1994 to the present day.

This particular dilemma relates to all aspects of the care planning process focused upon the promotion of independent functioning, ranging from episodes of non-compliance with medication, supporting the person through an individual journey from relapse to recovery to the more draconian aspects of practice related to a supervised discharge if a person fails to cooperate with aspects of the CPA care planning process and outcomes. Failure to cooperate could ultimately lead to a recall back to hospital. Yet even with the NSF (Department of Health, 1999b) it still remains unclear what sanctions people will have if services fail to honour or meet their part of the agreement. However, the essential skills of the care coordinator can be achieved through honouring their part of the agreement by building a therapeutic relationship based on a commitment to that individual, their CPA process and securing their trust. This can be achieved for people with mental health problems and their carers, through a practical realisation and collective belief that the care planning process will help to contribute towards the promotion of the recovery of independent functioning as an eventual goal.

They must also have within their repertoire of skills the capacity to deal with the aftermath of what may be perceived as the breaking of that trust, belief and commitment from the perspective of the person with mental health problems who they are supporting, when recall to hospital is the only safe, effective and efficient recourse that is initiated as an essential requirement for protecting the individual, their family and society generally.

Essential requirements can so easily be perceived as a controlling factor for the person with mental health problems, while providing a real ethical and moral dilemma for the care coordinator working within a therapeutic relationship with that person, their wider family and community. Such a therapeutic relationship would emphasise the promotion of recovery within that wider community, rather than a process of recall back into a hospital setting. Creating a further competing dilemma for the care coordinator's own personal moral code are those of their employing organisation and the Codes of Practice (General Social Care Council, 2002; Nursing and Midwifery Council, 2004) articulated by relevant professional bodies that govern their behaviour, professional conduct and practice.

Significant aspects of professional etiquette in terms of skills, knowledge and appropriate values are therefore required and clearly demonstrated throughout the forthcoming chapters and their subsequent themes, illustrating the extent of service development in the promotion of recovery and the link to collaborative working arrangements between individuals, their carers and community based resources and networks of support. This ensures that mental health practice continues to be delivered within the context of an accountable, integrated system of care coordination and is capable of being judged against a clear social work value base that is consistent with aspects of nursing practice that are equally underpinned by an ethical, legal and moral perspective. This would then equate to a mutual process of continuing to forge links between competent, confident and indeed creative mental health care planning processes that provide the hallmarks for the effective delivery of future mental health care services.

Conclusion

This chapter has attempted to demonstrate the importance of charting the historical foundations of mental health care planning, in order to understand aspects of current approaches that actively seek to promote the concept of recovery of independent functioning as a meaningful reality for people whose lives are touched by mental health problems and are delivered from within an integrated system of care coordination, provided via CPA.

Despite the acknowledgment *'that we are still a long way from a complete understanding of these disabling states of mind. It is important as a society that we make every effort to do so, both in the interests of the individuals and families affected and in the interests of society generally'* (Byrne & Padfield 1990:155). This illustrates that the preventative agenda is as much reliant upon this understanding being enacted into the heart of all interdependent partnerships between mental health practitioners as it is to the re-energising of the previous smouldering embers of enthusiasm being ignited within the intensity of continuing to deliver integrated collaborative working arrangements.

Collaborative working arrangements have continued to progressively emerge from a volcanic landscape of professional, societal, legislative and historical perspectives that have (over time) erupted into the current process of shaping the recovery of independent functioning as a practical reality for many people with mental health problems and their wider family throughout 20th and 21st century society.

This chapter has also consistently sought to strengthen the importance of strategic thinking and mental health policy from (1913–1999) and how these have provided a stimulant for developing essential links between integrated collaborative working arrangements prevailing conflicts, dilemmas and tensions aligned to a range of formal and informal networks of support coming together.

The combined commitment of avoiding hospital admission (or readmission), and the appropriate protection of the individual, society and others, and striving to secure a real presence for that individual, (by actively encouraging their engagement within a recovery process care planning process) have served to inform and influence the shape of future mental health care services. Such proactive arrangements (built on humane influences), have enabled the recovery of independent functioning to become an accepted way of life for many people with a mental health problem.

References

Anthony, A. (1991). Mirror Images, *Nursing Times*, **87(2)**, 35–6.

Audit Commission (1986). *Making a Reality of Community Care*. London: HMSO.

Beveridge, W. (1942). *Report On Social Insurance and Allied Services*. London: HMSO.

Biesteck, F. (1961). *The Casework Relationship*. London: Allen and Unwin.

Brayne, H. & Martin, G. (1999). *Law For Social Workers*. London: Blackstone Press. (6th edn).

Brown, R. (2006). *The Approved Social Worker's Guide to Mental Health Law*. Exeter: Learning Matters Limited.

Bulmer, M. (1987). *The Social Basis of Community Care*. London: Unwin-Hyman.

Butler, A. & Pritchard, C. (1983). *Social Work and Mental Illness*. Basingstoke: Macmillan Press.

Byrne, T. & Padfield, T. (1990). *Social Services Made Simple*. London: Butterworth-Heinmann. (4th edn).

Coulshed, V. & Orme, J. (1998). *Social Work Practice; An Introduction*. Basingstoke: Macmillan Press. (3rd edn).

Davies, M. (1994). *The Essential Social Worker*. Hampshire: Ashgate Publishing. (3rd edn).

Department of Health (1959). *The Mental Health Act 1959*. HMSO. London.

Department of Health (1983). *The Mental Health Act 1983*. London: HMSO.

Department of Health (1990). *National Health Service and Community Care Act*. London: HMSO.

Department of Health (1991a). *The Care Programme Approach For People With Mental Illness*. London: HMSO.

Department of Health (1991b). *Social Services Inspectorate Care Management and Assessment Guidance*. London: HMSO.

Department of Health (1993). *Mental Health Act 1983: Code of Practice*. London: HMSO.

Department of Health (1994). *Implementing Care for People: Care Management*. London: HMSO.

Department of Health (1995). *Mental Health (Patients in the Community) Act*. London: HMSO.

Department of Health (1996). *Building Bridges*. London: The Stationery Office.

Department of Health (1999a). *Effective Care Coordination in Mental Health Services*. London: The Stationery Office.

Department of Health (1999b). *National Service Framework For Mental Health: Modern Standards and Service Models*. London: The Stationery Office.

Department of Health (1999c). *Coughlan Judgement*. HSC 1999/180. London: The Stationery Office.

Department of Health (2006). *The Chief Nursing Officer's Review of Mental Health Nursing*. London: The Stationery Office.

General Nursing Council for England and Wales (1977). *Design of Curricula*. Circular 77/19A. London: GNC.

General Social Care Council (2002). *Code of Practice for Social Care Workers and Code of Practice for Employers of Social Care Workers*. London: GSCC.

Goldberg, D. & Huxley, P. (1980). *Mental Illness in the Community*. London: Tavistock.

Golightley, M. (2006). *Social Work and Mental Health*. Exeter: Learning Matters Limited. (2nd edn).

Griffiths, R. (1988). *Community Care; Agenda for Action*. London: HMSO.

Hafford-Letchfield, T. (2006). *Management and Organisations in Social Work*. Exeter: Learning Matters Limited.

Henderson, V. (1966). *The Nature Of Nursing: A Definition and Its Implications For Practice. Research and Education*. New York: Macmillan.

Hoggett, B. (1990). *Mental Health Law*. London: Sweet and Maxwell.

Horner, N. (2006). *What is Social Work? Context and Perspectives*. Exeter: Learning Matters Limited. (2nd edn).

Kratz, C.R. (1979). *The Nursing Process*. London: Baillière Tindall.

Martin, J.P. (1984). *Hospitals in Trouble*. Oxford: Blackwell.

Maslow, A. (1954). *Motivation and Personality*. New York: Harper and Row.

National Institute for Social Work (1982). *Barclay Committee Report: Social Workers Their Roles and Tasks*. London: Bedford Square Press.

Nursing and Midwifery Council (2004). *Code Of Professional Conduct: Standards For Conduct. Performance and Ethics*. London: NMC.

Olsen, J. (1982). A Qualified Success. *Community Care*. **December 23/30**, 19–20.

Orme, J. & Glastonbury, B. (1993). *Care Management: Tasks and Workloads*. Basingstoke: Macmillan.

Payne, M. (2002). Management. In: Adams, R., Dominelli, L. & Payne, M. (eds) *Critical Practice in Social Work*. Basingstoke: Palgrave. **(22)**, 223–235.

Peplau, H.E. (1952). *Interpersonal Relations in Nursing*. New York: GP Putnam's Sons. 1988.

Quinney, A. (2006). *Collaborative Social Work Practice*. Exeter: Learning Matters Limited.

Ramon, S. (2005). *Options and Dilemmas Facing British Mental Health Social Work*. Available at: http://www.crtpsynet.freeuk.com.Ramon.htm. (Accessed: 19 July 2005).

Renshaw, J. (1988). Care in the Community: Individual Care Planning and Case Management. *British Journal of Social Work.* **18**, 79–105.

Ritchie, J., Dick, D. & Lingham, R. (1994). *The Report of Inquiry Into The Care and Treatment of Christopher Clunis*. London: HMSO.

Social Services (1968). *Seebohm Report, Report of the Committee on Local Authority and Allied Personal*. London: HMSO.

The United Kingdom Centre For the History Of Nursing and Midwifery (2006). *Midwives and Midwifery*. Available at: http://www.ukchnm.org/midwives&midwifery.php

Wright, H. & Giddey, M. (1993). *Mental Health Nursing: From First Principles To Professional Practice*. Cheltenham: Stanley Thorne.

Chapter 2

The Ethical and Legal Implications of Care Planning in Mental Health

Graham Lyons

Introduction

This chapter will initially look at the ethical and legal implications of current legislation, policies and multiprofessional issues that can influence and impact upon the mental health care planning process.

In the first instance, therefore this chapter will look at society's perception of mental illness and health and how such perceptions combined with current mental health legislation can impact upon the professionals who work within such constraints. It will also explore the reasons why paternalistic policies such as the 1983 Mental Health Act (Department of Health, 1983a), the care programme approach (CPA) (Department of Health, 1996b) as well as the power base of the mental health practitioner (MHP) are all deemed to be necessary measures to monitor and control people with mental health difficulties.

It will highlight the reasons why the MHP plays such an important role when implementing the 1983 Mental Health Act (MHA) as part of the care planning process. This chapter will pay particular regard to how the MHP is part of the control ethos that is currently governing the way in which people with a mental illness receive treatment and care, therefore highlighting the dilemmas that such an ethos presents to the MHP when adopting a value base that promotes recovery within individualised care planning.

In a bid to place this work within a practical context, legislation and procedures will be looked at in detail, again giving particular regard to the implications of these in relation to the role of the approved social worker (ASW)

'For Society, Mental Health is intended to control deviant behaviour, for the individual, mental health law is intended to protect a person's interests and allow him or her to obtain treatment. In both instances, problems are theoretically solved and social order is maintained' (Cockerham 1996:319).

Obviously the idealist would purport that Cockerham's view does not allow for the individual and their choices and decisions with regards to society's view of their behaviour and their consent to or compliance with any subsequent treatment. One has to ask why it is that the individual deemed to have a mental illness is not allowed a fully autonomous role in their care and well being. Horowitz (1982) states in his discussion about labelling theory that the social response to individuals and their psychiatric condition, is the major determinant of whether they will be socially identified as mentally ill. Here, the social response involves measures ranging from, at the lower end of the spectrum, taking medication and consulting a GP through to coming under the controlling nature of the 1983 MHA with all its implications.

The context

Thompson (1993) feels that applying labels to people on the basis of dubious scientific objective is a process that has distinctly oppressive connotations. Atkinson (1991) goes on to say that anyone who draws attention to themselves by their behaviour will face social labelling and stigmatising; the more extreme the behaviour, the more censorious the label. It is easy to equate certain aspects of the 1983 Act with the oppressive connotations mentioned above, such as compulsory treatment and detention.

In order to understand why society has measures in place to ensure that those deemed as mentally ill have certain restrictions placed upon them, it is necessary to understand why, in the first instance, mental illness carries with it a web of stigma. It is clear that it is society's perception of a person's behaviour that leads to them being labelled as mentally ill. This behaviour is seen to be a product of the mental illness and the actions are perceived to be symptoms. Psychiatric services are in place to ensure that such behaviour (mental illness) is dealt with in an acceptable way, acceptable to society but possibly not to the individual concerned. Indeed one major criticism of psychiatric services, and there are many, is that it loses sight of the individual. Thompson (1993), when discussing the medical approach to mental heath, states that this is a view that concentrates on the generalities at the expense of specifics. A person who is suffering from schizophrenia is known as a schizophrenic, manic depression as a manic depressive and so on. Within such a way of working it is easy to concentrate on the illness (or label) and its treatment, losing touch with the individual and the complex nature of each situation especially their recovery.

The MHP when working within the statutory framework of the 1983 MHA (Department of Health, 1983a) and on a more routine basis as part of the multidisciplinary team (MDT) contained within the community mental health team (CMHT), must be able to recognise and convey, clearly and assertively, a social or wider perspective of the individual in order to contribute fully to the assessment process. Coulshed (1991) discusses social work values such as respect for the individual, honesty and client centeredness. However these values are (obviously) not the sole property of the social worker. It is however up to the MHP (in this instance, social worker) to ensure that these values and principles pertaining to the rights of the individual are upheld. She goes on to mention that conflict within these processes of assessment and decision-making are central to success. This perspective and understanding of the individual and their particular situation must be given, indeed Coulshed identifies offering different perspectives by placing the problem in a wider frame of reference and assertively challenging a dominant view as being key skills of the social worker (or MHP). It is clear that these skills translate to all professionals working in mental health.

The ASW carrying out the assessment under the 1983 MHA must actively demonstrate these skills. Specific reference is made to them in the MHA where it states that the ASW must take into account the views of others. The MHP whilst respecting the tactics and visions of the psychiatrist, must ensure that their views are articulated, for a failure to do so could result in a medically biased approach, which whilst dealing with any immediate behaviour difficulties or symptoms, could be more effective in the longer term if a wider biopsychosocial perspective had been offered and more importantly, adopted. Hudson (1982) favours closer workings with psychiatrists without becoming uncritical, and psychiatrists' aides (social workers) need to work alongside them in order to achieve more humane and better services. A total disregard for the psychiatrists and the medical model could only mean a poorer service to the individual.

Community care and growing pressure upon hospital beds has ensured that mental health has and is, still moving away from the traditional hospital setting. Indeed certain aspects of control in the community are at the forefront of the proposed changes in mental health legislation, which will incorporate treatment in the community. Consequently the medical model is being challenged so that it now must take into account the broader aspects of the individual. Hence the complexities of the problems experienced by the individual cannot so easily be dismissed in search for the quick cure. Relationships, finance, employment, housing etc. are seen not only as causes of the individual's difficulties but also as part of the cure. It is necessary to have a clear understanding of the medical model as it features greatly in the support of individuals with mental health problems and should work with biopsychosocial models of care. MHPs must ensure that they are fully knowledgeable and conversant in both in order to provide the holistic care necessary.

The 1983 MHA also places a duty upon the ASW to take into account the views of carers and others involved with the person. As mentioned earlier, this ensures that the wider perspective is viewed at the time of assessment. The ASW must concern themselves with the broader aspects of the individual and then make sure that these aspects are heard and taken heed of during assessments and decision-making processes. The medical model with its focus on the illness and search for a cure can overlook this crucial area. The Carers (Recognition and Services) Act (Department of Health, 1995b) places a wider duty on mental health services ensuring that carers' needs are fully assessed and that services are also in place to help meet any needs identified. MHPs must ensure they are able to work alongside individuals, their carers and families in an effective and sensitive manner. The MHPs' respective Codes of Practice identify the need for respect of differences as being key facets to professional practice. Differences in relation to ethnicity, gender, religion, culture and sexual orientation are included in this and as such demand respect, awareness and sensitivity (GSCC, 2002; NMC, 2004).

The behaviour of an individual in one culture may not be perceived the same as in other cultures. For example, Horowitz (1982) reminds us that people who fall into trances and claim to communicate with supernatural beings would be labelled schizophrenic in Western societies, but in others they are placed in the valued role of Shaman or some other prophetic role. This defines accepted ways of behaving for members of a particular society (Haralambos & Holborn, 1991). It is the variation between the different societies and cultures that has implications for the practice within the field of mental health and in particular the role of the MHP. An individual from a particular cultural religion may behave in a manner that differs from the norm of the society they find themselves in. This deviation could result in the label of mental illness being attributed to them and the consequences of such an interpretation could be that the individual is compulsorily detained and treated in hospital or at the very least have to endure the stigma that comes with being labelled mentally ill.

It is therefore crucial that the MHP operates in a manner that allows for differences in culture and adopts an ethically sensitive (Dominelli, 1988) approach that is able to recognise the differences between groups and the significance of such differences. Language and communication are key areas of difference in Britain's diverse society and the use of interpreters is a necessity when communication for whatever reason is problematic. A failure to ensure that this is done by the MHP would result in an intervention operating in a discriminatory and racist manner. The MHP therefore has a duty to make themselves familiar with the different cultures that exist within their area of practice and ensure that they access resources enabling them to communicate with the individuals and their carers and families at the point of assessment, remembering that MHA assessments can be lengthy processes which are often convened quickly and often take place out of hours. The MHP, when making a decision within the framework of the MHA for possible detention or within the care programme approach (Department of Health, 1996b), must also give due consideration to the area of risk and dangerousness.

When looking at the area of detention in hospital, the MHA is very specific and details the grounds for detention under Sections 2, 3, and 4 and lays down some very clear rules regarding the protection of others. The Code of Practice (Department of Health, 1983b) also gives the ASW guidance in this area but the question still remains as to why it is that there is such an emphasis on risk and dangerousness within mental health. Earlier, this chapter briefly looked at stigma and the labelling processes and it is here that the issues of risk and dangerousness will be addressed.

When discussing the reports of failures within community care concerning people with mental health problems Bingley (1997) states that this has given weight to the *'perception among the general public that most people with mental health problems pose a serious threat to others'*. Names like Christopher Clunis (Ritchie *et al.*, 1994) have become synonymous with such failures and have not only further stigmatised people with mental health problems but have actually brought about changes in legislation resulting in further control mechanisms such as Aftercare Under Supervision (Jones, 1983) aimed at the protection of society. Here the implications for all MHPs are fairly clear; the process of labelling someone as being a danger to themselves or others can be viewed as oppressive in itself. The Royal College of Psychiatrists exacerbated the issues in their *Confidential Enquiry into Homicide and Suicide by Mentally Ill People* (RCP, 1996) stating that the inquiry's findings indicate that there are situations where suicide or homicide has involved people who might well have been detained as the Act allows. The Code of Practice (Department of Health, 1983b) tells us that the ASW should consider the needs of others to be protected from the patient (Jones, 1983).

One would assume that in the blame culture that is inherent in the realms of mental health, the MHP would actually address the risks involved and lean towards compulsory admission to hospital in order for MHPs not to be deemed responsible for such incidents. It could therefore be argued that pressure placed upon MHPs as a result of recent events involving people diagnosed as having a mental disorder and portrayed as failures in community care and psychiatric services could result in MHPs practising in a defensive manner (Haralambos & Holborn, 1991). It appears to be implied that it is better to label the individual than to take responsibility for their actions. Unfortunately, as practitioners are only too acutely aware, the media and society would certainly be quick to apportion blame to those who have been deemed to have failed in their job.

Atkinson's (1991) discussion relating to autonomy and mental health, highlights that ethical reasoning must always underpin practical answers while everyday realities will always temper moral absolutes. It is within these everyday realities that the MHP find themselves and the conflict to their value base at these times only compounds the difficulties they face in making such decisions. Perkins and Repper (1998) suggest that at these times it is the rights of the individual versus public comfort and safety and, in the views of many clinicians, the scales are heavily weighed in favour of caution in this regards. The MHP therefore is forced to work within the conflict produced by the rights of the individual as well as the rights of society as a whole. Bingley (1997), when debating decisions about detention, highlighted that there is the need for professionals to balance the need to act in the interests of the community as agents of control and custody on the one hand and to serve the interests of the individual on the other.

Would any MHP like to be described as an agent of control and custody? Surely, when the MHP is making decisions they are being guided by the interests and well-being of the individual and that the actions of the individual (as a result of their mental disorder) could seriously affect their well being, or, as mentioned earlier, in the climate within which the MHP is now operating, ensuring that they are becoming over cautious. Bingley says that caution is inherent in risk assessment, blaming the way in which the medic and community responds to serious offences being committed by discharged patients and that this response should be tempered by the reality that risk assessment is not an exact science.

Mental health professionals' ability to predict risk or dangerousness is tempered by the unpredictability of individuals who behave at times outside the parameters that rating scales and risk assessment offer. During a statutory MHA assessment the responsibility regarding the application to hospital lies with the ASW. The ASW's decision can, on one hand, deprive an individual of their liberty due to the lack of risk assessment skills combined with the aforementioned defensive practice. On the other hand the ASW could make the decision not to detain the individual; again this could be a consequence of poor assessment and/or poor assessment skills, and consequently they shoulder the blame if anything goes wrong. The community psychiatrist nurse (CPN) who leaves at home a severely depressed or acutely psychotic client shoulders the same level of responsibility for such decisions.

If, as Perkins and Repper (1998) suggest, the psychiatric hospital takes on the role of a prison designed to keep the public safe, where does the MHP fit into this? It could be argued that the MHA, and those who ensure that society is given peace of mind, state that those assessed as being mentally ill and therefore dangerous require special powers to enable them to be dealt with appropriately. Indeed Perkins and Repper state that social explanations of deviant behaviour are rarely invoked, implying a need for major social change. Explanations in terms of individual pathology are favoured. Obviously society cannot be blamed for the difficulties a person may experience and how they cope with those difficulties. However, when they step outside what is accepted by society as its norms, they are seen as different, deviant and therefore a problem. The 1983 MHA and care planning can then be seen as a means to solving this problem. The MHP could be, if one continues to work with this argument, seen as a social policeman acting on society's behalf, helping to remove and solve problems in a way deemed appropriate, thus ensuring that society is allowed to continue functioning safe in the knowledge that challenges to its equilibrium are being dealt with.

The implications with regard to the MHP and their value base, as cited earlier, are governed by the conflict which exists between attempts to promote the needs of the individual and the oppressive nature of the legislative framework provided by society and its perceptions of mental illness.

How control is achieved

Cavidino (1989) states that the area of law that deals with compulsory admission to hospital and compulsory treatment is unarguably a means of society control. Mental health legislation provides a framework within which professionals operate and this legislation has changed over the years to encompass the changing perspectives on mental health by society. The current (1983) MHA is itself subject to forthcoming amendments that will incorporate the current shift in emphasis towards the protection of the public and increased control of people with mental health problems.

Cavidino describes the 1983 MHA as a professional discretion law, stating that it contains wide and vague definitions of mental disorder and criteria for detention that are to be interpreted and applied by professionals in the shape of doctors and social workers. The use of the MHA in compulsorily admitting people to hospital accounts for a small percentage of admissions and it is in fact the informal admission to hospital (1983 MHA:Section 131) that accounts for the majority of admissions. The Code of Practice (Department of Health, 1983b) defines the informal patient as someone who has arrived on the ward and who has offered no resistance to the admission procedure. It is in this area that issues such as capability and competence with regard to consent to treatment come to the fore. The most recent and notable of these was the Bournewood Judgement (O'Hanlon, 1998). In brief, this involved an autistic man with learning disabilities who was incapable of consenting to treatment and was an informal patient. It was felt that because of his lack of consent the man should have been detained under the 1983 MHA in order to receive treatment lawfully. The House of Lords however decided that treatment was justified by the common law of necessity and the judgement was overturned (Macgregor-Morris *et al.*, 2001).

One is able to distinguish that individuals detained under the MHA have certain safeguards and rights afforded to them, but that the informal patient does not, e.g. the provisions set out in part IV of the MHA relating to the issue of consent to treatment. It is clear therefore that the informal patient is potentially open to abuse from the psychiatric system and it is here that the MHP, once again, has a role in establishing that patients and their families and carers are fully involved in their treatment and participate in the decision-making processes concerned with their care.

Under existing mental health legislation doctors have holding powers that enable them to detain informal patients for up to 72 hours in hospital, in order for a formal MHA assessment to take place (1983 MHA:Section 5(2)). The holding powers are normally used when an informal patient is asking to be discharged from hospital, or is threatening to leave (Cavidino, 1989). When, during a mental health assessment, the MHP concludes that an informal admission to hospital is appropriate and acceptable to the individual, they should remember that this might change if the individual decides that they want to leave hospital once there. Is it right not to mention this to the individual who agrees to come to hospital informally? Surely the MHP with their biases towards the rights of the person, would make them fully aware of the facts or would it be seen to be more oppressive to have to use the MHA assessment as opposed to the individual deciding themselves to come into hospital informally and remaining ignorant of Section 5(2) of the 1983 MHA? Article 5(4) of the Human Rights Act states that *'everyone who is deprived of his liberty by arrest or*

*detention shall be entitled to take proceedings by which the lawfulness of this deten-
tion shall be decided speedily'* (Macgregor-Morris *et al.*, 2001). People detained
under section 5(2) MHA have no right of appeal and as such the use of this
holding power, it could be argued, is in breach of the detained person's basic
human rights.

Cavidino (1989) does argue in favour of informal admission saying that it is
usually preferable in every way to compulsory treatment. However does this
include the level of coercion that could be present when an individual agrees
to an informal admission to prevent being sectioned? Having already explored
the difficulties that exist for the MHP in presenting a different and often conflicting perspective to the medically dominated service, it is necessary to state
again that any failure to ensure the involvement of individuals and their carers
and families only lends weight to the oppressive practice that permeates the
psychiatric system. In 1996 the Department of Health published *Building Bridges:
A Guide to the Arrangements For Inter-Agency Workings For The Care and Protection Of Severely Mentally Ill People* (Department of Health, 1996a). This was
a response to the Inquiry surrounding the care and treatment of Christopher
Clunis (Ritchie *et al.*, 1994). The document provided a framework for agencies
working within mental health, in which the aim was for them to forge closer
working links, ensuring that clients did not slip though the net.

The main elements of *Building Bridges* were the guidelines for the care
programme approach (which was originally introduced in 1991) and the introduction of the supervision register. The care programme approach (CPA)
(Department of Health, 1996b) is still the mainstay with regard to procedures
governing the collaborative and inter-agency care of people with mental health
problems. Its implementation and practice differs from authority to authority.
The principles of CPA however, remain the same: multidisciplinary assessments, formulation of a care plan, appointment of a key worker/care coordinator to monitor the care plan and to keep in touch with the client and,
finally, regular reviews for the client's care. Although the significance given to
CPA may vary, it is the role of the key worker that contains implications for
the MHP within the community mental health team (CMHT).

There is a responsibility for the identified key worker to monitor the client
and this may be the only contact the client has with psychiatric services apart
from the occasional and brief outpatient appointment with the psychiatrist.
The MHP as care coordinator takes on the responsibility of monitoring the
mental health of the individual and feeding back any concerns to the CMHT.
In the current climate that exists within mental health, the work of the MHP
lies heavily on this monitoring of the client. A busy MHP with a varied and
complex caseload would, as mentioned earlier, possibly adopt a defensive stance
in relation to their work, invoking statutory powers in times of crisis etc. rather
than attempting to work through difficulties with the client in the community
because of the risks involved. Again the MHP is in conflict with their value
base that respects the choice of individuals on one hand and has the heavy
weight of responsibility and accountability on the other.

In recent years there have been proposals and developments within mental health which have attempted to further legalise the control of individuals with mental health problems in the community. The Royal College of Psychiatrists (RCP, 1996) proposed the introduction of community treatment orders (CTOs), which would allow for the compulsory treatment of people outside of hospital or if such treatment was reduced, for patients to be brought into hospital to allow treatment to be administered. This, as one would expect, had and still has, many critics. Bean and Mounses (1993) felt that CTOs were an ill-considered attempt to transfer the whole of the hospital into the community. Whilst Cavidino (1991) felt that the proposal was flawed because of the Civil Libertarian concern that it would lead to unjustified infringements on the freedom of individuals to decide for themselves whether or not to accept medication. Cavidino's argument equates nicely with the MHP position, in that, a patient who requires active treatment should be in hospital for this and once they are discharged from hospital can they not have the choice as to the need for continued treatment? The arguments against were strong enough to stop the proposal. Cavidino (1989) also argued that just because the care of psychiatric patients is moving out into the community it does not mean that powers of formal control have to move out with it. Surely this is an argument that remains valid in light of current thinking around the control of people with mental health problems in the community.

In the early 1990s there were calls for a community supervision order similar to the CTO and in 1995 the Government put forward the Mental Health (Patients in Community) Act (Department of Health, 1995a) and with this came aftercare under supervision or the supervised discharge order. This amended Section 25 of the 1983 MHA. In brief, this allowed the responsible medical officer (RMO) to complete an application for a supervised discharge order (SDO) after receiving one recommendation from the ASW and another from a community responsible medical officer (normally the GP). It requires a person subject to the SDO to reside at a specified place, attend specified places at certain times for training, treatment etc and allows access to their place of residence to an authorised person. These powers are similar to those laid out in section 7 (Guardianship) of the 1983 MHA; however, the supervisor under the SDO, who would normally be a MHP, also has the power to take and convey a person to a specified place. It is this power that has caused most concern among mental health professionals. For example, surely one cannot expect a MHP to forcibly convey an unwilling client to a place for an appointment. The SDO like the guardianship order can specify that an individual must attend a place for treatment, however once at the place there is no requirement for the individual to take any treatment offered. A failure on the part of the individual to comply with the SDO can result in a review of their care and possible compulsory readmission to hospital under the 1983 MHA.

The position of the supervisor under SDO, like the key worker under CPA, presents the MHP as some kind of social policeman or, as suggested earlier, an agent of control and custody: a role so far removed from the aspects of social work and nursing, that it is difficult to equate the two.

Prior to its introduction Eastman (1997) felt that such legislation would fail in its stated purpose because it attempts to substitute legal rules for resources. The intention of the Bill is clinically unachievable because legal control of treatment and living arrangements cannot practically be extended into the community. With regard to the power to take and convey, he felt that this was anti therapeutic; believing that no matter who was tasked with such a power the result would be inconsistent with properly exercised assertive care. The use of the SDO has been limited and the reasons for this may be a testament to some of the arguments suggested above. He gives a possible reason for this by suggesting that a core problem is that it is not practically possible to exert legal control over patients in the community. If MHPs were willing to exert such controls over a client the difficulties brought about by such actions would negate any level of effectiveness for the service, the MHP and, more importantly, the client. Surely adequate resources would diminish the need for legal powers or further aspects of control. What people need is, according to Cavidino (1989), appropriate accommodation and good psychiatry that they will accept. Eastman goes on to say that there should be a reciprocal arrangement and that current services and legislation are failing to offer the right to adequately resourced care in exchange for further infringement of civil rights. MacPherson *et al.* (1997) in their work looking at drug refusal amongst long term patients in the community concluded that rather than developing additional sanctions, this most disabled group of patients are in need of more intensive support, support which may in itself be an effective intervention.

It could therefore be seen that what is needed is a properly resourced mental health service, which would allow individuals to exercise choice and control with regards to their care, working in conjunction with services instead of against them. In view of continued pressure for some form of CTO and events involving people with mental health problems being portrayed negatively in the media, the Government was, at the time of writing, reviewing the Mental Health Act. Paul Boeteng (Labour MP and former Health Minister) when announcing the review, stated that: *'the law must make it clear that non compliance with agreed treatment programmes is not an option. New legislation is needed to ensure a proper balance between the interests of the public and the rights of the individual'* (MIND, 1998). The review of the existing legislation governing Mental Health services was a long drawn out process resulting in an, initial, ill fated Mental Health Bill. This contained a number of proposals – some more controversial than others. However the most controversial of them all was once again the notion of compulsory treatment in the community. This was widely and vigorously criticised by all the mental health agencies from user organisations such as MIND through to the Royal College of Psychiatrists. Other proposals included widening the definition of mental disorder to make the legislation more inclusive as well as change to the role of the ASW and allowing other professions to become approved mental health practitioners.

Earlier in 2006 the Government finally announced that the new Mental Health Bill was not to be introduced and in its place would be a number of amendments to the existing 1983 Mental Health Act. The broadening of the definition of mental disorder is one of these amendments as is the removal of treatability for people diagnosed with personality disorders. This will allow for the Mental Health Act to be used without the clause *'any such treatment is likely to alleviate or prevent a deterioration in the condition'* (Jones, 1983) having to be considered.

However of greatest concern to MHPs must be the use of compulsory treatment in the community, which as discussed earlier in this chapter, will significantly change the relationship between MHPs and the individuals subject to such powers. Its implementation can only lead to a more potentially coercive and controlling system when in truth mental health services are attempting to move towards a more collaborative and empowering method of care delivery. What's the point of the Advance Directive if the individual it concerns knows that failure to comply with treatment at home will be monitored and acted upon by the MHP who is meant to be encouraging them towards recovery? What use is the care plan that is drawn up as part of an engaging process if some members of the team have more power and control than others? What value does society place on a legislation that coerces individuals experiencing mental health difficulties in order to make them fall into line and comply?

Not only will MHPs have to contend with the current conflicts with existing legislation during MHA assessments and as key workers/supervisors under CPA and supervised discharge orders respectively, they will also have to monitor the treatment compliance of individuals and act accordingly when such compliance is in doubt. The age of the therapeutic relationship will be long gone. Such duties will challenge key elements of their training whereby they will be working in a manner that could be perceived as being overtly oppressive and coercive, which is at the extremes of the current remit of social workers and nurses in other areas of practice.

Conclusion

This chapter has illustrated why the MHP forms a crucial part in the care planning process and the delivery of care and support to those individuals experiencing mental health difficulties, it also highlights the conflict that exists between the MHPs statutory duties, their training and their respective professional, inherent value base. The oppressive nature of mental health legislation and the blatant disregard for the individual's autonomy with regards to control and compulsion are the key components in the difficulties that face the MHP. The pressure in terms of risk assessment and dangerousness coupled with the blame culture that exists within the media and society further compound these difficulties.

Leff (1997) suggests that not all violence by psychiatrically ill people is predictable and therefore avoidable. There will inevitably be a price to pay for a system of care that gives patients the degree of autonomy and freedom they seek and appreciate. The alternative is to lock up large numbers of people to secure a very small minority who cannot be identified with any certainty. The choice between these alternatives is a societal one. It appears that society is indeed choosing its alternative. It would also appear that the mental health professional would continue to manage the balance between care and control, attempting to balance the basic needs and human rights of individuals experiencing mental health problems with the wider needs of control and order placed upon them by society. This ethical dilemma exists in current practice and will continue to exist with changes to legislation only compounding the situation.

The value bases underpinning the practice of MHPs are key to this balancing act and ensure that in whatever shape or form mental health services are delivered, the MHP will continue to practise and respond to risk to the person, others and society, in the least judgemental, least oppressive and least discriminatory manner possible.

References

Atkinson, J. (1991). Autonomy and Mental Health. In: Barker, P.J. & Baldwin, S. (eds). *Ethical Issues in Mental Health*. London: Chapman and Hall. **(7)**, 103–126.

Bean, P. & Mounses, P. (1993). *Discharged from Mental Hospitals*, Macmillan. London.

Bingley, W. (1997). Assessing Dangerousness: Protecting The Interests Of Patients. *British Journal of Psychiatry (Supplement).* **(32)**, 28–29.

Cavidino, M. (1989). *Mental Health Law in Context*. Aldershot: Dartmouth.

Cavidino, M. (1991). Community Control. *Journal of Social Welfare and Family Law.* 258–268.

Cockerham, W.C. (1996). *Sociology of Mental Disorder*. London: Prentice-Hall.

Coulshed, V. (1991). *Social Work Practice*. London: Macmillan Press. (2nd edn).

Department of Health (1983a). *Mental Health Act*. London: HMSO.

Department of Health (1983b). *Mental Health Act: Code of Practice*. London: HMSO.

Department of Health (1995a). *Mental Health (Patients in Community) Act*. London: HMSO.

Department of Health (1995b). *The Carers (Recognition and Services) Act*. London: HMSO.

Department of Health (1996a). *Building Bridges: A Guide to the Arrangements For Inter-Agency Workings For The Care and Protection Of Severely Mentally Ill People*. London: The Stationery Office.

Department of Health (1996b). *Care Programme Approach (CPA)*. London: The Stationery Office.

Dominelli, L. (1988). *Anti-racist Social Work: A Challenge for White Practitioners and Educators*. London: Macmillan Education.

Eastman, N. (1997). The Mental Health (Patients in the Community) Act 1995: A Clinical Analysis. *British Journal of Psychiatry*. **(170)**, 492–496.

General Social Care Council (2002). *Code of Practice*. London: GSCC.

Haralambos, M. & Holborn, N. (1991). *Sociology and Themes and Perspectives*. London: Collins Educational. (3rd ed).

Horowitz, A. (1982). *Social Control of Mental Illness (Studies on Law and Social Control).* Oxford: Academic Press.

Hudson, B.L. (1982). *Social Work and Psychiatric Patients.* London: Macmillan Press.

Jones, R. (1983). *Mental Health Act Manual.* London: Sweet and Maxwell.

Leff, J. (1997). *Care in the Community: Illusion or Reality,* Wiley & Sons, Chichester.

Macgregor-Morris, R., Ewbank, J. & Birmingham, L. (2001). Potential Impact Of The Human Rights Act On Psychiatric Practice: The Best Of British Values? *British Medical Journal.* **(322)**, 848–850.

MacPherson, R., Jerrom, B. & Hughes, A. (1997). Drug Refusal Among Schizophrenic Patients Treated in the Community. *Journal of Mental Health.* **6(2)**, 141–148.

MIND (1998). *People in Mind.* London: Mind Publications.

Nursing and Midwifery Council (2004). *The NMC Code of Professional Conduct.* London: NMC.

O'Hanlon, K. (1998). R.V. Bournemouth Community and Mental Health NHS Trust. *All England Law Reports.* 289–293.

Perkins, R. & Repper, J. (1998). *Dilemmas in Community Mental Health Practice.* Abingdon: Radcliffe Medical Press.

Ritchie, J., Dick, D. & Lingham, R. (1994). *The Report of the Inquiry into the Care and Treatment of Christopher Clunis.* London: HMSO.

Royal College of Psychiatry (1996). *Report of the Confidential Inquiry into Homicide and Suicides by Mentally Ill People.* London: RCP.

Thompson, N. (1993). *Anti-Discriminatory Practice.* London: Macmillan Press.

Chapter 3

Therapeutic Risk and Care Planning in Mental Health

David Duffy

Introduction

Risk can be defined as the probability that negative consequences will follow an action or as the likelihood that particular adverse events will occur (Woods, 2001:85). A therapeutic risk simply involves weighing the likelihood of such negative consequences against potential therapeutic benefits. It is a rational decision made with the potential for either positive or negative outcomes and which seems worthwhile not only because of the possible benefits but also because it is believed to be reasonably predictable that the outcome will be positive.

This chapter will explore the concept of therapeutic risk in the context of mental health care planning. The historical and cultural background to therapeutic risk will be briefly summarised, approaches to measuring and predicting risk will be outlined, and the chapter will conclude with a consideration of therapeutic risk taking in relation to the care planning process.

Risk and litigation

It is often said that we live in an increasingly risk averse society. Tony Blair has himself stated that

'Public bodies, in fear of litigation, act in highly risk-averse and peculiar ways. We have had a local authority removing hanging baskets for fear that they might fall on someone's head, even though no such accident had occurred in the 18 years they had been hanging there. A village in the Cotswolds was required to pull up a seesaw because it was judged a danger under an EU Directive on Playground Equipment for Outside Use. This was despite the fact that no accidents had occurred on it' (Blair, 2005).

How has such a situation arisen? It can be seen positively, as an outcome of greater public awareness of personal rights and a greater assertiveness in challenging abuse and neglect. It is essential that complaints against public services are effectively investigated, not least because consumer (patient, service user or client) feedback plays a vital role in quality assurance. On the other hand, the compensation culture is facilitated by the fear of costly litigation and the readiness of lawyers to support claims. In the field of mental health care, Mr Blair's words are pertinent: '*A risk-averse public sector will stifle creativity and deny to many the opportunities to be creative while supplying a few with compensation payments*' (Blair, 2005).

Clinical negligence

The scale of clinical negligence litigation today illustrates Tony Blair's comments about the growing compensation culture. In 1997–98, £50 million was paid out in response to clinical negligence claims. Only a few years later, in 2003–04, the NHS Litigation Authority states that this had risen to no less than £422.5 million. These figures include both damages paid to patients and the legal costs borne by the NHS. For settlements up to £50 000, the legal costs of reaching the settlement were usually greater than the damages awarded. Incidentally, many clinical negligence claims never actually reach court. The NHS Litigation Authority reports that since its inception in 1995, 35% of the clinical negligence claims that it handled were abandoned by the claimant, 43% were settled out of court, while only 1.5% were settled in court in favour of the patient. A further 0.5% of claims were settled in court in favour of the NHS and 20% remain outstanding (NHS Litigation Authority, nd a).

Clinical negligence litigation hinges on the legal test for the standard of care known as the Bolam Test. This derives from a famous mental health issue that came to court in 1957, the case of Bolam v Friern Hospital Management Committee (Jones, 2003). In 1954, Mr John Bolam was admitted to Friern Mental Hospital suffering from depression. Electro-convulsive therapy (ECT) was carried out without the administration of any relaxant medication or manual restraint and Mr Bolam sustained hip fractures as a result. Mr Bolam alleged that the hospital was negligent in failing to administer him a suitable relaxant drug before the electric current was passed through his brain, failing to provide manual control whilst he was fitting and failing to warn him of the risks of ECT. Both parties obtained expert reports. Both medical experts agreed that there were many doctors opposed to the use of relaxant drugs on the basis that, in some cases, the more restraint there was, the greater was the likelihood of sustaining a fracture.

The judge had to decide whether the hospital had been negligent as Mr Bolam claimed. Displaying the male-oriented language of that time, he stated that, where a situation occurs which involves the use of some special skill or competence, as in the issue of the appropriate use of ECT, then the test as to whether there has been negligence or not is *not* the test of the man on the top of a Clapham omnibus, because he does not have the special skill, but is the test of a man who does have the skill.

Accordingly, a doctor was not guilty of negligence if he acted in accordance with a practice accepted as proper by a responsible body of medical men skilled in that particular art even though some others would take a different view. In today's language, the requirement would be for a responsible body of clinicians to accept a practice as proper. However, although the Bolam Test became accepted in law, the later case of Bolitho v City and Hackney Health Authority in 1993 (Jones, 2003) determined that judges had the power to choose between different clinical opinions and to reject an opinion that seemed to them to be logically indefensible. In other words, as well as showing that an action would be accepted by a responsible body of peers, a defendant against a claim of clinical negligence would also have to be able to demonstrate that the action was logical in the circumstances.

One positive outcome of clinical negligence litigation is that health services are ever more aware of the need to demonstrate that clinical decisions are made reasonably and that, if challenged, they would stand up to legal scrutiny informed by Bolam and Bolitho (Hewitt 2004:156–158). This means that permanent written evidence has to be provided and maintained through accurate and complete clinical records that document evidence of reasonable practice (NHS Litigation Authority, nd b).

Risk and regulation

It is not only the fear of litigation that can impact on attitudes to therapeutic risk. Regulation of clinical activity has also markedly increased in recent years. One of the main ways in which risk is managed in any context is through regulation. This is true of society in general, which uses laws and policing to minimise potential harm to its citizens; it is true of professional bodies such as the General Medical Council, the Nursing and Midwifery Council and the General Social Care Council which have the power to strike individuals from professional registers if they are found guilty of professional misconduct; and it is also true of organisations, which will seek to ensure cost-effectiveness by regulating the behaviour and performance of their employees. Organisations that provide public health care are now more intensively regulated than at any time in history, and it is in this context that therapeutic risk must be considered.

Mental health patients have not always been stereotyped as a risk to others. In a mainly rural society, people with mental illness were often accepted and treated charitably (for a history of mental health care, see Roberts, 1981). As the number of people living in cities increased, a large population of urban mentally ill developed. In this environment they had a greater chance of causing disruption or simply failing to blend in. This led to the building of the early asylums that simply removed the mentally ill from society in the same way that prisons did with criminals. By the 18th Century, institutions like

Bethlehem Hospital, Bedlam, were allowing visitors to pay a penny to observe their patients as a form of freak show. This outsider status aroused fear and rejection and a long-standing belief, still evident today, that people with mental health problems are automatically a risk to others.

Along with continuing social prejudice, however, insanity came to be medicalised, seen as a disease to be diagnosed and potentially cured, and in 1948 the asylums were absorbed into the newly formed National Health Service and became large psychiatric hospitals. These total institutions have in turn given way in recent decades to a wide range of community-based provision, of which in-patient care is now only one aspect. As part of a major public service, mental health care is nowadays subjected to the same kinds of centralised quality control as other public services such as education. This is partly in response to continuing Government drives to ensure standardised, cost-effective health care in response to demands from the electorate. In pursuit of this aim, targets are set and their achievement is monitored by central bodies such as the Healthcare Commission. Regulation is also driven by the requirements of the clinical negligence scheme for Trusts (CNST), which is a pay-as-you-go mutual pooling scheme aimed to assist Trusts to meet the costs of clinical negligence litigation. CNST will only provide financial cover for services that can practically demonstrate that they meet a wide range of standards that must be met to confirm that risk is being effectively managed (Table 3.1). Currently, mental health Trusts are required to meet 8 standards before they

Table 3.1   Clinical negligence scheme for Trusts standards.

Standard 1	Learning from experience	Trusts must show that the organisation learns from adverse incidents
Standard 2	Response to serious incidents involving/ relating to service users	Emphasising the need to engage effectively with service users and carers following an incident
Standard 3	Communication between professionals and service users	Ensuring that service users are fully informed about treatments and procedures
Standard 4	Clinical information and care records	Record keeping must be appropriately maintained
Standard 5	Induction and staff procedures	Ensuring staff competency
Standard 6	Training	Demonstrating that staff are able to fulfil their function safely and effectively
Standard 7	Care processes	Systematic development of organisational policies and procedures
Standard 8	Communication between professionals involved in the care of service users	Ensuring that staffing levels are appropriate and care is effectively coordinated.

can be accepted by CNST. These standards reflect the areas where Trusts are seen as most vulnerable to litigation (NHS litigation authority, nd c).

Inquiries

CNST standards are in turn based on national guidance on managing risk. Such guidance has often emerged as a result of major inquiries into mental health care associated with tragedies involving homicide or suicide. One of the most influential was the inquiry into the care and treatment of Christopher Clunis (Ritchie *et al.*, 1994). Christopher Clunis killed Jonathan Zito when he was waiting for a tube train at Finsbury Park. The subsequent inquiry identified a long list of errors and missed opportunities in the care of this patient, stretching back over many years. He had a long history of violence, institutional care and non-compliance with treatment programmes (Ritchie *et al.*, 1994). The inquiry report was particularly scathing in its criticism of the poor co-ordination between all agencies involved in Christopher Clunis' care despite the introduction of the care programme approach (CPA) in 1991, which was intended to ensure seamless planning and provision of healthcare between services and agencies. The report led to renewed attempts to operationalise the CPA effectively. The main elements of the CPA are:

- systematic arrangements for assessing the health and social needs of people accepted into specialist mental health services
- the formulation of a care plan which identifies the health and social care required from a variety of providers
- the appointment of a care coordinator to keep in close touch with the service user and to monitor and coordinate care
- regular review and, where necessary, agreed changes to the care plan.

Problems in implementing the CPA were addressed in 1999, as part of the Government's reform of mental health services. Case management, the approach to mental health care used by local authorities, was integrated with the CPA into a single system featuring:

- a single point of referral
- a unified health and social care assessment process
- coordination of the respective roles and responsibilities of each agency in the system
- access, through a single process, to the support and resources of both health and social care.

There have been many other important inquiries that have influenced attitudes to risk. One such was the report of the Committee of Inquiry into the events leading up to and surrounding the fatal incident at the Edith Morgan

Centre, Torbay, on 1 September 1993 (Blom-Cooper *et al.*, 1995). The incident involved a mental health patient, Andrew Robinson, who stabbed to death an occupational therapist, Georgina Robinson. The inquiry found that:

- the fatal incident was inherently unpredictable
- for reasons connected with Andrew Robinson's unlawful absence from the Edith Morgan Centre, the homicidal attack was preventable
- there was a likelihood of some dangerous conduct by Andrew Robinson as a consequence of the removal of a previous Restriction Order by a Mental Health Review Tribunal
- a previous guardianship application could and should have been renewed
- there were deficiencies in the mode and manner of communication.

The report also contains a significant chapter on the role of risk assessment and management in care planning. Having shown that the staff in this case had failed to detect Andrew Robinson's risk of violence through their failure to explore his past history, it emphatically states that past behaviour is the best predictor of future behaviour and recommends that the circumstances of any past violence should be rigorously examined.

A further, highly influential example of the inquiry process is provided by the five yearly *Report of the Confidential Inquiry into Suicide and Homicide by People with Mental Illness, Safety First* (Department of Health, 2001). Information about every case of suicide or homicide by mental health service users is reported to the confidential inquiry team, which has now compiled an extensive database of evidence and used it to provide recommendations for safe practice in mental health care. Since this is the best evidence available on what makes a safe service Trusts are now audited annually on their compliance with the recommendations of Safety First by the Healthcare Commission.

Among the many standards which must now be met as a result of this inquiry, all mental health staff who work with people at risk must be trained in risk management every three years, while, because most suicides have been found to occur in the period after discharge, in-patients who have been at risk must be followed up within seven days of discharge. The inquiry finding that the main suicidal method is hanging has led to a requirement that likely ligature points in in-patient areas must be removed or covered. This addresses impulsive suicidal acts that make use of immediate suicidal means rather than planned suicides that need to be prevented by effective risk assessment and therapeutic relationships.

Managing therapeutic risk

The aim of mental health care and treatment is to help to restore the person as far as possible to independent functioning. The recovery of independence inevitably involves a degree of risk. However, risk can be reduced as far as possible without compromising the need to allow the person appropriate opportunities to act independently.

Staff

Mental health staff themselves can reduce therapeutic risk by ensuring that their own practice is of an optimum standard. Service users have a right to expect that the risks involved in their care and treatment are minimised by the fact that they are in the hands of staff who are skilled and knowledgeable in their field. It is reasonable for them to expect that staff receive clinical supervision rather than practising in a vacuum; that they are continually developing as professionals through appraisal and learning; that their practice is supported by evidence, via clinical guidelines and protocols; that they communicate effectively with each other and record their actions and observations; that they will involve service users themselves as far as possible in their own care; and that they take note of and learn from adverse incidents.

Systems

Effective multi-disciplinary and multi-agency working is essential if risks are to be minimised. Team development can be used to promote effective communication and decision-making that makes best use of the varied skills, knowledge and experience of the different team members. This was a lesson that the Georgina Robinson Inquiry Report (Blom-Cooper *et al.*, 1995) drew – had information from all the professionals in the team involved been heeded, the tragic outcome might have been avoided. If the care programme approach is to be used effectively to minimise risk, it is essential that involvement and communication between mental health workers and primary care workers such as the GP, together with other agencies such as housing and the police, is a reality rather than a paper exercise.

The risk management cycle

Given this context of increased regulation and concerns about complaints and litigation, mental health practitioners face a challenge in seeking to balance the imperatives of safe and defensible care and treatment with the need to avoid paternalistically over-protecting the mental health service user, for whom recovery of functioning can only be achieved by appropriate therapeutic risk-taking. Defensible practice, proceeding responsibly on the basis of evidence, is not defensive practice, aimed at avoiding harm at the expense of the person's recovery of independence, which would be the opposite of therapeutic. Mental health staff can achieve this balance by approaching therapeutic risk systematically (Table 3.2). The process can be seen as a simple and logical cycle.

Table 3.2 Systematic risk identification.

Identify the potential for risk	Mental health service users are at risk not just for suicide or self-harm but also for violence, self-neglect, abuse and other kinds of harm. Each person must be approached as an individual who may face a particular and fluctuating range of risks in different circumstances.
Assess the risk	Risk assessment is not an exact science. While a wide range of risk assessment tools have been produced and published, in themselves they will yield too many false positives (i.e. predict too many people to be at risk who are not) and so are more of a help rather than an alternative to subjective decision-making. However, risk assessment should always be approached systematically to ensure that all potential risk factors are considered. Both actuarial risk factors, such as social group, gender or age, and clinical risk factors related to the person's mental health problem, past history and mood need to be included in any comprehensive risk assessment.
Rate the risk	Quantitative risk assessment tools do exist in mental health. More usually, however, risk assessment is descriptive and levels of risk may be expressed as being high, medium or low. If this is so, it is essential that understanding of the meaning of these adjectives is shared among a clinical team, since subjective interpretations of particular words vary widely and there is a danger of misunderstanding.
Take preventive action	Action plans to address risk need to be integrated with the rest of the person's care, and for mental health service users should come within the standards of the Care Programme Approach – the care plan should be co-ordinated and monitored by a single co-ordinator and it should be shared with the service user. This is the stage where the balance between care and control can be responsibly addressed. Preventive actions need to be considered in the context of therapeutic actions: for example, a period of home leave may seem to be essential for the person's recovery, but at the same time a risk may well be involved in allowing the person to spend time away from the clinical setting.
Evaluate the success of preventive action	Risk management measures must be continuously monitored for effectiveness and if they are not effective must be changed.
Re-visit the potential for risk	The risk management cycle always needs to return to its beginning. Risks vary and fluctuate, one risk may be replaced with another, or risks may have permanently reduced.

(Doyle, 1999).

Many of the factors involved in therapeutic risk and care planning which have been discussed in this chapter can be illustrated using a case study:

Case study 3.1 Peter: therapeutic risk.

Peter has a 2-year history of severe treatment resistant depression. He has a past history of self-harm, including two suicide attempts, involving trying to throw himself in front of a car (2 years ago) and apparently trying to hang himself (a year ago), although on this occasion he did so when he could be interrupted by his wife.

Peter has had several admissions to the ward, and each time has made sufficient progress to be discharged back home. However, he quickly becomes challenging to his family, who fear that he will take his own life and his wife had been threatening to divorce him during his present admission.

Peter has now been on the ward for 3 months. He is detained under Section 3 of the Mental Health Act. He has been under varying levels of observation during that time, including several periods of constant observation to prevent him harming himself and several periods of intermittent observation. He continues to say that his life has no meaning, that he is a burden to everyone and that he should be allowed to kill himself. As he has been relatively stable in recent days, staff have been trying to take therapeutic risks by allowing him unescorted time off the ward but not out of the building in order to go to occupational therapy sessions. Yesterday the nurse in charge, with the agreement of the responsible medical officer, allowed Peter to go for a short walk on his own in the grounds. Although there is a busy road nearby, he returned at the agreed time with no apparent problems and reported having enjoyed the fresh air.

On arriving on duty today Peter asks the nursing staff if he can have another walk on his own. He appears to be relatively calm in mood.

Discussion

In terms of the risk management cycle:

1) There is a risk to Peter: he has a number of risk factors for self-harm and suicide.
2) The risk is immediate and has the potential to be fatal.
3) From the information available, the risk appears to be medium. However, his calm mood may be assumed in order to secure an opportunity to leave the ward, or he may genuinely be feeling calm because he intends to end his problems soon by taking his own life.
4) Preventive options available include refusing leave, allowing escorted leave only, or seeking further assessment before making a decision.
5) Whatever decision is made, the decision must be evaluated. At some stage Peter will have to be allowed leave and a full record must be made of what happened to inform his future care.
6) The multidisciplinary team should discuss the issue and plans made for the next time Peter asks for leave.

In order to recover independent functioning, Peter needs to be allowed graduated periods of autonomy. He could be protected from self-harm to a large extent by being obliged to remain on the ward, but this would probably be at the cost of his confidence and it is likely that it would become increasingly stressful for him. The staff have a duty to try to promote Peter's recovery of independence while at the same time ensuring that the risks to him are minimised. As a self determining individual, it is possible that Peter could use a period of leave to harm himself, for example by hanging or throwing himself in front of a car as he has in the past. If he did the staff could claim that they were acting in his best interests and that any reasonable body of mental health practitioners would have acted as they did (the Bolam Test). However, in order to justify their claim, the staff would need to demonstrate that, like any reasonable body of practitioners, they had tried to minimise the risks inherent in allowing him a period of leave. They could do this firstly by ensuring that the decision to allow him leave complied with the terms of the Mental Health Act: as Peter was a detained patient, the responsible medical officer would have to sign a section 17 form specifying the conditions of his leave. There may be other Trust policies that would need to be considered. Further, the staff should carry out and record an individual risk assessment, since risks fluctuate and they could not rely only on his behaviour the previous day or on the actions of other staff. It would be essential that the staff member who made this assessment had up-to-date training in risk management. Finally, in terms of managing the risk, staff have the option of refusing leave (with an explanation to Peter), of agreeing to leave with an escort, or of allowing unescorted leave. In the end, a decision has to be made, and it is possible that the decision could have tragic consequences. Nonetheless, the staff are acting responsibly and in Peter's interests if they take a therapeutic risk which they can demonstrate was justified.

Conclusion

As this chapter has shown, despite the pressures of potential litigation and the demands of national guidance and regulations, it is always in the interests of the well being of mental health service users that appropriate therapeutic risks are not compromised by defensive practice. By approaching care and treatment systematically, with an awareness of legal, professional and policy requirements and through constantly maintaining their own professional competencies mental health staff can ensure that care planning across professional and organisational boundaries has the potential to be both therapeutically effective and – not defensive but *defensible*.

References

Blair, T. (2005). *Common Sense Culture Not Compensation Culture*. Available at: http://www.number-10.gov.uk/output/Page7562.asp

Blom-Cooper, L., Hally, H. & Murphy, E. (1995). *The Falling Shadow: One Patient's Mental Health Care 1978–1993*. London: Duckworth.

Department of Health (2001). *Safety First: Five-Year Report Of The National Confidential Inquiry Into Suicide and Homicide By People With Mental Illness*. London: The Stationery Office.

Doyle, M. (1999). Organisational Responses To Crisis and Risk: Issues and Implications For Mental Health Nurses. In: Ryan, T. (ed). *Managing Risk in Mental Health Nursing*. London: Stanley Thornes. **(4)**, 40–56.

Hewitt, D. (2004). Assisting Self-Harm: Some Legal Considerations. In: Duffy, D. & Ryan, T. (eds). *New Approaches to Preventing Suicide*. London: Jessica Kingsley Publishers. **(10)**, 148–166.

Jones, M. (2003). *Medical Negligence*. London: Sweet & Maxwell. (3rd edn).

NHS Litigation Authority (nd a). *About the NHS Litigation Authority*. Available at: http://www.nhsla.com/home.htm

NHS Litigation Authority (nd b). *Clinical Negligence Litigation* Available at: http://www.nhsla.com/Clinicians/

NHS Litigation Authority (nd c). *Risk Management*. Available at: http://www.nhsla.com/riskmanagement

Ritchie, J., Dick, D. & Lingham, R. (1994). *The Report Of The Inquiry Into The Care and Treatment Of Christopher Clunis*. London: HMSO.

Roberts, A. (1981). *Mental Health History Timeline*. Middlesex University. Available at: http://www.mdx.ac.uk/www/study/mhhtim.htm

Woods, P. (2001). Risk Assessment and Management. In: Dale, C., Thompson, T. & Woods, P. (eds). *Forensic Mental Health Practice: Issues in Practice*. London: Baillière Tindall. **(5)**, 85–98.

Chapter 4

Care Planning across Professional and Organisational Boundaries

Alan Pringle and Richard Brittle

Introduction

This chapter focuses on the differences and common features of the professions as they contribute to mental health care planning. The acquisition of the ten shared essential capabilities will be explored in relation to practitioners developing the necessary skills and competence in multidisciplinary care planning.

The organisational and professional differences that minimise effective team working shall be highlighted and the features of effective teams shall be identified. It will be argued that an integrated team approach to care planning in mental health will improve the experiences for service users and carers.

Government documents such as the NHS Plan (Department of Health, 2000) and the National Service Framework for Mental Health (Department of Health, 1999) promote the importance of effective inter-professional working to ensure a high quality of care. Jefferies and Chan (2004) suggest that the general commitment to this concept is because multidisciplinary team (MDT) working has been shown to be the main mechanism to ensure truly holistic care. This, they feel, is because it helps provide patients with a seamless service throughout their disease trajectory and across the boundaries of primary, secondary and tertiary care. This view of MDT working providing the most effective model for intervention is supported by literature in such diverse fields as pain control (Lemstra *et al.*, 2002), elderly care (Tanaka, 2003; Ross *et al.*, 2005), cancer care (Tripathy, 2003) and learning difficulties (Yerbury, 1997).

In mental health the idea of multidisciplinary working has been a mainstay of care for many years and proven to be an effective way of working (Hall, 2001; Beardsall *et al.*, 2002), but Barker and Walker (2000) caution that what is often described as MDT working in psychiatric care settings actually remains largely a medical–nursing activity.

Jones (2006) feels that the shift towards greater team working has had a blurring effect on professional boundaries between the different disciplines involved in care. Cott (1998) agrees but is positive about this change and feels that multidisciplinary professionals have subsequently had to develop complex role-sets that have resulted in greater involvement by teams in genuine decision-making. Frost *et al.* (2005) suggest that to work effectively in this way professionals have had to find a common language to make knowledge accessible to their colleagues from other disciplines and that although this can be a painful process it ensures real MDT working.

Atwall and Caldwell (2005) note, however, that ever since the National Health Service (NHS) was introduced problems around deficits in inter-professional collaboration have been identified and according to Davies (2000) this remains the case today. Davies claimed to have found both medical and nursing staff intransigent in working towards collaborative ways of working and the Sainsbury Centre for Mental Health (1997) suggested that the extent to which mental health workers were pulling together appears open to question. Frost *et al.* (2005) suggest that if we are to develop true multidisciplinary working the challenge for professionals in multi-professional, multi-agency teams is to contain and embrace diversity while not sacrificing those beliefs that underpin their commitment.

One way of doing this is to build care upon a foundation that is able to identify and enhance those aspects of care that offer all of those involved in mental health care shared ground, shared language and a shared philosophical foundation. A clear step towards this end is the development of the *Ten Essential Shared Capabilities; A Framework for the whole of the Mental Health Workforce* (Department of Health, 2005).

The ten essential shared capabilities

The ten essential shared capabilities (ESC) describe the underpinning values and principles which should be evident in the delivery of services for all people who have mental health problems (Table 4.1). They were developed by the National Institute for Mental Health in England and the Sainsbury Centre Joint Workforce Support Unit and are seen as the core skills and attitudes that all qualified and non-qualified mental health staff working in the NHS, social care, voluntary and independent sectors should acquire as part of their primary training. These values and principles are about attitudes, behaviours, expectations, and relationships and, as such, reflect how people who use mental health services, and those who support them, want and expect to be treated. They should, therefore, shape the behaviour of people working in mental health services.

The aim of the ESC is to set out the shared capabilities that all staff working in mental health services should achieve as best practice as part of their pre-qualifying training. Thus the ESC should form part of the basic building blocks for all staff who work in mental health whether they are professionally qualified or not and whether they work in the NHS, the social care field or the private and voluntary sectors (Department of Health, 2005).

Table 4.1   Ten essential shared capabilities.

Working in partnership	Developing and maintaining constructive working relationships with service users, carers, families, colleagues, lay people and wider community networks. Working positively with any tensions created by conflicts of interest or aspiration that may arise between the partners in care.
Respecting diversity	Working in partnership with service users, carers, families and colleagues to provide care and interventions that not only make a positive difference but also do so in ways that respect and value diversity including age, race, culture, disability, gender, spirituality and sexuality.
Practising ethically	Recognising the rights and aspirations of service users and their families, acknowledging power differentials and minimising them whenever possible. Providing treatment and care that is accountable to service users and carers within the boundaries prescribed by national (professional), legal and local codes of ethical practice.
Challenging inequality	Addressing the causes and consequences of stigma, discrimination, social inequality and exclusion on service users, carers and mental health services. Creating, developing or maintaining valued social roles for people in the communities they come from.
Promoting recovery	Working in partnership to provide care and treatment that enables service users and carers to tackle mental health problems with hope and optimism and to work towards a valued life-style within and beyond the limits of any mental health problem.
Identifying people's needs and strengths	Working in partnership to gather information to agree health and social care needs in the context of the preferred lifestyle and aspirations of service users their families, carers and friends.
Providing service user centred care	Negotiating achievable and meaningful goals; primarily from the perspective of service users and their families. Influencing and seeking the means to achieve these goals and clarifying the responsibilities of the people who will provide any help that is needed, including systematically evaluating outcomes and achievements.
Making a difference	Facilitating access to and delivering the best quality, evidence-based, value-based health and social care interventions to meet the needs and aspirations of service users, their families and carers.
Promoting safety and positive risk taking	Empowering the person to decide the level of risk they are prepared to take with their health and safety. This includes working with the tension between promoting safety and positive risk taking, including assessing and dealing with possible risks for service users, carers, family members, and the wider public.
Personal development and learning	Keeping up-to-date with changes in practice and participating in life-long learning, personal and professional development for one's self and colleagues through supervision, appraisal and reflective practice.

Implementation of the ESC

It is claimed that the adoption of the ESC is an important step towards embedding MDT working as the norm for all mental health care (Department of Health, 2005). In reality however, they are somewhat vague and short of detail and in a nebulous way reflect the philosophy of care for all health care professionals at their lowest possible common denominator. It would be very surprising to find a mental health professional, for example, who did not respect and value diversity, who did not attempt to develop and maintain constructive working relationships with service users, carers, families, or did not attempt to provide care that is accountable to service users and carers within the boundaries prescribed by national (professional), legal and local codes of ethical practice.

All mental health professionals, indeed every health professional would hopefully agree with the ESC and support the sentiments contained within them regarding the desire and need for effective, integrated team working and agreed care planning i.e. agreed by all relevant members of the MDT. So let us assume for a moment that it is true i.e. that every health professional believes that team working and integrated approaches improve the experiences of users and carers. Most of you reading this will be mental health professionals or someone who has had, or will have, experience of a MDT either as a professional or a user of mental health services. Now answer this question. In your experience of mental health services have you always witnessed effective team working and agreed care planning? Be honest.

The answer, sadly, is almost certainty no. But is it realistic to expect effectiveness in every situation? After all MDTs consist of many professionals from different backgrounds and organisations, with differing professional beliefs and values, as well as varying responsibilities and accountabilities, all of which will inevitably result in differing opinions and ideas of what is right and, of course, what is not. Then there are the service users themselves each with their own priorities and needs. Not forgetting too (and more frequently in contemporary health services) interactions with providers other than those specific to mental health. Fatchett (1998) in examining reforms for the desired new, modern and dependable NHS acknowledges that: *'collaboration with other potential NHS competitors, and indeed with wider agencies, whatever the depth of their relationship previous to the reforms, appears to have taken a back seat in recent times'*. She continues however to say that *'it would be unfair to blame a lack of multidisciplinary collaboration in care on organisational and structural changes alone'* (Fatchett 1998:137). Correctly she recognises that the individual practitioners, who represent the various organisations at every level, play a significant part in making effective collaborative partnerships difficult to initially establish and subsequently maintain.

All of which begs the question that whilst effective team working is desirable, is it actually achievable? Well if you believe in doing the best for your users then the answer is absolutely and definitely yes. It is not only, however, desirable but is also a necessity because no one profession, agency or individual can provide sufficient diversity to meet all the demands of contemporary services nor, more importantly the needs of the users themselves.

In order to provide the desired effective integrated working there is a need for the various organisations and their respective employees to work in partnership. Kappeli (1995) recognised that no one discipline is sufficiently equipped to meet the demands of effective care delivery and that *'acting on the theoretical basis of our own discipline must not prevent us from seeing what it does not cover'* (Kappeli 1995:253).

However, it takes more than simply recognising that no one discipline is enough, it also means that each discipline involved must suspend any professional prejudices held against the other services and to break down the various barriers that can and do interfere with effective multidisciplinary care planning. Genuine partnerships in care are not merely about working alongside one another, they are about working together. Partnership working should get all interested parties working together to promote optimum and equitable health care. To achieve this in the real world of mental health provision a number of conditions and attributes must be fostered. These will be explored shortly, but first an examination of ineffective multi-professional working. Sadly in current health care provision this is sometimes happening. What follows is an abridged true case study that portrays an example of multidisciplinary interactions.

Case study 4.1   An example of poor multidisciplinary working.

A 29-year-old man had a long and well documented history of depression, drug and substance abuse. He lived alone in a small flat but normally had almost daily contact with his family. On the weekend in question he did not answer the phone or open the door to his flat despite his Mum and sister's numerous efforts. On the Monday, at his mum's request, the emergency services broke into his flat. Her son was found lying in faeces and urine with several pressure sores developing. He was admitted to the local district hospital.

During his hospitalisation he stated he was seeing aliens who were telling him to kill the other patients. In his more lucid moments, usually talking to his sister, his terms of reference about events, people etc. were from some 6 years previously. Sleep did not come easy to him and one night his sister was called at 10 pm to *'come in and calm him down'* after he had punched a nurse who, he claimed, was trying to poison him with sleeping tablets.

Eventually his sister did calm him and demanded to see the senior house officer (SHO) because, in her words, *'enough was enough'*. The SHO came and referred her brother to the on site emergency crisis mental health team (MHT). In the meantime the SHO administered a sedative to the patient and at approximately 6.30 am for the first time in some time, he fell into a deep sleep. At 9 am a psychologist from the MHT arrived. As the patient was asleep he chose not to wake him and said he would return later. He did not return until several days later when he undertook a 15 minute assessment.

The following week an MDT meeting, including representatives from the community learning disability team (CLDT), drug and alcohol team (DAT) (who were there at the request of the crisis team), the community mental health team, the SHO, the psychologist who had carried out the assessment, the patient's mum and his sister, took place. The psychologist's evaluation was that the patient did not meet the criteria for generic mental health services but perhaps was eligible for the DAT or maybe the CLDT. Having read the report and listened to the various opinions both the CLDT and DAT felt he did not meet the criteria for their services, whilst the CMHT felt he should be with the DAT. After 90 minutes no decisions regarding a specialist service had been made and he remained in hospital. When his physical condition improved he was discharged back to his flat. He and his family continue to fight for him to receive a suitable service but fear that only another crisis incident will provide any hope of this happening.

This particular MDT meeting took place in 2006 and, at time of writing, this young man continues to receive no specialist input and his mental health continues to deteriorate.

Before examining how inter-professional working can be proactive and complementary, take a moment to reflect upon this scenario. Now answer this question – if this happened in my locality what would be the outcome? It is hoped your answer is a more positive one. Whatever your response, it is a fair assumption however that every one of the readers of this text can think of situations where users have been ignored, neglected, passed from service to service because agencies and organisations could not, or would not, make and/or take decisions that would have provided, if only in part, access to a useful service and begin to provide constructive planned care. Take a moment to think about the scenario and ask yourself if most of the problems were avoidable. Clearly this real life scenario is lacking some of the ideas outlined in the literature that are the hallmarks of good partnership working.

What is clear, however, is that there are some areas across the country where great strides have been taken and where partnerships are beginning to function. In these areas partnership working is built securely on a combination of the following components:

- Cooperation
- Collaboration
- Communication.

These three Cs need to be fostered on two levels. Firstly these components need to be active in the relationship between agencies and organisations. Secondly they need to be in place between the individuals who represent the various agencies and organisations. The NHS Plan (Department of Health, 2000) emphasises that partnerships between agencies and organisations are required throughout the entire gambit of service commitment ranging from strategic planning to commissioning through to actual provision at the point of contact with users, it stated that:

'Over the next ten years the NHS will concentrate on getting people to work together for the benefit of the patient not the system . . . There will be a greater emphasis on partnership working by all parts of the NHS and other organisations involved in health care such as local authorities' (Department of Health, 2000 section 1.3:20).

Fundamental to the success of these ideals will be the overcoming of the numerous barriers that exist between agencies and organisations. It is the implementation of the three Cs that is paramount to both achieving the ideals and breaking through the barriers. Before moving on to the three Cs and their benefits to delivering effective care a little time will be spent identifying the main barriers, most of which have (arguably) in some way been created through our own prejudices towards each others respective professions and organisations.

Barriers to partnerships in care

Like most barriers there is no one single causative factor that leads to the breakdown of MDT working. A review of the literature suggests that there area range of factors that can impact negatively the development of good MDT working. Some barriers to effective partnerships are:

- Ignorance of other professionals, particularly their roles, responsibilities, rules, regulations and limitations
- Narrow vision that fails to understand, appreciate or acknowledge what other people do or what other organisations can and will provide
- Lack of contact between organisations or individuals involved in providing the care
- The difficulty of access is a key barrier to integrated partnerships not just for users but also for professionals
- Allied to problems of access are communication problems
- Differences between providers, even between professionals within the same organisation.
                    (Hornby and Atkins (2000); Crawford *et al.*, 2001; Kappeli, 1995).

The most common differences found within MDT working are those on application of practice, priorities and protocols, many of which are entrenched in the respective professional education each professional has received. This can lead to some of the often repeated clichés that exist in the field of mental health care such as nurses stating that social workers know nothing about mental illness, social workers stating that mental health nurses know nothing about social care and both stating that psychiatrists and psychologists are irritating because they think they are superior beings! Unfortunately the education of professionals tends to either overtly or covertly reinforce the negative, thereby creating subjective prejudices.

This is arguably the most damaging aspect to overcome because each profession will promote a culture of we're right and, whilst not openly stating it, there exists, perhaps, the implication that other professions are not so competent or knowledgeable. This does not have to be the case. There is strong evidence that inter-professional learning during a professionals pre-qualifying education reduces the negative effects of these barriers and creates improved understanding of each profession's unique culture (D'Amour and Oansden, 2005; Fealy, 2005; Oansden and Reeves, 2005).

Overcoming the barriers to MDT working

Many university courses, including health and social care, are moving towards greater use of inter-professional education and the sharing of curricula, so it may well be that in the years to come the barriers identified here will be considerably less obvious than today. The Department of Health (1999) acknowledges that joint education and training between different organisations is a necessity to break the barriers and organisational cultural differences which can impede partnership working. These notions of collaborative and cooperative approaches are, as stated previously, the main considerations for improving current partnerships in care, so that they are not merely words in mission statements, but practical and achievable objectives. This is achievable if the three Cs can be developed to become the normal way of delivering mental health care. This leaves people with the need to define exactly what collaboration and cooperation mean when applied to partnerships in care.

Collaboration

The Concise Oxford English Dictionary (Soanes & Stevenson, 2004) defines collaboration as *'(to) work jointly on an activity or project'*, which in a sentence neatly sums up what partnerships in care should be constantly striving to promote. The dictionary also provides a second definition *'Cooperate traitorously with an enemy'*, which a cynic may say is how some professionals view the notion of joint working with other organisations. But, and this is a big but, is not the idea and practice of collaborative approaches in partnerships about facilitating a holistic care package? As identified earlier no one professional or organisation can provide every user their needs, therefore collaboration is not simply an idealist fantasy it is a practical necessity.

The evidence suggests that collaboration between individuals from the various organisations does result in a more comprehensive and individualised care package. El Ansari (1999) describes how collaborative approaches and partnerships are important and are particularly relevant within mental health practice. Hornby and Atkins (2000) concur stating that several reports during recent years supported the importance of collaboration to promote optimal care. Collaboration is seen as by Henneman *et al.* (1995), Whitehead (2001) and others as vital because it actively develops teams (Box 4.1).

Leathard (2003) suggests various models for inter-professional collaboration. However the starting point for any collaboration concerned with establishing commonality and within the MDT, indeed any multi-professional service the most common element is the people the MDT provide care for i.e. the reason for the team's formation. Therefore each team should establish areas of commonality:

Box 4.1 Effective collaboration.

- Establishes shared identity
- Offers creative practice and innovations
- Uses shared experiences and knowledge to increase team strengths and assists in identifying shared needs
- Uses differing perspectives to identify service gaps more readily
- Reduces mistrust and professional rivalry
- Promotes inter-professional cohesion.

- Agreed purpose and function (criteria) of the team
- Agreed purpose and function of individual members
- Team terms of reference, policies and protocols
- Clearly defined roles and responsibilities of individual team members in respect of services they can provide (as well as identifying what each cannot provide) and organisations they represent
- Agreement on a clearly defined team structure, including hierarchical responsibility
- Agreed referral systems between professional disciplines represented within the team
- Agreed contact details for individuals (as applicable for other professionals and service users).

The team that can achieve this can now begin to develop a cohesive and, importantly, a cooperative approach. This is easy in theory however in practice it does require effort and negotiation to reach the agreements noted above. Yet if MDTs are supposed to be teams then it makes sense that these issues should be jointly agreed i.e. every member and the service they represent will have been able to have they say in an atmosphere that fosters equality. Contrary to Jones's (2006) assertion that the move towards greater team working blurs boundaries, agreed roles and responsibilities within MDTs actually strengthen professionals' positions by clearly defining who they are and what they can and cannot do. This in turn helps to clarify and identify case and care management principles, which otherwise have the potential to become grey areas of responsibility and practice that result in situations such as those highlighted in the scenario. This benefits no one, least of all the user and only serves to reinforce damaging stereotypes.

Cooperation

The definition of cooperation is: '*Action or process of cooperating*,' and cooperate is: '*Work together towards same end. Help someone to comply with their wishes*' (Soanes & Stevenson, 2004).

The notion of helping someone to comply with their wishes gives greater emphasis than ever before to the desire for cooperation within and between mental health services as service user involvement becomes a desired objective (Department of Health, 2005), not to mention that without cooperation between relevant organisations the various national service frameworks (NSFs) will never be achievable. Whereas collaboration is a collective concept, co-operation errs toward an individualised concept that takes place often on a personal level between members of the team, which has both benefits and drawbacks. Benefits include fewer people to satisfy (or upset), increased time, more accessible, greater personal recognition, and potentially easier to reach satisfactory agreement to name but a few. Drawbacks may include personality clashes, unresolved differences leading to altercations and alienation, increased tensions and so on. To avoid the drawbacks MDT members must move from being a group of individuals who have come together with different skills, attributes and attitudes to being one team with a collective identity made up of people with individual skills and attributes, who share similar attitudes.

Most importantly a cooperative approach recognises two specific issues, firstly that no one individual can do everything him/herself and secondly that the differences between members e.g. social worker, nurse, and so on are not negative attributes but are in fact positive thereby breaking down yet more barriers to effective partnership working. Henneman *et al.* (1995) recognise that cooperation with others should be utilised to solve issues, rather than placing emphasis on the competitive nature of working alongside another professional. Lets be honest, everyone reading this will, at some point in their careers, have relied on another professional in order to achieve a desired outcome and whether you like it or not you will have cooperated together to ensure the outcome was met. Therefore it makes sense to develop an atmosphere of cooperation from the beginning. So what is required to develop cooperative approaches within multidisciplinary environments?

Arguably the single most important need is to have open systems of communication within the team and for each team member to promote freedom of information and interaction (see the section on communication). This however is not sufficient by itself and can only be achieved if the following conditions are also achieved:

- Recognition of each individual's unique contribution
- Awareness of own expertise, strengths, needs and limitations
- Confidence in own abilities
- Confidence in other team members' abilities
- Sharing of knowledge, responsibility, values, language and team objectives for future developments
- Willing to actively participate in team activities
- Trust and respect
- A desire to get to know each other as professionals and as individual people, so that identity is not just rooted in an organisation or job title.

These conditions result in partnerships built on mutual trust and under-standing, as they erode the prejudices of inter-professional rivalry and suspicion. Whitehead (2001) argues that collaborative and cooperative alliances produce a more effective way of distributing and utilising resources, the latter only being recognised when the team knows exactly what each individual member can actually give to the collective effort.

Assuming the above can be established then other potential barriers can begin to be brought down. The team, and therefore the organisations they represent, can begin to draw up an agreement on some of the more sensitive issues that influence partnership working. Below are some of the more obvious issues that can be resolved:

- Agreed access to files by devising an *acceptable to all* team policy, which is also acceptable to the represented organisations
- Recognition of individual practitioners' professional responsibilities
- Policies for sharing responsibilities, casework, disclosures and so on that do not infringe on the above
- If casework is not shared then individual practitioners should agree levels of involvement with each other if necessary to benefit care delivery.

Once these are agreed then not only can there be an increased awareness of individual responsibilities but also a recognised collective responsibility within the team and more importantly a collective ownership of the partnership itself. From these cooperative agreements a more open, flexible and collaborative approach to care planning will develop. This is easily said and even the cynics would probably say this is obvious and sensible. But if is it that easy, obvious and sensible why is it, for example a) not witnessed in every MDT, CMHT? and, b) necessary to reinforce it within this publication? Before moving on to communication it is worth reinforcing that it is the individuals within the MDTs who are responsible for making the team efficient and effective, and therefore it is the very same individuals who are responsible for the team being or becoming inefficient and ineffective.

Communication

So much has been written regarding communication needs for effective care planning, team working and care delivery that it may seem to be unnecessary to add to existing information available. However, without effective commun-ication nothing is achieved least of all an appropriate care plan. With these considerations in mind this section will be relatively short, but, and yet again this is another big but, without the willingness to promote effective commun-ication in practice then readers will have wasted their time reading this chapter because without effective communication neither collaboration nor coopera-tion are attainable. Wilson (1997) recognised that within mental health MDTs communication is particularly important because of the diverse nature of care planning and the need for feedback.

According to Hornby and Atkins (2000) there are four main communication difficulties:

- Failure to establish adequate lines of communication that promote collaboration and, equally important, feedback, the latter being necessary within any MDT, but especially where the MDT is in the business of providing health and social care
- Incomplete communication e.g. not providing all the details necessary to make decisions, or lack of relevant information and so on
- Confused communication often to the point of not making complete sense, which frequently lacks definition and/or purpose
- Inadequacy or feelings of inadequacy to convey thoughts and feelings effectively, which can lead to indecision, isolation and so on.

The single most important aspect of communication within any MDT is freedom of expression and every member, irrespective of their profession or position in the MDT should feel free to be able to say what they want with regard to care, without worrying about the potential repercussions. This is most notable in the fourth of Hornby and Atkins' difficulties outlined in the table above but it is also applicable to the other three. This is as much about creating an environment that fosters openness as it is about communicating in a practical way. The environmental component owes much to the way individuals interact with each other and how well they get on together both personally and professionally. Unfortunately the former is difficult to control, however, a good professional should put aside any personal issues that get in the way of effective team working. Also, as previously noted, it is unfortunate that some people find it difficult to put aside professional prejudices. Assuming these issues can be put aside, hopefully with the intervention, if necessary, of other team members (particularly the team leaders) the following are needed to create a communicative MDT.

A common language

This is particularly necessary when collaborating across organisations. Social services and the NHS are the two most obvious examples of a different language. Therefore a common language for care must be developed and agreed to aid understanding and to bring the team together.

Shared understanding

This covers several issues such as goals, aims, objectives, problems and understanding of organisational structures. These need to be openly discussed, debated and resolved. In order to do this, practitioners must be willing and able to talk to each other in freedom. As El Ansari (1999) states this should embrace the different cultures of the stakeholders.

Clear purpose of the MDT

Clarifying the purpose of the team enables members to express themselves within accepted boundaries without fear of offending others. The purpose needs to be especially clear for any new team members to feel comfortable. Obvious? Think back to when you were interviewed for your position within the team, did you know what was expected of you? Did you know what the purpose of the MDT was? Could you immediately hit the ground running and take on case work? You probably did but this does not make it right. Clarifying the purpose means there is less likelihood of confused, unclear communication.

Willingness to resolve conflict

Whether this is in respect of care issues or between individuals, the failure to resolve conflict will fester and inevitably lead to serious problems, including even more ineffective communication. Most conflict remains unresolved because people feel unable or unwilling to discuss the differences. Conflict will only be resolved if people are willing to talk through the differences. A good team allows people to articulate their differences openly and differences will occur in any MDT.

Returning briefly to the clinical scenario it is reasonably obvious what the problems were and how they arose. Ineffective communication is a key issue, but so too is a lack of cooperation, assumptions regarding collaboration and an unwillingness to suspend a range of prejudices. Willingness to accept professional differences, to acknowledge no one professional or organisation can provide all the required elements for an effective plan of care and to recognise the one thing that all members of the MDT should have in common i.e. the user's best interests. These are the keys to effective collaboration all of which were notably absent in this particularly case, but all easily achievable. With this in mind, many of the suggestions made here are to all intents and purposes common sense, but has it not been said that the only problem with common sense is that it is just not that common?

Conclusion

It appears to all intents and purposes that the commitment the Government has to effective inter-professional working outlined in such documents as NHS Plan (Department of Health, 2000) and the National Service Framework for Mental Health (Department of Health, 1999) will be a feature of legislation to come.

The challenge for all staff involved in mental health care is to turn the rhetoric of MDT working into a reality that underpins service delivery at every stage of care. If the optimistic outlook suggested by Cott (1998), that multidisciplinary professionals have been successful in developing complex role-sets which have resulted in greater involvement by teams in genuine decision making, is to continue then staff have to integrate this way of working into both their thinking and their actions.

The adopting of the ten essential shared capabilities and the adherence to the three Cs of effective teamwork might, to some, seem idealistic and utopian but in reality the ideas contained in these concepts are achievable by a committed, engaged and motivated workforce. A team characterised by effective leadership, a concordance of values, respect and high quality communication can have each member maintaining their own separate, professional identity whilst at the same time embracing the essential shared capabilities (Department of Health, 2005).

In the end care is simply too big and too complex for a single person or service to deliver well. It is only by a genuine multidisciplinary team approach that we, as professionals, can have confidence that the services we provide across the domains of children and adult services, and care planning in mental health are the best that they possibly can be when working together to safeguard the needs of children adults and society generally.

References

Atwall, A. & Caldwell, K. (2005). Do All Health and Social Care Professionals Interact Equally: A Study Of Interactions In Multidisciplinary Teams In The United Kingdom. *Scandinavian Journal of Caring Sciences.* **19(3)**, 268–273.

Barker, P.J. & Walker, L. (2000). Nurses' Perceptions Of Multidisciplinary Teamwork In Acute Psychiatric Settings. *Journal of Psychiatric & Mental Health Nursing.* **7(6)**, 539–546.

Beardsall, L., Gough, J. & Pringle, A. (2002). Developing an ECT Integrated Care Pathway. *Practice Development in Healthcare.* **1(1)**, 21–35.

Cott, C. (1998). Structure and Meaning in Multidisciplinary Teamwork. *Sociology of Health & Illness.* **20(6)**, 848–873.

Crawford, P., Brown, B. & Darongkama, J. (2001). Boundaries and blurred roles: interdisciplinary working in community mental health. *Mental Health Care.* **4(8)**, 270–272.

D'Amour, D. & Oansden, I. (2005). Interprofessionality As The Field Of Interprofessional Practice and Interprofessional Education: An Emerging Concept. *Journal of Interprofessional Care, (Supplement).* **1**, 8–20.

Davies, C. (2000). Getting Health Professionals to Work Together. *British Medical Journal.* **320(7241)**, 1021–1022.

Department of Health (1999). *The National Service Framework for Mental Health.* London: HMSO.

Department of Health (2000). *The NHS Plan: A Plan for Investment: A Plan for Reform.* London: HMSO.

Department of Health (2005). *The Ten Essential Shared Capabilities; A Framework for the Whole of the Mental Health Workforce.* London: HMSO.

El Ansari, W. (1999). Partnerships In Mental Health: Guidelines To Good Practice, *Partnerships in Mental Health.* April, 19.

Fatchett, A. (1998). *Nursing in the New NHS Modern, Dependable?* London: Baillière Tindall.

Fealy, G. (2005). Sharing The Experience: Interdisciplinary Education and Interprofessional Learning. *Nurse Education in Practice.* **5**, 317–319.

Frost, N., Robinson, M. & Anning, A. (2005). Social Workers In Multidisciplinary Teams: Issues and Dilemmas For Professional Practice. *Child & Family Social Work.* **10(3)**, 187–196.

Hall, J. (2001). A Qualitative Survey Of Staff Responses To An Integrated Care Pathway Pilot Study In A Mental Health Care Setting. *Nursing Times Research.* **6(3)**, 696–705.

Henneman, E.A., Lee, J.L. & Cohen, J.I. (1995). Collaboration: A Concept Analysis. *Journal of Advanced Nursing.* **21**, 103–109.

Hornby, S. & Atkins, J. (eds) (2000). *Collaborative Care: Inter-professional, Intragency and Interpersonal.* Oxford: Blackwell Science. (2nd edn).

Jefferies, H. & Chan, K.K. (2004). Multidisciplinary Team Working: Is It Both Holistic and Effective? *International Journal of Gynaecological Cancer.* **14(2)**, 210–211.

Jones, A. (2006). Multidisciplinary Team Working: Collaboration and Conflict. *International Journal of Mental Health Nursing.* **15(1)**, 19–28.

Kappeli, S. (1995). Interprofessional Cooperation: Why Is Partnership So Difficult? *Patient Education and Counselling.* **26**, 251–256.

Leathard, A. (ed) (2003). *Interprofessional Collaboration: From Policy To Practice In Health and Social Care.* Hove: Brunner-Routledge.

Lemstra, M., Stewart, B. & Olszynski, W.P. (2002). Effectiveness Of Multidisciplinary Intervention In The Treatment Of Migraine: A Randomised Clinical Trial. *Headache: The Journal of Head and Face Pain.* **42(9)**, 845–854.

Oansden, I. & Reeves, D. (2005). Key Elements For Interprofessional Education, Part 1: The Learner, The Educator and The Learning Context. *Journal of Interprofessional Care, (Supplement).* **1**, 21–58.

Ross, F., O'Tuathail, C. & Stubberfield, D. (2005). Towards Multidisciplinary Assessment Of Older People: Exploring The Change Process. *Journal of Clinical Nursing.* **14(4)**, 518–529.

Sainsbury Centre for Mental Health (1997). *Pulling Together: The Future Roles and Training of Mental Health Staff.* London: Sainsbury Centre for Mental Health.

Soanes, C. & Stevenson, A. (2004). *Concise Oxford English Dictionary.* Oxford: Open University Press.

Tanaka, M. (2003). Multidisciplinary Team Approach For Elderly Patients. *Geriatrics and Gerontology International.* **3(2)**, 69–72.

Tripathy, D. (2003). Multidisciplinary Care for Breast Cancer: Barriers and Solutions. *The Breast Journal.* **9(1)**, 60–63.

Whitehead, D. (2001). Applying Collaborative Practice to Health Promotion. *Nursing Standard.* **15(20)**, 33–37.

Wilson, J. (1997). *Integrated Care Management: The Path To Success?* Oxford: Butterworth-Heinemann.

Yerbury, M. (1997). Issues In Multidisciplinary Teamwork For Children With Disabilities. *Child: Care, Health and Development.* **23(1)**, 77–86.

Chapter 5

Safeguarding Children when Care Planning in Mental Health

Karen Bibbings

Introduction

The aim of this chapter is to provide mental health practitioners with a greater understanding of the impact of parental mental health on children and young people. It will go on to explore the role of mental health practitioners in safeguarding children they come into contact with as well as identify the roles, responsibilities and policies pertaining to those working with children and their families.

The impact of mental health on parenting capacity

Parenting is a challenging task even when carried out under ideal circumstances. Parents are required to demonstrate the ability to have enough emotional space to meet their children's needs be they physical, social, psychological or emotional. They also have to demonstrate the ability to adapt to the changing needs of their children throughout the span of their childhood.

   As parents we must have the ability to contain a child's anxiety. This in turn assists the child in developing the internal working models required to enable it to regulate its own emotions. We must also appreciate that a child needs to encounter a broad range of experiences to enable it to develop the skills it will need to successfully negotiate adult life. So, if our basic premise is that the above description represents somewhere near the ideal, what do we understand about the effect that any deviation from this ideal can have on children? Green (2002:1) reminds us that, *'parental mental illness takes many different forms and that its impact on children varies according to a number of factors'*. He explains these factors as being, *'the severity of the illness and the length of the episode of illness'*. Rutter (Green, 2002) goes on to tell us that the child's age and resilience and the presence of a well parent or carer are significant as is the extent to which the illness pervades all aspects of family life. Three decades ago researchers were beginning to explore the links between maternal depression, parenting capacity and outcomes for children (Bowlby, 1988). More recently a study by Murray (1992:543–61) demonstrated that, *'the infants of post-natally depressed mothers performed worse on object concept tasks, were more insecurely attached to their mothers and showed more mild behavioural difficulties'* and Flynn and Starns (2004) suggest that post-natal depression may not only cause difficulties in the attachment between the mother and the child but may also cause later difficulties in adult relationships.

Pound (Reder *et al.*, 2000) goes on to explain further a number of difficulties experienced by children whose parent(s) suffer from a depressive illness; he suggests that the children of depressed parents, and particularly depressed mothers, are at high risk of developing psychiatric disorder either currently or in the future. They also have poor interpersonal skills, few friends and suffer either from dysfunctional levels of guilt, poor self esteem and clinical depression or from detachment, aggression and conduct disorder, while cognitive impairment and attention deficits interfere with learning skills such as reading. Warner *et al.* (1999:289–96) consider the wider family perspective and demonstrate that, *'children in families with multiple generations of depression are at particular high risk from some form of psychopathology'*.

So what of children whose parents have schizophrenia or other major mental health issues? A study by Riordan *et al.* (1999) suggests that women with schizophrenia show greater interaction deficits (with their infant) than those with affective disorders, being more remote, insensitive, intrusive and self-absorbed. The four-month-old infants of women with schizophrenia were more avoidant and the overall quality of mother–infant interaction was poorer. Dermot *et al.* (2003) demonstrate that greater impairment in parenting capacity is related to the caregiver being diagnosed with a major mental health problem. However, there are numerous factors that often accompany mental health problems that will impact on a person's ability to parent effectively. Adults with mental health difficulties are statistically more likely to be lone parents, suffer divorce and relationship breakdown and have reduced opportunities in securing the employment necessary to enable them to enjoy a good standard of living and housing. Therefore, adults with mental health difficulties and their children are more likely to experience a higher degree of socio-economic disadvantage than those who experience good mental health.

It is also important at this point to acknowledge that not all children who have a parent with a mental health problem will suffer adverse effects from this. Many parents with mental health issues will be able to raise their children in a warm, loving supportive environment. A whole host of risk, resilience and protective factors within the child, the family and the wider community will influence outcomes for children. A summary of studies carried out by Haggerty *et al.* (1996) is represented in the Table 5.1. These findings enable us to understand the many factors which impact on children at an individual, systemic and community level which may either increase risk or, alternatively, promote resilience.

Table 5.1 Study summary.

	Risk factors	Resilience factors
Child	Genetic influences Low I.Q. and learning disabilities Specific developmental delay Communication difficulty Difficult temperament Physical illness especially chronic and/or neurological	Being female More intelligent Easy temperament when an infant Secure attachment Positive attitude, problem solving approach Good communication skills Planner, belief in control Humour/religious faith Capacity
Family	Overt parental conflict Family breakdown Hostile or rejecting relationships Inconsistent or unclear discipline Failure to adapt to a child's changing needs Abuse – physical, sexual or emotional Loss or separation from an attachment figure Parental psychiatric illness Parental criminality, alcoholism or personality disorder Death or loss – including loss of friendship	At least one good parent–child relationship Affection Supervision, authoritative discipline Supportive marriage Support for education
Community	Socio-economic disadvantage Homelessness Disaster Discrimination	Wider supportive network Good housing High standard of living High school morale and positive attitudes Schools with strong academic and non-academic opportunities Range of sport, leisure opportunities.

(Haggerty, *et al.*, 1996).

From a service provision perspective, Haggerty *et al.*'s (1996) work appears to have set the groundwork for the DfES (2004) document, *Every Child Matters*. This clearly states that there were to be five major outcomes to ensure that children and young people do not slip through the service provision net. This document detailed five outcomes that services would work towards: being healthy, staying safe, enjoying and achieving, making a contribution, and economic well being.

To enhance understanding and enable us to apply theory to practice, the framework above can be used to assist in considering the following case examples.

Case study 5.1   The first young mother.

Paula is a 21-year-old female who has just had her first baby. Zara is a healthy, happy, placid infant born at full-term weighing 4 kg. Paula has been married for two years and describes her marriage as happy, loving and supportive. The couple are buying their first home in an affluent part of town and have no major financial difficulties. Paula's mother and father live in the same road as Paula and visit everyday. They have described to you their great delight at the birth of their first grandchild. Paula was referred into adult mental health services after her health visitor had noticed that Paula seemed low in mood, lethargic and lacking motivation. Paula had also described to her health visitor that she had feelings of both sadness and guilt and had considered suicide.

Consider:

1) What might be the risk factors relating to baby Zara in the above situation?
2) What are the resilience factors which may afford baby Zara a degree of protection?
3) Begin to consider what your role and responsibilities might be when considering the above scenario.

Case study 5.2   The second young mother.

Sue is the mother of Jack, an 18-month-old boy. She is a lone parent but has some support from her own mother who she sees most weekends. Obsessive compulsive disorder has affected Sue since late adolescence. Sue has a fear of dirt and germs and has developed a number of behaviours and rituals that she carries out in an attempt to reduce her anxiety. These include hand washing and bathing (this can consist of up to eight baths a day), cleaning of the house, particularly the kitchen and bathroom, and avoidance of the outside world and social situations. Sue also avoids having visitors to the family home as she is fearful of the dirt and germs that they may transport into the house. When visitors do come to the house they are asked to remove their shoes, walk on magazine pages and sit in one particular chair on a towel. When they leave she embarks on a cleaning schedule that can last several hours. Jack spends the majority of the day in a playpen in the living room or in a high chair positioned over a sheet of plastic in the kitchen, he is fed by his mother to avoid mess, has access to one toy at a time as the others are in a weak bleach solution, has no contact with other children and rarely sees other people besides his maternal grandmother. Sue describes Jack as a miserable, whining child.

Consider:

1) What might be the risk factors relating to Jack in the above situation?
2) What are the resilience factors which may afford Jack a degree of protection?
3) Begin to consider what your role and responsibilities might be when considering the above scenario.

Case study 5.3   A young carer.

Hannah is a 15-year-old girl whose father has schizophrenia. She is the eldest of four children, the youngest being 5. Hannah's mother also had mental health problems and she committed suicide 2 years ago. Since her mother's death Hannah has taken on the responsibility of caring for her siblings. In the last 2 years her school attendance has fallen to 25% and she has not submitted any course work for her GCSEs despite being described as having above average intelligence. Hannah has lost contact with her friends and is reluctant to invite them to her home as she is often embarrassed by her father's behaviour. The family lives in a two bedroom council house, are benefit reliant and live in an area identified as one of the most deprived wards nationally. There is limited contact with extended family and Hannah no longer attends the local youth club as she is fearful that her siblings will not be adequately cared for if she is not at home.

Consider:

1) What might be the risk factors relating to Hannah in the above situation?
2) What are the resilience factors which may afford Hannah a degree of protection?
3) What your role and responsibilities might be when considering the above scenario.

Safeguarding children

In all three case examples above the adult is our client and as mental health practitioners our care planning will have the adult at its centre, however, the Children Act, (Department of Health, 2004) states very clearly that the welfare of the child is paramount. By law, The Children Act takes precedence over all other legislation including the Mental Health Act (Department of Health, 1983), and states clearly that we all have a duty and responsibility to safeguard children from risk or harm. *Working Together to Safeguard Children* (Department of Health, 2006) leaves us in no doubt as to our responsibility toward children and clearly outlines the role of adult mental health services when working with parents experiencing mental health problems. Section 2.92 states that:

'Adult mental health services – including those providing general adult and community, forensic, psychotherapy, alcohol and substance misuse and learning disability services – have a responsibility in safeguarding children when they become aware of or identify, a child at risk of harm. This may be as a result of service's direct work with those who may be mentally ill, a parent, a parent-to-be, or a non related abuser, or in response to a request for the assessment of an adult perceived to represent a potential or actual risk to a child or young person' (Department of Health, 2006 section 2.92:60).

This document goes further in advising us not only of our duty toward the child but also guides our practice when considering the welfare of children.

'Close collaboration and liaison between adult mental health services and children's social services are essential in the interests of children. This may require sharing information to safeguard and promote the welfare of children or to protect a child from significant harm. The expertise of substance misuse services and learning disability services may also be required. The assessment of parents with significant learning difficulties, a disability, or sensory and communication difficulties, may require the expertise of a specialist psychiatrist or clinical psychologist from a learning disability service or adult mental health service' (Department of Health, 2006 section 2.94:61).

Our responsibilities as adult mental health practitioners therefore are clear. We should have a clear understanding of the legislation pertaining to the protection of children and have access to and knowledge of the local policies and procedures regarding child protection. Be able to demonstrate the ability to carry out a mental health assessment whilst considering how the adult's illness impacts on their children or children that they may have contact with. Be able to liaise and collaborate with those services whose client is the child, i.e. health visitors, school nurses, paediatricians, social workers etc. and discuss any concerns with line managers or the named nurse or doctor for child protection. We must also be able to follow the procedures for making appropriate referrals into child protection agencies and engage in multi-agency information sharing.

It is of paramount importance that we have a full understanding of the impact of mental health issues on parenting capacity, as we are more likely now, more than ever before, to witness children being cared for by adults experiencing a range of mental health issues. Gould (2006) informs us that population studies indicate that there is a prevalence rate of 23% or just over 9 million adults in England with moderate to severe mental health problems. He also demonstrates that there is a higher rate of mental disorder among lone parents than for adults living as a couple with a child and concludes by stating that there are approximately 946 000 children in England and Wales living with a lone parent with a mental disorder and approximately 1 333 500 children living in a two-parent household where at least one parent has a mental disorder.

Adults with mental health issues now receive the majority of their care within the community as directed by the NHS and Community Care Act (Department of Health, 1990). Children are increasingly taking on the role of carer as mental health services have moved from a hospital to a community setting in accordance with legislation. Community based interventions enable families to remain together during episodes of parental illness but this approach also places children in the position where they are more likely to witness and experience their parent's illness and in some instances be relied upon to participate in caring for their ill relative.

Children acting as carers

There is no doubt that children often do act as carers and will do so seemingly willingly, capably and competently. However taking on a caring role can often place the child in a situation that requires them to make decisions outside of their level of understanding and emotional maturity. They will frequently negate their own needs in carrying out this role.

Within the new provisions from the Carers (Recognition and Services) Act (Department of Health, 1995) to the Carers and Disabled Children's Act (Department of Health, 2000a) there is a requirement for local authorities, in certain circumstances, to inform carers that they may be entitled to an assessment under both of these Acts. This is designed to ensure that carers get all information about their rights at the appropriate time. Amendments to the Carers (Recognition and Services) Act now mean that when a local authority is carrying out an assessment of a person's community care needs and it appears that an individual may be entitled to ask for (but has not requested) an assessment of his ability to care, the local authority must inform the carer of this right before they go on to make any decision about services.

Children will often outwardly express no resentment with their situation, apportion no blame for their circumstances and show great love and loyalty toward their parents. Children can appear to be wise, worldly, strong and responsible but the impact of assuming responsibility for adults and often siblings on a child's physical, educational and emotional well being is worthy of further consideration. Within the amendments to the Carers and Disabled Children's Act provision has been made whereby any decision about services for the carer by the local authority must consider whether a carer works or wishes to work, is undertaking or wishes to undertake any education, training or leisure activity.

There would seem to be a scarcity of research that enlightens us as to the feelings and experiences of the child when being parented by an adult experiencing mental health problems, or when assuming a caring role. However the summaries in Table 5.2 give us a greater understanding of the issues affecting children at specific ages when their parents have mental health issues. This not only enhances our understanding when assessing risk but also assists us in considering the impact of assuming responsibility for others on a child or young person's development.

The information in Table 5.2 also demonstrates that risk per se does not necessarily diminish as the child ages; it just changes.

So what of the child's perspective and lived experience? To assist us in understanding how children feel when parented by an adult experiencing mental health problems Claire Armstrong on behalf of Young Minds (Armstrong, 2002) has published a report based on the evaluation of a young carers project specifically for young people living with a parent experiencing mental ill health. The key findings of this qualitative study are shown below where young people are reporting a range of concerns and difficulties. They

Table 5.2   Age related issues for children.

0–2 years	Physical and emotional neglect to the detriment of their health Impact on cognitive development due to parents under-stimulating, inconsistent and neglecting behaviour Identity issues due to rejecting relationships Attachment difficulties due to parental unhappiness, tension irritability and inappropriate responses.
3–4 years	Child placed in physical danger due to parents' limited physical capacity to care Neglect of physical needs Delayed cognitive development due to a lack of stimulation and failure to access early educational opportunities A post traumatic stress type response when parents' behaviour is unpredictable or frightening Children taking on responsibilities beyond their years due to parental illness A child may not have the communication skills to clearly articulate their distress.
5–9 years	Children may be at increased risk of physical injury, and show symptoms of extreme anxiety and fear Academic attainment is negatively affected and children's behaviour in school becomes problematic Identity, age and gender may affect outcomes. Boys more quickly exhibit problematic behaviour but girls are also affected if parental problems endure Children may develop poor self-esteem and may blame themselves for their parent's problems Inconsistent parental behaviour may cause anxiety and faulty attachments Children's fear of hostility Unplanned separation can cause distress and disrupt education and friendship patterns Children may feel embarrassment and shame over parent's behaviour. As a consequence they curtail friendships and social interaction Children may take on too much responsibility for themselves, their parents and younger siblings.
10–14 years	Children have to cope with puberty without support Children are at increased risk of psychological problems Children fear being hurt Children are at increased risk of actual injury Children are anxious about how to compensate for physical neglect Children's education suffers as they find it difficult to concentrate School performance may be below expected ability Children may miss school because of looking after parents and siblings Children reject their families and have low self-esteem Children are cautious of exposing family life to outside scrutiny Friendships are restricted Children fear the family will be broken up Children feel isolated and have no one to turn to

Table 5.2 *(Continued)*

	Children are at increased risk of emotional disturbance and conduct disorders including bullying An increased risk of sexual abuse in adolescent boys The problems of being a young carer increase Children may be in denial of own needs and feelings.
15 years and over	Teenagers have inappropriate role models Teenagers are at greater risk of accidents Teenagers may have problems relating to sexual relationships Teenagers may fail to achieve their potential Teenagers are at increased risk of school exclusion Poor life chances due to exclusion and poor school attainment Low self-esteem as a consequence of inconsistent parenting Increased isolation from both friends and adults outside the family Teenagers may use aggression inappropriately to solve problems Emotional problems may result form self-blame and guilt, and lead to increased risk of suicidal behaviour, and vulnerability to crime Teenagers' own needs may be sacrificed to meet the needs of their parents.

(Cleaver, *et al.*, 1999).

describe economic disadvantage, unemployment being a major issue for their parents; this in turn often renders them unable to take part in leisure activities due to financial constraints. Children report social isolation, spending limited time outside of the home or with friends and being reluctant to discuss their situation with peers for fear of being ridiculed. They also describe having a limited understanding of mental health problems and of themselves experiencing feelings of anxiety, worry and emotional pressure, this escalating to fear when the parent was unwell. They also explain their efforts to constantly maintain stability and protect their parents from added stress. Many children report that they worry about their own mental health, being fearful of catching or inheriting their parent's illness and will often normalise their chaotic lifestyles and describe feeling that they did no more than others of their age when they clearly did. The researcher concludes by stating that:

'in order to provide young people with effective support, it is imperative that whenever a parent has mental health problems, adult mental health services recognise the presence and needs of young people in the family. Without that recognition, young people's needs are likely to go unnoticed, because in many cases no other service is involved with such families' (Armstrong 2002:4).

The Carers (Recognition and Services) Act acknowledges the part that children play in supporting their parents or significant others during times of illness. Young carers are entitled to an assessment of their ability to care under Section 1 of this Act and this assessment should guide agencies with regards to the delivery of community based services for parents. Additionally it must be acknowledged that young carers may be classed as a child in need in respect of the original Children Act (Department of Health, 1989) and that the young carer should not only be supported in their role as carer but that they are enabled in and encouraged to do the things that are important to them, hence the importance and relevance of the Children Act (Department of Health, 2004) and the explicit expression of the aforementioned five outcomes.

The care programme approach (Department of Health, 1996) and the Carers (Recognition and Services) Act (Department of Health, 1995) collectively recognise the importance of those who undertake caring responsibilities and, as care coordinators, adult mental health practitioners will be expected to facilitate the assessment of carers needs. This should include their own written care plan showing the support they are entitled to receive and thus enable carers to have a clear understanding of who to contact if the person they care for has a mental health crisis. Many organisations now produce Charters of Standards for users and carers that outline clearly what they can expect from those delivering mental health services and information outlining local and national support services for service users and carers. Increasingly these guidelines acknowledge the role of children as carer and will have information specifically geared to those under the age of eighteen. However, it is worth noting that the National Service Framework for Mental Health (Department of Health, 1999) acknowledges that, *'young carers are a particularly vulnerable group and that few authorities had implemented the Carers (Recognition and Services) Act, 1995 within their mental health services when inspected by the Social Services Inspectorate'* (Department of Health 1995:70). It is therefore of paramount importance that the needs of children are acknowledged by those responsible for the care of their parents and that children are included when care planning for adults with mental health difficulties.

Conclusion

Children often demonstrate a remarkable level of resilience as shown earlier by Haggerty *et al.* (1996) even when presented with the most difficult sets of circumstances and parents with mental health issues frequently parent their children in an extremely loving and effective manner. However, there is evidence to suggest that a child's physical, emotion, social and psychological health and development can be influenced by their parents' mental health and that children often assume the role of carer for their parent(s). This is graphically illustrated with The Framework For The Assessment Of Children In Need and Their Families (Department of Health, 2000b). As adult mental health practitioners it is not only our responsibility to address the health needs of our adult service users but to have a clear understanding of the impact of parental mental illness on children and be guided in our practice by the legislation intended to safeguard children and promote independent functioning.

References

Armstrong, C. (2002). *Behind Closed Doors – Living With A Parent's Mental Illness.* Available at: http://youngminds.org.uk/magazine/61/armstrong

Bowlby, J. (1988). *A Secure Base. Clinical Application of Attachment Theory.* Hove and New York: Brunner Routledge.

Cleaver, H., Unell, I. & Aldgate, J. (1999). *Children's Needs Parenting Capacity: The Impact of Parental Mental Illness, Problem Alcohol and Drug Use and Domestic Violence on Children's Development.* London: The Stationery Office.

Department for Education and Skills (DfES) (2004). *Every Child Matters: Next Steps.* Nottingham: DfES Publications.

Department of Health (1983). *The Mental Health Act (1983).* London: HMSO.

Department of Health (1989). *The Children Act.* London: HMSO.

Department of Health (1990). *The National Health Service and Community Care Act.* London: HMSO.

Department of Health (1995). *The Carers (Recognition and Services) Act.* London: HMSO.

Department of Health (1996). *Care Programme Approach (CPA).* London: The Stationery Office.

Department of Health (1999). *The National Service Framework for Mental Health.* London: The Stationery Office.

Department of Health (2000a). *The Carers and Disabled Children's Act.* London: The Stationery Office.

Department of Health (2000b). *The Framework For The Assessment Of Children In Need and Their Families.* London: The Stationery Office.

Department of Health (2004). *The Children Act.* London: The Stationery Office.

Department of Health (2006). *Working Together to Safeguard Children: A Guide To Interagency Working To Safeguard and Promote The Welfare Of Children.* London: The Stationery Office.

Dermot, J.H., Chiodo, D., Leschied, A. & Whitehead, P. (2003). *Correlates of a Measure of Parenting Capacity with Parent and Child Characteristics in a Child Welfare Sample.* Ontario, Canada: King's College London & The University of Western Ontario.

Flynn, H. & Starns, B. (2004). *Protecting Children. Working Together To Keep Children Safe.* Oxford: Heinemann Educational Publishers.

Gould, N. (2006). *Mental Health and Child Poverty.* York: Joseph Rowntree Foundation.

Green, R. (2002). *Mentally Ill Parents and Children's Welfare.* NSPCC, Practice Development Unit. Available at: http://www.nspcc.org.uk/inform/onlineresources/informationbriefings/mentallyillparents

Haggerty, R.J., Sherrod, L.R., Garmezy, N. & Rutter, M. (1996). *Stress, Risk and Resilience in Children and Adolescents: Processes, Mechanism and Interventions.* Cambridge: Cambridge University Press.

Murray, L. (1992). The Impact Of Postnatal Depression On Infant Development. *Journal of Child Psychology and Psychiatry.* **33(3)**, 543–61.

Reder, P., McLure, M. and Jolley, A. (2000). *Family Matters. Interfaces Between Child and Adult Mental Health.* London: Routledge.

Riordan, D., Appleby, L. & Faragher, B. (1999). Mother-Infant Interaction In Post-Partum Women With Schizophrenia and Affective Disorders. *Psychological Medicine.* **29(4)**, 991–995.

Warner, V., Weissman, M., Mutson, L. & Wickramaratne, P. (1999). Grandparents, Parents, and Grandchildren at High Risk for Depression: A Three Generation Study. *Journal of the American Academy of Child and Adolescent Psychiatry.* **38(3)**, 289–296.

Section 2

Personal Experiences of Care Planning

Chapter 6

Care Planning and the Carer

Molly Halford

Who is a carer? Being a carer does not refer to how much you care for (or love) a person. You can love someone greatly and for a variety of reasons, not be a carer. The concept of who is a carer is variable and legal definitions are hard to pin down for ordinary people who often find that they have to become one of these individuals without being asked – as I did.

In the mental health context, a carer is someone who gives practical and emotional support to a person experiencing a mental health problem – but this is outside a professional capacity. In the carer's assessment a carer is *'an individual who provides or intends to provide a substantial amount of care on a regular basis for the relevant person'* (Carers (Recognition and Services) Act, Department of Health, 1995). However, you are not a carer if you act as a volunteer for a voluntary organisation, if you have a contract of employment or another contract with any person. This Act gives carers the right to ask for an assessment of their own needs and their capacity and willingness to provide care.

Figures distributed by the National Institute for Mental Health in England (NIMHE) suggest 10% of the adult population of England and Wales identified themselves as carers in the 2001 census. This is because they provide unpaid care to support family, friends or neighbours due to long-term physical or mental ill health, disability, or old age. This percentage involves 5.2 million people but excludes a sizeable group of young carers who are often unnoticed outside their families and immediate communities. Schools and colleges often have no idea if their members, staff or students, are carers. At a recent mental health event celebrating involvement together for mental health service users, carers, and mental health professionals, one carer pointed out that she was care in the community for 23 hours 50 minutes a day following the 10 minute professional visit.

I am a member of a large family (I stopped counting first cousins at 50) and so it is unsurprising that some of my family suffer from severe mental illness. Rethink (the national charity formerly called the National Schizophrenia Fellowship) estimates that in the general population 1 in 4 suffer mental ill health at some time and 1 in 100 globally develop schizophrenia. In 1994, my life experienced an earth-shaking change when a close relative (whom I will refer to as Jack) developed a psychotic illness, eventually diagnosed as schizophrenia.

My husband and I had become carers although at the time we did not know it. This chapter describes and reflects on my experience as a carer, together with the support, or more frequently lack of support, from mental health professionals or social workers, that I have encountered.

Three distinct epochs can be identified in the story. For the first three years Jack was suffering acute problems. I felt the situation was out of control, chaotic and desperate. Advice and assistance that could have been useful was absent: no structures were in place to offer these to carers and the professionals probably never thought in such terms. From 1996 to 2002, Jack's circumstances improved in various ways but, despite the legislation that was in place from 1995, during these years little help was available to me in my role as a carer, and I remained in ignorance of what support might be available. Only after 2002 did this change. I became actively involved in organisations that were aware of the problem and increasingly became aware of initiatives to support carers.

In 1994 Jack was initially admitted to hospital in a confused state and was, when I first visited, under severe sedation. Jack remained in hospital for a few weeks, although was soon transferred between hospitals because of his postcode. We only learned of the transfer after it had taken place when we arrived at the first hospital for one of our daily visits. Schizophrenia was not mentioned. We know now that it is not a diagnosis that would be given on the basis of a single psychotic episode, but this does not seem an adequate reason for not mentioning the possibility. Nobody talked to us about Jack's condition: what he was suffering and what was meant by psychosis. I later learned from my GP that the hospital doctor had noted I was an awkward or obstructive relative because I had encouraged Jack to ask questions and query the medication. In fact, our interaction with staff at either hospital was minimal, nothing on: diagnosis and what we might expect or do, the effects of medication, effects on our lifestyle, effects on day by day living, and so forth. When he was discharged with a provisional diagnosis of epilepsy, Jack came to stay with us and received good medical care from our GP and an experienced community psychiatric nurse.

The immediate practicalities for my husband and I were devastating. Events had been an enormous shock – not unlike a sudden death because lots of people and organisations had to be informed (e.g. Jack's tenancy had to be ended and his flat cleared) but different because care had to be given to a relative sometimes too ill to be left while we went to work. I had real time-management and reliability issues to face. This is where I could have really used some help and support from mental health professionals. In the end, I gave up my job with consequent loss of salary and, long term, my pension. I was very lucky to have an endlessly supportive GP who listened to me forever but help over carer's issues like money or the possibility of arranging leave of absence from work did not get discussed. We were also fortunate in having a number of supportive friends, some of whom were informed about mental health issues, although none had experienced actual carers' problems.

Jack remained at home: difficult, often depressed, sometimes hostile. Another, more severe, psychotic episode occurred a few months later and a further period of hospitalisation. His anti-psychotic medication was increased and he was also given the ubiquitous Prozac. But from this nadir, a gradual improvement did occur. He began a postgraduate course, living with us, travelling daily. We provided everything we could to minimise life's stresses – it was teamwork. Even so, eventually the stress of the course caused a further relapse, hospital admission and, finally, the diagnosis of schizophrenia. We were fortunate in that the hospital was a leading psychiatric centre and the psychiatrists were ready to discuss issues involving the illness in an informed and sympathetic way. However, they did not see as part of their brief the need to give us any specific consideration as carers. I remember that the hospital registrar's advice was to get some books and go on a steep learning curve – we have been doing this ever since but on our own – not with mental health professionals.

In 1994 support for us, as carers, from mental health professionals or social workers, did not happen. On a social level, our lives at home became quite severely restricted. One of us had to be at home when Jack was really ill. We found it best to avoid turning on television or radio. Newspapers were kept away. All these had messages. Figurative use of language caused confusion, everything was understood on a literal level. In general we did not invite or visit many friends or relatives. It was too painful and difficult. People would not have understood. On an employment level, we both had demanding jobs with extensive out of hours work. No mental health professional enquired how we would restructure our lives to continue working. To be fair, at the time, everything was so chaotic that I did not realise that we needed help or even could be helped. Perhaps I could have negotiated a leave of absence but instead I felt I could not cope and resigned. We just felt that other family members had been supported inside the family and they had coped. We had not realised how difficult this must have been or what the personal costs had been. We felt we would have to do the same. If only we had known about Rethink and carers' groups for information and support. The mental health professionals should have told us about this.

Further hospital contacts brought no support for us as carers and no information that there were mental health charities. This in spite of the 1990 NHS and Community Care Act (Department of Health, 1990) which recognised that public bodies should be doing more to support carers. After 2002 I received a list of the details for carers' groups in our area which came from Rethink. We needed this information with the explanation of how much help we could receive, when Jack first became ill. I understand from my knowledge of a Rethink support group that some mental health professionals now do this.

Mental health carers are lonely people. When the one you care for becomes ill, it is not like getting bronchitis or breaking bones. Everything is confidential. Many carers have difficulty in finding out what is thought to be wrong with their relative; they are not informed about medication or how they can best help. I was not told about nearest relatives although this is a legal position with practical implications. It would help reduce the isolation and shock if relatives were given information and the possibility of choice of immediately accessing support for themselves. It was only many years later, when we were having a particularly bad time, that my husband returned from work having rung MIND who had recommended Rethink to him.

There are many ways in which we could have been helped through this phase as carers. I would have benefited from real, detailed advice sessions on how to help and handle Jack, a person whom I had known all his life and yet who now was very different. Written information and advice on psychosis would have provided a reference point for us – and I might have done or not done things differently had I been better informed. I learned through trial and error how to get through seemingly endless days; that it was morale boosting for us all to have a daily achievement, for example, walked the dog, made something, etc. This marked our progress and was normal and inclusive. It was something to tell family and friends. In addition to the written information provided with medication, it would have been helpful to be able to talk about the prescription drugs, what to give when, the hoped-for effects, the possible side effects and, most importantly, tips on taking them. For example, a simple, but extremely useful tip was when we were recommended to give a drug at night. This was really helpful as its drowsy factor was reduced by the night's sleep. I made lists of medications. I still have these lists reminding me of the efforts I made to try to master the mysteries of drug action.

Even when things were relatively good, numerous problems emerged relating to getting Jack's life back onto an independent course. The carer's goal must be the independence of the cared for but there is no guarantee that a mentally ill person can achieve this. As recovery progresses, the major areas that emerge are finance, employment and social inclusion. Friendships are often casualties of mental illness. We were relatively fortunate in being in a position to provide accommodation and some financial support. An important breakthrough came when the psychiatric social worker found a voluntary part-time job with a charity that led subsequently into paid employment. Another breakthrough came when, as a result of contacts through our friends, Jack developed new friendships and eventually established a relationship.

Our experience was probably quite typical but it is interesting to note that during this period the Carers (Recognition and Services) Act (Department of Health, 1995) was passed, which gave carers the right to request assessment of our ability and willingness to be carers. That is fine, but as the Rethink report *Under Pressure* (Pinfold & Corry, 2003) points out, to obtain an assessment you have to know of your entitlement and have to ask for one. The same document makes depressing reading about how few carers receive assessments and how little difference assessments actually make to carers even now. *Under Pressure* examined the impact that caring for someone with mental health problems had on the carers. It succinctly summarises what has improved and what remains to be tackled.

The years from 1996 to 2002 were difficult and sometimes lonely for us but not without hope. The good news is that for some people with psychosis, recovery and inclusion are possible. As Jack recovered he was helped back into voluntary work with a charity by a good community psychiatric nurse. By October 1996 Jack had independently managed to obtain a job. Moreover new friendships emerged, and in 1998 a relationship developed to the point at which he married, providing a considerable and much needed boost to his self-esteem. Even though Jack's marriage broke up in 2000, he was able to continue living independently from that point.

Marriage entailed a change of address and a different community mental health team (CMHT), although the latter seemed almost non-existent. Perhaps because of poor communication, moving away seemed like falling into a mental health black hole. For a time, until a relapse in 2003, there was little mental health service support apart from occasional visits to a psychiatrist. This individual appeared content that Jack was in a stable condition but, as far as we were able to tell, did not probe beyond his immediate medical condition to examine, for example, whether the side effects of the medication were interfering with job performance. Jack had been on the same medication for several years during which time the new anti-psychotic drugs had arrived. As a carer, I believed that both diagnosis and medication should have been reviewed and a second opinion arranged. As a consequence, Jack was transferred to one of the newer anti-psychotic drugs with the consequence that he became much less drowsy.

This was important because an employment pattern had emerged whereby Jack could cope with a job over a short period but, in part because of drowsiness from the medication, failed to progress from short-term contracts to a permanent one. Such a pattern is very stressful because it is not financially secure and it is very difficult to maintain social networks made through work. These are all known typical problems for mental health service users, which can only be resolved by a combination of sympathetic employers and empowering disability legislation in the workplace. Jack moved between a number of jobs, none lasting more than a year.

The financial difficulties of temporary and part-time employment patterns are considerable and provide additional stress both for the cared for and the carers. Employment legislation is cumbersome and although there are signs that mental health considerations are being taken into account the view is often encountered that either you are fit to work or you are not. Nevertheless, disabled living allowance and working tax credit are available and can provide much needed support for individuals with mental health conditions. In Jack's case they would not have been achieved without considerable persistence from his social worker who took the issue to a tribunal. These benefits are, however, time limited and Jack is already worrying about how he will cope when they expire. Pensions are another major concern. Jack has no pension provision. There are large gaps in his National Insurance contributions and to this day this is a continuing source of anxiety. It is not yet sorted and is on hold because I cannot face it.

As far as we were concerned, from 1994 until 2002, the following legislation affecting mental health carers might never have happened:

- The National Health Service and Community Care Act (Department of Health, 1990) which recognised public bodies should do more to support carers.
- The Carers (Recognition and Services) Act (Department of Health, 1995) that gave us the right to request assessment of our ability and willingness to be carers – if someone had told us about it!
- The National Service Framework for Mental Health (Department of Health, 1999a) in which standard 6 asks health and social services to assess carers' needs and provide care to meet them.
- The Caring about Carers: National Strategy for Carers (Department of Health, 1999b) in which the government made a commitment to carers with policy packages and funding to inform, support, and care for carers.
- The Carers and Disabled Children's Act (Department of Health, 2000) allowed local councils to provide specific services to carers after assessment of their health and social care needs.
- The Developing Strategies for Carers (Department of Health, 2002) to develop carers' support services which are person centred and view carers as co-experts.

Jack suffered a relapse in 2003, effectively losing two months of his life, probably because of lack of care with medication. He spent several days in a very distressed, although not psychotic, state. More positively, soon after this, following a further painful termination of employment, he obtained a part-time post in the speciality of his graduate course. At present he has decided to earn less, to job share, and work part-time. This is frustrating for a young person but shows that Jack has gained some insight into managing his condition and realistically pacing himself. He currently (2007) still holds this job and no longer has a psychiatric social worker because he is regarded as coping well.

In my active caring role, which has provided continuous support of a fluctuating level, practically, emotionally and sometimes financially from 1994 to the present day, June 2002 was an important turning point.

Up to that point, I genuinely did not know that I was something called a carer nor did I know that I had some legal carer's rights because no one had told me. In May 2002, the local press ran an article on mental health and the charity Rethink. This was coincidentally soon after my husband had been given their name. Rethink was the new name for the National Schizophrenia Fellowship. The new name was chosen to be inclusive of anyone suffering from any severe mental illness and their family and friends. It exists primarily for members to support each other. In some parts of the UK, it provides mental health services and some branches campaign actively to promote improvements to mental health care. The establishment of a countywide branch was suggested. I joined.

That was when I discovered that I am a carer as defined in the Carers Act (Department of Health, 1995) with an entitlement to request my own assessment but it took Rethink to tell me. The National Service Framework for Mental Health (Department of Health, 1999a) standard 6 also lays a duty of assessment of carers' needs on mental health professionals/social workers. Again, I only heard of this through Rethink meetings and publications. I cannot stress too much how valuable Rethink's information has been. Although I learned in 2002 that I could request my own assessment, I have not asked for one because between 1994 and 2002 we learned how to cope. When the 1995 Act is properly fulfilled it should be of tremendous help and support to new carers, provided they are told about it.

Individuals with a diagnosis of schizophrenia should have a personalised care plan. Jack is willing for us to be involved in caring but we have never seen or been consulted over a care plan, unless the document described below counts. We have never been to a meeting with mental health professionals to plan care. In July 2004, we did receive a carer advice plan for the first time. This consisted of a pre-printed sheet of A4 paper.

The left hand side has three boxes concerning crisis information. Box 1, concerning self-harm, advises ringing 999. Box 2, about potential self-harm, or danger to others advises contacting the community mental health team by day and the GP or NHS Direct by night. Box 3, if the person has become unwell, recommends as for Box 2. The right hand side concerns carer support information and has four boxes. Box 1 emotional needs advises to contact the community mental health team by day and the GP or NHS Direct by night. Box 2 physical needs advises do as Box 1. Box 3 caring needs advises to ring the CMHT. Box 4 if you are unable to care further ring the CMHT by day or GP/NHS Direct by night. Below these boxes relevant names and telephone numbers are added.

We managed to exist for ten years before we received even this information from a mental health professional. I am not sure if this is a care plan or not. It certainly is not personal, it has not been agreed, and it has not been reviewed annually. We have had one or two meetings with Jack's psychiatrist at crisis points. After the 2003 relapse, we did have some contact and useful discussion with a psychiatric social worker. These meetings were helpful in dealing with issues involving Jack, but did not touch at all on our needs as carers.

Rethink made me aware that carers' support groups exist. I was lucky enough to go on a carers' education course in 2005 run by Rethink and our local community mental health team. I really could have benefited from this excellent course, had it existed, in 1994. We were in the wilderness about so many carers' issues concerning ourselves: management, isolation, loss of our own lives, effect on our employment and others. Above all I felt we needed information. The carers' course in 2005 lasted 10 weeks and covered multiple carers' issues.

Rethink carers' one to one link (COOL) gave me details of local groups and information on NHS user-carer involvement. Supported by the NHS user and carer involvement structure, both user and carer groups have written their own mental health charters. In front of me, as I write, I have three excellent short publications produced in 2000 by the Carers' Advisory Group for Mental Health in London. The group have produced *Valuing Carers*, which is a carers' charter with two clear and helpful workbooks: *Guide for Carers* and *Working with Carers*, which is a handbook for professionals working with mental health carers. Their common foreword states that the publications are the direct result of the National Service Framework, the Carers' Act, and the NHS Plan, all recognising the role of carers. Similarly the NHS Executive London and the Social Services Inspectorate for London social care region established *A Strategy for Action* (Heron, 2000).

These documents are intended to assist agencies, in particular health and social services, to provide better care and support to carers, with the overall aim of improving care and support to people with mental health problems. The professionals' guide makes good clear reading also for carers. I hope it is put into practice and used. It has a clear definition of mental health carers and their needs. It informs about carers' assessment under the Carers and Disabled Children's Act (Department of Health, 2000) and in standard 6 of the National Service Framework for Mental Health Caring for Carers (Department of Health, 1999b). It also has a practical, comprehensive 10-point checklist to ensure standard 6 is implemented, together with guidance on confidentiality and sharing information with carers.

Working through this document, bearing in mind that Jack became ill in 1994, prior to *Caring about Carers* (Department of Health, 1999b), I think we are identified as carers because in 2003 the social worker phoned us and knew that Jack comes to us during a relapse. Also Jack's GP knows that we support him. I have been with him many times to the GP when he has been ill. We have now the confidence to ask for the information we need in order to provide care. We did not have this in 1994.

Mental health professionals do listen now to what we say. With Jack we obtained a second opinion review from a hospital psychiatrist. We enquired about cognitive behaviour therapy and then paid for it, which possibly shamed the mental health services into providing some sessions on the NHS. Jack reported that he did not feel it was useful. I do not know whether, according to the agreed criteria, we provide regular and substantial care. We provide unlimited care, both emotional and practical, as and when it is needed – this fluctuates. We provide rent-free accommodation. We are not involved with the mental health services in what they do for Jack. Indeed currently they are not involved with Jack at all. Disabled living allowance and working tax credit would not have been achieved without the social worker taking the issue to a tribunal. Jack has no pension provision. There are large gaps in his National Insurance and this worries him, and me. Jack is unable to sort this and he now has no social worker to assist because he is coping so well.

Although I am not consulted about what help Jack does or does not receive, independently through Rethink I have become involved in the planning and development of mental health services. I meet and interact with the local NHS user-carer involvement team and have attended forums. Rethink encouraged me to ask to join the local improvement group (LIG) of my Primary Care Trust and I did this for four years up to their disappearance in the NHS reorganisation of 2006. With other Rethink members, I have been a member of a nursing collaborative at a local psychiatric hospital aiming to improve their services to carers. Through Rethink I was the carer representative on a group looking at a vision for the development of NHS mental health services in the future and their relationship with the voluntary sector.

As a carer, Rethink and the CMHT have educated me via their carers' course and given me confidence to talk for other carers as their friend. Rethink encouraged me to train as a mental health advocate with the local community service volunteers (CSV). Rethink has involved me in training for trainers. I am currently being trained in order to train Rethink staff. Also I have been involved in putting a carers' perspective to second year health and social work students at a local university and to diverse groups undergoing raising mental health awareness. Currently with a colleague I am running a short community awareness programme on the importance of early intervention in psychosis for secondary school and college staff. There is hope that, if treatment begins early enough in the prodromal stage, thus reducing the duration of untreated psychosis (DUP), as many as one third of suffers may only experience a single psychotic episode.

The greatest help I personally have had as a carer has come from Rethink. Being involved with mental illness is like entering a parallel world. Rethink gives you the information and confidence to cope. It gives you hope. You support and are supported by other families who have dropped out, sometimes for years, because of the effects of mental ill health. Many carers live quietly, keeping themselves to themselves. Traditional stigma about the mentally ill, sadly to say often reinforced by media stereotyping, does not encourage you to advertise your problem.

I believe support to carers is crucial – it saves the country millions of hidden pounds – in keeping those cared for out of hospital. While social services are rightly now supporting carers in many ways unheard of in 1994, I believe carers can support themselves and their cared for by borrowing and adapting an idea from British Columbia. Vela Microboards were originally a device supporting learning disabled citizens and are support networks made up from, amongst others, family and friends who help enhance the quality of life of an individual. This idea could be adapted to support any vulnerable citizens. In their different ways a circle of committed friends or family support an individual who will always face challenges. Making provision for a time my husband needed to work away and I wished to take the chance to accompany him, we set about making our own arrangements to support Jack. Half a dozen trusted friends offered to become a support team. Jack's GP, psychiatrist, social worker and employer were all given contact details. During our absence, Jack survived job loss and a benefits tribunal. People gave support in different ways: weekends away, meals out, walks, cinema and shopping. They acted normally and Jack was socially included. This gives me great reassurance, which I do not get from the mental health professionals, that Jack will be supported if I should die or otherwise become unable to support him.

References

Department of Health (1990). *NHS and Community Care Act*. London: HMSO.

Department of Health (1995). *Carers (Recognition & Services) Act*. London: HMSO.

Department of Health (1999a). *The National Service Framework for Mental Health*. London: The Stationery Office.

Department of Health (1999b). *Caring about Carers: National Strategy for Carers*. London: The Stationery Office.

Department of Health (2000). *Carers and Disabled Children's Act*. London: The Stationery Office.

Department of Health (2002). *Developing Strategies for Carers*. London: The Stationery Office.

Heron, C. (2000). *A Strategy for Action: NHS Executive London and the Social Services Inspectorate for London Social Care Region*. London: Jessica Kingsley Publishers.

Pinfold, V. & Corry, P. (2003). *Under Pressure*. London: Rethink.

Chapter 7

Experiencing the Process

Edward Smith, Julie Smith, Mark Hopps,
and Victoria Lumley

Stanza 1: the son's tale
Edward Smith

It was a couple of weeks before I came home from university after I first started to feel ill. I was not sleeping and I had my long hair cut off. I started seeing spiders on the ceiling and I started seeing messages in names. Everything became even scarier. I didn't tell anyone about my thoughts. I started smoking cigarettes. I thought different makes of cigarettes had different effects. I thought people had infrared lights on me and someone was aiming a gun. So I decided to go home. I felt really bad on the train and a lady gave me a cigarette and talked to me, which made me feel a bit better. When I was going out of the station I kicked over a dustbin.

When I got home I took the video recorder to pieces because I thought there was a camera in it. The GP came to see me. Everything was very frightening. I was put on to trifluoperazine and then fluoxetine was added and lithium but I can't remember in which order. I soon felt a bit better and I got a job away from home but I thought the trainer was from Star Trek. I was suspicious of people. I went out for the night with work colleagues and I was arrested. Mum came and got me and I went home. I got a new community psychiatric nurse (CPN) and I could talk to him.

I started drinking to get friends but I just drank. I was on depot injections and had cramps in my stomach for two or three months. The CPN told me about the medication but he did not tell me about the illness or what was happening to me. Then the voices started, at first it was lots of voices talking but now it's fewer. These *people* were hassling me all the time. If they come now I can tell them to come back later. I went in to hospital. Talking to people and hearing other people's views of their illness helped me get better. The hospital gave me a safe environment. I was so busy talking to the other patients that I did not hear many voices. I had a named nurse in hospital but find it difficult to remember. The staff observed me carefully to see if I needed any medication or anything like that. We had meetings every month with all the staff and my family. I thought everyone was friendly. My CPN was friendly and I could tell him my thoughts. I couldn't confide in any of the nurses in the hospital. On a number of occasions, I thought my heart had stopped for a few minutes. I couldn't swallow for fear of choking and I was very frightened. Another time I thought I was coughing up embryos and I didn't have anyone to tell.

After six months I began to get better, I got less afraid. I think the stable environment helped. The people I could talk to were the other patients. There was not a staff member that I could confide in. The monthly meetings with the psychiatrist, staff and mum and dad were very useful because I got some feedback about how I was. I would have liked to have had someone to talk to me, like a friend to whom I could talk about my experience and talk about recovery and what it would be like. I could not even get soft drinks in the hospital – only tea and coffee. All I could do during the day was talk and smoke.

It was eventually decided I should go home and that the CPN should visit me there. I have to have my bloods checked once a month and then go to the hospital for other checks and to collect my pills. At first the CPN came once a week and asked me about my voices. I could confide in him and talk about them all. My new CPN talks to me differently.

I don't think that my CPN discussed my future with me, we only talked about the present although I was with him when he wrote a care plan. He wrote a letter to the council and I got a flat in the town. He supported my decision and talked to me about it. He got me started on 'exercise on prescription' to give me something to do during the day. When I spend time on my own the voices are much busier. It was good having someone to check on me. No one explained how the voices happened until the last time I saw my psychiatrist; it was very helpful and interesting. Having contact with someone outside the house is important. My new CPN explains things more to me.

I have no worrying voices now. I have learnt to deal with them. My pills were changed when I was in hospital. I like working on my computer, I go for a walk in the fields, like listening to music, going to art and other classes and I help old people with computers. I like watching TV now, when I was ill I didn't watch it at all. Some things are still scary; for instance, I am frightened of getting lost.

Recovery is being happy. I am getting happier! It's like climbing a mountain, you always think that you're at the top but you're not. If I were better I would be at the top of the mountain, in control of myself without hearing any voices.

My medication has been reduced and I take omega 3 fish oil and vitamin supplements because of information that was shown to me by my new CPN. I need someone watching me to make sure I'm not getting ill because when you are ill you don't know that you are ill. I have talked about early warning signs with my CPN, we wrote them down but I don't know where the paper is. I am very worried that I might be trapped in hospital again. The CPN has written a crisis plan for me but I can't find it – it should be on my notice board.

I feel quite positive now and perhaps I will get my life back again. The voices are getting quieter now but it's hard work climbing mountains. It is possible to get your life back again and I think that it has helped getting all this down on paper.

Stanza 2: the mother's tale
Julie Smith

The early years

I first realised that Edward was ill, when, in the spring of 1996, he telephoned me sounding very strange. We had a long talk and I was able to persuade him to come home for a while. A few days later he caught the train and a bus to our town, could not remember our telephone number but rang a friend of ours who rang me. I drove to pick him up. He looked grey and thin with big startled eyes. His hair was short and he was wearing a cap on which was written *no fear*. He did not look the same son that we had sent back to university, wearing a ponytail and looking relaxed.

We knew something was wrong when he said that he was going to take the video player to pieces to find out how they were watching and listening to him. Television was not allowed to be on in his presence. He was still helping by doing jobs around the garden for us but he was frightened. I phoned our GP, who, on a pretext, called into the house and talked to him. Nothing much was done straight away because it was assumed that it was a temporary psychotic episode perhaps due to taking drugs at university.

However, things got worse. He was sure that people had been putting something in his coffee at his part-time clerical job while at university. When one of his brothers came home having been away on holiday Edward believed his brother was in a secret service and that the daffodils on the table had microphones in their trumpets and were recording him. So we called the doctor again and Edward eventually became involved as a patient with the mental health team. The psychiatrist eventually put him on lithium and gradually other medications such as fluoxetine were added.

He became more ill and was crawling around the floor so that *they* could not see him through the windows. My mother was visiting us and sat with him holding his hand for days because he said that he wanted to lie in the road and let a car run over him. More pills were added and we thought that he was better, but he wasn't. In the summer he got a good job using his computer skills, but after three weeks he thought that his work colleagues were from outer space. Whilst working he was staying with my parents and on one occasion, my father said that Edward stared at him and made him feel very uncomfortable. He was sure that there was something wrong. Edward went out for a meal with his office one evening, ending up in a police cell. I went to bring him home and because our GP kindly wrote to the police explaining that he had been mentally ill no charges were made.

When he got home he was put onto depot injections, the psychiatrist was of the old school. Although he saw us with Edward he seemed to think that it would breach confidentiality if he talked to us 'behind Edward's back'. Looking back, we think that Edward's CPN took the easy course and followed the psychiatrist's lead. Edward began to drink because he said that he had an empty space and an ache in his tummy. On my way home from work I was trawling the pubs to find him and bring him home. He was meant to be attending a class or a meeting but instead was spending the day in one of the many pubs in the town. He would go out on the town in the evening and be brought home by some kind taxi driver. We were desperate for help. All the GP was able to suggest was that we should see a counsellor when one was in the village, but what we wanted was to talk to someone who knew about the illness.

Things became more and more difficult. Eventually, one afternoon Edward had drunk too much and ended up being arrested in a shop. He was taken to the police cells handcuffed. Police came to our house in the evening and asked us if it was true that he needed to take his medication. The policemen told us that we should get our GP to see him and they would release him if he went to hospital. Having seen the GP with Edward he was referred to the town general hospital where we sat for two hours in a waiting room with an ill son lying on the floor. The young A&E doctor did not seem to know what to do and we were eventually told that the hospital's psychiatric ward would not take him. We were told to take him to the regional psychiatric hospital out in the country. We had never heard of it, far less knew where it was, but eventually found it at two in the morning. It was raining and very dark. We could not even find the ward entrance door at first and we felt intimidated. Eventually we were admitted and were given a very friendly welcome by the staff nurse. In there he seemed to blossom with the care and activities that were available. We think that he was there for about six weeks, late in 1996.

The psychiatrists there were open and ready to talk to us and to discuss Edward's treatment. One psychiatrist said to us that Edward was probably suffering from schizophrenia and could have it for the rest of his life. This, instead of upsetting us, gave us something to latch onto and was almost comforting because we had a name for the illness, we could learn about it and perhaps know what to expect. After his discharge from hospital things were better for a while.

In the summer of 1997, a year or so into Edward's illness, when we thought he was recovering, some work placement agency organised a work scheme for him which we thought was just what we wanted. It was to be for a short period and looked on as a training event. At first he enjoyed the job as it was with computers and his degree had been in IT. We were able to drop him off at the workplace and pick him up in the evening. He was paid and they asked him to stay on for a little longer. This was when the work experience person should have stepped in and said stop. Working that extra week caused him to lose all his benefits for another six months, luckily, we were able to support him. He became progressively more ill when working there, presumably due to stress, and he was not being monitored by anyone. We now realise that the whole thing should have been very carefully planned and supported. After this Edward went downhill.

The middle years

When Edward was really ill we wrote letters and diaries that we gave to various professionals. We seldom got any response. When we wrote to the local head of social services with a series of questions about the type of support that he could expect it was thought to be a complaint and received a quick response resulting in a couple of meetings with senior people but failed to answer our basic questions. Without knowledge it is difficult to ask the correct questions. Talking is important, as the old saying goes *a trouble shared is a trouble halved*.

When we were at our wits' end, and desperately trying to get more help for Edward, we kept a diary. Here are a few excerpts from October to November 1998, when I was trawling round the pubs on my way home from work.

Diary entries:

Saturday 23rd October: Phoned the mental health team at their clinic at 5 pm to see if there was an emergency number. The answer phone gave another number that I rang. A recorded message gave me an emergency number. There, the phone was answered by a human who told me to phone the hospital since she knew nothing about an emergency number and that it had happened before and something needed to be done about it! I phoned the hospital and got through to the psychiatric unit. The man that I spoke to told me to phone my GP. I spoke to the doctor's answering service and within ten minutes a locum was at our house and gave Edward some pills to calm him. All these calls were made surreptitiously because Edward was behaving very strangely and denying the need for help. He has spent two weeks' spending money on drink in two days. (At this point we were two and a half years into Edward's illness and in an emergency were still unaware of how to obtain expert advice. Since the locum was untrained in psychiatry she was unable to give us such advice.)

Sunday 24th October: Edward asked for half an extra pill because he was feeling paranoid.

Monday 25th October: He agreed to go to hospital with me. Refused to be admitted. The psychiatrist said 'No more than two beers a day'!

Wednesday 28th October: Went to writing class. Did not come home. Could not find him in the pubs at 5 pm but went back for another trawl at 7.30 pm and found him very drunk.

Friday 30th October: Took him to mental health group meeting at 10.30 am and he promised to come home at 1.30 for lunch. The social worker would give him a lift. (Edward had a social worker who was not at all forthcoming and who we only glimpsed occasionally). Edward rang to say that he was staying out. Rang at midnight from town, very drunk. When we found him a man was looking after him.

Saturday 31st October: Called doctor this evening because of strange behaviour.

Sunday 1st November: Drank half a bottle of vodka and some lager at home.

Tuesday 3rd November: 'To computer class in morning. Spent day in pub. Collected him at 7 pm'.

Thursday 5th November: Promised to be at home at 4 pm but we found him in the pub in the evening.

Friday 6th November: Dad stayed at home from work to support Edward and in the morning, having dropped him at his mental health group, phoned his new CPN. He phoned to say he did not need a lift home as he was going to 'see friends'. So once again he missed his lunchtime pills. The CPN arrived at 2.30 pm to see Edward but he was missing. It transpires that the social worker has told the CPN that Edward and his parents didn't really talk to each other. Dad told the CPN that we had not met the social worker for two years and that he did not seem to want to be involved with us and had obviously accepted Edward's tales. Dad told the CPN that Edward had said that the social worker thought that his parents can afford to look after him. (Was he implying that Edward's case was not high priority because we scooped up Edward when he was in trouble?) Dad said that this was an irrelevance and that if his reported comments are true the social worker was just justifying his position. The CPN said that he wished to have a relationship that involved us and would make an early appointment for us with the psychiatrist. At 6 pm found Edward in a pub very drunk.

Edward's consultant psychiatrist changed. This one was very approachable and would ring in the evening or at the weekend if we were worried. He even answered our letters.

We could not talk to friends and most of our relations because people tend to become embarrassed, frightened and are unsure how to react when you tell them that you have a son who suffers from schizophrenia. Nowadays we use the term psychosis that seems to have less of a stigma attached to it. It is akin to when someone has died. I remember my mother-in-law telling me just after her husband died that people crossed the road and walked on the other side when they saw her coming along.

One afternoon when we were at work Edward rang a friend because he was lonely and was at a loose end. He persuaded his friend, a pillar of society in the village, to pick him up and take him down to the pub for a cider. After half an hour or so they returned to our house and noticed that the burglar alarm had been activated. They entered through the back door and found that the outside front door had been smashed in and the glass in the inside door had been smashed enough for someone to get through. The telephone was next to the front door so Edward lent on the door while his friend called the police. A scene of crimes officer took our fingerprints and found prints on the glass left in the inner door. The next thing was that we were asked to take Edward to the station where two large policemen interviewed him. They told us that he was first suspected because he was sweating and shaking when the prints were taken and that his prints were on the door glass and that there were no exit fingerprints. The DC (detective constable) came to see us and suggested that if we abandoned the insurance claim, which totalled £6000 for stolen goods and property damage, they would not charge Edward. By abandoning the claim we would have been accepting Edward's guilt. We trusted our son's and his friend's honesty and knew that there was no way that he could have got through the little hole, especially as he was on medication. We employed a solicitor who hired a fingerprint expert who found exit prints that were not Edward's. The police dropped the case and we eventually received an apology by word of mouth. What would have happened if we had not kept the damaged inner door in the garage? We got our insurance claim settlement. The solicitor summed up the case in a letter saying, *'Although this has been a costly experience for you and a time consuming one for me, the result was that your trust in Edward was justified and his honesty confirmed. I have seldom been involved in a more rewarding case'.*

The drinking continued and the voices became vicious and really frightening. As a result, Edward was admitted to the psychiatric ward in the town general hospital.

In there he spent his time chain smoking and there was little encouragement for him to take part in any activities. His medication was changed to olanzapine and he was discharged after about six months to a house run by a charity near the hospital. We felt at the time that perhaps it would be better for him to be more independent. However, it was not right for him as the carers were not on duty twenty-four hours a day and they were not expected to check that he took his medication. His period of independence lasted six weeks even though we were visiting nearly every day. He started drinking again and stopped his medicine. The carers there were very kind and worried about his strange behaviour. I got a call to meet them at the house and was able to encourage him to return to hospital.

The watershed

He was on a ward for some time then became a day patient living with us when a nurse whispered into my ear that I should ask about clozapine and gave me an article on it. His mental state was deteriorating again so he was admitted full time again and this time was eventually put onto clozapine.

Before leaving hospital Edward was helped by a psychologist who was very interested in recovery and early warning signs. When Edward was due to be discharged this psychologist spent a few sessions with us, sometimes without Edward being present, talking about early warning signs and psychosis. These sessions were very valuable and we appreciated him spending time with us and treating us as part of the team. Before this we did not really feel that we were valued members of the team and on many occasions during Edward's treatment we would have liked to have received more information and had it discussed. Edward has generally wanted us present at his meetings with psychiatrists. We know the professionals may have been concerned about confidentiality but it is quite possible to discuss an illness rather than a named person. I read an article written by a consultant psychiatrist who holds a weekly clinic for carers. They enquire about the illness, how best to cope with the effects it has on the person who is being cared for and how to clarify issues that are causing stress. He does this without breaching confidentiality. I think that it is much easier to cope and live with an illness if one has knowledge of it and of what possible outcomes there could be. It is so helpful if there is someone to talk to who knows about the illness.

Recovery

Here I use recovery as a relative term. What has been achieved is far from full recovery nor is it a completely level plateau.

Once Edward got home from hospital about the middle of 2000 he wanted no alcohol but still smoked about fifty a day. Eventually, though, with the help of a stop smoking clinic run by our GP's surgery he stopped completely and has never smoked again. He had support from his CPN to whom we could all talk and who was ready to respond. Edward still hears and talks to his voices but now they are friendly. He goes to mainstream activities such as photography evening classes and creative writing, intended to help people with mild mental health problems. He has continued in this situation for about six years without major crises but with some fluctuations in his state of health.

He needs structure to his day because we think that his levels of self-confidence and self-motivation are quite low. Even if we are away for a day, things become a bit pear shaped unless we have left a very tight schedule for him, detailing who he is to meet, when and where he is going.

His span of concentration is short and because of his voices and thoughts he misses chunks of conversation, with the result that we often have to explain what was said a few minutes earlier. He now expresses interest in how we are feeling and will say, 'What can I do to help you?' This gives us hope.

Care plans need careful management and following through. Edward has had a couple of care plans written but there has really been no attempt to implement or manage the project plans. Perhaps it would need too big an investment to manage it.

Our son has, for most of his time when not in hospital, attended local courses and now has a file full of certificates. He has voluntarily helped at the adult education centre, teaching people about computers and helped with IT teaching in village halls, which has helped him enormously to socialise and to have something to do. A group was started in our village when Edward first became ill which still meets one morning a week and is for people with mental health problems. It is now supported by a charity and has been the only consistent activity in the ten years that he has been ill. He gets really keen on an activity, such as a creative writing class and then it closes because of lack of funds and so he has another day free with nothing to do. He does now have an outreach support worker from the charity who does something with him on one day per week and this is absolutely marvellous. He really looks forward to those days when they generally go to exercise on prescription.

Here is a record of a typical week that we kept last year to record his activities.

A typical week:

Sunday 8th May: 'Edward stayed in bed till 1 pm. We gave him lunch, drove him to his flat with his supper, having checked that he had his sports clothes and pills. We later phoned him with income information that he had forgotten'.

Monday 9th May: Bill, Edward's outreach worker, picked him up from his flat and took him to the gym where they spent an hour. They then went to the carers' centre where they discussed Edward's income support and disability benefits to establish if he was receiving the correct amounts. In the afternoon Edward walked round to the adult education centre to help coach computer skills. We collected him at 4 pm from his flat, brought him home and fed him so that by 5.15 he was ready to be picked up by some neighbours who he accompanied to an art class about 25 miles away. Home at 9.30 and straight to bed.

Tuesday 10th May: Edward got up at 10.30, watched a James Bond video, had lunch with us and later tried to help install our broadband. After supper a friend of his, Roger, who teaches an evening class, picked him up and dropped him off on his way home at about 10 pm.

Wednesday 11th May: Roger picked Edward up at 11 and they went to the writing group that is run locally for people recovering from mental illness. (A predecessor to this group published a small book of poetry and Edward was proud to have contributed because his psychiatrist and his wife came to the evening launch of the book). At 4 pm his father took him to the village hall to help set up a digital projector and laptop for a talk and during the talk in the evening he operated the mouse. He went straight to bed when he got home.

Thursday 12th May: Got Edward up and gave him breakfast. Took him into the town at 9.30 where he visited his grandmother (who had recently moved down to a care home). In the early afternoon he went to the adult education centre for a short one-to-one class. We then brought him home and he again tried to sort out our broadband but found that our operating system was too early a version. He watched some TV and went to bed at about 10. During the day I made an appointment for him to see his consultant and to chase up his bus pass.

Friday 13th May: At 10 am a minibus called to pick Edward up on the way to the local mental health group and dropped him off after lunch. He went to bed in the afternoon. When I got home at 6 pm he helped me unpack the shopping.

Saturday 14th May: Got him up by noon. I was able to persuade him to do some painting in the afternoon that he enjoyed for about an hour. To bed at 10.

Looking at this diary even I am amazed to see how much help he receives from friends and relatives who go out of their way to support and encourage him. A few changes have occurred. His grandmother has died and some activities are no longer run. Two years ago Edward was given a housing association flat in our market town, which has given him freedom and a feeling that he has his own place, just like any other man in his thirties. He does spend most of the time at home with us but he has his bolthole. He says that he feels lonely in his flat and we notice that even after two days there he is talking with his voices much more than he would have been had he been at home. We feel that he needs something meaningful to do every day, something that does not dry up because of funding and stop because it is the school holidays. The welfare to work people had him on their books for a few years but they have now taken him off their list, *'because he is happy how he is'*! Obviously because it is difficult to get a mentally ill person back in to employment. They did, however support him in a course he was doing but soon everyone realised that it was not suitable for him. People that he has helped with their computer skills at the adult education centre stop me in town and tell me how helpful, kind and what a good instructor Edward is. So there must be someone out there who would be able to give him a little chance even if he was to be supported.

He has applied for the new direct payment scheme. An employee from Rethink is helping him with the forms and the organisation. He needs someone to give him some help with his housework, it's so much easier if there is someone there to give support and have someone to talk to in the flat, even for an hour a week. So at the moment we are waiting for the outcome of this request.

One day a fortnight, not in the school holidays though, a friend takes him with her, as she is training people who have or have had mental illness, in advocacy for the mentally ill. Edward enjoys this and comes home with a feeling of worth.

He has a few school friends who call when they come home and support him with emails but are now working in other parts of Britain.

Both Edward's younger brothers are now working in other parts of Great Britain, but he is very interested in their careers and housing etc. One of Edward's dreams is to own a house in the southwest near my family and one of his brothers and he is patiently waiting *for his ship to come in*. I suppose that everyone needs a dream. Who said *'hope is the waking dream of all men'*? My husband's family are in the far northeast of Great Britain and so, we have no family in this part of the country to give us support but to move with Edward would be as if we were taking him into deep space, almost frightening not knowing what sort of support would be available.

Edward is now willing to be put on a flight and be met by his brother so that he can stay with him for a holiday, but having to catch a series of three buses each way to attend the clozapine clinic at the hospital, taking most of the day, would be too much for him because he would be worried about becoming lost. So life has to be arranged around him to a certain extent. Now that we are in our sixties we want to do things for ourselves, before we are too old. I know that it may seem selfish but we would like to go off for a week without feeling mean and ashamed of ourselves for not taking him with us. He does come with us for holidays. We had a lovely week skiing when the whole family and his brothers' girl friends were together. When we go away with him we avoid hotels and stay in a friend's house or rent a place, as we have noticed, on the few occasions when we have stayed in a hotel, that Edward found it rather confusing.

He is much more stable now since he has been on clozapine. He neither drinks nor smokes. He is now interested in how we are feeling. We believe that there are opportunities for further improvements in his life. We would like him to try cognitive behavioural therapy and he agrees with this. However, his new CPN says that she has to gain his trust before embarking on it, but time is pushing on and he has now been ill for over ten years.

It is now clear to us looking back that if he had been on his own and not received our help in dealing with the NHS, police, social services, housing association etc., he would now very likely be in prison or a mental institution or living on the streets or dead.

My involvement with carer support

One thing that our son's illness has taught us is that, *'shy bairns don't get treats'*. So we decided to try to be more assertive than we were early on when we were grateful for any small attention given to Edward or ourselves.

I joined Rethink, which was formerly called the National Schizophrenia Fellowship, and began to meet other carers, some with horrendous stories of how the system had failed their relatives, and activists who undertook advocacy. Three years ago Rethink asked if I would train to deliver a course entitled family education and training programme. The idea of the initial training programme was that over three days Rethink would teach social workers and nurses working in mental health and carers of people with psychosis how to deliver the course to other carers. A team of three of us eventually ran a course of thirteen weekly sessions of two and a half hours. The three of us (a psychiatric nurse from the hospital, a mental health social worker and myself) were supported by a Rethink employee. The course content focused on education and problem solving. About ten carers took part, being recruited by a variety of means. Some were recommended by CPNs, some by social services and some by myself, through personal contact. The participants were very appreciative and some said that they had been unable to talk about the illness outside the house for over ten years. As a follow up we three trainers wrote to the local Primary Care Trust and it was funded to run again. We have modified the content in light of our experience and shortened the course. We now hope that the course will be run regularly.

The outcomes from the courses have been positive and many. For example, carers have felt empowered to go and discuss the treatment of the person they care for with psychiatrists. Housing and benefits have been sorted and a rural bus stop was the outcome of one problem solving session. All this is because the carers have been given information and feel that they can talk to the professionals. In the course we invite mental health professionals to talk on topics such as early intervention, medicines and benefits.

When caring for someone really ill, one's initiative feels as if it has been sapped and to make decisions or ask questions is very difficult. So preparation and discussion before a meeting with professionals is very helpful. If only we had been offered something like this in the early stages of Edwards's illness, when all our GP said might be on offer to us was a general counselling service. We wanted and needed information, a map to get us out of the wilderness and a guide to lead us through. I myself have learnt so much since being involved with the training for carers programme.

Stanza 3: the CPN's tale
Mark Hopps and Victoria Lumley

Mark Hopps

I first met Eddie and his family in November of 1998. I had succeeded in establishing myself within the local mental health team having achieved a promotion to a higher grade of nursing. I had previously worked at a lower grade within a different team. This was to be my first opportunity at managing my own caseload of clients. Previously I had worked in the community alongside a senior colleague who generally managed the more complex work. I envisaged that this new role would be both challenging and rewarding, particularly as my previous community experience was within an urban mental health team and based predominantly within a primary care setting. Indeed as a community mental health nurse, my experience of working with people suffering from psychosis was limited at that stage in my career. The other significant challenge within my new work would be managing the transition and challenges of working within a rural area such as where Eddie and his family lived.

Upon commencing my new role I adopted a large caseload of individuals who lived across a broad area of rural County Durham. At the time I recall being introduced to the majority of my new client group only once by my predecessor. As a result of this, upon reflection, I recall that the process of engagement with my clients was gradual as I endeavoured to ascertain from case notes and colleagues a hierarchy of engagement, based upon the general needs and risks associated with my client group.

I recall that I met with Eddie comparatively early within this process. This was as a result of him experiencing what had been described to me as a significant mental health problem, however his depot injection was also due, which clearly necessitated a visit. Upon first meeting Eddie it became apparent that I was the most recent addition to a considerable line of clinicians with whom Eddie had been associated since he had suffered his first episode of psychosis three years previously. As a means of establishing a rapport we spoke, at times with humour, of his experiences with my predecessors and less jovially of the psychosis that he was trying so hard to manage and understand.

Unfortunately, as a result of the size of the caseload that I had adopted, the process of engagement with Eddie was gradual as I endeavoured to establish a rapport with him. This process was eased, as it was apparent that generally his previous experiences of mental health services, particularly my predecessors had been fairly positive in nature. As a result of several sessions with Eddie and following consultation with his parents and his case notes, I managed to establish a degree of clarity regarding what had occurred in his life over the previous few years.

Eddie had first come to the attention of the mental health services in April of 1995 following a referral by his general practitioner. At that time he had stated that his difficulties had commenced one month earlier when out socialising with friends whilst completing his university course. He stated that as the evening had progressed he had become increasingly suspicious of others and recalled feeling angry and upset by this. A few days later he had felt physically unwell after a few pints of beer and believed that friends had put salt into his drink. He had recently lost a temporary job with an accountancy firm as a result of the difficulties he had been having with his concentration and ability to sleep and had felt particularly 'slowed down'. Eddie had discussed how such paranoid thoughts had become worse over a 3–4 week period, believing that he was being filmed for a practical joke for a television programme and that ultimately he was being persecuted. Recognising that perhaps he was unwell Eddie travelled home to his parents' house. Unfortunately the persecutory thoughts continued to occur and Eddie also experienced thoughts that aliens were controlling him and the television. Eddie had recognised that this early episode was likely to have been caused by his repeated use of cannabis and amphetamine over an extended period of time while at university; indeed it was apparent that this was part of the culture among some students.

Positively, with the intervention of my predecessors Eddie responded well to the use of low doses of medication and in September 1995 was offered employment in Jersey.

From the information gained it was apparent that Eddie's care plan through-out this first episode of psychosis centred upon the need for continued assess-ment. The aim of the care plan was to endeavour to understand what had been occurring prior to him experiencing the initial symptoms of psychosis, so that hypotheses could be established regarding the nature of his presentation. Naturally the need for monitoring of his treatment with medication was re-cognised within the care plan, as was the need to be optimistic regarding the potential for Eddie achieving an early recovery. Indeed he had progressed to the point where he had felt able to consider accepting employment.

Unfortunately while working only for 2–3 weeks in his new role Eddie lost the job as a result of being arrested by the police on a charge of drunk and disorderly. Again he returned to his parent's home requiring treatment. Eddie has resided in the northeast of England since that time.

Initial assessments that were carried out upon Eddie's return to his parents suggested that he had been experiencing fluctuation in his mood level along with a preoccupation with inventive ideas regarding the use of computers. I learned that Eddie had eventually agreed upon a need to take a longer period of time to work towards recovery. The mood swings that he had experienced had necessitated the use of a mood stabilising medication to work in conjunc-tion with the anti-psychotic treatment that he was already prescribed. As a result of this recognition of patience within his recovery the evidence would suggest that some consideration had been given to his psychosocial needs. Eddie's care plan now included the need for him to attend a local mental health group and a creative writing group. It is anticipated that the rationale for this would have been to ensure that Eddie continued to maintain some contact with individuals away from his home environment. It would help to prevent him from withdrawing socially.

In the January of 1996 Eddie experienced his first admission to hospital for his mental health problems. It is apparent that this was exacerbated by his excessive use of alcohol. It is argued that at this juncture his use of alcohol and previously other substances were making the underlying mental health problems difficult to treat and the use of an addictions worker was being considered at that time. Ultimately this admission lasted for a period of two months and he was discharged from hospital with an uncertain diagnosis of bipolar illness or schizoaffective disorder.

Upon discharge he was seen to progress comparatively well. In July 1996 his mental health problems deteriorated a little and Eddie acknowledged that he had not been taking his anti-psychotic medication for a while. He is reported to have had insight into the link between him not taking this and the deterio-ration in his well being. He was agreeable to commence on a depot prepara-tion of an anti-psychotic medication, with the aim of ensuring that his treatment was fully sustained.

The evidence would suggest that Eddie went on to progress comparatively well once established on depot medication. This continued to be in conjunc-tion with oral mood stabilising medication. He continued to attend social groups regularly and participated well within these. In response to potential side effects that Eddie was experiencing, he was prescribed anti-cholinergic medication to try and reduce the incidence of this. Within his reviews it was apparent that aspects of his mental health had a tendency to fluctuate and his medication was adjusted accordingly. Clearly an issue of concern for his parents was a behavioural tendency Eddie had to gulp large quantities of fluid. It was reported that Eddie believed that the purpose of this was to fill a large void inside him. Other concerns raised by his parents were that he had continued to use alcohol and had not accepted any connection between his use of alcohol and fluctuation within his general mental health. It was also apparent that he had been experiencing potential negative symptoms of a psychotic illness. Reference was made to a general lack of motivation and ability to concentrate effectively. Eddie's parents had written several letters of concern regarding this issue to Eddie's consultant psychiatrist. Ultimately his response to this was an increase in his medication to resolve what was considered to be residual features of Eddie's psychosis.

Ultimately when I became involved in Eddie's care, his care plan remained similar to that which had been implemented by my colleagues. He was receiving visits at home on a fortnightly basis, predominantly for the purpose of administering his depot injection and monitoring of his mental health and treatment regime. He also received contact from clinicians while in attendance at the mental health group, which a member of the mental health team usually attended. As a result of this attendance Eddie was well known to most members of the team. On a three-monthly basis he attended the local surgery for blood testing to ensure optimum efficacy and safe use of mood stabilising medication. He also continued with attendance at a creative writing group in which he was a valued and resourceful member. Unfortunately his use of alcohol had continued to present as a problem and following engagement with Eddie, I endeavoured to reinforce a potential link between this and the impact it had upon his mental health and efficacy of his treatment regime. Positively, the impact of these discussions was an overall reduction in his alcohol intake and ultimately he was able to reflect upon feeling comparatively well. Indeed at this time he was agreeable to giving some consideration to future vocational needs.

Unfortunately, an appointment arranged with the disability employment advisor had coincided with a further deterioration in Eddie's mental health, it was apparent that he had been using alcohol to excess and not taking his oral medication. He had spoken of a *'waveband'* in his head controlling his thoughts involving government forces. At the time he believed that the only way to resolve this was to have his eardrums removed. This series of circumstances had resulted in him being admitted to hospital again. While in hospital, Eddie responded well to a change in treatment and a period of rehabilitation. It was felt by the care team and his parents that Eddie would benefit by continuing his rehabilitation in sheltered accommodation. Ultimately, Eddie was discharged to a facility where he would be supported by staff. As this was in a different locality I met with Eddie on two occasions to ensure that he was effectively settled in and his care was transferred to the local mental health team in May 1999.

I had no further involvement with Eddie until November 1999 when again he had returned to hospital, on this occasion he had been detained under the Mental Health Act. Again, this occurred following deterioration in his mental health brought about by alcohol use and non-compliance with his treatment. The plan upon him being discharged from hospital was for him to return to his parents' home on the condition that he accepted complete abstinence from alcohol and ensured absolute compliance with his treatment. While Eddie was not completely discharged from hospital until March of 2000, I participated in his rehabilitation by seeing him at home while on leave and accompanying him to the mental health group. His treatment regime had been adjusted significantly. Eddie was now only prescribed clozapine that required routine, regular monitoring in clinic at the hospital. Positively, he had responded well to this and had not been experiencing the disabling side effects that he had struggled with previously.

Upon complete discharge from hospital the following few years of my involvement did not feature any further, negative incidents. On the contrary it was apparent that Eddie had adopted a more mature, optimistic approach towards his personal needs. Generally, he adhered to his parents' request regarding abstinence from alcohol, only occasionally having a supervised glass of wine when appropriate. He also ensured that he complied with his treatment regime and I regularly transported him to clinic to ensure that his needs were met regarding clozapine monitoring. He discussed on many occasions being prepared to do anything to prevent a return to hospital. This was to be a significant motivating factor for him. Eddie had spoken regularly of residual voices that had occurred and as they were not causing him any obvious distress we reflected upon alternative ways of managing these. Indeed he learned with time how to distract himself from these or allocate time, at his convenience, to allow them to occur. He reported that one voice that he experienced fulfilled a social role for him by keeping him company. We agreed that further increases in medication to eliminate these experiences would be potentially counter therapeutic as a result of the likely increase in disabling side effects that he might experience.

With regard to Eddie's vocational needs, as his confidence improved a fulfilling programme of activities were established to ensure that he had structure and pleasure within his week. This included the mental health group, creative writing group and time at the local gym. Eventually he assisted in running a local group teaching computer skills and spent social time with a support worker from an allied organisation. Using his local contacts he also voluntarily assisted a friend with administrative duties within a neighbouring mental health trust.

As a result of the gradual progress that Eddie was making this allowed me to spend more time with his parents. Within each session I was able to assist them in understanding the nature of the difficulties which Eddie had been experiencing as well as hearing, and sharing their own experiences. I believe that whilst the content of these sessions was predominantly psycho-educational they also allowed the opportunity to problem solve as appropriate.

When I eventually ended my interventions with Eddie in February of 2005 he had been living in his own rented accommodation successfully for over one year, routinely sharing his time between his own flat and his parents' home. He was maintaining his programme of activities, whilst continuing to experience some residual mental health symptoms. His consultant psychiatrist had commenced the process of reducing his medication a little and he had not experienced any negative effects of this. At the time I recall feeling confident that in the future he had the potential to establish himself with some form of paid employment. I also believe that the eventual progress he made was as a result of a combination of maturity, compliance, education and ultimately acceptance.

Victoria Lumley

My interest in promoting mental well being became apparent many years ago whilst working as community support worker with clients who were labelled severely mentally ill. This experience inspired me to do my nurse training and my ultimate ambition was to become a community practitioner.

Once qualified, I was able to consolidate my theoretical knowledge and clinical skills, working on a busy acute admissions ward. The experience was valuable, providing me with the opportunity to develop engagement skills working with clients who were acutely unwell. I soon began to feel frustrated from the pressures of working within a medical model, observing the approach to be creating iatrogenic mental health issues for the majority of service users and families.

Negative perceptions of severe mental illness that have been maintained for many years have arguably contributed to the development of stigma, social exclusion and unemployment, which are contributing factors of poor outcome (Gamble & Brennan, 2000). This has influenced the view of people diagnosed as mentally ill as being unable to take control over their lives and ultimately as dangerous, resulting in negative public responses. Conversely the medical concept is one of society's portrayals as chronic 'mental person' which is influential in terms of recovery.

In October 2005, the opportunity arose for me to join a community mental health team. Although a little apprehensive I was motivated by enthusiasm and the need to break free from the dominance of attitudes, values and beliefs that were indoctrinated by a medical approach to care. I instantly inherited a caseload of service users, all of which had been informed that they would be allocated a new care coordinator.

I first met Eddie at one of our carers training programme launches; throughout our conversation he informed me that he had been mentally unwell whilst at university. As the conversation progressed I tentatively explored his hopes for the future. He suggested that he was quite happy and comfortable with the way his life was, but expressed at some point he would like an opportunity to *get back to normal*. Eddie appeared to be fearful of the consequences this might have on his mental health.

The Social Exclusion Unit Report (Office of the Deputy Prime Minister, 2004) identifies the vicious cycle of social exclusion with which individuals with mental health difficulties are faced. Underlying causes include stigma, discrimination, unclear responsibilities, lack of coordination between agencies, a narrow focus on medical symptoms and limited support to return to work. A quote from a service user encapsulates this perfectly: 'Everybody needs something to do, somewhere to live and someone to love.'

Eddie's care coordinator left the team soon after I joined them and it was agreed that I would take over this role. I was very delighted by this decision partly due to the awareness of the challenges I envisaged in supporting him through his journey of recovery. The engagement process was further facilitated by my close relationship with his mother that had flourished through developing a carers' training programme specifically for carers supporting individuals experiencing psychosis.

During my initial contacts with Eddie we talked extensively about his perception of what had happened to him when he came into contact with mental health services. I felt that to develop a therapeutic relationship I needed understanding of his experiences to enable me to work within his model of illness.

Eddie described becoming unwell whist studying at university, he was working at a book shop, student life was such that it involved late nights, alcohol and drugs. Eddie described feeling unable to sleep, racing thoughts, high moods and voices talking to him. At one point he found the experience overwhelming and unbearable, describing a feeling of detachment and a search for peace and tranquillity. Eddie's recollection of voices was when he first heard the voice of a university friend (Emma), he gained emotional comfort from engaging with her and felt honoured by her presence.

Eddie rejects his diagnosis of schizophrenia primarily because of the stigmatising views held by society. He described a sense of loss and bereavement from when he became unwell which he feels has prevented him from achieving his personal aspirations. If he were to think of a diagnosis for his unique experiences then he would prefer the term bipolar disorder and he believes this to be a more accurate reflection of his mental health difficulties.

A problem with the concept of schizophrenia is that schizophrenic symptoms are reported to exist in the 'normal' population (Bentall, 1993; Romme & Escher, 1993) and are listed within the *Diagnostic and Statistical Manual of Mental Health Disorders Version IV* (American Psychiatric Association, 1994) and the *Internal Classification of Diseases Version 10* (WHO, 1990) as key features of schizophrenia. This research was helpful to Eddie as the findings are that schizophrenia is a disease and offered an alternative explanation.

In clinical practice service users entering into community mental health teams have traditionally been advised not to work and to apply for disability living allowance, which supports the idea that the condition is lifelong. On the other hand there are some clients who feel that it reduces their financial stress, in this case it would be good if professionals discussed the implications of benefits and perhaps suggest they apply until reaching recovery.

Explorations of his concept of schizophrenia opened up the debate and guided Eddie in discovering other people's experiences. Normalising his experiences alleviated his own model of madness and feelings of not being normal. Eddie soon became aware that many people heard voices and described psychotic experiences and despite this went on to lead relatively normal lives. This suggests that experiences such as hallucinations are not at all confined to people with any kind of psychiatric diagnosis (Bentall, 1996).

Using a continuum of normal experiences such as sleep deprivation, bereavement and solitary confinement helped socialise Eddie to the stress vulnerability model (Zubin & Spring, 1977). We looked at stressful life events prior to his onset of psychotic symptoms using an analogy of a bucket, to share an integrated biopsychosocial formulation. I began drawing a bucket suggesting to Eddie that his biological makeup and past experiences demonstrate the shape of the bucket and how much water it could hold. I described the stressful life events as water filling the bucket and once the bucket reaches capacity water will overflow resulting in the symptoms he experienced. Eddie was able to identify stressors that may have contributed to him becoming unwell and is conscious of the impact that stressful thoughts and feelings have. At such times Eddie is able to apply coping strategies.

I encouraged Eddie to think about people he knew that had experienced similar things. We began to discuss automatic thoughts. Eddie was very accepting that everyone's brain produces all sorts of automatic thoughts that we have no control over, sometimes pleasant and sometimes unpleasant ones. I was able to share my experience of odd ideas, which appeared valuable in developing a therapeutic alliance and demonstrating that having strange ideas is quite normal.

Many recovery stories describe the devastating effects of patients being told by mental health professionals that they have schizophrenia and that the prospects for recovery are slim or even non-existent. Normalising Eddie's psychotic experiences appeared to help him accept his voices as a normal part of him. It is said that the single most powerful element of recovery is hope (Deegan, 1993).

Talking about previous episodes of psychosis was difficult for Eddie. I believe it is easier for him to seal over his experiences to enable him to think about his future life, despite the presence of psychotic phenomena. One may argue that Eddie avoids talking about his deepest thoughts for fear that disclosure may lead to relapse or hospital admission. Eddie recalls a previous occasion of disclosure that resulted in admission to hospital and depot medication. We have both agreed that creating a trusting relationship can take time and hopefully when Eddie feels comfortable and safe he may choose to disclose his inner beliefs. However, his choice to validate his psychotic experiences has to be respected as this process alone may be enabling him to focus on activities of living that are often taken for granted by many individuals.

During the sessions with Eddie and his family we were able to develop a needs and strengths list:

Eddie's needs list:

- Spend more time in his flat
- Be independent to go into town shopping, and attend gym
- Develop a 'clear mind'
- Build confidence to explore social relationships
- Explore employment opportunities
- Develop a staying well plan.

The following strengths were recognised:

- Eddie's motivation and determination to recover
- Willingness to engage in therapeutic interventions
- Supportive family
- Contentment with relationship with Emma, his voice.

Collaboratively, this led to the development of a care plan based on addressing Eddie's needs and strengths. Eddie started to set himself goals and expressed interest in exploring interventions to help him develop a clear mind and lose invasive thoughts. Further explorations revealed that in actual fact he was very happy with the majority of his thoughts, although as I mentioned earlier there are still thoughts he chooses not to disclose. It was apparent that Eddie was experiencing sedating side effects from his medication, clozapine, which he has been prescribed since his last admission six years ago. Eddie described feeling very tired, forgetful and unable to think clearly and cognitively.

Initially, Eddie was very shocked by this discovery but this may be due to years of culturing compliance with medication and feeling the need to continue with medication and tolerate side effects. On reflection, Eddie originally believed the origins of his psychosis to be as simple as a chemical imbalance. It may be proposed that his beliefs were indoctrinated by the medical model.

A large proportion of patients would do better if they were never exposed to neuroleptics. Frequently patients report horrific side effects from their medication, in particular weight gain, salivation, lethargy, sexual dysfunction, cognitive blunting, tremor and increased sleep. May (2002) in his experience of psychosis talks about when he took neuroleptics, describing a feeling of detachment that decreased his ability to think creatively, problem solve and decreased his motivation, therefore hindering the recovery process.

Eddie was very eager to reduce his medication and his family was very supportive of this request. He had also started to take omega fish oils in response to the growing evidence base for improving outcomes for individuals with psychosis. Research indicates that people with mental health problems are at greater risk of having diabetes, heart disease, respiratory diseases, stroke and hypertension (Sayce & Owen, 2006). The Government is attempting to bridge the gap of health inequalities and the Department of Health has produced guidance on promoting physical health (Department of Health, 2006). Promoting Eddie's physical well being has been a priority for some time; he has regular access to a leisure centre and enjoys walking and finds that exercise benefits his physical and mental well being. Eddie is also cautious of the effects of antipsychotics on physical health and tries to monitor his eating/living regime in recognition of these factors.

During Eddie's outpatient appointment we discussed reducing his medication. Initially the psychiatrist was reluctant, rationalising this by the fact that Eddie still had residual symptoms but he reluctantly agreed to reduce his clozapine and eventually prescribed omega fish oils after we had provided him with the appropriate evidence base. Since this appointment, the psychiatrist has further reduced his medication at his request. Both Eddie and his family are able to observe the positive effects this has had. He is now more motivated during interactions, and concentration and self-care have improved dramatically. The medical model tends to define recovery in negative terms and the philosophy of symptoms from a medical perspective need to be eliminated so that patients can return to a healthy state of living.

The standards of care for people with schizophrenia recommend that patients are maintained on antipsychotic drugs; however, there is consistent evidence that reveals that maintaining all patients on antipsychotics produces poor long-term outcomes. Medical models attempt to treat the illness then rehabilitate the person and recovery is delayed while medical cures are being sought. Psychiatrists appear to abandon patients, whose symptoms fail to respond to medication, labelling them treatment resistant. Debatably, is medication alone the answer? Are psychiatrists viewing recovery as being symptom free?

Guided discovery helped Eddie and his family to move forward from this position of learnt helplessness. Eddie was able to discover alternative approaches to psychosis. Eddie's parents have requested that Eddie engages in cognitive therapy in an attempt to alleviate his voices and beliefs, which they informed me are to do with the Government. As I mentioned earlier in the text Eddie has never confided in me about these beliefs, but I acknowledge his parents' concerns. Talking to them about their perception of his voices revealed that they are troubled by his responses to his voices whilst in the company of others and observe that Eddie can be very preoccupied and distant and sometimes mutters to himself. Ultimately, their anxiety is about social inappropriateness and how this may be perceived as stigmatising for him.

In contrast to their concerns, Eddie finds talking to his voice (Emma) very interesting, and his thoughts provide a world of discovery that at times distracts him from the reality of life and perhaps unstimulating conversations. Eddie illustrates his relationship with Emma (voice) as a positive experience that provides him with company and contentment. In an attempt to address the issue highlighted by his parents, Eddie agreed to try to engage with Emma when he was on his own and set a time limit in an attempt to reduce the inappropriateness that was observed by others.

I spent time with Eddie's mum helping her to understand the relationship he has with Emma and the function of his secret beliefs. It is my understanding that she is now more aware of the emotional comfort that he experiences from this process and his relationship with Emma. Eddie had no motivation to engage in therapy and it was agreed that engaging him in cognitive therapy to try altering the way he thinks and feels at this stage would be detrimental to his mental well being. It may be proposed that his beliefs and relationship with Emma are maintaining his self-esteem, confidence and core beliefs. One could argue that perhaps when Eddie feels able to achieve these feelings through alternative ways, for example, a girlfriend or employment, then his need to engage in conversation with Emma may decrease and allow him to feel more comfortable with himself, others and the world. It may be at this point that consideration for cognitive therapy is discussed again with the primary aim to focus on core beliefs.

The interventions that Eddie is presently engaging in are attempting to help him address his needs. Direct payments have been accessed to provide opportunities to build his self-esteem and confidence and to increase his social networks.

The National Institute for Mental Health in England (NIMHE, 2003) supports the development of recovery services for people who experience mental illness. They have recently appointed Piers Allott who is working with others to develop a national framework of values for mental health. NIMHE talk about recovery as a process, instead of focusing on the medical symptomology; the philosophy is of helping individuals in their own personal experiences and developments. Building self-esteem and finding a meaningful role in society are key principles identified by NIMHE.

Recovery was an alien concept to Eddie, possibly one that he had not been allowed to consider. Talking about other service users' experiences of recovery and providing information, promoted feelings of optimism, demonstrating that *there is some light at the end of the tunnel.*

An empowering description of recovery is given by Fisher (1998). His emphasis is that full recovery is possible for everyone but that doesn't mean they no longer require support. Contending that despite being labelled as schizophrenic the individual can carry out important social roles and learn to take control of their own life. Recovery described by people who have experienced it demonstrates key themes including self-empowerment, a sense of being in control, optimism and hope. Recovery models appear to be presented as an alternative to the treatment of schizophrenia, by what is often called the medical model.

Eddie has weekly contact with a local housing project worker whose primary aim was to work with Eddie to help him maintain his tenancy. However, the project worker has also been providing a secondary role attempting to provide emotional and practical support based on needs highlighted during engagement with Eddie and his family. These needs were regularly discussed and reviewed and a care plan was developed based on Eddie's needs. Goals achieved so far:

- 'Feeling' and observed to be more independent
- Spends majority of time in his own flat
- Accessing mainstream education and leisure courses
- Eddie feels more confident to socially interact with others
- Takes pride in personal appearance
- Developed relapse prevention plan/staying well plan.

On reviewing Eddie's progress and journey of recovery so far it is fair to say he has achieved many of the goals that he set out to achieve. It may be argued that without the adoption of a psychosocial approach to Eddie's care the process of recovery or outcomes may have been substandard. Providing hope, optimism and positive beliefs to facilitate the recovery process have been fundamental. Interventions to help Eddie normalise his psychotic experience appear to have promoted acceptance and contentment allowing him to move forward in his life.

Eddie is presently accessing mainstream educational courses. He still has goals that he wants to achieve in describing his journey of recovery, which he equates to climbing a mountain. In conclusion of his progress so far his words were: *'I'm getting to the top of the mountain now and it feels as though I'm ascending'*.

The emphasis of the disease/medical model and assumption of the condition as chronic deterioration appear to be unhelpful in developing care that hopes to improve recovery from schizophrenia. Changing mental health services to be led by recovery based interventions would have to be founded on understanding individual recovery experiences, fostering hope, equality and social inclusion, recognising self determination, acknowledging and supporting the service user and family.

Working with Eddie and others on my caseload demonstrates that despite a diagnosis of schizophrenia it is possible to recover. The journey of recovery is a unique and personal experience. A question proposed is, who has the right to define recovery? What one person may consider as being recovery may not be acceptable to another. One may reveal a variety of definitions of recovery all applicable.

It is clear that those who have experienced mental health distress and have overcome their difficulties and have recovered to an individual optimum are leading the recovery movement. It is my opinion that hope, positive attitudes, values and beliefs are key components in the recovery process. As professionals we should demonstrate and maintain these attributes to help individuals through their process of recovery however it is defined.

References

American Psychiatric Association (1994). *Diagnostic & Statistical Manual of Mental Disorders Version IV*. Washington DC. American Psychiatric Association.

Bentall, R.P. (1993). Cognitive Models Of Voice Hearing. In: Romme M. & Escher, S. (eds). *Accepting Voices*. London: MIND Publications.

Bentall, R.P. (1996). From Cognitive Studies Of Psychosis To Cognitive Behaviour Therapy For Psychotic Symptoms. In: Haddock, G. & Slade, P.D. (eds). *Cognitive Behavioural Interventions with Psychotic Disorders*. London: Routledge. **(1)**, 3–27.

Deegan, P.E. (1993). Recovering Our Sense Of Value After Being Labelled Mentally Ill. *Journal of Psychosocial Nursing.* **31**, 7–11.

Department of Health (2006). *Choosing Health: Supporting The Physical Health Needs Of People With Severe Mental Illness*. London: The Stationery Office.

Fisher, D. (1998). A New Vision Of Recovery: People Can Fully Recover From Mental Illness. It Is Not A Life Long Process. *National Empowerment Newsletter.* **Spring/summer**, 12–13.

Gamble, C. & Brennan, G. (eds) (2000). *Working With Serious Mental Illness. A Manual For Clinical Practice*. London: Baillière Tindall.

May, R. (2002). *Making Sense of a Psychotic Experience & Working Towards Recovery*. Bradford: Bradford Community District Care Trust.

National Institute for Mental Health in England (2003). *A Framework For Primary Mental Health Care*. London: NIMHE.

Romme, M. & Escher, S. (1993). *Accepting Voices*. London: MIND Publications.

Sayce, L. & Owen, J. (2006). Bridging The Gap: Results Of The DRC's Formal Investigation Into Physical Health Inequalities. *Mental Health Practice.* **10(2)**, 16–18.

Social Exclusion Unit (2004). *Mental Health and Social Exclusion: Social Exclusion Unit Report*. London: Office of the Deputy Prime Minister.

World Health Organization (1990). *International Classification of Diseases. Version 10, (ICD-10)*. Geneva: WHO.

Zubin, J. & Spring, B. (1977). Vulnerability: A New View Of Schizophrenia. *Journal of Abnormal Psychology.* **86**, 260–266.

Section 3

Promoting Recovery

Chapter 8

Recovery as a Framework for Care Planning

Jim Campbell, Theo Stickley and Sarah Bonney

'What matters is not whether we're using services or not using services; using medications or not using medications. What matters in terms of a recovery orientation is, are we living the life we want to be living? Are we achieving the life we want to be living? Are we achieving personal goals? Do we have friends? Do we have connections with the community? Are we contributing or giving back in some way?' (Deegan, 1993)

Introduction

Pat Deegan's statement captures the essence of recovery, of how anyone who has experienced mental distress could be living. In this chapter we discuss how the mental health practitioner might provide an environment where the individual is supported and facilitated in achieving a life that is meaningful for them. With the growing concept of recovery within mental health services, there needs to be a change in the way mental health professionals work in the future with people who have experienced mental distress. We aim to provide mental health practitioners with a broad understanding of the many issues around successfully developing recovery focused work and we aim to provide ideas for developing frameworks needed for care planning that promote the true essence of recovery.

We approach this whole subject with temerity. As authors, we have all been trained as mental health professionals. Although we may acknowledge our own mental distress, none of us has been hospitalised under the Mental Health Act (Department of Health, 1983) or been diagnosed with an enduring mental health problem. While some authors on recovery have their feet in both camps, we do not. We recognise from the outset therefore that we are not the most qualified people to write about this subject. As professionals though, we are able to appreciate the service user discourse on recovery and act as translators, interpreters or advocates to the world of mental health practice. What we are blatantly aware of is the potential for the concept of recovery to be hijacked by the professional discourse. Already in the UK there are recovery teams and even a Fellow for Recovery at the University of Wolverhampton. What is understood by some as a service user movement is all too quickly becoming a statutory vehicle for service delivery. What began its life as a movement or paradigm is fast becoming a method for systems. We do not wish to contribute to that process, rather, we wish to encourage mental health workers to appreciate the depth of meaning of the concept of recovery and apply this meaning to their work. Furthermore, the notion of recovery carries with it a set of values that puts the position of the service user as paramount within the hierarchy of care. If our chapter contributes to this in some small way then we will have achieved much.

The chapter will consider the concept of recovery with its values and principles, providing the reader with a foundation upon which they might be able to practise mental health care in a more meaningful way. This is largely achieved through a review of the recovery literature, paying particular attention to what writers have been saying in recent years. We consider recovery in the light of social construct theory and discuss the implications of this understanding for mental health practice. We draw on service users' experiences and some of their concerns and fears. Examples of recovery philosophies, models and approaches will then be addressed, providing questions on whether working within the particular frameworks captures the essence of recovery. Finally, the chapter considers some alternative approaches drawing on examples from New Zealand for the reader to consider. It is hoped that the reader will begin to understand some of the complexities and issues around developing a recovery framework, enabling them to reflect on their own practices within the future.

Recovery debated

Recovery is being increasingly debated within mental health discourse. It appears to have a multitude of meanings, being an idea, a movement, a philosophy, a set of values, policy and a doctrine for change (Turner, 2002a). It has split opinion, on the one hand being viewed as simplistic, on the other revolutionary. Various models of recovery are being postulated, for example, Barker, (2001); Copeland, (2006); Fisher, (2005); Heather, (2002); May *et al.*, (1999); the National Institute for Clinical Excellence, (NICE and NHS, 2002b); the National Institute for Mental Health in England (NIMHE, 2004); Repper & Perkins (2003); Rethink, (2005). Furthermore, recovery teams have been operating within the United Kingdom for some years (Department of Health, 1999).

The concept of recovery in mental health services is well established in other parts of the world, especially in New Zealand and America, however, in the UK it is still a relatively new concept. From recovery literature, it is clear, that there will need to be a dramatic change in the way mental health professionals work if the ethos of recovery is to be maintained. The traditional role of providing individual services, based on what the professional thinks to be most appropriate, will need to be replaced with a comprehensive system to support the service users to achieve their chosen goals:

> *'Adopting a recovery approach in a community mental health system (as contrasted with simply incorporating language about recovery in policy documents) necessitates fundamental changes in the ways that needs are assessed, and how services are planned, delivered and evaluated'* (Grierson, 2001:4).

The voice of the service user will need to be at the centre of their own care, they will be seen as the expert on their experiences, deciding on the form of their care and support, whether it is social, medical, psychological and/or educational. The mental health professional's role will shift from the traditional role of being the expert, to working alongside service users and carers as peers in supporting them to make these choices and decisions. This will give the service user hope and empowerment for their future, from their often, poor experiences of the psychiatric system (Mead & Copeland, 2000; Coleman *et al.*, 2001). What perhaps is most challenging for mental health workers is not the necessary change to systems and approaches, but rather the change that is required within one's self. For the whole business of recovery is intrinsically tied up with our personal beliefs and values.

The key to the recovery concept is the simple premise that recovery from enduring mental health problems is possible. Historically, people who have been diagnosed with a mental illness have been told that their symptoms are incurable and that they will have to take medication for the rest of their lives, they will never work, get married or have children. With the growing literature from personal experiences of service users, professionals and research, over the last few decades, it has been clearly demonstrated that recovery is possible (Mead & Copeland, 2000; Deegan, 2001).

> *'The consumer/survivor movement has shown that through empowerment and peer support even people with the most 'hopeless' diagnosis, schizophrenia, can recover fully'* (Ahern & Fisher, 2001:24).

These are not merely theoretical postulations, rather, writers including Coleman (2000) and May (2000a) have demonstrated, from their own experiences, that people who have been hospitalised, heavily medicated and felt despair and hopelessness for the future, can recover. They have shown that people can confront their experiences and live meaningful functional lives within society.

Historical context

The idea of recovery in mental ill-health can be traced back more than 200 years and was instrumental in informing the philosophy of the Tukes at the

York Retreat. It has been suggested that R. D. Laing and the anti-psychiatric movement planted a seed that helped propel people with schizophrenia towards recovery (Kelly & Gamble, 2005). Rethink (2005) cites Dr Abraham Low as having developed the first recovery approach in 1930 when he set up post in-patient self-help groups to enhance self-determination and develop self-confidence. The physical disability movement and de-institutionalisation within psychiatry led to the emergence of a recovery vision in America in the 1990s. New Zealand has also followed this philosophy and in the United Kingdom recovery has followed on from disability legislation, anti-discrimination and consumerism, and the civil rights movements of the 1960s and 1970s. The sharing of personal accounts has further developed this concept and helped to reduce stigma (Roberts & Wolfson, 2004).

The concept of recovery emerged from those people who had first-hand experience of mental health difficulties (Repper & Perkins, 2003) and is arguably a political response to an unsatisfactory mental health system that focuses on maintenance (Turner, 2002a). The National Schizophrenia Fellowship in Powys compiled a report on the recovery approach in 2001 (Turner & Frak, 2001). Their review identified three models of modern care:

- Medical – we can treat you/we can cure you.
- Social – you have needs that we should meet.
- Recovery – I have a problem that I can grow beyond with help.

The purpose of the review was to explore the perspectives and meaning associated with the concept of recovery. The promotion of recovery was thought to involve the worker assuming a non-expert role, with the service user as the expert of their own experience. This was a shift away from the medical paradigm. It was possible that issues of risk, responsibility, choice and policy-making were at odds with current systems. The question was therefore to explore whether service delivery was complementary to the experience of recovery for individuals. From this, the paper went on to identify conflicting and common views and demonstrate potential areas of service shortfall. While it may be useful to identify models of care to promote recovery (we develop this later), firstly we need to understand more about how the concept of recovery is constructed.

The mental health literature regarding recovery could be divided into what may be referred to as discourses. In other words, the meaning of the word recovery is largely dependent on the perspective of the person who is defining it. People's perspectives are determined by their life experiences. Each of us constructs our own versions of the world. In the case of recovery, understandably the person with a diagnosis of mental health problems will have a very different perspective to the person who has given the diagnosis. Collectively, we could identify a service user discourse and a service provider discourse. However, the distinctions are not that straightforward as some people who provide services are also people who have used services.

There is a branch of social science that deals with this concept that is called Social Constructionism. Later in this chapter we consider the concept of recovery from a social constructionist perspective. Before this, we will look at what the recovery literature actually tells us about recovery and mental health. Recent literature has been analysed and we present the themes from this analysis.

Recovery concepts in the literature

A review of the recent recovery literature reveals six broad themes:

1) The intra-personal domain
2) The service provision agenda
3) The social domain
4) Power and control
5) Hope and optimism
6) Risk and responsibility.

However these are indistinct at times, and could be said to inter-weave, not necessarily fitting wholly to one particular theme. Each of these themes is considered in turn.

The intra-personal domain

Recovery described intra-personally is a theme dominated by service users. Recovery is often defined in terms of an ongoing process requiring a change in attitudes and values (Repper & Perkins, 2003). It is also identified with learning and growth (Fisher, 2000; Turner, 2002b; Whitehill, 2003) and a conversion from coping to healing (Fisher, 2000; Repper & Perkins, 2003). Barker (2003) elaborates further by speculating that the healing may be discovered during the journey itself, rather than upon reaching any final destination.

Flexible services are considered essential in order to provide individually tailored care, but it is recognised that views will be competing and conflicting and therefore at best difficult and at worst impossible for services to incorporate. Furthermore a national approach can fail to account for local and personal needs (Department of Health, 2003). People's experiences are considered fluid (Barker, 2000) and seen as uniquely individual journeys (Fisher, 2000; Turner & Frak, 2001; MacDonald, 2005). The significance of recovery for Deegan (1993) was not to attain normality but to embark on the recovery journey to realise one's calling. Recovery here does not stand still, but is an ongoing process of personal discovery (Turner, 2002a; Wimberley & Peters, 2003; Kelly & Gamble, 2005).

The personal aspect of individual recovery defined, lived and managed by service users, whilst highlighted within policy rhetoric, can become filtered and diluted as the practicalities of service provision are meted out, focusing on outcomes (Department of Health, 1999; Reid *et al.*, 2001; Blair, 2004). The language can become paternalistic, with providers seeking to stabilise people's conditions (Lester *et al.*, 2005), with preferred service user behaviour being modelled from universal and generic practice (NIMHE, 2004). The development of such models, whilst enabling service providers and policy makers with measurable evidence and statistics, may inadvertently stifle the individuality and creativity they are seeking to promote (Turner & Frak, 2001) unless measurement of success remains firmly within the service user domain (Holloway, 2002).

Service provision agenda

Despite there being a general consensus around placing service user needs first (Department of Health, 1999, 2001, 2002, 2005; Sainsbury Centre for Mental Health, 2001; NICE and NHS, 2002(a); NIMHE, 2003, 2004, 2005; WHO, 2005) one might question whose best interests are served by maintaining a model that promotes the ill–cured dichotomy. To attempt to eradicate and at best manage an individual's experiences not only retains a strong marriage to the pharmaceutical industry but also influences society and community in terms of acceptability and what is permitted.

Groups who describe recovery in terms of a biomedical model, seek an absence of symptoms. Campbell (2001) describes providers wanting to eliminate problems as opposed to expose or integrate them. Crucially recovery is considered to be achievable without cure. The Sainsbury Centre for Mental Health, (2001:3) declares that *'mental health services aim to cure or ameliorate ill health'*. The NIMHE website provides information booklets in association with a pharmaceutical company. Chalmers (2001) argues that the pharmaceutical industry has hijacked mental health care with biomedical frameworks increasing their domination in education and research. Some observers argue that hidden promotion can be located in research funding, with pharmaceutical companies infiltrating hospitals and universities who are short of public funding, by providing contract based research, often not open to public scrutiny (Mansfield & Jureidini, 2001).

If recovery is referred to in terms of complete cure or getting back to normal, then few people will recover (Roberts & Wolfson, 2004). The Department of Health and Hope (2004) state that *'recovery is not about eliminating symptoms or the notion of cure'* and Harrison *et al.*, (2001) define complete recovery as no longer requiring any treatment. Policy, however, tends to focus on these very issues (Roberts & Wolfson, 2004). NICE (2003) states that medication is viewed as indispensable for most people in a recovery phase and Travis *et al.*, (2001) record its efficacious role in prevention. Buckingham (2001) and May (2001) argue that medication only serves to suppress symptoms and hinder recovery as a result of dissociation unless one can confront the unconscious world in order to make sense of what has happened.

Recovery is not only described as the way in which one manages the experience of mental health but also how one redefines mental illness, for example to see mental ill-health as meaningful (as opposed to biochemical) and a creative opportunity (not a brain malfunction) (Chadwick, 2002). Mansfield and Jureidini (2001) argue that the pharmaceutical industry influences the manner in which health is defined, notably as an absence of symptoms as opposed to optimal functioning.

Coleman (1999) argues that recovery occurs within the context of complex relationships. It involves every aspect of the human condition and thus is truly holistic (Turner, 2002a). Coleman states that the mental health system can destroy the fragile sense of self by explaining experiences and problems as biological, labelling attempts to find a voice as lack of insight and seeing anger and fear as aggression and deterioration. Thus the essential components of recovery that Coleman outlines as the four 'selfs' are, he believes, undermined by the very system set up to help. He notes that this often subsides into a loss of identity and eventual compliance, leading to denial of the experience.

Warner (2004) argues that 114 follow-up studies of outcome in schizophrenia (conducted in the developed world since the beginning of the 20th Century) showed recovery rates were no better for those admitted post the introduction of anti-psychotic medication than for those predating this period. Despite this, a model of deficits and pathology has been in the ascension for many years, with a present emphasis on maintenance and relapse prevention (May, 2000b).

There is great diversity of feeling around the philosophy of recovery even amongst those who use services, with recovery and the medical model exhibiting significant tensions (Roberts & Wolfson, 2004). Jacobson (2004) argues that these tensions can be alleviated by accepting the individuality and uniqueness of recovery, but goes on to state that this approach presents difficulties for policy makers. There are, however, numerous providers within the literature who advocate recovery in its wider terms and Nolan (2000) states that recent scholarship points to a middle way that recognises the value of both. Recovery appears hotly contested within the service provision arena with money, power and control underpinning decision-making. Groups may have an invested interest in maintaining the status quo, thus challenging attempts to seek a middle way.

The social domain

Coleman (1999) states that one cannot become whole if isolated from society. Barker and Buchanan-Barker (2003) argue that recovery can and does take place in the absence of treatment and can occur with the right kind of social support. Here recovery is seen as being dependent on a variety of other external factors, such as the environment, civil rights, and opportunities for inclusion (Sayce, 2000). However, Coleman (1999) questions the reality of social recovery, arguing that the mental health system in effect robs people of opportunities to develop social and economic independence through stigmatisation and institutionalisation. Campbell (2001:16) describes his experience: *'Ever since I was catapulted from the status of under-graduate scholar to that of long term mental patient questions about who I am now have been central'*.

This is further explored by the British Psychological Society (2000) who talk of the need to recover from prejudice, stigma, low expectations and the pressure to adhere to a sick role.

The language of providers incorporates the notion of living well in either the presence or absence of illness (Wimberley & Peters, 2003; Kelly & Gamble, 2005). Bradstreet and Connor (2005) write about the Scottish Recovery Network's definition of re-establishing a fulfilling, meaningful and satisfying life with or without symptoms. Recovery therefore involves finding new meaning and purpose beyond mental illness.

There may be incongruity between the rhetoric of policy makers and providers around the importance of these factors and the actual lived experience where service users find difficulties in accessing meaningful work, living in an environment conducive to health, overcoming prejudice and being genuinely included in the formation of services.

In Martyn's (2002) research, in conjunction with Rethink, 48 service users were approached. Lost homes, education, jobs and careers were all common experiences. Deegan's (2001) personal experience was of others seeing schizophrenia before they saw her or her potential to work. Furthermore, she outlined the importance of living in an environment tolerant of difference. Even if policy and service provision promote social inclusion, resistance may occur within communities. Additionally, if full integration is realised for some, stigma may prevent the true attainment of potential and lost career years may never be recouped unless education, careers and financial support can be tailored to the individual's needs and discrimination abolished. Stanton (2001) found an application to enter Australia failed due to the applicant being sectioned under the Mental Health Act in the past. It could therefore be argued that beyond the rhetoric of social inclusion and the value of homes, work and careers, (ordinary things that many take for granted) a number of obstacles stand in the way and serve to filter out opportunities for recovering a social life. The whole business of recovery therefore cannot be separated from people's social issues including their social problems. Mental health problems are intertwined with social problems such as poverty, poor housing, racism, abuse, relationship breakdown and possible subsequent issues such as substance misuse and dependency.

Power and control

The study of the literature illuminates underlying shifts of power, ownership and control around the emergence of recovery in contemporary health care. Coleman (1999) sees service users as a commodity that agencies bid for, vying to provide services and obtain funding. He says that it will be essential for service users to reclaim power as a vital part of the recovery process. This view is mirrored by Barchard (2005) who argues that self-management is very often commandeered by the establishment.

Kendell (2000), speaking at a Royal College of Psychiatrists' annual meeting, expresses concerns over psychiatrists' perceived loss of power to other professions and service users. He considers that the way of retaining power is through the continued management of medication and fears the loss of the sole right to prescribe. Power is also retained through the promotion of the medical model with Kendell (2000) seeing no fundamental difference between physical and mental illness. Furthermore, he offers a prediction that psychiatry will become more biological in future and begin to catch up with other physical illnesses in terms of biochemical knowledge. The motivation behind the desire to listen to service users is not necessarily philanthropic, as Kendell states that to refuse to listen to, or fall out with, service user organisations could damage psychiatrists' reputations badly. Finances are also cited as being a driving force behind the choice and delivery of services, with the suspicion that funds will follow psychological services seen to be taken over by clinical psychologists. Kendell expressed further concerns about a rise in consumerism, which he believes equates to a reduced deference towards the medical profession.

The control of symptoms often remains in the provider/policy-maker domains. The 12-year follow-up study of those regarded as heavy users of psychiatric services by Reid *et al.*, (2001) focused on assessing problems, deficits and needs. The authors concluded that to improve outcomes for this group further active treatment strategies would be required, with the criteria for minimum levels of functioning set by experts. This explanation by health care providers has implications for service users on a number of levels. Firstly, the language utilised suggests a generalised approach rather than a personalised or specific one. Secondly, it looks at recovery in terms of outcomes. Thirdly, the focus is on deficits and problems as opposed to strengths and potential (Morgan, 2004). Fourthly, it suggests external treatment and monitoring have to be imposed upon service users by experts in order to attain benefit. One assumes 'experts' here means health care professionals, but the term expert is itself a contested concept. Barker (2003) sees health care professionals often casting themselves in the role of expert by empowering themselves at the expense of the service user. Subtle phraseology can expose where the management of recovery lies. According to Altschul and Millet (2000:xxiii), '*The role of psychiatry has historically been to judge the validity of patients' accounts and to correct them, via therapy.*'

The National Institute for Mental Health in England (NIMHE, 2004) has commended a recovery model from the Ohio Department of Mental Health (Townsend *et al.*, 1999). The model describes how a person may be dependent/unaware. At the beginning they may have difficulty identifying needs and accepting a diagnosis, lack experience in the development of relationships, lack insight, be resistive and be totally dependent. The clinician is cast in the role of demonstrating, promoting, explaining, informing, helping, encouraging and assisting. The idioms suggest control and expertise remain with the clinician and the service user is in a position of ignorance, lacking understanding and education, and being unable to take control and to comprehend complicated aspects of medication.

Arguably, recovery should not be about meeting gold standards of achievement. Neither should it be about a tick-box approach in order to monitor, standardise, evaluate and organise (Blair, 2004; Kitson, 2005), which is perhaps not where policy makers and health care practitioners would wish to sit. Legitimate choice may not always be afforded service users. People in receipt of services may well have different priorities from those delivering them. A top down, one approach fits all philosophy will lack flexibility and sensitivity (Mental Health Foundation, 2004). The work around recovery styles (Tait *et al.*, 2003) demonstrates the need to recognise and respect the individual response to coping and adjustment. Treatment should therefore match the recovery style. May (2001), as both a practitioner and service user, believes choice should be offered to people as to how and when they explore beliefs or whether they in fact choose to live alongside or indeed seal over them (Tait *et al.*, 2003).

Perkins (2002) considers the conflict in evidence between professionals and service users, with professionals very often labelling, separating and excluding people with mental health problems and service users arguing for a right to define their own wishes and needs. Barker *et al.* (2000) state that people need fellowship as opposed to treatment and someone to join with them, as opposed to act upon them. Repper and Perkins (2003) argue that when mental difficulties are seen within the context of illness they become the province of professional experts. Jacobson (2004:161) provides a USA perspective with regard to a shift from *'power over, to power sharing'*, stating that *'recovery expertise occurs in the absence of professional qualifications, and is possibly only available to those with personal experience and insights'*. Kelly and Gamble (2005) agree that recovery can occur in the absence of professional intervention and this has the potential for creating challenging new ways of working.

Recovery does not mean that service users will cease using services or indeed become independent of services (Turner & Frak, 2001; Martyn, 2002; Perkins, 2003). What is of utmost importance is how these services are built and delivered. Repper and Perkins (2003) argue for a shift whereby recovery is not seen as a professional intervention like medication or therapy and therefore workers need to change their role from one in authority to that of coach. This is a challenge to workers who cherish the sense of power that comes with the role. Repper and Perkins furthermore refer to the need for workers to develop *'hope-inspiring relationships'*. When workers struggle to work in systems that are under-resourced and when morale reaches rock-bottom, providing hope-inspiring relationships may sound a tall order. Arguably however, without this quality of relationship it is impossible to provide the value-based care that is required to promote recovery.

Hope and optimism

Whilst hope and optimism are largely valued by all stakeholder groups, the British Psychological Society (2000:14) suggests that clinical practitioners often only see those experiencing acute periods thus getting a skewed view they describe as a *'clinician's illusion'*. This outlook can leave the clinician thinking recovery is rare. Warner (2004) suggests that mental health workers may inadvertently label problems as biological deficits in order to cope with their own frustrations. It could therefore be argued that the work of hopefulness and optimism needs to be addressed from within practitioners as well. In addition, diagnostic labels can have a devastating effect upon one's sense of hope (Longden, 2001). The outcome of Harrison and colleagues' 15 and 25-year international follow-up study of recovery from psychotic illness (Harrison *et al.*, 2001), offered a direct challenge to the traditional views of chronicity and pessimism. Furthermore evidence of late recovery suggested rehabilitation and employment should be encouraged in long-term illness.

Under *Helping You Recover* in the NICE guidance on schizophrenia (NICE, 2002a), a negative picture of schizophrenia with a poor prognosis is painted; one that will need constant vigilance from professional teams to avoid crisis, with implications for both physical and mental health. Barker and Buchanan-Barker (2003) question what has happened to the person within the NICE guidelines on schizophrenia. They state that the guidelines are about pathology, not people, arguing that they fail to refer to peer support, the importance of recovery and the reclamation of lives or indeed the lived experience of schizophrenia. It is therefore important not to lose the person within the milieu of guidelines.

The life-affirming experiences of service users do not necessarily bear out the pessimistic prognosis postulated by some stakeholders. Buckingham (2001) describes being able to relax with schizophrenia once she had overcome stigma, guilt and shame. Perkins (2001) advocates the 'normal to be different' approach.

It seems that service users may not only need to hold hope for themselves but also promote hope and confidence in some practitioners and policy makers. Believing in people's potential does not require specialist professional qualification. Indeed those general practitioners who offered encouragement and willingness to support recovery in practical ways were highly regarded in Lester *et al.'s* (2003) study. No amount of rhetoric around hope, it seems, can substitute for the reality of those actions that truly provide a catalyst for hope to flourish. These include embracing the empowerment of service users, peer support, self-help and management (Ahern & Fisher, 2001; Roberts & Wolfson, 2004; Stewart & Wheeler, 2005).

Risk and responsibility

Much of practice and policy concerns itself with risk, which is viewed differently by the stakeholder groups. The medical model offers a gloomy prognosis with emphasis on the suppression of symptoms and the safety of society (Turner & Frak, 2001). From this viewpoint, crisis should be anticipated or prevented and risk reduced (Department of Health, 1999). Fakhoury and Prebe (2002) argue that any government drive for safety-orientated practices will continue to alienate and stigmatise the mentally ill.

From the service user perspective Coleman (1999) writes of recovery requiring a degree of development, trial and error. It is also argued that recovery involves learning from experience (Turner, 2002a). If this is truly the case, practitioners who intervene to prevent difficulty may actually have a negative impact on this very process by acting as rescuer. Whitehill (2003) therefore argues for a paradigm shift from that of containment to one of therapeutic experience. This involves taking risks and accepting failure (Coleman, 1999; Romme & Escher, 2000; Turner, 2002a; Gould *et al.*, 2005).

Drayton *et al.* (1998) conclude that successfully coping with psychosis is linked to a person's own subjective appraisal of it as opposed to its objective severity. Dilemmas are evident when providers attempt to juggle the demands of assuming professional responsibility for risk, and the perceived protection of society with the desire to provide optimism to enable change to occur and the opportunity to nurture recovery (Stickley & Felton, 2006). Different interest groups hold different versions of any true situation. Contradictory truths may lie side by side and reach consensus with differing perspectives.

There is a general consensus amongst the groups that service users ought to be central to their own recovery, that mental health services are undergoing significant changes in order to accommodate the notion of recovery and that service users must be involved in their future development and sustainability. However, tensions exist within the policy-maker and health care practitioner groups. It also became noticeable that several factors could effectively act as filters to frustrate a service user's influence in their own recovery. From the intra-personal domain, service delivery and organisation could be seen as oppositional to the personal individualistic needs; and national policy to local needs and diversity (Service Delivery and Organisation Research Development Programme, 2003). It was also noticeable that policy makers were talking in wider terms of the provision of services *'The British Government's primary interest in health is with the performance, economy and acceptability of the NHS'* (Baker, 2000:214), whilst service users were talking in terms of personal human experience *'I felt so miserable . . . not a girl anymore, just a thing'* (Longden, 2001).

Service users record the experience of accepting psychosis and recovering in spite of it (Campbell, 2001). The challenge may lie in policy makers and health care practitioners being able to accept psychosis and to recover themselves from past patterns that may feel secure. *'Many professionals are not yet ready to think in terms of a comprehensive modern service – they are still focused on the hospital out-patient clinic-type model'* (Sainsbury Centre for Mental Health, 2001:4). Again, it was not easy to know how and where these two experiences could find solidarity.

The drive for measurable and uniform services could be seen to filter out the creativity of individual expression (Turner & Frak, 2001; Blair, 2004; Kitson, 2005). The hidden influences of the pharmaceutical industry and their promotion of a biomedical model were also demonstrated by Mansfield and Jureidini (2001) and the way in which recovery is defined can act to filter and compete with the service user experience. The service provision agenda highlighted the gulf between the biomedical perspective (defined by the elimination of symptoms) and recovery as an accepted and lived alongside experience. Examples included differing messages and language concerning advice and warnings of possible long-term suffering and breakdowns and bothersome symptoms (NICE and NHS, 2002a).

Lack of hope and optimism can affect delivery of services (Longden, 2001). A pessimistic starting point is likely to frame the way in which services are provided, not only at a policy level but amongst practitioners who deliver care. Finally issues around risk and responsibility are likely to have a direct influence on how much service users will be enabled and supported to manage and dictate the terms of their own recovery. Turner (2002a) sees this as the ability to experience one's own psychosis and develop skills in self management.

The social construction of recovery

Social Constructionists take the stance that human beings construct their world through language in different social settings. People therefore make sense of their experiences in the world through constructions of reality and meaning. Through daily interactions different frameworks of understanding and meaning are constructed from the experience. There are an unlimited number of descriptions and explanations for any form of representation, depending on the group. The construction of recovery, as already shown in this chapter, is specific and unique to the individual's experience. The variety of definitions each use their own language and fit different disciplines, models and frameworks. It is clear that there are unlimited definitions and meanings to recovery, none of which are right or wrong, yet all unique to the individual.

However, Burr (1995) and Parker (1999) explain that the concepts of social construction is not as simple as just about language. Historical, cultural and social processes and power are all important influencing factors. In relation to recovery an important aspect to consider is the effects of power in which, *'words and phrases have meanings that are organised into systems and institutions, what Foucault (1969) called "discursive practices" that position us in relation of power'* (Parker, 1999:6). Discursive practices therefore allow individuals to position themselves within different frameworks. The use of words such as symptoms, delusions, hallucinations and medication are essential to carry out the practice of psychiatry and similarly, for practitioners, assessments, care plans and interventions construct their reality. Without these shared words, these specific disciplines would not exist, yet these words construct our reality. As Harper

(1999:131) explains, as soon as interventions are described as treatment it *'automatically introduces a whole range of discursive positions (e.g. illness, diagnosis, recovery and cure) and a range of subject positions (e.g. of doctor and patient)'.*

The challenge for policy makers is how not to construct recovery as another model that practitioners can work within. Although this fits into the constructs and understandings of practitioners this may destroy the essence of recovery. The challenge for the practitioner, as already discussed in this chapter, is for the worker to find the meaning of recovery for the individual and not hijack their experience (with their own discursive practices) that have been constructed from their training and practices. For example, because a person may never have heard of the concept of recovery as presented in this chapter and in this book, does not mean that he/she will not respond to a hope-inspiring relationship. In as much as the concept of recovery is understood by the worker, so the worker may construct a negotiated understanding of the concept of recovery for the person. For example, service users are all too familiar with established language within the psychiatric discourse e.g. assessment, care planning, review meetings etc. What we are suggesting therefore is that workers can (and should) contribute to a shared understanding of the concept of recovery (thus constructing meaning) because the construct is inherently positive. This is arguably far more positive than the more traditional constructs of risk-assessments, care planning, compliance with medication etc. The introduction of the constructed language of recovery and a focus upon recovery concepts is intrinsically good for the client. We would also assert that this approach is intrinsically good for the worker too. For the language of recovery is inherently optimistic. So much of 21st century mental health care is focused upon negative constructs such as protecting the public and subsequent risk-assessment. The focus of much of the care programme approach is about disability, symptoms and illness. A recovery approach to care planning will focus upon wellness, the person's wishes, aspirations, hopes, plans, dreams, ideas and furthermore the resources they possess to achieve these goals.

Models for recovery

The remaining section in this chapter focuses upon specific models of mental health care that may promote recovery.

Wellness recovery action plan

The wellness recovery action plan (WRAP) developed by Mary-Ellen Copeland (2001, 2006) is a simple self-help tool enabling the individual to identify early warning signs and triggers whilst encouraging the development of coping strategies and supports. It has a resemblance to a relapse signature, which *'seeks to identify the earliest signs of impending psychotic relapse and offer timely and effective intervention'* (Birchwood *et al.*, 2000:93). However, WRAP can be developed by

Table 8.1   Six stages to developing a wellness recovery action plan.

Stage 1	Wellness toolbox	Tools and strategies I use each day to stay well
Stage 2	Daily maintenance plan	What I do each day, when I am feeling well
Stage 3	Dealing with triggers	What are my triggers and what is my response to each one?
Stage 4	Early warning signs	What are my early warning signs for me, and what is my action plan?
Stage 5	When things are breaking down	How do I know? Breaking down list and responses/action plan.
Stage 6	Crisis plan – to be seen by others	How do I know when I am well, crisis symptoms, supporters' phone list, medications, treatments, treatment facilities & respite care, supporters roles, what to do if I am in danger to myself of others, and how to know when my supports no longer need to use this plan?

(Copeland, 2001).

anyone '*to relieve symptoms and/or enhance their wellness*' (Copeland, 2001:127). An individual develops a WRAP plan, which involves working through six sections, providing guidance in developing tools, strategies and a crisis plan (Table 8.1). The key to the plan, is that the individual writes the plan entirely for him/herself, with the support of practitioners, family and friends.

Strengths model

The strengths model of recovery was developed by Charles Rapp following his frustrations regarding the current culture of understanding the human condition as a set of problems, abnormalities and disorders, which is how most therapeutic approaches are undertaken. The construction of perceiving a person as sick, with a disorder that needs changing by a practitioner who does not have problems is often very harming. The strengths model takes the opposite approach to this deficit model. It places the individual in an equal position with the professional, society and the environment, empowering the individual to look at their positive attributes rather than the negative.

The individual identifies their strengths, aspirations and dreams and then works towards achieving them. The aim of the practitioner is to work in collaboration with the individual, using their language in order to build a relationship, gather information, undertake a strengths assessment, identify resources in the community, so short and long terms goals can be achieved (Rapp & Goscha, 2006). The 6 principles of the strengths model are:

1) Focus on the individual's strengths, not their weaknesses, problems or deficits
2) The community is not an obstacle, but an oasis of resources

3) Interventions are self determined by the individual
4) The client–practitioner relationship is the foundation of mutual collaboration
5) Seeing the individual in their preferred environment rather than the practitioner's office
6) Individuals with serious mental illness can continue to grow and change.

Tidal model

The tidal model, developed by Phil Barker arose from research undertaken by Chris Stevenson and Sue Jackson concerning what people need psychiatric and mental health nurses for, drawing on the theoretical work of Peplau (1952). The philosophy of the model is based on six principles (Box 8.1) and focuses on personal experience human needs forming, and thus creating new narratives and allowing the restoration of the sense of self that has been lost due to everyday traumas or distress. The model acknowledges the fluid nature of human experience, which changes with unpredictable events, '*Life is a journey undertaken on an ocean of experience.*' (Barker, 2001:235).

The models, philosophies and approaches to recovery presented here, all have similar themes running through them. This demonstrates that recovery is not so much a model as a set of values or attitude that practitioners need to adopt to work with individuals within recovery. The human experience is so fluid and complex that simply implementing any of these models would not achieve recovery, instead practitioners need to have a number of tools and values which are adaptable to the individual's needs and beliefs. This leads to the question of whether an effective recovery-orientated service can be

Box 8.1   Six principles of the tidal model.

Curiosity – the professional knows nothing about the person and his/her experience. The individual is the expert of their experience and the role of the practitioner is to explore the individual's experience with curiosity.

Resourcefulness – instead of focusing on diagnosis, symptoms or illness, the individual is encouraged to focus on their resources, using a solutions focused approach.

Respect for the person's wishes – the role of the practitioner is to take the individual's wishes seriously.

Crisis as an opportunity – a crisis is seen as an opportunity for change, to rethink the life path and do something differently, rather than seeing a crisis as something to cope with or control.

Think small – following the solution focused approach, individuals are encouraged to take small steps forward and not set bigger, less achievable goals.

Elegance – care plans are simple, with simple interventions.

(Barker, 2000).

integrated within the current mental health system. As already demonstrated within this chapter, recovery cannot stand alone within mental health services and there still needs to be large changes in practice and services for recovery values and principles to be fully embedded. Although, there are a number of models, concepts and views on developing recovery, it is still unclear how recovery orientated services can be formed across whole services. Within New Zealand a recovery orientated acute mental health service has been established within the current mental health system, acting as a good example to demonstrate that this is possible.

Recovery orientated acute mental health service

The home based treatment team model adopts its own aims, objectives and philosophies according to the team and service, which therefore acts as a good approach to incorporate recovery work. The capital and coast home based treatment service within New Zealand has adopted a philosophy that although people experiencing a crisis are in danger, they are also presented with an opportunity. By working in partnership as a collaborative approach with the service user, clinician and family, the crisis can be turned to an opportunity for self determination, self efficiency and an opportunity for personal growth, while minimising risks (Goldsack *et al.*, 2005). The service does not act as a replacement to hospital treatment, rather an alternative, providing the individual with a choice of support. The team encourages an open communication policy, in which family/partners are fully involved in the support. By being upfront with the individual's crisis there are no privacy issues, which provide power imbalances. The main emphasis of the work is based on relationships and building relationships. Once open communication is formed, families and individuals can trust the team a lot more and the distress decreases. The underlying work of the team is encouraging the individual in crisis to identify how the team can help them. This helps the practitioner return to simple levels of caring, enabling a connection.

The Mental Health Commission (New Zealand) has recently published a report evaluating this service and looking to see if it offers a recovery orientated service. Following a narrative methodology, the results stated that although recovery research is in its infancy, this service offered all the aspects of recovery identified in other research (Goldsack *et al.*, 2005). The study found that service users and families were very positive in the way they were offered practical help, advice and information. Visits, often several times a day, provided reassurance and support, as the team formed strong supportive relationships to both service user and their family. People felt they were treated as individuals, were included in decisions with hope and encouragement of recovery. Team members were also very positive about their work, with their nursing skills being drawn upon, clearly being able to articulate a recovery philosophy.

Conclusion

In this chapter, we have explored the complex world of recovery by considering the social construction of recovery and its historical developments. By analysing recent literature, we have identified key themes relating to the subject. We have looked at models of recovery and considered how the mental health worker might authentically work within such models whilst retaining their integrity. For some people who have used mental health services over a period of years, the language of service providers has affected them. They may see themselves as hopeless. Working in a recovery promoting way may be hard for the person to accept. There are those that may no longer be confined within the brick walls of the asylums, but psychologically have become institutionalised to the psychiatric discourse. For they may see little hope for themselves beyond reduction of symptoms by changing medication. A challenge to mental health workers who wish to work within a recovery paradigm is to let the client define what recovery means to them, and to use their language. It is all too easy to restrict people by our own language and approach.

The individual worker will need to decide for themselves if it is possible to work with individuals towards recovery without destroying the concept. We argue that it is possible but this largely depends upon the worker's willingness to listen to the person's hopes, dreams and aspirations and genuinely work with the person to achieve these. Understanding of mental health problems needs to go way beyond the bio-medical definitions and approaches. For much of what we refer to today as mental illness is more to do with the pathology of society than the pathology of the person.

It can be argued that services require a degree of structure and organisation in order to delivery quality care and retain accountability to public funds. Despite this, it will be important for those who deliver these services to be able to demonstrate flexibility, which includes being able to effect any necessary paradigm shift (Sainsbury Centre for Mental Health, 2001). Workers will need to believe that recovery is possible (Kelly & Gamble, 2005) and accept a shift in authority to that of working alongside (Repper & Perkins, 2003). To work with a recovery philosophy in mind will require workers to allow service users to define recovery for themselves and to work collaboratively with the service user's own style. This is likely to throw up dilemmas for workers with implications at policy level, not least in the domain of risk-taking.

We acknowledge that there is currently a fear amongst many people that recovery will be destroyed and colonised by professionals, becoming another thing *done to them*. It is our hope that this chapter has not contributed to that problem. What we have endeavoured to demonstrate is that the positive construction of recovery can be used as a vehicle for good practice. Arguably, unless the worker has experienced mental health problems themselves, the true essence of recovery cannot be captured. However, with a change in attitude and approach to a belief that there is hope for the seemingly hopeless, that there are endless opportunities for change and growth, the careful art of care planning can be part of a person's journey to recovery.

(*Editors' note*) Readers may be interested to note that Jim Campbell (Campbell, 2006) recently engaged in a research study tour of New Zealand and Australia, some of the findings of which influenced and informed some of the content of this chapter.

References

Ahern, L. & Fisher, D. (2001). Recovery At Your Own Pace. *Journal of Psychosocial Nursing and Mental Health Services.* **39(4)**, 22–33.

Altschul, A. & Millet, K. (2000). Foreword. In: Barker, P.J., Campbell, P. & Davidson, B. (eds). *From The Ashes Of Experience: Reflections On Madness, Survival and Growth.* London: Whurr Publishers. xi–xv.

Baker, M. (2000). *Making Sense of the NHS White Papers.* Oxon: Radcliffe Medical Press. (2nd edn).

Barchard, C. (2005). *Voices forum.* Kingston on Thames. Available at: http://www.voicesforum.org.uk/ideasma.htm (Accessed 22 November 2005).

Barker, P.J. (2000). Turning the Tide. *Open Mind.* **106**, 10–11.

Barker, P.J. (2001). The Tidal Model: Developing An Empowering, Person Centred Approach To Recovery Within Psychiatric and Mental Health Nursing. *Journal of Psychiatric and Mental Health Nursing.* **8(3)**, 233–240.

Barker, P. (2003). The Primacy Of Caring. In: Barker, P. (ed). *Psychiatric and Mental Health Nursing: The Craft Of Caring.* London: Arnold

Barker, P. & Buchanan-Barker, P. (2003). Not So NICE Guidelines. *Open Mind.* **121**, 14.

Barker, P.J., Campbell, P. & Davidson, B. (2000). *From The Ashes Of Experience: Reflections On Madness, Survival and Growth.* London: Whurr Publishers.

Birchwood, M., Spencer, E. & McGovern, D. (2000). Schizophrenia: Early Warning Signs. *Advance in Psychiatric Treatment.* **6**, 93–101.

Blair, G. (2004). The New GMS Contract and Its Implications for Mental Health, *Community Mental Health.* **3(2)**, 12–14.

Bradstreet, S. & Connor, A. (2005). Communities Of Recovery. *Mental Health Today.* **May**, 22.

British Psychological Society (2000). *Recent Advances In Understanding Mental Illness and Psychotic Experiences.* Leicester: Division of Clinical Psychologists. **184**, 176–181.

Buckingham, C. (2001). Schizophrenia: The Biological and Social. *Open Mind.* **111**, 11.

Burr, V. (1995). *An Introduction to Social Constructionism.* London: Routledge.

Campbell, J. (2006). *Mental Health Recovery: A Way Forward. What can the UK learn from the New Zealand and Australian Expereince?* Scottish Recovery Network. Available at: http://www.scottishrecovery.net/content/mediaassets/doc/JCampbell%20study%20tour%20report.pdf

Campbell, P. (2001). It's Not The Real You. *Open Mind.* **111**, 16–17.

Chadwick, P. (2002). How to Become Better After Psychosis than You Were Before. *Open Mind.* **115**, 12–13.

Chalmers, F. (2001). *Psychiatry 'Hijacked' By Big Pharma.* Available at: http://healthmatters.org.uk/issue45/bigpharma. (Accessed 07 July 2006).

Coleman, R. (1999). *Recovery; An Alien Concept*. Gloucester: Handsell Publishing.

Coleman, R. (2000). The Politics Of The Illness. In: Barker, P.J. & Stevenson, C. (eds). *The Construction of Power and Authority in Psychiatry*. Oxford: Butterworth-Heinemann. **(4)**, 59–66.

Coleman, R., Baker, P. & Taylor, K. (2001). *Working To Recovery, Victim To Victor 111: A Guide To Mental Well Being, A Personal Planning Tool*. Gloucester: Handsell Publishing.

Copeland, M.E. (2001). Wellness Recovery Action Plan: A System For Monitoring, Reducing and Eliminating Uncomfortable Or Dangerous Psychical Symptoms and Emotional Feelings. *Occupational Therapy in Mental Health*. **17(3 & 4)** 5–21.

Copeland, M.E. (2006). *Mental Health Recovery and Wellness Recovery Action Plan (WRAP)*. USA: West Dummerston. Available at: http://www.mentalhealthrecovery.com/art_aboutwrap.html

Deegan, P. (1993). Recovering Our Sense Of Value After Being Labelled Mentally Ill. *Journal Of Psychosocial Nursing*. **31(4)**, 7–11.

Deegan, P. (2001). Recovery As A Self-Directed Process Of Healing and Transformation. *Occupational Therapy Mental Health*. **17(3 & 4)**, 5–21.

Department of Health (1983). *The Mental Health Act 1983*. London: HMSO.

Department of Health (1999). *A National Service Framework For Mental Health. Modern Standards and Service Models*. London: The Stationery Office.

Department of Health (2001). *The Journey To Recovery: The Government's Vision For Mental Health Care*. London: The Stationery Office.

Department of Health (2002). *Developing Services For Carers and Families Of People With Mental Illness*. London: The Stationery Office.

Department of Health (2003). *Continuity Of Care For People With Severe Mental Illness*. Service Delivery and Organisation Research Development Programme. Briefing paper. London. Available at: www.sdo.ishtm.ac.uk (Accessed 13 May 2005).

Department of Health (2005). *New Ways Of Working For Psychiatrists: Enhancing Effective, Person-Centred Services Through New Ways Of Working In Multidisciplinary and Multi-Agency Contexts*. London: Royal College of Psychiatrists, National Institute for Mental Health in England and Changing Workforce Programme.

Department of Health and Hope, R. (2004). *The Ten Essential Shared Capabilities: A Framework For The Whole Of The Mental Health Workforce*. London: The Stationery Office.

Drayton, M., Birchwood, M. & Trower, P. (1998). Early Attachment Experiences and Recovery from Psychosis. *British Journal of Clinical Psychology*. **37**, 269–284.

Fakhoury, W. & Prebe, S. (2002). The Process Of Deinstitutionalisation: An International Overview. *Current Opinion in Psychiatry*. **15(2)**, 187–192.

Fisher, D. (2000). Hope, Humanity and Voice In Recovery From Mental Illness. In: Barker, P.J., Campbell, P. & Davidson, B. (eds). *From the Ashes of Experience: Reflections on Madness, Survival and Growth*. London: Whurr Publishers. **(8)**, 127–133.

Fisher, D. (2005). *A New Vision Of Recovery: People Can Fully Recover From Mental Illness; It Is Not A Life-Long Process*. Lawrence: National Empowerment Centre. Available at: http://www.power2u.org/who.html (Accessed 18 November 2005).

Foucault, M. (1969). *The Archaeology of Knowledge*. London: Tavistock.

Goldsack, S., Reet, S., Lapsley, H. & Gingell, M. (2005). *Experiencing a Recovery-Orientated Acute Mental Health Service: Home Based Treatment from the Perspectives of Service Users, their Families and Mental Health Professionals*. Wellington, New Zealand. Mental Health Commission.

Gould, A., DeSouza, S. & Rebeiro-Gruhl, K. (2005). And Then I Lost That Life: A Shared Narrative Of Four Young Men With Schizophrenia. *British Journal of Occupational Therapy.* **68(10)**, 467–473.

Grierson, M. (2001). *Emerging Best Practice In Mental Health: User-Based Outcomes and Recovery.* Available at: http://myweb.tiscali.co.uk/recovery/reading/reports/directional.htm (Accessed 10 May 2004).

Harper, D. (1999). Tablet Talk and Depot Discourse: Discourse Analysis and Psychiatric Medication. In: Willig, C. (ed.). *Applied Discourse Analysis: Social and Psychological Interventions.* Buckingham: Open University Press. 124–144.

Harrison, G., Hopper, K., Craig, T., Laska, E., Siegel, C., Wanderling, J., Dube, K., Ganev, K., Giel, R., Der Heiden, A., Holmberg, W., Janca, A., Lee, P., Leon, W., Malhotra, C., Marsella, A., Nakane, Y., Sartorius, N., Shen, Y., Skoda, C., Thara, R., Tsirkin, S., Varma, V., Walsh, D. & Wiersma, D. (2001). Recovery from Psychotic Illness: A 15 and 25 Year International Follow Up Study. *The British Journal of Psychiatry.* **178**, 506–517.

Heather, F. (2002). Pro-motion: A Positive Way Forward For Clients With Severe and Enduring Mental Health Problems Living In The Community, Part 1. *British Journal of Occupational Therapy.* **65(12)**, 551–558.

Holloway, F. (2002). Outcome Measurement In Mental Health, Welcome To The Revolution. *The British Journal of Psychiatry.* **181**, 1–2.

Jacobson, N. (2004). *In Recovery: The Making Of Mental Health Policy.* Nashville: Vanderbilt University Press.

Kelly, M. & Gamble, C. (2005). Exploring The Concept Of Recovery In Schizophrenia, *Journal Of Psychiatric and Mental Health Nursing.* **12(2)**, 245–251.

Kendell, R.E. (2000). The Next 25 Years. *The British Journal of Psychiatry.* **176**, 6–9.

Kitson, C. (2005). Roads To Recovery. *Mental Health Today.* **May**, 16.

Lester, H., Tritter, J. & England, E. (2003). Satisfaction With Primary Care: The Perspectives Of People With Schizophrenia. *Family Practice.* **20(5)**, 508–513.

Lester, H., Tritter, J. & Sorohan, H. (2005). Patients' and Health Professionals' Views On Primary Care For People With Serious Mental Illness: Focus Group Study. *British Medical Journal.* **330**, 1122.

Longden, E. (2001). Suspended Animation. *Open Mind.* **111**, 12–13.

MacDonald, A. (2005). *Milestones On My Recovery Road.* Glasgow: Scottish Recovery Network. Available at: http://www.scottishrecovery.net (Accessed 23 November 2005).

Mansfield, P. & Jureidini, J. (2001). *Giving Doctors The Treatment.* Available at: http://healthmatters.org.uk/issue43/givingdoctors (Accessed 07 July 2006).

Martyn, D. (2002). *The Experiences and Views Of Self Management Of People With A Schizophrenia Diagnosis.* London: Rethink.

May, R. (2000a). Psychosis and Recovery. *Open Mind.* **106**, 24–25.

May, R. (2000b). Routes to Recovery from Psychosis: The Roots of a Clinical Psychologist. *Clinical Psychology Forum.* **146**, 6–10.

May, R. (2001). *Understanding Psychotic Experience and Working Towards Recovery.* Bradford: Bradford District Community Trust.

May, R., Risman, J., Kidder, K., Campbell, J., Caras, S., Dumont, J., Fisher, D., Johnson, J., Kaufmann, C., Knight, E., Loder, A., Penny, D., Townsend, W. & Van Tosh, L. (1999). *Recovery Advisory Group Recovery Model. A Work In Process.* Recovery Advisory Group. Available at: http://www.mhsip.org/recovery (Accessed 28 March 2006).

Mead, S. & Copeland, M.E. (2000). What Recovery Means To Us: Consumers' Perspective. *Community Mental Health Journal.* **36(3)**, 315–328.

Mental Health Foundation (2004). *Response To Consultation Document: New Vision For Adult Social Care (SCIE 2004).* London. Available at: http://www.mentalhealth.org.uk (Accessed 21 November 2005).

Morgan, S. (2004). Strengths Based Practice. *Open Mind.* **126**, 16–17.

National Institute for Clinical Excellence and National Health Service (2002a). *Treating and Managing Schizophrenia (Core Interventions) Understanding NICE Guidance: Information For People With Schizophrenia, Their Advocates and Carers and The Public.* London: NICE.

National Institute for Clinical Excellence and National Health Service (2002b). *Core Interventions In The Treatment And Management Of Schizophrenia In Primary and Secondary Care. Clinical Practice Algorithms and Pathways To Care.* London: NICE.

National Institute for Clinical Excellence, National Health Service and National Collaborating Centre for Mental Health (2003). *Full National Clinical Guideline on Core Interventions in Primary and Secondary Care.* London: Gaskell and British Psychological Society.

National Institute for Mental Health in England (2003). *Recovery and Change: Mental Health Into The Mainstream.* Leeds: NIMHE/DoH.

National Institute for Mental Health in England (2004). *Emerging Best Practice in Mental Health Recovery.* Leeds: NIMHE/DoH.

National Institute for Mental Health in England (2005). *Making it Possible: Improving Mental Health and Well-being in England.* Leeds: NIMHE/DoH.

Nolan, P. (2000). History of Psychiatry, Patients and Hospitals. *Current Opinion In Psychiatry.* **13(6)**, 717–720.

Parker, I. (1999). *Critical Textwork: An Introduction To Varieties Of Discourse and Analysis.* Buckingham: Open University Press.

Peplau, H.E. (1952). *Interpersonal Relations in Nursing.* New York: Putman.

Perkins, R. (2001). Stigma or Discrimination. *Open Mind.* **112**, 6.

Perkins, R. (2002). The Right to Define Reality. *Open Mind.* **116**, 6.

Perkins, R. (2003). The Altar of Independence. *Open Mind.* **119**, 6.

Rapp, C.A. & Goscha, R.J. (2006). *The Strengths Model: Case Management with People with Psychiatric Disabilities.* Oxford: Oxford University Press.

Reid, Y., Johnson, S., Bebbington, P., Kuipers, E., Scott, H. & Thornicroft, G. (2001). The Longer Term Outcomes of Community Care: A 12 Year Follow-Up of The Camberwell High Contact Survey. *Psychological Medicine.* **31(2)**, 351–359.

Repper, J. & Perkins, R. (2003). *Social Inclusion and Recovery: A Model For Mental Health Practice.* London: Baillière Tindall.

Rethink (2005). *Recovery: A Brief Introduction to the Recovery Approach.* London. Available at: http://www.rethink.org/recovery (Accessed 19 November 2005).

Roberts, G. & Wolfson, P. (2004). The Rediscovery of Recovery: Open to All. *Advances in Psychiatric Treatment.* **10(1)**, 37–48.

Romme, M. & Escher, S. (2000). *Making Sense of Voices.* London: MIND Publications.

Sainsbury Centre for Mental Health (2001). *Mental Health Policy: The Challenges Facing The Government.* London: SCMH.

Sayce, L. (2000). *From Psychiatric Patient to Citizen.* Basingstoke: Macmillan Press.

Service Delivery and Organisation Research Development Programme and National Health Service (2003). *Continuity Of Care For People With Severe Mental Illness?* London: SDORD.

Stanton, S. (2001). Inescapable Past? *Open Mind*. **111**, 15.

Stewart, L. & Wheeler, K. (2005). Occupation for Recovery. *Occupational Therapy News* **13(11)**, 20.

Stickley, T. & Felton, A. (2006). Promoting Recovery through Therapeutic Risk Taking. *Mental Health Practice*. **9(8)**, 26–30.

Tait, L., Birchwood, M. & Trower, P. (2003). Predicting Engagement with Services for Psychosis: Insight, Symptoms and Recovery Style. *The British Journal of Psychiatry*. **182**, 123–128.

Townsend, W., Boyd, S., Griffin, G. & Hicks, P. (1999). *Emerging Best Practices in Mental Health Recovery*. Columbus, Ohio: Ohio Department of Mental Health.

Travis, M., Peters, E. & Kerwin, R. (2001). *Managing Relapse in Schizophrenia*. London: Science Press Ltd.

Turner, D. (2002a). Mapping The Routes to Recovery. *Mental Health Today*. **July**, 29–30.

Turner, D. (2002b). *The National Voices Forum: The Regaining Control Conference* (2002). Oxford: National Voices Forum and UK Advocacy Network.

Turner, D. & Frak, D. (2001). *Wild Geese: Recovery in National Schizophrenia Fellowship*. Powys: Green Gauge Consultancy and NSF Wales.

Warner, R. (2004). *Recovery From Schizophrenia*. Hove: Brunner-Routledge. (3rd edn).

Whitehill, I. (2003). The Concept Of Recovery. In: Barker, P.J. (ed.). *Psychiatric and Mental Health Nursing: The Craft Of Caring*. London: Arnold. **(6)**, 43–49.

Wimberley, L. & Peters, A. (2003). Recovery in Acute Mental Health. *Occupational Therapy News*. **July**, 25.

World Health Organization (2005). *Mental Health Declaration for Europe. Facing The Challenges, Building Solutions*. Available at: http://www.euro.who.int/HEN/syntheses (Accessed 09 December 2005).

Chapter 9

Engagement within the Care Planning Process

Mike Firn

Introduction

There is little doubt that engagement in a central therapeutic relationship between provider and service user is a reliable predictor of outcome in mainstream psychiatric care (McCabe & Priebe, 2004). This chapter examines how practitioners can relate to service users and their carers to encourage engagement within the care planning process and beyond. This will include scoping what is included in engagement related activity and what we know from qualitative studies of the reasons that service users give for engaging and not engaging. How do we effectively engage carers in care planning? Are their needs necessarily the same as that of the service user? To what extent do psychology, culture, recovery style, beliefs, demographic factors, and insight affect engagement or the experience of coercion? Addictions, eating disorders, depression, anxiety and psychosis present different challenges and motives for service user engagement with or avoidance of care. Case examples and care plan examples will be used throughout to demonstrate real life applications.

There are many facets to engagement. An eclectic understanding will enable practitioners to operate across the spectrum of mental health care from an outpatient primary care focused clinic, a secondary care community mental health service or a forensic secure unit.

Modern mental health services increasingly deliver home based care in an environment where the service user uses informed choice to be an active partner in care planning. In their own homes people have choices, they are more individual, they have lovers, children, bills, jobs, unemployment, drugs, alcohol and a variety of mental and physical health needs. The service user may not be ready or willing to discuss drug use or mental health. Child protection and welfare may be another threatening area. We can see already that the process of engagement requires skill, life experience, team work and support, patience and the ability to negotiate conflicting demands. In essence it requires the practitioner to be genuine in displaying a sense of working for the patient's best interest and to perform their professional role competently.

What is engagement?

We need to recognise that the term engagement may not always be well understood by service users, relatives and colleagues – it is jargon. Normal language would talk about rapport, motivation, trust, commitment, keeping or missing appointments and dropping out. We all consider changing our dentist or GP when we have a long wait, a short and dismissive consultation or don't get what we want or expect. The same and more are true for mental health services. Additional obstacles occur in the guise of stigma, and the effect of more serious mental health problems on judgement, beliefs and behaviour. In addition some of the pharmaceutical treatments for depression or psychosis are associated with negative side effects.

Within mental health, engagement is used to describe both a process and goal. Process as being the activities undertaken towards developing long-lasting and trusting relationships, and goal as an idealised, steady state of collaborative, positive interaction between the service provider and the service user. The ultimate purpose is to provide the optimal conditions within which to deliver health and social care interventions, whether treatment, rehabilitation or support. So engagement is not an end in itself, but a necessary precursor.

The difficulty for services is encapsulated in the quote: *'very few people seek help for mental health problems with enthusiasm'* (Onyett, 1992).

The conditions for swinging the balance towards better engagement are choice, respect, understanding, ease of access and tolerability of treatment. Statutory mental health services have traditionally been poor in these respects but the rise of consumerism and advances in models, frameworks and under-pinning values of care (National Institute for Mental Health in England, 2004) have been evident in recent years.

There is best practice in the attitude and activities of staff within mental health services and there is structural and operational best practice such as ease of referral and accessibility and acceptability of treatment locations. This chapter concentrates mainly on the behaviours and practices of staff, but successful outcomes depend on both aspects being in place.

Diagnostic groups and individuals vary in the degree to which they tend to engage with services. Later sections deal more thoroughly and provide case vignettes. For now let us consider a simple classification (Table 9.1) which covers the scope of engagement related staff activities of care adapted from Burns and Firn (2002). We will expand on these strategies in later sections through case vignettes and discussion.

Constructive engagement and care planning

Given that few service users will be care planning and treatment enthusiasts in mental health, some ambivalence to services is usually present. For the majority engagement will be about persuading the persuadable. Allaying fears,

Table 9.1 Classification of engagement related activity by degree of collaboration.

Constructive approach	Informative approach	Restrictive approach
C1 **Collaborative or patient led agenda** Can you tell me what has brought you here today? Where would you like to be this time next year? How do you see your problems? What would you like to do about this problem? Joint crisis plans WRAP plans Advance agreements	**I1** **Frequent and persistent attempts to visit or arrange appointments** For example a new referral for severe depression has missed several appointments. Are they going to work? Has the GP seen them? Have they had home visits to see if they are in but not opening the door?	**R1** **Use of statutory powers under 1983 Mental Health Act** Patients can be discharged from hospital with conditions to allow access, to facilitate treatment and to ensure they get appropriate aftercare services. e.g. Section 25a aftercare under supervision. This is likely to be replaced by a full community treatment order to be called Supervised Community Treatment under proposals to amend legislation. Section 17 long leave of absence. Section 37/41. Criminal Court Hospital Order.
C2 **Strengths focused interventions** Focus on normalising, mainstream and abilities rather than disabilities. Allowing positive risk taking. A rehabilitation approach to maximising strengths.	**I2** **Regular contact with the family or carers where no direct contact with the patient** Do the family have current concerns about behaviour or symptoms?	**R2** **Leverage** More informal attempts to encourage compliance rather than engagement. Linking treatment to potential sanctions. In the UK this can involve becoming the appointee for a person's welfare monies where they are judged incapable. Some residential care involves a commitment to receive prescribed treatment.
C3 **Non-judgemental approach** For example in the management of self-harm or personality disorder.	**I3** **Contact with GP** Are they picking up prescriptions, have they seen the GP?	**R3** **No drop out policy** Assertive outreach teams in particular will adopt a policy of not discharging patients in need however much the patient refuses their help.
C4 **Practical assistance and problem solving** Debts, welfare benefits, housing	**I4** **Contact with probation** e.g. forensic services	**R4** **Drug treatment/testing or rehabilitation orders** Court prescribed and probation monitored conditional community sentences.

Table 9.1 (*Continued*)

Constructive approach	Informative approach	Restrictive approach
C5 **Advocacy and self-advocacy** Advocacy in welfare benefit appeals, criminal justice system, education or work difficulties. Empowering approach. Promoting personal responsibility.	**I5** **Contact with housing and benefits office** Are they behind with the rent, collecting benefits? e.g. where history or concern about self neglect and exploitation this may be an indicator of relapse.	
C6 **Home-based care or a non-stigmatising environment** Remove the barriers to attendance. Clinics in normal health centres or anonymous premises.	**I6** **Evidence of self neglect or violence when visiting the premises** Broken window, door, mail piling up, and rubbish piling up.	
C7 **Support and involvement of family members and friends** Where appropriate and permitted by the client involve and engage their support system.	**I7** **Use of telephone contact in between or instead of visits to increase frequency of contact.**	

normalising, genuine concern and a flexible, human face to the service you are providing.

If we look at the annual English National Mental Health Patients Survey responses from 25 500 users of secondary mental health services, we can see that simple care planning steps and behaviours are important (Healthcare Commission, 2005). Questions cover trust, respect, being listened to as well as specifics about services like: were you given a copy of your care plan? Some useful quotes illustrate the sentiments of the respondents. *'My psychiatrist is excellent, a good listener who has never patronised me. I trust him implicitly'* (Anon in Healthcare Commission, 2005).

The English National Service Framework for Mental Health (Department of Health, 1999a) recommends that all those people whose care in secondary services is coordinated by the care programme approach (CPA) (Department of Health, 1999b) receive a copy of their written care plan. The 2005 survey reports results as an average for Mental Health Trusts in England. On average 50% of respondents were offered, or received a copy of, their care plan (70% of those on enhanced CPA and 41% on standard CPA). Of these on average 58% said that they definitely understood what was in it, 32% understood it to some extent and 10% didn't understand it at all. Only 59% definitely agreed with what was in their care plan, with 35% agreeing to some extent. This leaves 6% disagreeing, perhaps reflecting the degree of involuntary care, or care that does not match their preferred choice, still occurring in mental health. Given that an average of 23% of respondents said that they were not involved in deciding what was in their care plan, this figure could have been much higher.

Similar problems were highlighted by this annual survey for care review meetings. 5% of respondents from the average Mental Health Trust said that they were not given a chance to express their views at the meeting. Simple things are important and obvious. Asked whether they had trust and confidence in the psychiatrist they saw, significantly more respondents replied yes definitely when they saw the same psychiatrist on the previous two occasions than a different one each time (64% and 45% respectively). Interestingly when seeing different psychiatrists only 59% of respondents felt that they had definitely been listened to carefully, rising to 73% when they saw the same person both times.

It is hardly surprising given these findings that attendance rates at review meetings and follow up appointments are problematic. We cannot treat care planning as a bureaucratic exercise that doesn't meaningfully involve the recipient of care or their families. The written care plan needs to be a living document that frames what the service user can reasonably expect and to some extent their aspirations. The same survey gives us a quote from a respondent about the review of his care.

'Promises are made in your care review but never seem to happen, like when I was promised more support by a social worker and I'm still waiting since my review and meeting' (Anon, in Healthcare Commission, 2005).

Case study 9.1   Primary care – Colin.

Colin was highly anxious and had given up his job as a warehouseman and become increasingly withdrawn and avoided social interaction. He had low self esteem and was reluctant to share or speak about the extreme discomfort and shame he experienced. He had consulted his GP about a series of physical ailments such as palpitations, nausea and sleeplessness. His GP had started to suspect a psychological cause and prescribed an anti-depressant with anxiolytic properties. Fortunately the GP practice had some psychological therapy sessions available and Colin was persuaded with some reluctance to see a primary care mental health worker. Sensing at the first consultation that Colin was going to be easily scared off by any follow up treatment the practitioner avoided a diagnostic assessment approach initially since the background history was available. Instead the session concentrated on what it felt like to be anxious in normal situations, how it was normal to be anxious about aspects of work, life, and death. That anxiety has harmless, but unpleasant, physical manifestations that recede as the anxiety diminishes. These physical manifestations can be positive in certain situations speeding up the thoughts and improving blood flow to muscles. In excess they can be disabling. Visual aids and written material were given and the session terminated when the practitioner sensed that Colin was becoming tense again. Colin completed the talking therapy over six sessions and learned valuable techniques to manage and understand his anxiety that gradually receded.

This case vignette demonstrates a common primary care presentation. It demonstrates how male reaction to psychological distress can differ from female. More importantly it describes tailoring the treatment package to suit the individual. Colin could not tolerate long sessions. He could not tolerate much in the way of probing the underlying cause of his anxiety if any. Positive reframing of anxiety as a normal but occasionally dysfunctional response helped Colin to overcome the shame and stigma that he felt. The intervention was delivered in a mainstream primary care setting not at a mental health out-patients facility. Colin was equipped with the knowledge and skills to manage future episodes.

Informative and restrictive approaches

In Table 9.1, informative approach number I1, we gave the secondary care example of a GP referral to the specialist mental health team of a man with severe depression who had defaulted on a number of appointments. Let us expand on this and the responsibilities of the care team to engage this person and their support network. Some refer to these responsibilities as a duty of care.

Case study 9.2   Secondary care – Ranjit.

Ranjit had lost his business that he had spent many years building up. He initially didn't disclose this to his wife and family and carried on going out in the mornings to sit in the library. By the time the family had found out and tried to support him, he was severely depressed and had stopped his pretence and all contact with others outside the house. Indeed he started to express overvalued ideas about his own role in the collapse, characterised as deep self-loathing and guilt to the extent that he believed that his ex-workers wanted him and his family dead. His family GP was also an associate and came to see Ranjit at the request of his wife after Ranjit had refused to go to the surgery. The GP told Ranjit that he was referring him to the mental health services and that he was concerned he would harm himself. The GP was also concerned for Ranjit's wife and family and advised them to call him or the police if they were concerned. Ranjit disposed of the medication his GP had left.

The community mental health team (CMHT) usually performed first assessments at home. They also followed up written appointment letters with telephone calls. Ranjit refused the offer of an appointment and said that the depression was his punishment for letting everyone down. The team phoned again the next day and got the same response. They then rang the GP who spoke to Ranjit's wife. She arranged an appointment and arranged for Ranjit to be in. The team were able to conduct an initial assessment with Ranjit although he was a little guarded. He refused any follow up visits saying he wasn't worth it. The team also spent time assessing his wife's needs and concerns separately. She agreed to keep in daily contact with the allocated worker at the CMHT. She also agreed to remove all harmful medication, rope and tubes from the house and garage even though Ranjit had denied any suicidal ideation. The care coordinator continued to make telephone contact with Ranjit even though he refused visits. Eventually Ranjit agreed to take medication for the depression 'to please his wife' but continued to refuse visits. The care coordinator made the deliberate decision to deliver the medication personally in seven days supplies as a way of establishing some contact, minimising the risk of overdose, and monitoring progress and side effects. His wife was in regular contact and reported that she was watching Ranjit take the tablets.

In this case vignette would Ranjit ever agree with a care plan item stating, *'remove all accessible means of self-harm or suicide'*? Probably not. How could we write an acceptable care plan detailing frequency of contact, use of anti-depressant medication and assessment of mental state, suicidal ideation, and risk assessment? In the acute phase this is more of a challenge.

Patient choice includes legitimately refusing care and treatment. In physical health patients regularly refuse life enhancing or prolonging treatments whether it be for diabetes or for chemotherapy and the patient is discharged to primary care. Providing mental capacity is assessed and evident individual choices must be respected. In mental health the nature of some illnesses can impair judgement. Clinical assessments according to legally defined criteria for compulsion, or legally defined mental incapacity, must be made before any intervention against the individual's stated choice.

In the absence of such overriding evidence, and in the presence of concerns that withdrawing care and follow up would be potentially hazardous a watching brief is the next best alternative. This is described as the informative approach. This is only really acceptable practice where there are legitimate causes for concern about significant and harmful deterioration or risk. These are decisions and conundrums best discussed with teams. Otherwise undue persistence could be construed as harassment and indeed it has been described as therapeutic stalking (Speight & Denoual, 2005).

How then can Ranjit and his family be involved to some extent in deciding what is in his care plan? Consider the simplified example in Figure 9.1. The care plan includes stated problems of risk and difficulty in contact; it also includes a diagnosis. To ignore these would be potentially negligent in a care plan but they may be areas of conflict with Ranjit. Figure 9.1 attempts to frame these difficulties in language more acceptable to Ranjit and allows for his comments to be placed on the record and for his signature. To some extent the care plan forces Ranjit and the service to openly share their concerns and reach an agreed compromise. The plan avoids phrases like suicidal ideation and uses Ranjit's own words to describe his mood. Likewise it does not state risk of self harm or suicide as a problem but positively rephrases this as maintaining safety and again uses his words of ending it all.

In Table 9.1 the restrictive approach describes strategies and activities where positive engagement and informative approaches have consistently failed despite numerous and often long-term attempts. Usually this applies to managing a small number of people with a serious mental illness who refuse any form of care and who present risk or ethical challenges to withdrawing care, or standing by and watching avoidable and predictable deterioration. It is retention in treatment, and is about getting people to comply rather than engage. In other words this is about persuading the non-persuadable.

Leverage and coercion are other terms used. Leverage describes the informal powers that are brought to bear on an individual to get them to co-operate with treatment. This can come from services and family members. Persuasion, pressure and coercion can derive from incentives or sanctions such as access to or refusal of housing, giving or withdrawal of support and attention, financial assistance, and especially the perceived threat of involuntary commitment to hospital or granting of hospital leave (Monahan *et al.*, 2005).

R1 and R4 in Table 9.1 describe some legal powers that can be brought to bear in prescribed circumstances in English jurisdiction. All countries have

Enhanced CPA/Section 117(2) Review (delete as applicable)	
Patient's name: Ranjit Singh Address: Phone: Date of birth: GP: Phone:	CMHT: West Sector Phone: .... New patient: YES If NO, date of review: .... Diagnosis: 1. Severe depressive episode F 32 .2 2.. F__ __.__

You must consider the following:

1) Mental health, including indicators
     of relapse
2) Physical health
3) Medication
4) Daytime activity
5) Personal care/living skills
6) Carers, family, children and social network
	7) Forensic history 8) Alcohol or substance misuse
	9) Cultural factors 10) Housing/finances/legal issues
	                                            and
	a) make sure a risk assessment is done
	b) include: i) a crisis plan ii) a contingency plan
	     i.e. what should be done if part of the care plan can't be
	     provided (e.g. the care coordinator is on leave or ill)?

Assessed needs or problem	Intervention	Responsibility of:
1. Feelings of worthlessness and failure. Feels it would be better for everyone if he were dead and that others would wish this.	1. Ranjit does not wish to receive psychiatric help for this problem. Allocated worker Phillip Jones to maintain regular contact in order to offer care to Ranjit and his family. 2. Invite and attempt daily contact from family members by telephone. 3. Provide weekly home visits to assess mood, potential risk and offer support and treatment. 4. Ranjit is prescribed anti-depressant medication and does not wish to start this treatment at this time. Continue to provide information, reassurance and weekly supplies of medication. 5. Provide structured opportunity for Ranjit to question and test his beliefs that others want him dead. Contrast with concern that others are showing for his welfare. Discuss hopes and future solutions for real life problems concerning business, family and livelihood.	PJ Ranjit and Family. PJ
2. Family coping difficulties.	6. Support family coping and maintaining a safe environment. Support family in their caring role and provide information and assistance in dealing with Ranjit's low mood and thoughts of 'ending it all'.	Ranjit and Family.
3. Maintain safety.	7. See item 6. Involve family in maintaining a safe environment and contingency planning should perceived risk or identified risk factors occur. See risk management and contingency plan.	

Client Comments: I would never hurt myself or my family, I am a religious man and I am being rightly punished	
Care co-ordinator (signature) .... Job title: Community Mental Health Nurse	Date of next review... Patient's signature..

Figure 9.1   A care plan for Ranjit.

recourse to similar types of legislation and procedures for care and control in recognition of this difficulty between personal autonomy and mental incapacity. Forensic community teams face particular challenges as do services for tuberculosis, probation officers, teachers and tax collectors. Experience is that monitoring and coercive strategies are not however a satisfactory or particularly effective strategy in the longer term.

Evidence for enablers and barriers to engagement

Subjective factors impact on engagement. These include personal or cultural beliefs about the nature of mental illness, personality traits, past experiences with services, insight and psychological adjustment to a major illness. Capturing these factors in a systematic way has been attempted through in depth interviews and the use of scales and questionnaires.

Tait *et al.* (2003) concluded that, for the 50 patients diagnosed with schizophrenia they interviewed, recovery style contributed more to engagement than insight. By recovery style they utilised two concepts to describe enduring personality traits, and a recovery style questionnaire, both developed by McGlashan (1987). The two concepts of recovery are the integration recovery style characterised by acknowledgement, ownership and curiosity about the illness, and the sealing over style characterised by cognitive and behavioural avoidance of the diagnosis and its treatment. Sealing over is not the same as lack of insight since some people with a sealing over style knew they were ill. *'I know I am ill but it was just one of those things and I want to forget about it and move on'* (McGlashan, 1987).

Priebe *et al.* (2005) used independent in-depth interviews with a culturally and ethnically varied group of 40 patients from 9 assertive outreach teams in London. They were interested in subjective accounts of the factors involved in engaging and disengaging from these services, particularly as assertive outreach teams are set up to serve hard to engage and revolving door patients. Three main themes were identified as enabling engagement:

- Social support and engagement without focus on medication
- Time and commitment
- Partnership model of therapeutic relationship.

'He wants to know about everyday things, not just how are your pills. . . . It is broader. That makes up you know, it's a better relationship and you feel oh, you know I wouldn't mind sharing what I do. . . . But when it was very patronising I just put shutters up' (Priebe *et al.*, 2005).

This study also identified three themes in the accounts of reasons for disengagement:

- Desire to be an independent and able person
- Lack of active participation and poor therapeutic relationship
- Loss of control due to medication and its effects.

Twenty six patients identified a difficulty in accepting mental illness and the patient role or identity as reasons for disengagement. This correlates with the sealing over recovery style. Secondly the therapeutic relationship and staff behaviour was important.

'it's like just general gestures they give out with their body language and their posture, it just suggested they didn't want to hear what you had to say. . . . Start answering the question and you'd be in the middle of what you were saying and they'd catch on to one particular word out of what you were saying and start talking about something they want to talk about, which was very insulting' (Priebe *et al.*, 2005).

And importantly drowsiness, weight gain and other side effects of anti-psychotic medication were reported by 15 patients as a factor in disengaging. This would suggest that care plans need to address the importance of treating and minimising side effects from medication to the same degree as medication adherence.

In a study of perceived coercion among mental health service users (Monahan *et al.*, 2005) a third of legally detained patients do not report a sense of coercion. Justice and fairness means that some people understand why the system detained them and they do not feel coerced, but a significant proportion of voluntary patients do consider themselves coerced. They are technically free but do not perceive this to be the case. This suggests that treatment expectations, perceived procedural justice and the nature of the therapeutic relationship influence the sense of coercion. This study is important in that it exposes the myth that the use of legal measures will always damage an established therapeutic relationship.

Taken together these three recent studies are complementary in their implications for practice and understanding the dynamic interplay of personal and interpersonal factors.

Promoting positive risk taking, self-determined WRAP plans and advance agreements

A working relationship may include being prepared to support someone through decisions that might contradict evidence based treatment or received wisdom in relation to mental health. This is sometimes termed positive risk-taking. For example a person well maintained on medications that have some undesirable side effects may wish to reduce the dose, stop the medicine or reduce contact with services due to a new life circumstance. Pregnancy, relationships, work, holidays all present new challenges and potential reasons to change.

The ten essential shared capabilities (National Institute for Mental Health in England, 2004) is a framework and a set of values for all staff in mental health settings to support education and training. Promoting safety and positive risk taking is the 9th capability and described as empowering the person to decide the level of risk they are prepared to take with their health and safety. The capability required is to work with the tension between promoting safety and positive risk taking, including assessing and dealing with possible risks for service users, carers, family members, and the wider public.

Morgan (2004) describes positive risk-taking as:

'Weighing up the potential benefits and harms of exercising one choice of action over another. Identifying the potential risks involved, and developing plans and actions that reflect the positive potentials and stated priorities of the service user. It involves using available resources and support to achieve the desired outcomes, and to minimise the potential harmful outcomes'.

A useful tool that is becoming widespread in use internationally is the wellness recovery action plans (WRAP) developed in the USA by Mary Ellen Copeland (Copeland, 2001, 2006) within the self-help and peer support movement. The underpinning values are of hope, recovery, personal responsibility and self-advocacy. Clinical, medical and diagnostic language is avoided and the focus is on strengths rather than disability or deficit.

A personal WRAP plan would usually be constructed by a person living with persistent mental illness and their support system. It would be a comprehensive document or folder containing a personal toolbox of resources and actions to maintain wellness. Self discovered and refined they may be taking responsibility to get 8 hours sleep, maintain a healthy diet, avoid stimulant drugs, take regular exercise, or socialise every day with peers. The WRAP plan contains pages for recognising and recording early warning signs of relapse, triggers for relapse, and remedial action of what to do at different stages such as early warning signs or crisis points. Peer support would be included and specific advance directives to others in the event of loss of judgement.

Advance statements refer to the writing of expressed instructions concerning actions or inactions around treatment and care, should the person's judgement and mental capacity become impaired in the future. These can also be termed advance agreements, or joint care plans, where they are written in conjunction with treatment service providers. One British randomised controlled trial of 160 patients (Henderson *et al.*, 2004) reports that those patients who had a jointly agreed crisis plan were significantly less likely to be subject to compulsory admission and treatment than the control group (13% versus 27%) and had a mean of 14 days compulsory detention compared to the control group's mean of 31 days. There was no significant difference between the groups on the overall bed days used.

Participants had a psychotic diagnosis or non-psychotic bipolar affective disorder and had an admission to hospital in the last two years. They were randomly allocated to two groups of 80. The joint crisis plan group had plans using their exact words and were collated with the input of carers, friends and advocates where possible. Crucially in this study a third party independent of the patient and the treating team mediated, chaired the planning meeting and produced the written joint crisis plans. Plans detailed negotiated plans of what to do in a crisis, and resources. The control group received written information leaflets on local services and resources, and written copies of their traditional CPA care plans.

Joint crisis plans are informal agreements based on Trust. They offer an excellent example of a collaborative approach to care planning providing demonstrable service and service user benefits. By also involving the carer where possible, their concerns about managing acute episodes at home can be incorporated and acted on by compensatory intensive home based support for user and carer.

Such jointly prepared care plans are a tool to help us to bridge the gap between staff perceptions of engagement or therapeutic alliance and the service users.

Working with carers and families

Not before time families and carers are being enrolled as active partners in care rather than being viewed as dysfunctional contributors to an individual member's pathology and in need of family therapy (Mohr *et al.*, 2000). Social service departments in England are now required to offer carers an assessment of their own needs. This does not extend to the duty to provide for identified need such as respite care. The requirement to assess does however mean that gaps such as access to information and support are visible. The NHS Plan (Department of Health, 2000) introduced carers support workers as champions and an additional support for carers. Many more carers are now involved in planning services and are more vocally supported in challenging service obstructions to helping shape the care plan and content of care.

Typically carers report exclusion on the grounds of inaccurate staff beliefs about patient confidentiality. If carers are expected to be partners in delivering care they need to be partners in care planning processes and products. The British Medical Association (BMA, 1999) guidance on confidentiality is helpful in clarifying the scope of confidentiality where implied or expressed consent has not been given:

> *'It is not a breach of confidentiality to discuss the medical implications of general information that is already known to the recipient. Where relatives, for example, are already aware of an individual's condition or diagnosis, an explanation of the possible options for that patient does not breach confidentiality, but revealing the person's views of those choices would do so'.*

Therefore excuses that confidentiality requires the service provider not to engage with the carer at all over care planning and giving is not valid (Machin, 2004).

An understanding of the stages and emotions that families and carers go through in coming to terms with what happens to their loved one is important in tailoring support. The stages for families and carers living with persistent mental illness are described as dealing with the catastrophic event, learning to cope and moving into advocacy (Mohr *et al.*, 2000). They may move through denial, acceptance, guilt, blame, apathy and empowerment. They do not need therapy but individual support, group and peer support, information, education and training and cooperation from the mental health system.

Cultural determinants

For schizophrenia, cultural and ethnic differences exist in explanations or models of illness. These in turn influence help seeking behaviour, satisfaction with care received and engagement, even amongst second generation migrants (McCabe & Priebe, 2004).

In this study set in the UK, service users were asked about the primary cause of their illness. The responses differed significantly according to ethnicity. White service users utilise a biological model of illness more readily than did those of Bangladeshi, West African or African-Caribbean heritage. African-Caribbeans were more likely to cite social causes than West Africans, and West Africans and Bangladeshis reported supernatural causes more frequently.

The clinical implications of these differences in causal attribution are in the influence of these causal beliefs on preferences for treatment and satisfaction. So Bangladeshis were less likely to want any form of treatment than Whites or African-Caribbeans, and Whites were more likely to want medication. Regardless of ethnicity respondents with a biological causal model were more likely to report that they were receiving the right treatment for them than those with a social model. This reflects the predominantly biological model used in western psychiatry.

Less scientifically a culturally capable team and an ethnically representative workforce would be expected to provide and plan care with greater cultural sensitivity. Where care coordinators are employed in longer term relationships there may be some value in matching the selection of workers to clients ethnically although this is simplistic. Would you ascribe a female care co-ordinator to a female referral? Well no, only if it was relevant to the circumstances of that referral. Indeed for some Asian families it might not be acceptable for a man to treat a young female client. In any culture for a referral of a young manic woman with indications of over-familiarity and impaired inhibitions it would be unwise to have a male worker visit alone. So it is with ethnicity and culture. Some circumstances will indicate that relationship forming and outcome will be enhanced by ethnically or culturally matching the service user and their primary contact with services.

Measuring engagement

A plethora of instruments exist measuring therapeutic alliance, and engagement from the point of view of the service user, the therapist or care provider or an observer. Some have developed from counselling and psychotherapy, other from addictions and general psychiatry. A few instruments have achieved a degree of recognition and have been utilised in numerous studies and settings. The older working alliance inventory (WAI) (Horvath & Greenberg, 1989) derives from psychotherapy and has a therapist version and a client version and it asks a series of questions which are rated, for example, '*my therapist and I are working towards mutually agreed upon goals*'. The client is asked to rate this statement to the degree to which it corresponds with their experience.

The helping alliance questionnaire (HAQ) is a 19 item instrument also with a therapist and patient version (Luborsky *et al.*, 1996). The use of this questionnaire together with measures of symptom severity in opiate dependency yielded a clear finding. Among those with moderate and severe psychiatric problems 50% of patients who reported relatively weak alliances completed treatment versus 85% of those who reported relatively strong alliances (Petry & Bickel, 1999).

The helping alliance scale (HAS) was developed to assess the quality of the therapeutic alliance in working with people with severe and enduring mental illness (Priebe & Grutyers, 1993). It is shorter, comprising only 5 questions, and the original client rated version has been complemented latterly with a clinician rated version. Questions are simple and to the point such as '*how much is your key worker committed to and involved in your treatment?*' and '*is the treatment you are currently receiving right for you?*'.

Of relevance to collaborative care planning are the findings of Bale *et al.* (2006) who looked at the validity and consistency of the WAI and HAS client version in a community care setting for people with severe and enduring mental health problems. The shorter HAS provides as good a measure as the WAI of the client's view of the relationship but clients' and key-workers' views on the WAI are not strongly related. In other words the client's assessment of the relationship is not reliably correlated to the key worker's assessment. Given the ease and simplicity of the HAS it would be worthwhile using this in routine clinical practice to identify the baseline for engagement within the care planning process and any discrepancies with the care coordinator's assessment.

Conclusion

Engagement in a meaningful therapeutic relationship offers a significant advantage in planning and delivering care. Despite attempts to define it we have seen how engagement and care planning are complex, multi-factorial concepts and activities. Factors include the service setting and the attitudes and beliefs of service users and service providers. Using the language of service users themselves, rather than professional jargon, is one theme that has emerged in this review. Development such as WRAPs plans and joint crisis plans offer collaboration and a recovery approach to care planning. The importance of language is emphasised in the following quote:

> *'Engagement is a term used exclusively by professionals and regarded with suspi-cion by some patients. Patients may not share our positive associations with phrases such as "preventing people falling through the net". Is this the sort of net that fish are caught in or the one that saves the trapeze artist? It is important that we are sensitive to alternative perceptions – our "conscientious persistence" may be our patients' "harassment"'.* (Burns & Firn, 2002)

Assessment, therefore, guides the essential forum for engaging with and addressing these differing perceptions as a component of building a skilful, sen-sitive, therapeutic and accountable relationship. For the interchange of engage-ment to be successfully facilitated between service users, carers and colleagues, all parties must be mutually committed to engaging with this relationship.

Assessment and engagement are intertwined as each weaves around each other, growing off each other; the greater the engagement, the more compre-hensive the assessment. Recovery orientated assessment will be a collaborative process which is essentially person-centred and thus lead to an agreed under-standing of the person's priorities.

References

Bale, R., Catty, J., Watt, H., Greenwood, N. & Burns, T. (2006). Measures of the Therapeutic Relationship in Severe Psychotic Illness: A Comparison of Two Scales. *International Journal of Social Psychiatry.* **52**, 256–266.

British Medical Association (1999). *Confidentiality and Disclosure of Health Information.* Available at: http://www.bma.org.uk/ap.nsf/Content/Confidentialitydisclosure

Burns, T. & Firn, M. (2002). *Assertive Outreach in Mental Health: A Manual for Practitioners.* Oxford: Oxford University Press.

Copeland, M.E. (2001). Wellness Recovery Action Plan: A System for Monitoring, Reducing and Eliminating Uncomfortable or Dangerous Psychical Symptoms and Emotional Feelings. *Occupational Therapy in Mental Health.* **17(3 & 4)**, 5–21.

Copeland, M.E. (2006). *Mental Health Recovery and Wellness Recovery Action Plan (WRAP).* West Dummerston, USA. Available at: http://www.mentalhealthrecovery.com/art_aboutwrap.html

Department of Health (1999a). *National Service Framework for Mental Health.* London: The Stationery Office.

Department of Health (1999b). *Effective Care Coordination in Mental Health Services. Modernising the Care Programme Approach. A Policy Booklet.* London: The Stationery Office.

Department of Health (2000). *The NHS Plan – A Plan For Investment, A Plan For Reform.* London: The Stationery Office.

Healthcare Commission (2005). *Survey of users 2005. Mental Health Services. Appendices.* Available at: http://www.healthcarecommission.org.uk/_db/_documents/04020345.pdf

Henderson, C., Flood, C., Leese, M., Thornicroft, G., Sutherby, K. & Szmukler, G. (2004). Effect Of Joint Crisis Plans On Use Of Compulsory Treatment In Psychiatry: Single Blind Randomised Controlled Trial. *British Medical Journal.* **329(7458)**, 136–140.

Horvath, A.O. & Greenberg, L.S. (1989). Development and Validation of the Working Alliance Inventory. *Journal of Counseling Psychology,* **36(2)**, 223–233.

Luborsky, L., Barber, J.P., Siqueland, L., Johnson, S., Najavits, L.M., Frank, A. & Daley, D. (1996). The Revised Helping Alliance Questionnaire (HAQ-II): Psychometric Properties. *Journal of Psychotherapeutic Practice and Research.* **5**, 260–71.

Machin, G. (2004). *Carers & Confidentiality – Law & Good Practice.* A paper presented to the Carers Council Conference on Carers & Confidentiality in Mental Health, held on 23 April 2004. Available at: http://www.mhcarers.co.uk/confidentiality-conference

McCabe, R. & Priebe, S. (2004). The Therapeutic Relationship in the Treatment of Severe Mental Illness: A Review of Methods and Findings. *International Journal of Social Psychiatry.* **50**, 115–128.

McGlashan, T.H. (1987). Recovery Style from Mental Illness and Long-Term Outcome. *Journal of Nervous and Mental Disease.* **175**, 681–85.

Mohr, W.K., Lafuze, J.E. & Mohr, B.D. (2000). Opening Caregiver Minds: National Alliance for the Mentally Ill's (NAMI) Provider Education Program. *Archives of Psychiatric Nursing.* **XIV(5)**, 235–43.

Monahan, J., Redlich, A.D., Swanson, J., Robbins, P.C., Appelbaum, P.S., Petrila, J.J.D., Steadman, H.J., Swartz, M., Angell, B. & McNiel, D.E. (2005). Use of Leverage to Improve Adherence to Psychiatric Treatment in the Community. *Psychiatric Services.* **56**, 37–44.

Morgan, S. (2004). *Health Care Risk Report.* **10(10)**. Available at: http://www. practicebasedevidence.com/risk_health_care_risk.htm

National Institute for Mental Health in England (2004). *The Ten Essential Shared Capabilities: A Framework For The Whole Of The Mental Health Services.* London: National Institute for Mental Health in England and The Sainsbury Centre for Mental Health.

Onyett, S. (1992). *Case Management In Mental Health.* London: Chapman Hall.

Petry, N.M. & Bickel, W.K. (1999). Therapeutic Alliance and Psychiatric Severity as Predictors of Completion of Treatment for Opioid Dependence. *Psychiatric Services.* **50**, 219–227.

Priebe, S. & Gruyters, T. (1993). The Role Of The Helping Alliance In Psychiatric Community Care: A Prospective Study. *Journal of Nervous & Mental Disease.* **181(9)**, 552–557.

Priebe, S., Watts, J., Chase, M. & Matanov, A. (2005). Processes of Disengagement and Engagement in Assertive Outreach Patients: Qualitative Study. *British Journal of Psychiatry.* **187**, 438–443.

Speight, G. & Denoul, I. (2005). *Assertive Community Treatment or Therapeutic Stalking?* Available at: http://www.uclan.ac.uk/facs/health/nursing/research/documents/conference/10speightmay2005.ppt

Tait, L., Birchwood, M. & Trower, P. (2003). Predicting Engagement with Services For Psychosis: Insight, Symptoms and Recovery Style. *British Journal of Psychiatry.* **182**, 123–28.

Chapter 10

Assessment

Angela Hall and Joy Trotter

'Understanding the perspective of another person is essential if we are to be able to put our expertise at the disposal of that individual in a constructive way'. (Repper & Perkins, 2003:21)

Introduction

It is acknowledged that a comprehensive assessment is essential when planning care for people experiencing any form of mental illness. It is also the starting point of any client involvement and sets the foundations for the future development of the therapeutic alliance. The information gathered is used to form the basis of the client's future care, so it is essential that all the necessary information is available on which to make informed decisions for future care. If the assessment is inaccurate or incomplete then it follows that the care given will be inappropriate or lacking.

This chapter aims to examine the nature of recovery and its implications for the mental health practitioner (MHP) when they are assessing an individual's mental health. The term assessing raises issues for those attempting to adopt a more recovery focused approach as historically and organisationally assessing is done by the *experts* to others. However, this chapter will identify how the assessment process can be utilised by practitioners to shape and improve the experience for service users and how certain methods that are more person focused than others, can contribute to the gathering of relevant information. Recovery models are briefly highlighted to alert readers to their existence and possible use in mental health practice. Finally a composite case example and practical strategies are presented in order to assist practitioners with their challenge of promoting recovery.

The nature of assessment

When we attempt to make sense of and understand a person's experience of mental illness we begin on a journey of discovery. Whether assessment is the right term for this journey, in which one person learns about another, how they have experienced life, what their dreams and desires are as well as their ghosts and demons, is debatable. According to the American Psychological Association, the term assessment is defined as *'assess. (nd): to judge or estimate the value, character, etc of. . . .'* (APA, 2007).

It is something which everyone is familiar with, we assess everything constantly – what brand of baked beans to buy, which car will be the best, when is it safe to cross the road? However, when we use the word assess in relation to mental illness it can be perceived as very clinical and professional where one person judges the worth of another or makes judgements regarding that person's ability. This approach reinforces a medical model and is based on professional power/expertise, the expert decides what is wrong with the person and decides how this can be put right.

The common practice of MHPs to focus on a person's symptoms or problems can often leave the person feeling negative and hopeless about themselves and their lives. Repper and Perkins (2003:13,14) warn MHPs of the *'limits of our expertise'* and encourage us to *'listen to people with mental health problems'*. It sounds simple and most professionals would argue that they do listen, so why then do service users and carers continue to report that *'they never listen'*? (Lindow, 1996:14).

Watkins (2001) emphasises the need for practitioners to gain a more balanced view of the person by also valuing the richer narratives that they can offer including their qualities, strengths and achievements. This in turn can lead to a more hope inspiring perspective. *'This is where assessment and recovery become interwoven in the helping process'*.

This discourse is compatible with the concept of recovery and the promotion of collaborative working. If we deconstruct the word assessment and analyse what it means in terms of human interaction, it is a relationship in which one person facilitates the other to tell their story. The information provided forms the basis of a shared understanding and explanation of the person's world. In mental health it is mainly subjective and relies on the person being able to disclose the information. To assess means to make a judgement about, but what judgements are we trying to make, is it in relation to their illness, their ability or inability, problems, strengths or weaknesses? It is all of these and more as we are trying to put together a jigsaw that represents the whole person, but often without all of the pieces.

Assessment is not a one off process although at times it can be presented as such, often referred to in practice as *the* assessment (Figure 10.1). The initial contact with a person is often the beginning of this ongoing process, which leads to the collection of extensive data. It may be helpful to think of assessment as a snowball that grows as it rolls along. As each new piece of information is received (added) then this contributes to the *'decision making process'* (Barker, 1997:6).

The aim of assessing someone's mental health is to enable the person and the people involved in their care gain insight and understanding of the person's

Figure 10.1 The assessment process.

lived experience. This enables the person to be involved and be an active partner in the care planning process. So assessment should not be done to people rather it should be done with people in a collaborative way.

Policy guidance

Assessment within adult mental health services has become an integral part of the care coordination framework (Department of Health, 1999a). It was introduced in April 2001 following a review of the care programme approach (Department of Health, 1990) and the incorporation of care management (Department of Health, 1991) systems that had been established in the early 1990s (Department of Health, 1993). Care coordination, which incorporates the care programme approach (Department of Health, 2006a) is a way of co-ordinating community health services for people with mental health problems. According to the Government's website (http://www.direct.gov.uk), it means that *'once you have an assessment detailing your needs one person will be able to coordinate all aspects of your care, for example your medical and social care and community services available to you'* (Department of Health, 2006b). It goes on to outline that the assessment might include:

- your personal history, including any previous treatments that have worked for you
- your social history, including family details, your income, whether you are employed
- looking at the symptoms of your illness
- how long the doctor thinks you will need treatment, particularly if it is likely to be long-term
- what your needs may be (both health and social).

The care programme approach (CPA) has become an accepted part of practice, despite the continuing lack of strong direct evidence of its value or morality (Sapey, 2004; Kingdon & Amanullah, 2005). Guidance from the Department of Health has refined the original requirements, and now specifies that care plans include provision, as necessary, for risk assessment and management, employment, leisure, accommodation and plans to meet carers' needs (Department of Health, 2006c). Integrated services, a central requirement of current government thinking, can often be hard to achieve in ways that are respectful and meaningful to service users (Parker, 2001) especially when they employ methods which are bureaucratic, procedurally complex or repetitive (Commission for Social Care Inspection, 2006). Government guidelines maintain however, that:

> '*Access to services provided by the NHS or Local Authorities is based on an assessment of need. A joint assessment process prevents duplication for the user and carer but, as appropriate, ensures the services allocated from whichever source match need . . . a single assessment should facilitate access to both health and social services'.* (Department of Health, 1999b, paragraph 38)

Trevithick (2005), drawing on Coulshed and Orme (1998), suggests that assessment should be collaborative (between practitioners, service users and carers) and should incorporate social and environmental factors. Trevithick goes on to add that assessments, whether they are referred to as one-off events or ongoing processes, are likely to be similar in practice as '*most acknowledge the importance of monitoring events, updating information and responding to new developments'* (Trevithick, 2005:127).

Organisational issues

While all MHPs are involved in assessments the terms and approaches used to describe the process can be very different. Currently there is no single approach to assessment that is agreed. Perhaps we should be thankful that this is not the case, as all individuals are different and require different approaches. In fact Wright (1986) warns about the limitations of universal assessment tools in that they can be inappropriate for individual need. Having said that, the development of a common assessment framework exists for all agencies working with children and families, and is now being considered for adult services. It is proposed that the CPA would be incorporated into a common assessment framework (CAF) for adults as a specialist assessment to be used by all MHPs and the principles of person-centred planning would inform personal health and social care plans.

In developing CAF it will be important to build on experience to date from implementing CPA, the single assessment process (SAP) for older people and person-centred planning. In particular, there has been significant investment in SAP in many local organisations since 2002 and this investment must not go to waste. A policy collaborative to support the development of a common assessment framework for adults and guidance on personal health and social care plans was launched on 11 October 2006. It is intended that this will support the development of two important commitments given in the Government White Paper: *Our Health, Our Care, Our Say* (Department of Health, 2006b).

Assessment for nurses and social workers

Historically, assessment within nursing was introduced formally when the nursing process as a framework for organising nursing care emerged from the USA in the 1970s. It was disseminated as a philosophy of individualised care, which would ultimately improve the quality of care delivery for the person. Unfortunately, as already alluded to in Chapter 1, too many nurses viewed it as a *'paper exercise . . .'*. *'Managers approached the implementation of the nursing process in an autocratic way; it was seen as another management task to be completed'* (Nichols, 1993). Ironically, this has led to the gradual improvements in how nurses assess people including:

- increasing involvement with the person and relevant others as part of the information gathering process
- focusing on the person's strengths and achievements
- utilising an evidence based approach (including assessment tools as appropriate)
- developing formulations/nursing diagnosis
- utilising theoretical models to develop/enhance assessment process.

'The voice of the nursing process movement urged all nurses to show concern for the person behind the label, reminding us to look for "worth" amid what might seem like insurmountable problems' (Barker, 1997:5). It presented an alternative approach to the dominant medical model of the time. Nurses began to be person-centred and aimed to assess the whole person as opposed to focusing on symptoms and ailments. The situation in social work practice is not dissimilar to that of nursing. Although assessment is now seen by those in social work as an *'integral part of the social work process'* (Parker & Bradley, 2003:8), especially since Climbie (Department of Health, 2003), social workers have not always considered it to be so pivotal in their work. In the 1970s social work practice was largely informed by medical practice and diagnostic techniques, which identified and responded to dysfunctions and problems, often in terms of treatment (Hollis, 1967). Over the following decade few texts referred to assessment in any detail (Reid & Epstein, 1972; Specht & Vickery, 1977). However, it is likely that, even though not specifically referred to, some sort of assessment was taking place. Indeed, Reid and Epstein (1972), who greatly

influenced social work practice in the last quarter of the 20th century, interestingly reveal the ambiguous and insincere assessment of whose perspective, whose priorities and whose judgement should take precedence.

> *'The practitioner's primary role is to serve as the agent to help clients satisfy their requests within limitations of his resources and skills, the mandate of his agency and the laws of the land. Thus a high value is placed on helping the client obtain what he asks for, even though we may have reservations about the worth of his requests, may regard other goals as more important or may even suspect that at some deeper level he "really" wants something else'.*

Although the fundamental principle of Reid and Epstein's task-centred model was to focus on the the problem which the client is most anxious to resolve as the primary target of intervention, it was often abandoned in practice.

Some of these ideas were challenged by a number of radical texts that highlighted social workers' judgemental, prejudiced and authoritarian decisions and interventions which systematically failed to include the clients' own assessment of their circumstances and wishes (Mayer & Timms, 1970; Bailey & Brake, 1975; Rees, 1978). By the 1980s most social work texts, including those specifically focused on mental health, included at least one section or chapter on assessment (Butler & Pritchard, 1983; Huxley, 1985). These emphasise validity, accuracy and reliability in assessments and despite the work of the radicals, continue in their ambiguity about the value of the clients' (or informants') perspective and judgement.

> *'The accuracy of the assessment depends on many things: having a reliable informant, asking the right sort of questions, probing for evidence of the opinion given by the informant, looking for evidence from other sources or in other ways, by direct observation, or by observation of non-verbal information given during the interview through posture, tone of voice, reactions to the interviewer, etc. – this has been referred to as the "leakage" of information . . .'* (Huxley, 1985:29).

More recently, key texts refer to defining (Pritchard & Hackman, 2006), decision-making (O'Sullivan, 1999), exploring and judging (Bailey, 2002) rather than assessing.

According to Baldwin and Walker (2005:36) the starting point for any assessment is individual *'need . . . in order to maximise well-being in all key areas of . . . life'* and these authors advocate an ecological framework, supported by robust systems, including time for reflection, in order to make judgements about effective services. Milner and O'Byrne (1998) provide a comprehensive discussion of social work assessment, something they suggest is an *'increasingly burdensome and complex task'*.

As outlined by Parker and Bradley (2003) personal values and beliefs affect professionals' approaches to assessment as much as their theoretical or methodological standpoints. Social workers share many of the views of the society they live and work in, and although educated and perhaps more aware of the injustices of prejudice and discrimination, are still likely to overlook and forget subtler inequalities and avoid working with less common (and therefore seemingly more difficult) issues. Perhaps one of the most challenging of these currently relates to work with asylum seekers and others subject to immigration control. Assessments in this area need to balance political and personal tensions and ethical issues, as well as offer good practice (Hayes, 2005).

Methods of assessment

The assessment process is generally ongoing in that the MHP is continuously observing for any changes or additional information to evaluate the person's mental health. This is vital as even the smallest of detail can indicate a change in the person's health requiring possible intervention. Each time the MHP engages with the person, on each contact or at each visit they are alert to that interaction and the meaning and value of it. There are a number of key terms that highlight a range of different methods of assessing.

Global assessments include any method that gathers general information about the person. They are about assessing the whole person or whole phenomenon or overall functioning. It can be achieved using unstructured or semi-structured interviews or global assessment tools such as the Krawiecka, Goldberg and Vaughn (KGV) assessment scale (Krawiecka *et al.*, 1977).

Clarifying or specific assessments focus on particular aspects of the person's life or experience that has been identified during the global assessment. These assessments allow a deeper exploration of a single issue. For example, measuring distress relating to delusional ideas or investigating the consistency of family relationships and support. The methods used can be varied from a more structured or focused interview to the use of specific assessment tools or questionnaires, such as the Liverpool university neuroleptic side effect rating scale (LUNSERS) (Day *et al.*, 1995).

Another dimension to the assessments is the nature of the information that is gathered. It can be:

Qualitative (subjective) or informal information (Figure 10.2)

This kind of information is likely to be gained from less structured interviewing and from a person's self-assessment. It is subjective in that it is the person's perspective of their lives, their story and thus has meaning to them. It is as Barker (2000) acknowledges, *'their words, their story'*. It would be this rich and meaningful information that would be valued with a recovery orientated approach as in Barker's tidal model and it is the basis on which the remainder of the assessment is focused. However it may be valuable for the person's own insight and search for meaning that so called objective information is sought.

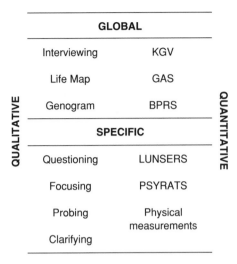

Figure 10.2 Two domains of information. (Barker, 1997)

Quantitative (objective) or formal information (Figure 10.2)

Information is gained from using more research based assessment tools and rating scales. They attempt to provide a quantifiable measure of a particular area such as anxiety or depression levels as well as measuring overall functioning or symptomatology. The use of such tools has inherent difficulties, as they tend to compartmentalise aspects of complex human behaviour that is then quantified leaving the assessor to tick the correct box.

In some cases the actual method of assessment that is used is determined by the person for instance it may be that some people could become anxious and agitated with any of the above methods. In our experience however it is often with the more complex and comprehensive assessment tools like KGV that it is more likely to happen. Therefore it is important to begin with an approach that will encourage the engagement process and encourage the person to express their perspective. The assessment method must be relevant to the person being assessed and it is also important that they understand the rationale and purpose of the method being used.

The collection of information that contributes to the assessment can be achieved by these main methods:

- Direct observation
- Logs, diaries and records
- Questionnaires and rating scales
- Interviewing.

(Barker, 1997)

Direct observation

By observing a person the mental health practitioner can gain valuable information about the person sometimes it may be information that the person is not consciously aware of but is being demonstrated in their non-verbal communication. Observation skills can be used generally or more specifically (Trevithick, 2005). However it is often a neglected method and the relevance of observations are often ignored. By rigorous observations of the person a pattern of behaviour can be identified and shared with the person to enhance understanding of their experiences.

Observations can be made by:

- Any involved practitioner
- By relevant others, family, friends and carers
- By the person themselves.

(Barker, 1997)

The frequency and duration of specific behaviours can be measured and noted i.e. how often and for how long a person spends talking to non-existent voices. Self-monitoring is a useful way of involving the person more actively in the assessment process. Following on from the initial assessment, together with the MHP, they can agree what behaviours, thoughts or feelings are to be monitored. The person may agree to count the number of times they experience a specific thought, feeling or behaviour (frequency). For other aspects of the person's behaviour it may be more appropriate to measure how long an experience lasted i.e. a panic attack (duration). By involving the person in their own assessment it gives them a sense of responsibility and usefulness. It can empower them to be active rather than passive and can help them to gain further insight and understanding of their experiences. This in turn helps them to reframe their sense of self as they begin to recognise strengths they perhaps were unaware of.

Logs, diaries and records

Another method, which can empower the person and engage them in the collaborative process of assessment, is to encourage them to keep a diary. A diary or log can record a person's daily activities and any related thoughts or emotions. The format of the log can be arranged to suit the person's preference for structured or unstructured formats. It should be agreed and the rationale discussed and how to enter information. An example of a simple cognitive diary can be seen in Table 10.1.

Questionnaires and rating scales

The majority of standardised assessment tools have been developed from research. Therefore, they are tried and tested to ensure that they are valid and

Table 10.1 An example of a cognitive diary.

Day	Activity	Thought	Emotion
Monday	Going to the shop for milk	People are looking at me	Become anxious
Tuesday	Talking to a friend	She thinks I'm mad	Afraid and embarrassed

reliable tools. Tools have been developed to measure both global and specific aspects of mental health, and Gamble and Brennan (2000) have developed a useful glossary of some of the key assessment tools for people with serious mental illness. Choosing and using the most appropriate assessments can lead to an enhancement of the collaborative process as both the person and the mental health practitioner search for meaning. *'Using and choosing appropriate assessments is the foundation on which successful, collaborative intervention is built'* (Gamble & Brennan, 2000:83).

Interviewing

An interview is the most common and most effective way to gain information and an overall assessment of the person. Not only can an interview gain information from questioning but also from observing the person's non-verbal responses and their interaction with the interviewer. An interview is a two-way process in which each person has a specific role, the person is there to explore their experiences and the MHP to facilitate the person's story telling. Not only is it about the mental health practitioner asking appropriate questions, it is also about *'credulous listening'* in believing what is being communicated (Feltham & Dryden, 1993:105). This is particularly important when listening to someone whose sense of perception is altered, it can be difficult to accept what the person is saying but it is essential that any judgements are withheld. Most would consider that they are good listeners but this is not the case, many people and practitioners fail to listen, that is, *really* listen to what is being said. When this happens then people can feel undervalued, judged and even worse worthless; as MHPs we can prevent this from happening by giving our full attention and actively listening to the person and their story.

Interviews can be structured or unstructured, an unstructured or reflective approach is more likely to yield richer, more meaningful information as it is gathered in a less systematic way; rather it is done in an empathic and intuitive way (Trevithick, 2005:73). This approach is usually preferable if promoting a recovery focused assessment as it gives the person the responsibility of identifying their hopes, beliefs, feelings and strengths rather than focusing more on problems or deficits. However it may be intimidating or overwhelming to have such little structure and they may feel they need more prompting from the mental health practitioner, this is when a semi-structured interview may be more appropriate.

A semi-structured interview has certain key areas that the practitioner would use as prompts for the person to respond to, thereby reducing any pressure they may feel. A structured interview is more likely to be used, with set questions that require an answer, when more specific information is needed – usually following a less structured approach.

Formulation

Bellack and Hensen (1998:4) state that '*a formulation is designed precisely to fit the individual and is intended to help therapists to derive theoretically-based hypotheses about factors that contribute to causing and maintaining their specific problems*'. A formulation then is preferential to diagnosis as it offers a hypothetical frame-work for interventions that may produce change or benefits for the client. It is within the formulation process that the concepts of recovery and evidence based approaches can be drawn together to ensure that a shared explanation of the person's experiences is agreed and the potential/desirable interventions are identified and selected. Formulation is not just about signs and symptoms but involves arriving at a useful understanding of the person's experiences that is meaningful to them; this is termed the treatment utility (Hayes *et al.*, 1987).

Assessing risk

'*Risk assessment is an essential and ongoing part of the CPA process. Risk assessment, therefore, is about weighing up both the possible beneficial and harmful outcomes of an intervention or procedure and stating the likelihood and extent of either occurring*' (Department of Health, 1999a).

The ability to assess risk remains a central task for MHPs. However, there may be different views between colleagues on how best to approach positive risk taking (Carpenter *et al.*, 2003) and it is quite common for both health and social work professionals to regard risk to different groups of people, quite differently. For example, in relation to older people, it is often regarded as a threat to their welfare and rarely as an acceptable stimulant or diversion. It is more likely in this context, for service users' choices and behaviours to be seen as leading to dangerous incidents or serious harm (Stevenson, 1999). These views of risk and risk taking, as undesirable and negative, are often influenced by stereotypical and prejudicial views of older people, and should be avoided (Titterton, 2005).

Risk assessment is not a one off process, rather it is integral to the ongoing care planning process. It must involve a collaborative exploration of the person's potential to harm and their vulnerability to harm. It is essentially, an interpersonal process and often the level of collaboration can be a predictor of risk behaviour. Generally, an effective therapeutic alliance will lead to reduced risk and a poor working alliance is indicative of a higher risk, but of course risk assessment is not an exact science and variations do occur; there is no guarantee, as the chance of risk (harm) occurring is multi-dimensional and dynamic.

The occurrence of risk behaviour is difficult to prevent but it can be minimised and strategies to improve the quality of a risk assessment are:

- A comprehensive person focused assessment
- Development of an effective therapeutic alliance
- Encourage an open and honest debate of issues
- Valuing of the person's perspective
- Utilise appropriate assessment tools
- Share information to increase collaboration
- Involve the person in taking responsibility for their actions and the possible consequences
- Be aware of the risk situations/behaviours
- Discuss early warning signs and strategies for self-help
- Demonstrate a collaborative approach to care plans/crisis plans.

Sayce (2005:176) shows how current social care provision is *'utterly permeated by risk-thinking'* and how this discriminates against people with mental health problems in particular. Although risk does not always signal danger or urgency, nor necessarily require an emergency response, it may indicate problems – even suicidal thoughts and intentions. For example, risky behaviour is often regarded as normal for young men, in contrast to older people, and health and social work professionals might make incorrect assumptions and misinterpret evidence (Oliver & Storey, 2006).

Models/theories used in assessment

Ixer (2000) points out both students and experienced workers need opportunities to reflect and develop in order that they might re-think bias and subjectivity. Health and social work practitioners should also attend to more theoretically and personally reflective methodologies if their work is to be truly meaningful, relevant and inclusive (Cox & Hardwick, 2002; Fook, 2001). It is suggested (Trotter & Leech, 2003) that what is often missing from health care practice is a theoretical perspective, or what Fook (2002) refers to as critical reflection. Fook argues that this is essential for contextually relevant practice because *'it constitutes an alternative approach to our understanding of knowledge and knowledge creation'* (Fook, 2002:157). Fook advocates that students and practitioners should develop theory from their own experience and, like she has done, learn to bend formal theories to fit their own context, for their own use. Others have worked in this way to develop theoretical and practice models as mechanisms or aide-memoirs to assist them more readily in practice. According to Cutting (1997:21) models can help practitioners by suggesting:

- Reasons for observed behaviours
- Therapeutic treatment strategies
- Role enactment for service user and practitioner.

There are a prolific number of models and theories that can be employed to shape the assessment process and the subsequent care delivery for people experiencing mental health problems. Traditionally practitioners have been directed to the use of evidence-based models; models that have been subject to systematic review and have been shown to be effective. There has more recently been a move to more recovery orientated models such as the wellness recovery action plan (WRAP), tidal model, strengths model and solution focused model. These models have already been described in Chapter 8, so only minimal reference is made here.

Wellness recovery action plan

This model was developed by people dealing with mental health problems. It is essentially a guide to self management and recovery, it was designed to:

- Decrease and prevent intrusive or troubling feelings and behaviours
- Increase personal empowerment
- Improve quality of life
- Assist people in achieving their own life goals and dreams.

(Copeland, 2001)

Copeland has shared the model with many people and she believes it can be adapted to many other illnesses. The person is given responsibility for developing their own WRAP but they may choose relatives, friends or mental health practitioners to help them.

Tidal model

This is one of the most well known models for promoting recovery with projects established in many countries and was developed in the late 1990s in the UK by Barker (2000). It focuses on enabling people to tell their stories, so that they can begin to make sense and derive some meaning from them. The tidal model helps people to reclaim their lives as detailed by professionals which Barker believes is the first step to recovery (Barker & Buchanan-Barker, 1999; Barker, 2000).

Strengths model

At the core of this model is *'a deep belief in the necessity of democracy and the contingent capacity for people to participate in the decisions and actions that define their world'* (Saleebey, 1992:8). It has the opposite approach to most evidence-based models, which tend to identify problems or deficits; instead it values people's strengths and abilities, hopes and aspirations.

It has several underpinning assumptions:

- Respecting the person's strengths: all people have strengths that they can mobilise to make their lives better
- Motivation to change is enhanced by building on and acknowledging strengths
- Cooperation is essential and is a process of exploring strengths
- Focusing on strengths focuses the work on survival and how this can be achieved
- The client in their environment is the key to change as the environment contains the resources.

The strengths model also underpins the solution focused model approach, which is also core to the tidal model. All have at the core an unconditional valuing of the person experiencing mental health problems and all believe that it is the person themselves who possesses the resources and abilities to shape their own lives and recover what they can from their experiences. While the more recovery focused models have as the core an emphasis on the value of the person's experiences, more focus is needed when working within an evidence-based model that puts theory at the fore. The work with Peter below has been based on the framework provided by Kingdon and Turkington (1994) who identify a systematic approach to cognitive therapy.

Case study 10.1   Promoting recovery within an evidence-based model.

Peter is a 46-year-old man who lives alone in a rented house, in a deprived area of a northeast town. He was one of six children. Peter describes his childhood as normal and his school days as uneventful; he was a good mixer of average intelligence. He left school and found work driving, before working in a factory for 10 yrs. He can't remember having any girlfriends.

His first hospital admission was when he was 24 years old, he was said to have hypo-chondriachal delusions, he believed that a gadget inside his head was making him ill and was given a provisional diagnosis of schizophrenia-delusional ideas.

He had further hospital admissions over the years, not usually being in for any more than 2 months and the problems appear to reoccur. In that each admission is due to the threat of, or actual, overdose, he feels at a point that he can not cope any longer with the gadget. The development of the delusion appeared over the years and was presented when he was readmitted to hospital following an overdose. He felt that there was some outside force trying to control him via the gadget and that somebody is spying on him all the time.

Peter now lives alone in a run down area where several houses are boarded up and local youths often vandalise the area. Peter has experienced some harassment from them. The house is reasonable in that it is furnished and he has basic essentials, however it is not clean and Peter himself at times is dressed in dirty clothes. Peter finds it hard to go out of the house alone. He still has occasional admissions to hospital when he becomes suicidal.

Peter is prescribed antipsychotic medication. Peter is grateful for his medication and he believes it is helping him sleep and reducing his depression. He reports no side effects and is overly compliant with his treatment plan in that he does not query or question the need or purpose of his medication.

Engagement

Chadwick *et al.* (1996) acknowledge that engaging with people with serious mental illness can be one of the biggest challenges facing the mental health practitioner. They also identify two prerequisites for practitioners in order to utilise a cognitive approach, basic counselling skills and acknowledgement of the cognitive-behavioural approach (Chadwick *et al.*, 1996). The basic counselling skills would be used to develop a trusting therapeutic relationship. The MHP would display the core conditions as identified by Rogers (1951). The rationale behind the cognitive and stress vulnerability model (Neuchterlein & Dawson, 1984) would need to be explained and that the aim of the work would be to reduce his distress. It is important to set the scene at the first contact to encourage a joint understanding of how the work can be useful. There can be an assumption by practitioners that the client knows why we are there, they know our approach and that they know what they want.

Engaging with Peter would be essential to encourage Peter to express his distress and anger directed towards the people he believes are controlling a gadget inside him. While his belief may not be consistent with the practitioner's belief system it is possible to bridge this discontinuity gap (Jaspers, 1962) by acknowledging that part of Peter's experience is beyond them, but that his response to it is not. Rogers (1978) himself acknowledged the limits to achieving empathy *'I am often impressed by the fact that even a minimal amount of empathic understanding ... a bumbling and faulty attempt to catch the confused complexities of the client's meaning ... is helpful ...'*. The core conditions as described by Rogers (1951) are seen as fundamental to any therapeutic relationship and are in fact considered as indicative of a positive outcome in therapy rather than the particular model used (Truax & Carkhuff, 1967; Luborsky *et al.*, 1985).

Assessment

The assessment of an individual with a serious mental illness presents a huge challenge (Gournay, 1996) but has become a major aspect of effective clinical practice (Department of Health, 1999a). Gathering relevant information by selecting the correct process and tools (Gamble & Brennan, 2000) is crucial to understanding the nature of Peter's experiences and his life.

Global assessment

Being comfortable and familiar with interviewing people is essential to gain Peter's story. Gamble and Brennan (2000) reinforce the use of semi-structured interviews as the first step in the assessment process for people experiencing a serious mental illness. However it may also be necessary to gain a baseline global assessment of Peter, so the global assessment scale (GAS) and health of the nation outcome score (HoNOS) (Wing *et al.*, 1995) could both be considered for this purpose. To gain an overall assessment of his psychiatric symptoms the brief psychiatric rating scale (BPRS) (Overall & Gorham, 1962) and the KGV assessment scale (Krawiecka *et al.*, 1977) could be utilised, however the rationale for each should be carefully considered prior to use, particularly as Peter seems overly compliant. It is important to select relevant tools rather than indiscriminately apply all tools available (Gamble & Brennan, 2000) and this might be done in consultation with Peter.

The BPRS is a well validated tool for general psychiatric symptoms while the KGV is a standardised tool for rating chronic psychotic patients (Gamble & Brennan, 2000). The KGV scale is useful to get an accurate overview of symptomatology and establishes a baseline, prior to then exploring aspects in more detail. Because of the extensive questioning required for some of the tools practitioners should be aware of taking the person's pace and check with the person if they are alright to continue with the questions.

Risk assessment

The suicidal thoughts would require further exploration to establish whether Peter had any actual intent and that he had not made any plans of how he might act upon his ideas. The risk factors associated with Peter indicate a risk because of his age, gender, his previous attempts and his social isolation together with the distress caused by his delusional beliefs (Ryan, 1999). Therefore it is necessary to continually review his mental state, life events and levels of distress in order to monitor the risk in addition to checking out his intent. The suicide risk interview (Barker, 2000) provided the structure for assessing the suicide risk. Other practitioners involved in his care should be consulted and collaboratively it should be agreed the level of risk Peter presents. A crisis plan would be required in case of increased risk, detailing necessary actions.

Specific assessment

The hallucinations and delusional symptoms could be followed up with further assessment using the psychotic symptom rating scales (PSYRATS) (Haddock *et al.*, 1999), which is considered as a useful tool that is complimentary to the KGV. These tools can also be used to review the outcomes of interventions.

Formulations

The initial formulation for Peter could be based on the stress vulnerability model (Neuchterlein & Dawson, 1984) using information gained regarding his past, his experiences and his current symptoms and problems. It may provide an explanation of the maintenance of his illness and indicate some genetic vulnerability relating to his first episode, with evidence of stressful life events linked to his first episode. This formulation would be related back to Peter to check out if he related his life to this explanation. The formulation is vital in creating a shared meaning of the client's experiences and symptoms and has been shown to provide a key role in planning interventions.

From the information obtained links can also be made at various levels between Peter's thinking, feelings, his behaviour and the maintenance of his current symptoms.

Current thinking affect and behaviour

Cognitions expressed by Peter:

'This thing (gadget) is bloody killing me'
'What have I done to deserve this'
'The gadget causes all my problems'

Affect

Peter describes being worried all of the time and his *'nerves are bad'*. If he goes out of the house he has panic attacks. He also complains of a moderate degree of depression with some suicidal ideation but without intent.

Behaviour

Peter refuses to go out due to the *'stalking by his persecutors'* although on occasion he has gone to the telephone or the shop when necessary. He will not attend appointments unless accompanied and therefore has not attended several. He is visited by mental health services and friends who do his shopping, cleaning and put his bets on for him.

Themes

- Anger at people persecuting him (youths and gadget)
- Afraid of what might happen
- Depressed at being unjustly blamed for something and that he is unable to do anything about it.

Problems identified with Peter:

- Inability to sleep, eat or concentrate
- His nerves: the depression, anxiety and distress associated with his beliefs
- Physical effects: headaches, pains in stomach and back

- Gadget being responsible for the above, controlled by the Department of Social Security.

The central principle of introducing cognitive approaches is that there is a strong connection between thoughts and feelings, and the way we interpret (think about) situations is influenced by our beliefs about the world and ourselves. Nelson (1997) also suggests that in schizophrenia physiological responses of anxiety may be given a delusional explanation, which then exacerbates the anxiety, thereby creating a maintenance cycle.

Peter's assessment will be gained over a lengthy period of time ensuring that observations and information gained from him is as comprehensive as possible and that he has collaborated in the discovery of the information. It may be possible to introduce self-assessment as a way of further involving Peter but his motivation would need to be estimated to increase his self-esteem. In promoting recovery Repper and Perkins (2003) identify three areas to be tackled: loss of power, loss of meaning and loss of hope. As MHPs we need to be mindful of how our interactions and interventions can serve to counteract these effects of being diagnosed with a mental illness. We can see from the example here that Peter was given some hope that had previously been about maintenance. The evidence-based approach offered a new way of understanding his experience that gave room for new interventions. The formulations described identified key areas where the MHP may intervene.

Stress management strategies could be employed such as breathing techniques and relaxation tapes especially at night as this could help him to sleep. His medication would also be a key factor in ensuring 5–6 hours sleep. Relapse prevention could be introduced to identify with Peter what indicators he can recognise from the times when he felt suicidal and was admitted to hospital, a rating scale could be used to identify at what level he is likely to act on his suicidal feelings. Coping strategy enhancement would be used to build on the strategies Peter had employed over the years to reduce his distress. Coping strategies used which, consisted of positive and negative strategies, can be seen in Table 10.2.

Being involved in decisions about the assessment process would enable Peter to feel he was valued and that he had some control or power in relation to his care also it would increase his understanding of his experience. The relationship is central to the process of recovery and while mental health practitioners cannot recover people they can contribute in many ways.

Table 10.2 Peter's coping strategies.

Positive	Negative
Medication Watching TV Contact with workers	Avoids going out Physically inactive

Practical strategies for promoting recovery focused assessment

Preparation for the assessment interview

Preparation and planning are important prior to the interview, whether the person is in a community or a hospital setting as this is often the initial contact with the person and influence the future development of a working relationship. There may be more arranged distractions (Kadushin, 1990) in the home environment that can interfere with the engagement process (a television turned on playing loudly, children playing in the room). The MHP needs to balance the importance of such distractions against empowering the person to be in control of the situation. It would be fine to ask the person if they would mind turning down the TV or asking the children to play in another room, as this would involve a person in the decision making process, however the practitioner would then need to respect whatever decision was made. Other potentially empowering considerations can be:

- Where and when the assessment interview will take place
- Who may be present other than the practitioner (student nurse, social worker or other colleagues)
- People who the person would like present (friend, carer or advocate)
- How long the interview may last
- What issues are likely to be covered
- What, if any, notes will be made or shared and whether they will be recorded during the interview or not.

These can all be discussed at the initial contact so that the person is shown respect and given responsibility in the care planning process. It may be that the person is too unwell in which case the practitioner can consult with the person's carer or advocate who may know of the person's preferences.

The interview

The environment needs to be arranged to promote a physically and psychologically safe feeling for the person, wherever the interview is being held. If in an unfamiliar setting the person should be reassured regarding privacy and that there will be no interruptions.

Greeting the person and whoever is accompanying them is a way of establishing rapport and demonstrating respect for each individual and also introducing yourself and saying a little about where you work and your role. Also give the person the opportunity to ask any questions from the start, check out their understanding of what will be happening so that they feel as much in control as possible. Another way to initiate the conversation and help the person feel at ease is with small talk: a social chat about their house, how they travelled here or the weather. Any non-controversial topic is suitable and while this social chat should not continue throughout the interview. It can serve as an icebreaker and allows the person to adapt to the situation, but can be counterproductive if dragged out too long.

The person should then be asked what their priorities or expectations are regarding the meeting and the mental health practitioner should acknowledge whether or not they can be addressed or if there are any other alternatives that may be useful but allowing the person the final decision. Anyone accompanying the person (friend, relative or advocate) should be acknowledged and their needs identified; also their role within the interview should be agreed.

Relationship development

It is essential to demonstrate the following skills in relationship development, during the interview:

- Demonstrating a concern for the issues of the service user and their self determination
- Showing an interest, conveying warmth, generating an atmosphere of trust
- Demonstrating a respect for the service user's individuality
- Conveying an acceptance of the individual
- Demonstrating an empathic understanding
- Conveying a sense of genuineness and authenticity
- Drawing boundaries on information which may need to be disclosed as necessary and agreeing what may be shared and with whom.

(Kadushin, 1990:39–57)

Explain the role of the interview and its likely format, encourage the use of an unstructured approach initially although this may need to be changed if the person is struggling to tell their story. Intuition will play a large part in that the practitioner should observe for non-verbal cues and respond or adapt their approach accordingly. An opening, inviting question may be sufficient to begin the process followed by occasional encouragement or more specific questions may be appropriate at times. The assessment should cover the areas detailed in Box 10.1 but this is not an exhaustive list as the assessment will also be influenced according to which specific model is being used.

Once you have completed the assessment, ensure that you review any notes you have taken with the service user and be prepared to make changes or additions at the user's or advocate's request. Watch your language! Avoid jargon as much as possible and use language that makes the service user an active partner in the planning process rather than the passive recipient of professional decisions. Arrange for the fully written up assessment to be counter-signed by the service user and if appropriate, the carer.

Box 10.1   Areas for consideration during an assessment.

Previous history/life map
Previous family relationships
Previous illness – physical/mental
Education and work history/aspirations
Current relationship, family and support networks
Child care/child protection issues
Housing/finance and benefits
Neighbourhood and community networks – if any
Religion/spiritual/cultural issues of importance
Physical health needs
Hygiene, diet and lifestyle
Services used currently or in the past as well as the service
   user's and carer's views about these services
Any experiences that may be considered risky
Psychological experiences/presenting issues
What are their personal goals and aspirations
What ways of coping are being used already

Disengaging/terminating the interview

Preparation for ending should begin at the start of the interview so that the person is prepared for and expecting the ending. Kadushin (1990:206) suggests that *'preparation for termination of the interview begins at the very beginning of the interview'*. An appropriate ending would be to ask what the person feels has been achieved and what they are able to take away with them that is useful. If there are any unresolved issues then these should be acknowledged and where appropriate, highlighted as priorities for the next meeting.

Conclusion

In this chapter we have tried to explore the complex and huge area of assessment. The nature of assessment has been discussed in terms of what it is and how it may be experienced by service users as quite clinical and how it is more appropriate to consider it as an opportunity for the person to tell their story.

However at policy and organisational levels we can witness a current discourse of evidence-based assessment. It has been argued that the recent developments of objective, accurate and scientific procedures in nursing and social work are part of the historical context of modernist empiricism (Iverson *et al.*, 2005). Mental health practitioners are caught in a dichotomy between the policy, organisational demands, users of services and their carer's needs and aspirations. If MHPs are to promote recovery then the challenge is to let the person define what their recovery is and to collaboratively plan on how that can be achieved. While constrained to some degree with policy guidance practitioners can minimise the extent of how much of this restricts the person in achieving their recovery. The assessment methods and process can all influence the person's experience so practitioners need to choose wisely how assessment is carried out and documented. Subtle changes in practice can lead to a more collaborative approach to assessment and care planning.

All these recovery focused models offer systems for promoting recovery. However, as already alluded to, recovery should not be another model that becomes professionalised (see Chapter 8 in this text) but one that ensures that people are respected and is implemented according to individual need. Evidence-based models continue to contribute to improvements in mental health practice but perhaps they should be under-pinned with the recovery principles – however, we acknowledge that we have a long distance to travel!

References

American Psychological Association (APA) (2007). *Dictionary.com Unabridged (v 1.1)*. Available at: http://dictionary.reference.com/browse/assess (Accessed 02 April 2007)

Bailey, D. (2002). Mental Health. In: Adams, R., Dominelli, L. & Payne, M. (eds). *Critical Practice in Social Work Practice*. Basingstoke: Palgrave Macmillan. **(17)**, 126–143.

Bailey, R. & Brake, M. (eds) (1975). *Radical Social Work*. London: Edward Arnold.

Baldwin, N. & Walker, L. (2005). Assessment. In: Adams, R., Dominelli, L. & Payne, M. (eds). *Social Work Futures: Crossing Boundaries, Transforming Practice*. Basingstoke: Palgrave Macmillan. **(3)**, 36–53.

Barker, P.J. (1997). *Assessment in Psychiatric and Mental Health Nursing: In Search of the Whole Person*. Cheltenham: Stanley Thornes.

Barker, P.J. (2000). *The Tidal Model: From Theory to Practice*. Newcastle: University of Newcastle.

Barker, P.J. & Buchanan-Barker, P. (1999). *The Tidal Model: Recovery and Reclamation*. Available at: http://www.tidal-model.co.uk/recovery.htm (accessed 30 March 2007).

Bellack, A.S. & Hensen, M. (1998). *Comprehensive Psychology*. New York: Pergamon Press.

Butler, A. & Pritchard, C. (1983). *Social Work and Mental Illness*. Aldershot: Macmillan.

Carpenter, J., Schneider, J., Brandon, T. & Wooff, D. (2003). Working In Multidisciplinary Community Mental Health Teams: The Impact On Social Workers and Health Professionals Of Integrated Mental Health Care. *British Journal of Social Work*. **33(8)**, 1081–1103.

Chadwick, P., Birchwood, M. & Trower, P. (1996). *Cognitive Therapy for Delusions, Voices and Paranoi*. Chichester: Wiley and Sons.

Commission for Social Care Inspection (2006). *Key Lines of Regulatory Assessment (KLORA): Adult Placement Schemes*. Available at: http://www.csci.org.uk/Docs/klora_aps_080606.doc (Accessed 26 April 2006).

Copeland, M.E. (2001). Wellness Recovery Action Plan: A System For Monitoring, Reducing and Eliminating Uncomfortable Or Dangerous Psychical Symptoms and Emotional Feelings. *Occupational Therapy in Mental Health*. **17(3 & 4)**, 5–21.

Coulshed, V. & Orme, J. (1998). *Social Work Practice: An Introduction*. Basingstoke: Macmillan/BASW.

Cox, P. & Hardwick, L. (2002). Research and Critical Theory: Their Contribution to Social Work Education and Practice. *Social Work Education*. **21(1)**, 35–47.

Cutting, P. (1997). Concepts, Models and Theories In Psychiatric and Mental Health Nursing. In: Thomas, B., Hardy, S. & Cutting, P. (eds). *Stuart and Sundeen's, Mental Health Nursing, Principles and Practice UK Versio*. London: Mosby. **(2)**, 19–32.

Day, J.C., Wood, G., Dewey, M. & Bentall, R.P. (1995). A Self Rating Scale for Measuring Neuroleptic Side Effects: Validation In A Group Of Schizophrenic Patients. *British Journal Of Psychiatry*. **166(5)**, 650–653.

Department of Health (1990). *The Care Programme Approach for People with a Mental Illness Referred to the Special Psychiatric Services*. Joint Health/Social Services Circular, HC (90) 23/LASS (90) 11, London: HMSO.

Department of Health (1991). *Social Services Inspectorate: Care Management and Assessment Guidance*. London: HMSO.

Department of Health (1993). *Services For Mentally Disordered People*, LAC93/10. London: HMSO.

Department of Health (1999a). *Effective Care Coordination in Mental Health Services: Modernising the Care Programme Approach, A Policy Booklet*. London: The Stationery Office.

Department of Health (1999b). *National Service Framework for Mental Health*. London: The Stationery Office.

Department of Health (2003). *The Victoria Climbie Inquiry, Report Of An Inquiry. (The Laming Report)*. London: The Stationery Office.

Department of Health (2006a). *Community Care Assessments and Plans*. London: The Stationery Office.

Department of Health (2006b). *Our Health Our Care Our say: A New Direction for Community Services*. Available at: http://www.doh.gov.uk/ourhealthourcareoursay (Accessed 26 June 2006).

Department of Health (2006c). *Common Assessment Framework*. Available at: http://www.socialcare.csip.org.uk/index.cfm?pid=7 (Accessed 26 June 2006).

Feltham, C. & Dryden, W. (1993). *Dictionary of Counselling*. London: Whurr Publishers.

Fook, J. (2001). Identifying Expert Social Work: Qualitative Practitioner Research. In: Shaw, I. & Gould, N. (eds). *Qualitative Research in Social Work*, Sage. London. **(8)**.

Fook, J. (2002). *Social Work: Critical Theory and Practice*. London: Sage.

Gamble, C. & Brennan, G. (eds) (2000). *Working With Serious Mental Illness A Manual For Clinical Practice*. London: Balliere Tindall & RCN.

Gournay, K. (1996). Schizophrenia: A Review Of The Contemporary Literature and Implication For Mental Health Nursing: Theory, Practice and Education. *Journal of Psychiatric and Mental Health Nursing*. **3(1)**, 7–12.

Haddock, G., McCarron, J., Tarrier, N. & Faragher, E.B. (1999). Scales To Measure Dimensions Of Hallucinations and Delusions: The Psychotic Symptom Rating Scales (PSYRATS). *Psychological Medicine*. **29**, 879–889.

Hayes, D. (2005). Social Work with Asylum Seekers and Others Subject To Immigration Control. In: Adams, R., Dominelli, L. & Payne, M. (eds). *Social Work Futures: Crossing Boundaries, Transforming Practice*. Basingstoke: Palgrave Macmillan. **(13)**, 182–194.

Hayes, S.C., Nelson, R.O. & Jarrett, R.B. (1987). The Treatment Utility Of Assessment: A Functional Approach To Evaluating Assessment Quality. *American Psychologist*. **42**, 963–974.

Hollis, F. (1967). Exploration in the Development of a Typology of Casework Treatment. *Social Casework*. **48**, 335–41.

Huxley, P. (1985). *Social Work Practice in Mental Health*. Aldershot: Gower.

Iverson, R.R., Gergen, K.J. & Fairbanks, R.P. (2005). Assessment and Social Construction: Conflict Or Co-Creation? *British Journal of Social Work.* **35(5)**, 689–708.

Ixer, G. (2000). Assessing Reflective Practice: New Research Findings. *Journal of Practice Teaching.* **2(3)**, 19–27.

Jaspers, K. (1962). *General Psychopathology.* Manchester: Manchester University Press.

Kadushin, A. (1990). *The Social Work Interview.* New York: Columbia University Press. (3rd edn).

Kingdon, D.G. & Amanullah, S. (2005). Care Programme Approach: Relapsing or Recovering? Making Care Programming Work. *Advances in Psychiatric Treatment.* **11**, 325–329.

Kingdon, D.G. & Turkington, D. (1994). *Cognitive Behavioural Therapy of Schizophrenia.* Hove: Guildford Press.

Krawiecka, M., Goldberg, D. & Vaughn, M. (1977). A Standardised Psychiatric Assessment Scale for Rating Chronic Psychotic Patients. *Acta Psychiatrica Scandinavica.* **55**, 299–308.

Lindow, V. (1996). What We Want From Community Psychiatric Nurses. In: Reid, J. & Reynolds, J. *Speaking Our Minds.* Milton Keynes: Open University Press. 186–190.

Luborsky, L., McLellan, A.T., Woody, G.E., O'Brien, C.P. & Auerbach, A. (1985). Therapist Success & Its Determinants, *Archives of General Psychiatr.* **42(6)**, 602–611.

Mayer, J.E. & Timms, N. (1970). *The Client Speaks: Working Class Impressions of Casework.* London and Henley: Routledge and Kegan Paul.

Milner, J. & O'Byrne, P. (1998). *Assessment in Social Work.* Basingstoke: Macmillan Press.

Nelson, H. (1997). *Cognitive Behavioural Therapy with Schizophrenia: A Practice Manua.* Cheltenham: Stanley Thorne.

Neuchterlein, K.H. & Dawson, M.E. (1984). A Heuristic Vulnerability/Stress Model of Schizophrenic Episodes. *Schizophrenia Bulletin.* **10(2)**, 300–312.

Nichols, R. (1993). Nursing Interventions. In: Wright, H. & Giddey, M. (eds). *Mental Health Nursing: From First Principles to Professional Practices.* Cheltenham: Stanley Thornes. **(19)**, 205–230.

Oliver, C. & Storey, P. (2006). *Evaluation Of Mental Health Promotion Pilots To Reduce Suicide Amongst Young Men: Final Report.* London: Thomas Coram Research Institute.

O'Sullivan, T. (1999). *Decision Making in Social Work.* Basingstoke: Macmillan.

Overall, J.E. & Gorham, D.R. (1962). The Brief Psychiatric Rating Scale. *Psychological Reports.* **10**, 799–812.

Parker, J. (2001). Integrating Person-Centred Dementia Care In Social Work and Social Case Practice. *Journal of Social Work.* **1(3)**, 329–345.

Parker, J. & Bradley, G. (2003). *Social Work Practice: Assessment, Planning, Intervention and Review.* Exeter: Learning Matters Limited.

Pritchard, C. & Hackmann, A. (2006). *Mental Health Social Work.* London: Taylor and Francis.

Rees, S. (1978). *Social Work Face to Face.* London: Edward Arnold.

Reid, W.J. & Epstein, L. (1972). *Task-Centred Casework.* New York: Columbia University Press.

Repper, J. & Perkins, R. (2003). *Social Inclusion and Recovery: A Model for Mental Health Practice.* Edinburgh: Baillière Tindall.

Rogers, C.R. (1951). *Client Centred Therapy.* London: Constable.

Rogers, C.R. (1978). *Carl Rogers on Personal Power.* London: Constable.

Ryan, T. (1999). *Managing Crisis and Risk in Mental Health Nursing.* Cheltenham: Stanley Thornes.

Saleebey, D. (1992). *The Strengths Perspective in Social Work Practice*. New York: Longman.

Sapey, B. (2004). Practice for What? The Use of Evidence in Social Work with Disabled People. In: Smith, D. (ed.). *Social Work and Evidence-Based Practice*. London: Jessica Kingsley Publishers. **(8)**, 143–160.

Sayce, L. (2005). Risks, Rights and Anti-Discrimination Work In Mental Health: Avoiding The Risks In Considering Risk. In: Adams, R., Dominelli, L. & Payne, M. (eds). *Social Work Futures: Crossing Boundaries, Transforming Practice*. Basingstoke: Palgrave Macmillan. **(12)**, 167–181.

Specht, H. & Vickery, A. (eds) (1977). *Integrating Social Work Methods*. London: George Allen & Unwin Ltd.

Stevenson, O. (1999). Old People At Risk. In: Parsloe, P. (ed). *Risk Assessment in Social Care and Social Work*. London: Jessica Kingsley Publishers. **(8)**, 201–216.

Titterton, M. (2005). *Risk and Risk Taking in Health and Social Welfare*. London: Jessica Kingsley Publishers.

Trevithick, P. (2005). *Social Work Skills: A Practice Handbook*. Maidenhead: Open University Press.

Trotter, J. & Leech, N. (2003). Linking Research, Theory and Practice. In: Personal and Professional Development: Gender and Sexuality Issues In Social Work Education. *Social Work Education*. **22(2)**, 204–214.

Truax, C.B. & Carkhuff, R.R. (1967). *Towards Effective Counseling and Psychotherapy*. Chicago: Aldine.

Watkins, P. (2001). *Mental Health Nursing: The Art of Compassionate Care*. London: Butterworth-Heinemann.

Wing, J., Curtis, R. & Beevor, A. (1995). *Measurement for Mental Health: Health of the Nation Outcome Scale*. London: Royal College of Psychiatrists Research Unit.

Wright, S.G. (1986). Patient-Centred Practice. *Nursing Times*. **83(38)**, 24–7.

Chapter 11

Promoting Inclusivity in Care Planning

Jenny Weinstein

'Somewhere to live, something to do, someone to love' (Anon).

Introduction

'Somewhere to live, something to do, someone to love – I want a whole life, not half a life'. This quotation from a service user who prefers to remain anonymous underpins the philosophy of this chapter. Inclusive care planning means, in the phrase coined by Kitwood (1997) that 'the person comes first'. When we meet someone who has mental health issues, we must engage with that person as a human being with their own identity, culture and aspirations before we focus on their illness.

If you watch any of the medical dramas on TV (such as Holby City, Casualty or ER) you will notice that when we are introduced to patients we are immediately invited to relate to them not as the *heart condition* or the *cancer patient* but as people – the single parent, the father estranged from his children or the beloved grandma etc. The drama usually relates to how their illness impinges on their life and their family; but it is the story of their life and their family that engages us and makes us care about whether the medical staff can help them to get better.

With mental illness, the media tends to focus first on the bizarre behaviour or way in which a person is different or not functioning normally and only later, if at all, do we meet the human being who is suffering from the illness. Unfortunately, many professionals approach people with mental health issues in a similar way. For example a research study undertaken by Stanley *et al.* (2003) found that mothers with mental health issues felt they received little support in their role as parents – rather they were branded as mentally ill and given labels which were often used to justify their inability to care for their children. The problems are eloquently outlined by Laurance (2003:72):

'People with mental health problems are discriminated against at work, and locked up even when they have committed no crime. Comedians joke about them, headline writers demonise them . . . A psychiatric diagnosis acts as a bar to relationships,

employment and key services such as insurance and mortgages. Unlike a physical diagnosis it is often for life. Since the diagnosis is made primarily on the basis of a judgment about a person's conduct there is a risk of it invalidating their whole identity and sense of self.

The chapter will begin by contextualising an inclusive care planning model by discussing the social aspects that are critical factors in the recovery and inclusion of people with mental health issues. The first section will focus on addressing problems such as poverty, discrimination, racism, unemployment and homelessness; the next section will address current government policy as it relates to these issues and in particular to care planning; the third section will focus on the importance of service user and carer involvement; and the chapter will conclude by offering specific guidance on good practice in inclusive care planning using a range of case examples from different settings. There is not space here to offer examples from in-patient units, care of older people or forensic psychiatry but it is suggested that the same good practice principles should apply in these settings.

Person centred planning: promoting recovery

The model of care planning (Figure 11.1) promoted in this chapter is one that has the person, not the mental illness, at its centre. The next consideration is the person's immediate family or significant other(s) who may be their carer, their children, their partner or the absence of significant others. The model then moves outwards to consider the person's cultural identity, spirituality and aspirations before taking account of the social and practical aspects of finance, housing and employment.

Having clarified the person's perspectives on these and any other key issues, the final stage is to look at how the person's mental health and physical health may be impacting on their situation and agreeing a plan of access to both mental health services and/or relevant community resources that the person feels would help them to recover. The term recovery does not necessarily mean cure the illness (Anthony, 1993), it is defined as a '*continuous process of growth and adaptation to disability as opposed to time-limited interventions directed at symptom removal*' (Perkins & Repper, 1998:18). The individual is empowered to take responsibility for their own recovery (Deegan, 1997) through a process that has to be unique to the particular individual and their circumstances and aspirations (Young & Ensing, 1999). This process will be more possible when a person comes to terms with their illness to some degree and develops hope for the future (Russinova, 1999; Carpenter, 2002; Warren, 2003). The fundamental principle underpinning this model is that the care planning process is both user led and seamlessly multidisciplinary (Leiba & Weinstein, 2003). If this is achieved, it could contribute to meeting the challenges set out by Bracken and Thomas (2001:725):

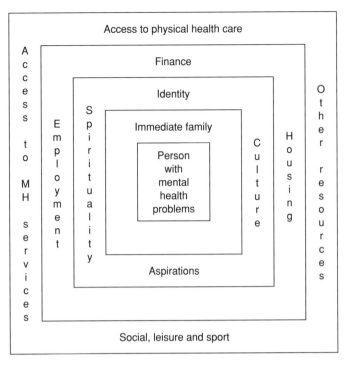

Figure 11.1   An ecological model of person centred care planning (Jones and Ramchandani, 1999).

- Can we imagine a different relation between medicine and madness from that forged in the asylums of a previous age?
- How apt is western psychiatry for ethnic groups who put greater value on spirituality, the family and community?
- How also can we uncouple mental health from the agenda of social exclusion, coercion and control to which it has become bound over the last 200 years?

Social exclusion

Poverty

The World Health Organization (2000) defines health inequality as *'differences in health status or in the distribution of health determinants between different populations'*. In mental health the situation and environment in which some people live can either be detrimental to their mental health or can promote their well being as suggested by Myers *et al.* (2006) so that mental illness is more or less prevalent in particular groups. For example, studies consistently show an association between poverty and mental illness whereby mental health problems are more common among poorer communities and people who have

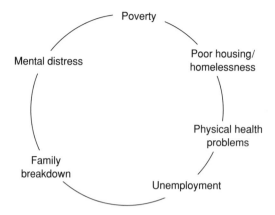

Figure 11.2   The cycle of poverty and mental distress (Myers *et al.*, 2006).

mental health problems are more likely to be poor. This can be seen as a cycle (Figure 11.2). At whatever stage the person enters the cycle, the subsequent problems may occur.

Myers *et al.* (2006) identify both risk and resilience factors that should be considered when supporting people towards recovery. In adverse circumstances, risk factors are those likely to make someone more vulnerable to becoming mentally ill while resilience factors may enable people to face difficulties/trauma without their mental health being affected.

Resilience

Box 11.1   Resilience factors.

Safe and secure in family or other intimate relationships, environment, work and finances
Sense of self determination and control of own life
Life skills and coping skills
Meaningful activities and roles
Access to social support
Access to resources and services that protect mental well being.

(Myers *et al.*, 2006).

Risk Factors

Box 11.2   Risk factors.

Structural – poverty, homelessness, unemployment, discrimination and deprivation
Social isolation and exclusion
Negative life events – abuse, illness, domestic violence, separation, bereavement
Physical health – physical disability, learning disability, chronic illness, substance abuse.

(Myers *et al.*, 2006).

Racism

Research studies over the last two decades have consistently found higher rates of diagnosed mental illness, particularly schizophrenia among black African-Caribbeans (McGovern & Cope, 1987; Fernando, 2003; Nazroo & King, 2002).

The first ever census of psychiatric patients in hospitals in England and Wales conducted by the Healthcare Commission, the Mental Health Act Commission and Care Services Improvement Partnership/National Institute for Mental Health in England (HCC/MHAC/CSIP/NIMHE, 2005) recorded information on 33 828 patients in all 102 NHS Trusts and in 110 of the independent providers. This constituted a 99% response rate of all providers. Admission rates were three times the average for black men, double the average for black women and there were high admission rates for Asian men but not for Asian women. For all patients 46% of men and 29% of women were admitted under section but for black people, black men were 25% to 38% more likely to be admitted on section and the compulsory admission rate for black women was between 56% and 62% above average. Black men were also less likely to be referred to the services by their GP and more likely to come via police and to be held on secure wards.

Fearns (2005) argues two possible hypotheses to explain the statistics. One is that black people in Britain will be subject to many of the risk factors identified above and are therefore more likely to be vulnerable to mental illness. The other is that the prejudice and ignorance of society and professionals will lead to black people being picked up by the police and diagnosed as mentally ill when there is no real justification for this. Outcomes of this kind can be the result of institutional racism defined in the MacPherson report (MacPherson, 1999:6.4) as:

'The collective failure of an organisation to provide an appropriate and professional service to people because of their colour, culture or ethnic origin which can be seen or detected in processes; attitudes and behaviour which amount to discrimination through unwitting prejudice, ignorance, thoughtlessness and racist stereotyping which disadvantages minority ethnic people'.

A subsequent enquiry into the death of another black male, David 'Rocky' Bennet (Department of Health, 2003a), who died while being restrained on a psychiatric ward, branded the British mental health services as institutionally racist and prompted the Government to develop a new action plan to promote race equality within mental health services (Department of Health, 2003b). This proposes to employ 500 community development workers (CDWs) across England by 2010 to provide a bridge between the statutory services and black and ethnic minority communities.

Campaigners such as Bracken and Thomas (2001) or Fernando (2003) have called for genuine alternatives to mainstream mental health treatments: options that are not simply medical or westernised models revamped and provided by black led community projects, but real options to use non-western and non-medical approaches to healing and well being that recognise the central role of the faiths, cultures, families and socioeconomic circumstances of black and ethnic minority communities.

Achieving this kind of radical development would require not only structural changes, but also the training of culturally competent mental health practitioners – a concept that is widely used in the USA (Goode & Harrisone, 2000) and is being more widely introduced in UK – for example, promoted by the Royal College of Nursing (RCN, 2005) in their trans-cultural communication foundation module. As part of the action plan referred to above (Department of Health, 2003b), the National Institute for Mental Health in England (NIMHE) has been asked to develop a framework of cultural capability to underpin the preparation of mental health practitioners.

Person centred planning: confident and competent practice

Cultural competence means *'a dynamic process of framing assumptions, knowledge and meanings from a culture different from our own'* (Bartol & Richardson, 1998). It does not mean developing in depth knowledge and expertise about a wide range of different religions and cultures because this can lead to stereotyping and making assumptions about individuals because of their background, failing to acknowledge that individual beliefs and practices vary enormously within cultures and are in constant flux within and between generations. Cultural competence means respectfully approaching each individual without any prior assumptions and enabling that person to share what *they* feel is important about their lifestyle, culture or religion, how this impacts on *their* lives and how it should be incorporated into making plans for the future.

Case study 11.1   Good practice.

Sunitha (24) has lived in Ealing in London for a year having come over to England to get married. She speaks very little English and is very home sick for family and friends in India. Her older sister Chitra (30) is married and living in Birmingham with her own two children; Sunitha's husband's family live in Canada and she does not really know them. When she was pregnant with her first child, her husband was killed in a car accident and Sunitha went into a deep depression. When the child was born, Sunitha was still too depressed and upset to be able to care for the child. It was feared that Sunitha was suicidal and that the child might be at risk. Chitra, Sunitha's sister in Birmingham agreed to care for the baby and to finance Sunitha to go into a private mental health hospital.

   With a combination of medication and therapy, Sunitha began to make a recovery and once she was a little better constantly asked about her baby and expressed the wish to have him back and to care for him. Chitra brought the baby back to London and they were transferred to a mother and baby unit where Sunitha was supported to bond with and care for her baby. A case was made to find accommodation for Sunitha and her baby in Birmingham where she would receive support from her sister and the network that she had developed there. She was also referred to an Asian women's mental health project and to a scheme for learning English.

Sometimes in situations like this, the baby is taken into care rather than making efforts to find relatives. If Sunitha had been discharged back into the community isolated from family and without any support network, she could easily have become ill again and she and the child would both have been at risk.

Gender issues

In spite of radical changes in the roles and opportunities for women over the last forty years, the continued inequalities in status, life experiences and family roles between men and women are reflected in mental health statistics. For example

> '. . . *women are more likely to self harm, suffer from depression and anxiety; men are more likely to receive a diagnosis of anti-social personality disorder, experience an earlier onset and more disabling course of schizophrenia; women are more likely to attempt suicide and men are more likely to succeed*' (Department of Health, 2003c:10).

Women's mental health is likely to be adversely affected by experience of abuse or neglect as a child or adolescent, lone parenthood, poor housing, poverty, domestic violence, asylum seeking, being part of an ethnic minority group, anxiety about body image and being overwhelmed by the pressures of parenting or other caring responsibilities. Care planning must take account of all these aspects of women's lives rather than focusing only on the mental illness. Government policy commends a vision in response to what women say they want.

An holistic approach to care planning with an emphasis on hope and recovery encompasses the need for women to be safely accommodated (with their children where appropriate), have access to training and employment, receive their full benefit entitlement, receive support in their mothering and caring roles, establish social networks and have their physical health care needs met (Department of Health, 2003c:12).

But Government also acknowledges that '*mental health service provision often fails to recognise the social context of women's lives*' (Department of Health, 2006a). Doing so would require joined up care planning between mental health services and social care; significant resources to build social networks and provide the support that many isolated women need; and, as recommended by Barnes *et al.* (2002) women-only and women-sensitive mental health services.

It is ironic that guidance on care planning insists on careful risk assessment and yet when female patients are actually in hospital they can be at the greatest risk of being assaulted. A report published in 2006 by the National Patient Safety Agency (NPSA) identified over a hundred patients on NHS mental health wards who were raped, sexually assaulted or sexually harassed *and the*

NPSA acknowledges that these figures represent probable under-reporting. The majority of the victims were women and the perpetrators were other patients. Complacency about this kind of abuse experienced by female psychiatric patients is further illustrated by the refusal of health professionals to listen to complaints made by numerous women abused by two psychiatrists over a 40 year period (Jackson, 2006).

Case study 11.2   Poor practice – medical model.

Claudette, a black British lone parent, was admitted to hospital under section 2 following a suicide attempt. Claudette had four children under eight. She lived on the fourth floor of a block of flats in inadequate accommodation. Her youngest child had a physical disability and her oldest child was beginning to manifest behavioural problems at school. She was in serious debt. Claudette was cut off from her Jamaican family because her children's father was a white man and she had abandoned the strongly held Christian faith of her parents. When she was admitted to hospital, the children had to be taken into care. The older two were separated from the younger ones.

Claudette made a good recovery and regretted her action saying that she had been feeling absolutely desperate and her problems had got on top of her. At the discharge meeting, the social worker responsible for Claudette's children wanted to discuss arrangements for supporting Claudette when she returned home. She wanted advice about whether or not she could discharge the children from care. The psychiatrist who was chairing the discharge meeting told the social worker that this meeting was about Claudette and her mental health and other issues should be discussed elsewhere.

Case study 11.3   Good practice – holistic woman-sensitive care planning.

Claudette (situation described above) was admitted to a women only ward in the community following her overdose. The ward is based in an ordinary 5 bedroom house in the community near where Claudette lives. At a therapeutic group meeting, Claudette talked about the rift that had occurred with her family and admitted that she had been too proud to contact them when the situation became very serious. The group persuaded Claudette to contact her mother who visited and agreed to take the children out of foster care and look after them together at home. Claudette's parents had not realised that the children's father had left or how much stress Claudette was experiencing.

When Claudette recovered from her overdose, a multidisciplinary meeting was convened in the women's unit including the social worker, health visitor, Claudette, her parents and the mental health staff. They considered all the different problems that had led to Claudette taking an overdose and agreed a strategy to support Claudette to address her problems.

Employment

Like poverty, unemployment can be both a cause and a consequence of mental illness and this is reflected in the high rates of depression and suicide associated with unemployment (Office of the Deputy Prime Minister, 2004). Employment rates for people engaged with mental health services are between 10 and 15% and those people with mental health issues who do work earn less than two thirds the average rate (Office of National Statistics, 2002; Meltzer, 2003).

From the service user's perspective, as for anyone else, the most important aspect of employment is earning money. This gives the person a sense of dignity, status and purpose. Having a job can lead to a reduction in symptoms. However, there are a number of barriers to overcome if the 35% of mentally ill people in the UK who say they would like to work are to be enabled to do so.

First there are fears about security. People become dependent on their welfare benefits and fear being left high and dry if they start to work but then become ill again. Second there is the need for self-confidence, training and support required by people with mental health issues returning to work. Third it will be necessary to challenge attitudes and prejudices of employers who do not want to take the risk of employing someone with mental health issues. According to the social disability and access model described by Perkins and Repper (1996), the aim is not necessarily to change people to prepare them for work but to change workplaces to prepare them to accept people with disabilities. Work environments need to be re-designed so that work stresses are identified and reduced and discrimination and prejudice addressed.

Fourth, for health professionals working with people with mental health issues, employment is often not on their agenda; they tend to focus on symptoms and impairments rather than social factors (Office of the Deputy Prime Minister, 2004). Work is considered in terms of an activity or therapy that does not involve wage earning. For employment to be achieved as part of effective care planning, vocational advisers would need to be part of the multidisciplinary team as a matter of course.

Research in the US found that up to 58% of adults could be rehabilitated using the individual placement and support approach (Bond *et al.*, 1997). This model demonstrates that high expectations, encouragement and support can enable people to return to the workplace.

Case study 11.4 Employment – a necessity (1).

A successful charity replaced its sheltered employment schemes with the following opportunities or pathways back to work:

- Education and training opportunities including interpersonal skills and IT training
- Volunteering placements supported by a development worker
- Work placements supported by a development worker
- Real jobs with ongoing support from a development worker.

The support provided was offered to both the employer and the employee. The development worker helped the employer and employee agree a contract at the beginning of the placement or job that included a strategy for dealing with problems that might arise. The development worker visited at monthly intervals at the beginning to iron out any problems and then less frequently. If this was a work or voluntary placement the development worker would visit towards the end and facilitate the employee receiving feedback about their performance and advice about further training they might need to progress to the next stage of their aspiration. More often than not, feedback was extremely positive and this was very affirming for the employee and helped them to regain self confidence.

Case study 11.5   Employment – a necessity (2).

An administrative placement was offered to a highly intelligent service user who had been institutionalised for more than three decades. The manager was concerned that the service user would feel bored and insulted by the routine nature of the work. However, at the feedback stage the service user said how much she had enjoyed the placement because she felt like '*a normal human being*' coming into a normal workplace each day and having a cup of tea in the works canteen.

The experience of the project described in the above practice examples replicated the outcomes of the American research (Bond *et al.*, 1997) which was that with appropriate support, double the number of service users were involved in real work experience than had used the previous sheltered schemes.

The Government White Paper *Our Health, Our Care, Our Say* (Department of Health, 2006b) encourages businesses to establish social enterprises where the goal is to improve communities socially and environmentally.

Case study 11.6   Employment – a necessity (3).

In 2005, Novas Housing Association established a chain of four social enterprise cafés employing service users. Each café staff member receives training and an hourly wage in line with that of employees in similar settings. They develop social and communication skills that help them reintegrate into the community (Sale, 2006).

The Government intends to address concern about loss of benefit through proposals set out in the Green paper entitled *A New Deal for Welfare* (Department for Work and Pensions, 2006). This aims to reduce unemployment among people with disabilities by replacing incapacity benefit with an initial employment and support allowance and a subsequent support allowance conditional on them attending a rehabilitation programme aimed to enable them to return to work. The *Pathways to Work* project (Department for Work and Pensions, 2002) will be extended to private and voluntary sector organisations, as well as primary care settings, all of which will be encouraged to support people back into the workplace.

While these measures have been cautiously welcomed, there is some cynicism that the policy is more about cutting expensive benefits such as the Disabled Living Allowance than about social inclusion. There is also concern that rehabilitation programmes will be a waste of time unless they are accompanied by significant changes in the workplace culture to reduce the stigma associated with mental health. Progress on this aspect should be supported by the implementation of the employment-related clauses of the Disability Discrimination Act (Department of Health, 1995). This requires employers to make reasonable adjustments within the workplace in order for disabled people, with suitable qualifications for the job, to be enabled to work.

Case study 11.7   Ahmed.

Ahmed, a very able 22-year-old computer technician working for a large company experienced a mental health crisis following a family trauma. He recovered quite well but the medication he was taking meant that he was very slow getting started in the mornings and he had less energy than before. Previously, Ahmed used to arrive at work at 8 am and work through until 6 pm. In consultation with his manager and the HR department at the firm, Ahmed returned to work on a basis of reduced working hours of 10 am until 4.30 pm. He was also given time off each week to attend a one hour counselling session and he had an employment support worker who helped him and his employer to make the arrangement work. Being able to work again helped to improve Ahmed's confidence and self esteem and aid his recovery. From the firm's perspective they retained a valued employee.

Homelessness

Having somewhere to live is a basic human need and for many people with mental health issues having their own home represents a key step on their path to recovery. However, maintaining a home both in terms of finance and day to day practicalities can be a real challenge. Unfortunately, even when housing has been acquired, mental distress can severely affect a person's ability to sustain a tenancy unless care and support are readily available. Some vulnerable and homeless people may become trapped in a revolving door of settling in their accommodation but then losing it if they are admitted to hospital, thus the cycle of exclusion illustrated in Figure 11.2, where mental health issues lead to homelessness or homelessness exacerbates mental health issues is hard to interrupt.

The report on *Mental Health and Social Exclusion* (Office of the Deputy Prime Minister, 2004) paints a depressing picture of the current state of homelessness for people with mental health issues with 30–50% of homeless people having mental health problems and very few having access to a GP or other health services.

Many hostels for homeless people will not accept people with mental health problems because there is no one to provide for their support needs. Those who have both mental health issues and alcohol/drug problems face particular difficulties in finding accommodation or services because hostels have strict rules about use of substances.

The options for homeless people with community care needs relating to mental health, drug or alcohol problems are very limited because of pressures on social services budgets. The current models of accommodation fall within a spectrum of:

- Residential hostels with staff available 24 hours per day
- Group homes with day time staff
- Group homes with access to off site staff

- Supported housing with independent units and staff on site 24/7
- Supported housing with off site staff available on call
- Residential hostels with staff available 24 hours per day.

Older service users, especially those who spent significant time in psychiatric institutions before moving into the community, may be more comfortable in communal living environments such as hostels or group homes. On the other hand, younger people, in the experience of this author, are seeking their own room, preferably with en suite facilities or even their own self contained flat with support available. These facilities are few and far between and tend to be provided by the voluntary sector with limited support from statutory funds.

Case study 11.8 Joshua.

Joshua, aged 26 had a severe mental health crisis when his marriage broke down and he lost his job. He was able to move into a 12 bedroom therapeutic short stay hostel for Jewish young people. Each room has en suite facilities and the resource provides dining room, living room, games room and kitchen. Staff are on the premises 24/7 and offer one to one counselling, therapeutic groups and support with participation in outside activities. All Jewish dietary customs and festivals are practised. Joshua was able to begin the recovery process while he was in the hostel and was supported to move out to a more independent living situation within 18 months.

Joshua moved into a small apartment block with six self contained one bedroom flats, each with its own kitchen, reception room and bathroom. A member of staff has her own flat on the premises and is on call to provide support to the tenants. She also facilitates social events and outings for the tenants and helps them with daily living problems such as budgeting and home maintenance.

Care planning, social exclusion and government policy

The care programme approach (CPA) (Department of Health, 1990) was first implemented in 1991 and extended to include everyone who is in contact with specialist mental health services. The expectation in terms of good practice (Department of Health and Welsh Office, 1993) was that a multi-professional assessment would take place in partnership with the service user and that this assessment would take into account both health and social care issues. A plan would be formulated to meet the identified needs and a key worker would coordinate the implementation and regular review of the plan.

In 1999 CPA was revised and integrated with care management to form a single coordinated approach for all adults of working age with mental health issues (NHSE and SSI, 1999). A distinction was created between standard CPA – for people whose needs could be met by one agency or professional and who did not constitute a risk to themselves or others – and enhanced CPA for people with more severe and complex needs who required multi-agency involvement and where there may be a degree of risk. The National Service Framework for Mental Health (NSF) (Department of Health, 1999) emphasised the importance of service users being involved in the development of the plan and receiving a written copy. Section 6 of the NSF also required greater information for and involvement of informal/family carers.

The user perspective

The Government's expressed commitment to user-centred services is illustrated in the title of its White Paper – *Our Health, Our Care, Our Say* (Department of Health, 2006b) and in its framework *Our Choices in Mental Health* (CSIP/NIMHE, 2006). These documents are the outcome of detailed consultations with service users and patients and claim to be person-centred rather than focused on either health care or social care services. For people with mental health issues, implementation would mean that many of the demands that have been made by service users over many years would actually be met. For example the White Paper promises:

- Improved quality of initial contact in primary care where it would be possible to speak directly with a mental health professional rather than having to wait for specialist services
- Easier access to talking therapies
- Support to remain in or find employment
- More access to mainstream leisure and sports facilities
- Better advice on nutrition and diet
- Better access to physical health care and advice
- Encouragement and support to stop smoking or using other harmful substances
- Improved collaboration between health and social care services
- Better support for carers.

And the Choice Framework advocates four choice points:

- Promoting and supporting life chances
- Accessing and engaging with services
- Assessment
- Care pathways.

Some cynicism about this panacea has to be expressed when in the same year that the White Paper was published mental health services were, as ever, bearing the brunt of severe cuts (Rethink, 2006) in order to bail out acute NHS Trusts with massive overspends. As service users from an affected Trust told this author, *'You can't make choices if there is nothing to choose from'.*

Between 1997 and 2004, this author regularly sought the views of mental health service users about the services they received in a large voluntary agency. She found that service users were unenthusiastic about the care planning process, did not enjoy attending review meetings, especially when a large number of professionals were in attendance, and often felt disempowered rather than empowered by the procedures. When asked to set their own agenda for a quality review, care planning did not feature as a priority (Weinstein, 2006). Rather, service users wanted to focus on holidays, day centre opening hours, interesting activities and breaking down their sense of isolation by feeling that they were part of a warm and welcoming community.

In 2004 a group of service users carried out their own survey (Hounsell & Owens, 2005) and found that less than half of their respondents had a care plan that they had seen and signed and a third did not know that they had a care coordinator. A more positive study by Carpenter *et al.* (2004) found that service users within the community felt that they did have a say in their care plan and were involved in the process. However, this contrasted with a sense of powerlessness that users said they experienced as in-patients. In her review of the literature on CPA, Warner (2005) indicated limited service user involvement in CPA although where service users were effectively engaged they were more satisfied with the process. The largest survey was undertaken by the Healthcare Commission with others in 2005. About half the respondents said they had been offered a copy of their care plan and three quarters were satisfied with the content. Two thirds knew who their coordinator was and had seen the coordinator recently.

Leiba and Weinstein (2003) outline some of the barriers faced by both professionals and service users in achieving genuine partnership and equal involvement. These include factors such as power relations, professionals' preoccupation with risk management and service users' fear about the consequences of challenging professional judgements and decisions. Langan and Lindow (2004) suggest that independent advocacy would be helpful to overcome these barriers and enable genuine service user involvement because service users need a full understanding of options and services in order to be meaningfully involved. It is the contention of this author, in agreement with Evers *et al.* (1994) that users are the experts in their own needs and must therefore be fully involved, if not leaders in the care planning process. This approach can sometimes lead to conflicts with close family carers who are the subject of the next section.

Informal or family carers

Informal or family carers play a critical role in the lives of people with mental health problems. Their needs were acknowledged in standard 6 of the NSF (Department of Health, 1999), which gave every carer the right to an independent assessment of their needs. Unfortunately, this provision has not improved the day to day experience of many carers nor their sense of being left with the fear and frustration involved in caring for someone with a severe and enduring mental illness. *'Carers complain consistently that their cries for help are ignored or rejected'* (Laurance, 2003:160). The key issues for a carers' group consulted by this author were support for emergencies to be on hand 24/7, a familiar, named professional who could be contacted on a need for support basis and a wider more flexible range of services available in a crisis.

Case study 11.9   Poor practice.

Maria is 66 years old. Her daughter Sylvia (33) has suffered from depression since she was in her early teens. This is a chronic condition and from time to time the situation becomes acute and Sylvia harms herself or attempts suicide. Maria is the main carer for her daughter who has her own flat but who frequently finds it impossible to manage and comes back home to live. Hospital admissions are sometimes inevitable but, rather than offering respite, these are extremely stressful for Maria because Sylvia is placed on a mixed ward where she feels frightened and harassed. When Maria, who, as a care professional is knowledgeable about mental health issues, sought a carers' group for mutual support, she was offered training as the only option. She feels totally alone and unsupported – seeing no end to caring for her daughter, even though she herself is getting older.

When trying to promote the interests of carers with mental health professionals, this author often experienced hostility to the carers who were perceived as negative, hostile, over involved or as treating adults with mental health problems as though they were children. Although the British Psychological Society (2000) agrees that relatives who behave as described above can be potentially damaging to the patient's recovery, this is not a reason to cut the relative out of the care planning process. On the contrary, the relative needs to be informed and involved in such a way as to enable the relative to find ways of being that will support recovery rather than exacerbating the mental health problem.

A carers' survey undertaken by Rethink (2003) suggests that the carer/user relationship can be used as an excuse for not involving the carer and that fewer than 1 in 10 respondents to the survey said that the service user they cared for forbade contact with their care professional. The authors conclude that *'the underlying reason for not involving carers in care planning . . . must often lie within the relationship between mental health professionals and carers'* (Rethink, 2003:4). In the same survey, 37% of carers surveyed reported that patient confidentiality was cited as the reason for their exclusion.

In the experience of this author whose role involved responding to complaints and concerns expressed by carers of people with mental health problems over a number of years, excluding relatives is counter-productive because it raises tensions. Thus for example relatives become extremely distressed when their son or daughter will not get up or attend to personal hygiene or eat healthily etc. As carers' anxiety mounts, they may become increasingly hostile or critical towards their offspring whose mental health will worsen. Involvement in the development of a care plan can help to reduce the carer's anxiety and help them to understand and play a positive role in the recovery programme. Douek (2003) stresses that carers want to be kept informed about and involved in their relative's treatment; they need someone to talk to; and they need to be supported in their role and provided with respite care.

Good practice in inclusive care planning

In order to engage in a productive, trusting relationship, it is essential to start where the service user is at and to include the service user at all stages in the care planning process. The illustration in Figure 11.3 was drawn by a service user, Kevin Chettle and entitled *The Experts of the Case Conference*. The picture graphically expresses Kevin's feelings about being excluded from discussions about his welfare.

It is suggested here that many service users will be preoccupied first and foremost with social issues such as housing, benefits, employment and relationships. If this is the case, this is the place to start. On the other hand, some people may wish to discuss their symptoms. McCabe *et al.* (2002:1148) analysed conversations between psychiatrists and patients with mental health issues. They found that when patients tried to discuss their symptoms, *'doctors hesitated, responded with a question rather than an answer . . . indicating that they were reluctant to engage with patients' concerns about their psychotic symptoms'*. The authors contend that a willingness to engage with the patient would result in more effective engagement of patients with services. In order to ensure that your care planning process is inclusive you need to think beyond referring the person to services. Are there ways that the person can be supported to participate in mainstream activities such as education, work or leisure if the right support is offered? Make sure that the plan acknowledges the priorities of the service user. Even if they may be unrealistic for the immediate future do not make the service user lose hope for future possibilities and do not forget to explore personal, social, cultural and spiritual needs as well as any practical or health needs.

Case study 11.10   Marvyn – how *not* to write up a care plan.

The patient continues to suffer from a drug induced psychosis but this is now partially controlled by medication and he will be permitted to live in the community with appropriate supervision. Although his mother is not keen for him to return home because of his disruptive behaviour, it has been explained to her that he could attend the local day centre to take the pressure off. Because the patient has a history of non-compliance, medication will be administered monthly by depot.

Figure 11.3 The Experts of the Case Conference (reproduced with permission of the artist, Kevin Chettle).

Case study 11.11   Marvyn – how *to* write up a care plan.

Marvyn says that the most important thing on his mind at the moment is for him to have his own flat. However, he acknowledges that, although he is feeling a lot better, he still hears voices and sometimes gets very angry or upset and that taking responsibility for a flat at this time in his life might be very stressful. He also accepts that it might take some time to find the right flat for him but his key worker will support him in liaising with housing agencies.

Marvyn's mother feels that she cannot take him back in to the family home at the moment because she has many other pressures in her own life and cannot give him the support he needs. She feels that her relationship with Marvyn would be better if they did not live together at the moment but kept in touch in other ways.

Marvyn's second choice in terms of housing would be to live in a hostel with young people of his own age, preferable run by a black voluntary organisation and not by the local authority or health service. His key worker will help Marvyn to secure a place in this kind of resource.

Marvyn understands that he will need to take medication for the time being and, realistically, he thinks that having the community psychiatric nurse (CPN) to come round with a depot would be better than relying on him to take medication because he knows that this can be erratic when he is not well. However, he would also like the opportunity to talk about his life and his frustrations so arrangements are being made for him to access a black mental health counselling service in the locality. Marvyn hates going into hospital so he has signed an advanced directive asking the CPN to ensure that if he becomes unwell, he continues to receive his medication even if, at the time, he appears reluctant to cooperate.

Marvyn is very keen to go to college and pursue his interest in music and he would like to get back to the gym for his fitness but it is rather expensive. He was very pleased to hear that the GP could prescribe gym membership for him.

Case study 11.12   Good practice.

Eileen is a 59-year-old Scot who has suffered with mental health issues since she was a young woman. She lived in a council estate in a ground floor flat but received daily abuse and taunting from gangs of youths on the estate who call her '*local loony*'. She had a care plan that involves a visit from a home carer twice a week to support her with managing her flat and attendance at a day centre twice a week.

When her care plan came up for review, it emerged that Eileen was very dissatisfied with her current living arrangements. Her first priority was to get off the estate. She was not happy with her home carers over whom she felt she had no control and who constantly changed. She no longer wanted to attend the day centre but she would like to do a computer course. Her niece gave Eileen her old computer and set it up for her and Eileen has become fascinated by the internet and email etc.

A new care plan is agreed with Eileen whereby she is helped to make an application for an urgent transfer to a new flat.

Her day centre and home help are replaced with a direct payment that Eileen can use to purchase her own cleaning lady and to attend a computer training course. Eileen becomes so adept with the computer that she goes back to her day centre and runs a training course in computers for other members for which she is paid a fee. This significantly enhances her self esteem and, through the day centre, she is recommended to get involved at a local university, helping to select and train mental health nurses. Employing her own cleaning lady gives her control back over her own home and she takes a greater interest in keeping it nice. Eileen says that she has never felt so 'normal' and, because she is out so much, the taunting on the estate had virtually disappeared so she withdraws the transfer application.

Bad practice

The care plans of people who have severe and enduring mental health problems are often reviewed in a cursory way – sometimes done in the office with a few phone calls. Undertaking a user-led review leading to a user-led care plan changed Eileen's life.

Conclusion

As a professional working in the 1970s, this author recalls the social work role incorporating community work – i.e. engaging with tenants' associations, nursery campaigns, women's struggles and anti-discrimination projects. These activities were crushed in the 1980s and damned by critiques of political correctness, community work jobs were eradicated and social workers were forced back into individual casework. Thankfully the wheel has turned full circle and now the whole mental health workforce (Department of Health, 2004) is required to be involved in enabling people to meet their social needs; building on strengths and resilience rather than focusing on problems; looking outwards to the community as well as inwards to health and social care services.

A key concept evolved by the Disability Rights Commission (2003) promotes the creation of inclusive environments whereby schools, colleges, workplaces, leisure centres, shops and businesses become places where disabled people, including people with mental health problems, can participate as equal citizens.

Case study 11.13   An education project.

Service users in a voluntary sector mental health service were surveyed by the quality assurance department about their satisfaction with services. Although the users expressed high levels of satisfaction with the organisation's services they felt that they were excluded from the local community and wanted to participate more and feel accepted.

An education project was established whereby a group of staff, volunteers and service users developed drama based presentations to raise awareness about mental health and social exclusion. These presentations were made to local schools, colleges and other organisations and initial evaluation indicated improved understanding within the community. Service users who participated gained confidence and self esteem through the process.

Inclusive care planning is about empowering service users to take control over their own lives and to address their aspirations in an optimistic way rather than focusing on mental illness. The last word comes from a service user: *'My psychiatrist thought that he only had to think about me from the neck up and my GP was only interested from the neck down – why don't they understand that I am a whole person?'*

References

Anthony, W.A. (1993). Recovery From Mental Illness: The Guiding Vision Of The Mental Health Service System In The 1990s. *Psychosocial Rehabilitation Journal.* **16(4)**, 11–24.

Barnes, M., Davies, A., Guru, S., Lewis, L. & Rogers, H. (2002). *Women Only and Women Sensitive Mental Health Services: An Expert Paper.* Report for the Department of Health. Available at: http://www.csip.org.uk (Accessed September 2006).

Bartol, G.M., & Richardson, L. (1998). Using Literature To Create Cultural Competence, *Journal of Nursing Scholarship,* **30**, 75–9.

Bond, G.R., Drake, R.E., Mueser, K.T. & Becker, D.R. (1997). An Update On Supported Employment For People With Severe Mental Illness. *Psychiatric* Services. **48(3)**, 335–346.

Bracken, P. & Thomas, T. (2001). Postpsychiatry: A New Direction for Mental Health. *British Medical Journal.* **322**, 724–727.

British Psychological Society (2000). *Recent Advances in Understanding Mental Illness and Psychotic Experience.* London: BPS.

Carpenter, J. (2002). Mental Health Recovery Paradigm: Implications for Social Work. *Health and Social Work.* **27(2)**, 453–462.

Carpenter, J., Schneider, J., McNiven, F., Brandon, T., Stevens, R. & Woolf, D. (2004). Integration and Targeting of Community Care for People with Severe and Enduring Mental Health Problems: Users' Experiences of the Care Programme Approach and Care management. *British Journal of Social Work.* **11(3)**, 281–293.

CSIP/NIMHE (2006). *Our Choices in Mental Health.* Available at: http://www.csip.org.uk (Accessed September 2006).

Deegan, P.E. (1997). Recovery and empowerment For People with Psychiatric Disabilities. *Social Work in Health Care.* **25(3)**, 11–24.

Department for Work and Pensions (2002). *Pathways to Work: Helping People into Employment* Cm 5690. London: The Stationery Office.

Department for Work and Pensions (2006). *A New Deal for Welfare – Empowering People To Work.* Available at: http://www.dwp.gov.uk/aboutus/welfarereform/ (Accessed May 2006).

Department of Health (1990). *Caring for People: The Care Programme Approach For People With A Mental Illness Referred To Specialist Mental Health Services.* Joint Health/Social Services Circular C(90) 23/LASSL. London: HMSO. **(90)11.**

Department of Health (1995). *Disability Discrimination Act.* London: HMSO.

Department of Health (1999). *National Service Framework for Mental Health.* Available at: http://www.dh.gov.uk (Accessed May 2006).

Department of Health (2003a). *An Independent Inquiry into the Death of David Bennett.* London: The Stationery Office.

Department of Health (2003b). *Delivering Race Equality: A Framework for Action.* Available at: http://www.dh.gov.uk (Accessed August 2006).

Department of Health (2003c). *Mainstreaming Gender and Women's Mental Health Implementation Guidance.* London: The Stationery Office.

Department of Health (2004). *The Ten Essential Shared Capabilities: A Framework For The Whole Of The Mental Health Workforce.* London: The Stationery Office.

Department of Health (2006a). *Supporting Women into the Mainstream: Commissioning Women Only Community Day Services.* London: The Stationery Office.

Department of Health (2006b). *Our Health Our Care Our Say: A New Direction for Community Services.* Available at: http://www.doh.gov.uk/ourhealthourcareoursay (Accessed May 2006).

Department of Health and Welsh Office (1993). *Mental Health Act 1983 Code of Practice.* London: HMSO.

Disability Rights Commission (2003). *Fair For All – Disability: Positive Action Positive Change.* Stratford upon Avon: Disability Rights Commision.

Douek, S. (2003). Collaboration or Confusion? The Carers' Perspective. In: Weinstein, J., Whittington, C. & Leiba, T. (eds). *Collaboration in Social Work Practice.* London: Jessica Kingsley Publishers.

Evers, H., Cameron, C. & Badger, F. (1994). Interprofessional Work with Old and Disabled People. In: Leathard, A. (ed). *Going Interprofessional: Working together for Health and Welfare.* London: Routledge.

Fearns, P. (2005). Finding a Way Forward: A Black Perspective. In: Tew, J. (ed). *Social Perspectives in Mental Health.* London: Jessica Kingsley Publishers.

Fernando, S. (2003). *Cultural Diversity, Mental Health and Psychiatry: The Struggle against Racism.* London: Routledge.

Goode, T. & Harrisone, S. (2000). *Cultural Competence in Primary Health Care Partnerships for a Research Agenda.* Washington DC: Georgetown University Child Development Centre, National Centre for Cultural Competence.

Health Care Commission, Mental Health Act Commission & NIMHE/CSIP (2005). *National Census Of Inpatients In Mental Health Hospitals and Facilities.* Available at: http://www.healthcarecommission.org (Accessed May 2005).

Hounsell, J. & Owens, C. (2005). User Research in Control. *Mental Health Today.* **May**, 29–33.

Jackson, C. (2006). Out of Sight: Are Trusts Doing Enough To Prevent Rape and Sexual Assault On Psychiatric Wards? *Mental Health Today.* **Sept**, 8–9.

Jones, D.P.H. & Ramchandani, P. (1999). *Child Sexual Abuse: Informing Practice from Research.* Oxford: Radcliffe Medical Press.

Kitwood, T. (1997). *Dementia Reconsidered.* Berkshire: Open University Press.

Langan, J. & Lindow, V. (2004). *Living with Risk: Mental Health Service User Involvement In Risk Assessment and Management.* York: Joseph Rowntree Foundation/the Policy Press.

Laurance, J. (2003). *Pure Madness: How Fear Drives the Mental Health System.* London: Routledge.

Leiba, T. & Weinstein, J. (2003). Who are the Participants in the Collaborative Process and What Makes Collaboration Succeed or Fail? In: Weinstein, J. Whittington, C. & Leiba, T. (eds). *Collaboration in Social Work Practice.* London: Jessica Kingsley Publishers.

MacPherson, W. (1999). *The Stephen Laurence Inquiry: Report of an Inquiry by Sir William MacPherson of Cluny.* London: The Stationery Office.

McCabe, R., Heath, C., Burns, T. & Priebe, S. (2002). Engagement Of Patients With Psychosis In The Consultation: Conversation Analytical Study. *British Medical Journal.* **325**, 1148–51.

McGovern, D. & Cope, R. (1987). The Compulsory Detention Of Males Of Different Ethnic Groups, With Special Reference To Offender Patients. *British Journal of Psychiatry.* **150**, 505–512.

Meltzer, H. (2003). *Further Analysis Of The Psychiatric Morbidity Survey 2000 Data Prepared For The Social Exclusion Unit.* London: Office of the Deputy Prime Minister.

Myers, F., McCollam, A. & Whitehouse, A. (2006). Breaking The Cycle of Injustice. *Mental Health Today.* **Mar**, 23–26.

Nazroo, J. & King, M. (2002). Psychosis: Symptoms and Estimated Rates. In: Sproston K. & Nazroo, J. (eds). *Ethnic Minority Psychiatric Illness Rates in the Community.* London: National Centre for Social Research.

NHS Executive and Social Services Inspectorate (1999). *Effective Care Co-ordination in Mental Health Services: Modernising the Care Programme Approach. A Policy Booklet.* London: NHSE and SSI.

NPSA (2006). *With Safety In Mind: Patient Safety Observatory Report.* Available at: http://www.npsa.nhs.uk (Accessed September 2006).

Office of the Deputy Prime Minister (2004). *Mental Health and Social Exclusion.* London: Office of the Deputy Prime Minister.

Office of National Statistics (2002). *Labour Force Survey 2002.* London: HMSO.

Perkins, R.E. & Repper, J.M. (1996). *Working Alongside People with Long Term Mental Health Problems.* London: Chapman Hall.

Perkins, R.E. & Repper, J.M. (1998). *Dilemmas in Community Mental Health Practice: Choice or Control.* Oxford: Radcliffe Medical Press.

Rethink (2003). *The Experience Of Mental Health Carers Accessing Services and Information.* Available at: http://www.rethink.org/how_we_can_help/carers/publications/html (Accessed August 2006).

Rethink (2006). *A Cut Too Far.* Available at: http://www.rethink.org/how_we_can_help/publications/html (Accessed August 2006).

Royal College of Nursing (2005). *Transcultural Communication and Health Care Practice: Foundation Module C.* Available at: http://www.rcn.org.uk/resources/transcultural/foundation/sectionthree.php (Accessed Oct 2005).

Russinova, Z. (1999). Providers: Hope-Inspiring Competence As A Factor Optimising Psychiatric Rehabilitation. *Journal of Rehabilitation.* **65(4)**, 50–58.

Sale, A.U. (2006). *Enterprise and Shine, Community Care 8–14th June 2006.* Available at: http://www.communitycare.co.uk/Articles/2006/06/08/54386/enterprise-and-shine.html?key=SALE (Accessed May 2006).

Stanley, N., Penhale, B., Riordan, D., Barbour, R.S. & Holden, S. (2003). *Child Protection and Mental Health Services.* Bristol: The Policy Press.

Warner, L. (2005). Review of the literature on the Care Programme Approach. In: Sainsbury Centre for Mental Health, *Back on Track*? Available at: http://www.scmh.org.uk (Accessed May 2006).

Warren, K. (2003). *Exploring the Concept of Recovery from the Perspective of People with Mental Health Problems.* Norwich: University of East Anglia.

Weinstein, J. (2006). Involving Service users in Quality Assurance. *Health Expectations.* **9**, 9–109.

World Health Organization (2000). *Health Impact Assessment: Glossary of Terms Used.* Available at: http://www.who.int/hia/glos/en/index.html (Accessed August 2006).

Young, S.L. & Ensing, D.S. (1999). Exploring Recovery from the Perspective of People with Psychiatric Disabilities. *Psychiatric Rehabilitation Journal.* **22**, 127–134.

Chapter 12

Physical Health and Serious Mental Illness: Promoting Good Health

Debbie Robson and Mary Bragg

Introduction

The World Health Organization (1991) defines the concept of health as a state of complete physical, mental and social well being and not merely an absence of disease. For centuries the notion that physical health and mental health were somehow separate from each other was commonplace. This mind–body dichotomy that dominated healthcare for many years has, in theory, been replaced by a more holistic and integrated concept of physical and mental health. When mental health care was delivered in institutions, the assessment and management of the physical health needs of patients with serious mental illness (SMI) was once the remit of mental health nurses and psychiatrists. Large mental health institutions had onsite dental, ophthalmology and chiropody services as well as gymnasiums and opportunities to engage in physical and occupational activities. Although the move from institutional to community settings was undoubtedly necessary, what followed in some areas in the UK was the fragmentation of physical health and mental health care.

Despite efforts over the past two decades to provide holistic and integrated health services for people with SMI, the physical health care needs of this population have continued to be overlooked by both primary care and mental health practitioners (MHPs) in secondary care (Cohen & Hove, 2001; Phelan *et al.*, 2001). Pre-registration nurses and qualified MHPs face the challenge of meeting mental health needs alongside the physical health needs of people we work with. However in order to do this we need to understand the causes of physical health problems as well as feel confident in preventing, assessing, monitoring and managing potential and existing physical health conditions.

In this chapter we will begin by highlighting recent UK policy guidance about meeting the physical health care needs of people with SMI in both primary and secondary care. We will then explore the context of the global increase in physical health conditions and how common co-existing medical conditions are in people with a SMI. We will then look at some of the reasons to explain the poor physical health of people with SMI and the complexities for promoting health and managing co-morbid conditions. We will then discuss some practical care planning skills that may enable the mental health practitioner to work collaboratively with service users to promote physical health and well being. Case examples are included to illustrate the complexity of integrating evidence-based recommendations into real life clinical practice.

Policy

The Department of Health (1990) recommended that health services should adopt a holistic view of the assessment and development of care plans for mental health service users. However for many years there has been confusion and doubt over whose role it is to provide health promotion, detect potential physical problems and manage existing physical health problems in people with SMI (Phelan *et al.*, 2001).

Recent health policy in the UK has included recommendations for the physical health care of people with SMI (Department of Health, 2005, 2006). Guidelines from the National Institute for Health and Clinical Excellence for the treatment of schizophrenia in primary and secondary care (NICE, 2002) recommend that routine physical health checks should be carried out in primary care services. Where this is not possible either through service user choice or where the user has no GP, the responsibility for physical health monitoring must be taken up by secondary services. People admitted to psychiatric wards should also have physical health checks undertaken. It can be argued that there remains a lack of clarity about where the responsibility for physical health care lies in this population and that there is a risk that services which are not working in close partnership may assume that responsibility lies elsewhere.

The chief nursing officer's review of mental health nursing (Department of Health, 2006) places a strong emphasis on mental health nurses having the necessary skills to assess the physical health problems of service users and to ensure that any identified needs are met. This may involve supporting service users to access appropriate physical health care services or nurses arranging for further investigations to be undertaken locally. Mental health nurses should also be actively involved in health promotion. Underpinning this focus on the physical assessment and intervention skills of the mental health nurse is the aspiration that service users should be viewed holistically rather than being seen fundamentally as recipients of treatment for a mental health problem. This refocusing towards holistic health care delivery is key to the Government's drive to reduce health inequalities, support people to make informed healthy choices and to improve partnership working across services (Department of Health, 2005).

Box 12.1   Six key priorities for health improvement.

Six key priorities for health:

- Tackling health inequalities
- Reducing the numbers of people who smoke
- Tackling obesity
- Improving sexual health
- Improving mental health and well being
- Reducing harm and encouraging sensible drinking.

(Department of Health, 2005).

The UK Government have identified six key priorities for health (Box 12.1) which aim to focus on longer term health improvement and illness prevention in addition to medical treatment (Department of Health, 2005).

The Government recognises that improving access to health care for disadvantaged groups will be essential in order to address the current health priorities and that the knowledge and skills of mental health practitioners need to be improved if health targets are to be achieved (Department of Health, 2005).

The next part of the chapter is aimed at providing MHPs with useful knowledge about the most common physical health problems people with SMI experience and possible reasons for this.

What physical health problems do people with SMI experience?

People with SMI have higher morbidity and mortality rates for cardiovascular disease than the general population; they also have higher than expected rates of infectious diseases, non-insulin dependent diabetes, respiratory diseases and some forms of cancers (Dixon *et al.*, 1999). It has been estimated that the life expectancy of people with schizophrenia is reduced by 10 years (Newman & Bland, 1991), although recent research suggests that the rate may have accelerated to 25 years (Parks *et al.*, 2006). These higher rates of morbidity and mortality do however need to be viewed within the context of a global increase in the rates of chronic diseases (Robson and Gray, 2007).

Cardiovascular disease

People with SMI have rates of cardiovascular disease (CVD) 2–3 times higher than the general population (Brown *et al.*, 2000; Osby *et al.*, 2000). More recent studies suggest that women with SMI have a higher risk of developing coronary heart disease (Goff *et al.*, 2005). CVD includes conditions such as coronary heart disease, hypertension and high cholesterol and is caused by obesity, smoking, diabetes, lack of exercise and poor diet. These are all conditions and behaviours seen more commonly in people with SMI (Brown *et al.*, 2000; Harris & Barrowclough, 1998).

Respiratory disease

Up until 50 years ago respiratory diseases such as pneumonia and tuberculosis accounted for the majority of deaths amongst people with SMI who lived in institutions (Brown, 1997). Respiratory diseases are still more prevalent in people with SMI, which are thought to be as a result of the high rates of smoking or passive smoking. People with SMI are more likely than the general population to suffer from asthma, chronic bronchitis and emphysema (Sokal *et al.*, 2004).

Cancers

Researchers have consistently reported higher rates of digestive and breast cancer in people with schizophrenia (Schoos & Cohen, 2003); however, the research on lung cancer in people with schizophrenia is contradictory. Brown *et al.* (2000) and Lichtermann *et al.* (2001) found mortality rates for lung cancer twice as high in people with schizophrenia as one would expect in the general population, whereas in other studies rates for lung cancer have been similar or lower compared with the general population (Mortenson, 1989, 1994). Tobacco use is the single largest causative factor for lung cancer, followed by poor diet and physical inactivity.

Diabetes

The relationship between diabetes and schizophrenia has been discussed and investigated more than any other co-occurring physical and mental health problem. Controversy exists about how common diabetes is and the causes of it in people with SMI (Holt *et al.*, 2004). The association between schizophrenia and diabetes was first observed in the 1800s by the famous British psychiatrist Henry Maudsley (Koren, 2004) who observed that *'diabetes is a disease which often shows itself in families in which insanity prevails'*. Insulin resistance and glucose dysregulation have been observed in psychiatric patients since the 1920s. We have therefore known that diabetes occurs independently of antipsychotic medication for over a century. Diabetes occurs in approximately 15% of people with schizophrenia (Holt & Peveler, 2006) and possibly even higher in people with mood disorders compared to approximately 5% in the general population (Busche & Holt, 2004). It is influenced by a family history of diabetes, physical inactivity, poor diet, smoking and the metabolic effects of antipsychotic medication (Gough & Peveler, 2004). There are two main types of diabetes, type 1 and type 2. In type 1, the pancreas can no longer produce insulin because the insulin producing cells have usually been destroyed by the body's immune system. Type 1 has a rapid onset, usually days to weeks. In type 2 the insulin cells are not able to produce enough insulin or the body does not use it properly. Type 2 diabetes has a much slower onset. It often goes undiagnosed for 9–12 years (Department of Health, 2001), in the meantime prolonged exposure to raised blood glucose causes visual impairment and blindness, damage to kidneys, which can lead to renal failure, damage to nerves which can lead to loss of sensation in feet, foot or leg ulcers, amputation, difficulties in emptying bladder, impotence, cataracts and cardiovascular disease (Department of Health, 2001).

Glucose intolerance and diabetes

Typical antipsychotics, in particular the low potency ones such as chlorpromazine, may induce or make existing diabetes worse (Newcomer *et al.*, 2002). With regard to the atypical antipsychotics clozapine and olanzapine have been most frequently associated with new onset or exacerbating type 2 diabetes, not just through their propensity to cause greater weight gain than other newer agents but because of their effects on glucose regulation. There are case reports linking respiridone and quetiapine to impaired glucose intolerance, diabetes and ketoacidosis (Taylor *et al.*, 2005). Although the research on the use of antipsychotics and its association with diabetes is copious, some argue that the quality of the research is methodologically weak and at this point in time more controlled prospective studies are needed before a definite causal link between antipsychotics and diabetes is confirmed (Taylor *et al.*, 2005; Holt & Peveler, 2006).

Diabetic ketoacidosis (DK), a potentially fatal condition, may be the first obvious symptoms of type 2 diabetes. It is related to metabolic stress such as an infection, trauma, myocardial infarction or stroke (Jin *et al.*, 2004). Mental health nurses need to be aware that DK has a rapid onset (often <24 hours) and symptoms include polyuria, polydipsia, polyphagia, vomiting, abdominal pain, dehydration, potentially leading to coma and death (Expert Panel, 2004). Emergency treatment includes rehydratation, insulin therapy, electrolyte correction and treatment of the underlying condition. Case study 12.1 gives an example of care planning for a client with poorly controlled type 1 diabetes and a history of ketoacidosis.

Case study 12.1   Care planning for a client with type 1 diabetes.

History
Bernard is a 50-year-old man with a 30-year history of schizo-affective disorder. He also has a history of type 1 diabetes. His diabetes can become poorly controlled when he is mentally unwell. Bernard was admitted to an acute mental heath unit following a period of elation and increasingly erratic behaviour. On admission Bernard appeared to be physically well with the following physical observations: temperature 36.9 °C,

pulse 106, BP 140/92 mmHg, respirations 16, BM 12 mmols/L. Ketones were present in his urine.

He was prescribed sodium valproate 1000 mg, risperidone 4 mg, benzodiazepine 5 mg TDS and for his diabetes: insulin glargine 24 u nocte, insulin lispro 8 u TDS and metformin 500 mg BD.

Presenting problem

A client with a history of poorly controlled type 1 diabetes, particularly when mentally unwell

Assessment

- Current treatment for diabetes confirmed with GP
- Full physical assessment on admission
- BM monitoring
- Urinalysis.

Goal

To maintain blood glucose at recommended levels of 4–7 mmols/L before meals and less than 9 mmols/L post meal (NICE 2004).

Implementation

A plan was put in place for nursing staff to:

- Monitor BM 3 times daily pre meal
- Give actrapid 2 units if BM was more than 20 mmols/L
- Repeat blood glucose monitoring after 2 hours
- Inform duty doctor if BM level remains >20 mmols/L

Outcome/Evaluation

Three days following admission Bernard's BM had consistently been in the range 20–25 mmols/L. Nursing staff followed the suggested diabetic management plan and Bernard was reassessed by medical staff. Unfortunately a detailed care plan had not been completed. Nursing and medical staff failed to recognise signs of ketoacidosis e.g. thirst, nausea and drowsiness. Bernard was found one morning to be having difficulty breathing, was not responsive and was showing signs of cyanosis. Oxygen and actrapid were administered. He was transferred to A&E as an emergency and was admitted to intensive care where he required ventilation. He made a full recovery. This incident was investigated resulting in the development of a protocol for the management of clients with diabetes in mental health services.

Clinical implications

Mental health professionals may assume that the care of the person with diabetes is not primarily their concern. This case example illustrates that poor recognition of symptoms and complications of diabetes can have serious consequences in the mental health setting. Mental health professionals need to be able to recognise the signs and symptoms of diabetes and seek prompt advice from medical and nurse specialists in the event of poorly managed blood glucose levels. (NICE 2004)

NICE (2004) recommends that there should be a clear plan about how to respond to signs and symptoms of hypo or hyperglycaemia. In Bernard's case such a plan, communicated to all team members, may have prevented a potentially very serious complication of diabetes.

In Bernard's case a more thorough history taking would have revealed that he had a history of rapidly developing ketoacidosis necessitating admission to intensive care.

Other recommendations from NICE (2004) include:

- Input from specialists in the care of people with diabetes regarding medication management, nutritional information and monitoring.
- Routine monitoring of blood glucose. NICE (2004) recommend BM levels of 4–7 mmols/L pre meal and less than 9 mmols/L post meal.

- Provide information about the longer term risks of prolonged exposure to raised blood glucose levels, which include kidney damage, visual impairment and cardiovascular disease.
- Monitoring at least annually for the signs of late complications of diabetes as above.
- Physical monitoring at least annually for other risk factors for cardiovascular disease including body mass index, blood pressure, lipid profile, waist measurement.
- Collaborative discussion between the client and healthcare worker about the role of the client, mental health worker and diabetes specialist in managing the condition.
- A collaboratively drawn plan that details what should happen if the client is temporarily unable to manage his diabetes. Ideally this should involve the client's family member/carer.

Complexities to promoting physical health care

There are a number of complex reasons why people with SMI have poor physical health (Table 12.1).

Table 12.1 Reasons for poor physical health in people with SMI.

Health behaviours	Smoking Diet Physical inactivity Alcohol and substance misuse Sexual behaviour
Illness	Positive symptoms Negative symptoms Cognitive and mood symptoms Poor spontaneous reporting of physical health problems
Health service	Lack of knowledge of mental health workforce Lack of training Attitudes and confidence of mental health staff Attitudes of primary care staff Confidence Lack of integrated care
Adverse effects of medication	Extrapyramidal side effects Weight gain Glucose intolerance and diabetes Cardiovascular effects Sexual dysfunction Neuroleptic malignant syndrome
Environment	Poverty Poor housing Social exclusion

Health behaviours of people with SMI

The most commonly cited reasons for the increased morbidity and mortality rates in people with SMI are their high rates of smoking, poor diet, lack of exercise, co-morbid substance use and unsafe sexual practices (Lambert *et al.*, 2003). In a survey of 102 service users with schizophrenia, McCreadie (2002) identified that 70% were smokers, 86% of females and 70% of males were overweight, and 53% had raised cholesterol, all significantly higher rates than in the general population. These behaviours are often referred to in the literature as *lifestyle choices*. Services users, however, would probably argue that these are not choices at all, but the physical, psychological, social and environmental consequences of having a severe mental illness and the treatments prescribed for them (Robson & Gray, 2007).

Smoking

People with schizophrenia and bi-polar disorder smoke up to three times more than the general population (Hughes *et al.*, 1986; de Leon *et al.*, 2002). They are heavier smokers, smoking more than 25 cigarettes a day (Kelly & McCreadie, 2000) and are more likely to smoke high tar cigarettes. The reasons why people with SMI may have such high rates of smoking are well researched and include neurobiological, psychological, behavioural and social. This makes it extremely difficult (though certainly possible) to alter smoking behaviour in this population. An increase in dopamine through inhaling nicotine has been shown to alleviate certain psychiatric symptoms (e.g. negative symptoms, cognitive dysfunction, side effects of antipsychotic medication) and therefore smoking has been viewed as a means of self-medication (Dalack *et al.*, 1998). Smoking may also improve the attention and selective processing of information that is normally impaired in people with schizophrenia (Alder *et al.*, 1998). Qualitative studies have found that people with schizophrenia smoke out of habit and routine, for relaxation purposes, as a way of making social contact, for pleasure and as a way of gaining control in their lives (Luckstead *et al.*, 2000; Lawn *et al.*, 2002). Smoking is ingrained in the culture of psychiatry. Health professionals often doubt this client group's motivation to stop smoking and promote smoking by using cigarettes to manage service users' behaviour (McNeill, 2001).

Diet

In a national survey on behalf of the Food Standards Agency and Department of Health in the UK, Marriot and Buttris (2003) report that although the overall diet of the British public has improved in the past 10 years, the consumption of fruit, vegetables, oily fish, wholegrain products and fibre are still below the recommended intake levels. In a survey of the dietary habits of 102 people with SMI by McCreadie (2003) the average fruit and vegetable intake for these people was 16 portions a week, compared with recommended intake of 35 per week (Department of Health, 2004). The physical health consequences of a poor diet include coronary heart disease, CVD, high blood pressure, diabetes, obesity, some cancers, osteoporosis and dental caries. There is also evidence to suggest that saturated fats from dietary intake of meat and dairy products are associated with worse outcomes in schizophrenia (Peet, 2004). There is a particularly strong association between sugar consumption and poorer outcome in schizophrenia whereas consumption of fish and sea food, particularly omega 3 fatty acids, has been associated with better outcomes (Peet, 2004).

Physical activity

The World Health Organization, (WHO) identifies physical inactivity as one of the leading causes of death in developed countries (WHO, 2003). People with SMI have been shown to be less physically active than the general population (Brown *et al.*, 1999; McCreadie, 2003). Encouraging people to follow national recommended guidelines to improve their physical health through activity is a major public health challenge. People with SMI face additional challenges to lead a more active lifestyle. The sedating effects of some medications make it more difficult to be active. Depression or negative symptoms of schizophrenia may make it difficult to get motivated. The financial cost of joining a gym may be off-putting or the lack of confidence to do so may also influence a person's decision to participate in exercise. However, the benefits of exercise are well documented and can prevent, delay the onset of, or help with, the management of a number of physical and mental health problems.

Illness related factors

In addition to health behaviours and the limitations of the health service, we need to take into account the effect severe mental illness has on help seeking behaviour. It has been suggested that people with schizophrenia are less likely to spontaneously report physical symptoms (Jeste *et al.*, 1996). They may be unaware of physical problems because of the cognitive deficits associated with the schizophrenia (Phelan *et al.*, 2001), because of a high pain tolerance (Dworkin, 1994) or due to reduced pain sensitivity associated with antipsychotic medication (Jeste *et al.*, 1996).

Health service factors

The physical health care needs of this population have long been overlooked by both primary care and MHPs in secondary care (Phelan *et al.*, 2001). This may be due to lack of clarity and guidance about whose role it is to assess and manage the physical health care of this group. It may also be due to lack of training and the attitudes and confidence of the mental health workforce.

Differences in opinions have been reported about what mental health nurses regard as important areas for their education and training and what mental health service users consider to be important.

Jones and Lowe (2003) carried out a training needs analysis of 235 mental health nurses working in acute in-patient settings throughout the UK. Twenty-four nurses generated a list of topics they believed were important for post registration training. Two thousand mental health nurses who were registered with the Royal College of Nursing were sent a questionnaire asking them to rate the most important areas of training. Two hundred and thirty five mental health nurses working in acute in-patient settings returned the questionnaire. Training in physical health was not a topic generated in the focus groups. This sample of nurses rated risk assessment and the management of violence as the most important areas for training.

Simpson (1999) interviewed 52 patients and 24 carers as part of a larger project to identify the education and training needs of community mental health nurses (CMHNs). Whilst users and carers were mostly positive about the current practice of CMHNs, they identified that nurses should receive more training in providing information and advice about physical and medical problems. Nash (2005) undertook a training needs analysis of 168 qualified mental health nurses in the UK mental health trust. He found that 45% (n = 168) of mental health nurses had no formal training in physical health care, though 96% (n = 161) said they would be willing to attend physical health training. These nurses also reported lack of managerial support, staff shortages and lack of resources as potential barriers to attending training. Hyland *et al.* (2003) examined the attitudes and practice of 27 case managers working in Melbourne, Australia. Although 90% of the sample believed that they had responsibility to improve the physical health care of people with SMI on their caseloads, a third of the sample believed that physical health needs were of secondary importance to mental health needs. Hyland *et al.* (2003) also reported that case managers did not systematically review health behaviours of the people on their caseloads, with preventative health checks receiving less attention.

There is evidence about the lack of assessment, monitoring and recording of the physical health status of people with SMI. In a study by Patton *et al.* (2004) case notes of 606 in-patients with SMI were reviewed to determine if weight, cholesterol and triglycerides had been assessed during admission. Only 18% (n = 113) of patients had their weight recorded and 3.5% (n = 21) had their lipids monitored during their admission. In a survey of case notes of 63 patients in a community mental health service, 24% (n = 16) had their blood pressure recorded in the previous 5 years and 16% (n = 10) had their weight recorded (Greening, 2005).

Treatment related factors

Psychotropic medication has undoubtedly improved quality of life for many people with SMI and enabled people to live in the community rather than spend long periods of time in hospital. The National Service Framework for Mental Health (Department of Health, 1999) placed pharmacological therapies at the heart of modern psychiatric care. However we have known for many years that antipsychotic medication has a deleterious effect on physical health. For example, in the late 1950s, within a year of its introduction, there were reports that chlorpromazine, one of the older antipsychotics, was linked to hyperglycaemia, glycosuria and weight gain (Koren, 2004). With the reintroduction of clozapine in 1991 and the subsequent novel agents risperidone, olanzapine, quetiapine, and most recently aripiprazole, there has been heightened interest in the relationship between antipsychotic drugs and physical health. Antipsychotics, antidepressants, mood stabilisers and benzodiazepines all have an impact on physical health. The assessment, management and evaluation of side effects of psychotropic medication need to be an integral part of the mental health practitioner's role during the care planning process. Treatment related factors that have an impact on physical health include extrapyramidal symptoms, weight gain, insulin resistance and diabetes and sexual dysfunction.

Extrapyramidal symptoms

Acute extrapyramidal symptoms (EPSs) refers to pseudo-parkinsonism, dystonia and akathisia. It has been estimated that 50–90% of service users treated with conventional antipsychotics (e.g. chlorpromazine, haloperidol) develop acute EPSs (Casey, 1991). There is a variation in the course of each EPS. Dystonia commonly occurs within 12–48 hours of starting treatment, akathisia starts within a few hours to a few weeks of starting medication or increasing the dose, pseudo-parkinsonism takes days to weeks after starting medication or increasing the dose (Taylor *et al.*, 2005). EPSs can have a negative impact on satisfaction and adherence with medication. It is therefore important that mental health practitioners are vigilant in identifying EPSs. In a survey by Gray *et al.* (2001) 80% of community mental health nurses reported that they routinely asked patients about side effects, however very few assessed side effects in a systematic way using valid and reliable assessment tools. Table 12.2, later in the chapter, gives further information about the presentation, assessment and management of EPSs.

Weight gain

There is conflicting evidence whether people with SMI have higher rates of obesity than the general population. What appears to be emerging in the recent literature is that women with SMI appear to be more obese than men (Allison *et al.*, 1999; Cohen *et al.*, 2002). It is also increasingly recognised that people with SMI have higher rates of upper body obesity (i.e. visceral fat), which is more of a risk factor for developing cardiovascular disease and diabetes than overall body fat (Ryan & Thakore, 2001). The impact of obesity on one's health can lead to a number of disabling conditions such as increased blood pressure, insulin resistance, respiratory difficulties, chronic musculoskeletal problems, increased risk of diabetes, and an increased risk of heart disease (WHO, 2003). Both typical and atypical antipsychotic drugs have an effect on dopaminergic, serotonergic, histaminergic, cholinergic and adrenergic neurotransmitters, all of which are associated with the aetiology of weight gain. Clozapine and olanzapine are commonly associated with weight gain compared with other antipsychotics and initially cause insulin sensitivity leading to hypoglyceamia and food cravings (Werneke *et al.*, 2003). The noticeable difference in body composition between service users with SMI and healthy controls of a higher waist to hip ratio and more visceral fat has also been found in people with schizophrenia who have never taken antipsychotics (Thakore *et al.*, 2002). Antipsychotics, some mood stabilisers and antidepressants increase one's appetite and make people thirsty. Fast food and carbonated drinks that are high in saturated fats and sugar are a quick way of relieving these problems and an affordable and easy option for people on a low income. Weight gain added to schizophrenia or bipolar disorder increases the social stigma people have to endure and increases the risk of people stopping their medication (Robson & Gray, 2007).

Sexual effects

All antidepressants (particularly the selective serotonin reuptake inhibitors, SSRIs), mood stabilisers (particularly lithiuim and carbamazepine), typical and atypical are known to cause sexual problems (Taylor *et al.*, 2005). The adrenergic and anticholinergic effects of antipsychotic medication affect sexual functioning and the antagonism of dopamine caused by antipsychotics in the tuberinfundibular part of the brain leads to hyperprolactinaemia (raised levels of the hormone prolactin). A consequence of raised prolactin levels is a decrease in testosterone in both men and women leading to sexual dysfunction and a decrease in oestrogen in women. Most studies have shown that the older antipsychotics are associated with a two- to ten-fold increase in prolactin levels and usually develop over the first week of treatment and remain high throughout the period of use. Once treatment stops, prolactin levels return to normal within 2–3 weeks (Hummer & Huber, 2004). The atypicals that have been associated with increased levels are amisulpride and risperidone (Halbreich & Kahn, 2003). Prevalence of hyperprolactinaemia in females taking risperidone has been reported to be as high as 88% compared with 47% in people taking typicals (Kinon *et al.*, 2003). In adolescents treated for childhood-onset schizophrenia 6 weeks of olanzapine raised prolactin levels beyond the upper limit of the normal range in 70% of patients (Wudarsky *et al.*, 1999). There are numerous clinical effects of hyperprolactinaemia seen in people with SMI who are taking antipsychotic medication. Women experience amenorrhoea, disturbed menstrual cycle and anovulation. Both men and women experience galactorea (leaking milk from the breasts), gynaecomastia (painful and swollen breasts) and sexual dysfunction (Dickson & Glazer, 1999; Halbreich & Kahn, 2003). There is contradictory evidence that the reduction in oestrogen caused by raised prolactin levels is associated with increased rates of breast cancer (Halbreich *et al.*, 1996) and osteoporosis (Halbreich & Palter, 1996; Hummer & Huber, 2004).

Case study 12.2   An example of integrated physical and mental health care planning for a female client with suspected hyperprolactinaemia.

History
Maureen is a 34-year-old woman who was admitted under section 2 to a mental health unit. She is the mother of three children and prior to her admission her husband had been finding it increasingly difficult to cope with Maureen's aggressive and chaotic behaviour. On admission Maureen presented as hypomanic with pressure of speech and expressed that she believed she was pregnant. A pregnancy test performed on admission and again over subsequent weeks was negative. Maureen was commenced on a mood stabiliser (sodium valproate) and an antipsychotic (risperidone). After six weeks in hospital Maureen's mental state stabilised, her speech became more coherent and she had greater insight into her situation. However, she continued to believe that she was pregnant.

Presenting problem
A client believes that she is pregnant despite negative pregnancy tests. It is possible that she is experiencing side effects of antipsychotic medication (risperidone). This was expressed in the client's own words as: '*I have not had a period for 3 months and feel that I am pregnant but the pregnancy tests have been negative. I am very upset that no-one believes me.*'

Assessment

- Menstrual history enquired about
- Sexual health history enquired about as clients are unlikely to spontaneously report sexual dysfunction
- Assessment of current physical symptoms
- Assessment for side effects of antipsychotic medication carried out using a recognised assessment tool – the Liverpool University Neuroleptic Side Effect Rating Scale (LUNSERS) (Day *et al.*, 1995)
- Blood test to establish prolactin levels
- Further assessment of Maureen's beliefs regarding pregnancy.

Goal setting
In the client's own words: '*I want to understand why I feel pregnant but the tests are negative*'.

Implementation
The primary nurse to explore Maureen's beliefs and exchange information.

Exploring beliefs about medication
Ask Maureen to rate how strongly she believes that she is pregnant on a scale of 0%–100%
(0 = not convinced, 100% = absolutely convinced)
Ask Maureen what has happened/is happening for her to think this. Then ask her is there anything that has happened to make her think it might not be the case.

Exchanging information

- Find out from Maureen what she currently knows about the effects and side effects of her prescribed medication.

- Ask her what she would like to know.
- Primary nurse to provide information based on Maureen's information.
- Ask her how this new information has affected her.
- Ask Maureen to predict what it would mean to her if blood tests reveal that her medication is causing the physical symptoms she is experiencing.
- Re-rate how strongly she believes she is pregnant.

Pharmacological management:
Consider switching to a prolactin sparing drug if blood tests reveal hyperprolactinaemia and Maureen continues to believe that she is pregnant.

If switching to a prolactin sparing drug family planning advice should be given as this will stop the anovulation and she will be at an increased risk of pregnancy. Sodium valproate is a contraindicated medication during pregnancy (Taylor *et al.*, 2005).

Outcome/Evaluation
Maureen revealed that she believed she was pregnant, despite several negative pregnancy tests, because she had not had her menstrual period for 3 months and 'felt pregnant'. She elaborated by telling her primary nurse that her breasts felt swollen and she had been producing milk. This was to her incontrovertible evidence that she was to have a child. Maureen was able to identify some evidence for not being pregnant however, e.g. she had not put on weight, she had not felt sick, 7 pregnancy tests could not all be wrong. Blood tests revealed a significantly raised prolactin level. The nurse and Maureen discussed how her prescribed medication worked and why her periods had stopped and she was experiencing the other unpleasant symptoms. Maureen requested that her medication was changed and she was prescribed quetiapine. Her periods returned 2 months later.

Following the implementation of the care plan Maureen's conviction in her belief reduced from 95% to 50%.

At her next care plan review meeting it was agreed that Maureen would continue with her new medication that the multidisciplinary team would regularly monitor side effects of the medication and continue to have discussions about her occasional belief that she is pregnant.

Clinical implications
This case example highlights the importance of information exchange between client, prescriber and other members of the multidisciplinary team. Some professionals may believe that giving information about medication may result in non-compliance. However, Taylor *et al.* (2005) caution that being economical with the truth is unethical and may ultimately damage the therapeutic relationship or result in litigation. Clients who are very unwell should be consulted about their choice of drug as soon as reasonably possible.

Neuroleptic malignant syndrome

Neuroleptic malignant syndrome (NMS) is a rare though potentially fatal consequence of all antipsychotic drugs or any drugs that induce dopamine-2 receptor blockade. Reported incidence and mortality rates with the use of typical drugs are 0.2% to 1%. There are case reports of NMS occurring with the use of atypicals but this is less common than with the older drugs. NMS usually occurs when people are taking drugs within the therapeutic range, though studies suggest that people are more likely to experience it if they take high doses or they are rapidly increased. Some studies suggest that greater risk is posed if the patient is catatonic, is exhausted and dehydrated or has a previous history of NMS. Signs include hyperthermia and profuse sweating, fluctuating blood pressure and tachycardia, muscle rigidity (often referred to as lead pipe rigidity), coarse tremor, confusion, mutism and stupor leading to coma and death if not treated. Blood tests reveal elevated creatine kinase, leucocytosis and altered liver function. If NMS is suspected liaison with medical colleagues is essential. Antipsycotics need to be withdrawn in the first instance and temperature, pulse and BP monitored until a diagnosis is confirmed through blood tests. Patients will need rehydrating and the high temperature treated. Moderate to severe cases will need to be referred to an emergency unit where dopamine agonists and muscle relaxants may be prescribed. Patients usually recover in one to two weeks and antipsychotic medication can be restarted with very close monitoring of physical and biochemical issues (Taylor *et al.*, 2005).

Environmental related factors

One also needs to consider the socio-economic consequences of suffering from a mental health disorder, such as poverty, poor housing, reduced social networks, lack of employment and meaningful occupation opportunities, and social stigma, all of which impact on physical health and health behaviours of people with SMI.

Now we have an understanding of the challenges faced by people with SMI and mental health services we will discuss the role of the mental health practitioner in the assessment, monitoring and management, and evaluation of the physical health of people with SMI.

Assessment

There is currently no consensus about the type and frequency of physical health assessment and management of people with SMI, although a number of guidelines and recommendations exist that can guide our current practice (NICE, 2002; Marder *et al.*, 2004; Phelan *et al.*, 2004; Department of Health, 2006). In the assessment phase of the care planning process a number of factors should be included.

Current physical health status of the service user should be assessed e.g. blood pressure, pulse, temperature, weight, body mass index and waist circumference, condition of skin, dental health and eye health (Table 12.2). It should be established if the service user is receiving any current treatment for physical health conditions. We need to ask the service user if they have a family history of any illnesses, e.g. diabetes or heart disease. A health behaviour assessment should include dietary intake, nutritional status, amount of physical activity undertaken, smoking behaviour, alcohol use, illicit drug use, sexual health and side effects of medication (Robson & Gray, 2007).

Table 12.2   Some useful assessment tools.

Health behaviour	Assessment tool	Description
Overall physical health	The physical health check (Phelan *et al.*, 2004)	27 items divided into 4 sections: Section 1: current medication, known illnesses, lifestyle, diet, exercise and smoking Section 2: current physical symptoms Section 3: physical investigations and health screening Section 4: action plan
Exercise	International physical activity questionnaire (IPAQ) (Craig *et al.*, 2003)	A brief questionnaire that can be self administered or administered over the telephone. Five questions about the user's levels of vigorous, moderate, gentle and sedentary activities over the past 7 days are assessed. Questionnaires and scoring criteria can be found on www.ipaq.ki.se/ This questionnaire has been validated for people with schizophrenia (Faulkner *et al.*, 2006)
Smoking	Fagerstrom test for nicotine dependence (Heatherton *et al.*, 1991)	A six item questionnaire about smoking behaviour and dependence. Validated for use in schizophrenia (Weinberger *et al.*, 2007)
Diet	Food diaries Body weight Body mass index (BMI) Waist circumference	BMI = weight in kg ÷ height in m^2 BMI over 25 kg/m^2 = overweight BMI over 30 kg/m^2 = obese A waist circumference of more than 35 inches in women and more than 40 inches in men is predictive of future risk of heart disease or diabetes (Ryan & Thakore, 2001)

Goal setting

When negotiating with the service user and carer how to improve or maintain a good level of physical health, the MHP should facilitate the process of setting goals that are specific, measurable, achievable, realistic and time orientated (SMART) (Egan, 2001). It is very easy for service users and their carers to be overly ambitious about changing health behaviours and either try and do too many things at once e.g. change their eating habits, start exercising and stop smoking or set unrealistic goals e.g. to loose 4 kg in a short space of time. It is also important that the goal is sufficiently challenging and outcome focused to motivate the client. The goal also needs to focus on an outcome that is important to the client rather than focusing on the needs and concerns of the professional or the service. Progress towards a goal is unlikely to be successful if the client does not feel that the goal belongs to them (Egan, 2001). It may be useful to work with the client on reframing goals to be positively focused e.g. rather than framing the goal statement in terms of *'giving up smoking'* it could be reframed in terms of a positive outcome that this may lead to, *'I would like to be able to walk to the shop daily to buy my groceries without having to stop due to breathlessness'*.

Interventions

NICE (2002) have produced an algorithm to guide one's practice about promoting the physical health of people with schizophrenia (Figure 12.1).

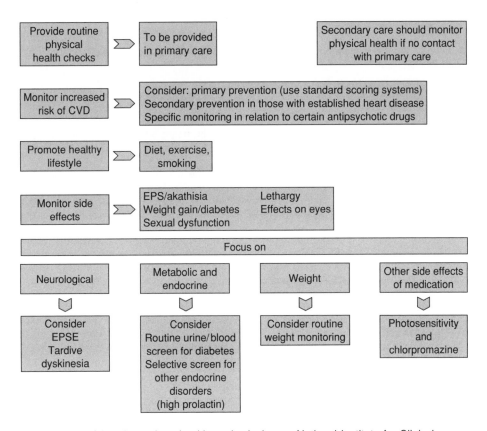

Figure 12.1   Clinical practice algorithm: physical care. National Institute for Clinical Excellence (2002). Schizophrenia: Core Interventions in the Treatment and Management of Schizophrenia in Primary and Secondary Care (NICE 2002). London: NICE. Available www.nice.org.uk. Reproduced with permission.

These recommendations have training implications for mental health practitioners who work in primary care, in-patient units and in community teams, who may lack the knowledge and confidence to carry out these recommendations. This next part of the chapter aims to fill some of the gaps in knowledge and give suggestions of what mental health practitioners can do to work collaboratively with people with SMI to promote optimal physical health.

Interventions to help service users manage their weight through healthy eating and exercise and how to minimise the use of substances such as tobacco should be integrated into routine mental health care and should begin when the service user first comes into contact with mental health services (Robson & Gray, 2007). Most mental health services have access to dieticians, physiotherapists and smoking cessation specialists. Mental health practitioners could actively collaborate with these professionals to design specialist health promotion programmes for people with SMI. There are also many simple interventions that practitioners can incorporate into routine care planning with regard to both increasing physical activity (Box 12.2) and promoting a healthy diet (Box 12.3).

Box 12.2   What can mental health practitioners do to promote increased physical activity in people with SMI?

- For general health benefits, adults need to be achieving at least 30 minutes of moderately intense activity on at least 5 days of the week (Department of Health, 2004).
- Service users may need explanations of what is meant by moderate intensity (i.e. working hard enough to be breathing more heavily than normal, becoming slightly warmer but still be able to talk).
- Service users also may need explanations of the different types of exercise one needs to do to improve and maintain overall health. For example, endurance or aerobic activities that improve cardiovascular health could include brisk walking, cycling, jogging, swimming and dancing. Activities for improving flexibility and mobility could include gardening, housework and walking. Strengthening exercises can improve balance, muscle tone, bone health and increase the rate at which the body burns calories, can be achieved by climbing stairs, carrying shopping or walking uphill.
- Most in-patient mental health services have access to gyms and physical training instructors, and practitioners can act as a link between such services.
- Building confidence in a hospital gym may help people feel more at ease with accessing public gyms once discharged, whilst acquiring personal information about the best way to exercise.
- For those people who lack the confidence, motivation and finances to attend public gyms, there are still many ways of increasing one's activity that can be incorporated into people's lives without any disruption or much more organisation or effort. For example, breaking up the period of exercise into three 10 minute bouts of brisk walking throughout the day is initially more appealing than 30 minutes all at once and more manageable for in-patient staff trying to promote healthy behaviours on busy acute wards. Brisk walking is good for endurance and also strengthening bones and muscles.
- Nurses can help people with SMI explore their beliefs about exercise and help people problem solve barriers to increasing activity.

Box 12.3 What can mental health practitioners do to promote healthy diets in people with SMI?

- Food choices for people with SMI not only depend on individual choice but also on cost and affordability of food, kitchen equipment and storage, skills and confidence in budgeting, shopping and cooking, and knowledge of nutrition.
- It makes sense to start with helping people sort out any practical problems they may have with kitchen equipment, storage and accessibility of food.
- Acquiring skills and confidence in budgeting, shopping and cooking could be done in partnership with other members of the multidisciplinary team, such as occupational therapists and support workers.
- Nutritional educational information can be shared with people in a way that is understandable and meaningful to people with SMI. There are many readable and easy to follow educational leaflets (for example, produced by the British Heart Foundation) that are freely available to members of the public.
- Diets that are low in sugar, simple carbohydrates and saturated fat but high in whole grain products, complex carbohydrates, fibre, fruit, vegetables and omega 3 fatty acids should be encouraged. Some people may need more practical help with how to actually modify eating habits, for example suggesting recipes, menu plans and how to read food labels.
- Personal clinical experience also suggests that creative solutions need to be found for users on in-patient units who often order in extra food from local take-aways because of increased appetites and lack of alternative food options to meet this need.

There are a number of simple health promotion strategies mental health workers can safely use to help people with schizophrenia who wish to stop smoking. Smoking cessation guidelines for health professionals recommend the four 'A's approach to smoking cessation i.e. ask, advise, assist and arrange (West *et al.*, 2000) which can be adapted to meet the needs of people with schizophrenia (Box 12.4).

Conclusion

It is well established that people with severe mental illness (SMI) have higher rates of death and physical illness compared with the general population (Harris & Barrowclough, 1998) and die at a younger age (Newman & Bland, 1991). The causes of poor physical health in people with a severe mental illness are complex and interactive. The adverse effects of medication have a significant impact on physical health, as do health behaviours of people with SMI. Not only has the physical health care of people with SMI been neglected in the past, the training health professionals receive to assess, monitor and manage physical health care in people with SMI has also been lacking. Mental health practitioners have an opportunity to improve the physical and mental health of people with SMI through systematic monitoring and collaborative health promotion interventions initiated at the onset of people's illness. Poor physical health in people with SMI does not have to be inevitable.

Box 12.4 What can mental health practitioners do to promote smoking cessation in people with schizophrenia?

- **Ask** all people with schizophrenia about their smoking status as a matter of routine.
- **Assess** the smoker's level of nicotine dependence perhaps by using the Fagerstrom Test for nicotine dependence (Heatherton *et al.*, 1991). Although not validated for use in people with schizophrenia it is a quick and reliable way of measuring levels of tobacco dependence. The person is asked 6 questions such as how many cigarettes they smoke in a day and how soon after waking up do they have their first cigarette? The sum of the answers predicts how dependent the person is.
- **Assess** readiness to quit. When the person is not acutely ill, or in a state of relapse, their readiness to quit can be assessed. Mental health workers can simply ask how ready the person is to quit, i.e. not ready, unsure or ready. Some people will not be interested in stopping, others will be ambivalent and some people will be keen.
- **Advise** smokers who are not ready to quit about smoking and the benefits of cessation. Information should be provided in a balanced, non-judgemental way at a time when the service user is ready to accept it.
- For people who are not sure about quitting **explore** this ambivalence. This can be done by asking the user the good and not so good things about smoking as well as the not so good things and good things about quitting. At this time, information can also be given about local specialist smoking cessation services.
- If the person is ready to stop then the worker needs to **assess** the risks of that person stopping. It is important to understand if the person has had any previous attempt at quitting, how they managed it and how it affected their mental health. Mental health workers could work alongside the specialist practitioners in their local smoking cessation service, to **assist** the service user with the pharmacological (e.g. nicotine replacement therapy) and **arrange** for any psychological support that may be needed to make a successful quit attempt and prevent a relapse of the service user's mental health condition.

References

Alder, L.E., Olincy, A., Waldo, M., Harris, J., Griffith, J., Stevens, K., Flach, K., Nagamoto, H., Bickford, P., Leonard, S. & Freedman, R. (1998). Schizophrenia, Sensory Gating and Nicotinic Receptors. *Schizophrenia Bulletin.* **24(2)**, 189–202.

Allison, D.B., Fontaine, K.R., Heo, M., Mentore, J.L., Cappelleri, J.C., Chamdler, L.P., Wieden, P.J. & Cheskin, L.J. (1999). The Distribution Of Body Mass Index Among Individuals With and Without Schizophrenia. *Journal of Clinical Psychiatry.* **60(4)**, 215–220.

Brown, S. (1997). Excess Mortality of Schizophrenia: A Meta Analysis. *British Journal of Psychiatry.* **171**, 502–508.

Brown, S., Birtwistle. J., Roe, L. & Thompson, C. (1999). The Unhealthy Lifestyle of People with Schizophrenia. *Psychological Medicine.* **29**, 697–701.

Brown, S., Inskipp, H. & Barraclough, B. (2000). Causes of Excess Mortality of Schizophrenia. *British Journal of Psychiatry.* **177**, 212–217.

Busche, B. & Holt, R. (2004). Prevalence Of Diabetes and Impaired Glucose Tolerance In Patients With Schizophrenia. *British Journal of Psychiatry.* **184**, S67–S71.

Casey, D. (1991). Neuroleptic Drug Induced Extra-Pyramidal Syndromes and Tardive Dyskinesia. *Schizophrenia Research.* **4**, 109–120.

Cohen, A. & Hove, M. (2001). *Physical Health of The Severe and Enduring Mentally Ill.* London: Sainsbury Centre For Mental Health.

Cohen, M.E., Dembling, B. & Schorling, J.B. (2002). The Association Between Schizo-phrenia and Cancer: A Population–Based Mortality Study. *Schizophrenia Research*. **57**, 139–146.

Craig, C.L., Marshall, A.L., Sjostrom, M., Bauman, A.E., Booth, M.L., Ainsworth, B.E., Pratt, M., Ekelund, U., Yngve, A., Sallis, J.F. & OJA, P. (2003). International physical activity questionnaire: 12-country reliability and validity. *Medicine & Science of Sports Exercise*. **35**, 1381–95.

Dalack, G.W., Healy, D.J. & Meador-Woodruff, J.H. (1998). Nicotine Dependence in Schizophrenia: Clinical Phenomena and Laboratory Findings. *American Journal of Psychiatry*. **155**, 1490–1501.

Day, J.C., Wood, G., Dewey, M. & Bentall, R.P. (1995). A Self Rating Scale For Measur-ing Neuroleptic Side Effects: Validation In A Group Of Schizophrenic Patients. *British Journal Of Psychiatry*. **166(5)**, 650–653.

de Leon, J., Becona, E., Gurpegui, M., Gonzalez-Pinto, A. & Diaz, F.J. (2002). The Association Between High Nicotine Dependence and Severe Mental Illness May Be Consistent Across Countries. *Journal of Clinical Psychiatry*. **63(9)**, 812–816.

Department of Health (1990). *The NHS and Community Care Act*. London: HMSO.

Department of Health (1999). *National Service Framework for Mental Health*. London: The Stationery Office.

Department of Health (2001). *Diabetes National Service Framework*. London: The Station-ery Office.

Department of Health (2004). *At Least 5 A Week*. London: The Stationery Office.

Department of Health (2005). *Choosing Health: Making Healthy Choices Easier*. London: The Stationery Office.

Department of Health (2006). *From Values To Action: The Chief Nursing Officer's Review Of Mental Health Nursing*. London: The Stationery Office.

Dickson, R.A. & Glazer, W.M. (1999). Neuroleptic-Induced Hyperprolactinaemia. *Schizo-phrenia Researc*. **35**, S75–S86.

Dixon, L., Leticia, P., Delahanty, J., Fischer, P.J. & Lehman, A. (1999). The Association Of Medical Co Morbidity In Schizophrenia With Poor Physical Health. *Journal of Nervous and Mental Disease*. **187(8)**, 496–502.

Dworkin, R.H. (1994). Pain Insensitivity In Schizophrenia: Neglected Phenomena and Some Implications. *Schizophrenia Bulletin*. **20**, 235–248.

Egan, G. (2001). *The Skilled Helper: A Problem-management Approach To Helping*. Belmont, Ca: Wadsworth Publishing.

Expert Panel on the Diagnosis and Classification of Diabetes Mellitus (2004). Diagnosis and Classification Of Diabetes Mellitus. *Diabetes Care*. **27**, S5–S10.

Faulkner, G., Cohn, T. & Remington, G. (2006). Validation of a physical activity assess-ment tool for individuals with schizophrenia. *Schizophrenia Research*. **82**, 225–31.

Goff, D.C., Sullivan, L.M., McEvoy, P., Meyer, J.M., Nasrallah, H.A., Daumit, G.L., Lamberti, S., D'Agnosino, R.B., Stoup, T.S., Davis, S. & Lieberman, J.A. (2005). A Comparison Of Ten Year Cardiac Risk Estimates In Schizophrenia Patients From The CATIE Study and Matched Controls. *Schizophrenia Research*. **80**, p45–53.

Gough, S. & Peveler, R. (2004). Diabetes and Its Prevention: Pragmatic Solutions for People with Schizophrenia. *British Journal of Psychiatry*. **184(supp47)**, S106–S111.

Gray, R., Wykes, T., Parr, A.M., Hails, E. & Gournay, K. (2001). The use of outcome measures to evaluate the efficacy and tolerability of antipsychotic medication: a com-parison of Thorn graduates and CPN practice. *Journal of Psychiatric and Mental Health Nursing*. **8**, 191–196.

Greening, J. (2005). Physical Health of Patients in Rehabilitation and Recovery: A Survey Of Case Note Records. *Psychiatric Bulletin.* **29**, 210–212.

Halbreich, U. & Kahn, L.S. (2003). Hyperprolactinemia and Schizophrenia: Mechanisms and Clinical Aspects. *Journal of Psychiatric Practice.* **9(5)**, 344–351.

Halbreich, U. & Palter, S. (1996). Accelerated Osteoporosis In Psychiatric Patients: Possible Pathophysiology Processes. *Schizophrenia Bulletin.* **22(3)**, 447–454.

Halbreich, U., Shen, J. & Panaro, V. (1996). Are Chronic Psychiatric Patients At An Increased Risk For Developing Breast Cancer? *American Journal of Psychiatry.* **153**, 559–560.

Harris, E.C. & Barrowclough, B. (1998). Excess Mortality Of Mental Disorder. *British Journal of Psychiatry.* **173**, 11–53.

Heatherton, T.F., Kozlowski, L.T., Frecker, R.C. & Fagerstrom, K.O. (1991). The Fagerström Test for Nicotine Dependence: a revision of the Fagerstrom Tolerance Questionnaire Addiction. *British Journal of Addiction.* **86(9)**, 1119–1127.

Holt, R.I.G., Peveler, R.C. & Byrne, C.D. (2004). Schizophrenia, The Metabolic Syndrome and Diabetes. *Diabetic Medicine.* **21**, 515–523.

Holt, R.I.G. & Peveler, R.C. (2006). Association Between Antipsychotic Drugs and Diabetes. *Diabetes, Obesity and Metabolism.* **8**, 125–135.

Hughes, J.R., Hatsukami, D.K. & Mitchell, J.E. (1986). Prevalence Of Smoking Among Psychiatric Outpatients. *American Journal of Psychiatry.* **143**, 993–997.

Hummer, M. & Huber, J. (2004). Hyperprolactinaemia and Antipsychotic Therapy In Schizophrenia. *Current Medical Research Opinion.* **20(2)**, 189–197.

Hyland, B., Judd, F., Davidson, S., Jolly, D. & Hocking, B. (2003). Case Managers Attitudes to the Physical Health of Their Patients. *Australian and New Zealand Journal of Psychiatry.* **37(6)**, 710–714.

Jeste, D., Gladsjo, J., Lindmayer, L. & Lacro, J. (1996). Medical Comorbidity In Schizophrenia. *Schizophrenia Bulletin.* **22(3)**, p413–430.

Jin, H., Meyer, J.M. & Jeste, D.V. (2004). Atypical Antipsychotics and Glucose Dysregulation: A Systematic Review. *Schizophrenia Research.* **71**, 195–212.

Jones, J. & Lowe, T. (2003). The Education and Training Needs Of Qualified Mental Health Nurses Working In Acute Mental Health Services. *Nurse Education Today.* **23(8)**, 610–619.

Kelly, C. & McCreadie, R. (2000). Cigarette Smoking and Schizophrenia, *Advances in Psychiatric Treatment.* **6**, 327–332.

Kinon, B.J., Gilmore, J.A., Lui, H. & Halbreich, U.M. (2003). *Psychoneuroendocrinology.* **28**, 55–68.

Koren, D. (2004). Diabetes Mellitus and Schizophrenia: Historical Perspective. *British Journal of Psychiatry.* **184(supp 47)**, S64–S66.

Lambert, T.J.R., Velakoulis, D. & Pantelis, C. (2003). Medical Comorbidity In Schizophrenia. *Medical Journal of Australia.* **178**, S67–S70.

Lawn, S.J., Pols, R.G. & Barber, J.G. (2002). Smoking and Quitting: A Qualitative Study With Community-Living Psychiatric Clients. *Social Science & Medicine.* **54**, 93–104.

Lichtermann, D., Ekelund, J., Pukkala, E., Tanskanen & Lonnqvist, J. (2001). Incidence Of Cancer Among Persons With Schizophrenia and Their Relatives. *Archives of General Psychiatry.* **58(6)**, 573–578.

Luckstead, A., Dixon, L.B. & Sembly, J. (2000). A Focus Group Pilot Study of Tobacco Smoking among Psychosocial Rehabilitation Clients. *Psychiatric Services.* **51(12)**, 1544–1548.

Marder, S.R., Essock, S.M., Miller, A.L. & Buchanan, R.W. (2004). Physical Health Monitoring Of Patients With Schizophrenia. *American Journal of Psychiatry.* **161**, 1334–1349.

Marriot, H. & Buttris, J. (2003). Key Points From The National Diet and Nutrition Survey Of Adults Aged 16–64 Years. *Nutrition Bulletin.* **28**, 355–363.

McCreadie, R.G. (on behalf of the Scottish Co-morbidity study group) (2002). Use of Drugs, Alcohol and Tobacco By People With Schizophrenia: Case Control Study. *British Journal of Psychiatry.* **181**, 321–325.

McCreadie, R.G. (2003). Diet, Smoking and Cardiovascular Risk In People With Schizophrenia. *British Journal of Psychiatry.* **183**, 534–539.

McNeill, A. (2001). *Smoking and Mental Health: A Review Of The Literature. Smoke Free London.* London: ASH.

Mortenson, P.B. (1989). The Incidence Of Cancer In Schizophrenia Patients. *Journal of Epidemiology and Public Health.* **43**, 43–47.

Mortensen, P.B. (1994). The Occurrence Of Cancer In First Admitted Schizophrenic Patients. *Schizophrenia Research.* **12**, 185–194.

Nash, M. (2005). Physical Care Skills: A Training Needs Analysis Of Inpatient And Community Mental Health Nurses. *Mental Health Practice.* **9(4)**, 20–23.

National Institute for Clinical Excellence (2002). *Schizophrenia: Core Interventions In The Treatment and Management Of Schizophrenia In Primary and Secondary Care.* London: NICE.

National Institute for Clinical Excellence (2004). *Type 1 Disabetes in Adults: National Clinical Guidelines for Diagnosis and Management Primary & Secondary Care.* London: NICE.

Newcomer, J., Haupt, D.W., Fucetola, R., Melson, A.K., Schweiger, J.A., Cooper, B.P. & Selke, G. (2002). Abnormalities In Glucose Regulation During Antipsychotic Treatment Of Schizophrenia. *Archives of General Psychiatry.* **59**, 337–345.

Newman, S.C. & Bland, R.C. (1991). Mortality In A Cohort Of Patients With Schizophrenia: A Record Linage Study. *Canadian Journal of Psychiatry.* **36**, 293–245.

Osby, U., Correia, N., Brant, L., Ekbom, A. & Sparen, P. (2000). Mortality and Causes of Death in Schizophrenia in Stockholm County, Sweden. *Schizophrenia Research.* **45**, 21–28.

Parks, J., Svensden, D., Singer, P. & Foti, M.E. (2006). *Morbidity and Mortality In People With Serious Mental Illness.* Virginia, USA: National Association of State Mental Health Programme Directors.

Patton, C., Esop, R., Young, C. & Taylor, D. (2004). Obesity, Dyslipidaemias and Smoking In An In-patient Population Treated With Antipsychotic Drugs. *Acta Psychiatrica Scandinavica.* **110(4)**, 299–305.

Peet, M. (2004). Diet, Diabetes and Schizophrenia: Review and Hypothesis. *British Journal of Psychiatry.* **184(supp 47)**, S102–S105.

Phelan, M., Stradins, L., Amin, D., Isadore, R., Hitrov, C., Doyal, A. & Inglis, R. (2004). The Physical Health Check: A Tool for Mental Health Workers. *Journal of Mental Health.* **13(3)**, 277–284.

Phelan, M., Stradins, L. & Morrison, S. (2001). Physical Health Of People With Severe Mental Illness. *British Medical Journal.* **322**, 443–444.

Robson, D. & Gray, R. (2007). Serious Mental Illness and Physical Health Problems: A Discussion Paper. *International Journal of Nursing Studies.* **44**, 457–466.

Ryan, M.C. & Thakore, J.H. (2001). Physical Consequences of Schizophrenia and Its Treatment: The Metabolic Syndrome. *Life Sciences.* **71(3)**, 293–57.

Simpson, A. (1999). Creating Alliances: The Views Of Users and Carers On The Education and Training Needs Of Community Mental Health Nurses. *Journal of Psychiatric and Mental Health Nursing.* **6**, 347–356.

Schoos, R. & Cohen, C.I. (eds) (2003). *Medical Illness and Schizophrenia.* Vancouver: American Psychiatric Publishing.

Sokal, J., Messias, E., Dickerson, F.B., Kreyenbuhl, J., Brown, C.H., Goldberg, R.W. & Dixon, L.B. (2004). Co-morbidity Of Medical Illnesses Among Adults With Serious Mental Illness Who Are Receiving Community Psychiatric Services. *Journal of Nervous & Mental Disease.* **192(6)**, 421–7.

Taylor, D., Patton, C. & Kerwin, R. (2005). *The South London and Maudsley NHS Trust and Oxleas NHS Trust, 2005–2006 Prescribing Guideline.* London: Taylor and Francis. (8th edn).

Thakore, J.H., Mann, J.N., Vlahos, I., Martin, A. & Reznek, R. (2002). Increased Visceral Fat Distribution In Drug-Naïve and Drug Free Patients With Schizophrenia. *International Journal of Obesity Related Metabolic Disorders.* **26**, 137–141.

Weinberger, A.H., Sacco, K.A., Creeden, C.L., Vessicchio, J.C., Jatlow, P.I. & George, T.P. (2007). Effects of acute abstinence, reinstatement, and mecamylamine on biochemical and behavioural measures of cigarette smoking in schizophrenia. *Schizophrenia Research 2007.* **91(1–3)**, 217–25.

Werneke, U., Taylor, D., Sanders, T.A.B. & Wessley, S. (2003). Behavioural Management Of Antipsychotic Weight Gain: A Review. *Acta Psychiatrica Scandinavica.* **108**, 252–259.

West, R., McNeill, A. & Raw, M. (2000). Smoking Cessation Guidelines for Health Professionals. *Thorax.* **55**, 987–999.

World Health Organization (1991). *Implications For The Field Of Mental Health Of The European Targets For Attaining Health For All.* Geneva: WHO.

World Health Organization (2003). *Global Strategy on Diet, Physical Activity and Health.* Geneva: WHO.

Wudarsky, M., Nicolson, R. & Hamburger, S.D. (1999). Elevated Prolactin. In: Paediatric Patients On Typical and Atypical Antipsychotics. *Journal of Child and Adolescent Psychopharmacology.* **9**, 239–245.

Chapter 13

Integrated Care Pathways for Mental Health

Dennis Cross and Joan Murphy

Introduction

The purpose of this chapter is to explore the evidence for the development and proliferation of integrated pathways of care in mental health settings. Integrated models of service delivery have been developed to create integrated care based on population and patient need. The NHS Confederation (2006) states that integrated care pathways (ICPs) will provide a focus for clinical leadership and create viable hospital services for relatively small populations. Most of all, care pathways will make best use of all the resources that can be used to promote health and well being. One of the main challenges facing healthcare professionals, managers and administrators in the UK today, is trying to make the best use of limited resources, whilst providing high quality, timely, evidence-based, best practice. The ICP tool has much to offer, yet the many potential benefits often fail to be realised due to poor project planning and management. The ICP know-how information set out in this chapter aims to provide you with knowledge of ICP tools and the ICP Conceptual Framework, as well as access to further resources for ICP information, training and support.

The history and proliferation of ICPs

According to the National Library for Health (2005) critical path and process mapping methodology was first used in industry, particularly in the field of engineering from as early as the 1950s. In the 1980s, clinicians in the USA began to develop the pathway tool within managed care; they were re-defining the delivery of care and attempting to identify measurable outcomes that were focused on the patient rather than the system. The reason for this was that they needed to demonstrate efficient processes in order to fulfil the requirements of the US insurance industry.

In the early 1990s the NHS in the UK funded a patient focused initiative to support organisational change. This resulted in the investigation and development of concepts such as care pathways. In 1990 a team from the UK visited the USA to investigate the use of these pathways, or anticipated recovery pathways as they were then called. As a result of this visit, 12 pilot sites for pathways were set up in Northwest London in 1991/92. The West Midlands pathway development work also got underway. By 1994, the anticipated recovery pathway had evolved into the integrated care pathway (ICP), in the UK ICPs were clinician led and driven, locally agreed, had service user involvement and had best practice at their heart.

According to the National Library for Health (NLH) in response to the demand for a coordinated ICP users' group, the national pathways user group (later re-named the national pathway association) was set up in 1994. The NLH pathways database was launched in 2002 to enable the free sharing of ICPs and ICP projects across the U.K. The international web portal dedicated to ICPs was launched in 2002 to enable the free sharing of ICP information and to provide ICP user forums for discussion and sharing of best practice and development skills. Since 1992 ICPs have been developed and implemented across all healthcare settings in the UK (acute, community, primary, mental health, private, independent, NHS). ICPs are now used all around the world including the UK, USA, Canada, New Zealand, Australia, Germany, Belgium, and the Netherlands.

Definitions of integrated care pathways

Naidoo and Bullock (2001) consider that care pathways have been developed in a number of clinical areas and in many different ways. Basically, a care pathway could first be described as a pre-determined plan designed for service users or patients who have a specific diagnosis. This is usually a multi-disciplinary agreed route, based on research evidence where it is available or based on consensus where it is not. The consensus approach has some definite advantages in that both service users and professionals gain ownership of ICP implementation.

Every ICP needs an identified start point and end point but they usually vary in the way they are implemented. In a Scottish Executive Publication (2004) an ICP for the care of people with drug problems in acute psychiatric settings should begin on the day of admission to an acute psychiatric in-patient ward and end when the patient is discharged from the ward. In relation to an integrated care pathway for dementia, Naidoo and Bullock (2001) state that it includes the time from early diagnosis of dementia up to and including continuing care.

The purpose of introducing integrated care pathways in mental health is to introduce tools to improve the quality of mental health care. ICPs are usually developed for local use, often following an incident or a perceived local need within a particular group of service users. The term integration has many meanings and interpretations, and Hall and Howard (2006) consider that over recent years the term care pathway has been used in a variety of ways with various intentions. Hall and Howard go on to say that it has been used to describe various concepts from guidelines and protocols to general descriptions of a patient's journey or high-level process maps of services and processes of care. Consequently, they consider that it has become difficult to interpret the expression of integrated care pathway in a consistent way.

Integrated care can be conceived as client or consumer driven care and as such, it is similar to strategies in industry, agriculture, commercial services, or other public sectors such as education, town and country planning, youth care or public transport (EHMA, 2006). In all these sectors, supply-driven management systems are gradually being replaced by integrated, demand-driven systems. Goodwin *et al.* (2003) believe that these systems are being developed because of service user demand, but also because they are cost effective and efficient, as well as offering employees more job satisfaction.

In 1999 the National Pathways Association mental health subgroup defined a number of criteria a care pathway should meet and these are listed in Hall and Howard (2006). First, the pathway should be developed for a specific condition, process or patient group. This could be related to a diagnosis such as schizophrenia, symptoms such as persecutory delusions, or a health care need; it also includes the interventions detailing expected care. The care pathway should have expected start and finish points. However, not all pathways will have a physical matrix appearance but could be structured on the concept of having two axes: one based on time or stages of care, and the other on interventions, goals or standards. Outcomes, goals or aims are identified and wherever it is appropriate they should be agreed with the service users, and their families. The care pathway can be used as all or part of the clinical record and in most cases will include multi-professional input. The pathway is used as a tool for the clinician, or users/carers, in making decisions about the agreed care and provides the ability to track care given against care planned. If there is variance from this agreement this must be recorded and the reasons for this must be stated. The pathway document should comply with standards for record keeping and must include the date that it was developed and the date of any review. In this way evidence of accountability for recorded clinical care should be provided.

Furthermore, relevant guidelines and/or protocols should be incorporated within the care pathway. Outcomes, goals or aims can be for the service users to achieve, or for the staff to achieve on behalf of the service user, or may be process outcomes such as an administrative procedure. The care pathway should be a tool for identifying where decisions about care and treatment are being made, and when it is appropriate to include the service user and/or carer in that process. The ability to track care can be separate from the ability to track care that is planned. Tracking assists with the management of care for both the individual service user and groups of users. It is also used for audit and review, and for other analytical purposes. Finally, having a place to record variation on the care pathway meets the basic level of expectation. However, a more detailed care pathway can provide specific information about the process, and identify why there is variance and/or action taken in response to this.

ICPs are both a tool and a concept that embed guidelines, protocols and locally agreed, evidence-based, patient-centred, best practice, into everyday use for the individual service user. In addition, and uniquely to ICPs, they record deviations from planned care in the form of variances. An ICP aims to have the right people, doing the right things, in the right order, at the right time, in the right place, with the right outcome, all with attention to the patient experience and to compare planned care with care actually given. It is this last point that sets ICPs apart from the myriad of other tools supporting best practice.

The ICP conceptual model

The integrated care pathway (ICP) is a document that describes a process within health and social care, and that collects variations between planned and actual care (Venture, 2002). Venture goes on to state that an ICP is a document that must be used within the ICP conceptual framework to realise its potential. An ICP is a document that describes the process for a discrete element of service. It sets out anticipated, evidence-based, best practice and outcomes that are locally agreed and that reflect a patient-centred, multi-disciplinary, multi-agency approach. The ICP document is structured around the unique ICP variance tracking tool. When used with a patient/client, the ICP document becomes all or part of the contemporaneous patient/client record, where both completed activities and outcomes, and variations between planned and actual activities and outcomes, are recorded at the point of delivery.

An ICP framework

An ICP framework incorporates a systematic cycle of activities based around the development and use of an ICP document to ensure continuous improvements to practice and outcome. These activities include selecting ICPs to use with patient/client groupings, developing ICP content and layout, using ICPs as the contemporaneous patient/client record, recording, analysing and comparing any variations from planned activity and outcome, and continuously updating practice as a result.

A number of definitions of ICPs have been around since the late 1990s. Some confusion has been created because they all link ICPs directly to patient groupings or case-types. A single ICP rarely covers the full span of a patient journey for a particular condition; the patient's package of care is commonly built up from a group of ICPs, each of which describe a component/phase of the care e.g. an admission or assessment phase, a set of interventions, a discharge phase.

Further definitions

Commonly quoted definitions:
  An ICP:

'amalgamates all the anticipated elements of care and treatment of all members of the multidisciplinary team, for a patient or client of a particular case-type or grouping within an agreed time frame, for the achievement of agreed outcomes. Any deviation from the plan is documented as a 'variance'; the analysis of which provides information for the review of current practice' (Johnson, 1997).

An ICP determines locally agreed:

'multidisciplinary practice based on guidelines and evidence where available, for a specific patient/client group. It forms all or part of the clinical record, documents the care given and facilitates the evaluation of outcomes for continuous quality improvement' (National Pathways Association, 1998).

Contents of ICPs

An ICP should contain all multidisciplinary, multi-agency, clinical and administrative activities involving a specific client group. It should be evidence based wherever this is possible, it must be locally agreed, and must represent best practice for the service user. The ICP should represent both local and national standards and contain variance tracking which is essential to all ICPs. There must be sections related to tests, charts, assessments, diagrams, letters, forms, information leaflets, satisfaction questionnaires etc. Scales for measurement of clinical effectiveness must be devised and included. An ICP should be outcome based and these must be constructed and agreed locally. There should also be space to add activities or comments to a standard ICP to individualise care for a particular patient and space for freehand notes. Freehand notes include the multi-disciplinary template for recording and variance tracking an individual patient's problems, goals, and plans.

Designing ICP documentation

The description as to what ICPs look like is simply anything that the development team would like them to look like. ICPs rarely look the same in any setting or between departments and organisations, in the same way as notes, assessments, charts etc. are very different in different places. It is not the layout of the ICP document that is critical; rather that it makes sense and can be clearly followed by those who have to use it. However, developing rules and guidance for corporate ICP templates assists in standardising a corporate look within a particular organisation.

Protocols developed by the National Library for Health (2005) state that how the variance tracking and continuous improvements framework is embedded within the ICP will be critical to the success of useful data capture and its subsequent analysis. The layout of the variance tracking tool within the ICP will influence whether or not the service users record variances as they occur. If variances are not recorded, there will be no information available to inform the multidisciplinary team as to whether or how activities were unmet.

The design of the variance tracking tool should be quick and easy to complete, meaningful and accessible to all relevant people. It must be part of the routine of clinical/administrative record keeping and be clearly linked with the relevant activity by a unique identifier. However, it should not involve duplication of recording, the need for searching for variance tracking sheets or needing to search for information on how to complete the record. It should not involve having to describe the related activity longhand in order to identify it on the variance tracking sheet.

Differences between ICPs and protocols

ICPs may go by many names, but there is only one way to be sure that a document is a true ICP – it will contain structured variance tracking. An ICP is not just a protocol, a flow chart of events, a care map, a process map, a decision tree, a guideline or a care plan. ICPs may contain protocols and guidelines and they may start their developmental histories as a process map, flow chart or decision tree, but unless they have a mechanism for recording variations/deviations from planned care/activities when used as the record of patient care, then they are not a true ICP.

Other names that are sometimes used to describe ICPs include anticipated recovery pathways (ARPs), multidisciplinary pathways of care (MPCs), care protocols, critical care pathways, pathways of care, care packages, collaborative care pathways, care maps and care profiles.

The authentic ICP is constructed in such a way that it records systematic action for consistent best practice, continuous improvements in patient care, all with attention to the patient experience. It must be patient centred, and built into packages of care for identified groupings. It must be able to provide continuous feedback via variance tracking and analysis, and be multidisciplinary in that it is based on roles, competence and responsibility rather than discipline alone. It must incorporate order and priorities including guidelines, protocols, maps and models of clinical and non-clinical care processes. An authentic ICP will also include standards and outcomes.

Differences between an ICP and a package of care

The National Library for Health (2005) point out that confusion often arises over the differences between ICPs and packages of care. They state that this may have arisen because there has been, and still is, a tendency to call ICPs by the patient group they serve rather than by the service that they provide to that group. ICPs are elements, or bite-sized chunks of service or care. Each bite-sized chunk of service is developed into an ICP, setting out detailed processes i.e. a collection of activities, done by a role, that uses one or more kinds of input, often in an order, and which creates an output that is of value to a patient/other.

A package of care (often called the patient pathway or pathway of care) may contain one or more ICPs selected for a particular patient or target group. It describes the whole range of care given to that patient or patient group, usually for one episode of care. A package of care is also sometimes represented in the form of a flow chart, process map or decision tree. In this case, each item (or small group of items) in the map could represent a discrete ICP.

It is essential during the ICP project planning stage to define the scope of each ICP so that it has a clear start and finish point. Well-scoped ICPs will facilitate the building up of these bite-sized chunks of service into seamless packages of care for each target patient group. Keeping the ICPs discrete also makes it possible to tailor care more closely to an individual patient by adding or removing ICPs from the patient's anticipated package of care in response to their particular or changing needs. It also provides opportunities for including distinct patient/carer ICPs as part of the package of care.

In summary, the National Library for Health (2005) states that this bite-sized chunk approach enables the use of ICPs with complex patient groups. It helps to avoid duplication of effort such as when the same pre-admission process is written into numerous longer ICPs instead of being written once only and selected for each appropriate package of care. It enables tailoring of the package of care for individual patients by adding and removing ICPs and facilitates the development of patient/carer ICPs. Furthermore, this approach supports a framework for the development of electronic ICPs.

Integrated care pathways in mental health: some examples of the need for development of ICPs

Pathways to care for patients with bipolar disorder

This example of an ICP relates to bipolar disorder which is a debilitating, recurring psychiatric illness characterized by alternating episodes of depression and mania or hypomania. The original article by Bhugra and Flick (2005) stated that despite the availability of effective therapies fewer than half of the affected patients in the USA receive appropriate treatment. They state that this unfortunate statistic reflects the presence of medical, financial, legal/governmental and cultural barriers to patients gaining access to appropriate care. Users of mental health care services described a treatment environment that relies too heavily on crisis response rather than comprehensive, on-going, long-term illness management.

Improving access to care among the bipolar community required multi-lateral strategies to influence the actions and attitudes of patients, communities, providers, health care systems, and state/national governments. In other cultures, barriers to care differ according to a number of factors such as type of services, explanatory models of illness, misdiagnosis and perceptions of care givers. Bhugra and Flick (2005) state that it is essential that clinicians are aware of pathways and barriers so that appropriate and accessible care can be provided. They state that there are also two additional problems associated with bipolar disorders. These include an increased relapse rate and the problem associated with sub-threshold diagnoses. In a follow-up study Angst (2004) concluded that the relapse rate of bipolar disorder was twice that of depressive disorder. Angst has also persuasively argued that the burden related to bipolar disorders is significantly underestimated.

Quality of life is significantly altered in patients with bipolar disorder. The enormously disruptive nature of bipolar illness extends to the patient's family, social relationships, finances, and career. Studies have found that bipolar patients have a greater likelihood of experiencing separation, marital problems, or divorce. They are also more likely to remain single throughout their lives. Goldberg and Huxley (1980) described a model of access to health care that identifies the sequential referral filters through which a patient passes to reach specialist care. The model assumes that patients generally initiate care with a general practitioner (GP) and are subsequently referred to psychiatric specialists and the effectiveness of this approach depends upon symptom presentation, the primary care physician's ability to diagnose mental disorders, and his or her willingness to refer the patient to a specialist. Access to services is defined as the possibility of being seen in the services in a clinical context.

In 1999 the Government put forth its National Service Framework for Mental Health (Department of Health, 1999) which outlines national standards for mental health including their goals and how they should be delivered and evaluated. This document has been criticised for its lack of specific considerations for bipolar patients (Morris *et al.*, 2002) despite its admission that one person in 250 will have a psychotic illness such as schizophrenia or bipolar affective disorder. The National Service Framework sets seven standards including the accessibility to services 24 hours a day for 365 days a year. The accessibility therefore has to be, not only geographic, but also emotional in that the place where services are delivered should be acceptable to the patients and their carers.

Pathways to care in first episode psychosis

Etheridge *et al.* (2004) explored pathways to care for people experiencing a first episode of psychosis. They state that these people often suffer for months or years before their condition is recognised and treated. They argue that it is widely believed that delay in treatment of psychosis results in a worse outcome (McGlashan & Johannassen, 1996; Birchwood *et al.*, 1998). The causal relationship between the long duration of untreated psychosis and poor prognosis has been questioned as it is possible that both could be related to social variables or some other independent factor (Barnes *et al.*, 2000). They state that it would be ethically impossible to conduct a prospective study in which people with early psychosis were denied treatment at random for prolonged periods of time in order to assess subsequent outcome (McGorry, 2000). Despite such reservations, it is clearly desirable to deliver treatment as early as possible to this seriously needy group of people, if only to alleviate suffering and to minimise adverse secondary psychological and social consequences of the psychosis. The concept of early intervention in psychosis has now been embraced in official Department of Health policy guidelines (Department of Health, 1999, 2000, 2001) as well as in treatment guidelines for schizophrenia (Department of Health, 2002). Etheridge *et al.* (2004) argue that in order to deliver treatment early to people developing psychosis, it is necessary to identify those factors which lead to delay. They include delay in recognition of symptoms, seeking help and receiving appropriate treatment. Early symptoms of psychosis are difficult for professionals to distinguish and recognise, pathways to care are complex and carers often find appropriate services are not available when needed (Larsen *et al.*, 1998; Lincoln *et al.*, 1998).

As part of the process of investigating local need for an early intervention service for psychosis in Rotherham, Etheridge *et al.* (2004) conducted surveys of both service users and carers, who were asked about their experiences of obtaining care when they first developed symptoms of psychosis. The aim was to assess whether duration of untreated psychosis in Rotherham reflected that reported nationally and internationally, and if so, to identify potential obstacles to early identification and treatment. This survey was conducted by the Rotherham service user monitoring team (RMT), which is an independent group made up of people who have all used or are still using the statutory mental health services. The carer survey was conducted by the project manager for early intervention in psychosis in Rotherham. Consultation exercises were held with the two main carers' groups, which highlighted common themes and difficulties which carers had experienced with the services. The results of this small local survey echo data from larger studies and have the added advantage that the direct personal accounts of service users were obtained. The striking feature of this is the similarity of the experience of service users and those of their carers. Several major themes arise which are of direct practical importance to setting up local services.

The first was the need for early recognition; the fact that there was a problem recognised very early by both carers and service users. However, attempts to find help were thwarted by lack of knowledge of who to approach and unhelpful responses from professionals. This appears to indicate that awareness raising, not only for school students and the general public but also for front line professionals including teachers, GPs and school nurses, would be appropriate. However, Etheridge *et al.* (2004) state that it must be appreciated that behavioural changes in young people are very common. Attempts to identify prodromal schizophrenia is very difficult even for trained research teams, and is therefore subject to a lot of false positive identified cases which could lead to inappropriate stigmatisation (Birchwood *et al.*, 1998).

This survey also emphasised that many service users are below the age that is normally dealt with by acute mental health services when problems first become apparent. Therefore, strong cooperation between child and adolescent services, and adult services is essential in the management of early psychosis. The GP was an early point of contact in the majority of cases, and was often found to be unsatisfactory both in the identification of psychosis and the subsequent treatment that was given. Awareness raising for GPs and the availability of a fast track assessment service by secondary mental health services is recommended.

Etheridge *et al.* go on to state that there has been recent emphasis on the importance of providing adequate services for people with dual diagnosis (Department of Health, 2002). The need for this is highlighted in the survey, in that the diagnosis and appropriate treatment of schizophrenia appear to have been significantly delayed in some service users with a history of substance abuse. This is an issue of education and awareness raising within secondary services, and supports the need for the appointment of specialist dual diagnosis workers to promote good practice and earlier recognition and treatment.

Hospital admission to a general acute psychiatric ward was widely regarded as inappropriate by both service users and carers. However, it was the first course of treatment for all but one of the sample. They state that this is worrying in view of the evidence that highlights the adverse psychological effects of young people being placed on general adult psychiatric wards (Lincoln *et al.*, 1998). Any service focusing on early intervention needs to have effective alternatives to hospital admission available, including home treatment services. If some form of 24-hour care away from the home is essential, then they recommend that this should be provided in a separate unit, which is appropriately focused on the needs of this group of clients including the fact that they are a very young group.

Etheridge *et al.* concluded that comments from the carers and service users reinforced locally the findings of the international evidence base which highlights the fact that for young people experiencing a first episode of psychosis pathways into secondary services are often suboptimal, unhelpful and tangled. Additionally, it reveals the inconsistent and inappropriate nature of routine local service provision for these people. They consider that information that was collated will be extremely useful to enable them to plan future early intervention in psychosis services that are carer and user focused. This will enable them to positively address some of the issues that have caused stress and difficulty and therefore build bridges for future joint working and better service engagement.

Determinants of outcome in the pathways through care for children hearing voices

Escher *et al.* (2004) consider that auditory hallucination, or hearing voices, is generally associated with psychopathology. In psychiatry it is interpreted as a symptom of an illness, with no connection to the individual's life history. Voice hallucinations in childhood occur in a variety of contexts and have variable long-term outcomes but little is known about the course of the experience. In this study, 80 children and youngsters hearing voices were interviewed on four occasions over a period of three years about the content of the voices and their overall experience of voices, focusing on the determinants for a promising outcome in the pathways through care. The results indicated that the need for care in the context of the experience of voices is associated not only with high levels of problem behaviour and associated negative symptoms of psychosis, but also, independently, with an appraisal of the voices in terms of anxiety, depression, dissociation and frequency of occurrence. In 60% of the participants the voices disappeared during the three-year research period. The relationship between the disappearance of voices and the course of mental health treatment was considered to be ambiguous.

For hallucinating children in the general population such experiences are non-pathological (McGee *et al.*, 2000). A small group of children may, however, develop persistent symptoms and subsequent psychotic disorder in adult life. Their study concerned the characteristics that influence the continuity or discontinuity of hearing voices in children. Voice persistence was also associated with a high score on the dissociative experience scale (DES) (Bernstein & Putnam, 1986), older age and lack of clear triggers in time and place (Escher *et al.*, 2002). Developing delusional ideation had no influence on voice continuation/discontinuation. Having professional mental health care did not in itself influence the probability of voice discontinuation (Escher *et al.*, 2002). They identified problems because the voices often had a major influence on daily life. In the first year most of the children reported problems at home (70%) and problems at school (82%) because of the voices (Escher and Romme, 1998). Children reported that the voices evoked emotions such as anxiety (80%) and confusion (68%), or that the voice-hearing resulted in aggression (54%), sadness (50%), feeling lonely (49%) or uncertain (46%). The influence of the voices resulted in such problems as difficulty paying attention in class at school (59%). Children reported problems at home that irritated the other family members, such as '*doing things they did not want to do themselves*' (50%), stealing, running up and down the staircase, touching tiles. Because of the voices, some children reported talking out loud in public, smashing things, being provoked into quarrels or being disturbed while doing homework. Many children also said that they were punished because of their behaviour connected with the voices (41%). In the second year fewer problems related to the voices were reported. Of the 57 children still hearing voices, 35% reported voice-related problems at home and 42% at school.

The need for care was defined as having received professional mental health care because of hearing voices. Children who received professional mental health care generally had higher scores on social and psychopathological dysfunction than did the children who were not receiving care. Children in care reported more emotional triggers to the voices and greater childhood adversity. Emotional appraisal of the voices was more often negative, and the voices influenced their emotions and behaviours more. Lastly, children in care used specific coping strategies (Escher *et al.*, 2002) such as passive problem-solving. Being in care was further related to receipt of special education (of the 18 children placed in special schooling, 12 were in care). Children in care reported more traumatic events. Children who acted out aggressively, hit their siblings, broke things or shouted at their parents also ended up in care more often. Sometimes it was the child's behaviour at school that forced the parents to look for care, for example when a child started to talk out loud to the voices during class.

Results from this study on children hearing voices were in agreement with contemporary epidemiological population surveys and with recent research into individual recovery. The results of this and similar studies should have consequences in three areas: hearing voices as a signal of serious problems in daily life; the construction of illness from the phenomenon of auditory halluci-nations; and the kind of mental health care offered. Auditory hallucinations as a signal of serious problems in daily life and in the last decade several popu-lation surveys (Eaton *et al.*, 1991; Tien, 1991; Bijl *et al.*, 1998) have shown that psychotic experiences such as hallucinations and delusions occur in the nor-mal population without illness. These studies make it quite clear that there is no clear dichotomy between health and illness; illness/health is not an either/or situation. They also found elements in care that children and parents found not to be helpful. These included first, not accepting the voices as real for the child, and calling it a fantasy or delusion. The fact that neuroleptics were usually the only therapy provided. The emphasis was on constructing an illness instead of focusing on complaints and treating the illness instead of helping to solve the problem. There was a problem that the child became too dependent on the treatment and not given enough influence of his/her own. The child often had to choose between two negative possibilities and not enough attention was given to underlying problems in daily life. The children also reduced activities in order to adapt to illness.

The kinds of care that were experienced as helpful were mostly oriented to providing social support, promoting development and helping to work through social problems. In keeping with the findings is data that shows that 20% of the children who heard voices were not in need of care and seemed to be able to solve their problems within their family setting. This suggested that nor-malising the experience and supporting the natural resources of the child and the family might be important elements in the process of learning to cope. These elements are part of a process and require time rather than immediate professional action. This raises the question of which elements of mental health care are effective or helpful. Parents and children mentioned the following as being effective and helpful: accepting the voices; recognising the experience; making the experience concrete; reducing anxiety; focusing on problems resulting from voices such as the problem of sleep deprivation; developing techniques for coping with the voices, techniques that promote coping with emotions and working through problems that trigger the voices. Mental health care seemed more promising when it was oriented toward helping the person to feel safe, being supportive and was directed toward learning to cope with the voices; a very important element seemed to be working through the problems and emotions involved.

This is logical when hearing voices is seen as a reaction to problems in daily life and not as an illness in itself. When hearing voices is interpreted only as part of an illness, diagnosing and treating that illness is the only consequence. In general, the subjects in their study did not experience the kind of mental health care that follows from this perspective as being of much help. Parents and children mostly discontinued that kind of care and looked for other kinds of care such as those they have described in this study. The data shows that those who sought care elsewhere did find helpful care, their voices disappeared and their development was positive. On the other hand, the data also shows that those children who stayed in the same kind of care continued to hear voices and did not develop well. It is the authors' aim to promote a more open view regarding the phenomenon of hearing voices. They state that voices are often messengers and relate to the individual's life history. By interpreting them in light of that history, the experience itself and the meaning of the experience for the voice hearer become of greater interest. It is their experience that this interest could stimulate the natural resources of the child and his/her family to successfully cope with the voice-hearing experience.

Pathways into care and satisfaction with primary care for black patients in south London

Bhugra *et al.* (2004) state that there is evidence in the literature to suggest that black patients access different pathways to mental health care. These pathways are influenced by clinical diagnosis as well as previous satisfaction with services. The authors aimed to study pathways into care of both black and white patients to the Maudsley Hospital who had come into contact with secondary care services for the first time or after a gap of one year.

After identifying the ethnicity and mode of entry into psychiatric services, patients were approached to participate in the study. In addition to socio-demographic details, pathways to care encounter and GP satisfaction scales were given to the patients. As expected black patients were less likely to come through primary care services and were are also more likely to be dissatisfied with primary care compared with white patients. They were also more likely to suffer from schizophrenia. It is likely that dissatisfaction with primary care services may have led to more coercive pathways into secondary care.

The authors state that there is now a substantial body of research from the UK that indicates black and ethnic minority people with mental illness appear to have different patterns of service utilisation, service accessibility, different diagnoses and treatment packages compared to white people (Bhui, 1997). An interest in the pathways into care across different groups arises from two main factors. Firstly, the widely different pathways taken in some groups may reflect attractiveness, cultural appropriateness and attitudes towards services due to health beliefs, previous experiences and culturally defined lay referral systems. In the UK, once the points of access are identified, the weak points in pathways through care can be strengthened. For example, if African Caribbean men make contact with mental health services in crisis, through the police and the criminal justice systems, rather than through their general practitioner (Moodley & Perkins, 1991), the service challenge is to explore reasons for this. General practitioners can support the delivery of effective interventions by ensuring access through closer working relationships with the voluntary sector. Data from forensic settings, hospital inpatient settings, and the community settings all indicate an over representation of African Caribbean men in compulsory care as well as in the criminal justice system (McGovern & Cope, 1991; Thornicroft *et al.*, 1999). It has also been shown that South Asians are under represented in inpatient admission statistics, have shorter hospital stays and are less likely to be detected as having a mental disorder by their general practitioner (Gupta, 1991; Bhui *et al.*, 2000).

Angel and Thoits (1987) point out that the perspective of the individual and his or her interpretation of physical and emotional states have been neglected by researchers, who have tended to favour sociological/anthropological style examinations of the impact of the wider culture on these factors. Zola (1972) found that in consultation, Italians are more likely to report a number of symptoms, in contrast to the Irish, who report only a few. Tendencies towards introspection are more common amongst females and Jews. Therefore, it is possible that culture plays a role at stage one, i.e. in sensitising the individual to physical and emotional states especially at the time of recognition of distress. Many studies suggest that irrespective of ethnicity, people will turn to their natural support systems first – turning to statutory organisations only as a last resort (Gourash, 1978; Zola, 1972). Kleinman (1980) observes that although the popular sphere of health care is the largest part of any system it is the least studied and most poorly understood. Studies undertaken in the US and Taiwan indicate that the order of 70–90% of all illness episodes are managed within the popular sector (Zola, 1972). It is at this level that cultural factors come into play, since the person's friends and relatives will express beliefs and standards that are representative of the worldview of the larger social group. In countries where psychiatric services are less well resourced patients may use traditional healers as first port of call (Gater *et al.*, 1991). The role of patient pathways into care are worth remembering while establishing services (Bhugra, 1997). Neighbors (1985) found that nearly 20% of the black people in his study sought help from a minister in the first instance. Bhui and Bhugra (2002) modified the Goldberg and Huxley (1980) model to include a level six for forensic patients. Furthermore, they point out that the patient's cultural appraisal of their problem, and perhaps their preferred interventions, may differ from those of their GPs that will push them into non primary care pathways.

Their study attempted to uncover the reasons why primary care services are being under-utilised by black patients. White patients experienced better continuity of care offered by their GP, with the satisfaction of white primary care patients being considerably higher than the rest. Scores relating to a patient's satisfaction with the depth of his/her relationship with their GP received the lowest scores of all the other measures. A comparison of black and white patients who followed the primary care route highlighted significant differences between the level of satisfaction experienced by patients from the two ethnic groups, when it came to three aspects of the care they received from their GP. In three areas white patients were more satisfied, these were: general satisfaction with the GP; satisfaction with the GP's premises; and satisfaction with the accessibility of the surgery (Mann–Whitney U test). There were also some significant differences between the levels of satisfaction expressed by black and white non-primary care patients.

The authors state that the data for the study needs to be interpreted with caution. Firstly there were smaller numbers of black patients than white patients, which may have influenced the outcome of some of the results. Secondly, as the data was being collected from a western style psychiatric facility it is possible that individuals were reluctant to come forward with the non-medical pathways they may have used. Furthermore, no data is available on inter-rater reliability and the effects of the interviewer's ethnicity in relation to patient ethnicity. This needs to be kept in mind when interpreting the results. Thirdly, by identifying patients by the source of pathway may have biased some of the findings. The sample reflects the representative nature of patients who were already in contact with western style facilities but the generalisability of findings elsewhere may prove to be problematic.

The time between problem identification and reaching psychiatric care was longer for both black and white primary care patients (median delay 25 and 23 weeks respectively). This could be explained by the fact that non-primary care patients by-pass their GP services and go straight to psychiatric services (such as the emergency clinic) which is a local facility available 24 hours a day. Whilst this is a possibility, this does not explain why, when those using the emergency clinic were compared by ethnicity, within this group, whites had longer delays than black patients did.

It was shown that black patients were more likely to have a case note diagnosis between schizophrenia, schizotypal and delusional disorders whereas whites using the emergency clinic were more likely to have a case-note diagnosis of affective disorders. It may be that the black patients with case note diagnoses of schizophrenia, schizotypal and delusional disorders were in greater need of treatment so that cases were prioritised and the time it took them to reach psychiatric care was thus less. This also confirms previous suggestions that there may be a diagnostic bias for certain diagnoses in black patients (Bhugra, 1997; Bhui, 1997).

Conclusion

Trowbridge and Weingarten (2001) argue that there are a number of evaluations of ICPs which report little or no improvement in the quality of health care as a result of introducing an ICP. Thus, there needs to be both appraisal and assurance of the quality of an ICP on behalf of the organisation. The organisation needs to ensure that ICPs have also been adequately tested locally to increase the likelihood of successful implementation. The development of ICP programmes requires consideration of the organisational frameworks in which they will have to operate or they may fail to be established. This chapter describes a systematic approach to developing ICPs and suggests a framework in which they can be standardised within mental health care organisations.

References

Angel, R. & Thoits, P. (1987). The Impact Of Culture On The Cognitive Structure Of Illness. *Culture, Medicine and Psychiatry.* **11**, 456–494.

Angst, J. (2004). Bipolar Disorder: A Seriously Underestimated Health Burden. *European Archives of Psychiatry and Clinical Neuroscience.* **254**, 59–60.

Barnes, T.R.E., Hutton, S.B. & Chapman, M.J. (2000). West London First-episode Study of Schizophrenia: Clinical Correlates Of Duration Of Untreated Psychosis. *British Journal of Psychiatry.* **177**, 207–211.

Bernstein, E.M. & Putnam, F.W. (1986). Development, reliability, and validity of a dissociation scale. *Journal of Nervous and Mental Disease*, 174, 727–735. Available at http://www.ncbi.nlm.nih.gov/sites/entrez?cmd=retrieve&db=pubmed&list_uids =3783140&dopt=Abstract

Bhugra, D. (1997). Setting Up Services: Cross Cultural Issues. *International Journal of Social Psychiatry.* **43**.

Bhugra, D. & Flick, G.R. (2005). Pathways to Care for Patients with Bipolar Disorder. *Bipolar Disorder.* **7**, 236–245.

Bhugra, D., Harding, C. & Lippett, R. (2004). Pathways Into Care and Satisfaction With Primary Care For Black Patients In South London. *Journal of Mental Health.* **13(2)**, 171–183.

Bhui, K. (1997). Service Provision for London's Ethnic Minorities. In: Johnson, S., Ramsey, R., Thornicroft, G., Brooks, L., Lelliott, P., Peck, E., Smith, H., Chisholm, D., Audini, B., Knapp, M. & Goldberg, D. (eds). *London's Mental Health.* London: Kings Fund.

Bhui, K. & Bhugra, D. (2002). Mental Illness in Black and Asian Ethnic Minorities: Pathways into Care and Outcome. *Advances in Psychiatric Treatment.* **8**, 26–33.

Bhui, K., Bhugra, D. & Goldberg, D. (2000). Cross-Cultural Validity of the ADI and GHQ Amongst English and Punjabi Primary Care Attendees. *Social Psychiatry and Psychiatric Epidemiology.* **35**, 248–254.

Bijl, R.V., Ravelli, A. & Van Zessen, G. (1998). Prevalence of Psychotic Disorder in The General Population: Results from the Netherlands Mental Health Survey and Incidence Study. *Social Psychiatry Epidemiology.* **33**, 587–596.

Birchwood, M., Todd, P. & Jackson, C. (1998). Early Intervention in Psychosis: The Critical Period Hypothesis. *British Journal of Psychiatry.* **172(supp 33)**, 53–59.

Department of Health (1999). *National Service Framework for Mental Health.* London: The Stationery Office.

Department of Health (2000). *The NHS Plan.* London: The Stationery Office.

Department of Health (2001). *Mental Health National Service Framework Policy Implementation Guide.* London: The Stationery Office.

Department of Health (2002). *Mental Health Policy Implementation Guide – Dual Diagnosis Good Practice Guide.* London: The Stationery Office.

Eaton, W.W., Romanonski, A. & Anthony, J.C. (1991). Screening for Psychosis in the General Population with a Self-Report Interview. *Journal of Nervous and Mental Disorder.* **179**, 689–693.

EHMA (2006). *Integrating Services for Older People: a Resource Book for Managers.* Available at: http://www.ehma.org/carmen/is_01.html

Escher, A., Morris, M., Buiks, A., Delespaul, P., Van Os, J. & Romme, M. (2004). Determinants of Outcome in the Pathways through Care for Children Hearing Voices. *International Journal of Social Welfare.* **13**, 208–222.

Escher, A. & Romme, M. (1998). Small-Talk: Voice-Hearing in Children. *Open Mind.* **July/August**.

Escher, A., Romme, M., Buiks, A., Delespaul, P. & Van Os, J. (2002). Independent Course of Childhood Auditory Hallucinations: A Sequel 3-Year Follow-Up Study, *British Journal of Psychiatry,* **181(supp 43)**, S10–S18.

Etheridge, K., Yarrow, L., & Peet, M., (2004). Pathways Of Care In First Episode Psychosis, *Journal of Psychiatric and Mental Health Nursing.* **11**, 125–128.

Gater, R., de Almeido-e Sousa, B.B.G., Caraveo, J., Chandrashekar, C.R., Dhadphale, M. & Goldberg, D. (1991). *The Pathways To Psychiatric Care: A Cross Cultural Study.* London: Tavistock.

Goldberg, D.P. & Huxley, P. (1980). *Mental Illness in The Community.* London: Tavistock.

Goodwin, N.P., Peck, E., Freeman, T. & Posaner, R. (2003). *Managing Across Diverse Networks of Care: Lessons from Other Sectors.* Birmingham: Health Services Management Centre.

Gourash, N. (1978). Help-seeking: A Review of the Literature. *American Journal of Community Psychology.* **6(5)**, 413–424.

Gupta, S. (1991). Psychosis in Migrants from the Indian Subcontinent and English Controls. *British Journal of Psychiatry.* **154**, 222–225.

Hall, J. & Howard, D. (2006). *Integrated Care Pathways in Mental Health.* London: Churchill Livingstone.

Johnson, S. (1997). *Pathways of Care.* London: Blackwell Science.

Kleinman, A. (1980). *Patients and Their Healers in the Context of Culture.* Berkeley, CA: University of California Press.

Larsen, T.K., Johannessen, J.O. & Opjordsmoen, S. (1998). First Episode Schizophrenia with Long Duration of Untreated Psychosis Pathways to Care. *British Journal of Psychiatry.* **172(supp 33)**, 45–52.

Lincoln, C., Harrigan, S. & McGorry, P. (1998). Understanding The Topography of Early Psychosis Pathways. *British Journal of Psychiatry.* **172(supp 33)**, 21–25.

McGee, R., Williams, S. & Poulton, R. (2000). Hallucinations in Nonpsychotic Children. *Journal of American Academic Child and Adolescent Psychiatry.* **39(1)**, 12–13.

McGlashan, T.H. & Johannassen, J.O. (1996). Early Detection and Intervention with Schizophrenia Rationale, *Schizophrenia Bulletin.* **22**, 20–22.

McGorry, P.D. (2000). Evaluating The Importance of Reducing the Duration of Untreated Psychosis. *Australian and New Zealand Journal of Psychiatry.* **34(supp)**, S145–S149.

McGovern, D. & Cope, R.V. (1991). Second Generation of Afro Caribbeans and Young Whites with a Diagnosis of Schizophrenia. *Social Psychiatry and Psychiatric Epidemiology.* **26**, 95–99.

Moodley, P. & Perkins, R. (1991). Routes To Psychiatric Inpatient Care In An Inner London Borough. *Social Psychiatry and Psychiatric Epidemiology.* **26**, 47–51.

Morris, R., Marshall, M. & Harris, A. (2002). Bipolar Affective Disorder: Left Out in the Cold: Too Late for the National Service Framework but Local Initiatives May Be Possible. *British Medical Journal.* **324**, 61–62.

Naidoo, M. & Bullock, R. (2001). *An Integrated Care Pathway for Dementia: Best Practice for Dementia Care.* London: Harcourt.

National Health Service Confederation (2006). *Creating Integrated Models of Service Delivery.* Available at: http://www.nhsconfed.org/connecting/creating_integrated_models_of_service_delivery.asp

National Library for Health (2005). Available at: http://www.library.nhs.uk/Default.aspx

National Pathways Association (1998). NPA Definitions of a Pathway of Care. In: *Protocols & Care Pathways.*NHS National Library for Health. Available at: http://www.library.nhs.uk/pathways/page.aspx?pagename=ICPS.

Neighbors, H.W. (1985). Seeking Professional Help For Personal Problems: Black Americans' Use Of Health And Mental Health Services. *Community Mental Health Journal.* **21**, 156–166.

Scottish Executive Publication (2004). Effective Interventions Unit: Integrated Care Pathways. Available at: http://www.scotland.gov.uk/Publications/2004/01/18739/31555

Thornicroft, G., Davies, S. & Lees, M. (1999). Health Services Research Into Forensic Psychiatry: A Black and White Case. *International Review of Psychiatry.* **11**, 250–257.

Tien, A.Y. (1991). Distribution of Hallucinations in the Population. *Social Psychiatry and Psychiatric Epidemiology.* **26**, 287–292.

Trowbridge, R. & Weingarten, S. (2001). Critical pathways. In: Eisenberg, J. & Kamerow, D. (eds) *Making Health Care Safer – A Critical Analysis of Patient Safety Practices,* Evident *Report/Technology Assessment No. 43.* Rockville, MD: AHRQ Publications. Available at: http://www.ahcpr.gov/clinic/ptsafety

Venture Training and Consultancy (2002). *Integrated Care Plans (ICPs).* Available at: http://www.venturetc.com/messagereply.asp?ID=51&Reply=51&forum=DG_W

Zola, I.K. (1972). Medicine as an Institution of Social Control. *Sociological Review.* **20**, 487–504.

Chapter 14

Evaluation

Joan Murphy and Dennis Cross

Introduction

This chapter explores the concept of evaluation in nursing and its role in the promotion of recovery for those with mental health difficulties. Evaluation represents an integral and dynamic component of individual care planning. It is recognised as possessing fluidity, as it may permeate any aspect of a care plan. In particular, its intimate and often indivisible links with the process of assessment are explored. It may also be delineated into 5 broad stages, including the collection and reviewing of information and the modification of the care plan thereafter. These are described in some detail with reference to case examples, where appropriate. Evaluation requires various strategies to support it. The underpinning collaborative process is explored along with the use of various tools facilitating the measurement of progress therein.

On progressing from evaluation within the context of individual care planning, the various frameworks and strategic policies underpinning the broader evaluation of mental health services are explored. In this context, the dissonance that often exists between professional and user evaluations is explored, and in particular this chapter aims to elucidate what it is that service users desire from mental health services. This includes an analysis of the various means by which service users are canvassed for these evaluations, whether it is consumer satisfaction surveys or the use of focus groups. This moves logically on to exploring some of the outcome criteria or benchmarking that services use for standard setting and auditing purposes encompassing, for example, the essence of care framework (Department of Health, 2001a).

There are a number of factors, which can be equally applied to personal or service evaluation, that either prevent it from taking place or at least make it less effective that it might be. Some are seemingly obvious, such as the availability of sufficient information, time or will to enable evaluation to be successful. Others involve multi-factorial elements; personal, ethical, legal, organisational and societal that may serve to restrict the process of evaluation. At the other end of the spectrum, there is a great deal of discussion looking at the concept of the service user as expert regarding his/her care. This has implications for looking at the relative worth of such expert opinion in relation to evidenced based practice where it resides at the bottom of the pile at level five in the hierarchy of evidenced based practice (Sackett *et al.*, 2000).

What is evaluation?

Evaluation literally means assessing the value of something (Bruce & Paxton, 2002). It is an integral part of the care planning process that helps to determine the effectiveness of nursing interventions. It is usually associated with assessing whether a problem identified has improved and goals have been met as planned (Norman & Ryrie, 2004). However, in its broadest sense evaluation permeates all aspects of nursing care and any part of a care plan can be reviewed as long as there are changes to be considered. It may be that the initial assessment failed to generate sufficient information upon which to base a plan of care. Indeed, the terms assessment and evaluation are interlinked and often used interchangeably in the literature in the context of judging whether problems are diminishing, increasing or remaining at the same level (Barker, 2004). It may be that the needs identified in collaboration with the service user need to be reviewed in the light of a reshaping of priorities, aided perhaps by the availability of more information. Finally, the nurse needs to be cognisant of the need for on-going review when implementing interventions as these may need to be revised over time or as new problems need to be addressed. Other areas to evaluate include the extent of the client's participation, sense of self-efficacy and assumption of self responsibility. These will be further described within the five inherent stages of evaluation.

The process of evaluation

Identifying goals to be achieved

At the outset, it is important to be clear about what is being evaluated and how this is been operationalised. For example, a service user with a poor sleep pattern may have a goal of being able to sleep 6 consecutive hours without waking up. Alternatively, someone with anxiety may wish to be sufficiently relaxed to be able to read the daily newspaper for a period of 5 minutes. This provides very clear measurable outcome criteria facilitating evaluation. It also allows for the provision of both short and long term goals, as the goal of reading the newspaper may be evaluated at a later stage and re-formulated as a goal of being able to read the paper for 20 minutes, or indeed read a chapter of a book.

Collecting relevant data

In order to be able to ascertain whether identified criteria have been achieved or not relevant information must be collected. This may be enabled in a number of ways including the use of interviews, personal journals or diaries, questionnaires and rating scales, self monitoring and staff observations. For example, data relating to hours slept may be collected through observation and the completion of sleep charts by staff, families or through self monitoring by service users. Meanwhile, degrees of anxiety and its effects on activities lends itself to the use of a personal journal and self monitoring where the service user would be asked to record levels, duration and effects of anxiety over a specified period of time. Finally, the Liverpool university neuroleptic side-effect rating scale (LUNSERS) (Day *et al.*, 1995) is a standardised questionnaire that specifies all potential side effects of neuroleptic medication and rates their severity based on patient response to each item. These methods need not be used in isolation and should at all times be supported by effective engagement in the interview process, be that formal or informal.

Comparing the information with other selected criteria

Information collected is now compared with other criteria, for example, previous baselines from rating scales, self monitoring, staff observation in order to obtain a sense of what has been happening over a period of time. Is the service user's goal nearer to being achieved, has progress levelled out or, for whatever reason, has a further deterioration taken place in this area? For example, on identification of the goal, the person may have had a broken sleep pattern averaging 3 hours in the course of the night. Information now collected shows an improvement, showing that this individual has now slept 4 consecutive hours, for 5 of the last 7 nights. Alternatively with the use of LUNSERS, comparing the user's rating against a specified cut-off point could tell the nurse and client whether neuroleptic medication has produced an excess number of side effects (absolute measurement). On an on-going basis, comparing ratings can indicate whether side effects are actually occurring to a lesser extent, or at least being better tolerated.

Judging the client's response which is reflected by this comparison

This stage involves collaboration with the client and his family and carers, to discuss, where appropriate, the data collected and listen to their interpretation. This emphasises the importance of having a working alliance with users, of working with rather than for clients (Barker, 2004). Thus problem statements should reflect a shared understanding of what the problem/needs are, if such exist. Ultimately should changes be required to the individual care plan, the options available must be openly discussed with the user having access to sufficient information to enable that decision.

Feedback and modifying the care plan

The final stage in this particular cycle involves the provision of feedback to the relevant stakeholders and modifying the care plan accordingly. For example, it may be that the service user has reached a stage where they wish to seek employment as part of their recovery. This may be incorporated as an aim of seeking employment two days a week initially and the interventions will obviously be adjusted accordingly to include consultation with relevant personnel who may facilitate this aim.

Practical strategies that facilitate evaluation

Central to the care planning process is collaboration with the service user since a working alliance is central to any meaningful evaluation and to the individual definition of recovery for that individual. Indeed, many researchers and theorists consider the formation of working partnerships between service users and nurses as central to best practice (Peplau, 1988; Christensen, 1993). In Ireland, the strategic plan as outlined in the document *A Vision for Change* (Department of Health and Children, 2006) speaks of the need for service users to be viewed as active participants in their own recovery rather than as being passive recipients of expert care. This appears to be highly logical, since service users are in fact the experts of their own illness. The concept of service users being experts is congruent with the philosophy of recovery, since this promotes both enhanced self-management and the development of services that facilitate the individual's personal journey towards recovery.

To assess this journey it is important to have measurable goals or specified outcome criteria against which an evaluation of progress can be made. We speak of having SMART goal statements: specific; measurable; achievable; realistic and time limited. These provide the detail on what should be achieved and within what timeframe and thereby, the means by which a care plan can be evaluated and when. Even when goals are not achieved within defined limits, much can be learned from the experience that will benefit both service users and staff in formulating alternative care plans.

Evaluation is also facilitated by having access to the knowledge of various professionals who comprise the multidisciplinary team. In the future this strategy is likely to be utilised to a much greater extent as suggested by the proposed development of a substantial framework of community mental health teams in Ireland (Department of Health and Children, 2006). Significantly, the proposed operational guidelines of these multidisciplinary teams are underpinned by a spirit of collaboration in the context of the needs of each service user being discussed jointly, in consultation with users and carers. Consequently, the strategy envisages that the care plan be agreed between all parties, including time frame, goals, strategies and resources to support these goals and crucially, the development of clear criteria for assessing outcome and user satisfaction. This will demand that the concept of user involvement in evaluating care be embraced fully be all members of the team and that a consensus of outcome criteria is achieved. In this context there is evidence to suggest that collaboration between professionals can improve outcomes that are important to both clients and healthcare managers (Zwarenstein & Bryant, 2002).

Conversely, it is likely that the degree of involvement in care planning that service users encounter will be variable if members of the health care team fail to reach consensus on how the concept will be operationalised within, what will be, for the most part newly operating teams. A further aspect of evaluation includes the need for the provision of facilities to seek feedback from service users, their families and carers on their experiences of care and support from the multidisciplinary team as an ongoing quality assurance measure.

When should evaluation be done?

Evaluation is a continuous active and dynamic process that begins early in the relationship with the service user and continues throughout. Thus, the care plan is very much a living document that is developed and refined throughout the process of care. Evidence of this on-going evaluation is inherent in nursing handovers, multidisciplinary team meetings and clinical reviews and should also be implicit in nursing documentation.

At other times, evaluation may be triggered by specific events such as a care programme approach meeting, a case conference or in the event of an aggressive outburst. A defined date may also be decided upon as a cut-off point at which decisions have to be made based on the outcome of that evaluation. For example, the service user may wish to assess the side effects of a particular medication for a further 2 weeks, when an ultimate decision will be made as to whether to proceed with this pharmacotherapy or not.

On moving to the broader basis of evaluation of mental health services on a macro level, a framework is useful to identify the dimensions of the service to be evaluated. A very influential early framework was that of Donabedian (1988) who created a distinction between an evaluation of structure (the settings in which care is given), process evaluation (of the giving and receiving of care) and outcome evaluation (the effects of care on the health status of patients and populations). Outcome evaluation tends to predominate occurring in a climate of pressure from government and health economists to justify the cost of health care, and the desire by professionals to provide a quality service. However, Donabedian emphasises that outcomes are only flags that must be used to examine causal antecedents and are meaningless if viewed in isolation from structure and process analysis.

As regards process analysis current Irish health strategy, as outlined in *Quality and Fairness, a Health System For You* (Department of Health and Children, 2001), recommends that the health system become more person-centred with the interests of the public, patients and clients being given greater prominence and influence in decision-making at all levels. This central value of person-centeredness is further operationalised in the recent strategic plan of the Irish mental health services: *A Vision for Change* (Department of Health and Children, 2006), where the concept of individual recovery is endorsed. A number of its underpinning principles include: the promotion of respect, inclusion, citizenship, community care, continuity of care, equity and effective service, accountability and quality. Significantly, the Irish mental health commission, whose aim it is to foster and promote high standards of care and best practice in the delivery of mental health services has also endorsed the recovery approach as an effective basis of care and support.

Historically methods of evaluating mental health care have been driven by professional perspectives (Prince & Prince, 2001). This occurred despite marked differences noted between these and consumers' concepts about what is desirable or indeed effective (Perkins, 2001). Notably, service users mostly want choice, accessibility, advocacy, equal opportunities, employment and self-help. Meanwhile many psychiatrists and mental health nurses still prefer to concentrate on a more traditional approach to treatment that involves professional support, treatment and monitoring (Repper, 2000).

Increasingly, means of incorporating expert opinion of service users are being discussed in the clinical audit literature. A prime example is the use of consumer satisfaction surveys that have been widely used recently. These provide both a means of collecting data to measure against standards and a way of identifying concerns that then inform the selection of topics for clinical audit. It is obviously important that service users are facilitated to describe and discuss such concerns. Examples of such facilitation include the recent work of the Irish mental health commission who designed a consultation process aimed at gathering the views and perspectives of all stakeholders as to what constitutes quality in mental health services (Mental Health Commission, 2005). Perkins (2001), meanwhile, criticised the use of some consumer satisfaction surveys. He described these as being token attempts at including service user views, frequently asking questions based on professional views of what is important in services, rather than those of users. Malins *et al.* (2006) agree, stating that surveys often face the problem of consistently high satisfaction levels that may not represent the reality of the services for many service users. Thus, the validity of satisfaction as a concept must be questioned.

A number of other methods of evaluating patient experience have been used. These include the critical incident technique (Powell *et al.*, 1994), consumer audit (Fitzpatrick & Boulton, 1994) and the use of focus groups (Kelson *et al.*, 1998). A degree of consumer audit was evident in the evaluation of mental health services (Malins *et al.*, 2006) by basing methods and tools for evaluation around the experiences of service users and also by the incorporation of service users in the overall research work. Thus, service user researchers conducted the interviews, with the proposition that a greater sense of empathy was generated and thus, may have produced more valid and reliable findings. Meanwhile, the purpose of focus group discussion is to provide a comfortable and non-threatening situation where individuals with a particular experience in common can discuss their views, feelings, beliefs or opinions, so that these can be recorded and used to inform future practice (McIver, 1995). This method of data collection was chosen by O'Toole *et al.* (2004) for the purpose of exploring the experiences of a first episode intervention in psychosis among twelve service users with an ultimate aim of informing future service planning and provision. They found the use of such groups provided a continuous audit cycle incorporating service improvements, centrally informed by service users' and caregivers' perspective.

We have already discussed the value of outcome criteria in relation to individual care planning. These also exist in the form of benchmarks for improvement on a service level. A particular example, and one that fully embraces the principle of service user involvement, emanates from New Zealand where service users developed a list of recovery-based competencies for attainment by mental health services staff (New Zealand Mental Health Commission, 2000; Allott & Loganathan, 2002). A further example of the benchmarking process to identify best practice and to develop action plans to remedy poor practice is the use of the essence of care framework. This was launched as part of the NHS Plan (Department of Health, 2001b) to enable healthcare personnel to take a structured approach to sharing and comparing practice, enabling them to identify best practice and to develop action plans to remedy poor practice. Service users, carers and professionals worked together to produce benchmarks covering nine fundamental aspects of patient care. These included the provision of best practice in relation to: communicating with service users, ensuring privacy and dignity of service users, as well as guaranteeing the safety of service users with mental health needs. The aim of this benchmarking process is to improve and ensure consistency in the quality of care and where necessary to implement change and disseminate good practice (Department of Health, 2001b).

Discussion of outcome criteria for evaluation as part of collaborative process with service users

The fact that adopting a recovery approach is, by definition, an individualistic process, has implications for evaluating care since some attempt needs to be made to establish important elements of care from whence specific criteria for auditing can be extracted (National Institute for Clinical Excellence, 2002). Thus, Anthony (1993) in his review of the recovery literature found that a common denominator of recovery is the presence of people who believe in and stand by the person in need of recovery. In this context, there is a growing body of evidence that indicates that there are two linked basic interpersonal processes that appear to be vital for mental health nurses in providing care for service users: engagement and inspiring hope (Barker, 2003). Engagement serves as the grounding for all other interventions but is also a powerful intervention in itself as the core of the working alliance between health professionals, service users, their families and carers. Such an alliance is a prerequisite to the sensitive and effective assessment of the person's needs, and the planning and implementation of suitable interventions. Engagement is also at the core of evaluating with the service user whether these needs are being met or not.

As regards the inspiration of hope, this appears to be a very subtle, discrete and multidimensional process. According to Turner (2002) an environment of hope is characterised by some of the following: taking risks, failing and trying again, access to objective information, validation of coping strategies and experience, (re)establishing skills for work, self management, social inclusion and support of family and/or friends. Meanwhile Cutcliffe and Grant (2001) found that the presence of another human being who demonstrates unconditional acceptance, tolerance and understanding as he or she enters the caring practice inspires hope. This is similar to the themes of mentorship, being treated as an individual, capturing the sense of the person beyond mental illness, giving assistance in developing a sense of self-worth, fostering connectedness with their community, recognising potential for growth and the importance of spirituality that emerged from recent studies (Kelly & Gamble, 2005; Malins *et al.*, 2006) as essential components of the recovery process. It is suggested, that collectively, these may be represented by the theme that emerged in a recent consultative exercise with Irish services users, as one of the most important features of a quality mental health service, that of being treated with dignity and respect (Mental Health Commission, 2005).

Negative influences on achieving an effective evaluation process

Peplau (1988) views the nurse as having a pivotal role in encouraging patients to make their own decisions, and assisting them by providing the necessary background information. This particular theme of lack of sufficient information is commonly encountered in user evaluations of services (Malins *et al.*, 2006). McDermott's (1998) study of the care programme approach found that patients had little knowledge regarding their care, and felt that their opinions regarding care planning and decision-making were less valued than those of their relatives and health professionals. This is supported by the recent British mental health service user survey (Healthcare Commission, 2005) which found that only a half were given a copy of their care plan, while one third did not know who their care coordinator was. This enforces the need for all stakeholders, staff and service users alike to be equipped with all necessary information to inform the evaluation process and subsequent decision making.

Interestingly, even where sufficient information is available, Rogers and Pilgrim (2003) dispute the concept of service user choice and make a valid point that expertise in all its forms is a form of disempowerment of service users although it is difficult to envisage how this could be totally eliminated. This is echoed in the observation of Campbell (2001) who notes that:

> *'the rhetoric of partnership implying as it does a large measure of equality and a close identity of interests and objectives is usually much more comfortable for those with the power, than those handing out the invitations'* (Campbell, 2001:7).

Thus, it is accepted that there is always potential for tension between the directive role of mental health professionals and the need to authentically maintain the user's role as the expert in how to manage their lives.

A further crucial variable here is time, with research by Anthony and Crawford (2000) identifying the problem of limited resources in terms of time and staffing as a major factor inhibiting service user involvement in care planning. This unfortunately is not an isolated finding (Robinson, 1994; Gijbels, 1995; Lepola & Vanhanen, 1997; Moore, 1998). In this context, it is essential that an organisational commitment to user involvement is reflected in adequate staffing levels and resource provision. An example of this is embodied in the process of refocusing (Bowles *et al.*, 2002) which endorses the need for more structured meaningful engagement with service users and their families, carers and significant others as appropriate. In facilitating this, it is the responsibility of mental health nurses to prioritise their available time to make their relationships with service users as collaborative as possible. Indeed, Bowl (1996) spoke of the necessity of staff training to facilitate successful implementation of user involvement in all aspects of their care including evaluation.

A further inhibiting factor in the process of collaborative evaluation may be the fact that the directive role of the mental health services is partially embedded in the delegated legal power that mental health workers have. Thus, mental health professionals have the power to detain and treat individuals who have been admitted on an involuntarily basis, through the powers of the Mental Health Treatment Act 1945 (Pilgrim, 1997). Thus it is hardly surprising that in situations where, as Happell *et al.*, (2002) found, choice is removed and the client is subject to involuntary treatment this impinges negatively on the development of the trust required for effective and therapeutic interactions and consequently it is argued, the necessary evaluation of same. Without such trust the partnership highlighted by successive governments, as an essential ingredient for a mental health service, will remain a challenge.

This challenge may be offset by the increased availability of advocacy services to support and guide those with mental health problems. The emergence and growth of mental health advocacy has been a major force behind the improvement of services (World Health Organization, 2001). It has been shown to improve the manner in which service users are able to articulate their vision of the services they require and their ability to make informed decisions about these services (World Health Organization, 2003). Obviously, meaningful involvement of service users in such shaping of the mental health services they desire requires the requisite access to information technology, training and administrative help and, where required, emotional support.

Service user evaluation can engender greater understanding and respect for the diversity of people's experiences and perspectives, increase awareness of users' and carers' resources and ultimately improve the quality of service delivery itself (Brooker *et al.*, 2005). It can provide true insights into the meaning and significance of illnesses that are culturally defined and socially mediated. Nowhere is this more blatant that in those with mental health problems. A recent evaluation of service users in Ireland (Expert Group on Mental Health Policy, 2004) found that 70% were dependent on welfare payments or had no income, while similar research in he UK (Office for National Statistics, 2003) found that only 24% of people with long-term mental health problems are in work. Since unemployment and poverty are interrelated, it is worth noting the clear evidence that poverty affects the experience of people with mental health problems in a variety of ways including not being able to afford accommodation, being stigmatised and being socially isolated (Rankin, 2005).

Being stigmatised in particular deprives people of their inherent dignity and interferes with their full participation in society and is a significant obstacle to fulfilling one's potential in life. To optimise user involvement in evaluating care requires that more be done to tackle stigma and discrimination, including the provision of a legislative framework to tackle such discrimination. It is well known that endeavours that facilitate social contact with individuals with mental health problems have the most impact in changing attitudes and behaviour towards such individuals (Gale *et al.*, 2004). This needs to be augmented by supportive communities and adequate financial backing if actions are to be taken to address basic needs such as the provision of adequate housing, vocational and employment opportunities with an emphasis on social inclusion.

As regards the relative worth of service user evaluations in the context of determining best practice, expert opinion appears at the bottom of the pile at level five in the hierarchy of evidence for evidenced based practice (Sackett *et al.*, 2000). That this should happen has formed the basis of some critical discussion in the literature. Significantly, the use of the randomised-controlled trial, at level one, has been criticised as the basis for nursing interventions in the mental health arena. The criticism, expressed by Rolfe (1996), proposes that, unlike what pertains to medical practice, mental health nurses should not be concerned with putting people into diagnostic categories, providing treatment appropriate to that diagnosis, and assessing the effectiveness of this through a randomised controlled trial. Indeed, the art of interpersonal relationships inherent in mental health nursing is not amenable to such reductionist measurement. Therefore, it is suggested that the hierarchy needs to be turned on its head and expert opinion be given priority in ascertaining the subjective experiences of those involved in receiving mental health interventions including service users, family, friends and carers, particularly in the current climate of change.

Conclusion

In summary, the process of individual care planning has been explored and some key points emerged:

- Evaluation is not a stand alone entity. In effect it permeates all stages of the nursing process but has particularly close links with the process of assessment.
- It can be a formal process in the context of completing measurement tools, or informal where it is taking place on a more on-going basis.
- The process of evaluation involves five stages: identifying goals to be achieved, collecting data, comparing this data with other selected criteria, judging the client's response (which is reflected by comparison and feed-back) and modifying the care plan.
- Practical strategies that facilitate evaluation include the process of col-laboration, the use of measurement tools, formulated outcome criteria and access to relevant underpinning knowledge.

On a more global basis a number of frameworks and strategic ideologies have been explored to ascertain broad national and international benchmarks of best practice in the mental health services. Perhaps the most notable factor has been the embrace of, and drive towards, a more holistic, person-centred and recovery based service embedded in desirable process and outcome measures such as respect, inclusion and citizenship. These are broad, often abstract precepts both to define and measure. However, a number of studies have been described that highlight how these principles are operationalised in the delivery of care and support. This information has been harvested using a number of data collection methods, some used with greater success and validity than others. Currently focus group interviews are proving quite effective, and have at times been facilitated by service users themselves with the aim of placing participants at ease with the process and enhancing rapport. Mean-while, the principle of consumer satisfaction surveys has being critiqued for the wooliness of the concept of satisfaction particularly in the context of a recurrent theme of dissonance between what service users and mental health professionals deem to be an optimum desirable outcome from contact with mental health services.

What is clear from the literature surveyed is that service users do not as a whole seem to be seeking complex interventions. Rather, in evaluating their care it would appear that many are searching for what may be termed, nebul-ous concepts such as the inspiration of hope, meaningful engagement, respect and the promotion of self-determination. The point was made that these values defy more conventional positivistic evidence-based measurement. In this context, traditional frameworks need to be modified to elevate the relative worth of expert service user opinion, thus appreciating the multiple personal constructions and different meanings inherent in defining these concepts.

The degree of service user involvement in the evaluation of care is influ-enced by a number of driving and restraining forces. These restraining forces may be individual to the service user, for example, role expectations, stage of illness, disempowering effect of self-stigma and adverse social circumstances. On a global basis meanwhile, systems vary nationally and internationally in their interpretation and embrace of service user evaluation and involvement. Therein, mental health professionals may use different benchmarks to evaluate the success or otherwise of contact with the mental health services. The negotiation and partnership required for such evaluation of care may be further compounded by the diminution of service user choice and freedom in situations where such users are legally detained within the mental health system and may be the subjects of compulsory treatment.

From a positive perspective much has happened to promote service user involvement in the evaluation of their individual care and that of mental health services generally. This includes the increased emphasis on the need for engagement and a working alliance with users, the growth of the advocacy services, the promotion of research involving service users and generalised strategic support of service user involvement. These elements are crucial to moving evaluation beyond rhetoric and into a meaningful reality.

References

Allott, P. & Loganathan, L. (2002). A New Paradigm for Delivering Recovery Oriented Services for People with Serious Mental Illness. *The Mental Health Review*. **7(2)**, 6–13.

Anthony, P. & Crawford, P. (2000). Service User Involvement in Care Planning: The Mental Health Nurse's Perspective. *Journal of Psychiatric and Mental Health Nursing*. **7**, 425–434.

Anthony, W. (1993). Recovery From Mental Illness: The Guiding Vision of the Mental Service In The 1990s. *Psychosocial Rehabilitation Journal*. **16**, 11–23.

Barker, P.J. (2003). *Psychiatric and Mental Health Nursing: The Craft Of Caring*. London: Arnold.

Barker, P.J. (2004). *Assessment in Psychiatric and Mental Health Nursing: In Search Of The Whole Person*. London: Nelson Thornes.

Bowl, R. (1996). Involving Service Users In Mental Health Services: Social Services Departments and The National Health Service and Community Care Act 1990. *Journal of Mental Health*. **5(3)**, 287–303.

Bowles, N., Dodds, P., Hackney, D., Sunderland, C. & Thomas, P. (2002). Formal Observations and Engagement: A Discussion Paper. *Journal of Psychiatric and Mental Health Nursing*. **9**, 255–260.

Brooker, C., Curran, J., James, A. & Readhead, E. (2005). Developing and Auditing an Audit Tool for Mental Health Education and Training: The National Mental Health Education Continuous Quality Improvement Tool. *Journal of Interprofessional Care*. **19(3)**, 280–293.

Bruce, S. & Paxton, R. (2002). Ethical Principles For Evaluating Mental Health Services: A Critical Examination. *Journal of Mental Health*. **11(3)**, 267–279.

Campbell, P. (2001). Surviving Social Inclusion. *Clinical Psychology Forum*. **150**, 6–13.

Christensen, J. (1993). *Nursing Partnership: A Model For Nursing Practice*. Edinburgh: Churchill Livingstone.

Cutcliffe, J. & Grant, G. (2001). What Are The Principles and Processes Of Inspiring Hope In Cognitively Impaired Older Adults Within A Continuing Care Environment? *Journal of Psychiatric and Mental Health Nursing*. **8(5)**, 427–436.

Day, J.C., Wood, G., Dewey, M. & Bentall, R.P. (1995). A Self Rating Scale For Measuring Neuroleptic Side Effects: Validation In A Group Of Schizophrenic Patients. *British Journal Of Psychiatry*. **166(5)**, 650–653.

Department of Health (2001a). *Essence Of Care*. London: The Stationery Office.

Department of Health (2001b). *The NHS Plan, a Plan for Investment, a Plan for Reform*. London: The Stationery Office.

Department of Health and Children (2001). *Quality and Fairness, a Health System for You*. Dublin: Stationery Office.

Department of Health and Children (2006). *A Vision for Change: Report Of The Expert On Mental Health Policy*. Dublin: Stationery Office.

Donabedian, A. (1986). Criteria and Standards For Quality Assessment and Monitoring. *Quality Review Bulletin*. **12**, 99–108.

Donabedian, A. (1988). The Quality Of Care: How Can It Be Assessed? *Journal of the American Medical Association*. **260**, 1743–1748.

Expert Group on Mental Health Policy (2004). *What We Heard: A Report On The Service User Consultation Process*. Dublin: Department of Health and Children.

Fitzpatrick, R. & Boulton, M. (1994). Qualitative Methods for Assessing Healthcare. *Quality in Health Care*. **3**, 107–113.

Gale, E., Seymour, L. & Crepaz-Keay, D. (2004). *Scoping Review on Mental Health Anti-Stigma and Discrimination: Current Activities and What Works*. Leeds: NIMNE.

Gijbels, H. (1995). Mental Health Nursing Skills In An Acute Admission Environment: Perceptions Of Mental Health Nurses and Other Health Professionals. *Journal of Advanced Nursing*. **21(3)**, 460–465.

Happell, B., Manias, E. & Pinikahana, J. (2002). The Role Of The Inpatient Mental Health Nurse In Facilitating Patient Adherence To Medication Regimes. *International Journal of Mental Health Nursing*. **11(4)**, 251–259.

Healthcare Commission (2005). *Service User Survey Access and Waiting*. London: Healthcare Commission.

Kelly, M. & Gamble, C. (2005). Exploring The Concept of Recovery in Schizophrenia. *Journal of Psychiatric and Mental Health Nursing*. **12(2)**, 245–251.

Kelson, M., Ford, C. & Rigge, M. (1998). *Stroke Rehabilitation: Patients and Carers' Views*. London: College of Health.

Lepola, I. & Vanhanen, L. (1997). The Patients Daily Activities in Acute Psychiatric Care. *Journal of Psychiatric and* Mental *Health Nursing*. **4(1)**, 29–36.

Malins, G., Oades, L., Viney, L. & Aspden, S. (2006). What's In A Service? Consumers Views Of Australian Mental Health Services. *Psychiatric Rehabilitative Journal*. **29(3)**, 197–204.

McDermott, G. (1998). The Care Programme Approach: A Patient Perspective. *Nursing Times Research*. **3**, 47–63.

McIver, S. (1995). Focus Groups and Discussion Groups: Are They The Same? *Journal of the Association of Quality in Healthcare*. **3(2)**, 43–48.

Mental Health Commission (2005). *Quality In Mental Health: Report On Stakeholder Consultation On Quality In Mental Health Services*. Dublin: Mental Health Commission.

Moore, C. (1998). Admission to An Acute Psychiatric Ward. *Nursing Times*. **94**, 58–59.

National Institute for Clinical Excellence (2002). *Principles For Best Practice In Clinical Audit*. Oxon: Radcliffe Medical Press.

New Zealand Mental Health Commission (2000). *Realising Recovery Through The Education Of Mental Heath Workers, Recovery Based Competencies and Resources*. New Zealand: New Zealand Mental Health Commission.

Norman, I. & Ryrie, I. (2004). *The Art and Science Of Mental Health Nursing*. Glasgow: Open University Press.

Office for National Statistics (2003). *Labour Force Survey*. London: Office for National Statistics.

O'Toole, M., Ohlsen, R., Taylor, T., Purvis, R., Walters, J. & Pilowsky, L. (2004). Treating First Episode Psychosis – The Service Users' Perspective: A Focus Group Evaluation. *Journal of Psychiatric and Mental Health Nursing*. **11(3)**, 319–326.

Peplau, H. (1988). *Interpersonal Relations in Nursing*. London: Macmillan.

Perkins, R. (2001). What Constitutes Success? The Relative Priority Of Service Users and Clinicians Views Of Mental Health Services. *British Journal of Psychiatry*. **179**, 9–10.

Pilgrim, D. (1997). *Psychotherapy and Society*, Sage, London.

Powell, J., Lovelock, R., Bray, J., & Philip, I. (1994). Involving Users In Assessing Service Quality; Benefits Of Using A Qualitative Approach, *Quality in Mental Health*, **3**, p199–202.

Prince, P. & Prince, C. (2001). Subjective Quality Of Life in the Evaluation of Programmes for People with Serious and Persistent Mental Illness. **21(7)**, 1005–1036.

Rankin, J. (2005). *Mental Health and Social Inclusion*. London: Institute for Public Policy Research.

Repper, J. (2000). Adjusting the Focus Of Mental Health Nursing: Incorporating Service Users' Experiences Of Recovery. *Journal of Mental Health*. **9(6)**, 575–588.

Robinson, D. (1994). *Developing Clinical Quality Indicators in Psychiatric Nursing*. PhD Thesis. Chelmsford: Anglia Polytechnic University.

Rogers, A. & Pilgrim, D. (2003). *Mental Health and Inequality*. Basingstoke: Palgrave Macmillan.

Rolfe, G. (1996). What To Do with Psychiatric Nursing. *Journal of Psychiatric and Mental Health Nursing*. **3(5)**, 331–333.

Sackett, D., Straus, S., Richardson, W., Rosenberg, W. & Haynes, R. (2000). *Evidence Based Medicine*. Edinburgh: Churchill Livingstone. (2nd edn).

Turner, D. (2002). Mapping The Routes to Recovery. *Mental Health Today*. **July**, 29–31.

World Health Organization (2001). *The World Health Report 2001, Mental Health: New Understanding, New Hope*. Geneva: World Health Organization.

World Health Organization (2003). *Health Report: Adherence to Long-Term Therapies Project*. Geneva: World Health Organization.

Zwarenstein, M. & Bryant, W. (2002). Interventions To Promote Collaboration Between Doctors and Nurses (Cochrane Review). *The Cochrane Library* Oxford. **2**.

Chapter 15

Reflections on the future

Angela Hall, Mike Wren and Stephan D. Kirby

It has become evident that throughout the previous chapters of this text, three main threads appear to run through what we euphemistically call contemporary mental health care. These being: the statutory demands of policy, law, professions and organisations; the developing evidence base, theoretical perspectives and models; and the person, the service user and carer perspectives and their focus on recovery. However if we had just logical frameworks and theories then the future would be bleak indeed, but we are all human beings and thankfully there is faith and hope and it is to these we turn for the future.

While Barker and Buchanan-Barker (1999) acknowledge that recovery has existed for over 70 years, it has transformed itself from the medical model notion of cure to the current service user owned and defined concept that encompasses hope, collaboration and positive optimism. There is evidence that in even the earlier work of both Bleuler and Kraeplin (in the late 1800s and early 1900s) there is the notion of recovery (Warner, 1997); however the rhetoric of these previous recoveries were usually created by professionals and bear little resemblance to today's service user defined concept of recovery.

Recovery when spoken about by mental health practitioners (MHP) tends to mean cure or at least an absence of symptoms. However recovery has been reclaimed and redefined by those service users who have lived the process for themselves and now new definitions have emerged:

'Recovery refers to the lived or real life experiences of people as they accept and overcome the challenge of the disability . . . they experience themselves as recovering a new sense of self and of purpose within and beyond the limits of the disability' (Repper & Perkins, 2003:45).

It is clear from the accounts of service user experiences within the chapters and from Eddie's story in Chapter 7, that being given a label of mental illness (schizophrenia) is destructive and disabling for the person and also their relatives and carers. The impact of discrimination in the form of stigmatisation can leave people feeling useless, worthless and with no hope. According to Sayce (1998), service users are most likely to shed their sense of shame if we succeed in attaining a society in which they are treated with greater value than at present. Stigma is often due to stereotypical images of mad people and the often exaggerated media accounts that fuel public ignorance and fear of people who experience mental health problems.

Graham Lyons in Chapter 2 referred to the oppressive connotations of labelling and how this oppressive behaviour became more extreme the more censorious the label. As Julie Smith notes in Chapter 7

> *'We could not talk to friends and most of our relations because people tend to become embarrassed, frightened and unsure how to react when you tell them that you have a son who suffers from schizophrenia. Nowadays we use the term psychosis, that seems to have less stigma attached to it'.*

We can also see how Eddie Smith in Chapter 7 has chosen his own diagnosis of bipolar disorder as he believes this more accurately reflects his mental health difficulties and is less damaging to his sense of self than his other possible diagnosis of schizophrenia.

Another message appears clear, one that service users and carers wish to be listened to, acknowledged and supported on their road to recovery, but at the same time they also have lives to live and deal with the same issues as every other person.

> *'Recovery is a process, a way of life, an attitude, and a way of approaching the day's challenges. It is not a perfectly linear process. At times our course is erratic and we falter, slide back, regroup and start again. . . . The need is to meet the challenge of the disability and to re-establish a new and valued sense of integrity and purpose within and beyond the limits of the disability; the aspiration is to live, work, and love in a community in which one makes a significant contribution'* (Deegan, 1988:15).

The concerns expressed in Chapter 8 by Jim Campbell and colleagues include the worry that this, service user, discourse on recovery will be hijacked by professionals and policy makers in an attempt to improve services. All of which rather dilutes or flattens the service users' original meaning and devalues their contributions to the act of recovery. This act of recovering needs to be left for the service user to define and have ownership of, while MHPs can assist by minimising and protecting their service user partners from the kind of destructive labelling, language and service experiences which can prevent the person's recovery process.

> *'Once recovery becomes systematised, you've got it wrong. Once it is reduced to a set of principles it is wrong. It is a unique and individualised process'* (Deegan, 1999).

If, as service providers, we are to promote the recovery of individuals then this would require a massive shift in the way services operate and assess local need. For those of us who remember the *taking over the asylums* fear as service users gained more control of their care, we can probably predict that the essence of recovery as a service model may well be a pipe dream. The fear created by the media presentations of people with mental illness and the current risk obsessed society in which we live are likely to stifle any major moves by the policy directors and organisations to actively promote recovery.

As David Duffy points out in Chapter 3, Mr Blair's words are pertinent: '*A risk-averse public sector will stifle creativity and deny to many the opportunities to be creative while supplying a few with compensation payments*'. It is against this wall of fear that promoters of the recovery concept are fighting. Not wanting to be too pessimistic, however, we know that given the right conditions, a recovery focused model of care can thrive, as is clearly shown in evaluations of the tidal model (Gordon *et al.*, 2005).

In order to improve mental health services we need to look at the users of these services to guide us and not at the services themselves. The chief nursing officer's review of mental health nursing (Department of Health, 2006b) puts the service user at the centre of the best practice competencies and capabilities for pre-registration mental health nursing in England. Along with *Our Health, Our Care, Our Say* (Department of Health, 2006a) the right messages are coming from Government sources; however these are accompanied with more paternalistic approaches proposed in the draft Mental Health Bill (Department of Health, 2004) and that of the care programme approach (CPA) (Department of Health, 1991).

Each aspect of these legislative and policy directives will have direct implications for the future delivery of collaborative care planning processes in mental health; collaborative care planning processes that are capable of providing a coordinated response to political and societal pressures. Such pressures are calling for the delivery of safe, effective and efficient practice, which is only effective if it continues to co-exist alongside the passionate petitioning from service users and their carers for a truly seamless and person-centred 21st century mental health service. This will involve:

'. . . balancing rights, responsibilities and risks creates situations where the views of individuals, the community, wider society or the media are in conflict (and) as with services for children, young people and their families integrated assessment across agencies is seen as important, along with preventative work and early intervention to facilitate people to remain better integrated in their communities, prevent social isolation and maintain independence (by strengthening) joint working between health and social care services, which will involve radically different ways of working, redesign of job roles and reconfiguration of services so that they are people-focused and more integrated across social care and health boundaries' (Department of Health, 2005a:11–13).

We have seen that the Mental Health Act (Department of Health, 1983) requires agencies to work together to devise after care plans for discharged patients previously detained under Section 3 of this Act. Equally the themes for working together within the NHS and Community Care Act (Department of Health, 1990) when contrasted with the current political and social policy directives clearly strengthen the argument that future practice and requirements to work together are essential factors that could yet prove to be crucial opportunities for the further development of a seamless, person-centred and proactive recovery focused approach to care planning within future mental health services.

Accommodating differences is therefore at the heart of sustaining and maintaining effective inter-professional working relationships and networks that is essential to the delivery of a seamless, person-centred and proactive CPA through the coordination of an efficient care coordinator. This can be efficiently carried out by the adoption of the ten essential shared capabilities, as cited by a number of authors in this text (e.g. Alan Pringle, Richard Brittle, Jim Campbell and colleagues), through particularly promoting recovery; service user centred care; making a difference and promoting safety and positive risk taking (Department of Health, 2005b).

Such improvements will require skilful navigation and interpretation of a very steep service development curve for all MHPs, their respective organisations and professional bodies as they ascend through this paper mountain of legislation, policy directives, White Papers, competing funding initiatives, service delivery objectives and targets intended to join up the strategic thinking of inter-professional mental health care planning practices for the future. Inter-professional practices are aimed at providing a collaborative base camp for delivering a seamless, person-centred and recovery focused approach to CPA (Department of Health, 1991) against a backdrop of control, effective risk management and the protection of the public.

Equally we propose that the ideal of inter-professional working (that is underpinned by effective education and developmental opportunities across the professional boundaries and domains of mental health nursing and social work) is now (more than ever) worth striving for. Particularly when striving to respond sensitively to the multiplicity of individual needs of people with mental health problems and their carers, working in close collaboration with a variety of colleagues and service providers who collectively acknowledge that working together is easy when things are going well, but it takes time, effort and commitment to stay together during tough times (Glasby, 2006:33).

How can individual practitioners promote recovery for service users whilst working within the frameworks of their organisational/professional constraints? It demands a return to the basics using 21st century style complementing 20th century rhetoric. Essentially underpinning the concept of recovery with the philosophy of respecting the individual human value and their potential. The humanistic values in the original work of both Maslow (1954) and Rogers (1951) are without doubt the fundamentals on which to base any interaction with another person. Maslow's (1970) theory of human needs and the belief of self actualisation, brings in his theory of motivation, linked into the growth, happiness and satisfaction of every person.

> 'The assumption that the subjective human being has an importance and a value that is basic: that no matter how he may be labelled or evaluated he is a human person first of all and most deeply' (Rogers & Stevens, 1967:2).

This, therefore, places all human beings as equals, on an equal level and assigns them equivalent rights and responsibilities based on the assumption that as persons they have a degree of worth which transcends that of other creatures and objects within the world.

Today we are clearly aware of the fact that the interpersonal relationship represents the key focus and that the practitioner's therapeutic strength lies in their ability to enhance a person beyond the restoration of rationality towards life enhancing growth – that is, empowerment. The only way MHPs can be of real service to the person is to learn from the person's experiences and facilitate a dynamic learning process whereby the practitioners learn what to do *for* the person, *from* the person.

This learning process is one of the most crucial elements in building relationships with anyone, be it service users, colleagues, friends, lovers, or relatives. We must develop and enhance our ability and a willingness to understand the life of the other person from where they stand, from their perspective. Although it is never possible to know what life is exactly like for someone else, a willingness to explore the way the person sees their situation is all important. It is the client who knows what hurts, what directions to go, what problems are crucial, what experiences have been deeply buried (Rogers, 1961).

To totally understand another's world involves being that person (Burnard, 1992). Yet, Gilmore (1980) stresses that from an existential perspective we are all alone, in that no other person can have total understanding of another. This is supported by the following quote *'For when horizons grow or diminish within a person, the distances are not measurable by other people'* (Axline, 1964). Understanding then can be seen to develop from the depths of our own experiences and while we can never experience totally the experiences of others, we can acknowledge that each person's behaviour is as a result of their unique experiences of life and the subsequent development of self, as are our own.

This idea of relating to another in relation to them as another self rather than an object is what Buber (Bragan, 1987) espouses in his work on I-IT and I-THOU relationships: *'I-THOU relating is active participation in the current of reciprocity that is empathic relatedness'*.

It is (and has been) proposed that effective therapeutic relationships are distinguished by a dynamic mutual learning process. This is one which is utilised by both parties in the alliance, the person who helps the practitioner to understand (in their own use of words) how they conceptualise, rationalise, explain and cope with their mental health problems (e.g. hearing voices, depression, anger/aggression problems, behavioural problems, sexual dysfunction) and the practitioner who learns from the person's experiences, both positive and negative. This will allow them to enter into care planning which is more meaningful and contextual and promotes deeper learning through their individuality and focus.

Recovery orientated practice does not demand that the frameworks of care that exist be abandoned recklessly, or that the developing evidence base be ignored. What it requires though is an emphasis on the person first and foremost and that the framework and theoretical perspectives are used in a way that enables the person to achieve their needs, desires and aspirations for living. Any theory or framework should not dictate what the person's needs are or how they will be achieved; they simply provide a vehicle through which they may be helped to achieve them. Deegan talks of how the strengths model (Rapp & Goscha, 2006) helped her to structure her life by assessing her strengths, planning goals, acquiring resources and gaining mastery and celebration (Deegan, 2003:372). Broadly defined, evidence based practice has a rightful place in the recovery paradigm for this very reason that some models/theories can resonate with the person's experiences and offer them hope for the future.

A recovery paradigm is each person's unique experience of their road to recovery. *'... My recovery paradigm included my reconnection which included the following four key ingredients: connection, safety, hope, and acknowledgment of my spiritual self'* (Long, 1994:4).

This will involve a primary focus by MHPs on what Barker (2000) refers to as the art rather than the science and will ensure that any framework or theory is adapted to the person not the person to fit the theory. This approach will enable practitioners to care for people rather than patients, clients or labels. We have witnessed from Eddie's account in Chapter 7, and from other service user accounts that hope, optimism and positive beliefs have been, and are, fundamental to the process of recovery. *'One of the elements that makes recovery possible is the regaining of one's belief in oneself'* (Chamberlin, 1997:9).

It is from within the human interpersonal relationship that hope can be drawn. As Deegan (1996:93) points out *'Hope is not just a nice sounding euphemism. Hope and biological life are inextricably linked'*. This relates to Seligman's (1975) proposition that the psychological state of helplessness increases the risk of death, he gives examples of when this has occurred with animals and humans and he concludes that the feelings of helplessness and hopelessness are the two pervading emotions linked to sudden death. While the scientific validity and reliability of such descriptions can be questioned and analysed, nonetheless it remains evident that it is a human phenomenon that when faced with no options, people will give up and become helpless and this can lead to what Deegan describes as the *'hardened heart'*.

> *'Giving up was not a problem. It was a solution. It was a solution because it protected me from wanting anything. If I didn't want anything, then it couldn't be taken*

away. If I didn't try then I wouldn't have to undergo another failure. If I didn't care then nothing could hurt me again. My heart became hardened' (Deegan, 1996:93).

Hope is the consistent thread running through many of the stories of recovery, it is also becoming a subject for detailed inquiry. Koehn and Cutcliffe (2007) have performed a systematic review of the literature focusing on hope as inspired within an interpersonal (counselling) approach in mental health nursing. They stated that being hopeful is viewed as an essential characteristic of mental health professionals who work with people with schizophrenia (Koehn & Cutcliffe, 2007). Another observation was that one's hope or hopefulness is contagious in that it can significantly affect the hope of other people, and they recommend that workplaces organise to increase hopefulness in both staff and clients.

'Having some hope is crucial to recovery; none of us would strive if we believed it a futile effort. I believe that if we confront our illnesses with courage and struggle with our symptoms persistently, we can overcome our handicaps to live independently, learn skills, and contribute to society, the society that has traditionally abandoned us' (Leete, 1989:607).

Finally we wish to ask you two key questions, as posed by Repper and Perkins, (2003:11) and leave the future to you!

'How different would services look if their primary focus was to enable people to use and develop their skills, make the most of their assets and pursue their aspirations?'

'Would this not change, for the better, the experience of using services, and the relationship between workers and those whom we serve?'

References

Axline, I.M. (1964). *Dibs In Search Of Self*. Aylesbury: Penguin.

Barker, P.J. (2000). Reflections On Caring As A Virtue Ethic Within An Evidence Based Culture. *International Journal of Nursing Studies*. **37(4)**, 329–36.

Barker, P.J. & Buchanan-Barker, P. (1999). *The Tidal Model: Recovery and Reclamation*. Available at: http://www.tidal-model.co.uk/recovery.htm (Accessed 30 March 2007).

Bragan, K. (1987). I and Thou: An Examination of Empathy. *Australian and New Zealand Journal of Psychiatry*. **21**, 575–579.

Burnard, P. (1992). *Counselling A Guide To Practice In Nursing*. Oxford: Butterworth Heinemann.

Chamberlin, J. (1997). Confessions of a Non-Compliant Patient. *National Empowerment Center Newsletter*. Lawrence, MA: National Empowerment Center.

Deegan, P.E. (1988). Recovery: The Lived Experience of Rehabilitation. *Psychiatric Rehabilitation Journal*. **11**, 11–19.

Deegan, P.E. (1996). Coping With: Recovery as a Journey of the Heart. *Psychiatric Rehabilitation Journal*. **19(3)**, 91–7.

Deegan, P.E. (1999). Recovery: An Alien Concept. In: *Proceedings Of The Strange Fish Conference: Recovery: An Alien Concept*. UK: Birmingham.

Deegan, P.E. (2003). Discovering Recovery. *Psychiatric Rehabilitation Journal*. **26(4)**, 368–76.

Department of Health (1983). *Mental Health Act*. London: HMSO.

Department of Health (1990). *NHS & Community Care Act*. London: HMSO.

Department of Health (1991). *The Care Programme Approach For People With Mental Illness*. London: HMSO.

Department of Health (2004). *Draft Mental Health Bill*. London: The Stationery Office.

Department of Health (2005a). *New Ways Of Working For Psychiatrists: Enhancing Effective, Person-Centred Services Through New Ways Of Working In Multidisciplinary and Multi-Agency Contexts*. London: Royal College of Psychiatrists, National Institute for Mental Health in England and Changing Workforce Programme.

Department of Health (2005b). *The Ten Essential Shared Capabilities; A Framework for the Whole of the Mental Health Workforce*. London: The Stationery Office.

Department of Health (2006a). *Our Health, Our Care, Our Say: A New Direction For Community Services*. London: The Stationery Office.

Department of Health (2006b). *The Chief Nursing Officer's Review of Mental Health Nursing*. London: The Stationery Office.

Gilmore, S. (1980). A Comprehensive Theory for Eclectic Intervention. *International Journal for the Advancement of Counselling*. 185–210.

Glasby, J. (2006). Joint working has many benefits. *Nursing Times*. **102(30)**, 22–3.

Gordon, W., Morton, T. & Brooks, G. (2005). Launching The Tidal Model: Evaluating The Evidence. *Journal of Psychiatric and Mental Health Nursing*. **12(6)**, 703–712.

Koehn, C.V. & Cutcliffe, J.R. (2007). Hope and interpersonal psychiatric/mental health nursing: a systematic review of the literature – part one. *Journal of Psychiatric and Mental Health Nursing*. **14**, 134–140.

Leete, E. (1989). How I Perceive and Manage My Illness. *Schizophrenia Bulletin*. **8**, 605–609.

Long, A.E. (1994). Reflections On Recovery. *Recovery: The New Force In Mental Health*. 1–16.

Maslow, A.H. (1954). *Motivation & Personality: Toward a Psychology of Being*. New York: John Wiley Publisher.

Maslow, A.H. (1970). *Motivation & Personality: Toward a Psychology of Being*. New York: John Wiley Publisher. (2nd edn).

Rapp, C.A. & Goscha, R.J. (2006). *The Strengths Model: Case Management with People with Psychiatric Disabilities*. Oxford: Oxford University Press.

Repper, J. & Perkins, R. (2003). *Social Inclusion and Recovery*. Edinburgh: Baillière Tindall.

Rogers, C.R. (1951). *Client-Centred Therapy*. London: Constable.

Rogers, C.R. (1961). *On Becoming A Person: A Therapist's View Of Psychotherapy*. London: Constable.

Rogers, C.R. & Stevens, B. (1967). *Person to Person: The Problem of Being Human*. Guernsey: The Guernsey Press Co. Ltd.

Sayce, L. (1998). Stigma, Discrimination and Social Exclusion: What's in a Word? *Journal of Mental Health*. **7(4)**, 331–44.

Seligman, M.E.P. (1975). *Helplessness: on Depression, Development and Death*. San Francisco: W.H. Freeman & Co.

Warner, R. (1997). *Recovery from Schizophrenia; Psychiatry and Political Economy*. London: Routledge. (2nd edn).

Index

MUS.

ANTONIONI

Antonioni

The Poet of Images

WILLIAM ARROWSMITH

Edited with an Introduction
and Notes by Ted Perry

New York   Oxford
OXFORD UNIVERSITY PRESS
1995

Oxford University Press

Oxford   New York   Toronto
Delhi   Bombay   Calcutta   Madras   Karachi
Kuala Lumpur   Singapore   Hong Kong   Tokyo
Nairobi   Dar es Salaam   Cape Town
Melbourne   Auckland   Madrid

and associated companies in
Berlin   Ibadan

Published by Oxford University Press, Inc.,
200 Madison Avenue, New York, New York 10016

Oxford is a registered trademark of Oxford University Press

Library of Congress Cataloging-in-Publication Data
Arrowsmith, William, 1924–1992.
Antonioni : the poet of images / William Arrowsmith :
edited with an introduction and notes by Ted Perry.
p.   cm.
Includes bibliographical references and index.
ISBN 0–19–509270–8
1. Antonioni, Michelangelo—Criticism and interpretation.
I. Perry, Ted.   II. Title.
PN1998.3.A58A77   1995
791.43'0233'092—dc20   94–35375

9 8 7 6 5 4 3 2 1

Printed in the United States of America
on acid-free paper

Acknowledgments

791, 4302
A779

NOV 03 1995

Without the support at Boston University of Gerald Gross, one of William Arrowsmith's literary executors, this book would not have been completed. I am very grateful to him, as well as to W. S. Di Piero, Seymour Chatman, Leger Grindon, and Rosanna Warren, who generously took the time to read the entire manuscript, providing many helpful suggestions and corrections. Don Mitchell, Miriam Perry, John Bertolini, and, particularly, Kirk Melnikoff have my gratitude for their invaluable editorial and research assistance. Special thanks go to Carrol Hassman, Arrowsmith's secretary, who found the original lectures and went over them again, deciphering some of the handwriting and otherwise providing inestimable aid in editing and interpreting Arrowsmith's essays.

I also wish to thank the following publishers for permission to use copyrighted material:

Bucknell University Press for its version of Arrowsmith's essay on *Red Desert*, published in 1980 in *The Binding of Proteus: Perspectives on Myth and the Literary Process*, ed. Marjorie W. McCune et al., pp. 312–37.

Humanities in Society, a journal published by the Center for the Humanities at the University of Southern California, for a version of Arrowsmith's

ACKNOWLEDGMENTS

essay on *The Passenger*, published in the summer of 1978 (vol. 1, no. 3, pp. 175–202).

The National Poetry Foundation for its version of Arrowsmith's article on *The Passenger*, which it published in 1985 in the journal *Pequod* (nos. 19–20, pp. 33–65).

Random House, Inc., for permission to reprint material from Oswald Spengler's *The Decline of the West*, vol. 2, trans. Charles Francis Atkinson (New York: Alfred A. Knopf, 1957).

Viking Press, a division of Penguin Books USA, for permission to reprint material from "Words from Confinement," in *Hard Labor*, by Cesare Pavese, translated by William Arrowsmith. Translation copyright © 1976 by William Arrowsmith. *Hard Labor* was published originally as *Lavorare stanca*, copyright © 1943 by Giulia Einaudi editore, Torino.

Excerpt from *Civilization and Its Discontents* by Sigmund Freud, translated by James Strachey, copyright © 1961 James Strachey. Reprinted with the permission of W. W. Norton & Company, Inc., and The Hogarth Press, London.

Excerpts from "Gerontion," *The Waste Land*, "The Love Song of J. Alfred Prufrock," and "East Coker" in *Complete Poems and Plays, 1909–1950* by T.S. Eliot. Reprinted by permission of Harcourt Brace & Company and Faber and Faber Ltd.

"Il passero solitario" (The Solitary Thrush), "L'infinito" (The Infinite), from *Giacomo Leopardi: Selected Poetry and Prose* by Giacomo Leopardi, translated by Iris Origo and John Heath-Stubbs, Translation copyright © 1966 by Iris Origo and John Heath-Stubbs. Used by permission of Dutton Signet, a division of Penguin Books USA Inc.

Excerpts from *Opere*, vol. 1, by Giacomo Leopardi, ed. Sergio Solmi. Copyright © 1966 by Riccardo Ricciardi, Milan.

Excerpt from *The Revolt of the Masses*, by José Ortega y Gasset, authorized translation from the Spanish. Reprinted by permission of W.W. Norton & Company, Inc., and HarperCollins Publishers.

Excerpt from "Eclipse" interview with Michelangelo Antonioni in *Theatre Arts*, vol. 46, no. 7 (July 1962). Reprinted by permission of Michelangelo Antonioni.

Excerpt from interview with Michelangelo Antonioni in *Sight and Sound*, vol. 33, no. 3 (Summer 1964) and *L'Express* (1964). Reprinted by permission of Michelangelo Antonioni.

"Did You Ever Have to Make Up Your Mind" by John Sebastian © 1965 by Alley Music Corporation and Trio Music Co., Inc. Used by permission of Freddy Bienstock Enterprises. All rights reserved.

Excerpt from "Zabriskie Point," performed by The Kaleidoscope on MGM record #SE-46668ST. Copyright Polygram Records.

Excerpts from *Blow-up* filmscript by Michelangelo Antonioni. Copyright Turner Entertainment.

Editor's Note

When William Arrowsmith died in 1992, he left an unfinished manuscript for a projected book on Michelangelo Antonioni; several years earlier he had written a letter asking me, in the event of his death, to prepare and edit that material for publication. We had been talking about the Italian film director since the 1960s, shortly after Arrowsmith had begun seriously thinking, lecturing, and writing about Antonioni. During those early years, Arrowsmith prepared and gave lectures on *Red Desert* and *Zabriskie Point*, and in 1977 he gave seven lectures at the Museum of Modern Art in New York City, one each on *Il grido*, *L'avventura*, *La notte*, *Eclipse*, *Red Desert*, *Blow-up*, and *Zabriskie Point*. In 1978 he published an early version of his essay on *The Passenger*, and in 1980 his essay on *Red Desert* appeared.

Arrowsmith's manuscript consisted of the eight essays contained in this volume, arranged here in chronological order according to the date of the film's release. The two published essays had obviously been revised extensively, but the others were still in a first draft form, typed and handwritten by Arrowsmith. These essays, most of which were probably his lectures for the Museum of Modern Art series, had been retyped but not examined by Arrowsmith. What I have done, with the help of Arrowsmith's secretary, is to compare the typed versions of each chapter with the first drafts and then to edit them. In one case (*La notte*) there was only a version done by a typist,

presumably working from an original Arrowsmith lecture which is now missing. In another instance (*Blow-up*) the original text had been revised, but it seemed to me that the revisions—mainly deletions—were done to prepare the essay for a lecture, and that it made sense to restore some parts of the first draft because the arguments there seemed more subtle and comprehensive.

I have done a fair amount of editing on the unpublished essays, often because neither I nor Carrol Hassman could make out Arrowsmith's handwriting, but mainly in order to clarify the text and to make some corrections, as well as to provide citations where Arrowsmith had not. I have resisted as much as possible the temptation to rewrite extensively, even where it was clear that an essay had been prepared to be spoken rather than published, because Arrowsmith's style was so distinctive that to rewrite it would have been not only presumptuous but to take away the sense of the writer. Arrowsmith is, after all, the person through whom Antonioni is being read, and to change the voice of the critic would be to alter unduly the sense of the argument. On the other hand, the published essays have been changed very little, and then primarily to correct some typographical errors in the printed versions, to provide some uniformity of spelling with the other essays, and to update some of the references and citations. The essay on *The Passenger* had been published in two versions, and I used mainly the more recent one, published in *Pequod*, presuming that it contained Arrowsmith's latest thoughts.

The titles utilized for the films are those most commonly used in the United States (the appendix provides alternate titles for each work). I should note, too, that I have not provided citations for each dialogue quotation that Arrowsmith uses, although I have checked the accuracy of the quotations against the versions of the films available in the United States and also, when necessary, against versions of the scripts; when a choice was to be made, I used the dialogue that is actually heard in the film rather than what appears in a script. Often the published scripts are erroneous (many are the screenplays produced before filming began), although in some cases the published scripts contain material that was never shot and/or does not appear in the film as released in the United States. Where there are important differences between script and film, or between an Arrowsmith quotation and that in the scripts or in the films, I have provided citations. Arrowsmith frequently quotes from the films, sometimes giving the original Italian, but for the sake of consistency I have translated everything into English, noting those places, as he often did, where the Italian was crucial to any real understanding.

Most of these essays were first given as lectures immediately following the screening of one or more of the Antonioni films; they thus assume detailed familiarity with the works being discussed. Readers of this book are at a disadvantage in not having recently seen all the Antonioni films. To

alleviate this situation I have included in the appendix a very brief synopsis for each of the eight films.

The essays on *Red Desert* and *The Passenger*, which Arrowsmith did rework extensively and publish, make it quite clear what we might have had if he had lived to finish this book; of all the essays, these are the most complex and substantial. They demonstrate most clearly the insight, sensitivity, and intelligence with which one of our most distinguished humanist critics illuminates and celebrates the work of Michelangelo Antonioni.

Contents

ANTONIONI

Introduction

What was there about Michelangelo Antonioni's films that ignited such a response in William Arrowsmith, noted literary critic and classicist, distinguished humanist and translator?[1] The complete answer requires reading this book, of course, for it makes quite clear why Arrowsmith thought that Antonioni's work was worth the critic's efforts. Yet there are reasons not readily apparent in the book. On a personal level, I think Arrowsmith identified with Antonioni; here was an artist who bravely and imaginatively enunciated those ideas that Arrowsmith himself found consequential. The act of criticism became an act of empathic impersonation, bringing Arrowsmith even closer to the filmmaker. Why else would a critic labor so enthusiastically if not because he saw the text of his own life in the text of the artist? An even more important reason for the effort on Antonioni's behalf was probably Arrowsmith's own understanding of what a critic is supposed to do: make revelatory judgments about texts—plays, poems, novels, speeches, films. What is crucial is not the medium but what is said, and how. If Arrowsmith discovered a body of work he thought beautiful and important, he stood on the highest ground he could find and loudly proclaimed what he discovered, explaining in great detail why the work was worth attention. Arrowsmith also relished a good fight, and he didn't suffer fools— not those of popular film criticism who he believed often unfairly dismissed

and stupidly misunderstood Antonioni's work, and not those of academic film criticism who he felt were so caught up in intellectual fads that they no longer gave a hoot about great texts, wouldn't know a great text if they stepped on one, or, if by some accident they did recognize a great text, wouldn't have the courage to say so. Timidity about texts and artists was not Arrowsmith's problem:

> Let me be clear about what I think: that Antonioni is one of the greatest living artists, and that, as a director of film, his only living peer is Kurosawa; and that he is unmistakably the peer of the other great masters in all the arts. As an innovator and manipulator of images, he is the peer of Joyce in the novel; in creating a genuine cinematic poetry, he stands on a level with Valéry and Eliot in poetry proper; and that his artistic vision, while perhaps no greater than that of Fitzgerald or Eliot or Montale or Pavese, is at least as great and compelling.[2]

At a time when much criticism thinks texts do not exist apart from readers of texts, when commentaries are overweeningly narrow and devoid of genuine appraisal, when analysis is frequently concerned with contexts more than with texts, we can delight in Arrowsmith's bold claim, not only because it declares so well his opinion of Antonioni but also because the declaration reveals clearly the degree of Arrowsmith's passion for the work of this filmmaker. Not an analyst laboring at arm's length from the work, and not a cultural theorist embroiled in a scheme that is indifferent to the quality and importance of the films, Arrowsmith was a writer who believed that the purpose of critical activity is to celebrate and illuminate films that are markedly innovative and that help us to live. This is a critic who thought that great films and great film artists are significant not because they contain useful concepts but because as felt experiences they enliven individuals. Arrowsmith's work is intimately bound up with understanding which texts and which artists hearten human beings and what that means. He asked the big questions: What are films for? Can films matter? How do great films inspire us?

These inquiries are closely connected to another question he also implicitly poses: What is an artist? Used so loosely now, the label "artist" needs clearer elaboration; Arrowsmith's case for Antonioni is based first upon an understanding of the great artist as someone supremely inventive in his or her expression, so much so that the resulting work constitutes a new definition of that artistic form. In the twentieth century such artists as Joyce, Picasso, and Cunningham gave us work the likes of which we had never seen, while at the same time also redefining the medium in which they worked. What Stravinsky and Webern and Cage did was at first thought not to be music, and the irate reaction to their initial work was repeated in the

enraged response to Antonioni's *L'avventura*. Many people were furious because it did not fit their notion of what a film should be.

We ask not only that the great artist have this distinctive and original "voice" but also that he or she use the medium to engage the fundamental issues of human experience; that there be a moral quality to the artist's distinctive vision. This is not to say that the artist tells us how to live, what is right and wrong, and what is good and what is bad, but that he or she describes the world uncompromisingly, thereby requiring us to see what is true. By energetically confronting the demons depicted for us by the artist—and rejecting the role of passive consumer of art—we can restore our confidence in the possibility of a vital human life. The resplendent originality and truthful insight of the artist's vision, wonderful and sometimes horrific, astonishes us. We marvel that a human being is capable of making something so unique. Seeing such a work revives our faith in human potential and reminds us all that creativity and imagination are essential to our lives; at best they inspire us to renewed action and at worst they make us feel less lost and confused.

Is there any truth to these generalizations, or are they simply platitudes that we mouth about "art" and the "artist," the last gasps of a dying elite? Arrowsmith thought not, as his study of Antonioni profoundly attests. Yet what does it mean to say that art, particularly if a film, actually serves some human purpose? Simply put, we understand better what is happening to us and in the world around us when someone organizes experience into an artificial structure that clarifies what is not readily apparent. We may not really know what we think or feel until we write or say it, or until someone does that for us, and we have a hard time seeing through the chaos of experience to determine what is actually happening, much less what it means. A film made by an artist can be a fabricated version of life that allows us to comprehend ourselves, the world, or something in it in a new way. Comprehending is not enough, of course. What we require from the film artist is nothing less than the impress of the self, a raging subjectivity presenting its revelatory vision not as lesson to be learned but as experience to be apprehended. Such a view of art doesn't account for everything, of course, and no definition ever will, for the artist's imagination is always involved in presenting things to us that we do not initially fathom and accept, but I think that this understanding of film as an art form underlies Arrowsmith's approach to Antonioni's work. The present study is, happily, not only a book *about* the films but also an explication—even a celebration—of what we as human beings can learn *from* them about who we are and what life is like.

The artist's role has its counterpart, then, in that of the critic, who comments upon and makes judgments about the work of the artist in the same way that the artist describes the world. The critic creates an artificial

structure that makes more apparent what the artist is saying, while celebrating the imagination manifest in the work. When an artist like Antonioni is examined by a critic like Arrowsmith, we see again how art is connected to life, life to death, and both art and life to meaning. These "stories"—in every sense of that word and including images and sounds and words—fundamentally change the way we see the world, and ourselves. We can live our lives without an Antonioni, but we cannot live as meaningfully and gracefully without something like the experiences he gives us. Our ability to know and understand this fact is enhanced by the critic who holds the great work up for us and shows how it is crucial.

I now want to recapitulate Arrowsmith's argument for Antonioni, although I do so with some trepidation, fearing that in trying to provide a summary I will give away too many details of the analysis. Yet a book of essays that began as lectures, written and delivered individually, with little thought of the whole, deserves an overview.

In what ways is Antonioni the innovator and manipulator of images that Arrowsmith claims him to be? The critic notes, as a small example, how in *La notte* the image of Lidia and Roberto driving off in the rain is an extraordinarily lucid presentation of the possibility for a feeling of oneness in a romance, however fleeting. The couple, cut off from the world, seems for a few moments to be one person, afloat on a sea of feeling—transcendent. In *Il grido* the expanse of emptiness that is the vast Po Delta becomes an analog for the state of Aldo's soul, just as his serial relationships—like those of so many Antonioni characters—tell again and again that he is permanently disconnected from himself, his home, true love, and a meaningful life.

One of the best examples of Antonioni's inventiveness, as revealed by Arrowsmith, is the scene in *Il grido* after Aldo puts his daughter, Rosina, on the bus and then leaves the woman, Virginia. We next see Aldo on the horizon, walking along the top of the Po embankment and flanked on one side by tall poplar trees; then, as a tree in the foreground is felled, Aldo too "falls" by running down the levee. The woods are being clear-cut; Aldo and the tree are both dying. The next moment reveals that porcupines are being easily killed because they are losing their shelter in the trees, just as Aldo's fall results from the original loss of his home. That one image of Aldo running down the embankment captures not only his desperate plunge, deeper and deeper into a spiritual death, but also connects the rampant clear-cutting to a culture intent on destroying its tree nest. Arrowsmith shows how every element of the scene—the horizontal embankment, the vertical trees, the tree felling, the loss of shelter for the porcupines and for Aldo, even a piece of dialogue in the original script that was not used in the film—all contribute to the import of the scene and connect it to the larger context of the entire work.

In *L'avventura* the image of Sandro in a fit of jealousy deliberately

spilling ink on the young man's drawing, and then racing back to force himself on Claudia, depicts what is happening to all those who have traded their souls for money and who try to fill the emptiness with various forms of a diseased Eros. In *Eclipse* the pervasive use of windows, walls, gates, fences, and other barriers is Antonioni's way of making it clear, visually, that this is a world in which people and their feelings are greatly confined. As Arrowsmith points out, "the imagery of enclosure that is so prominent in *Il grido* is [in *La notte*] already evolving into the imagery of imprisonment—caged feelings and suppressed realities—that will dominate *Eclipse*, hinting in that film of the violence lurking and looming under the deceptively placid surface of the world, with its solid appearances and stolid certainties."

Some of Antonioni's imagery is connected with psychogeographical journeys that fulfill an interior destiny—Aldo across the Po Delta, Locke through Europe, Claudia and Sandro looking for Anna, Mark and Daria going deeper and deeper into the desert. Lidia's walk in *La notte* is a revealing and imaginative pilgrimage toward those moments and places in her past when life seemed to have some vital essentiality. The hunger that animates Lidia's journey is also apparent in Vittoria's attraction to the fossil in *Eclipse*, and in the joyful lovemaking in the ancient desert at Zabriskie Point, and even in *Red Desert*'s Sardinian beach fantasy as imagined by Giuliana. Again and again Antonioni has found inventive visual means to express this longing for a past, for an Edenic time that is lost or can be revived only momentarily.

Antonioni's most phenomenal images ofter occur at the end of his films. In *Blow-up*, for instance, we understand quite clearly what is happening to Thomas as he is seduced back into the tennis game by the mummers who persuade him to loft an imaginary tennis ball. What he is really persuaded to do is to rejoin what Arrowsmith calls the Game, that is, to surrender his perceptions for the sake of belonging to a group and avoiding painful individuation. Nothing is said in this sequence; the image tells everything. Having confronted the shocking reality of a murder, Thomas still feels the need to join in the Game, although every aspect of his manner also suggests that this is a different Thomas. Perhaps he joins the Game because he is no longer sure what is real and what is imaginary, which is a new state of affairs for a photographer whose life has been ruled by appearances. This somewhat different Thomas, simultaneously more aware and yet still joining in the Game, then dissolves slowly into the grass, reminding us all how ephemeral is human existence. The final montage of *Eclipse*, depicting in detail the corner where Vittoria and Piero fail to show up for a promised meeting, presents with astute images a similar feeling of evanescence, as well as absence and the death of passion. The ending of *L'avventura*, with Claudia standing behind a seated and crying Sandro, with Mount Etna and a stone building in the background, forcefully captures the predicament of people who feel betrayed by emotions and attitudes out of kilter with their ideals.

Similary, near the end of *The Passenger* Locke meets his death—faces it in every sense of that word—in and through an image that is one of the most extraordinary in the history of cinema: during his death the camera floats out of his room, turns, and then comes back to witness the Girl and Locke's wife as they describe whom they see on Locke's deathbed. When Aldo, at the end of *Il grido*, climbs to the top of the tower and, like the porcupines watching from a tree the devastation of their shelter, looks out on his lost home being sundered by bulldozers and the fields burned to make way for an airfield, he seems incapable of dealing with this destruction; the loss of Irma is almost more that he can bear. This final disruption and displacement of his world are too much and, like one of the porcupines, he falls and dies. Is there a more poignant image of a person lost, detached from her world, than the scene near the end of *Red Desert* when Giuliana and the foreign sailor try to talk to one another? *Zabriskie Point* concludes with one of the more remarkable images of the plight of a world where things have become more important than people; the developer's house and all of materialistic culture are made to explode in a shower of goods. At the ending of *La notte*, Giovanni, listening to Lidia read his own old love letter, is suddenly confronted with the painful realization that his youth and his once-powerful love for Lidia have vanished. He tries to smother that excruciating awareness by forcing himself upon her. All of Antonioni's films end in sequences without parallel for their power and design. Where a lesser artist would wrap up the strands of the plot in a final verbal exposition, Antonioni gives each film a true coda of images that not only concludes the film but states its import in visual terms that cannot be adequately expressed in words.

Any attempt to appreciate Antonioni's ability to find and create images must be supplemented by an appreciation of how the director does such things as compose shots, use offscreen space, move the camera. Although primarily a literary critic, and therefore exceptionally sensitive to each film's themes and ideas, Arrowsmith also is well aware of Antonioni's mastery of the film medium. From such a critic we might expect his insightful declensions of color, and an appreciation of how color inflects idea, particulary in *Red Desert* and *Zabriskie Point*, but Arrowsmith goes beyond discussions of color into more cinematic aspects of Antonioni's work. In his analysis of the scene between the nymphomaniac and Giovanni in *La notte*, for instance, the critic proposes how the composition of shots expresses the meaning. Noting how she is framed next to expanses of wall, Arrowsmith writes, "What the nymphomaniac wants to shut out is any knowledge of the blank immensity . . . that we see exteriorized as she stands against the absolutely clinical white blankness of the wall, her own emptiness projected as the emptiness around her, threatening her." Arrowsmith also repeatedly elucidates Antonioni's use of shots where the image is held until a character enters, as well as those times the director holds on an image after a character

has exited. More often than not these are ways to lend weight to the material world, showing how frighteningly important objects and things have become, often eclipsing people. To capture in *Blow-up* the agitated feel of Thomas and his milieu, Antonioni frequently cuts on action. In *The Passenger* the director makes use of the long take, and even of autonomous camera movements, as a way of presenting the viewer with another perspective, one that is in fact the director's. "I no longer want to employ the subjective camera," said Antonioni, "in other words the camera that represents the viewpoint of the character. The objective camera is the camera wielded by the author. Using it I make my presence felt. The camera's viewpoint becomes mine."[3]

We not only should note the specific images and clusters of images within each film but also should be aware of the extent to which each work is itself a consequential image, depicting matters of importance in a fresh way. Before *L'avventura*, had there been a comparable expression of how a sick Eros is no longer strong enough to hold people, and perhaps humankind, together? Prior to *Il grido* was there a better expression of a man's inability to deal with the loss of the one thing that seemed to give his life some center? The death of middle-class marriage has hardly had a more effective expression than in *La notte*, and certainly one cannot imagine a more complete statement about the way in which money has affected human relations than that presented in *Eclipse*. Giuliana's neurosis in *Red Desert* seems wholly bound up with changes in technology and their impact on the human spirit; the engineering language of her husband has supplanted the song that surrounds Giuliana's imagined fantasy of the young girl on her Edenic beach. Never, before *Blow-up*, was there a clearer expression of the plight of a one-dimensional man confronted with something beyond his superficial ken, the traumatic reality of murder. The hunger for a significant self perhaps has never been shown as clearly as it is in *The Passenger*. The remarkable thing about Antonioni, well documented by Arrowsmith, is the extent to which the filmmaker has found not only individual images of uncommon vigor but entire stories that image, in fresh and evocative ways, ideas of consequence to human experience.

Antonioni's inventiveness is directed at making each created part contribute to the intent of the whole. Every square centimeter of every frame of film has been ruthlessly subjected to an artistic vision. The examples are endless. In *Blow-up*, when the old man asks Thomas what he is looking for in the junk shop, the photographer responds, "Landscapes." This is no throwaway gambit that leads only to the humor of the old man saying that he has no landscapes and Thomas then pulling one off a shelf. Rather, Thomas' word of dialogue expresses a deeper lever of unconscious desire that drives the photographer from the shop into the nearby park to find his "landscape." More than he realizes, Thomas is looking for landscapes, for he gets a metaphysical one that changes his life. In the same work, as Arrowsmith

9

points out, the opening credit sequence—gaudy letters floating over a sea of grass—expresses the dialectic of permanence and transience that is at the heart of the entire film. In *Eclipse* the little fossil that Vittoria brings back to her apartment is not idle "business" but is connected to a larger motif about the past, and about nature, to which Vittoria is drawn. Even the billboards in *Zabriskie Point* are inflections of another message: "You are what you look at." That Lidia in *La notte* twice passes people who are eating is central to that film's concern with a spiritual emptiness that animates a deep hunger. On the wall behind the *Zabriskie Point* developers is a case of pistols, linking them to the earlier Faustian tamers of the West. When Locke squashes the bug on the wall during *The Passenger*, he foreshadows his own death and its insignificance within the great scheme of eternity. The examples are numerous because Antonioni's artistic imagination is everywhere at work. Not only do these parts cohere in each individual film, they also suggest ways to understand how the films relate to each other. If we grasp the meaning of Vittoria's fossil in *Eclipse*, we can use that knowledge to comprehend the use of the desert in *Zabriskie Point* and what the trees mean to Lidia in *La notte*.

Antonioni's work is extremely complex, as Arrowsmith attests, a "compression of so much highly inflected detail into every frame that it is literally impossible to make words describe it." Typical is the use of the tree in *La notte*, beginning at the opening when the camera slides down the side of the Pirelli building, whose form was inspired by a tree. Then on to Tomasso in the hospital, looking from his deathbed out the window at a tree in the courtyard. Then to Lidia's walk and the tree that seems to be, in part, her destination. "She needs that tree," Arrowsmith notes, "for balance and also for shelter against a world that exalts mere present-mindedness, automatism, narcosis, somnambulism. The tree is her talisman." Lidia leans against the tree, listening, and that moment is described later, unbeknownst to her, in Valentina's voice on the tape recorder: "Put your ear against the trunk of a tree and if you wait long enough, you'll hear a sound. Maybe it comes from inside us, but I like to think it's the tree." Trees appear again, almost magically, inside Valentina's house in a glass-enclosed atrium and also in the wallpaper of the room in which she plays her game with the compact. She and Giovanni kiss among a group of trees. Several times we see Lidia on the balcony of the industrialist's house, looking up at the trees in the darkness overhead. Finally, having touched the leaves of one tree and while sitting near others, Lidia reads Giovanni's letter, and, as Giovanni forces himself on Lidia in the sandpit, trees fill the frame while the camera moves skyward. As Arrowsmith indicates, "The whole final sequence depends upon our perception of this tree life—first of the tree as metaphor, then the tree as subject in its own right, the great life of the enduring frame out of which the human participants have passed, or which moves past them, to its transcendent life incarnating the eternity of the recurrent seasons and the natural cycle."

The image of the tree recurs throughout the film, infuses it, inciting

not some abstract theme but a felt impression of the permanence which is juxtaposed with the impermanence of the games at the pool party, with the industrialist, and even with Giovanni. Lidia achieves balance and clarity by keeping in touch with trees because they allow her to recognize the perpetuity of the natural world and also to accept, clear-eyed and unafraid, her own fleeting life. The images of the trees in *La notte* are not casual but a pervasive expression of the very theme of the film. The manipulation necessary for Antonioni to place the final sequence on a golf course, among the trees and in the sandpit, as well as the work and expense necessary to have his opening shot careen down the side of a building whose form was inspired by trees—these efforts should be clear indicators of the importance of trees in *La notte.* Yet such labors, and complex motifs, are repeated manifold times as the artist, Antonioni, invents momentous images and fills every frame with his purposes. Density of expression is a truism in Antonioni's work. Bars on the windows. color of planes and cars and buildings and clothes, the coloration of Corrado's hair, the many and meaning-filled ellipses, the seemingly ceremonial bits of conversation, even choices in wallpaper and paintings, everything is determined by the director to serve his artistic ends. From tourists poring over a map in the background of a scene in *The Passenger,* to the shape of the vase that Vittoria touches in the opening of *Eclipse,* to the color of the portable toilets in *Zabriskie Point,* all is invented to support Antonioni's distinctive project.

As the use of the tree in *La notte* suggests, perhaps the clearest and most comprehensive example of Antonioni's inventiveness of expression is the way in which he uses background: physical locale, color, objects, and surroundings. For a minor artist, or no artist at all, the locale in which a scene takes place may be just that, a simple site. The costumes and the set design may be accurate and appropriate, even expressive, but that is all. For a major artist, the room is not just an appropriate place for a scene; rather, it *is* the scene—or at least an essential participant. The size and shape of the space, its color, the decor, are as important as what is said or done; indeed, in the case of a moving image artist such as Antonioni, the setting may say and do more than the people. In the exceptional episode that opens *Eclipse,* long before a word is spoken we feel the stifling confinement of the relationship between these very different people. Everything speaks to this sense of suffocation—the way the action is cut, the compositions, fans, placement of people, light, spatial geography, and objects that the characters touch. Making a point about color in his films which is also applicable to all the elements, Antonioni has said, "There are scenes and dialogue in my films which would not have been possible without the presence of walls or backgrounds of particular colors. . . . The image is a fact, the colors *are* the story. . . . The blue spread over Picasso's painting, evident during his blue period, *was* the painting."[4] Arrowsmith argues repeatedly for the role in Antonioni's work of the surroundings, not as pathetic fallacy but as the

choice by which characters reveal their authentic selves. Speaking of Aldo in *Il grido*, and by implication all of Antonioni's characters, Arrowsmith notes, "He *becomes* the landscape, expresses himself in his choice of it."

Background inflects foreground to such an extent that there is no "background" in the usual sense; all is foreground because, like a Möbius strip, there is no clear demarcation where one stops and the other begins. In *Red Desert*, when Giuliana makes her way about a house with tubular pipes and picture windows that show large ships going by outside, a residence more like an industrial plant than a traditional home, where is foreground and where is background? The Giuliana we know can't be separated from this environment, any more than this locale achieves its final statement without a human moving in its midst. In *Eclipse* Piero *is* the stock market; he is incapable of a love affair that extends beyond its parameters because those parameters define him. The lovemaking at the Zabriskie Point desert, like that of Piero and Vittoria in the "ancient" parents' apartment, is inextricably bound up with these locales, emblems of a past when sentiments were more stable and human beings more connected to their natural and man-made environment. The union between foreground and background generates these ideas.

An argument for Antonioni as a great artist depends not only upon his ability to merge foreground and background in a panoply of meaning but upon the depth and importance of the issues with which he deals; the questions he raises must be pertinent not only to his characters and their world but to most people and to our entire culture. What is the nature of Antonioni's artistic vision? How universal is its moral dimension? I want to quote Arrowsmith at some length because this passage clearly illustrates his facility for placing Antonioni's work in a larger context. Here he is speaking of *Zabriskie Point*:

Hence the bland, decent, torpid, mindless, innocent vacuousness of so many of these faces; they are not required to think, merely to consume. In this society, thought is subversive (hence the general anti-intellectualism, the fear of books amoung cops and guards). Hence too the general obesity, the result of that same imperative to consume. At Zabriskie Point the paunchy tourist with the blue camper, the fat wife, the ice cream–sucking kid imprisoned in glass, is simply the expression of what this nomadic, restless world culture (for it is not merely American, as any intelligent Italian or German or Frenchman knows) does to human beings, shaping them as they once shaped it. Medieval man thought the world's wheel was controlled by Fortune, goddess Contingency; Renaissance man, like Marlowe's Tamburlaine, thought he, not Fortune, turned the wheel. In the modern world the wheel controls the pilot, spinning where it wills, while permitting the helmsman the illusion of a firm hand on the rudder.

And the ramifications? The infinite stimulation of infinite desire is a

fatally divisive act, indeed a revolutionary one. The System spews out objects freighted with the only value there is, all other values being meaningless. Everthing is charged with *desire*. It was at Watts, Antonioni declared, that he first learned that a refrigerator was a revolutionary object, being loaded with desire (like the guitar stem in *Blow-up*).

Discussions at this broad level of insight are repeated in Arrowsmith's analysis of all the films, showing how each deals with larger issues than those on its apparent surface.

The characters, too, are to be seen as moving beyond the borders of the frame. In his discussion of *Il grido*, for instance, Arrowsmith observes, "All these are images that transcend the separation of Aldo and Irma; much more is at stake than one couple. All the people in Goriana, and we with them, are being expelled into a world in which the very capacity of the human psyche to adapt is under incredible strain." Antonioni's moral vision is presented through individuals who, while maintaining their particular feelings and circumstances, yet represent in some sense all of us. That this is evident in *The Passenger*, for example, is made clear by Arrowsmith: "Again it is the hollow man who, because he is hollow, can reveal the generic beneath the individual, the genotype that precedes the phenotype. Locke reveals, as his individual habits and old identity dissolve, the generic human hunger for transcendence and meaning. *We* are Locke."

Here too is a good example of an issue that permeates the Antonioni films, something specific to many of the particular characters, like Locke, and yet something with which every human being can identify. We all hunger for transcendence, which for Arrowsmith is "the ego's passage beyond the limits of the self, its merging with, or dying into, the larger world, the 'other' that lies beyond the ego." All Antonioni's characters, in one way or another, want the kind of otherness that allows them, as Arrowsmith points out, Dante's *trasumanar*—the process whereby the human transcends itself. Aldo and Locke perhaps are the clearest examples, but a similar need is evident in Lidia and Vittoria and Claudia—even in Giuliana—who find, however fleetingly, that love is a possible means to this transcendence. Mark and Daria's desert lovemaking is shown as going beyond the bounds of ordinary experience through the hundreds of couples cavorting seminude in the sand. *The Passenger*, of course, contains the supreme image of *trasumanar*, depicted by the camera as it floats out of Locke's room during and after his death. By the end of *Blow-up*, Thomas has become aware of the possibility of, and the need for, knowledge beyond what he can see with his camera. Mark, like Vittoria, finds such ecstasy momentarily in flight, which is a frequent image of transcendence in the films, although, like lovemaking, one that is very ephemeral. Locke in the tram "flying" over the Barcelona harbor, flapping his arms, is ecstatically happy because he thinks he has escaped—transcended—his old self and taken on a new identity. Such

images are everywhere in Antonioni's characters as their quest for a genuine self makes them tempted by flight and vicarious identity.

In *La notte* the image of flight is also related to the idea of escape when the amateur rocketeers shoot for the moon. Cars, too, provide means of escape, of entering another world that is more liberating. The trains in *L'avventura* are a similar image, although there and elsewhere these images of happy escape are also the penultimate image of the ephemeral. The train that awakens Claudia and Sandro after their delirious lovemaking in *L'avventura* is a clear premonition of the end of their love, and it is the same train, as presentiment of change, that appears in surrealist paintings, like those of De Chirico. The short-lived is just that. In *Eclipse*, when the drunk drowns himself in the car he has stolen from Piero, we see clearly how these images of escape are also closely connected with death. Aldo's flight from his hometown of Goriano, his escape through the empty Po Delta landscape, culminates in the "flight" from the tower that kills him. Mark flies his plane to his death. Locke's joyful tram ride ends in death when his car no longer works. In *Blow-up* the photograph of the parachutist is a glancing reference to this same notion, as is Thomas' use of his car and his desire to get out of town. Nomadism, too, is intimately joined with this idea of flight and escape. The clearest example is *Red Desert*'s Corrado Zeller, whose name is half German, half Italian, and who is a product of Milan and Bologna and Trieste. A man without a home, Corrado is trying to hire others to leave their habitats and go to distant places. Apparent in many ways, the same nomadism is certainly present in the boat travelers of *L'avventura* who wander about looking for excitement, but it is also suggested in less obvious places, like the English and Italian Berlitz records that we hear playing in Giovanni's apartment in *La notte*. The desire to go someplace else is really a desire to be someone else, to be another self.

Often this hunger for escape is expressed as an affinity for the lost world of nature and of Eden, a Pax Romana of the spirit. I've already mentioned Lidia and her tree, Vittoria in *Eclipse* with her fossil, the lovemaking in the ancient desert of Zabriskie Point, and to this list could be added a dozen other images where a lost past, and a harmony with nature are presented as ideals. "What imagination, what movement! . . . They were interested in theatrical effects! What extraordinary freedom!" Sandro exclaims effusively, looking at the baroque architecture in Noto, describing, really, a time when architecture was informed by a more coherent view of humankind's place in the universe. Arrowsmith points out that, at least since *Il grido*, one of Antonioni's most insistent artistic efforts has been to demonstrate the danger, for individuals and for society, in suppressing the reality of our biological and cultural origins. This story is apparent in the breaking of the ancient urn in *L'avventura*—dropped carelessly, with no regard for its significance—as well as in Vittoria's affinity with the African world, in Giuliana's beach fantasy, in the prehistoric bird that is Mark's plane, in

Thomas' verdant park, and in a myriad other moments. They all suggest that the break with the past and with nature can only undermine our psychic balance. This does not mean that Antonioni longs sentimentally for these missing elements, any more than he thinks technology and the city are monsters that must be destroyed; like all great artists he describes what he sees, and what he sees is that we have severed our relationship with our roots in ways that make us less human. As Arrowsmith says:

> The aim of Daria and Mark's Zabriskie Point journey is to bring back the missing dimension, the lost or forgotton sentiments, the reality suppressed by the Faustian city.
> That missing reality is essentially the earth life—the million-year-old life which *humans* share with plant and animal; and the lost sentiment is Eros, which the absolute city suppresses or sublimates, thereby redirecting it, by the dialectic I have described, into violence. Eros then becomes organized and syndicated aggression, that is, Thanatos, a force lethal to life.

This "lethal" direction, away from the past and nature, contributes to the overall crisis of the individual that Arrowsmith sees everywhere: "There is no more persistent theme in Antonioni's work than this intricate, culturally crucial diagnosis of the crisis of individual life." We may fault Aldo for being so unable to cope with the loss of his lover and the bulldozing of his community, but we all share his inability to adapt quickly to life's vicissitudes. "Change or die" is the refrain Arrowsmith hears in Antonioni's work, but the need for human beings to adjust is perhaps too urgent and, as Antonioni shows, few are capable of reckoning with this demand. Change, seen finally as transience, forever provoking the crisis of the individual, may be the quintessential Antonioni signature; certainly it is pervasive in the films that Arrowsmith considers. With the death of Tommaso and the collapse of Lidia and Giovanni's marriage, *La notte* is suffused with transience: as mortality, as vanishing youth, as the death of passion. Thomas' fading into the grass at the conclusion of *Blow-up*, Locke's adoption of Robertson's identity in *The Passenger*, the death of the drunk and the sudden collapse of the stock market in *Eclipse*, Anna's disappearance in *L'avventura*, the shooting of Mark in *Zabriskie Point*, all these and more are images of constant and relentless change. All is transience or, worse, all is the awareness of transience. Feelings and conditions fluctuate, people too; all that remains is the grass and the trees and the fossils and the desert. "But it is everywhere, this fact of change," Arrowsmith says, "not merely because it is a fact but because it is causally related to the compulsiveness of Eros, as well as to the ardors of individuation, in a time when man himself, like the landscape, is changing and therefore still clings passionately to the security, but above all to the group, like the players of the game in *Blow-up* or the rich pleasure-seeking nomads of *L'avventura*."

15

Society, too, is in rapid transition. The opening shots of *La notte,* with the steam shovel dropping with a threatening thump across from the older building, are typical. Out of touch with its past and yet not firmly established in a future, this world is too fragile to stand by itself, as we see from all the scaffolding and tree supports in *Eclipse.* As Arrowsmith remarks of Locke in *The Passenger:* "Hence also the parallel with evolving Pleistocene man, who dies as the forest creature he used to be in order to adapt to the dangerous void in which a changing environment, a changed world, required him—and us—to live. For that void is ours, the viewer's; now that our world has changed, we too must strip away the habits that bind us to the Eden we have lost. We must adapt or die, even when adaptation means dying out of oneself, dying into change."

But most of us are like Thomas in *Blow-up;* we often rejoin the Game because we are confused and because existence is too painful otherwise. We may want to learn how to fly around the poisonous fumes, like Giuliana in *Red Desert,* but that is easier said than done. Technology is here to stay, cities will remain the centers for human life, sentiments are no longer reliable, the values of the stock market will continue to pervade human relationships, the old institutions that held together our psychic interstices are no longer strong enough to perform that function; the world is out of kilter and humankind is destroying its nest in a madness that worships power and material objects. All of these realities threaten the individual. Like Mark in *Zabriskie Point* returning the plane to the airport, if we try to do the right thing we might be killed. Aldo, Claudia, Lidia, Vittoria, Giuliana, and Locke may try to live life as individuals but they will find it extremely difficult, if not impossible, and their striving will often lead to death. But the alternatives Antonioni describes are worse: somnambulism, serial eroticism, spiritual aridity, emotional coldness, self-centeredness, a morally empty existence, violence. Arrowsmith is fond of quoting Antonioni quoting Lucretius: "Nothing appears as it should in a world where nothing is certain. The only thing certain is the existence of a secret violence that makes everything uncertain."[5] The uncertainty, as Antonioni noted, is so present today that purposeful individual life is next to impossible.

Antonioni's persistent concern with the crisis of the individual leads to his depiction of individuation, which most of his characters avoid by giving their true self over to something else—sex or money or power or drugs or, simply, the drug of belonging, as in the death-in-life of playing the Game. The exceptions are Giuliana in *Red Desert,* Claudia in *L'avventura,* and Lidia in *La notte,* for example, who prefer to confront the relative solitude which is their painful fate because they refuse to lose themselves in the anesthetized life, like the partygoers in *La notte* or the stockbrokers in *Eclipse* or the pre-Robertson Locke or the Faustian developers of *Zabriskie Point.*

Those who choose some narcosis become morally bankrupt, and Arrowsmith points out "bad faith" as another important concern of Anto-

nioni's. Because people deliberately disavow accountability, we can't depend on them to keep their word or to assume responsibility because their first priority is to the pleasure of the moment and to the avoidance of pain. When Thomas needs his friend to go with him to the park in *Blow-up*, he finds him drugged and uncooperative. Claudia can't depend upon Sandro in *L'avventura;* despite his feelings for her, he goes with the first woman who offers herself. In *La notte* Giovanni flirts with Valentina right in front of his wife. Those who do try to live responsibly, to return planes, to reveal murders, to leave deadly relationships, to forge an identity of their own, to find some measure of truth and to act upon it, these people suffer immeasurably; they are the ones who actually feel and live the changes that are going on about them, rather than finding some addiction to ease the pain.

Nowhere is change more evident than in Eros, particularly in that form of Eros which commonly enlivens the relationship between two human beings. That old Eros, the one Freud wrote about, the one that was a life-informing and life-sustaining force because it held people together and animated life's work, seems so diseased that it is easily diverted into serial eroticism and, worse, into its opposite, violence. As Arrowsmith points out, there are no Antonioni films without a death or a suicide or a deathlike disappearance, such as Anna's in *L'avventura*. As early as *Il grido*, when Aldo slaps Irma, as well as when the motorcycle gang later surrounds Virginia and Aldo has to fight them off, Antonioni was showing the connection between love and violence, between Eros and Thanatos. In *La notte* we see in the brief vignette of the fight that Lidia watches, as well as in the victor's pursuit of her, a linking of the love–violence motif which Antonioni made so vivid later in the auspicious colors of *Zabriskie Point*, where the color red links love, violence, and blood.

Change can often become obsessive, as the normal processes of nature are annexed and hypostatized by human beings into destructive Progress. To describe many of Antonioni's characters and what they do, Arrowsmith frequently uses the term *Faustian*, which is his shorthand for the arrogant pursuit of power over objects, an endeavor which is disdainful of individuals, nature, and the past. As the industrialist Gherardini says, surrounded in his study by images of factories he owns, "I organize the future." In *Blow-up* Thomas' use of his car, his camera, his car telephone and his disrespectful treatment of his employees and models—all these show him to be supremely Faustian, as are the Sunny Dunes developers in *Zabriskie Point*, the stockbroker Piero in *Eclipse*, and Giuliana's engineer husband in *Red Desert*, who can't understand why Giuliana, like some machine, can't repair herself. All these characters might have said what Rod says in *Zabriskie Point*, when one of his colleagues suggests setting aside millions of dollars for contingencies, "What contingencies?" Such haughtiness is the hallmark of the Faustian spirit, one that recognizes not at all the possibility that nature holds surprises that cannot be easily overcome.

I could continue at some length about all the other aspects of Antonioni's realm that Arrowsmith illuminates, but such a recapitulation would be to repeat his undertaking. One summary remark is crucial, however. As Arrowsmith wrote in buttressing his case for Antonioni as an artist, the filmmaker's work is:

a true oeuvre; like the work of Pavese or Proust, one can enter it at almost any point and feel immediately at home. The themes of *Il grido* are present in *The Passenger*; you can understand *L'avventura* better by looking back from the vantage point of *Zabriskie Point* and knowing how *Red Desert* complements and qualifies *Il grido*. The image of the Game which so dominates *Blow-up* is implicit or explicit in every film of the director's career; one can only truly understand the Faustian nature of *Blow-up*'s Thomas, as photographer and therefore manipulator of appearances, by following the Faustian themes and characters from *Il grido* on, by observing the family resemblance that links all of Antonioni's intellectuals, whether they are writers, stockbrokers, developers, architects, or reporters. The invasion of the private house by the dynamics and functions of industry is unmistakably revealed in the set of *Red Desert*; but it is already implicit in *L'avventura* and *La notte*; in *Zabriskie Point* it is extended even further.[6]

The emphasis upon Antonioni's enterprise as a consistent oeuvre should not imply, however, that the work has not grown and changed; plainly it has. Antonioni has said that his films "are documents not of a finished thought but of a thought in the making,"[7] and also, "I don't want to be telling the same stories or dealing with the same theme."[8] *Zabriskie Point* and *The Passenger* present an attitude toward the possibility of human love that has changed since *Il grido* and *L'avventura*. Locke and Mark and Thomas aspire to be more responsible people than Sandro or Giovanni. Differences certainly exist between *Il grido* and *Red Desert*. Aldo's erotic malady has changed when it appears again in Giuliana; the burning fields and moving bulldozers, destroying the human habitat at the end of *Il grido*, surface again in *Red Desert*, poisoning the earth as expected, but by the end of that film Giuliana has learned that people must find a way to live in this new world; there is no going back. Antonioni's art, while circling about some persistent concerns, also moves forward and evolves. Aldo and Locke may both be on a journey that is really a quest for transcendence, but Locke's death is far more positive and hopeful than Aldo's.

I may have made Arrowsmith's effort sound too reductive, too driven by an obsession with themes and innovations of expression, or, worse, made the argument sound too simplistic. Nothing could be farther from the truth. Like the films themselves, Arrowsmith's appreciation of them is infused with the "tremulous vibration" he is fond of citing. Any sense of abstraction comes not from Arrowsmith's critical approach, and certainly not from the

films, but from my attempt to recapitulate it in an overview. If anything, Arrowsmith imbues Antonioni's films not with dead theory but with more life, the result of one passionate intelligence confronting another. The excitement in this confrontation comes in part from the sense of kinship, for this is Arrowsmith's oeuvre, too. The ideas in Antonioni are ideas that stimulated Arrowsmith his entire life, as one can tell from reading his translations and literary essays. The excitement also comes because Arrowsmith is able to place Antonioni in the broadest possible intellectual context, establishing an insightful dialogue between the film director's work and the ideas of Pavese, Spengler, Freud, Leopardi, Jung, and Eliot.

A covert statement about the nature and purpose of criticism also resides in this book on Antonioni, one in keeping with Arrowsmith's own definition of that task:

> My own hope is that we might achieve . . . *a poetry of criticism;* that is, a criticism designed to do more than report and judge its artistic object, but rather to respond to it antiphonally, to illuminate, even celebrate it. We need, not an autonomous criticism, as theorists seem to advocate, but a criticism that may affect us almost as deeply as the work itself; that tells us *how that work does to us what it does;* how, at its ultimate limits it may even make the work better by completing it in the act of comprehension.[9]

Arrowsmith once told me, quite proudly, that Antonioni had called him a creative critic, and no doubt Arrowsmith took that to mean that he had, in fact, achieved some measure of the very poetry of criticism he desired. This clearly seems to be the achievement of this study.

Il grido

At the 1960 Cannes Film Festival, the extreme reaction, both positive and negative, to the screening of *L'avventura* launched Michelangelo Antonioni's international reputation, but of course he had been making films since 1942, the year he started shooting *Gente del Po*. Several other short films followed and then, in 1950, Antonioni finished his first feature, *Cronaca di un amore*, which was succeeded by *I vinti* (1952), *La signora senza camelie* (1952–53), *Tentato suicidio* (an episode of *L'amore in città*, 1953), and *Le amiche* (1955).

Antonioni's next feature film, the one that immediately preceded *L'avventura*, was *Il grido*, which was released in 1956. Made with a very modest budget, it was shot, for the most part, under exasperatingly difficult conditions. Bad winter weather, above all. Long days of thick fog, followed by days of flooding rain plagued the shooting, dissipating the director's funds and forcing him to abandon whole scenes of a remarkably elaborate and ambitious script. As scripted, for instance, a scene that comes very quickly after Aldo has left home is the motorboat race on the Po near Elvia's house, which would have been a spectacular affair, clearly designed to give visual significance and immediacy to the theme of competition—of winners and losers—once so prominent in the film. For the scene in Ravenna, where Aldo and Virginia—the gas-station owner with whom Aldo stays briefly—consign Virginia's father to the old folk's home, the director intended an

elaborate sequence involving a motorcycle rally and race; of these important scenes of competition nothing now remains but the lone street fight
between Aldo and a group of young men who threaten him, Virginia, and
also Aldo's daughter, Rosina. Here is the relevant passage of that scene as
described in the original script, revealing clearly the weight of such competition sequences:

> Virginia turns her head and is shaken by a sudden shock of surprise. Next to
> her is a man dressed in a completely white uniform, with a thick black
> elastic band around his waist, a helmet strapped under the chin and a skull
> painted on the front. A knotted handkerchief is at his neck. Thick fencing
> gloves are on his hands. Noticing Virginia's shock and fright, the man
> smiles, an idiot smile. . . . The whole square is filled with more men of the
> same frightening type. They are helmeted, their uniforms are white, black,
> red, turquoise. . . . The participants are of every age. There are very small
> boys, also dressed in motorcycle uniforms. The women are wearing
> pants. . . . As they walk by, Virginia, Aldo and Rosina find themselves in
> the middle of this tide of motorcyclists. The sound is deafening. Virginia
> and Rosina succeed in reaching the sidewalk, but Aldo is prevented by a
> Lambretta which forces him to take a step backward. So he finds himself cut
> off by the procession, which has to open up and rearrange itself because of
> him. They begin to curse at him and eventually a fight breaks out.[1]

Included among the motorcycles is a large float bearing an outsized
model of the Italian Petroleum Agency (AGIP) emblem, a six-legged wolf,
from whose open mouth real flame is pouring. As described in the script,
this procession would have provided, first, an image of a world-in-motion—
at once a world of absolute mobility defined by deafening sound, but also a
masked and anonymous *mass* world, the group life in meaninglessly competitive motion. The wolf-emblem itself is used as an image of feral monstrosity
and as an epiphany of the sphinxlike terror suggested by the skulls painted
on the helmets of the riders. The blazon would presumably have been
cumulative as well, glancing back at the condition of the lunatics in the
field, earlier in the film, who so frighten Rosina. For these lunatics, like Aldo,
are all cultural casualties, victims of maladaptive response to change, men
confronted by a frightening reality with which they cannot cope, which
literally deranges them as it has physically altered the ground of their being.
Finally, the sequence in the original script would have effectively differentiated Aldo from Rosina and Virginia, who, in pointed contrast to Aldo,
succeed in reaching the safety of the sidewalk. Like so many of Antonioni's
women, they are "survivors," who somehow manage to adapt to, or at least
fail to be utterly overwhelmed by, change.

Except insofar as they help to define themes and the way in which the
director conveys them, unrealized intentions are of small critical interest.

But the danger with *Il grido* is that the viewer familiar with Italian neorealism will mistakenly assume that this film, because it is about an Italian worker, is a neorealistic motion picture whose authenticity lies in its evocation of psychological naturalism and working-class life. And the viewer will go on to conclude—wrongly, I believe—that it was not until Antonioni's next film, *L'avventura*, that his efforts came to maturity, breaking decisively with the director's earlier neorealism as represented by *Il grido*. Nothing, in fact, could be farther from the truth. Before *Il grido*, Antonioni was already making films of astonishing sophistication and complexity—above all *La signora senza camelie* and *Le amiche*, his version of Cesare Pavese's *Tra donne sole*—which have nothing to do with neorealism and indeed reject its premises. *Il grido* differs from Antonioni's earlier and later films *only* in having a working man as its principal character. The reason for choosing this protagonist is not a neorealistic penchant on the director's part but represents an extremely ambitious effort to *widen* his work, to demonstrate that his analysis of contemporary society is not limited to the middle-class but applies to all classes of Italian society and, by implication, to the world.

Among Italian left-wing critics, especially the communists, the film aroused almost as much hostility as some of Antonioni's later films would incite, such as *Zabriskie Point* among Americans or *China* among the Maoist Chinese. *Il grido* was, they charged, an inaccurate account of a worker's psychology; it had improbably imposed bourgeois problems, neuroses, and fashionable angst on an Italian worker. The premise of these criticisms was that Antonioni was unsuccessfully attempting to portray the psyche of the working man, and, just as the critics of *Zabriskie Point* assumed that Antonioni's subject was American and/or American youth culture, the left-wing critics of *Il grido* savaged it for disappointing a set of expectations that it was never meant to satisfy. Indeed, in some sense Antonioni was here, as elsewhere, trying to *distance* his work, pointedly refusing his audience the familiar pleasure of responding to a preinterpreted and prestructured reality. This may well be one of the reasons why most of the principal roles were given to non-Italians: Aldo was played by Steve Cochran, Virginia by Dorian Gray, and Elvia by Betsy Blair. The director wanted the parts not to be *pre*-interpreted by the stereotypes Italian actors would inevitably have brought to the parts; he wanted the parts to be perceived freshly, and this could only be done by avoiding the polished virtuosity of an actor professionally "playing a part," motivating it according to *his*, rather than the director's, sense of it. Antonioni has complained of Steve Cochran's stupidity, and Cochran evidently detested the director. Nonetheless, Cochran's performance, despite occasional unevenness, is one of the most successful of his career, and one of the parts in which Antonioni's strategy of forcing his actors to play unfamiliar roles has most strikingly succeeded.

Thematically, but also structurally and compositionally, *Il grido* is closely linked to the films which precede and succeed it. Aldo, for instance,

is clearly a male prototype of Giuliana in *Red Desert*, the later Antonioni film that also provides a penetrating study of erotic maladaptation. Rosina's relation to her father, Aldo, closely resembles Valerio's to his mother, Giuliana, the child providing at once a foil and a parallel to the parent's illness, though Rosina's role is more complex, since she not only informs us about Aldo but represents his inability to escape from Irma. The city–country polarity—the invasion of the rural world by the urban–industrial or even Faustian[2] city, so central to *Eclipse* and *Zabriskie Point*—is present in *Il grido*, too, in the motorboat race as originally planned, and the abortive motorcycle rally, but most powerfully in the closing expropriation sequence: the bulldozers waiting in the street of Goriano, the fields being burned to make way for the tarmac of an American military jetport. And the recurrent Antonioni theme of a private shelter—a world of the private self as embodied in a particular house and a specific *sentimento della casa*, constantly broached and invaded by an external or public reality—is no less central to *Il grido* than it is to *Eclipse* and *Red Desert*. The most striking resemblances, however, are those between *Il grido* and *The Passenger*, which share the same informing polarities of treescaped shelter and desert immensity and the same image of life as a fatal passage between one world and another—a passage in which the interior destiny of the main character is revealed as a psychogeographical journey. Even the germ of the theme of serial eroticism, so strong in *L'avventura* and *La notte*, is residually present in *Il grido*, as are the related themes of nomadism, primitivism and the Faustian extirpation of the wild.

Finally, in *Il grido* we also have, if in slightly less compressed and inflected a form than in *La notte* and *Eclipse*, the same concentration of themes, the same complex intrication of composition and motif. The density of these ideas is anything but neorealistic. Touch any detail and it will lead with rewarding inevitability to the whole complex work. Any part, any sequence of the film will bear the thematic weight and intricate coherence of the whole.

Consider, for instance, the shots that lead to Aldo's encounter with Adreina, beginning with the sequence of Gualtiero and his dredge. A long dissolve separates and connects this sequence to the preceding scene in which Aldo, desperate with grief, puts Rosina on the bus and returns to Virginia, who is waiting for him in a café. We see her through the glass door, there but *separated* from Aldo's point of view; then we see Aldo abruptly turn and leave, though the point of sending Rosina home was to allow the two lovers to make a life of their own, unencumbered by Virginia's old father and Rosina, her innocence already compromised by the adults. Abruptly, with Aldo's departure the scene dissolves. The next shot reveals a landscape of considerable complexity, the details of which are not immediately clear but will be revealed, detail by fragmentary detail, until, however glancingly or subliminally, the unifying whole is made clear.

The entire sequence has been composed with extraordinary craft and a scrupulous regard for *unfolding* meaning. That is, the whole *unfolds* visually, as cinematic images should, each of the details narrated by action and thereby, in their moving ensemble, revealing what the original landscape could not, of itself, declare. We see a landscape horizontally divided between earth and sky—a long balk of earth recognizable as the Po embankment. We first see the embankment because its straight horizontal is defined by the contrasting band of gray sky and because, along that line, a human figure—Aldo, we see—is moving. Vertically, the frame is divided almost exactly between a grove of trees—Lombardy poplars' slender trunks and leafless branches reaching up from the middle left foreground and filling the sky—and the embankment, which is not at all occluded by the trees. In the foreground we may perhaps be aware of fallen tree slash and a group of what look like white splotches, with three blackish human figures squatting or sitting to the right of the grove, almost in the middle of the frame. Suddenly voices are heard offscreen, cries of "Gualtiero! Gualtiero!" and two figures enter the frame from the right, cross diagonally down, and disappear at the bottom middle, shouting, "We caught two porcupines!" Then, as if to explain how the porcupines were caught, one of the poplars in the grove falls diagonally across the frame; at exactly that moment Aldo runs diagonally down the embankment in a line parallel to—and, as parallel, linked to—the falling tree. The metaphor could not be more pointed. Now we see that the grove is in fact being demolished, clear-cut. We are not told why, but the cutting of the grove is linked technologically to the dredging of the river, still another of those Faustian efforts at clearing away natual impediments, efforts which come to fulfillment in the scene of the bulldozers lined up in the street of Goriano, ready to clear the fields.

Here, in extremely compressed form, are the essential details—the polarities, the geography, the *ideas* of the film. The frame is, I remarked, almost equally divided above the black line of the embankment: between the poplar trees to one side, and the blank gray–white sky on the other. Wherever an Antonioni frame so divides, and when, as here, the division is repeated or inflected in imagery and detail, the point is to declare the opposed polarities, to make them *visually* available as controlling contrasts, as thematic foils. Thus, in one of the shots of the EUR in *Eclipse*, as Piero and Vittoria approach the jukebox in the restaurant, at this point the wall of the building fills exactly half the frame, while the park, all open space and greenery, fills the other half. It is into the park world that Piero and Vittoria now move, into *her* world and out of his. Then, as though to emphasize the point, Antonioni shows us the same division in horizontal manner: in the foreground trees and open space, then the abrupt balk of a kind of cliff or ridge of tufa, at the top of which, like an urban crest, we see the dome of a church and the citied world around it. Similarly in *Il grido*, we see Aldo's emergence from the edge of the grove and his entry into the blank sky

space on the right of the frame. This progress, so schematically defined and composed, tells us where Aldo now is, and to that degree inflects the larger compositional geography of the film, which in turn gives meaning to the detail. Narration of detail and the meaning of the whole are, as in painting, reciprocal in effect, mutually reinforcing.

Of the overall metaphysical pattern there can be no doubt. Aldo's odyssey is rendered in visual, geographical terms as a journey into landscapes of increasing desolation and spatial immensity. He moves from the comfortably enclosing world of his *casa* by the river in Goriano and finds himself near the end of the film living in a thatch hut which, like the landscape around him, will presumably vanish under water in the annual flooding of the Po. Around him on all sides, but above all in the scene with Andreina and the decoy ducks in the marsh, is the vast desert emptiness of the Po Delta. Following some obscure purpose of his own, a purpose which is in fact a kind of interior destiny gradually unfolding, he moves steadily toward an emptiness, a landscape and objects in which, among which, he can insert himself because they are what he is: a void. So, too, Locke in *The Passenger* begins the story of his unfolding destiny in the free flight over the water and the arbor shelter of Barcelona and its Gaudí buildings, and then moves by stages south into landscapes of increasing desolation, leaving behind him the world of trees, until he reaches the desertlike plaza of Osuna and the African textures, the open "desert" feeling of southern Spain—the beginning of the same desert which reaches from Gibraltar to Chad, where his journeying originally began. There is nothing here of the pathetic fallacy. The character reveals himself—his inward *destino*—by the objects and places among which he chooses, at the deepest subvocal level of choice, to situate himself. He *becomes* the landscape, expresses himself in his choice of it, its affinity with him. In *Il grido* we see Aldo, in a detail of his long odyssey, moving continuously away from the sheltered world of the grove, whose stability and density provide a kind of imagery of shelter and is everywhere opposed to, contrasted with, the treeless immensity of the delta.

Consider the tree. Aldo's house at Goriano is repeatedly revealed as a kind of shelter, the camera again and again pointing out the "fence" of pollarded willows and other trees, with the blank immensity of the moving river visible through the trees. It is *here*, among the trees, and defined against them, that Irma tells Aldo she is leaving him. Again and again we see her sitting or standing against a stalwart dark tree, while Aldo is defined by a slender poplar or profiled against the immensity of the landscape and the river, into which her decision now ejects him. The sturdy trees near Irma are at once the shelter of the house as well as a powerful image of the wall of privacy of the self, or the shared selves of two lovers, necessary for shutting out the intrusion into the fragile world of human space and time of those boundless vistas beyond the trees. Just as in *Red Desert* Giuliana tries to hide

25

in the trees and leaves of a slipcover or a chair, evading the terror that keeps seeping in, so Aldo and Irma have sheltered themselves for seven years against the river whose annual floods, as the milkman says, "carry away old things and bring new things." But the trees are also differentiated as images or metaphors of the individual who, by psychic affinity, "chooses" them. Antonioni suggests, I think, in the sturdiness of the tree against which Irma leans something of her own tough resilience; she is a strong woman. Aldo, by contrast, is defined by the pollarded willows, but above all by the Lombardy poplar—soft wood, frail, easily broken. So, too, in *La notte* are Lidia and Giovanni compared, in an extremely schematic metaphor, to a pair of trees, one straight and strong, the other stunted and misshapen. This is in part why Antonioni chooses to have Irma confront Aldo *outside* the house, among the trees, with the river beyond, at dawn.

Dawn is the time of sundered bodies, individuated by the light. The river slides by, immense and constantly moving, Antonioni's image of time—that time which Plato defined as "the moving image of eternity"—its vastness linked to the sky (and scored to music, a classicizing jazz piano), providing the theme of immensity and change and, as its human under-burden, the corresponding link to Irma. For in this film, as in *L'avventura*, there is a constant causal dynamic between the perception or knowledge of the immensities "out there," on the other side of our green, enclosing shelters, and the intensity of Eros and the love relationship. Discovery of the desert—the infinity of solitude, the recognition of human smallness in a post-Copernican universe or even an anonymous mass society, and then the consequent erosion of mere responsibility, automatism—leads the individual directly to the malaise of Eros. Love, as an enduring or even stable bond, disappears, replaced by serial affairs, the desperate effort to make Eros, by sheer quantification and repetition, an anodyne against reality, a shelter of human warmth against immensity. Or, as in the case of Aldo, the erotic sentiment is intensified, a cathexis fixed absolutely upon a single individual and therefore, in a world of relative, if not absolute, movement and flux, maladaptive. Marriage in such a world becomes a prison or a cage; and those who, like Aldo, remain unmovably rooted in their affections are destroyed by the very mobility of those they are doomed to love. The ground in which they are rooted—the ground of their being—disappears from underneath them; they lose their existential balance and die. Like wild things hunted down, they lose their habitat—a habitat that to them is everything. How, then, can they adapt?

It is like that with Aldo. He is rooted, like a frail tree, to one woman, Irma, the "ground of his being." She is contrasted with all the women whom he encounters—all of them, for him, only different faces of the same woman. Compared with Aldo, these women are adaptive and realistic; unlike the serial adventurers of *L'avventura*, they are capable of love, and in this respect are similar to almost all of Antonioni's women, except perhaps

Giuliana. Antonioni himself has made the point, speaking again and again of the greater adaptability of women in a time of change, something that struck him particularly about English women. "With so many changes," he said, "social, political, moral, happening so quickly, we cannot help but see that the rules we were taught as youngsters have become outdated. For me women can best portray this; they provide such a subtle and delicate measure. They are stronger, more realistic, closer to nature, the first to adapt themselves to changing times."[3]

Wherever Aldo stops, he tries, always unsuccessfully, to recreate his *casa*, his shelter. The women he meets are stronger than he is, and they are all mobile, each more mobile than the last. As he moves, the spaces keep opening up, his houses become smaller, shabbier, more open to the threatening immensities of reality. He is downwardly mobile—a man already falling—as the women all desire to be upwardly mobile. Elvia sees in him a husband; Virginia, a man worthy of love, someone she can escape with, with whom she can see all those places, above all those mountains, she has never seen—all those places which lie, as on the map of Italy, "beyond the frame." The gas station embodies, just as it services, a world whose only principle is mobility. The gas station itself is new, an outpost of the city world represented by the Boatti fuel truck from Milan, the rich signora from Rome with her *macchina di lusso*, the bespectacled and thieving city slicker on his Vespa, and the constant deedle-deedle of the passing buses. New, but also invasive, for the station is purchased by the sale of Virginia's father's farm. Of that farm all that remains are fields and farmhouse and a single tree. Why is the tree being pulled down? Presumably because it interferes with farm machinery, because it occupies tillable ground, because in modern agribusiness everything must be quantified and fitted to the measure of mechanization. We are not told why the tree has to come down, any more than we are told why the poplar grove by Gaultiero's dredge is being clearcut. The old *contadino*, Virginia's father—allied with Rosina, the two of them natural anarchists expressing their feelings, in league together against the world of the lovers and the owners, in which they are useless—protests the destruction of the tree; the new owner removes it presumably for profit, but also compulsively, as a needless nuisance.

Virginia sells the farm because she is unattached to the earth, as mobile as the world around her. Andreina is, if not quite a prostitute, also a woman who, like her money, is in constant circulation. She makes do with whatever comes to hand, and she sees in Aldo—who knows how to light a lady's cigarette—something better than Gaultiero and his hired hands. In each of these women and her house, Aldo sees only a surrogate Irma—Irma and the home he once had. And because they are not Irma, he finally rejects them all, thereby in his own way ironically setting in motion in others the very mobility which has destroyed him. The irony of his situation comes full circle when he tells Andreina, who refuses to stay and starve in the tempo-

rary thatch hut in the rain, to "come home" *(torni a casa)*—the very words he spoke to Irma after slapping her in the street. Then, acting on his own words while Andreina follows him sobbing, expelled from his love, he heads vaguely back, going nowhere, depressed and hopeless. Arriving at Virginia's he learns of Irma's postcard with the usual banal phrases, but also of something else; and something like a final hope breaks in him. He clenches his jaw, sits determinedly on the raised tailgate of the truck, and heads decisively for home.

Turn back now to the shot of Aldo on the embankment, emerging from the poplars, making for the blank space, the void on the right of the frame that is the Po Delta, with its enormous reach of treeless marsh, sand, and water. The void is in him, where he is and where he is headed. Aldo, like the porcupines, is a displaced creature. Now we see clearly the relation between the porcupines and the cutting of the grove—the destroyed habitat, the helplessness of tree-climbing creatures in a world without trees. One of the sequences cut in editing shows the men skinning the porcupines, then the exposed, "naked" bodies, and someone says, "It looks like a baby." The scene was presumably cut because it made the comparison of man and porcupine, and the idea of helplessness, too explicit. But it is this very helplessness of creatures deprived of a habitat, thrust from the shelters in which they have hitherto created and sheltered their humanity, which is encountered in the expropriation of the final scene, and the terrible sight that meets Aldo's gaze as he looks out from his tower, like a treed porcupine, at moving bulldozers and the smoke from the burning fields—at the image of the habitat, *his* and everyone else's now being destroyed.

For *Il grido*, too, like *Red Desert*, is not simply a narration of one person's pathos and death but an account of the expulsion of a world from the ground of its being. Expulsion into mere mobility and change, a landscape of dwarfing immensity, with its injured or hurt humanity, groping desperately for an elusive balance, equipped with a technology of such power that it can destroy the world itself as a livable habitat. The story of Aldo is, in short, a story about most of *us*—a *de nobis fabula*—like Giuliana's in *Red Desert*. We may not *be* Aldo, but in our rootedness—in possessing like him some fundamental reality which *is* the ground of our being, a life in which we are, like the trees around us, rooted—we are *like* Aldo. Irma and the more mobile or adaptable characters may be endowed with the talents for survival and the gift of balance; but that balance, as we know from *Eclipse* and *Red Desert*, *Blow-up* and *Zabriskie Point*, is increasingly hard to maintain in a world tilting rapidly out of control, in radical disequilibrium.

The unbalanced world of *Red Desert*, with its refineries poisoning earth, sky, and marsh, is, after all, precisely the world predicated in the final sequence of *Il grido*. The factory workers may speak of the solidarity of farmers and workers, but if the fields are buried under cement, what is left but the factory? In *Eclipse* we see the Faustian world invade the night, human

relationships, the Borsa, everything, just as in *Zabriskie Point* the city, Los Angeles, invades the desert and colonizes Phoenix; so in *Il grido* we *see* the creation of that world of universal disequilibrium postulated by all the later films. What, after all, can happen to Goriano after the bulldozers have flattened the fields and slabbed them with cement? What happens to a sugar-beet factory like the one in which Aldo works once the fields are destroyed? What, in fact, happens to Irma and the others—the milkman, the egg lady, the old woman in the vegetable stall—who live in Goriano surely for reasons of *their own?* All these are images that transcend the separation of Aldo and Irma; much more is at stake that one couple. All the people in Goriano, and we with them, are being expelled into a world in which the very capacity of the human psyche to adapt is under incredible strain. It is this strain, pushed to the breaking point and beyond, that we cannot help hearing in Irma's terrible scream as Aldo's body falls; and that we hear as only idiot silence and a child's whimper in the terrible scene in which Rosina, expelled from her own childish world, confronts the casualties of those who could not bear their expulsion from their habitat and went mad in consequence.

What does Aldo actually *see* from the refinery tower? We cannot say. A smoky haze. Smoke, it must surely be, from the burning fields, but smoke reminding Aldo of the mist and fog that fill the first sequence of the film—the fog in the streets, around Aldo's house, around Aldo and Irma as they walk, already half estranged, along the embankment. The smoky haze recalls also the drab blankness of the river, turned into fog, the gray, void sky at the end of the Po Delta were Aldo and Andreina, compared now to the decoy ducks, at odd, skewed angles to each other, are revealed to us as *lost together* in that immensity of sky and sea opening up around them. And now for Aldo, down below the refinery tower, as it was in the beginning, as it used to be, the face of Irma looking up at him. Once again, immensity and human closeness, the erotic bond, in dialectical relation—on the one hand the immensities enlarged in the nearness of the lost person, whose love sheltered him against the immensity, like a grove of poplars, or a child's magic circle of stones shattered by the wheel of a passing bus; further, the need of the *other* intensified and quantified beyond bearing by the very knowledge of the immensity it must somehow dispel, or distance.

The tension is absolute. Aldo has almost no wish to live, no desire to eat or drink. Everywhere in the film the hunger for life is expressed as hunger and thirst: Virginia's father with his bottle; Rosina, thirsty from watching the motorboat propellers; Andreina, always hungry and thirsty (as in *Red Desert,* with Giuliana buying the young man's roll and eating it greedily). Aldo's movements depend, he tells Virginia, on three things—money, desire, and work—and what he has least of is desire (*la voglia*). In fact, he has lost his desire to live. But loss of the desire to live is also expressed as transcendence, as the desire to *be* the other. Aldo's love of Irma is just such a hunger for

ANTONIONI

transcendence; because it cannot achieve its goal, it turns into a yearning for transcendence pure and simple, the lust for the void, for the immensity of sea and sky toward which, expressing his nature and his unfolding destiny, he blindly but purposively sets out, downriver, toward the delta where sea and sky meet in a single sheet of gray. A world of haze, smoke, fog—the same world, in fact, that Locke hungers for in the *The Passenger*, and which takes him to the desert in the first place; and then, in "a new life," takes him to the same landscape again at the point where Europe becomes Africa.

Here, however, in better words than I can contrive, is that passion for transcendence as it seemed to Pavese—a man who, like Aldo, fell in love with one woman so utterly that she fused with everything he saw, became cloud, mountain, sea, hill; and when he lost her, she turned into the things which Pavese had seen present in her. As we read Pavese's words, his account of the feelings that ended in his death, we should try to imagine Aldo at the top of the tower looking out at the gray haze, then looking down at the face of Irma he has just seen, forever barred away from him, but still *there*, and imagine how it was with him, standing there at the top of his treelike tower, his habitat gone, with nowhere to go, torn and teetering, wavering between two worlds he can no longer keep apart:

Lying stretched out on the ground, I sometimes feel a violent shock, a jolt that sweeps me away like a river in flood, as if it wanted to pull me under. A cry, a smell, is enough to snatch me up and whirl me who knows where. I become rock, rotting fruit, dampness, dung, wind. . . . I strain like a wild animal which once was man but has lost the power of speech. I pull back, resisting. Why? Because I know that this is not my nature. . . . I stand stock-still, oblivious, looking at a landscape. The sky is clear, there is a brook in front of me, a wood. And suddenly a frenzy seizes me—a frenzy not to be myself, to become that field, that sky, that wood, to find the word that translates everything, down to the very blades of grass, the smells, even the emptiness. I no longer exist. The field exists. . . . It is a crisis, a revolt of the higher faculties which, deceived by a shock to the senses, imagine they will gain by surrendering themselves to things. And these things then seize, overwhelm, and engulf us like an angry sea, in their own turn as unpossessable and elusive as foam.[4]

Pavese committed suicide: "No words. An act. I won't write any more"—these were the last words in his diary. And Aldo dies. How? Not surely by suicide. How, then? By loss of the desire to live. Is that it? Or is it precisely this teetering on the brink, all transcendence, torn, so torn that he can only resolve the tension in him by fusing with the void for which he hungers and also with the human features of the woman he has lost? Fusing them, and falling toward them both. Then a scream, a thud, and a pietá, and the film is over.

30

L'avventura

"The Malaise of Eros." The phrase is Antonioni's, not mine:

> Why do you think eroticism is so prevalent today in our literature, our
> theatrical shows, and elsewhere? It is a symptom of the emotional sickness
> of our time. But this preoccupation with the erotic would not become
> obsessive if Eros were healthy, that is, if it were kept within human propor-
> tions. But Eros is sick; man is uneasy, something is bothering him. And
> whenever something bothers him, man reacts, but he reacts badly, only on
> erotic impulse, and he is unhappy.
>
> The tragedy in *L'avventura* stems directly from an erotic impulse of this
> type—unhappy, miserable, futile. To be critically aware of the vulgarity and
> the futility of such an overwhelming erotic impulse, as is the case with the
> protagonist in *L'avventura*, is not enough or serves no purpose. And here we
> witness the crumbling of a myth, which proclaims it is enough for us to
> know, to be critically conscious of ourselves, to analyze ourselves in all our
> complexities and in every facet of our personality. The fact of the matter is
> that such an examination is not enough. It is only a preliminary step. Every
> day, every emotional encounter gives rise to a new adventure.[1]

This malaise is presented not merely as afflicting the protagonists but
as a pandemic disease, an erotic illness that touches all classes and countries.

In the foreground of *L'avventura* is Sicily, with its characteristic *gallismo*, its stereotyped macho sexuality, as in the near-riot scene with Gloria Perkins at Messina, or the crowd of unemployed Sicilian *pappagalli* ogling Claudia in the street in front of the hotel at Noto. But this is only the local version of the erotic disease which afflicts everyone: the wealthy leisure-class Italians on their yachting cruise, the Lampedusa princeling; the druggist at Troina, and the international world gathered in the fashionable salons of the San Domenico Palace Hotel at Taormina.

Parenthetically, it is important for Antonioni's work generally, but above all, as we shall see, for our sense of *Red Desert*, that we should observe the director's insistence upon generalizing the neuroses of his protagonists, of making their individual illness the detailed visible form of a general cultural infirmity. For the power of Antonioni's thought, and the comprehensiveness of his cultural diagnosis, is a direct function of this passion for moving beyond the individual; moreover, unless we mark the effort, often allusively deft and elliptical, much in the detail but also the structure of his films will seem accidental or superfluous. In *Red Desert*, for instance, Antonioni clearly wants us to observe that the neurosis of his middle-class female protagonist is one that afflicts the worker at the Medicina radar and the whole group of Italian workers being engaged for the South American enterprise. More impressive still, we are made to see that even the engineers and businessmen, who seem so otherwise immune to the disease, exhibit its operation unconsciously, by continual compensation.

The most apparent symptom of the emotional disease in *L'avventura* is, of course, the compulsive serial eroticism exhibited by Sandro and acknowledged in the film's title and its epiphany in the script. In this sense, Sandro is like Fitzgerald's Dick Diver: "He was in love with every pretty woman he saw now, their forms at a distance, their shadows on a wall."[2] Sandro's attitude is apparent when he returns to the hotel room in Noto and approaches Claudia with a kind of desperate, cold ferocity. Repelled, even frightened, she turns away and says, "I feel as if I don't know you." To which Sandro replies, "Aren't you glad? You're having a new affair [*un'avventura nuova*]." The exchange is a revealing part of the director's cool, clinical diagnosis of this diseased Eros, noting the ensemble of the symptoms— the phenomenology of the disease—not merely suggesting its ubiquitous operation.

The brief exchange also tells us that the chief symptom of this diseased Eros is the denial of the individual; this is what makes its serial compulsiveness possible. But the suppression of the individual in this sick Eros goes very deep; indeed it sometimes seems as though Antonioni were suggesting that one of the causes of the disease, as well as its symptoms, was precisely the elimination of the individual. Demoted to anonymity, deprived of individual and individuating features, the erotic "other" becomes precisely object to the lover's subject; becomes merely a collection of discrete sexual

fragments—those parts of the body, especially the legs, which are everywhere, obsessively, being looked at, *stared* at—fragments incapable of cohering into a distinct individual. Indeed, no sooner does the individual begin to emerge than erotic communication seems to stop. Why? Not because, as critics are fond of saying, communication is impossible in Antonioni's world, but because the erotic compulsion exhibits its diseased nature nowhere more vividly than in its desire to annul or disown individuality. This is what transforms Eros as Love—the love that, in traditional theory at least, makes a pair of lovers transcend themselves, realize themselves to the fullness of their individual powers—into the disease of mere erotic impulse. The disorder is not only a drug, narcotizing the individual, but the epidemic spread of the narcosis makes the individual less capable of resisting by making his individuality more and more precarious.

In the mass world, Antonioni suggests, then, that individuality is fragile; incipient individuality (those Antonioni "loners" always, at great cost and with great difficulty, detaching themselves from the group) is difficult precisely because the world is organized to suppress individuality, to coerce each person back into the Game, like the mummers at the close of *Blow-up*, the Faustian real estate developers of *Zabriskie Point*, and also like Antonioni's somnambulists, who try to coerce those waking into individual life back into the ranks of the sleepers. To play the Game is to live life in opposition to Reality and to avoid being an individual. The group is powerful against the individual precisely because it *is* the group; because it can suggest that the failure to conform to its norms is illness, neurosis, even madness.

I cannot stress the point too strongly. There is no more persistent theme in Antonioni's work than this intricate, culturally crucial diagnosis of the crisis of individual life. Hence the persistence of the erotic theme, for it is in relation to Eros—as in Eros' purpose, in Freud's words, to make one of two—that the fate of the individual is sealed or revealed. Again and again, from the earliest film, *Cronaca di un amore*, to *The Passenger*, Antonioni explores how, in the individual's encounter with Eros and death, both the individual and the culture that depends on the individual's health are made or unmade. Hence the series of loners in the films; hence too the emphasis upon the contrasting "hollow men," those borrowers of identity such as Locke in *The Passenger*, or the self-narcotized somnambulists of *La notte* and *L'avventura*; and, last but not least, the persistent theme of responsibility and "bad faith" (bad faith in its existential sense, *mauvaise foi*, the deliberate disowning of responsibility for one's own life and powers).

To some exent, I realize, the purport of these remarks is to put Antonioni into the moralist mainstream of modern Western thought, but that, I am convinced, is where he belongs. In Italy that is clearly not the company in which a modern director would like to find himself, since the company is often tedious and canting; hence perhaps Antonioni's constant disclaimers. But we should not be deterred from reporting what the films say, and how

they say it. For it is the fineness of the moral statement, founded upon absolute clinical candor in reporting reality, combined with astonishing cinematic powers, that makes Antonioni a great director.

This malaise of Eros has, of course, many causes, intricately related. Why, we have to ask, is such overwhelming weight placed upon Eros, why the disproportionate emphasis? Antonioni's answer, I have suggested, is that in the modern world, the eclipse or destruction of those institutions in which the individual once found security, as well as a consequential cultural context for his individuality and humanity, has meant that an inordinate burden has been placed upon Eros. And Eros is simply not strong enough to bear the weight of the burdens imposed upon it, to compensate man for all the failed institutions of his culture—*paese*, church, and family—vividly revealed to us in the uninhabited "ghost town" near Caltanisetta, where we see Claudia at the shutters of a house, and the strangely revealing vividness of her echoed voice from within; or the silent piazza, and the dead church to which the camera keeps returning. *Paese*, family, church; nothing is left; the planned *paese* is in fact *un cimitero*, a cemetery. And it is precisely for this reason that Antonioni's next sequence is via a jump cut linking that dead church and piazza to a close-up scene of Claudia and Sandro making love in what we come later to realize is a vast expanse of open plain above the sea. It is the depiction of the dead town that drives Sandro and Claudia together. Cause and effect, as so often, *are* sequence; and the thematic and emotional necessity of the link far exceeds any merely narrative necessity.

Look at Antonioni's plots in this way and one instantly sees that their narrative necessity is not that of the novel but of the *symboliste* poem; what matters is fidelity not to conventional expectations of "story" but to the emotional and intellectual necessities that *are* the story. The necessities are *there* and are, I think, compelling. Critics who complain of "Antoniennui"[3]—and they are many—impose the banality of their own expectations upon the director and then savage him for failing to meet their demands.

But I was speaking of Eros, the sickly form, which has other causes too. Change, for instance; the fact of change is depicted in every Antonioni film from *Il grido* on without exception, usually at the outset, with glancing succinctness. So here, at the opening of *L'avventura*, we see Anna coming down the path of the villa—a villa which will soon vanish to make room for those rows of apartment-slab palazzi we see rising on the left of the frame and deftly contrasted with the great Renaissance–baroque cupola of Saint Peter's on the right. Then we see father and daughter confront each other, with the palazzi behind them, informing their skewed understanding, with its revealing exchange—yachting caps equated with marriage, the theme of nomadism and rest, and generational impasse, the pathos of the father's obsolescence rendered in the relationship with his daughter and in the buildings that form the background of the shot. Change is everywhere in this scene.

In *Il grido* the same kind of change is evident when Aldo is expelled from the magic circle of home and family by the mobility of Irma's affections, a mobility likened to the Po sliding behind them; similarly, Giuliana in *Red Desert* feels as though she were sliding downhill, drowning, losing balance in a world constantly moving out from underfoot; in *La notte* we see, again at the beginning, the steam shovel at work, uprooting part of the landscape, and later the houses abandoned to make room for the high-rise slabs.

But it is everywhere, this fact of change, not merely because it is a fact but because it is causally related to the compulsiveness of Eros, as well as to the ardors of individuation, in a time when man himself, like the landscape, is changing and therefore still clings passionately to the security, but above all to the group, like the players of the Game in *Blow-up* or the rich pleasure-seeking nomads of *L'avventura*. As Patrizia says in the film, "My childhood was a merry-go-round; they kept jerking me around from here to there." She, too, for all her sensitivity, belongs to the Game that Antonioni so persistently describes in opposition to Reality, and to the players of Reality. Mark, in *Zabriskie Point*, illustrates this clearly by saying, "It's not a game. The day you people don't believe you're going to lose is the day I'll join the Movement." Later, to Daria, he adds, "I don't want to play any games." The mobility of the ground underfoot, the constant transformation of the landscape, the universal nomadism, the horror of the bomb, or un-acknowledged reality—all these inform and incite the players of the Game, their chronic, tormented restlessness, their compulsive activity and sad gaiety, even their automatism.

But there is more, and it matters. In *L'avventura*, for instance, the debility of Eros reveals itself against a background of informing immensity. An immensity of space, all those recurrent shots of wide-screen natural landscape, the infinity of sea scored by *scogli* and the cones of volcanic islands; huge frames of sky and sea in which the only sound is the roar and whine of the wind, or the sea pounding against the rocks below. In these landscapes the human figure appears in scale, as in the desert shots of *Zabriskie Point*, dwarfed and humbled by the environing vastness, man in nature, man against nature, no longer center stage but a small figure surrounded by a violence he cannot ignore, a mystery he cannot explain. The search for Anna across the barren landscape of Lisca Bianca *disperses* the group, breaks up the compactness which has hitherto buffered them from the sea, the terror of the shark. Almost for the first time, we see the humans in full figure (long shot after long shot) but also isolated from each other—indeed, it is their isolation which reduces their scale, just as their reduced size increases their isolation. It is this isolation and dispersal that in turn motivate and explain the merging attraction, the gradually surfacing erotic awareness and tension between Sandro and Claudia. Hence, I think, the lingering of the camera over details of the search, but above all the backdrop of immensity.

35

Again and again we hear the dead smallness of the voices shouting against wind and sea—"Anna . . . Anna . . ." The shouts proceed from helplessness, and the futility of the effort—apparent in the pathetic small-ness of the human voice in the void—only enhances the helplessness. The shark—really Anna's desperately playful description of her relation with Sandro, for he is the shark, as the images tell us—looms into nightmare reality, similar to the shot down into a ravine that shows the angry sea surging into the cavelike cleft full of limestone teeth. A small twister spirals down from the lowering blackness of the huge sky; a great boulder crashes into the sea. It is these images of latent violence surfacing, *seen* in their full potency from a viewpoint of unaccommodated, if not naked, man, made vulnerable by the group's sudden, individuated involvement in mortality or, at the very least, transience. For Anna is *gone*, which is what matters. She has *disappeared*, and her disappearance is unresolved because this serves Anto-nioni's purpose here—the impotence of human affection and reason in the presence of this vast landscape, with its revelation of a violent mystery at the heart of things.

"Lucretius," said Antonioni in an exceptionally revealing interview at the Centro Sperimentale in Rome in 1961, "who was certainly one of the greatest poets who ever lived, once said, 'Nothing appears as it should in a world where nothing is certain. The only thing certain is the existence of a secret violence that makes everything uncertain.' Think about this for a moment. What Lucretius said of his time is still a disturbing reality, for it seems to me that this uncertainty is very much part of our own time."[4]

Anna's disappearance, then, is left in deliberate uncertainty, and the search for her reveals the one certainty there is—the eruption into tangible, visible presence of the secret violence, the storm of reality and mystery, which it is the purpose of all our drugs and games to conceal, and which now, as if triggered by a sudden rift in the general pretense, discloses itself. For the rest of the film this same secret violence—if we have responded to the *meaning* of the storm as something more than the director's pathetic fallacy, that is, bad weather precipitated by human feelings of terror—will make its occasional but potent appearance as the image of the volcano, the volcano on which the action takes place, the volcano nature which, how-ever dormant, conceals a potential fury of staggering power. We see the volcano, in a lovely shot, between Sandro and Claudia; but the director's point is not, I think, to make the volcano an image of *their* smoldering passion but rather to suggest their participation in the world of organic nature of which the volcano is, on the island, the informing expression.

We cannot perhaps be certain of this, but there are impressive clues. Why, for instance, does Antonioni ask us to consider these islands as fish? The name of one island, Lisca Bianca, means "white fishbone," and another, Basiluzzo, is said by Claudia to "sound like the name of a fish [Sembra il nome di un pesce; merluzzo, basiluzzo . . .]." Why Anna's shark, apart

from the glancing allusion to the opening chapter of Fitzgerald's *Tender Is the Night* and Dick *Diver's* underwater, sexual world, and thence to Sandro, the erotic shark of these waters? Why, again, does Raimondo, in flippers and skin-diver equipment (an early image of Thomas' frogman photographs in *Blow-up*), ask, "Who said that man was originally an inhabitant of the seas?" The purpose of all these references, I suggest, is to make us see the cruise of pleasure seekers on the *Oriana* not only as a voyage toward immensities of sea and sky, the immensities of space, but as a trip backward into time, into geologic time. Just as in *Zabriskie Point* the descent of Mark and Daria into Death Valley is a descent into desert immensity, those vast spaces of desert opening up after the thing-cluttered cityscape, so too is it a journey back into time, 5 to 10 million years down to the dead stream at the bottom; and to the desert dust in which they seem, as it were, to disappear, and which expresses a vision of the animal and lizard (that saurian tongue lolling from the Chaikin dancer's mouth, which we see repeated in the face painted on Mark's plane).

So here in *L'avventura* we descend into sea time and sea space, back toward the fossil fish of our origins and the geology of the volcano. The suggestion might be resisted if it were not for the persistence with which Antonioni shows us this insistent backward look, this journey to our origins, back into absolute, unindividuated paradisal nature, back toward Eden, or *Sein*, or oceanic feelings, or the primitive.

In *Eclipse*, similarly, we see the white women unconsciously slipping into the black tribal world of an African night, just as in *La notte* we observe the sophisticated novelist watching with absorbed interest an insipid "primitive" nightclub act; the girl at the party in the sudden night rain kisses the hairy flank of a stone satyr; and the guests, eager to forget themselves, plunge, fully dressed, into the paradisal pool, all estrangement overcome. In *Red Desert* Giuliana's Tahitian world surfaces from the unconscious, a shimmering fantasy in which the brown girl becomes united with the water and rocks around her, their nature hers, just as we see Thomas in *Blow-up* lured by his own inward proclivity into the delusive peace and leaf life of the green park.

Antonioni's point is not, need I say it, a celebration of primitivism but rather a recognition of the revealing prevalence in the modern world of a profound, even obsessive, primitivism. Even while we obliterate the past everywhere, compulsively destroying every wild thing (the hunt is a strong theme in Antonioni—the porcupine reference in *Il grido*, the zebra poster in *Red Desert*), the past continues to live *us*; suppressed, the primitive goes underground and possesses us, as compulsive sex, as violence, as any activity in which we feel the blood flow, or seem to come upon *meaning*.

And so it is in *L'avventura* with these pleasure seekers, who are drawn, despite their resistance and decadence, to the past, to this sea, these islands, this serial sexuality, this drugged restlessness they all exhibit. Just as Swed-

ish and German girls swarm south to Italy, looking for dark lovers, once at Rimini and now everywhere else, so these luxurious pleasure seekers move steadily southward, drawn of course by sea and sun, the immensities of time and space, but also by the lure of the south, that suppressed reality of Italian life first revealed by Carlo Levi's *Christ Stopped at Eboli*, with its magical and pagan Basilicata, and also by Pavese, still another sophisticated Torinese, with his primitivist discovery of an ancient Greek world still alive in Calabria, the deep south of Italy.

Here is Pavese, at Brancaleone, reviving in poetry the feel and sense of old Reggio Calabria, home of Ibycus, and no stranger to the poetics of Sappho. A vanished, paradisal world, but *there*, still there:

Bright and early we went down to the fishmarket
to wash stale eyes alive. The fish were
scarlet, green, silver, color of the sea.
The sea was shining, all scales of silver,
but the fish were brighter. We thought of home.

Beautiful too the women, with jars on their heads,
olive green, and molded like their hips,
softly rounded. We thought of our women,
how they talk and laugh and walk down the street.
We all laughed. Out at sea, it was raining.

In vineyards, along ravines, grapes and leaves
glisten with rain. The sky is ruddy
with scattered clouds, colored with sun
and pleasure. On earth, smells; in the sky,
colors. . . .[5]

Into this world the modern Mediterranean nomads of *L'avventura* sink, to lose themselves in colors, in the immensities of space and time, dissolving night and day in the apparent pursuit of pleasure, but also in the profounder pleasure of losing *themselves*, consenting, with the pretense of purpose, to the suppressed life that really rules their every action, that makes them tourists of abandoned islands where life began, or even of the "great constructions of the dead" like Noto or other touristic attractions of the human past. Against the background of these immensities the erotic impulse becomes obsessive.

Am I overreading? In *Cronaca di un amore*, Antonioni's first feature film, we see the lovers meeting in the Milan planetarium; their affair is informed, intensified, by the constellations and the immense scale of light-years figured in the night sky overhead. A scene that appears only in the script of *Eclipse* showed two women discussing their affairs against a backdrop of fossil forms connecting them with the Eocene age, a perspective of 50 to 80

million years. In *Blow-up* Thomas' present-minded manipulations of appearance have, as their compensatory side, the same appeal as the past—all junk and antiques.

Now, in traditional humanist appearance, these perspectives on the immensities of the universe are functionally sobering, and in some sense they serve that function in Antonioni too, insofar as they reveal the reality suppressed or, in cinematic terms, normally driven to the fringes of the frame. But these perspectives also, more importantly, perhaps, serve to emphasize the compulsiveness of Eros; to tell us *why* men and women place themselves in the foreground, center stage, eclipsing the reality which, once perceived, dwarfs them and reduces them—like Thomas, in the final shot of *Blow-up*—to true human scale. The true, unfiltered sense of the modern night sky, is, God knows, sobering and humiliating; it no longer has, like the medieval or Ptolemaic sky, anything human about it. Even the beasts of the zodiac have withdrawn.

A friend of mine, recently turned sixty, spoke to me of the sadness of a world where old friends seemed to have vanished into nothing, receding from each other at accelerating speeds, into the void of an exploding universe; and even more graphically of one friend in particular, once a star of first magnitude, who was now a kind of human black hole, collapsing in on himself with frightening intensity. It is, I think, this universe that Antonioni means to invoke by the immensities of *L'avventura* and other films. We have, at any rate, his word for it, explicitly astronomical, in the Cannes statement that accompanied the appearance of *L'avventura*.

> Consider the Renaissance man, his sense of joy, his fullness, his multifarious activities. They were men of great magnitude, technically able and at the same time artistically creative, capable of feeling their own sense of dignity, their own sense of importance as human beings, the Ptolemaic fullness of man. Then man discovered that his world was Copernican, an extremely limited world in an unknown universe. And today a new man is being born, fraught with all the fears and terrors and stammerings that are associated with a period of gestation.[6]

It is the immensity of this post-Copernican universe, revealed by modern astronomy, and also the immensity of geologic or earth time, that are everywhere revealed as the hidden spring of the erotic disease depicted by the film. I have suggested that the whole sequence of the search for Anna on the island has its deepest aim in the vision of a limitless, and limitlessly violent, natural world; in the presence of this unknown world, and the experiences of human transience, the feeble bonds that link the group are ruptured, and we see each person, isolated (all islands enact Donne's sermon on each man) and dispersed, as in a desert. (To the Mediterranean-

enchanted American eye these islands are beautiful; to an Italian eye they are deserted and therefore desert, uninhabitable waste.)

In the presence of this desert, erotic need is violently ignited (think in *Blow-up* of Thomas' talk to Vanessa[7] about his failed marriage, while across the blank wall of the room, in a photograph, there marches the tiny black caravan, suggesting an erotic desert informs his words, his effort to reach Vanessa; think, too, of the desert in *Zabriskie Point*, and the lovemaking it provokes; think of Giuliana's paradisal "red desert" surfacing in the pink-suffused room where she sleeps with Corrado).

Hence we see here in *L'avventura*, as the *immediate causal* consequence of this vision of violent immensity, the incipient attraction surfacing, like a submerged volcano, between Sandro and Claudia. And so we also see an immediate causal link between inhuman emptiness and deadness of the prefabricated "ghost town" on the way to Noto and the sequence of the same two lovers embracing, all close-ups, no background visible except for the grass and a bit of blank sea on the fringes of the frame. Confronted with immensity (photographic long shots, with wide-angle lenses) or death (all medium shots and long shots) and the extinction in image of family, church, and *paese*, the visual effect is close-ups of the body in which, now, all attention is concentrated.

This diseased Eros puts all its emphasis on the body: the relation between person and environing reality is obliterated; and with it the person, too, is obliterated, becoming nothing but body, close-ups of cheeks, facial flesh, hair, hands touching, hair on hair, flesh on flesh, fusing, parting, fusing—and on the sound track nothing but a soft moan and the rustling of clothes. The camera tells us, in this close-up sequence, why it is that Eros is ill; why the whole person no longer matters and the individual is literally shattered into the parts that compose his body; why the men glance so obsessively at legs, Raimondo peering under the table, the ogling workers, the pharmacist glancing down. We know now why this diseased Eros is a matter of serial affairs, for the camera has told us. The compulsion seeks the oblivion of the close-up, as well as requires animal contact against the assault of immensity. For this, *any* body will do; and many bodies are better than one body; besides, the individual body has been deprived of meaning. All bodies fuse into one; all women become one woman, all men one man. Hence the theme of interchangeable bodies, of exchanged identities, in the film. Early in *L'avventura*, the camera shows us Anna and Claudia, backs to the camera, brunette and blonde—a first suggestion only. In the island search we see Claudia mistake Giulia for Anna—their forms fuse at a distance. Later we see the brilliant scene in which Patrizia and Claudia exchange wigs; "You look like a different person," says Patrizia—and we think surely of Anna—but then they discard the wigs and return to their own hair and identities. At Troina the mysterious girl is said to be brunette by the druggist, blonde by his wife. As Sandro assaults Claudia later in the Noto

hotel room, she says, "I feel as though I don't know you"—and she is right; it is not Sandro but precisely any man, *un uomo qualunque, un ignoto*, who might act this way. The individual ceases to exist, hence the theme of interchangeability, the diffused identity which reduces them all to mere sexuality, a body.

This, after all, is precisely the point of the sequence involving Giulia and the young princeling–painter, Goffredo. He insists that it is Giulia, not Claudia, who inspires him, but his incredible gallery of nudes tell us instead a story of simple promiscuity, which is itself merely the habit or incapacity for individual discrimination. The drawings and paintings are rich in information. Quite without exception, they show us precisely what this erotic malaise always aims at: an expanse of body filling the frame and which, apart from a few details—a few strokes of grass beside a Tahitian or primitive nude, for instance—has no relation to space or time, no environing "world." Filling the screen during the island search, the great natural world is almost utterly eclipsed in Goffredo's paintings; in precisely the same way the close-ups of the lovemaking near Noto confirm the lovers' intention of obliterating the world, forgetting space and time, or rather, finding all time and space in the erotic bond, cosmologizing Eros. This is the young painter's world, one similar to Sandro's. With Claudia it is different. In Goffredo's room, for instance, she is only momentarily curious about his work. A medium close-up shows her riffling through the painter's canvases. "They look like nudes to me," she says, diffidently turning to the window, which interests her much more, the interest indicated by a hold on the landscape. We see Claudia move into the foreground and look out, absorbed by the wonderful landscape which unfolds at the window, interior space and exterior space for one intermittent moment in perfect equilibrium. Then we crosscut to Giulia, who says, "But why only paint women?" And the painter replies, "No landscape is equal to a woman's beauty." And now, to conform his point, Antonioni show us Claudia still absorbed by the landscape, revealing the degree of her absorption by the abstracted "What?" she gives in response to a pointless question from Giulia. Tersely and brilliantly, the camera *shows* us, by revealing the landscape outside, what is absent from or suppressed by the young painter's sketches. At the same time, we see Claudia subtly distinguished from Giulia and Goffredo by her revealed affinity with the world outside, with organic life and the leaf textures to which she constantly turns as to a talisman.

Except for the body, the princeling–painter's world is a blank; there is no relation between internal and external space, between body and nature. There is therefore no human scale, no *background*. In *La notte* Antonioni gives us a graphic representation of the erotic disease at peak power—a nymphomaniac standing against the wall of her hospital room. She is dressed in a black nightgown, a black silhouette except for the white contorted face and clenching arms and hands against the clinical white expanse of the wall.

The wall is absolutely blank, a blankness which explains her nymphomania and her utter sick concentration on the body of the man standing before her. Reality itself has gone blank obliterated by the body. She herself is clinically ill, yet her illness is one which, in greater or lesser degree, is shared by almost everyone around her. The quality of her absorption, its appeal and totality, is in turn qualified by one of the most extraordinary images in all of Antonioni, the carapace of a car moving slowly through the rain, and inside it, a bubble sealing off the occupants from external reality, the silhouettes of a man and a woman, smiling, talking, though we hear nothing except the rain and the swish of the windshield wipers. The power of diseased Eros, its ability to cosmologize itself and drive environing reality to the fringes of the frame, has no more vivid expression in all of Antonioni, whose work explores the intensity of Eros with an obsessiveness that is obviously as personal as it is a matter of artistic urgency. And, finally, the nymphomaniac and the magic bubble of the car are brought into relation as Valentina (Monica Vitti) says to her would-be lover, in refusal: "Love makes an emptiness [*il vuoto*] all around," adding later, "Every time I've tried to communicate with someone, love has vanished. . . ."[8]

The disease of Eros has other thematic symptoms, too, all of which are persistent themes in Antonioni's work but which I will mention here only briefly. Somnambulism, for instance. The victims of Eros are all in some sense sleepwalkers. Hence their desire for sleep and peace, their emphasis, like Thomas' in *Blow-up*, on sleeping and waking; on the need to relax, on *tranquillità*. At the beginning of *L'avventura* Claudia tells us that she slept well; by the close she is overwhelmed with the need to sleep but then incapable of doing so. We see her tossing and turning restlessly, then counting sheep, reading. Raimondo tells us that he slept badly; Claudia tells Patrizia defensively that Sandro didn't sleep all night. These sleepwalkers turn night into day and day into night with their restlessness; the crew of the *Oriana* complain that the work is harder during pleasure cruises. Pleasure is obsessive, its pursuit an addiction, always in need of a "fix." Hence, in part, the film's insistence on the erotic disease as itself a drug. The girl reported to have appeared in the druggist's at Troina was in search of a tranquilizer; the druggist himself, we can see, is still another of Eros' addicted pushers (for why else make him a druggist?). It is the repressed reality, or the astral vision—the terror of immensities, of morality—that requires anodynes and drugs; the restlessness is the symptom of the disease and an effort to evade it, therefore self-exciting, radically incurable. The male victim of this Eros characteristically hopes to cure his own restlessness by the stability of marriage, by the simulation of traditional and normalized Eros, a solution that Anna and Claudia, with a recognition of the mobility of the affections, consistently refuse. All around them is the hideous story of middle-class marriage, with its Corrados and Giulias, and, for the Italian women, its imprisoned feelings—the idea of which lies at the heart of *La notte* and *Eclipse*.

Another consequence of a sick Eros is automatism, unmistakably linked to the demotion of the individual and personal responsibility, which are the obvious consequences of an Eros whose aim is denial of identity and refusal of it to others through serial attachment. We hear it announce itself in Sandro's response to Claudia's anguished shame at the absurdity of their situation. "Fine, it's better to be absurd. It just means there's nothing we can do about it." This, of course, is simply existential "bad faith," the refusal to accept responsibility by the pretense that necessity leaves one no choice. The individual abdicates his personal responsibility of exercising human choice by pretending that there is no choice to make. So the music in Rod's office in *Zabriskie Point* chants "Don't Blame Me," and Lidia in *La notte* envies the nymphomaniac because, as she says, "She's not responsible."

The refusal of choice is, of course, in moral terms a renunciation of individual life, for the mature individual is responsible for each choice and every act. The failure to choose is a form of infantilism. Patrizia asks Claudia how she would describe Raimondo's face, and Claudia says, "A bit corrupt." "Corrupt?" responds Patrizia, "No, on the contrary, he's a child." So, too, in the brilliant sequence at Noto before the Immacolata church, we see Sandro, in a fit of *ressentiment* against his own youth and lost idealism, spill ink on the young architect's drawing and, a moment later, as though still twenty-three himself, try to pick a fight; and then, distracted from the fight with his younger self by a group of schoolboys marching out of the church, we see him obediently fall into place alongside the parade and march out of frame. In a single vivid sequence we actually watch Sandro in a regression that takes him from a forty-year-old failure to an idealistic young architect of twenty-three, testy and feisty, to his final regression to a schoolboy of ten or twelve. It is this schoolboy, on the point perhaps of growing up again, whom we see at the end of the film, receiving from Claudia the compassion of an anguished caress. She is standing behind him, he is sitting, weeping, very much like a boy, as she raises her hand with a trembling effort and slowly runs her hand through his hair. It is compassion, for she too shares in his weakness. But even in their likeness, they are also differentiated. She gives, he receives; she stands, he sits; the caress is the caress one might give to a child, or to a grown man in whom the child is all too visible.

Nomadism, too, of course, is another thematic symptom of diseased Eros as shown in *L'avventura*, for Antonioni's characters are all erotic nomads. Gloria Perkins at Messina; the little Sicilian couple with their Chinese transistor we see on the train in revealing low-life foil to the situation of Claudia and Sandro who are nearby, and during this scene the revealing cuts to the surf on the beach beside the tracks with the reminiscence of the searchers wandering over Lisca Bianca; the girl from Viterbo; the old smuggler with his pidgin English and his Australian family; and, finally, the summation of these images in the San Domenico Palace Hotel, an uprooted,

nomadic, international, polyglot society recalling Eliot's atomized communicants of the European Eucharist:

De Bailhache, Fresca, Mrs. Cammel, whirled
Beyond the circuit of the shuddering Bear
In fractured atoms. . . .[9]

But the human past, like nature, has its immensities too, or at least its magnitudes, those memorials of human greatness and confidence—poems, paintings, buildings—created in defiance of the inhuman immensities of Nature and Time or in alliance with them. Hence, the male protagonist is an architect; and though he is a failed architect, who has turned to making estimates, he is not so much a failure that he cannot still feel envy as he looks at the baroque buildings of Noto. The film gives us abundant evidence of these human magnitudes, first with Saint Peter's, then in the splendid baroque of the Villa Grevina Palagonia at Bagheria (converted here into the police station of Milazzo) and finally, lingeringly and fully, in the magnificent plateresque classicizing baroque of Noto. Sandro gazes at it with expert admiration and envy: "What imagination, what movement! . . . They were interested in theatrical effects! What extraordinary freedom!"

That Sandro should admire freedom, given his bad faith, his pretense of not being free, is simply absurd. It is not the idea of freedom but his own sad impotence that leads him to envy these buildings. And we are meant to feel his nostalgia, indeed, perhaps, to feel it as our own. There, in that splendid square, he sees baroque confidence and exuberance, the confidence which, in fact, after the destruction of Noto by earthquake, rebuilt the entire town in accordance with the great surge in baroque town planning all over Europe. The baroque is not ornate or florid but rather classicizing, evoking the Renaissance and expressing a like confidence in the future. (If we look closely at the puzzle Patrizia is doing on the boat, we see that it too has a classicizing motif.) The baroque speaks, with bold theatricality, of faith in the future and optimism therefore in the powers of man, and even human nobility. For all this grand urban theater, all these stage effects, are designed to accommodate the Magnum Miraculum of Pico's hermetic vision, man the miracle.

The point, glancingly but fully made, need not be elaborated; it is, after all, these splendid buildings which give us the fullest measure of the impoverished creature for whom the earlier "ghost town" (actually an abandoned or never-used Cassa del Mezzogiorno project) was built; and whose exuberant vitality is so harshly contrasted with the spiritual deathliness (un cimitero) of the Cassa paese. If the point of view is unmistakably nostalgic, we need to remember that we see the great structures through Sandro's envious eyes. It is his sense of desecration we feel at Milazzo, and his sense of personal affront and diminishment before those great facades at Noto.

These magnitudes at first move him to emulation, then to resentment and conviction of impotence. He has no confidence in his own future or talent, no confidence in the future of man, no conviction of nobility in himself or in others. He cannot plan cities because he does not believe in life. As Siegfried Giedion observed, "The supine imagination evinced by our contemporary attempts to devise new features in town planning . . . is invariably condoned on the plea that we no longer have a manner of life it would be possible to express."[10]

Sandro, like the director, is astute enough to realize that emulation—not imitation—is the only possible response to the challenge of a great past; but the knowledge does not solve the problem. This, I think, is why Antonioni's camera moves in for a closer encounter and shows us Sandro looking at the detailed sketch of a shell niche from the facade of the Immacolata. It is exquisitely done, and we see it in close-up: a lateral niche, its curving interior scalloped like the shell it imitates or incorporates, and than the frieze of floral and leafy stone crowning the vault of the niche as it curves and peaks. Then we see Sandro, as though checking the accuracy, glance at the facade, and the camera gives us the real niche, the niche in relation to the whole of which it is a detail. In this way ensemble and detail are united; we have the sweep of the whole facade, but also a sense of the rich intricacy that the eye cannot take in when it is overwhelmed by the whole. And then we see the swinging chain and the straining ink, and the *ressentiment* spilling out against the age, the style, the church, the youth, the detail. Then, in swift succession, Sandro's regression back to childhood and bad faith, the desire to lose himself in the past, and then quickly back to the hotel room with Claudia, to conceal himself in her, to disappear. To disappear. Like Anna perhaps. But not for the same reasons.

Just before Anna disappears, she seals her decision—whatever that decision is—by putting her blouse into Claudia's bag. The blouse is dark and interwoven with what seems to me a network, or tracing, of leaves. These leaves are the link—the organic link—between the two women; Anna gives Claudia an amulet of leaves. In *Eclipse* Vittoria, falling in love, reaches up and touches the leaves overhead; in her apartment of stone, a fossil leaf softens the wall; a flower stands in a beautifully curving white vase on the table; a tracery of fibers is everywhere. So, too, in *L'avventura*, when Claudia dances in ecstasy to the music of the sound truck outside, we see her framed by a screen of leaves, to which the camera keeps returning. She moves and dances to those leaves, similar to the scene in *Zabriskie Point* where we see Daria, after Mark's death, swaying with the desert leaves moving in the wind. And finally, at the ending of *L'avventura*, when Claudia comes up behind Sandro, sitting on the bench, weeping, we see her look at the leaves trembling in the dawn breeze, and then a shot of the leaves, only the leaves. As if she had to touch something that stirred in herself before being able to confront Sandro. And it is these same leaves, stylized in stone,

that we see crowning the detail of the drawing of the shell niche that Sandro deliberately destroys.

What do these leaves represent? It would perhaps be wise to take Antonioni's word for it and leave them trembling in subverbal mystery. And it would clearly be wrong to freeze them in the amber of abstraction—like instinct or nature or the unconscious. But I see no harm, and some advantage, in calling the leaves an affinity with the organic, with the organic life of earth that is prior to us and therefore, like our past or our instincts, our affinities with animal and plant, still living in us, whether we acknowledge them or not. It is also the life of our feelings, the feelings which are prior to our reasons and logic, and, lacking rapport with which, our rational life, our wills, even our faith in life, are poor and stunted. Without this organic sense, we do not know ourselves, we cannot reach or act upon our feelings. Our grasp of reality is prosthetic, enabled by instruments at a remove; it is not ten-fingered. We have no sense of inner quiet, or tranquillity, unless we can touch the leaf life, the plant beneath the animal in us. We cannot know ourselves. Worse, we cannot *be* ourselves. Unlike Sandro, or Giulia, or Anna perhaps, Claudia can keep her equilibrium because she keeps in touch with this organic life. For a long lingering shot, her hair blowing in the wind on Lisca Bianca, we see her in profile, and beside her, sharing the frame, moving with the wind, we see a single stalk of grass, a reed, standing free and then resiliently returning as the wind bends it down.

My rhetoric may be too rhapsodic, but the problem here is evocation. We need to evoke the sense, the aura of the thing, not the thing itself, which, being mystery, is reduced by being named. Here, in these leaves and leafy feelings, in the evocation of this organic dimension, we come closest to Antonioni's central artistic purpose, and also to what he does best—the evocation of significant feeling, feeling as it feels before being transformed into will, decision, passion, or even reason. The ephemeral, glancing feeling; the tracery of *sottinteso*, the coming-into-being of the whole intricate texture of the preconscious, prevocal, feeling life. We can understand it best perhaps in an expressive passage from Ortega's account of the feeling moments that become personal and collective history: "I believe that all life, and consequently the life of history, is made up of simple movements, each of them relatively undetermined in respect of the previous one, so that in it reality hesitates, walks up and down, and is uncertain whether to decide for one or other of various possibilities. It is this metaphysical hesitancy which gives to everything living its unmistakable character of tremulous vibration. . . ."[11]

Instantly, I find myself thinking of Antonioni's Valentina, in *La notte*, saying, "I'm not intelligent, I'm just alert [*sveglia*]"—and also of the narcotized life of the somnambulists around her. And it is precisely this quality, I think, that Antonioni tries to reach with his constant images of hair blowing over the face, the talismanic links between leaves and the women whom he

chooses as the appropriate filters of this suppressed reality—the very quality of feeling prior to all words, and the *being*, as tremulous vibration—of transience.

The point, of course, is not to exalt feeling over thought, or the organic over reason. The reality Antonioni likes to evoke is not better because it has largely been suppressed by our culture. Hence, I suppose, the director's constant insistence that he prefers the city to nature and that he is not hostile to technology. He *must* say these things to audiences who persist in seeing the instinctual, the natural, the primitive as beneficent, and reason and technology as baleful. What matters is balance, and the prospect of discovering a human, even civilized, stance in which, at last, the organic can be integrated with the rational; in which Eros will recover human, even moral, features; and in which our cities and culture can absorb and humanize the immensities, as once the great artists of the baroque fused geometric line and the undulating arc, leaf and line, and built, like the Royal Crescent at Bath, or the great squares of Nancy, cities that confronted nature without defying or outraging it, creating a civil but natural world and by doing so healing Eros of its disease and deformity.

With great persistence, Antonioni has generalized this malady of Eros, forcing us to see it as a universal affliction, refusing to permit his critics (or so one would think) to dismiss it as parochially Italian or Sicilian. None of Antonioni's films lacks this passion to generalize the malady of modern man, to make us look beyond the individual case to the generic condition. The same ambition led Antonioni, I think, to leave Italy, first for England, then the United States and China, and finally for Europe again at the place in the south of Spain where Europe, as the West, confronts the "third world." No matter where he goes, the essential analysis does not change; rather, it undergoes qualification, refinement, intensification.

As early as *Il grido* Antonioni was exploring—although in small and modest ways—the relationship between love and violence; between Eros and Thanatos; between internal and external space; between psyche and world; between change and the human capacity to adapt or not to adapt; between technology and nature; between reality and paradise. The themes and the metaphors persist—the desert of Eros; the latent violence; fossil affinity and psychic balance; the definition of the individual in a mass society; the confrontation with death; bad faith and multiplication of evasion; the temptation toward flight and vicarious identity; the caged feelings and the suppression of reality.

The astonishing complexity of Antonioni's work—the compression of so much highly inflected detail into every frame that it is literally impossible to make words describe it—is in large measure dependent upon this coherence of his oeuvre and upon the director's adamant refusal to defer to the attendance habits of audiences. He simply refuses to accept the prevalent notion that a film, despite the incredible complexity of which it is theo-

retically capable, is, by virtue of its serial presentation, doomed to one or at most two viewings. Why, after all, should the director demand less of himself and his audiences than any painter or poet? There *may* be such a thing as "Antoniennui," but I suspect that what the term discloses is simply the refusal of conventionally conditioned audience members to recognize the demands being made on them—the real *respect* being proffered them— by an artist, and a great one, in a great medium, as *L'avventura* makes obvious.

La notte

La notte has seldom been assigned a high place in Antonioni's work. Critics have found it too literary, too dependent upon a highly verbal if exquisitely written script; the long letter that Lidia reads to Giovanni at the end has been censured as uncinematic; or the film has been thought too intellectual, too densely textured, with its allusions, visual or spoken, to Broch's Sleepwalkers, Calvino, Nervi, Hemingway, and Adorno. Nonetheless, La notte seems to me one of Antonioni's most flawless works, certainly one of the most comprehensive and concentrated, the film in which all of the director's themes are presented in their richest and most intricate form. Like Cesare Pavese, Antonioni is an artist whose thematic repertory—his tematica, as Italians like to say—is complex but also severely limited; the motifs are recurrent, even obsessive. This is why almost any Antonioni film reveals an extremely close affinity with any other. Red Desert is amplified or enriched by Il grido; and Il grido, made in 1956, strikingly anticipates The Passenger, released in 1975. The desert imagery and desert journey of Zabriskie Point make more sense when juxtaposed with the scenes on Lisca Bianca in L'avventura; the stock exchange sequences of Eclipse are refined and amplified in the Faustian themes and the Sunny Dunes sequences of Zabriskie Point. The predatory erotic adventurer Nardo, in La signora senza camelie, has his unmistakable successor in Corrado of Red Desert. This does not mean that Antonioni is simply repeating himself;

49

it means that his work is a true oeuvre, like Pavese's, in which the crucial themes keep recurring, even as they exhibit constant, obsessive refinement and intensive, shifting intrication. The single individual film finds its meaning and even its power in a single developing *body* of work, in the oeuvre.

Pavese's novels, for instance, are much more impressive in their ensemble than individually, because it is the ensemble that gives meaning and collective power to the individual work. To some degree this is true of all artists, of course. But there is a real difference between the artist who, like Antonioni and Pavese, works obsessively over a lifetime with a handful of chosen themes, and those who, like Ibsen or Bergman, exhibit a development in which they scrap old themes, old obsessions, and make fresh beginnings. There is a gulf between the early Bergman and the late Bergman that has no parallel in Antonioni, who seems, like Pavese again, to have made contact with his artistic world on the first day, and who endlessly revolves around this huge monolith—this unity of themes—chipping away at it, working at its pieces, studying them in every possible light. For an artist of this sort there is finally only the oeuvre—the effort to make the fullest, the most concentrated and intricated statement of his chosen themes possible to him; and whose every individual work assumes its place in the whole corpus only as a tentatively complete draft, doomed to be scrapped for a fresh assault on the monolith.

The themes persist; what changes is their intrication and, at times, their articulation, their juxtaposition; they are refined, reaffirmed in new juxtapositions, or seen in new aspects. But the themes persist, the unvarying residue of a compulsive vision and an obsessive reality. Of the individual films one can only say that they are more or less comprehensive than one of the other works, that they express, in satisfying intricacy, more or less of the artist's preferred reality than others, in more or less satisfactory form.

What is remarkable about Antonioni—as opposed to Fellini or even Bergman—is, I think, the extraordinary consistency of quality, the ability to produce, out of a limited repertory of themes and ideas, one masterpiece after another; to sustain the vision, constantly intricating it or refining it, while at the same time steadily improving his technical means for stating it. In the moral quality of that vision and in the miraculously effective cinematic techniques he has devised for expressing and enabling that vision— techniques that have become more and more cinematic, more and more relentlessly visual—Antonioni's work as director parallels, in innovation and achievement, the greatest modern masters: Valéry and Eliot in poetry, Joyce in the novel, Beckett in the theater, Picasso in painting. Someday perhaps that truth will be more acknowledged. One notes, with a kind of despair, that Antonioni had so much difficulty, particularly during the latter years of his filmmaking, in raising funding, the kind of backing that any young studio hack can instantly command; and that the same critics who praise

worthless films also consistently patronize and even abuse one of the greatest living directors.

La notte seems to me one of the works in which Antonioni achieved the
richest intrication of his themes—a film that expresses those themes with
extraordinary beauty, comprehensiveness, and precision. There is, it seems
to me, no black-and-white film by any director that can compare, in adequa-
tion of statement to technique, form to content, with *La notte*—none except
perhaps *Eclipse*. Everywhere one looks, the compositional sense, the feeling
for *significant*—that is, expressively meaningful—inflection in black and
white is astonishingly present. From the contrasting clothes—even the
wigs, blonde and black—of the characters, to the complex and dramatic
alteration of feeling and reality as the blacks deepen, or lighten, as black and
white intersect in intricate design: zebra stripes, chessboard squares, lights
glowing in the sable depths of the pool. From the diurnal movement of the
film—the early afternoon siesta, deepening to late afternoon, then dusk,
then night, and finally the waking into the gray light of dawn—everything
shows the same relentless, scrupulous attention to detail and compositional
unity, the same care for dramatic inflection that is exhibited by the beautifully crafted script and by the interaction between visual image and sound,
particularly as that intersection unfolds the story. A story, true, like so many
Antonioni stories, that has no plot or none of the conventional sort, but
whose structural and thematic unity, like its unity of feeling and its intense
preoccupation with the sequential motivation of feeling, is a kind of miracle
of cinematic poetry on a par with, and indeed of a piece with, the best
modern symbolist poetry. Everything has been attentively, painstakingly
composed, with a kind of fastidious schematism; yet the effect, I think, is, at
its best, miraculously simple and even natural: *curiosa felicitas*—that kind of
art whose happy effects are the results of laborious art, kept scrupulously
invisible. Flawless, superbly sustained, exquisitely beautiful to look at, a
tissue of continuous feeling and seeing, understanding *as* perceiving, *La notte*
is a miraculously lovely film.

Its themes will be instantly apparent to an audience that has seen any
four or five of the director's films. We can tick them off almost mechani-
cally: nomadism, for instance, in the English and Italian Berlitz record that
we hear playing in Giovanni's apartment; a society in transition, for another
example, as in those opening shots that show us a bus passing, then a truck,
and then, dividing the screen, an old brownstone building and the high
soaring modern column of the Pirelli Building, as well as in the later image
of the steam shovel dropping with a thud across the street from the Renaissance palazzo. Even the Faustian theme is implicitly present in the
industrialist Gherardini's study, with its photographs of the factories he
owns—the exterior world entering the private house—and his faith that he
organizes the future ("Io me lo organizzo il futuro"). And the corollary
theme of capital and province, so prominent in *Eclipse*, here rendered by the

roar of jets overhead, and Signora Gherardini's garter billfold, the image of the dollar conquering a new region, forcing us to see or at least recognize the world that lies outside the frame, the world of the great powers to which even Milan, the business capital of Italy, is nothing but a parish or a province. Here in *La notte*, too, we have as a theme the contrast of the quick and the dead, those who are awake and those who are asleep, the drifting somnambulists of Antonioni's limbo world, so close to Eliot's—and therefore to Dante's:

A crowd flowed over London Bridge, so many,
I had not thought death had undone so many.[1]

And with this theme we have, in close intellectual tandem, the theme of "bad faith," existential *mauvaise foi*—the deliberate disowning of freedom and responsibility by those who prefer a kind of erotic narcosis to the pain of becoming an individual, the pain of human beings adapting to change, the pain of tragic solitude in transitional time. Also in *La notte* we have the familiar imagery of escape—those Faustian rockets and amateur rocketeers, wanting the moon, that Lidia watches and from which she turns away to find the tree in the courtyard where she and Giovanni used to meet.

Present, too, in *La notte* is the imagery of enclosure that is so prominent in *Il grido*, but here already evolving into the imagery of imprisonment—caged feelings and suppressed realities—that will dominate *Eclipse*, hinting in that film of the violence lurking and looming under the deceptively placid surface of the world, with its solid appearances and stolid certainties. Here, too, in *La notte* we see in the brief vignette of the fight that Lidia watches, as well as in the victor's pursuit of her, the first linking of the Eros–violence theme so vivid in the bright red tonalities—blood as Eros, blood as violence—of *Zabriskie Point*. And here, too, is Antonioni's familiar polar geography—the comparison and contrast—of center city and countryside, as well as their interim world at the periphery, what the Italians call *la periferia*, that is, the neither–nor space where the city gives out, where the paving abruptly stops and the high-rise palazzi of the *quartieri nuovi* yield to shacks and open fields; *la periferia* is the point where city and country intersect in a momentary, fragile equilibrium. Every image is composed to declare the intersection of these two worlds, at the periphery, but also the looming imbalance that threatens them both.

The theme of transience is here, too, in *La notte*—indeed, no Antonioni film with the possible exception of *Blow-up* is more overtly concerned with mortality and transience than this one. *La notte's* whole mood and urgency precipitated by the dying and death of Tommaso, as well as by the tender but clear-sighted analysis of the death of middle-aged marriage and the death of youth. Here, surely, in the pathos of lost youth, Antonioni touches, almost audibly, I would think, to an Italian ear, the great theme of Leopardi,

as we hear it, for instance, in *Il passero solitario*, with its beautifully controlled recognition of vanished youth:

> mi fere il Sol che tra lontani monti,
> dopo il giorno sereno,
> cadendo si dilegua, e par che dica
> che la beata gioventù vien meno.
>
> (The sun's glance, which behind the distant hills,
> As ends this clear, calm day,
> Sinks down and vanishes, and seems to tell
> How youth's blest season, too, dwindles away.)[2]

To return to *La notte* again, what matters at this point is not a catalog of these themes but a sense of their intrication, of the way in which, in terms of technique and narrative, they are combined into the complex and comprehensive vision—I will not say "statement"—of the film. And, if only to note with what economy and by what means the director gives them weight and meaning, and thereby to glimpse his visual and thematic priorities, we ought perhaps to glance at a few distinct "images" and metaphors. Consider, for instance, the director's characteristic device of having his characters leave the frame, confronting us then with a kind of hold, long or short as required, on the abandoned vacancy. For in this way we are asked, even forced, to perceive that there is a world or an image, a meaning, which is not wholly contained in the characters and their story; that an effective part of the story lies precisely in the relation between the characters and the world around them. As I noted in the case of *L'avventura*, Antonioni constantly insists that there is a world which is occluded by normal modes of storytelling. Such fictional narratives place the characters center stage and close-up, and the environing world is shown only as human "prop." But this form of storytelling leaves unknown, unglimpsed, or unrepresented that world which is in fact the true source, as well as the cosmic scale, of all the human agitation in the foreground. This normal mode of storytelling eschews wide-angle immensity in favor of the erotic close-up that is designed to dispel and annul that vastness. We can call this immensity, missing in most films, the "enormity of time and space," as in the huge sea and sky of *L'avventura*. Or we can call it the "desert of vast eternity" that unfolds as the camera pans away from Locke in *The Passenger*. Or we can even call it the "suppressed reality" that appears with such threatening vividness in *Eclipse* and *Blow-up* and *Zabriskie Point*. Or we can call this immensity "geologic time," as in *Zabriskie Point*, or "astronomical time," as in *Cronaca di un amore;* or simply call it the "mystery looming in the nature of things," the "all" toward which human transcendence is directed. But it is *something*—above all something Other, indeed the *Other*—that Antonioni insists must be seen, and

that must not, for the sake of clarity about our condition, our mortality, and therefore our power of compassion, our humanity, be reduced to human backdrop, to mere prop.

The pre-Copernican universe (to which Antonioni alluded so revealingly in his famous Cannes statement) posits man's centrality on an earth that is his ornate, treed shelter; in that construct man lives, as it were, in a homey place that exists to serve him. Nature in such a universe becomes not something strange, unknowable, vast, and terrifying but a green gemütlichkeit; the cozy home of Ptolemaic man, mere background to his foreground situation. On the other hand, this is the very sense of nature, as something awesome and frightening, not at all homey, that Antonioni forces us, however elliptically, to see; and for precisely the same reason he avoids the normal modes of narrative, he avoids what might reasonably be called the pre-Copernican or Ptolemaic plot, in which the human character is the focus of all interest. Antonioni prefers instead to depict human beings in dynamic relation to an unknown reality, a world in which the only certainty is the absence of any certainty whatever. Antonioni depicts a world, in short, that cannot be narrated in a Ptolemaic setting, or according to an obsolete purposiveness in a known reality, but rather must be improvised from day to day. And this improvisation requires all our wits and powers of adaptation, requires, therefore, absolute clarity, and also responsibility. We have to be alive, quick, awake. Like Valentina, not so much "intelligent," as Giovanni suggests to her she is, but rather, in her words, *sveglia*—*wide* awake, with waking *life*. Valentina and Lidia matter to Antonioni not so much because they are women but because they have the talent for survival, human survival. Here, I suggest, is a part of the intrication of themes that makes this film, with its companions, so impressive.

Again and again in *La notte*—I counted at least five occasions—the characters leave the frame; what remains, as I indicated, is the abandoned vacancy. And this vacancy is not simply an image but a reality of its own, a reality that precedes and also survives the passage—the transience—of the human characters. The camera holds, as it were, and lets us see what *will* be or what *is*; the human figures in the foreground *reveal* their transience by disappearing from the frame, and the world that was once background becomes the subject. When Thomas dissolves in the final shot of *Blow-up*, the grass into which he dissolves becomes the subject. The great world that is not man, that is Other to him, reveals itself; just as in Shakespeare's more Ptolemaic world the canopy of the stage Heaven overhead gives the human action a cosmic setting and therefore a panoramic metaphysical view of human existence in a world theater. Two examples. Giovanni and Lidia stand looking at that part of the area where they first met, a world that, with its trees and baroque church, will soon disappear under the advancing concrete and macadam of the approaching city; then we see them come to the weed-covered tracks of the train that brought them there; then they

pass from the frame, leaving only the image of the tracks. And what we see as a result is not the obsolescence of *their* world, but an image of what nature will someday do to the city that now overwhelms it.[3]

That this is Antonioni's point, however elliptical and glancing, is confirmed, I think, by the clear, indeed stressed, words of the script—words fitted to a crucial image. In this doomed part of the terrain where Lidia and Giovanni use to come as young lovers, we see Lidia at the end of her walk. Her destination was a tree, the tree against which we see her standing, her head against the bark, listening. Later, in the tape recording that Valentina plays, we *hear*, from Lidia's younger foil, precisely what it is that Lidia was thinking: "The park is full of silence made of sounds. Put your ear against the trunk of a tree and if you wait long enough, you'll hear a sound. Maybe it comes from inside us, but I like to think it's the tree." Lidia, we know, moves from a world of sterile sounds—the traffic and roar of the center of Milan—steadily toward the *periferia*, that area where city meets country. She is moving toward that tree, although it is not a destination she knows in advance, but one which is revealed in the way all our true, unspoken destinations are revealed. She moves toward the tree, which is in some sense her destiny, and also toward the country, but she moves also, in a real sense, backward into time. The tree and its sound, a sound which is deepest in her memory, but also *prior* to her, are her destination. She needs that tree, like Vittoria in *Eclipse* and Claudia in *L'avventura*, for balance and also for shelter against a world that exalts mere present-mindedness, automatism, narcosis, somnambulism. The tree is her talisman because, like Vittoria's fossil flower,[4] it provides an ancient perspective of natural growth, of natural life and natural death. Lidia moves toward that tree because it is prior to her; it is the very pattern of transience, like the tree whose swaying leaves and branches the *Blow-up* photographer sees overhead in the dawn breeze, where the vanished body once was. Lidia moves toward that tree also because she is trying to cope with Giovanni's spiritual and emotional dying, and also the dying of her own youth, and the dying of her marriage, her love for Giovanni. That tree not only provides perspective; it *is* perspective.

Look now to the intrication of this idea or theme—I will not call it "image"—of the tree in the film's obsession with transience and immortality. Gherardini, the industrialist, is afraid of death—in fact, like some Milanese Trimalchio, obsessed by it. His French gardener is preferred because only he can arrange flowers in a manner that does not remind Gherardini of the cemetery. He wants to acquire a novelist–intellectual in order to immortalize himself and the firm he has built. Giovanni, author of an ephemeral novel appropriately entitled *La stagione*—a three-month success—is the person that Gherardini believes can confer immortality upon him: a *monumentum aere perennius*.[5] There is, needless to say, intense and extremely ironic wit in the confrontation of the immortality-seeking industrialist and the novelist who knows and even accepts his own weakness and lack of talent; who

55

desires nothing more than release from the anguish of creativity; who seeks, in a deep sense, to be imprisoned in the industrialist's gilded cage; and who seeks, even though with a certain residual pride and real self-loathing, to be "bought." At heart he, the ephemeral novelist, envies the industrialist, because, as Giovanni says to Gherardini, he admires the permanence and "reality" of the latter's enterprises, of working with "real people, real houses, real cities," of "holding the future in his hands."

And, of course, Valentina is right in suggesting that Giovanni's own conviction of crisis and failure is what sends him in search of her, a young girl, that is, in search of the vitality he has so lost, just as it sent him earlier to the insipid nightclub where, intellectual primitivist that he is, he sat watching the idiotic act, eager to drown his awareness of failure, just as he is eager to lose himself in the magic carapace of love. But Giovanni is obsessed by time, made frantic by the conviction of ephemerality, seeking some anodyne or release from death. This hunger for eternity is expressed as Gherardini's yearning for the immortality he believes Giovanni can give him, and also as Giovanni's desire to escape his own fear of interior death by a new affair or by release from his own creative anguish in the comforts of Gherardini's cage. Antonioni insists on showing us this hunger and pointedly contrasting it with the attitudes of Lidia and Valentina.

For the two women have in common the ability to live in time, the ability to accept the present; like Vittoria in *Eclipse* they are constantly improvising, adjusting, balancing, correcting their stance in a world that, if they sink into somnambulism or the extinction of Eros, will overwhelm them. For Lidia and Valentina this ability to live in the moment—like a leaf, like water, like grass blown by the wind but still resiliently rising back—is their power of being, expressed by an acceptance of time, living in it as a natural element, making themselves at home as best they can in the mortality and temporality whose emblem and sanction is the tree they share. They—and they alone—have the courage and grace to be themselves, which means, in Antonioni's world, the courage to be individuals, to live alone, in the fragility of the moment, responsibly free. Different from everyone else in the film, they have no overwhelming desire to drown, to drug their consciousness, to cage themselves in fictions and structures or roles. This does not mean they do not *desire* what the others cannot resist—the image of that extinction of consciousness, that *participation mystique*, beautifully visualized throughout the party sequence in that black pool so persistently visible, beckoning every eye, glimpsed at the edge of every frame.

The pool, as Euripides knew, beckons us all; we see Lidia soaking wet, cavorting and about to leap, just as we see Valentina later—in the rain—drawn by some part of her to the dark side of the frame where Giovanni is waiting, dark in the darkness, just like Roberto with Lidia later. They too desire it; paradise is, for all of us, desirable, and for most, irresistible. Deepest of all is the hunger for irresponsibility, the need, as the contrasting

wide-angle shots and close-ups of *L'avventura* so vividly declare, to eclipse the great background—that eternity which includes our dying and which we fear. This is why, I think, *La notte* so unrealistically juxtaposes the sequence of the dying Tommaso and Giovanni's encounter with the nymphomaniac in the room nearby. Unrealistically, because nymphomaniacs and cancer patients are surely not put in the same ward or on the same floor. The point is an oxymoron, the rhetorical juxtaposition of the two polar images which control our perception of everything that follows. The images are total, schematic opposites, schematically presented. What the nymphomaniac wants to shut out is any knowledge of the blank immensity—it is hard to give it a name, call it the infinite, immensity, the unlimited, the object of transcendence—that we see exteriorized as she stands against the absolutely clinical white blankness of the wall, her own emptiness projected as the emptiness around her, threatening her. And that is what she seeks to escape as she kneels before Giovanni as before a present god. It is Antonioni's most potent image of the malaise of Eros, of which he spoke in his Cannes address, that illness which, to a greater or lesser degree, afflicts everyone in *La notte*. Love, Valentina remarks later—by virtue of its very intensity, its compulsive purpose and need to conceal the threatening immensity—makes an emptiness all around.[6] Visually it is the blankness of the wall against which we see the nymphomaniac stand—her own emptiness externalized—that propels her into Giovanni, just as, at least in part, it makes him respond as he does. It is the same need that drives Roberto—a virtual adolescent of fourteen in comparison with the five-year-olds playing hopscotch and throwing themselves into the pool in the sudden downpour—to lead Lidia to his car, which in turn becomes the site for the most magical image of love anywhere in cinema: that carapace of Roberto's car, a magic bubble enclosing two silhouetted faces, laughing, talking, smiling, as the rain beats down and the car slides slowly along, lit now and then, but constantly veering into darkness, no sound but the rain and the windshield wipers moving back and forth.

In that image of Lidia and Roberto, happy in the womb of the car, everything converges: the nymphomaniac's need; the yearning for paradisal irresponsibility; the desire for a world immune from change—as in Giuliana's Sardinian beach, a single, sheeted tissue of pure being, all alienation from nature overcome; the African darkness of the nightclub; the black pool known only by the lights shimmering on its blank surface; and ultimately the night itself, absolute and total. The night from which Lidia, moved by Tommaso's death, wakens herself and tries to waken Giovanni—the unindividuated night yielding, as so often in Antonioni, to the dawn of the individuated world, with its solitude and tragic loneliness, and its sundered bodies. It is in the light of this dawn, reading the words from Giovanni's old love letter, that Lidia tells us exactly what she has awakened from—another past sleep, a finished sleep:

For a moment I understood how much I loved you, and it was a feeling so intense that my eyes filled with tears. For I felt that this must never end, that our whole life together would be like the waking of this morning, feeling you not only mine but an actual part of me [addirittura una parte di me], something that breathed with my breathing and that nothing could ever destroy except the torpor of habit which I see as the only threat.

And it is, of course, Lidia's rejection of Roberto that tells us why she now refuses to be pulled back by Giovanni and his reawakened need into a world she has wakened out of forever. That this is the only reading of the conclusion seems to me inescapable. We see it forming in the nightclub as her fingers move, in imitation of a dancer's movements, then reach out to touch things, as though to test their reality, to make contact with something real, something no longer like Giovanni, the person who is bemused by the dancing stripteasers. Then we see it again as she savors Tommaso's death, on the balcony alone—the point punctuated by the laughter of Signora Gherardini and her question to Lidia, "All alone, Signora Pontano?" Yes, alone, because the encounter with death isolates. Tomasso, dying, precipitates Lidia's separation from Giovanni, precipitates her own individuation. Just as Locke, knowing he is about to die, sends the Girl away; there are no passengers on that journey. And in *Blow-up*, as a result of the encounter with death, the photographer is shown as newly individuated, separated from those watching and playing the tennis game.

Isolated by her knowledge of Tomasso's death, Lidia looks down from the balcony with a kind of longing, a need for company, on the dancers below—a long, lingering look, which is stressed as she leaves the frame and we look at what she has seen. The rhythm moves her, her foot stirring under the piano. Then, asked to dance, she discovers herself on the dance floor with a partner who cannot dance, and so she does what she will do from now on, and what Valentina—at the age of eighteen and "many many months"—has already learned to do: to accept solitude as the price of individual, responsible existence.

Look at the fragile affair between Vittoria and Piero in *Eclipse* from this point of view and one instantly understands its brevity as necessary. Not only is there no real mesh between their psychic geographies, but also the erotic relationship itself is not sustainable; or, if sustainable, only at the cost of ceasing to be oneself. Individuality is precarious; sometimes it demands too much, demands we surrender too much of ourselves as the price of erotic accommodation. The experience of Eros, as we know from Plato or Freud or *Red Desert* or *L'avventura* or *La notte*, is very much like drowning—drowning into another's being. Because of the failure of modern cultural institutions—family, church, *paese*, community—Eros must bear the burden of the failed structures, and it is unequal to the task. Hence serial eroticism and the other maladies of Eros. Hence the hunger to drown, the spectacle of

a world filled with drowned figures, like the nymphomaniac or poor Resy, or with professional sharks, those experts in oceanic feeling like Roberto, who quote Adorno in order to justify their own unfreedom, their own rationalized irresponsibility: "Our age, my dear sir, is anti-philosophical and base. It lacks the courage to say what possesses value and what does not, and democracy, in so many words means 'Do what happens.'" That is, abandon responsibility. Such bad faith, because it aims at obliterating the pain of change, because its deepest purpose is to recreate the world of childish and paradisal irresponsibility, is in fact the hunger for immortality, for the divinity of shared being that Giovanni once felt with Lidia and that he described in the letter which she reads to him at the end of film.

The depiction of this paradisal irresponsibility is the purpose of the torrential summer downpour that sends the guests into the pool, an act that is intended to create just the release necessary to liberate these putative adults from their weary roles and let them play uninhibitedly. The guests are earlier attracted by the pool, lolling and playing; we see one girl near the pool playing hopscotch on the black and white squares made by the flagstones and the grass. It is the darkness, as I said, the pool and the night that they desire; and that darkness, that pool life is a group life, unindividuated. There they hope to lose themselves, to become one with the others, just as in Eros two lovers become one, each a part of the other in a night that lasts forever, or if not, that can be serially renewed with a new partner, over and over. Lidia and Valentina clearly, though not without regrets, refuse this world, refuse to become somnambulists. Their refusal is rendered in terms that are elliptical and visual, but nonetheless unmistakable.

Valentina, for instance, like Vittoria in *Eclipse*, constantly corrects for light, when the darkness becomes too thick, too enclosing. Standing in the patio with Giovanni, she senses his need to draw her toward the dark and the rain, and moves, on the pretext of a cigarette, toward the staircase, a tunnel of light. We see her in her room, speaking to the servant: "Angelo," she says, and we wait while she lights her cigarette from the candlestick. Then, the long pause stressing the director's intent, she continues, "bring some more candles," a request that shows her consciously correcting for light, counterpoising the darkness. In the pendant scene between Lidia and Roberto, it is a passing train and the red light—with its semiotic cry of "Stop!"—that makes Lidia pull back on the point of surrendering. Still later, we see Giovanni and Valentina about to kiss, when the lights suddenly go on, and Valentina says, withdrawing from his embrace, "You see? It's absurd." For the same reason—the nice chiaroscuro she achieves by moving from the blacks to the white, her ability to "play" the game with neither too strong nor too weak conviction—Valentina represents in visual terms precisely the balance that she shares with Lidia and with nobody else. Even in her clothes—black hair and white face, bare white shoulders and black dress—she is sharply contrasted with the men, especially Giovanni, his

participation in the black tonalities of the pool world indicated by the preponderant black of his clothing and his revealing preference for the darker sides of the frame.

In Lidia's walk toward the *periferia*—itself, as I have indicated, the revelation of her unspoken self, her *destino*—we have still another form of achieving balance, in this case by shifting one's location, inserting oneself among objects and places by means of which the disequilibrium that causes the walk is righted. We see her leave the publisher's cocktail party, with its harsh laughter and plastic politeness; we know her feeling of being imprisoned because of the grillwork on the gate by which she leaves. Steadily, without knowing why, she moves through the traffic and uproar toward ever-quieter streets—the whole walk amounts, in fact, to a montage of images central to the film: the fountain where she stops momentarily is itself the tears she feels;[7] the wailing child in the condemned building is a glancingly expressive image of the pain of change, the pain of the lost child in a world of the derelict past; the image of the broken clock, time stopped dead at quarter of one; the *feel*—tactile, not visual—of age, the texture of time, as Lidia touches the rust-flaking metal. We sense Lidia's body loosening, unwinding as she moves along, impressed by the simple spectacle of a parking attendant enjoying his food (who responds to her gaze with the usual Antonioni male gaze at the legs), then smiling in contagious response to healthy laughter; the child in Lidia walks *between* the stone posts on the sidewalk until confronted with an old woman eating ice cream, at which point she resumes, corrected, her normal walk; then the sweater coming off; the siren with its memory of Tommaso; and the jets overhead. Then into the taxi and—crosscut with scenes of Giovanni, imprisoned in his cage, buried behind books, or looking out at others imprisoned in their cages in buildings that are nothing more than cubicle cages—Lidia finally arrives by cab at a spot near her emerging, increasingly declared destination.

Like Valentina, Lidia is all eyes; she uses her eyes to take in the world. At the party, in fact, Lidia becomes the curious observer, open to the world around her, an openness everywhere suggested in her ability to touch her own feelings. She is able to admit the world that is excluded from Giovanni's vision, by his absorption in his work and in himself, and she is able to look beyond the narcotized, preinterpreting vision of most of the guests at the party, seeing only what they have programmed themselves (I think the metaphor is right) to see, utterly ignorant of the hidden reality which, unedited, not cut away, opens up around us every time we open our waking eyes. So Lidia moves, all eyes but also with active senses—hands touching, ears listening, wakefully acute—toward the point where city and country intersect, where in an expanse of green field beside the highway the Faustians, with their rockets, reach for the moon. Across the way she finds, like a tiny oasis of lost time, the church, and the churchyard, and the tree of her past and of her nature.

Lidia performs an improvised, unself-conscious balancing act. Like Valentina, Lidia is an equilibrist. Her alert, attentive senses quicken to take in the world, refusing to drown, moving steadily toward the individuation that means selfhood but also tragic solitude. Everywhere around Lidia and Valentina is a world in change, a tilting reality to which the individual must adapt or, by freezing himself into the pretense that change can be avoided by finding a paradisal shelter, creating a kind of divine or deathless permanence in the intensity of Eros, and the fiction of undying love or the shared illusions of the living dead. It is because reality is constantly changing everywhere, sweeping away certainties, destroying every landscape, the very ground of one's being—as in *Il grido*—that the temptation to succumb to makeshift stabilities or certainties, to blot out consciousness of change by refusing to look behind the human figure, beyond the erotic close-up, is so overpoweringly strong. Valentina and Lidia keep their balance by changing, by shifting ground when they must, by constantly growing, by swimming or floating instead of drowning. The point is precisely that made by Ortega y Gasset:

> What is really confused, intricate, is the concrete vital reality, always a unique thing. The man who is capable of steering a clear course through it, who can perceive under the chaos presented by every vital situation, the hidden anatomy of the movement, the man, in a word, who does not lose himself in life, that is the man with the really clear head [recall Tommaso's phrase: "Now I see things with a certain lucidity," as well as Claudia's passion for clarity in *L'avventura*]. Take stock of those around you, and you will see them wandering lost through life, like sleepwalkers. . . . The man with the clear head is the man who frees himself from these fantastic "ideas," and looks life in the face, realizes that everything in it is problematic, and feels himself lost. . . . Instinctively, as do the shipwrecked, he will look round for something to which to cling, and that tragic, ruthless glance, absolutely sincere because it is a question of his salvation, will cause him to bring order into the chaos of his life. These are the only genuine ideas, the ideas of the shipwrecked. All the rest is rhetoric, posturing, farce.[8]

Clarity comes when the transient comes into contact with the unchanging or permanent, when it recognizes its transience, thereby realizing its very nature, clear-eyed and unafraid. On this the whole film insists; all its intrication is founded upon it, everything converging here. The point is implied often by Antonioni in *La notte*. For instance, at one point Lidia and Signora Gherardini stand at the buffet, and Signora Gherardini asks Lidia if she will have something to drink. Lidia says, "Yes, a cognac." Then, both women turn and stare at something off the frame, and Signora Gherardini says, "He's been looking at that statue all day. He's looking right at its eyes. Who knows what that animal is thinking? Maybe he's waiting for him to

61

wake up? Just try figuring out cats!" Even at this point we do not see the event being described. The director delays, heightening his point, as a man approaches the buffet and takes a drink. Only then does the camera show us a cat, its back to the camera, staring at what looks to be an ancient Roman, perhaps Mithraic, head. In the foreground, pure feline transience, as emblematic a form of pure being-in-the-present, pure waking consciousness as one could imagine; the object of its stare, the face of permanence, fixed in its enduring and unwaking sleep. In the statuary head is concentrated all the film's preoccupation with monuments, with contrived eternity, with the induced drowsiness of eternity, as evidenced by Signor Gherardini's longing for a lasting memorial of his life, and Giovanni's addiction to words that, aimed at eternity, remain ephemeral because of what we *see* in Giovanni's study: his own anesthetized self-absorption in his drowsy, indeed drugged, addiction to his profession, his inattentiveness to everything around him—his inability to *see* his world, his wife, himself. Again and again the film shows us Giovanni's life-in-death; the image of him, caged among his books, is that of a mummy surrounded by a wall of dusty scrolls and files in which he has been buried alive. Gherardini has labored, as he says—pounding a wooden table for emphasis—"to leave something solid behind"; Giovanni, too, has labored at his compulsive vocation in order to evade death, to circumvent mortality by the artifice of words.

Confronting that eternity is the unblinking gaze of the fascinated cat, in whose transience and acceptance of the moment—the enduring present—we can see the meaning of Valentina and Lidia, their lithe, alert, catlike confrontation with eternity. It is their wisdom, like cats, like leaves, like trees, to live organically, to live not in opposition to time but with it, at home in it, precariously perched, ripening into awareness in every waking moment. At times, as when Valentina plays with the sleeping man, the two women help others to wake from their sleep. Lidia and Valentina are clear-sighted and open-eyed, which means they have no illusions. There is only the present, and the world that opens around them in every gaze, revealing to a seeing eye, but not perhaps to a focused or specialized eye, both foreground and background, both the transient and the permanent, the detail and the whole of which it is part. The two women live in time, live like a leaf, like a tree, growing in the moment, rooted in the earth.

Consider, for instance, the idea or theme or image—though it is not quite any of those things but something else, both image and theme—of the tree. As the film opens, even before the titles begin, we see a bus passing, then a truck. Between them appears a nineteenth-century brownstone, and now to the right of the brownstone the Pirelli Building in Milan. The camera moves up the brownstone, holding both buildings in the frame, then veers, it seems, to the top of the Pirelli Building, with a shot of the observation deck and the city in the distance; then an interior shot of structural steel tubing. Slowly, very slowly, we slide down the side of the building,

past frame after frame of steel and glass, reflecting city, clouds, trees. Always the city reflected below, becoming more and more clear as we sink; then the shot of an avenue lined with trees, and a bus, no movement of traffic, the whole city sunk in the summer afternoon torpor of the siesta. Why, we might ask, does the director show us the Pirelli Building? For the same reason he shows us Nervi's Palazzo dello Sport in *Eclipse* or the two Gaudí buildings in Barcelona in *The Passenger*. Because in the work of both architects the emphasis is on the fusion of natural and geometric in what Frank Lloyd Wright and others have called the properly "organic" mode of modern architecture, its mission of reconciling engineering function and natural form, mathematical calculation and natural rhythm. The Pirelli Building, built in 1958, was designed by Pier Luigi Nervi, who was led, according to Giulia Veronesi, to constant researches in rhythm as a structural element because of his commitment to the principle of "strength through form"; the architect studied this idea on the corrugated surfaces of shellfish, insects, and flower calyxes. Commenting on his building in Milan, Veronesi added, "In the construction of the Pirelli Skyscraper in Milan (1958, with Gio Ponti and the architects of his office), the principle on which its strength is based is derived from nature too, viz. from the example of a tree. This is the prototype of the building's sectional development, with its four main stanchions growing ever more slender towards the top. . . ."[9]

The tree whose example lies behind this building—itself used as part of a *La notte* image sequence designed to suggest a society in radical transition, furiously juxtaposing incongruent modes of life—is, as already noted, the ultimate destination of Lidia's long walk through Milan, as she and her feelings and history slowly unfold before us. We see her with her head against the tree, listening to the rustle within, far removed now from all the sterile sounds and caged feelings with which, from which, her walk began. Twice in the party sequence we see Lidia, alone on the balcony looking up at the mass of the trees in the darkness overhead, then down through the trunks where she sees, screened by three trunks, Giovanni and Valentina kiss.

In the exquisite scenes of Valentina's game with her cosmetic compact on the white-and-black checkerboard of the floor where she chooses to sit, the natural world is brought inside, for villas, trees, and a horse race, or foxhunt, are pictured on the walls. Here, the whole composition declares, she is happily at home, happy even when—and perhaps because she *is*— alone. Alone as we first see her, sitting at the foot of the steps reading *The Sleepwalkers*. And then we have the internal story of Valentina's tape recording, with its trees whose rustling has its source, its life, in the tree itself—not in us—and whose transience is transferred to Valentina by the simple device of having her erase the tape. Unlike Giovanni, she has no designs on eternity: her words are written the way she lives, like a leaf, here passing, then gone. The power of being that she shares with other Antonioni women derives from the real eternity of the present moment, always ripening.

The whole final sequence depends upon our perception of this tree life—first of the tree as metaphor, then the tree as subject in its own right, the great life of the enduring frame out of which the human participants have passed, or which moves past them, to its own transcendent life incarnating the eternity of the recurrent seasons and the natural cycle. This concluding scene begins at dawn, after the night and the party, as Giovanni and Lidia walk away from the Gherardini house, out onto the grounds that become a golf course. Before the couple this whole field opens up, revealing two trees in the far foreground, behind the other trees. The grass is wet with the dew in the gray dawn light, the musicians still playing sadly in a world whose brilliant black-and-white textures have melted into a uniform gray. Lidia and Giovanni walk slowly and sadly toward the trees, he telling her of Gherardini's offer, she offering him, to his surprise, not indignation but a kind of painfully compassionate understanding. He will be more comfortable working for Gherardini. They reach a point opposite the black trunks of the two nearest trees and there they stop, fixed uncomfortably, rigidly maintaining position near the trees, while the camera holds on them, forcing us to recognize the metaphor. But which is which? Which tree—the straight one or the twisted one—represents which person? We do not know; either tree could be either person, for they are a couple, these trees, a rooted pair, close but separate—separate from the other trees. Their roots, we suppose, must touch. Then Lidia tells him of Tommaso's death, tells him what Tommaso meant to her. And now we see Lidia alone in the frame flanked on the right by a single tree—the straight one—and then we see him, answering, and to his left the misshapen tree that defines him. A gulf, we see, has opened between them, a gulf whose reality—real distance— derives from her clear-eyed perception of him, and from her newly ripened recognition that they are no longer one thing but two, and that she no longer loves him. No longer loves him in the way he described in his letter to her, that is, no longer as though she were a part of him, fused in a single being, one flesh breathing with a single life. The distance is expressed as pain but also as firmness, that same edge of cruelty we heard in Irma's voice in *Il grido* when, at dawn, she tells Aldo she is leaving him. Harshness combined with compassion. What Lidia feels for Giovanni is no longer love; only compassion. *Soltanto pietà.*

As though to emphasize her removal—but also surely her fear of turning away—she looks now toward another tree, a gray birch whose white and black mottlings pick up the evening's chiaroscuro, as though to remind us of her affinity with black *and* white, and of her ability to hold her balance, to be alone, on her own, an equilibrist, combining two opposite worlds and rooted in the ground. As though in recognition of her affinity with *this* tree, she reaches out and touches its leaves, claims it as her own image and talisman. Then—I am compressing—we see her read him the letter, *his* letter (though the pained expression on his face tells us he sup-

poses it is written by a lover), and while she reads, now and then, the camera shows us the trunk of the gray birch at her side. Then we see him seize her and try to pull her back into the old erotic world she has left, while she protests that she no longer loves him, that he no longer loves her. We see him a black figure *on* her, around her, his blackness overwhelming her, drowning her, trying to make her drown with him, pushing her down into the emptiness, the desert, of the sand trap. Love, Valentina had said earlier, makes an emptiness all around, and the sand trap *is* that emptiness, still another of Antonioni's images of the erotic or transcendent desert.[10] Each viewer must decide for himself whether Giovanni succeeds in overwhelming Lidia, but to me there seems no doubt that he fails. Why? Because the scene has been so carefully prepared for in the party, in her ripening loneliness, in the sequence of her dancing alone, and in her rejection of Roberto's invitation to love—a rejection that has nothing to do with fidelity and everything to do with responsibility and solitude. The world changes, feelings change. Ripeness is all. We must endure our going hence, even as our coming hither.

And now the camera pans away, moving with meaningful slowness back to the gray birch, her talisman before but now, I think, having its own meaning, standing alone, beautiful, in the ground of its being. For if this tree were merely a metaphor of Lidia, the camera would hold there, affirming *her* decision, *her* strength to be alone. Instead it moves, keeps moving, on and on, showing us the woods that lie beyond in the distance. Like a great clearing, the golf course and the sky above open up, revealing all the vast reality of time and space, the limitless and humbling immensities that, after all, always lie outside the insignificant frame of human action and the busy arrogance of the human present.[11]

Eclipse

How can I tell you the story of *Eclipse*? A story of imprisoned sentiments if told in a few words is ruined. It can lose all its significance. . . . *Eclipse* . . . is about a young working woman who leaves a man because she no longer loves him, and then leaves another man because she still loves him.

The world today is ruled by money, greed for money, fear of money. This leads to a dangerous passivity towards problems of the spirit. Love is affected by this too, and the woman Vittoria of my film, who has just walked out on an unfortunate relationship[,] meets Piero, a stock-broker, who might be the one love of her life, but this man is locked up in his world of investments, speculations. He is lost in the convulsive activity of the market. The market governs his every action, even his way of loving.
—Michelangelo Antonioni, from an interview in
Theatre Arts (July 1962)

"A story of imprisoned sentiments." Image upon image confirms the theme: everywhere gates, gratings, bars, barriers, doors clanging shut with prison finality; the *saracinesche*, or shop gratings, through which Vittoria, after the love scene in Piero's office, sees the tall trees of the park across the street,

66

their tops stirring in the wind, and then the free, unimpeded vision of the same trees, as though to declare, by removing the bars, what has been imprisoned; or Vittoria seen, as in the cell of her apartment, peering out at Riccardo, himself framed in the grill of the fence outside; or the wistful pain of the woman in the concluding montage sequence gazing through the bars before her.

Or, the same idea of imprisoned sentiments, expressed as claustrophobia—in dead, stale air, the stifling enclosure of a musty, stuffy room; as in Riccardo's apartment, with its fan and trays of stubbed cigarettes; or Vittoria's sudden recoil before the mirror as she senses something like death in the catatonic features and posture of Riccardo; then the longing to escape as she peers through the curtains at the dawn world outside, only to find herself imprisoned by the window glass; or the musty darkness in the apartment of Piero's parents, with the silent square and church below at the dead of siesta—the image of a dead or stricken world—and the living entombment of middle-class marriage conveyed there by the shuttered windows, the massive black furniture; or the sudden image of a woman in the palazzo opposite, Vittoria's mirror image, appearing in the confining frame of the black window, then vanishing into the blackness; or, perhaps most impressive of all in this brief catalog of the imprisoned feelings expressed as claustrophobia, consider the animal reek of the stock exchange on a summer day, its futile fans turning listlessly overhead, with the grating that separates the frenetically shouting and gesturing brokers from the arithmetically contrasting calm of the tellers; but also that other grating which seals off the Parco Buoi,[1] behind which the clients stand to watch the rise and fall of their investments.

To this list of representations of confinement must be added dozens of images of human beings divided, distanced—separated by bars, poles, walls, glass, lattices, grills, doors; and, most insistent of all, the succession of barriers, real or symbolic veils and partitions, that Vittoria revealingly keeps setting between herself and her lover, Piero, as though defending herself from too violent an intrusion into the interior landscape of her world, or against her own desire and even need to lose herself in the being of another, to disappear in what Yeats called "the labyrinth of another's being."

The appearance and disappearance of these obstacles, the lifting and lowering of barriers, provide the essential tempo of the film; we measure the life of the imprisoned feelings by the tensing or relaxing of these restraints. The feelings *breathe*, as it were; interior feeling is instantly, with graphic accuracy, translated into visible terms. We perceive it as the way in which—to use the language of theater—a character "blocks" his movements, charts his own passage in his relation to the physical space and objects around him. But this blocking is not conscious; it expresses, rather, the interior, subvocal script of the feelings. The character places himself in a room or scene, in a chair, before a window or mirror, in a way that externalizes and

thereby makes visible—phenomenal—the texture and quality of his inner life, the tremulous vibration of feeling that, in the process of forming, becomes decision, clarity, and thought.

There is, I think, no scene in Antonioni richer in this kind of externalization through "blocking" than the opening sequence in Riccardo's apartment, as Riccardo and Vittoria end their relationship, surely one of the most exquisitely complex and perfectly composed accounts of emotional life ever registered in film. We see Vittoria touch objects—not only the *kind* of objects that she touches (that rounded bud vase, caressed through a frame) but also the *way* in which she touches them—and we see these objects and touchings contrasted with the objects that Riccardo has, in some deep sense of "choice," selected for his environment. The books, the lamp, the fan, an onyx pyramid, an electric razor—these express his own alternating feelings of need and defiance that *are* his relation to Vittoria. Then we see the couple defined in their relations to each other—Riccardo withdrawn into himself in a comatose silence; she, watching him in the mirror as though not daring to look him in the face, standing obliquely and steeling herself to be loyal to the *fact* that she no longer loves him, must not let herself *succumb* to compassion for the hurt she has caused him. The two then pass in the doorway like strangers. This whole oblique but intensely dramatic narrative of skewed emotional life is portrayed with scrupulous technical precision. The insistent point is not the physical room itself, which the director deliberately leaves undefined, but the way in which fragmented parts of the room— walls, windows, lamps, the rich compositional clutter of objects—define the oblique drama of the interior lives of the two participants. Above all, Vittoria's viewpoint gradually tends to predominate. It would, I think, be impossible to make a drawing of this apartment—though its size seems very modest—precisely because the director has refused to satisfy our demand for a diagrammatic view of the whole and rather concentrates on the *parts*. The segments are never permitted to compose a whole. We sense the fragmentation of the affair, and the couple's incongruous feelings, in a field or frame that always dissolves into objects and parts of human beings which are constantly juxtaposed and made to comment on each other. In one shot, for instance, we see Vittoria's legs from the knees down; her legs are defined by, and in turn define, the chair legs beside her. Then we see her legs and the chair legs reflected in the cold, polished marble sheen of the floor, that is, as if they were objects among other objects. The composition of the shot goes far beyond aestheticism or stylization.

Indeed, the *deepest* purpose of this opening sequence is, I believe, the consistent, concentrated effort to render the breakup of the affair and its fractured affections as a clutter of discrete objects that never cohere into a whole. The room dissolves into "things" and "surfaces"; these things and surfaces then divide and dissolve into the incongruous objects that define Riccardo and Vittoria—*his* rational and geometric or intellectual *ambiente*

(lamps, book, pyramid) at odds with *her* environing objects. The effect culminates in the later image of the couple standing at the window, his head crowned by the bulbous mushroom of the EUR[2] water tower profiled in air, and her blond hair surmounted by a large evergreen tree. Then, as though to cap the sequence of fractured objects and warring contrasts, we see him shatter the bud vase which she had earlier touched with abstracted fondness, her hands passing through an empty picture frame as though to enclose both vase and gesture. The film, of course, continues to inflect that bud vase, as in the large illuminated vase—at once a flower vase and a lamp—shown repeatedly in Vittoria's apartment. Moreover, in this opening scene she *touches* the vase, and this act of touching, of tactily apprehending, is repeated, confirmed, and extended during the African sequence in Marta's apartment, where we see the women "run their hands over" the Zambezi Falls and caress the gnarled trunk of a huge baobab tree—as represented in photographs.

Glancingly, but unmistakably I think, the camera is already, even at the outset, telling us something of the feelings that are imprisoned everywhere in the film—the suppressed or repressed reality, so persistently at the heart of *Eclipse.* Vittoria surrounds herself with objects of organic shape, as she everywhere surrounds herself with flowers, with vegetable texture and fibers (even that Paisley blouse). Her relation to these organic objects is profoundly and revealingly tactile, in sharp contrast to Riccardo, and later Piero, who tend to inhabit a world of rational, geometric objects, and whose relation to those objects is wholly visual, not tactile. The distinction of roles is never absolute; there is, for Antonioni too, only a single human psyche, not a male soul and a female soul. But that psyche may be differently compounded, according to the psychic balance, personal proclivities, or cultural conditioning of the individual.

Antonioni has said that he prefers to place women at the center of his films because they provide a better "filter of reality." By this he means, at least in part, that for him women provide less-impeded access to the realities suppressed by the Faustian organization of the world. Since the actual structure of the Faustian world, especially in the Italy of these earlier films, is a male affair, and since Antonioni has mostly depicted male intellectuals—architects, writers, art critics, even stockbrokers, all of them clearly Faustian intellectuals insofar as they are manipulators of abstractions—his men exhibit fairly consistent traits. They tend to inhabit a noisy world, expressed in rational geometries and often inhuman abstractions; their behavior is characteristically compulsive, marked by frenzied restlessness and constantly compensatory behavior. His women, on the other hand, temperamentally or culturally inhabit a quiet world and define themselves by affinity with organic forms, above all trees and flowers. If they are healthy (like Vittoria in this film), they seem to possess a kind of psychic balance; the senses are integrated with each other, the eye enjoying equal dignity

69

with the rest. Such women, free of the male routines of role and profession, are capable at their best of power and beauty of being, living like a leaf or a wave with the natural rhythm of their feelings, at home even in time.

Integrity, beauty of being, and psychic balance belong to Vittoria here, as to Valentina and Lidia in *La notte* and, to a lesser degree, to Claudia in *L'avventura*. But the balance is precarious, especially in a world organized by Faustians like Ettore and Sandro in *L'avventura*, or like Riccardo and Piero here, for *La notte* suggests the world is tilting toward greater and greater imbalance. The final shot of *Eclipse* shows the artificial or man-made light—a light in which there looms the implicit power and threat of atomic explosion—pushing the blacks of the natural night to the fringes of the frame. Man eclipses nature; day defeats night. More and more, the film suggests, Faustian organization invades and expropriates another older organization of the world, suppressing an old reality. The wild animal, as in Kenya, is hunted down and disappears; untamed societies vanish, while the primitive goes underground and slowly, through the unconscious, invades the Faustian invader and manipulator. (This, *in nuce*, is the theme of *Blow-up* and *The Passenger*.)

The modern world, Antonioni suggests, is a world out of balance, radically and rapidly tilting, its center of gravity constantly shifting, and therefore constraining individuals to ever more desperate efforts to keep their balance. More and more agility, incredible adaptive virtuosity, is required; and the temptation, under the shock of constant change, is to counter the world's reeling by anchoring oneself somewhere, somehow. This means, of course, the effort to escape by regression; by returning to the past; by somnambulism or drugs or aphrodisiacs; by annihilating consciousness or extinguishing individual identity; by the impulse to renew one's bond with nature and the natural world in a violent recovering of paradise. Hence serial eroticism as in *L'avventura* and *Il grido*; hence, too, an erotic hunger whose real purpose is to lose oneself in another's being, to transcend oneself. We yearn to escape the limits of our own miserable body, our being, by entering into or becoming someone else. Proust's Marcel possesses a gnawing dissatisfaction with himself, compounded by the feeling that he cannot fully possess the person he desires. The urge for self-transcendence burns a hole in our being without ever attaining its goal: true otherness.

Hence in *Eclipse* the ubiquitous barrier images that express the characters' contrivance in creating and arranging obstacles, as well as their need to cross them, that is, to transcend them. Typically, the character "places" himself in such a way that his position cuts himself off from another, as though to protect his own intimacy and privacy, or as a sign of unhappy solitude achieved, an awareness of something impeding his access to others, something needing to be transcended; or even as his effort to cut off others; to imprison them. The prison cage becomes a multiple image: a room of

cell-like or cubicle proportions, like the various modern apartments—Riccardo's, or Piero's, or even Marta's (though she symbolically escapes her confinement by turning her walls into African jungle, mountains, and savannas). These cells *may* be the sign of solitude, and even solipsism; but there is danger in reading Antonioni's images so unambiguously. We see Riccardo, for instance, outside Vittoria's apartment, through bars, and we *hear* him, like a prisoner, caged outside—caged *away* from *her* who by Eros has become his world—shaking the doors as though struggling to escape *out* of himself, *out* of his solitude, trying to break free into her world. But *his* hunger *imprisons her,* constricting her freedom of movement; and when she appeals to Franco for help, we see her once again confronted by the threat of a man's erotic need—that look of annoyance and frustration that passes over her face as she lets the receiver fall, precipitating the cut to the shot of the airplane wing clearing the ground as the plane lifts off from the confining city and its crisscrossing confusion of erotic need and solitude, its countless images of prison cells and jailed jailers. This flight to Verona is a flight for freedom—like Mark's for the desert in *Zabriskie Point,* or indeed like so many of Antonioni's depictions of the hunger to escape and the exhilaration of free flight.

All these images represent sheer transcendence: transcendence of the human condition, like Icarus in the emblem books and Platonic images, soaring out of himself and the frustration of being earthbound, into another dimension, a kind of divinity.[3] All of the escape imagery in Antonioni—and it begins as early as *I vinti* (the shot of a steamer, in a travel agent's window, with Whatton and Hallan in the foreground)—is, like the flight imagery, the unmistakable sign of this hunger for transcendence, for *annulment* of the pain of individual existence, solitude, and responsibility, into the paradise of the past, or into childhood, or into space, or into erotic love; but above all into the paradise of Eros that, once achieved, becomes the explanation of, or assumes into itself, all the other paradises—past, childhood, oceanic feeling, nature, instinct, and unconscious.

In a mostly Faustian world, unbalanced and tilting ever more severely toward an eclipse of the natural and organic, toward abstraction and thought, away from feeling (or any meaningful integration of feeling and thought), the desire for escape and transcendence becomes correspondingly stronger. Balance itself can only be achieved by strengthening in oneself the opposed polarity. If you are oppressed, like Vittoria, by the dead air and the artificial light of old feelings no longer felt, you go to the window and let in the dawn light, you lose yourself in the shadow of the organic, that is, in contact with leaves or leaning against a trunk. You move from the busy foreground to the quiet background. You move back into your own interior geography, away from the exterior city, or you strike out for the "desert," toward your own solitudes and wilderness; or you regress, sinking back into your former self, your past, your childhood, your psychic

territory, into the night world of your feelings, the senses you suppressed while you were penned in the cage of another's being. This means, of course, breaking with others, with those in whose being it was once your deepest need to lose and transcend yourself but with whom you now feel intolerably confined.

For Antonioni's women, marriage is resisted precisely because it imprisons them in the needs of others, and, more important, in others whose way of existing has become increasingly alien and constricting. Once, Antonioni seems to suggest in the scenes in Piero's parents' apartment, marriage implied a congruence of feeling, the possibility in a stable world of modest change and comparatively stable affections. Feelings lasted. Now, in a time of convulsive change, one can almost never find the necessary congruence of feeling; now, for whatever reason, between men and women the only constant is sexuality, and for women like Vittoria this is not enough. The men mostly want marriage, the women evade it. Why? Because, as we learn on the convent roof in *L'avventura*, it is only the bells that chime and answer each other, *rispondono*; for Sandro and Claudia, separated on that roof by the very ropes they pull, in revealingly skewed and oblique relation to each other, there is no real chiming of feelings and purpose; *non rispondono*. Marriage becomes a sexual cage; the other feelings and even the whole intricate life of feeling, the integrated sense of thought and feeling fused into one, are suppressed or thwarted. We see this frustrated life in the woman's face behind the bars, near the end of *Eclipse*, or in the image of the woman in the window across from Piero's parents' apartment, appearing briefly before disappearing into the darkness that is her world, an image that shows the obscurity and suppression of her emotional existence.

Life, in Ortega's phrase, has become "scandalously provisional," a matter of daily improvisation. A matter, too, of daily efforts at balance, ever more difficult to maintain, as the individual's equilibrium in a tilting, shifting reality becomes more and more precarious. The individual is driven violently toward transcendence by the need to obliterate all barriers in compulsive or serial intimacy. This drive is cinematically asserted by the yearning to escape the confines of the "frame," and by the camera's expulsion of the whole external world from the frame, concentrating instead on foreground, that is, on erotic close-ups of the human body. The danger, of course, is that the individual may lose himself in a solitude or solipsism like Ugolino's prison as described by T. S. Eliot:

> I have heard the key
> Turn in the door once and turn once only
> We think of the key, each in his prison
> Thinking of the key, each confirms a prison
> Only at nightfall. . . .[4]

Antonioni's characters believe that the prison can be obliterated through erotic transcendence.[5] On the one side, loneliness and self-incarceration; on the other, deliberate, obsessive immersion (another incarceration), in the destructive element of another's being, in the self-extinction of an Eros that *aims* at self-extinction, or that confuses self-extinction with otherness. The dangers of this destructive element are very real, especially for Antonioni's women; *Red Desert* is transparently an effort to deal with the neurosis, even pathology, of this Eros. In *Eclipse*, however, the alternatives are expressed as polar possibilities, each with its own landscape and attendant terms, between which the character Vittoria must find some balance.

Meanwhile, the world itself is violently displaying its own brusque alternations in reality and mood, its veering and unpredictable changes of tempo. We *see* a symbolic day—from dawn to dusk—into which are compressed a number of narrative days. Time is experienced as time *is* experienced in modern life, not as a natural serial unfolding of organic time but as a series of discontinuous moments or scenes. Just as the physical world is shattered into unconnected fragments, so time in *Eclipse* is exploded into dissonant tempi, each tempo enjambed against its opposite, cinematically expressed in jarring cuts. Thus we move abruptly from a shot of Vittoria in her apartment, looking out at the trees moving in the dawn breeze, to the scene at the stock exchange where, in the street outside, cars are honking, people rushing, and, inside, pandemonium. So, too, we move from the night world of the African sequence in Marta's apartment to the peaceful, interim world of Verona, and then, by another abrupt cut, back to the stock exchange. The purpose of this kind of cutting is not merely contrast but rather incongruity of mood and tempo, the effort to describe time itself as dissonant, discontinuous, disjointed. The reeling and tilting of the changing world, the shifting reality that makes life so provisional and difficult, are thus everywhere suggested by a violent alternation of landscapes—city, country, the planned suburban world of EUR, the African motifs of Marta's apartment—all brusquely enjambed. Rooms become not so much spaces but rather object-filled cubicles of indeterminate appearance; external space is exploded into bewildering landscape variety. The discontinuity of space is confirmed by temporal dissonance, for the rhythm of time is itself shattered. Reality, in short, is now structured discontinuity.

To this unknown, perhaps unknowable, reality the individual must adapt; the narcosis of Eros is attractive precisely because it provides the illusion of stability. Thus in *L'avventura* the glimpse of immensity and transience motivates the erotic compulsion that eclipses the characters. So in *Eclipse* the perpetual temptation is to resolve the tension in oneself and in reality by fleeing to one pole or the other; toward day or night; city or country; eye or touch; past or future; the organic or the rational. The men,

mostly Faustians, intensify their restlessness in the narcosis of meaningless, frenzied, compulsive activity; the women, perhaps in reaction, are increasingly drawn toward some African night world of the senses, toward a tribal extinction of the individual, toward the animal and plant worlds. The common existential dilemma is to find a balance and to accept the tension; the difficulty is that one lives in a world of discontinuous time and space, that Eros—both a solace and a torment—embodies the restlessness of life itself, the passion for transcendence and the opposed need for solitude, the need to be oneself. Like Eliot, Antonioni accepts as his premise a perpetual disassociation of sensibility in the modern world, revealed primarily in the very polarities that inhabit his world so obsessively, but above all in the division of thought and feeling, with the consequent eclipse of Love as *the* humanizing experience that ideally and physically fuses thought and feeling, mind and body.

In *Eclipse*, as so often in Antonioni, the crucial action begins at dawn, when the light declares the individual, sundering the bodies that in the darkness were indistinguishable, one flesh. "I'm not a woman alone," says Giuliana in *Red Desert*, "although at times . . . it's as though I were . . . separated. No, not separated from my husband. . . . The bodies . . . are . . . separate."[6] Dawn separates: as in the dawn at the end of *La notte*, when Giovanni and Lidia dissolve into a different relationship; as in the early morning light at the end of *L'avventura*, when we see Claudia and Sandro still together but also differentiated; as in the dawn at the end of *Blow-up*, when Thomas separates himself from the tennis game, refusing the coercions of the group, an incipient individual. So, too, in *Eclipse*, at dawn, we see Vittoria separate from Riccardo and withdraw into her own psychic landscape, refusing to be absorbed in his.

Dramatically, in fact, the whole film is structured around Vittoria's effort to maintain, against the potent threat of Eros, the integrity of her own reality. Like Anna in *L'avventura* (whose *"Perché . . . perché . . . perché"* shows her hostility to verbal explanations), Vittoria cannot explain her deep feelings to Riccardo, who, Faustian man that he is, insists that there *must* be a reason (*un motivo c'è*). Her feelings tell her that she no longer loves him, and that is enough. So we see her withdraw into her world, *touching* the objects that explain her, seeking out the reality to which she is affined, and which tell *us*, if not her, *why* she no longer loves him. Because she no longer *feels* him (in *L'avventura* Anna says to Sandro, "I no longer feel you"); because, as she says later, with unmistakable emphasis, "How can I explain? There are days when it seems holding a piece of cloth, a needle, a thread, a book, or a man are all the same thing." Indeed, she no longer feels anything; we know why from what the camera tells us of Riccardo's world—its fragmentation into discrete objects, mere thingness, a world in which a woman's leg is effectively turned into an object, an object like other objects, imprisoned. Later we shall see Piero sneak a look at Vittoria's momentarily exposed

breast, and at another moment we see him turn and look at the legs of a passing nursemaid (a shot repeated in *Blow-up*), and this just after Vittoria comments on the handsomeness of the face of a man passing, not handsome in the way of Piero's face, but *humanly* handsome.

The point is not merely that people can be treated as sexual objects, but rather that as a result reality is radically impoverished. Nature then turns into mere manipulable things, *dead* things, according to the object status imposed upon reality by the Faustian eye and its will to power. It is Vittoria's horrifed discovery of the deadness of this world—the corpselike immobility of Riccardo—that hardens her resolve and sends her out into a world that Riccardo's worldview kills or suppresses. So we see her pass, with relief and a gradual unfolding, into the real light and organic reality of the world outside the apartment. So, too, after Vittoria leaves Riccardo, the camera delicately shows her constantly correcting the imbalances in her life, making minute adjustments. We see her, for instance, as she leaves Riccardo's, walking down the *middle* of the road. At the end of the road we see, on the left, the outlines of slab apartments, while on the right, umbrella pines. Quite unconsciously, at the sight, she veers toward the pines, away from the buildings—not abruptly or dramatically, but revealingly. She is still in the road when Riccardo's car appears, wheels squealing, an unwelcome intruder and also, as we learn, an unfamiliar one in this natural dawn world of Vittoria's. His appearance threatens her balance, and we see her veer again—this time into the woods, under the umbrella pines, as though she were adjusting to Riccardo's intrusion by pursuing a deeper immersion into her own element. When Vittoria finally arrives at her apartment, we see her not from within the apartment looking out at the trees, but rather from *outside*. In the foreground is the frame of the building, and it is through a balcony door that she looks at the trees, quite as though it were the building itself, the building *we* see, that explained her looking out at the trees. For the same reason we first see, before she arrives in her apartment, a shot of the wall and stairs, an abstract image that becomes defined only when she enters into the frame.

Antonioni insists in *Eclipse* that we should view Vittoria's withdrawal into her own psychic landscape as healthy, intelligent, psychical navigation, not neurotic withdrawal. She may be *tempted* by the leaf life of her interior world, but again and again the camera shows us this leaf world contrasted with another world, which is at once modern, intellectual, even abstract, but one with which she is completely at home, which is a real part of her nature. Giuliana may, in *Red Desert*, retreat from the refinery buildings into the shelter of a leafy covert; but Vittoria in *Eclipse* walks easily and naturally through a world that shows us, in balanced equilibrium, functional modern geometries like the bulbous water tower and Pier Luigi Nervi's beautifully engineered Palazzo dello Sport, as well as clusters of trees—city world and nature, geometric and organic—in amicable coexistence. Vittoria's balance

is itself an integration, declared as such by the objects among which she "blocks" her life. She withdraws and advances as need requires but constantly, even when teetering, recovers her balance. Everything in her history suggests this psychic health: she is, as translator, an intellectual, a reader of Hemingway. Even in her girlhood room at her mother's house, she surrounds herself not only with flowers but with an abstract image that looks like a thicket of barbed wire—an image, like the airplane hanger at Verona or even the airplane itself, of an organic and functional geometry. Whatever else Antonioni is doing, he is warning us against sentimentalizing Vittoria, or perceiving her idyllically as a representative of the organic against the rational, or of Rousseauian nature against the city.

What she constantly seeks is equilibrium, poise, the feelings moving in conformity with, not subjection to, the environing world. This equilibrium is repeatedly presented as a matter of constant, alert improvisation; she has no ready-made defenses or screens; she adapts daily. Her apartment is small but not inhumanly small, a garden apartment in the recently built area of EUR. The perspective may be planned, but it contains both buildings and trees, expanses of parkland alternating with tall apartment buildings. We see the objects that define her: that oversized flower lamp, softly swelling; fiber matting enlivening the dead walls; a poster of a woman in period clothes, wasp-waisted, with flowers, at a window; a constant commerce of old and new. When Vittoria is threatened by the dead objects in Riccardo's apartment, she raps her knuckles on wood; later we see her subtly adjusting the psychic balance of her apartment with a fossil flower she has bought;[7] the organic world deepens into time, another intensification of the leaf life threatened by the death of objects, the death of the senses hovering over Vittoria in the aftermath of her stagnant affair with Riccardo. In the African sequence in Marta's apartment, for example, we have a brief but extremely revealing narrative of an immersion, deeper than any other, in the destructive night world to which she is so vulnerable in the trough of her postaffair depression. Marta's walls, covered with photographs, open up into African expanses, and we see the immensity of that natural world so occluded by the urban uproar of the stock exchange: mountains, savanna, a pride of lions, and the African geography moving on, out of the photograph frame and onto the wall. In Marta's apartment the suppressed senses speak: a susurrus of women's voices in the summer night, a polar remove from the mostly male cacophony of the Borsa; the feeling hands touching everything, felt nature "coming alive." Then, as the women put on native costume and as Vittoria dances, the disappearance into the primitive, the sound of the drums, the spiraling down and back into the darkness of time. Finally, precisely at that moment of danger, incipient violence and animal cries, Marta, habituated to the dangers of "going native," turns on the light. All around, in rich profusion, the chiaroscuro at which the whole scene aims: the alternating black and white stripes of the zebra skin; the blond hair and

the blackened skin of Vittoria. It is a night world still, but now with the lights on and the threat of "going native" passed, it is a night world in which the precarious human balance is kept; visually, it fuses the blacks and whites that, when balanced, become true chiaroscuro, the mingling of opposed polarities, the harmonious fusion of what is elsewhere, but above all in the stock exchange, dissociated and sundered.

In the plane trip from Rome to Verona, the same balance and harmony are achieved through polarities that are geographical and cultural: Rome versus Verona; urban beast versus human-scale city; man-made versus natural; capital versus province. As the plane takes off for Verona, we see the proliferating megalopolis, the endlessly sprawling high-rise buildings in the new quarters of Rome. There follows a brilliant sequence in the plane itself; the men and women are differentiated, with the two men up front, steering by means of instruments and numbers—altitudes and velocities radio-beamed at them by the control tower; in back the women fly by impulse, psychically, almost. "Fly thorough that cloud!" says Vittoria impulsively, and the plane enters the eery blankness of the cloud.[8] Anita feels the gooseflesh rising on her arm, precisely as we do in *Eclipse*'s final montage sequence when we see the children playing in the street and the cloud of water, spurting from the gunlike nozzle, obliterating them, followed later in the scene by the threat of another obliteration suggested by the newspaper's headlines: "The Atomic Race" and "The Peace Is Weak."

Having passed through the cloud, the plane descends for its landing at Verona, and beneath it we see the great oval of the Roman amphitheater and the *città vecchia*, glancingly contrasted with Rome, the sinister megalopolis that moves out from the telephone booths and communications network of the stock exchange to dominate and annex the provinces. The plane glides slowly down the runway, and we see with delight the open fields and the foothills of the Alps. As the plane taxis onto the grassy field surrounding the runway, Vittoria looks about with a kind of happy relish; so much space and light; man-made things—like the plane she pats affectionately—and the world of nature are momentarily in beautiful balance. Under an arbor two men are talking; technicians in a green world, but speaking to each other like men. She looks about. Then she looks up to see the contrails of the American army jets doubtless stationed at the air base in Verona; abruptly, and profoundly, but not vexatiously, she walks out of the frame. The jets speak, after all, of transience and imminent change; of a different technological scale of things, of giant machines, different men, and a more ominous world. This airport, too, in which she feels at home, is doomed to disappear; the small runway, surrounded by grassy fields, will vanish soon under asphalt. So she adjusts her balance, moving away from the future, toward the little airport building. Here she finds that a kind of simple, even corny, but impressive peace prevails. Two blacks—Americans, obviously—stand out against the white building; they recall the African

sequence earlier and the director's insistence that we must not impose the idyllic. The American jets which flew overhead now reappear, represented by air corps personnel, but they are in no way ominous, merely that perfect balance of white and black, past and present, man and nature, that chiaroscuro of feelings that Vittoria instinctively seeks. The music is old-fashioned, as though even these jet pilots and mechanics needed a kind of tranquillity or rest as well as she; they too seek balance and repose. Black and white report this balance, two pilots seated at a table, one in a black shirt, the other in white; overhead, the striped white and black of an umbrella against the sun; sunlight and shadow. Vittoria sits easily in a chair, a row of shrubs rustling in the wind behind her, and she says, "It feels so good here." She is simply enjoying the brief pleasure and miraculous balance of the moment, savoring its happiness in the knowledge of its transience.

Then a violently revealing contrast: a quick cut takes us to the stock exchange—to economic panic. The account of the stock exchange crash is not only technically brilliant but also the ideological—or perhaps intellectual—center of the film. As an account of a stock market collapse, it is obviously unsatisfactory, even repetitive and boring. But actually it is an impressive effort to force us to look—to really look—at the stock exchange and its denizens, to ask, and keep asking, "What is this place?" Again and again, using high-angle camera shots taken from no particular observer's point of view, Antonioni confronts us with a spectacle that is metaphysically absurd. The culmination is a single comprehensive shot that for the first time shows us the entire floor of the exchange, men gesticulating and screaming, all animal energy and aggressiveness, while overhead, at once the result and also the source of the inexplicable human behavior on the floor, is the Big Board, its acronyms and numbers constantly changing. This image, surely, is Antonioni's epiphany; he delays showing us this comprehensive shot almost until the end of the scene because it is, in fact, the full revelation and explanation of all the violent activity and deafening uproar that precede it.

"What is the stock exchange?" This question is explicitly raised in a conversation that takes place later in the apartment of Piero's parents:

PIERO: You don't like coming to the stock exchange, do you?

VITTORIA: I don't yet understand whether it's an office, a store, or a boxing match [*un ring*]. Is it necessary?

PIERO: You have to keep coming in order to understand it. Once you start [*entra nel giro*—another image of the Game], you can't stop. It grabs hold of you [*si appassiona*, literally, "it enamors you"].

Vittoria, moving away toward a dark wall, turns; in her white dress she is like a luminous stain. Her voice is sad as she says:

VITTORIA: *What* grabs hold of you, Piero? [*Si appassiona a che cosa, Piero?*]

The dialogue here is pointed, clearly designed in the original Italian to express the erotic quality of the action on the floor, that expenditure of passion which we see in shot after shot: Piero embraced in a bear hug by a broker colleague; the effeminate man who asks, "Who wants to go upstairs with me?"; the magazine gatefold of a naked woman; the short conversation in which Piero refers to a woman as a good "deal" and the elegantly dressed client responds, "Keep your mind on *this* deal." One stock does particularly well because it manufactures a new deodorant soap for the bidet.

After the crash, in his parents' apartment, Piero is asked by Vittoria whether he was with a call girl last night, and he responds, "No, I'm the call girl [*La squillo sono io*]." The analogies are, in fact, innumerable, all designed to culminate in our sense of the stock exchange, and exchange-induced thinking and feeling, as a place of unmistakable *erotic* frenzy—misplaced or transferred Eros but still Eros. The effect of this frenzy is to leach actual love of everything except basic, animal sexuality. When Vittoria asks Piero, "*What* grabs hold of you?" her voice is sad because she knows that the market is the governing *passion* of his life, an erotic attachment to an organization of reality which eclipses—I use the word deliberately—and threatens her own sense of human love. Piero's financial Eros, like that of the Faustian world generally, is invasive, arrogant, contemptuous of difference (that gesture of contempt with which Piero throws away the fat investor's drawing of a tranquilizing flower), and exploitative. Piero is concerned primarily with material things, like his car, and indifferent to death, or indeed to anything but the organized game of Money and the numerical abstractions of the Big Board.

All these things are a direct expression of the values expressed by the stock exchange, which, by its agency, are spewed out across Italy and the provinces in the form of consumer goods, in the stimulation of desire and consumption, and in the industrial quantification of all those desire-laden goods on which the market mentality of the modern world thrives. Piero's coarseness is not, of course, merely masculine; we see the same spirit in the portrayal of Vittoria's mother, with her peasant gestures and superstitious rituals, her perfunctory, distracted, rote affection for her daughter—indeed, her indifference to anything at all except what happens at the stock exchange and moves across its Big Board. Into the orbit of the Board all of society's constituents are drawn—those of peasant origins like Vittoria's mother, middle-class men and women, even patricians like the elegantly dressed client whom Piero treats with almost servile deference. The analysis here, repeated and deepened in *Zabriskie Point*, is unabashedly Spenglerian. It

is the emphasis on money, according to Spengler, that gives contemporary civilization its character, that makes it utterly different from all past cultures. The process is simple. Money is first uprooted from the land and finally becomes the supreme abstraction, completely divorced from the country world, even the products, from which it was originally derived. Fields turn into futures, industrial goods like steel turn into acronyms like FINSIDER, and these acronyms are then transformed into the numbers racing across the board, yoking to its use and glory the passionate erotic service that men once gave to other values and institutions, to art or country or religion. Or even to Eros.

Take, for instance, the stock exchange as architectural form. Antonioni once remarked that, after film, his favorite pastime was reading about architecture, then painting. And the films seem everywhere to confirm this interest, constantly stating cultural themes in architectural terms: as in the great baroque ensemble of Noto in *L'avventura*; or in the vertical skyscraper and corporate "lookout"—half aerie, half fort—of *Zabriskie Point*. But *Eclipse* is perhaps even fuller in its architectural inflection: we move with glancing incisiveness to the planned suburb of EUR, with its Nervi Palazzo dello Sport; then to the stock exchange; then to a glimpse of Saint Peter's seen from Vittoria's mother's apartment; on to mixed classical and Renaissance in the shots of Piazza di Pietra, the site of the café where Vittoria meets Piero; to the middle-class ambience of Piero's parents' apartment in *Roma vecchia*; and then finally to the half-finished building, its skeletal ferroconcrete still masked by the drying mats of woven reed, on the corner where Piero and Vittoria meet. Consider the stock exchange. Its back side contains the twelve columns of what were once the twelve columns of Hadrian, fronting on Piazza di Pietra. In form the stock exchange building, the Borsa, is unmistakably a basilica. In imperial Rome such basilicas were used for transacting public business, above all for financial transactions. When the empire was converted to Christianity, these basilicas were taken over by the church and converted to religious uses; and this basilica form is the dominant architectural style of the Roman Catholic church. Antonioni's point, I think, is precisely this cultural rhythm, the way in which certain forms tend to express dominant social organizations and values. As once the basilica of public business was converted to the service of God, so here we see the basilica form employed anew in the service of money. Everything about the stock exchange in Antonioni's film tells us that the director is conscious of, and bent on making us conscious of, its religious nature. He wants to make us see this strange world as the quintessential rite of Money, of abstractions enthroned on the Big Board overhead. The point is not, of course, religious nostalgia, nor irony; the point is precisely the religious epiphany of Money, the cult of the god of Faustian organization. Hence the great columns of stone; the railing that separates the congregation in the Parco Buoi from the officiating priests, the brokers gesticulating around the High Altar where

the Host is elevated as the ringing of the bell signals the resumption of trading. Vittoria's mother kneels—a genuflection, in fact, dimly remembered from her past—to the great power that fills the place, the awful presence of Money. And inside the chancel, at the High Altar, the great marvel is performed, the assumption of the products of the earth into pure abstractions, that is, the miracle by which something is made from nothing.

Why, looking back, we may ask, do we see everywhere in the film the demotion of human beings into things or objects, as in the person–object analogies of Riccardo's apartment, or in Piero's treatment of his girlfriend, whom he calls *la bestiola* (the little animal)? The answer is the great liturgy of the stock exchange, where we literally assist at the daily celebration whereby the goods of the earth are transformed into things, and things into abstractions; where the mind celebrates its mysteries in complete isolation from nature and the body. It is this quality of arithmetic quantification, the incredible Faustian calculus, that Antonioni wants us, I think, to observe. And if we notice that, we cannot fail to notice how the same values emanate from the great basilica, this Mother Church of Money, into the world at large, into every corner of ordinary life, so that in the end the market comes to govern almost every action, even Piero's way of loving, just as it creates the general passivity toward the problems of the spirit. In *Red Desert*, in precisely the same way, we see the values and geometries, even the dehumanization, of the industrial world represented by the refinery creeping into Giuliana's relations with her husband and son, invasively eliminating even the last intimacies according to its imperatives.

It seems to me that *The Decline of the West* is, in this film, as crucial a text as it was for the novels and stories of Fitzgerald. "F. Scott Fitzgerald, Spenglerian," he dubbed himself. But let Spengler speak:

> The City assumes the lead and control of economic history in replacing the primitive values of the land, which are for ever inseparable from the life and thought of the rustic, by the *absolute idea of money* as distinct from goods.
> . . . With this the notion of money attains to full abstractness. It no longer merely *serves* for the understanding of economic intercourse, but *subjects* the exchange of goods to *its own* evolution. It values things, no longer as between each other, but *with reference to itself*. Its relation to the soil and to the man of the soil has so completely vanished that in the economic thought of the leading cities—the "money-markets"—it is ignored. Money has now become a power, and, moreover, a power which is wholly intellectual and merely figured in the metal it uses.[9]

And elsewhere Spengler's discussion of city versus country sounds almost as if it were the inspiration for the very last sequence of *Eclipse*:

> It is the Late city that first defies the land, contradicts Nature in the lines of its silhouette, *denies* all Nature. . . . *Extra muros*, chaussées and woods and

pastures become a park, mountains become tourists' viewpoints; and *intra muros* arises an imitation Nature, fountains in place of springs, flower-beds, formal pools, and clipped hedges in place of meadows and ponds and bushes. In a village the thatched roof is still hill-like, and the street is one of the same nature as the baulk of earth between fields. But here [in the city] the picture is of deep, long gorges between high, stony houses filled with colored dust and strange uproar, and men dwell in these houses, the like of which no nature-being has ever conceived. Costumes, even faces are adjusted to a background of stone. By day there is a street traffic of strange colors and tones, and by night a new light that outshines [*überstrachten*] the moon.[10]

The Spenglerian analogies in *Eclipse*, and elsewhere in Antonioni's work, are simply too close, and at too many points, to deny direct influence. But the artist, as Svevo once pointed out, is not less original because he, like writers or painters, has been influenced by the philosopher's vision. Dante's *Divine Comedy* is not Thomas Aquinas set to music, nor is Antonioni simply celluloid Spengler. What deserves our attention and respect, I think, is the way in which the director coordinates and fuses—indeed humanizes—the Spenglerian vision according to his own obsessive vision of Eros, that vision which is first stated, in all its thematic richness and comprehensiveness, in *wholly* cinematic terms, in *L'avventura*. It is thanks to Spengler's *acuity* that Antonioni recognizes in the stockbroker the true intellectual—the abstract artist—of a world organized around the cult of money; and he shows us, by juxtaposing Vittoria's two lovers, Riccardo and Piero, the family resemblance that links aesthete–intellectual and materialistic broker. But Antonioni also redeems Spengler's vision from its own dreadful abstraction and fuses it with the texture of actual feeling, showing us, as Spengler never could, the *look* and *feel* of that "tremulous vibration," that texture of Being which the Faustian world everywhere systematically oppresses. All Spengler's dreamy phrases about "the sterility of civilized man" have no meaning unless refreshed by a *sense* of the real thing, the lost life, which is what Antonioni gives us.

The director's triumph as a thinking artist, of course, is that the lost life is portrayed with such breathtaking beauty, particularly in the scenes dealing with the paired and contrasted entries of Piero and Vittoria into each other's domains. As in *Zabriskie Point*, we see two personal worlds briefly and poignantly interact, then, abruptly, parting in their own opposed directions. For Vittoria the intersection is, like the scene on the airport veranda at Verona, an instant of utterly transient happiness, one in which she is free to be, precisely because the encounter is so brief, completely and compellingly herself. The encounter may be short-lived, but it is not casual, not another *avventura*. Vittoria loves Piero; we might wonder why, but there can be no doubt whatever about the reality of the love, expressed in a gaiety and

82

radiance of being that find the fullest expression in the face, in the intense, waking life so visible in her features and their consonance with the world whose being she expresses, the flower and the fossil reaching up, evolving, into the lovely features of the face. For this beauty is a power of integrated being, not simply physical allure. And this is how we sense it in Piero's response. For one brief moment, he is utterly changed; his face, otherwise tense and inexpressive, savors her presence after she leaves, and what we see in his face is that presence. It shows composure, even repose. And it, too, is integrated, fusing thought and feeling, the face of a man who for the first time in his life exhibits what Heidegger would call dasein, that is, *being there*, rooted in the world, rooted in Being.

They promise, as lovers will, fidelity—a fidelity almost belied in the desperate looks and words of their last embrace, as they promise to meet "Tomorrow. And the day after tomorrow. And tonight." Time resumes for Piero with a sound of telephones ringing, ringing but ignored; for Vittoria time returns as she braces herself, with a kind of shudder, for the rush-hour encounter with the street, the jostling, and the uproar. But she looks up, caged at first and then freed, into the trees swaying in the park opposite.

Then we cut to the unfinished building on the street corner, at eight o'clock some night, and the series of images which, in their sequence of recapitulation and inflection, tell us why the appointment is not kept. The images emerge *from* the film and *from* the site—there is nothing in the series that a camera could not see if placed upon the site. What do they tell us? First of all, transience—the uncompleted building itself, an image of transitional life, life as an interregnum. Transience and anxiety—all those tense, waiting faces. Imprisoned feelings. Fragments of perceptions that fold into each other without ever quite coalescing into a single coherent sentiment. The fragmentary, but subtly suggestive, sequencing of the images is a large part of their meaning. They give a sense of latent violence, of looming danger; even of Faustian angels, as in the images of those contrails of jets that tell us that Faustian Rome is merely an outpost of greater imperial powers, poised in cold war. From the barrel where a piece of wood and a matchbook float, put there by Vittoria and Piero, comes the sound of water flowing like time running out; human life or life itself is represented as a chip or flotsam in some larger world, giving the sense of impotence as well as anxious transience. And then the deepening into the dark, the forms growing more and more sinuous, like the music on a sound track, as the images move toward their revelation of a world where time, space, and people are tilting out of control, perhaps. Then the evening clouds, suddenly dark, appear, and the street is empty and waiting. Waiting for what?

The dark, ominous side of that suppressed reality—whose beauty we see enacted as Love, however transient—is the story of Vittoria and Piero. Transient and fragile; its fragility is also expressed and explained by those images of a world slipping away, its latent aggression largely but never wholly screened by the flow of mostly peaceful images. And the fragility of Love, in turn, partly explains the latent apocalypse implicit in these closing images of light and dark, which makes its epiphany in the image of Faustian Eros disclosing itself at last for what it is: the *other* suppressed reality of death, Thanatos, looming over all the arrangements and peaceful orders of a world organized for aggression—*aggressive* Eros—and almost incapable of Love.

Red Desert

Q: Can you explain the title, *Red Desert*?

A: It's not a symbolic title. Titles of this kind have an umbilical cord linking them with the work. . . . "Desert" perhaps because there are few oases left; "red" because there is blood. The blood-stained desert, full of the bones of men.

—Michelangelo Antonioni, from an interview in *L'Express*, January 16, 1964.

First, a few cautionary remarks. With a few notable exceptions, *Red Desert* has had a "bad press." Admired for its virtuoso camera work and remarkable technical use of color, it has otherwise been treated as an unsatisfactory clinical account, psychologically inept, of a woman's neurosis. The artistic problem here, however, lies not with the film but with audience expectations. With depressing regularity audiences and critics alike demand that films should satisfy their expectations of conventional narrative realism, perhaps because so few films require or suggest anything else. In the circumstances, a kind of lazy McLuhanite consensus that film is a serial "throwaway" medium has come to prevail. It is a rare director indeed who dares to challenge this consensus, as Antonioni has done. He, by the precision and

85

complexity of his composition, the coherence of his structure implicit in every scene, the functional beauty of his detail, and his unmistakable effort to think and feel in genuinely cinematic terms, has taken the great risk of demanding from his audience the kind of intellectual respect or attention it would willingly give to a poem, a play, or a painting. But not, it would seem, to a film. In this we have tangible evidence of the cultural lag that still separates film from the other arts. Equally revealing, I think, is the fact that the audience for films still demands from directors the "solutions" to the problems they analyze[1]—a demand that audiences have long ceased to make of poets, dramatists, or novelists.

Antonioni literally compels his audience to see his works again and again (and they will more than repay, as I hope to show, such reseeing). Needless to say, such compulsion is resented by those who prefer staged "happenings" or mere technical bravura; and it is this resentment that is at work in the constant "underreading" of Antonioni's films. Simply stated, it is dangerous, very dangerous indeed, for a director to ask his audience to think and feel in new ways, to treat them with real artistic respect.

But the respect is *there*—visible, audible, demonstrable. Each frame, each scene, I have suggested, contains the pressure and sense of the whole. If this is so, it means that, in critical discussion, we can begin literally anywhere and be certain of discussing, by implication, almost everything. What is needed is simply to choose the best *point d'appui*—not the scene that best illustrates the critic's reading but the one that best gives, to audiences in any way tainted by naturalistic expectations, access to the film as a whole, to the director's characteristic *tematica*, that is, his "thematic repertory."

At its simplest, *Red Desert* is not a story of neurosis but an account of individuation; a story of the emergence of the psyche in a time when individuation has become exceptionally difficult. This story is, for Antonioni, inherently tragic; any discrete gain in human awareness, any progess in becoming or remaining human, is won at the cost of very considerable pain. Pain can kill individuals, or it can make them human. In different ways, from *Il grido* to *Zabriskie Point*, this is Antonioni's most persistent and obsessive subject: small, discrete advances in awareness; the acceptance of tragic loneliness and pain as the price of human existence; becoming, remaining (or trying to remain) human in a world so unbalanced and strange that it means literally improvising, from day to day, one's own humanity. Again and again the protagonists of these films must discover their humanity by improvising the courage to accept their necessary loneliness (or, like Aldo in *Il grido*, "lose their balance" and die precisely because they cannot accept it).

In *Red Desert* all of these themes, explicit or implicit, are involved in, and developed by, the scene of the sad, abortive "orgy" in Max's shack by the sea. Near the close of that sequence Giuliana stands alone on the mole in the dense fog; the others stand around her in a mute, staring semicircle.

One by one their individual faces appear, each shrouded in his private envelope, before being obliterated by the swirling fog. Only Corrado, defined by Giuliana's need, stands out, nearer and clearer, a little less blurred than the others. Each character is now seen as Giuliana for the first time sees them, not huddling together in a warm, sleep-blurred group in the red-walled shack but suddenly *there*, seized in individual isolation before dissolving into the anonymous fog. For the first time she sees them alone and then as a group, "alone" together, discretely, in their separation from each other and from her; then she sees them together, linked by a common extinction, all slowly folded in the fog. It is the fact of *visible* separateness that suddenly overwhelms her. She feels the separation as pain, a pain so intolerable that she frantically drives her car toward the end of the mole, away from the ship, away from the land and the others, toward the fog and the sea. "I didn't see the ship, Ugo," she tries to explain. "I wasn't thinking about it." "I wanted to go home, just to go home . . . the fog confused me." By "home" here she means the sea that we see surfacing in her Sardinian fantasy—that expanse of maternal ocean whose blue, sheeted water is fitted to the girl's brown adolescent body like a glove, containing and enclosing, the same sea that she earlier says she fears "drowning in." The sea is "home," the only refuge from the unbearable loneliness she has come to feel in Max's hut and outside on the mole, a loneliness heightened now by the felt loneliness of the others, and her new perception of human isolation generally.

But if we note Giuliana's regression, we are also meant to observe her progress: the gradual emergence of that consciousness toward which, blindly and doggedly, something slowly drives her. More than anything else she fears separateness, both because it hurts and because it is the way she must, against her wishes, go. But again and again she falters, and the to-and-fro pattern of her progress and regression is presented in a severely stylized form, quite as though the director wanted, even at the cost of static naturalism, to provide not a clinical report of neurosis but the general existential and cultural malaise of which her mania is only a symptom. Giuliana's neurosis is a story about *us*, and the director's generic and metaphysical ambitions lead him to a psychology that is generic and ontological, rather than clinical and individual.

Giuliana's illness is presented as a generic disease of contemporary human nature; a tension of polar opposites between which she (and we) must somehow learn to live, and thus resolve. Both poles are rooted in her nature, though the pole toward which she is fatally attracted is what looms largest in her nature: her femininity, her instinctual life, her desperate need of others, and her hunger to be contained by a natural world of which she is an unseparated part, protected against any intrusion into her "oceanic feeling." Something in her (as in us all, though it is less repressed, more dramatically visible, in her) wants desperately to remain what and where it is, not to change, to be a natural, unthinking, passive part of the season, the winds,

87

and the waters, to "be" and not "to know," to be spared the anguish of "becoming." Her profoundest instinct is to build an unbreachable wall against everything that might change her world. This is why she tells Corrado that she would like to have "everybody who has ever loved me . . . here around me, like a wall"; why she instinctively closes doors and cupboards, protecting herself against what might emerge from them; why she persistently seeks the shelter of walls, crouching against them to screen herself from exposure. When she and Corrado visit the worker's house in Ferrara, for example, she huddles in the couch as though trying to lose herself in the leaves and branches figured in the slipcover, or to camouflage herself by finding a background into which she can merge and disappear. In the first scene, when she goes off to eat her roll, she instinctively screens herself behind the trees, trying to evade the reality that threatens her in the industrial landscape of Ravenna. But reality breaks through her screen; the smokestack emits its poisonous yellow vapor, while a few feet away, to her horror, the waste smokes and steams. The same need for shelter later drives her to her shop in Via Alighieri, out of the painful present into the dead past, a timeless street where today intrudes only as a torn newspaper floating down, and she can surround herself with the blues and greens of her own psyche. But despite her defenses, reality keeps intruding. No shelter is proof against it. Underfoot, the pollution spreads; a boat breaches the privacy of that island where she peers out with fear and wonder; industrial wastes poison the marshes so that even the eels taste of crude oil; epidemic arrives in the shack by the sea; paralysis finally seeps into her own home—a contagion she cannot seal off or expel.[2]

But with another part of herself, with the incipient consciousness of her newborn eyes, she resists her instinct to find shelter—an instinct that, in her more conscious moments, compares to drowning, to sliding down a slope, or sleeping on quicksand. Offered the containment of physical love, she instinctively, with one part of herself, resists, even while she hungers for it too. She is virtually torn to pieces, her psyche partly rooted in the old world of instinct and "oceanic feeling," partly straining to remain loyal to a vague but insistent sense of dawning selfhood. Whether she is with Ugo or Corrado, she responds to physical love with desperate need but equally desperate fear—fear of somehow losing herself in *their* need, of *becoming* them, at the same time that she wants nothing more than the warmth and security of their being, to be part of them fused in a single identity. Giuliana's problem here is like that of almost all of Antonioni's protagonists:[3] the tragic pain of those who, in order to become themselves, must suffer the loneliness of an individual destiny. The pain is intensified by the psyche's knowledge of how it was before suffering separation, before being expelled from the garden and entering time and history, that is, before becoming human. This primal knowledge is the content of the personal and collective fantasy that, in Antonioni, each carries about with him, the ground of his

being, like Giuliana's fantasy of the girl on the beach. But everywhere in Antonioni's films, the fantasy periodically irrupts into, and transforms, ordinary life; in the background-paper sequence of *Blow-up*; in the sudden summer cloudburst in *La notte* that sends the party into the swimming pool and Lidia and Roberto into the magic carapace of the car moving slowly through the rain; in the African sequence of *Eclipse*. The effect of such irruptions is always to intensify, by contrast, the loneliness of those cut off from a felicity of an eternal moment they can remember but cannot recreate. It is the desire to recover that same felicity that drives them to drink or drugs or aphrodisiacs or frantic amusement or simple somnambulism—to anything that might assuage the pain of consciousness and restore them their lost paradise.

Obsessively, in film after film, Antonioni explores this perennial fantasy of the paradisal world,[4] which contains so much of us that we are constantly in danger of thinking it our true selves, what we once were before being expelled from the bright garden of Being. Philosophically, its power and appeal are in our bones as the old human hunger of "Becoming" for "Being." It is Plato's sun, Spinoza's God, or Heidegger's dasein. Erotically, it is Freud's "oceanic feeling," the warmth and security of the womb. Culturally, it is animistic feeling—the individual's absolute "oneness" with nature and society, so irresistible to those who fear that they have fallen out of culture into mere fragmentary existence,[5] that nature and the "gods" are dead. Politically, it is the appeal of millennialism in any form, the ideal past projected as the future. Wherever we turn, we find it subtly, often grossly, shaping us, "living" us. But whether "archetype," "oceanic feeling," or *participation mystique*,[6] its tyrannical control can be challenged only by confrontation: by articulating it and "bringing its contents to the light." Even this is not enough, for nothing necessarily follows from perception and clarity.[7] The crucial task, for individuals and cultures alike, is to transform *fantasy* into *myth*, making myth conform wherever possible to the vectors of unconscious energy, even though this may mean correcting fantasy with consciously *lived* patterns, often of great difficulty and complexity. The alternative is bad faith: to remain less than human, to deny responsibility for oneself and the world.

The essential content of this primal fantasy is childhood and love. For obvious reasons. The child has no memory; he lives like a god in the eternity of the moment; he is wholly one with his world; his rapport with "things" is total. Indeed, he and his world are a single-sheeted, continuous "being." In love it is the same, since love transcends the person and makes of two lovers a single, all-contained world. "When a love-relationship is at its height," says Freud, "there is no room left for any interest in the environment; a pair of lovers are sufficient to themselves, and do not even need the child they have in common to make them happy. In no other case does Eros so clearly betray the core of his being, his purpose of making one out of

89

more than one."⁸ In Giuliana's fantasy—the Sardinian beach sequence—love and childhood are fused in the figure of the adolescent girl on her island. Dark, gawky, browned by the sun, she is both the adolescent and the primitive, standing on the edge of childhood as on the verge of consciousness; and the innocence and primordial coherence of her world are suggested in those Gauguin-like frames in which she peers out at the strange boat making its appearance in her Eden. With the arrival of the romantic invader, she senses for the first time the mysterious allure of "the other" in a world until now wholly bounded by her own being. Something new "swims into her ken," and she swims out to meet it, when it suddenly veers and vanishes. But then a second "mystery" follows the first—that high, sweet, singing voice that leads her out where she has never been before, around the promontory of golden rock, into a new inlet where the rocks are like "flesh" and where, in a stonescape of pinkish golden torsos and buttocks, she sees what looks like two human figures lying side by side, and "at that point the voice was especially sweet." Thus upon the primal landscape of childhood Antonioni imposes the landscape of love, or its erotic anticipation. We see a child's self-contained world complicated and extended by the arrival of the "other"; and then the same world enhanced and transformed again by the anticipation of love. As the sequence closes, everything, even the rocks, is singing to her, embracing her, everything united in one ecstatic voice in which nothing is missing, nothing separated. Blue sky, blue water, the singing voice, everything combined in the single intensity of the primal fantasy as remembered or colored by the yearning unconscious—and the whole screen goes blue blue blue.

Unless we feel the intense, vital coherence of this world where individual loneliness is annulled in universal community—this timeless, paradisal landscape of Chaos and "the eternal moment," alive with divinity—it is, I believe, quite impossible to make sense of the film or, I would add, of art generally. For fantasy and "ordinary reality" constantly inflect each other; neither can be understood without the other. Thus when the fantasy reaches peak intensity, ordinary reality is demoted and degraded; the quotidian becomes, as here, in Giuliana's neurotic vision, the nightmare: dingy or frightening or boring; oppressive and intolerable. And the fantasy reaches peak intensity precisely in times of great change, and therefore of great pain; for change—expulsion from old and familiar things—is pain. It is the crucial fact of change in modern man's condition that makes this fantasy of such obsessive power and allure. Change is now so violent, swift, and brutal that the fantasy becomes nearly omnipotent; the enhancement of fantasy leads to the further demotion of reality and the attenuation of responsibility. Men are literally estranged from themselves—from place, community, even their own humanity; and this estrangement makes them increasingly vulnerable to *possession* by fantasy in all its many forms, but by Eros in particular. As the old institutions of culture disappear one after

another—family, church, the web of environing "ways"—individuals are more and more tempted to imagine that Eros can perform all the tasks of the failed institutions of the culture. "Eros is sick," wrote Antonioni in 1960 at Cannes. "Something is bothering man. And whenever something bothers him, man reacts badly, only on erotic impulse, and he is unhappy." From the erotic misery that afflicts Aldo in *Il grido*, to the compulsive eroticism exhibited by almost everyone in *L'avventura*, to Giuliana's neurosis in *Red Desert*, to *Zabriskie Point*, with its stylized ballet of copulating dancers in Death Valley, the theme is obsessively and searchingly employed.

But the crucial irritants are uncertainty and change. By estranging men from themselves, they endow the primal fantasy with quite demonic powers of possession. Thus to the old human anguish of expulsion from the garden there is added the unbearable pain imposed by the change in our very condition, with all its attendant uncertainty. For much of history, the rate of change in the human environment was still so slow that it was hardly apparent in a person's lifetime, and very little psychological adjustment was required. Today the pace of this change is so rapid that it strains the human capacity to adapt. From *Il grido* to *The Passenger*, Antonioni has insisted that modern life makes the ultimate demand—that the human psyche itself should change.

He shows us this, above all, through the situation of a woman. He prefers, as he has said, to put women at the center of his films because "they are stronger, more realistic, closer to nature."[9] But also, because cultural change touches them first; men are insulated from change by activity, by fate, by profession—like Corrado and Max—and are therefore less "open." Women are also more rooted, at least in Italian culture, in nature, more bound to place and time, than men. Giuliana, of course, is a neurotic exaggeration. For her the central problem, both psychologically and culturally, is how to endure the separation imposed upon her—separation from the old cosmos, the old social order, from childhood and her own nature. Her nature is rooted in a sense of life that is everywhere opposed by an alien mode that she feels as a universal and invisible pollution. And her own hunger for "life," her submission to the fantasy that "lives" her (as opposed to living her own authentic "myth"), leads her to act in ways that inevitably sap her power of adapting or resisting. So she regresses, irresistibly drawn to those experiences that promise to end her separation by giving her security and love. Her plight in this respect is common, indeed nearly universal, and Antonioni intends that we should observe its pervasiveness, its application to *us*. This is why, I think, he shows us in the first scene the long, massed parade of striking workers and, contrasted with them, the lonely scab who dares to resist the coercion of the group and to act on his own—much as Giuliana will later emerge from the group in Max's shack, defining herself in contrast to them.

Antonioni's point here is Jung's: "All mass movements, as one might

expect, slip with the greatest ease down an inclined plane made up of large numbers. Where the many are, there is security; what the many believe must of course be true; what the many want must be worth striving for. . . . In the clamour of the many resides the power to snatch wish-fulfillments by force; sweetest of all, however, is that gentle and painless slipping back into the kingdom of childhood, into the paradise of parental care, into happy-go-luckiness and irresponsibility."[10] Giuliana's dangerous regressing, her instinctive need for the security of physical love, is thus paralleled by the situation of the strikers, who take comfort in anonymity and numbers. It is first the scab and then the individual workman—that isolated but healthy young man, seen in clear focus, eating his sandwich—who interest Giuliana because she unconsciously desires what they have, which is the courage to be themselves and to accept separation, against the coercion or comfort of the crowd. Finally, in the faces of the workmen whom Corrado has enlisted for his Argentine expedition, we see the general social equivalent of Giuliana's terror, the fear of the new world to which she must adapt, and her hunger for security—all those superbly troubled faces over which the camera moves, peasant faces with the color of the Italian earth, lined and stacked like so many baskets and bottles for export, while their voices tensely, anxiously, ask whether they will be supplied with the old familiar things—newspapers, journals, TV, and wives—in the strange world into which they are being expelled. Like Giuliana, they too want to protect themselves with a wall of the familiar against the terrors of the new. Nomadism, of course, is a persistent theme in Antonioni; in one way or another every film employs it. But Antonioni's point is not Eliot's—the image of an atomized, polyglot society, without roots and traditions—but is rather designed to give the *sense* and *degree*, the universality, of modern mobility. Mobility here is such that it makes all ages and cultures simul-taneously contemporary—for instance, American blacks in Italy (*Eclipse*), Italian smugglers in Australia (*L'avventura*), Italian workers in Argentina (*Il grido*)—and thereby fatally disorients the psyche. It paralyzes it, stupefies it, drugs it, or forces it to dangerous forms of compensation and, by nullifying its possibility of making its own myth, cuts it away from nature and the earth, imposing a new, "man-made" reality upon it.

This is surely why Ugo everywhere uses engineering and electronic metaphors for what, in Giuliana's world, are essentially psychical opera-tions. Moral and physical equilibrium becomes gyroscopic; adjustment to reality is a form of "shifting gears."[11] His new reality is, like ours, techno-logical, and we and the world must adapt to it. Antonioni has repeatedly said that he does not regard technology as baleful in itself, and that this film is not antitechnological.[12] But this is quite compatible with a fear that something indisputably human or animal or natural in us will be ignored or scanted by the frequently stunted engineers of our fate; the forsaken part may be crucial to our lives and humanity. In Antonioni, this scanted element

is precisely that instinctive part of the psyche which the modern world so elaborately represses, which Giuliana and Vittoria in *Eclipse* are attuned to and live by. I mean the natural, the primitive, the animal—whatever it is in us that is still, despite all our sophistication, bound to the natural world. This is their value and allure—and their most immediate danger: their "red desert."

Giuliana's plight, then, is her fear of separation—of being cut away from a landscape, from the past, from the "ground" of her own being. In the deepest part of herself (as opposed to the woman who wants to escape what is intolerable in reality) she does not want to embark on one of those ships whose sudden looming and passing suggest man's contemporary condition—a passenger on a voyage somewhere, God knows where, ripped from the harbor of our past and nature, and therefore terribly uncertain and anxious, confused in our very natures, forced to consent to adaptations and permutations whose terminus we cannot begin to guess, toward an unknown destination. For some, like Corrado, traveling is an activity that prevents self-exploration, a deliberately chosen "busyness." For others, like Giuliana, the voyage is ultimately inward-bound, like Thoreau's, to an unknown landfall, the slow, courageous exploration of a new or altered place, a new psychic geography. And her characteristic danger is to refuse identity, loneliness, and consciousness. She cannot bear to part from others, because they are part of her. Thus she tells Corrado that he is a "part of her" and that, if she went away, she would take him with her. If she loved him, she would eat him; she would somehow, anyhow, assimilate him, make him "hers." Typically, her own situation is revealed by her son. "Mommy," he asks, "how much is one and one?" "Two," she answers. "No," he says, and shows her that two blue drops coalesce on his microscopic slide into a single blue drop. "One and one is one," he says, at which she says, "You're right, one," and bends down to kiss him. For a brief instant we see the two heads together, mother and son, as though it were one head of tangled, orange-reddish curls. Then, suddenly, Giuliana's eyes ("two little black points") open, as she peers anxiously toward the other room, where Ugo is packing for his trip to London. One and one, seen as two, but then, miraculously, one again—and then, separated, again two. It is an extraordinarily condensed scene, which succeeds in stating with remarkable clarity the whole emotional situation: Giuliana's intellectual knowledge that one and one are two suddenly confronted with her emotional conviction that they are one, child and mother alike, at a single stage in their psychic histories; then, like a knife, the thought of separation makes her open her eyes, and we see that one has become two, that her "separation" has begun. Her own separation, of course, influences her son's, Valerio's, for his feigned paralysis is his way of compelling his mother to give him the affection she herself so desperately craves. Because of Giuliana's new closeness to Corrado, Valerio unconsciously feels abandoned and so resorts to a trick to compel his

93

mother to return. Valerio's trick in turn frees Giuliana from her dependence on Valerio, pushing her toward her last "defense," Corrado.

All this, and perhaps more, is contained in this extraordinary sequence, whose thematic import is revealed in the penultimate scene of the film. Standing on the loading dock at night, talking to a Turkish sailor who cannot understand a word she is saying, that is, in absolute loneliness, she struggles to "communicate" her new knowledge, the fact of the adult calculus—that one and one are two. *Participation mystique* is no longer possible. "I'm not a woman alone, . . . although at times . . . it's as though I were . . . separated. No, not separated from my husband, the bodies . . . are . . . separate. If you prick me, you're not the one who hurts." Here, stated with the compelling slowness of conscious realization and pained understanding, is the adult recognition of separateness and loneliness, which divides child from woman, neurotic from healthy, each from each. In one way or another, everything in the film has been a preparation for this scene.

As so commonly in Antonioni's work, then, Giuliana's predicament is "explained" by a series of pervasive polarities between which she must somehow live, resisting both her own nature and the unnatural world in which she lives. To assent fully to either—the "red desert" or the technological desert (represented by the poisoned marshland of the Ravenna coast)—is death. On one side lies the primitive, instinctive, unconscious sea, that "oceanic feeling" toward which her nature and needs constantly push her, a sense world of touch and sound where the eyes are of no earthly use, since nothing is really distinguishable; on the other side is the bright, divisive, fractured, thing-cluttered world of the eye and daily reality, of technologically manipulated nature, where human touch and sound become vestigial through disuse. "What," says Giuliana, "am I supposed to do with my eyes? What should I look at?" and Corrado answers, "You say, 'What should I look at,' and I say 'How should I live?'" "It's the same thing." It is the uselessness of her newfound eyes that Giuliana is protesting, so she "looks" at the restless sea ("It never stays still. Never . . .") and says, "I think my eyes are wet," meaning, "What good are eyes except for crying, since seeing is unbearable?" Unconscious sea, then, against conscious land; conscious eye pitted against the other repressed senses; sea fog as against industrial steam, technological death, and polluted air; dark against light; natural greens at war with sulfuric and lethal yellows; female versus male, and so on. Between these polar extremes lies a spectrum along which the characters are placed so that they constantly define one another. The interaction is too chromatically complex for close scrutiny here, but one example may suffice to illustrate the technique.

Time and again throughout his oeuvre, Antonioni depicts the sense of human loneliness by hinting at the envelope that surrounds each character, and the way in which that container literally seals him off from others,

cutting off his access to a common world. He also shows us the revealing reverse of this encapsulation—the rapturous, miraculous feeling, so close to religious transcendence, that explodes when an individual breaks out of, or momentarily penetrates into, another's *Umwelt*. The theme of *communication*, which critics have so persistently said is Antonioni's only theme, is merely, I think, a function of his insistence on this subjective reality, and what happens when these individual worlds do, or do not, intersect. But he is above all fascinated by the typical difference of *Umwelt* in man and woman, extrovert and introvert, conscious and unconscious. A central theme in *Eclipse*, for example, is that of psychological independence and subjection: how far can either Piero or Vittoria enter each other's world without sacrificing his, or her, own individuality? How much sacrifice of one's own nature can erotic dependence exact? How can one love and still remain himself unless he can resist this very appropriation of his soul, this merging with the person he loves, which is the very purpose of eros?

In *Eclipse*, for instance, this theme is stated visually, through an exquisitely rich and functional use of black and white. Thematically opposed throughout, these blacks and whites attract to themselves subclusters of associated images and ideas (e.g., night and day; country and city; nature and man-made artifice, or technology; silence and sound), constantly complicating as the film progresses. Only at the end, in the final shot, do these accumulated inflections reveal their summary meaning, as a streetlight suddenly goes on, flares in the gathering darkness, "eclipsing" the night and driving the natural blacks to the fringes of the frame; on the sound track, a blaring, ominous, electronic crescendo. So, in human terms, we watch as Piero's artificial and cerebral world increasingly threatens to "eclipse" and extinguish Vittoria's more natural world and her precarious psychic balance. On one side is the "blackout" world of pure sensation (the "erotic desert" of *Red Desert*, "full of the bones of men," which is even more vividly depicted in *Zabriskie Point*), with its chaos of the instincts and passions, without individuation, moral distinction, or tragedy (we recall the dark pool in which the drunkard dies; the dogs running loose in the black freedom of the park at night; the sudden murk of the cloud that envelops the airplane on its way to Verona). On the other side is the harsh Apollonian noise-and-light-world of the city, the stock market, and the manipulative mind, represented by the pure abstraction of money. In this universe figures are uprooted from the context of natural things and are moved down the "big board," reaching out across the *geographical* frame for the provinces, for Verona, Milano, and the world. Vittoria, unlike Giuliana, is not neurotic, and her psychic balance is expressed in *Eclipse* by her ability to find a visual "mean" between the lethal extremes of black and white; an emotional chiaroscuro whose varying inflections, now dark, now light, chart the rise and fall of her feelings, her lapses and achievements, as she struggles to find and keep her balance in a world constantly shifting underfoot and tilting toward disaster. This striv-

ing for balance is the reason why, for instance, she feels so much at home on the airport terrace at Verona, poised happily but briefly and precariously between old and new, country and city, plant and machine, between one "affair" and another. The mean she barely succeeds in finding is her existential ambience; and in its fused or interwoven whites and blacks, depicted as latticed light or zebra stripes, in that afternoon aura she carries around with her, and in her lovely mesh of feeling and thought, we come to recognize her personal, visual "music." Her whole effort is devoted to avoiding Giuliana's plight, to avoid falling into "oceanic feeling" and losing balance before her lover's needs and erotic invasion. Both health and balance, as Antonioni ominously observes, are increasingly difficult in a world already desperately unbalanced.

But whereas in *Eclipse* (1962) Antonioni had only black and white at his disposal, in *Red Desert* (1964) he has the whole chromatic scale, with all its possibilities of shade and intensity. And his craftsman's pleasure in the expansion of his technical means is no less apparent than Uccello's delight in perspective. But despite the stylized exuberance of these chromatic experiments, Antonioni's use of color here is wholly in keeping with his artistic purposes in black and white. Color may make for greater complexity, but it still serves the same obsessive themes, the same mode of seeing and thinking, and the same persistent ordering of reality in terms of polar opposites. Color provides, that is, a richer spectrum, in which individuals can be chromatically "placed" and defined; but the spectrum is essentially that which we see in *La notte* and *Eclipse*. (*Il grido* and *L'avventura* are clearly marked by a more naturalistic idiom.) Thus Giuliana temperamentally inhabits a world of earth colors, above all dark blue, vegetation greens, mauves, and ochers, more or less matte and pastel in tone, while Ugo's technological world is defined by bright, mechanical, sometimes strident yellows, blues, reds, and whites (corresponding to the functional colors of the refinery), without subtlety or depth. And just as the artificial streetlight of *Eclipse* invades and usurps the natural night, so here the refinery spills over into green nature, seeping like a poison into the lagoons and estuaries (all deliberately painted a dreary dun color to give the sense of a literal *nature morte*). But Antonioni's point is not ecology or a conventional anti-industrial idyll. Nature and technology are here opposed not as sentimental opposites but rather as the framing facts of life on this earth, the essential terms of his artistic geography of the human spirit. The point here is not the imbalance (which, Antonioni seems to suggest, may be inevitable) but rather the human *perception* of the imbalance and responsible reaction to it. It is *clarity* that counts, for the characters and the audience whose fantasy and myth the characters enact, and, ultimately, for the sake of the action to which clarity must finally lead.

Consider, for instance, the "chromatic" character of Corrado. The romantic engineer par excellence, he occupies a point midway between

Giuliana and Ugo, modulating easily between their poles just as he moves, chameleon-like, changing color as he passes, between the violent noise and bright colors of the refinery to the secretive silence and the ochers and gray-greens of Giuliana's hideaway on Via Alighieri. Color, that is, provides immediate psychic definition, which in turn guides and explains affinities, sympathy, antipathy, and affection. Corrado, with his reddish hair and pastel greens, his shades of straw and stone, is immediately admissible into Giuliana's world, without jar, as Ugo is not. Color declares him simpatico, just as his emotional and erotic coarseness link him to the vulgar Max, to the world of moneymaking and mere "busyness." What is suggested by color is confirmed by his psychic geography: the wanderer and escapist, lured constantly seaward and away, moving back and forth between sea and land, a peregrine and nomad, between one adventure and another, a mining engineer who, instead of going down, as he says, went up; a mobile and transitional man, always in flight.

In her relation to Corrado, Giuliana finds, as she comes to learn, a projection of her own psychic world and a sea sympathy, that regressiveness toward the unconscious and the erotic which is her special danger. What finally saves her is her confrontation with her own and most personal peril—the appeal of the "red desert"—represented in the film by Corrado and her brief affair with him. Giuliana has the courage to confront her fears, but Corrado is the perpetual escapist. In his own words, "One goes round and round and ends up finding himself just where he was. That's what happened to me. I'm no different now from what I was six years ago. But I don't know whether that's what makes me leave or stay." Antonioni has commented on Corrado's role, and his words deserve attention:

> The character played by Richard Harris is almost a romantic, who thinks about fleeing to Patagonia and has no idea at all about what he must do. He is taking flight and believes that he is resolving, in this way, the problems of his life. But this problem is inside him, not outside. All the more true is it that he has only to meet a woman to provoke a crisis, and he no longer knows whether he will leave or not. . . . When, at the breaking point, the woman needs someone to help her, she finds a man who takes advantage of her and her crisis. She finds herself face-to-face with old things, and it is these old things that shake her and sweep her off her feet. Had she met someone like her husband, he would have acted differently.[13]

It is Corrado's evasion—his flight to the sea, his casual, nomadic existence, erotic and peregrine—that Giuliana confronts in the penultimate scene, when in desperation she seeks passage on a Turkish tramp steamer. Here colors, symbols, and themes converge. The blaze of the ship's red hull below the waterline as the scene opens, the piles of industrial matériel, the derelict and foreboding steamer with its suggestions of death and Eros—all

these reveal the real meaning of the romantic sailboat in the Sardinian fantasy and make possible Giuliana's recognition of the tragic tension to which her individuation has finally led her.

It is herself she now confronts, as she confronts the colors that are, no less than the romantic colors of her Sardinian fantasy, her real world. Deep reds, blues, greens, and the rusting hull of the sinister ship—everything in the scene corresponds to, has its equivalent in, her Sardinian paradise, which is now revealed in another aspect. What the unconscious once presented in the intense colors and delicate pastels of fantasy now suffers a conscious translation, as the erotic and paradisal dream is revealed as a nightmare. Soft pinks are intensified to violent reds; the blaze of red bulwarks and red hull recalls the beginning of the scene in Max's shack—that blurred, pullulating pink, a rosy chaos of red coals not recognized as coals until a foot suddenly emerges from them. The focus widens to show a stockinged curve of leg. From the rosy coals to the pink legs to the woman stretched out languorously before the fire, and then to the plank walls, the same bright red as the coals from which the camera began its journey: here, in one brief sequence, we are given the whole intricate scale of colors that set the scene and declare its nature. Rose and red breeds a pink, a sinuous curve of flesh; out of rosy nothing a pink leg constructs the bright red walls that frame and define it.

In this way, by accumulation and echo, Antonioni inflects his chromatic scale. From the colors and events of the earlier scene in the red-walled shack by the sea, we know what Antonioni intends with the rusty hull and the red bulwarks on the waterfront: the erotic "signature" of red is attached, for the first time, to a ship, a ship no less sinister than the fever ship by the shack but with suggestions of the boat that, like Corrado, breaches Giuliana's island world, and then mysteriously veers away. Red, too, is what the whole scene in the shack *aims* at—at the ruddy passion, the red desert, which the group wants somehow, by drugs, by wine, by aphrodisiacs, to compel into existence. But here everythng is abortive, turns into mere words, as the worker's girl disgustedly observes. Only Giuliana genuinely feels anything resembling passion. The aphrodisiacs touch her, work on her, because of her participation in the same organic nature from which they derive. No aphrodisiac really works unless, like a true animist or primitive, one accepts the world as one continuous living whole, so that you and it—whether quail eggs or ground rhinoceros horn—are really one thing, fused in *participation mystique*. The others must artificially construct the red feelings that come naturally, instinctively, to Giuliana; it is consciousness she lacks and for which she must struggle. Red is her peril. Hence we are meant to understand the danger implied by those red bulwarks, but also Giuliana's courage in what she here confronts at its peak intensity. The pale pinks in the curving sands of Giuliana's fantasy island also reappear with ruddier force in the pink-suffused room of Corrado's hotel after their love-

making; and these romantic and rosy pinks are in turn subsumed in the red blaze of the hull, against which she stands, alone with her particular peril. Here, in short, is the "red desert," that is, a pink from which all white has vanished; pink darkened into unconsciousness, into instinctive bloodred. So, too, the romantic sailboat of the Sardinian island is transmogrified into a Turkish tramp, and the sense of mystery surrounding the yawl earlier becomes the deathlike quality of this sinister steamer.

Giuliana's world, then, is wholly defined by color; we know who she is from what she sees, the colors she chooses to wear and also be worn by, just as we know the others from what they see and cannot see, from the colors of their world. The same is no less true of the other senses. It is Giuliana, for instance, who hears, with certainty, the cry—*il grido*—from outside the shack: a cry that sounds, in fact, very much like the cry of a baby. The other women clearly hear it too—and so does Ugo, if the spectator is attending closely, even though Ugo consciously is unaware that he has heard it. But the other women are quickly persuaded to deny what they have heard. And the reason is not only the authority of male consensus, but the women's habitual deference to this authority. They are *accustomed* to denying the reality of their own perceptions, to disbelieve and even disown their own senses (or at least to act as though they did). Their very disbelief or denial is evidence of Antonioni's thesis of the one-sided domination of the conscious over the unconscious, to which the women have readier access than the men. Here too, then, the director provides a spectrum of possible responses to reality. At one end is Giuliana, who is so close to the unconscious, to "others," that she is in danger of drowning in them; to her the cry is unmistakable. The other women have heard it but less distinctly. Ugo has unconsciously heard it, but denies it. The gross Max and the others have heard nothing; in them the unconscious, the other senses, are deaf or dormant. This is why the compensatory power of the unconscious is so strong in them; why they project their libido in aphrodisiacs and sexual innuendo; why they want to drown their individual "identities" in a collective "life." The compensatory effort of the unconscious explains their moods of childish "play" and the weight of "adult" propriety (the sudden hilarious tearing down of the plank walls to feed the dying fire, followed by that sad, embarrassed, individuated silence). And so they act like unhappy somnambulists, determined not to awaken. They prefer instead to punish, through the coercions of consensus, anyone who, like Giuliana, brings the contents of the unconscious to consciousness, or succeeds in achieving a genuine childishness and primitivism they envy but cannot create for themselves. Thus each character defines the other. Giuliana, isolated by her illness, is terrified of being thought mad if she contradicts the male consensus; the alternative is to deny her own senses, to disavow reality. When she resists the group, she inevitably separates herself from it; resistance individuates her. The sudden pain of finding herself separated from the others, of finding

99

herself alone, drives her *seaward*, toward the fantasy world—those blue maternal waters of her island world—to annul the unbearable pain of her loneliness and "difference." Yet this same sense of "difference" is also crucial to her individuation.

Separation and containment: between these polar psychological worlds the film moves. Just as the beauty and clarity of Giuliana's fantasy world are our best evidence of her "neurotic" hunger for containment and her immersion in it, so the final scene unmistakably reveals her separation from it, her *conscious* decision to accept the tension and live it. She is "separated" but also "not separated"; she is still pained and surprised by the *discontinuity* of pain: as she says to the sailor, "If you prick me, you're not the one who hurts [Se lei mi punge, lei non soffre]." And she realizes, sadly, at the moment of articulate decision, that her life is what "happens to her"; that she is responsible for her own life—as she has not been until now.[14] This is the moment of conscious wakening toward which her life and her neurosis have steadily, despite constant regressions, been driving her. One after another, Antonioni deprives her of all emotional support—first her husband, then her child, then her lover. All in some sense desert her or fail her. With each fresh abandonment she feels a wound, a hurt like death; yet each desertion drives her toward her own identity, away from fantasy and toward a workable myth of her own. Almost at the end of the film, back in her shop on Via Alighieri, she can respond to Corrado's advice not to worry about infidelity by saying scornfully, "Just don't think about it! A fine solution!" Here moral consciousness, the sense of duties, the sense of *others* supervenes. And it is the consequence of this decision, combined with her recognition of her own loneliness in her "conversation" with the Turkish sailor, that finally brings her to her true human "home."

A word about structure. *Red Desert*, like all of Antonioni's films, is very tightly composed, but the structure is based upon a complex crisscross of correspondence and echo whose matrix is the fantasy of the Sardinian island. It should be stressed that this is a genuine psychological fantasy, the emergence, at a moment of diminished consciousness, of the contents of the unconscious. What has been repressed suddenly surfaces, and the power, beauty, and intensity of the fantasy unmistakably declare its unconscious origins. This, I am certain, is how we are meant to see it; not as a lyrical flashback intruded as a fairy tale to beguile a sick child but a genuine fantasy, rich with unconscious life. In harmony with psychoanalytic theory, it looks both backward and forward; it is at once an ordering of past experience and a guide to future action. Thus it controls the film throughout, gathering up earlier themes and visual images, transmuting them according to the new experience and psychic needs of the dreamer, and thereby giving fresh meaning to the "manifest material." By so doing, it also anticipates the dreamer's future behavior, projecting the structure of past and present on the future. The "meaning" of the dream ultimately depends

100

upon what the dreamer does with it. He can actively transmute his fantasy into conscious myth by understanding and, to some degree, controlling its patterns; or he can remain the passive victim of the recurrence imposed by old behavior and personal need, doomed to perpetual repetition. The difference is that which divides adult from child, health from neurosis, purposive behavior from mere somnambulism. What matters for the dreamer is his perception of the pattern and his courage in confronting its hold on his life.

Structurally, the film depends upon *our* perception of the pattern—a pattern that makes its full epiphany only in the Sardinian fantasy, that is, when the film is more than halfway over. Only then do we see how firmly the fantasy echoes, with the skeletal clarity of fable, earlier scenes. Only then do we see that earlier events are nothing but the manifest material of the fantasy; that *it* explains *them* as much as they explain it; that repetition is precisely the artistic and psychological point. The reader need merely recall the fantasy's chief features: a lonely, adolescent girl, at one with the landscape, then hiding behind the branch of a tree (a repeated motif); the arrival of the mysterious boat (in the distance, a glimpse of fabulous landfalls); and, finally, the girl's discovery of an erotic landscape in the rocks at a point where everything is fused, singing in a single ecstatic voice.

Formally, however, reduced to its simplest terms, this fantasy is not new but a repetition that has been radiantly transformed by the unconscious. Its "everyday" source or "manifest material" lies above all in the earlier scene in Giuliana's "shop" in Via Alighieri. We see a timeless street, deserted, all leached greens, grays, and ochers, and the room where Giuliana, like a lonely child, "plays" shopkeeper, sheltered from reality by the comforting blues and greens of her amniotic world. Into this street, as dead as the past, where nobody lives, slides the car of Corrado, the curious and mysterious invader. He gently pushes her door open, then retreats as she anxiously peers out to see who has broken into her isolation. They talk of boats, of Corrado's comings and goings. He is attentive, and this makes an impression, for she abruptly asks, apropos of nothing except the fact of his *arrival* in *her* world, "When did you arrive?" ("Quando sei arrivato?"—with the stress on *arrivato*). The scene closes, like the fantasy, on a note of romantic anticipation. And the high, singing voice of the fantasy has, as its visual precursor, the incipient love we see blooming—a pink carnation in soft focus—between Giuliana and Corrado in Ferrara.

Even Giuliana's "island" is more than a metaphor of isolation. It, too, has its own manifest material in the floating oil depot (*isola della Sarom*, in the Italian) where Giuliana and Corrado, alone together, surrounded by waves and gulls, talk of love and Corrado's imminent departure (each mention of departure visually stressed by shots of struts, spars, and bars between them). But this scene tells us why, in Giuliana's fantasy later, the invading boat suddenly veers away, off toward the fabulous world it brings with it. Indeed, throughout the film boats and ships are images of transient, nomadic life,

cut away from all locality and home—visible emblems of the possibility of flight and the hope of "getting away from it all." In the scene on the floating depot and in the Sardinian fantasy, boats also acquire an aura of erotic hope, of flight *from* loneliness. Thus, after Giuliana recognizes Corrado's coarseness and irresponsibility, she runs, in sudden regressiveness, desperate to escape her loneliness by taking passage on the Turkish tramp (just as earlier she drove her car suicidally toward the sea in which she sees the shining blue "home" of her fantasy lagoon). It is in her confrontation with the Turkish sailor, her halting, desperate recognition, as she is confronted by his utter incomprehension, that she knows what evasion means—not annulment of loneliness but simply a repetition of the pattern; that, for better or worse, she is on her own. Knowing this, she can at last return, for the first time, truly home.

The correspondences between Giuliana's fantasy and her behavior before and after are too complex for full discussion here. But the schematic intricacy with which they are developed, thematically, visually, and aurally, leaves no doubt about the director's strategy. A brief glance at one scene—the "seduction" in Corrado's hotel room—is enough to suggest Antonioni's meticulous craftsmanship. For instance, immediately after the seduction, the bedroom is suddenly suffused in pink—the same tonal pink we see in the curving sands of Giuliana's Sardinian beach. And in the writhing bodies of Corrado and Giuliana, Antonioni clearly *requires* his audience to see again those twisted torsos and buttocks discernible in the island's rocks (rocks that "seemed to be made of human flesh," as the subtitle says), and thus to recognize the actualization in the bedroom of the erotic suggestions so vivid in the Sardinian beach fantasy. To reinforce the point, the sound of the lovers' bodies moving in the bedsheets is made to echo that gentle plash of the small surf on the pink beach. Indeed, only an audience completely inured to the narrative conventions of conventional realism, blinded and deafened by its own expectations, could possibly miss the fineness and complexity and power of Antonioni's *poetic* composition, that is, the intricacy with which the bedroom and beach scenes echo and inflect one another. For *poetry* is precisely what it is, sustained poetry at that, and one of the very few valid cinematic poetries yet created.[15]

Finally, a word about neurosis. It is important if we are to recognize in *Red Desert* something more than an essay in neurotic psychology that we should understand what is involved in Giuliana's illness and the victory of individual courage, however hesitant and faltering, that Antonioni intends. We need go no further than Jung (though Freud or indeed almost any eclectic psychiatry would do equally well). By citing Jung I am not suggesting that this film is a doctrinaire or even consistent application of Jungian theories of neurosis; I mean merely that the neurosis depicted here follows the general lines of humanistic therapy in the twentieth century. For the film's "subject" is neurosis only insofar as it is a film about humankind's

102

contemporary neurosis, the "diseased Eros" (the phrase is Antonioni's, not mine) from which all suffer, as well as its cultural origins and universal pervasiveness. On Antonioni's view (as on Mann's or Eliot's) we can speak of individual neurosis only if we are prepared to view the world itself as a great sanatorium or hospital, of which we are all inmates, and the sickest of all may be those who think themselves most sane. In Jung's judgment, the courageous neurotic is the patient who copes creatively with his own life, who comes to terms with himself by confronting the reality of his own nature and his responsibility for his illness or health. The neurotic in this sense is of course only the classical hero in disguise; his antagonist is his illness, and his illness is ultimately himself. But in Jung's words:

> The neurotic has no need to feel himself beaten; he has merely misjudged his necessary adversary, thinking that he could give him the slip. The whole task of his personality lies in the very thing he sought to avoid. Any doctor who deludes him on that score is doing him a disservice. *The patient has not to learn how to get rid of his neurosis, but how to bear it.* His illness is not a gratuitous and therefore meaningless burden; it is *his own self*, the "other" whom, from childish laziness or fear, or for some other reason, he was always seeking to exclude from his life. . . .
>
> We should not try to "get rid" of a neurosis, but rather to experience what it means, what it has to teach, what its purpose is. We should even learn to be thankful for it, otherwise we pass it by and miss the opportunity of getting to know ourselves as we really are. A neurosis is truly removed only when it has removed the false attitude of the ego. We do not cure it— it cures us. A man is ill, but the illness is nature's attempt to heal him. From the illness itself we can learn so much for our recovery, and what the neurotic flings away as absolutely worthless contains the true gold we should never have found elsewhere.[16]

Jung insists in volume after volume that Western man's reason has long since outrun his instinct. The result has been to develop an overly rational, overly technical civilization that has conquered much of the organic world at the cost of contact with its own soul. Only by drawing on our unconscious creative powers can we hope to redress the balance. Such a restoration, Jung argues, can begin only with the creative and resistant individual. The value and allure of Giuliana for our one-sided and overrationalized civilization is clearly exemplary. She is, after all, the one genuine "individual" in the film, that is, the only one who accepts tragic loneliness as the normal condition of existence and who asserts responsibility for her own life. Even more important perhaps is what she (like each of the four women played by Monica Vitti in these films) contributes to the culture and to others: that is, her own irreducible femininity, still integral, still "unassimilated" by masculine modes, rich with the mystery and complex appeal of

103

what Jungians call the "anima."[17] She and she alone provides access to an unknown world, a world so strange that others can scarcely acknowledge its reality or its power, which, undetected and repressed, deforms them, turning them into mere sleepwalkers or claiming them in compensatory violence. She is the taproot to the past, the primitive and natural, recognizable by her affinity with old, forgotten things, with trees and plants, with her earthy aura of blue and green. Like Vittoria in *Eclipse* or Valentina and Lidia in *La notte*, she reveals what would otherwise remain concealed: dormant sense and instincts, eclipsed feelings, all the layered humus of the unconscious world. When she appears, we are meant to glimpse, if only for an instant, the presence of the eternal rhizome buried in the earth, informing the ephemeral leaves with their seasonal continuity, and giving life to "the great-rooted blossomer."[18]

The beauty of Giuliana's individuation is that she achieves it without loss of what she represents to others. She no more loses her aura and appeal than she surrenders her nature. And even though she may succeed in transforming her personal fantasy into myth, she can do so only by retaining access to her own internal landscape. She acquires a psychic balance by mapping and exploring, not obliterating or abandoning, the ground of her being. Admittedly, her balance is precarious, her consciousness tentative and insecure. Yet, at least for now, for the finale, the psychic pressures are under control, as the visual metaphor (underground pipes, their valves periodically venting and liberating the violent pressures they contain) and the last line of the script clearly declare. What counts here is the *discrete* achievement, the *incremental* but crucial advance, which, as so often, contains the hint, the arc, of the completed circle. These discrete advances are, of course, typical of Antonioni's endings: small, revealing clarities; a gesture of compassion; minute but significant distinctions of awareness. This preference for hints and tentative gestures lies partly in the director's notorious, even fastidious, disdain for heroics; but also, more to the point, in his clear-sighted, scrupulous concern for contemporary reality. This concern precludes the splendid quantum leap of the classical hero. Advances in Antonioni's world are discrete because he postulates a world of total and universal uncertainty, whose violence of change and flux means that any significant advance is a step into the moral unknown, a new human condition, not the courageous assertion of an old arête. And, as in *Red Desert*, the protagonist's advance is more difficult and painful because it is invariably made in a world almost paralyzed by fear of the new—that is, in opposition to the intimidated many and the conformist crowd.

It is above all Corrado's evasion and cowardice that give us the measure of Giuliana's achievement (just as in *La notte* Lidia's clarity in confronting the death of love is meant to be measured against her husband's effort, by physical love, to pull her back into a world she no longer emotionally inhabits). With Ugo, it is harder to say how she stands, since we see him

almost entirely through her neurotically needful eyes. Considerate, even kind, Ugo is also flat, one-dimensional, and uninteresting, perhaps because his adaptation is so effortless and perfect. Thus he lives in his formidable technological world with the same practiced ease and assurance of habit as the young girl in Giuliana's fantasy fits her blue lagoon. This may, in fact, be all that can be said of him. Yet I think Antonioni expects us, out of a humanity closer to Giuliana's, to find him dull, a man so assimilated by the technological world around him that he functions like a well-mannered robot. An engineer, a cerebral product of a pure Apollonian world, he lacks both psychic energy and depth. And, even from him, the unconscious exerts a kind of compensation that visibly affects his behavior. Not all of his nature is expressed by the conventionally purposive life he leads; he hears, after all, sounds that he will not let himself hear. And this tells us that he has driven a part of himself underground, where it waits its chance to claim him in neurosis or violence (image: the refinery boilers erupting, with a hideous roar, into great clouds of steam, curling around Ugo and Corrado until, like an explosion, they nearly obliterate the screen—which is to say, the world). It is a dangerous condition. "Whoever protects himself," warns Jung, "against what is new and strange and regresses to the past falls into the same neurotic condition as the man who identifies himself with the new and runs away from the past. The only difference is that one has estranged himself from the past and the other from the future. In principle both are doing the same thing: they are reinforcing their narrow range of consciousness instead of shattering it in the tension of opposites and building up a state of wider and higher consciousness."[19]

That this is Antonioni's view of the matter seems to me to be confirmed by *Blow-up*, that remarkable study of a one-dimensional man, far friskier and livelier than Ugo here but unmistakably of the same mold. And the whole purpose of *Blow-up* is surely to subject that restless, shallow, one-dimensional photographer, with his easy adaptation and his utter unwisdom, to a sudden, overwhelming involvement in mortality, an experience of death that leaves him shaken to the depths of his being, by the things he can no longer shut out, so that the photographer uses his human eyes for the first time, to cry at the transience and brief bravery of the flesh, made clear in the green grass, the omnivorous natural world that alone survives.

Blow-up

Begin, as we should, at the beginning: a frame filled with a grassy field—the matte green of natural vegetation. Superimposed are titles and credits in bright fluorescent or chemical blue-greens. Within the hollows of the block letters is the moving figure of what looks like a dancer, a brightly striped bikini, arms and legs moving up and down as though wriggling about inside the letters. The overall effect is that of a natural field of grass, a motionless "background," through which pass these transient words and colored names, each letter filled with a brightly colored, swaying, even "swinging," life that is appearing, disappearing.

The director, wasting no space or time, deftly sets the polar chromatic terms that will define the film. The natural green remains motionless, fixed, while over it the man-made blue-greens pass and change, swarming with fragmentary internal life. The effect is a visual *image* of the transience that haunts this film as it pervades all of Antonioni's work.

The initial code-chromatic effort suggests *visual value*. Because color conventions (apart from traffic semaphores and industrial or commercial chromatic "signs") are no longer shared, the convention has to be created from scratch, then inflected by the film. The chromatic "overture" sets out the thematic binaries: natural and man-made; vegetation tones and chemical lives. Thematically the credits are linked, as theme to variation, to the

106

opening scene—the "ragging" students with their motley harlequin costumes, the London streets with their jarring incongruities of color and style, blazing red phone booths beside aniline blue buses, of overpainted red and blue houses, the teenyboppers' commedia dell'arte pantyhose and striped synthetics, the fantastic Carnaby Street ménage of the fashion photographer. Everywhere contrasted with those carnival chromatics is the green field of the park—silent except for the soughing of the wind in the leaves—and the grass into which the photographer dissolves at the close. The contrast has been artistically heightened; the director not only has garishly repainted the brick row houses but even sprayed the park grass its matte green, in order to make the routinely seeing eye see these things *as though for the first time,* as if they had freshly surfaced from the unconscious.

The trouble with English grass is that it is *too* green; to a continental or Italian eye it looks artificial. In accord with the credits, the man-made city world is chromatically contrasted with the natural world of the park. The park becomes an island of relative peace; and peace is intensely appealing to the agitated people of the film, that is, to the restless Thomas, to Vanessa, to the flighty "birds," and, in a different way, to the peace marchers. The city is correspondingly *noisy,* the sound track confirming the chromatic contrast between the man-made and the natural worlds. And these basic contrasts in turn generate an intermediate spectrum of color and sound values by which the film modulates its statements. This method is Antonioni's essential technique for ordering the world that his camera reveals.

In *Zabriskie Point,* for instance, the central binaries are expressed as absolute city and absolute desert. On the one hand is Faustian Los Angeles, with its verticals and semiotic bombardment and violent chemical colors; on the other, the unmoving, silent, timeless desert at Zabriskie Point, all desert horizontals and continuous, unfragmented space, an immense "field" of leached lavender and whitened pinks in which the human voice is diminished and lost; and the status of the human beings themselves is revealed within the vast space of the environing desert—not center stage but reduced to their true diminutive position in a post-Copernican universe. Between city and desert, at the point where they intersect, is the interim world of Danville, neither city nor desert, incongruously combining the opposed chromatics, geometries, and sounds of both. So, too, in *Red Desert,* the dead oil-poisoned estuaries of industrial Ravenna (also overpainted by Antonioni to give the feel of chemical rather than natural death) are set in violent contrast with the paradisal "red desert" of the Sardinian beach which surfaces as a fantasy from Giuliana's unconscious. And in *Eclipse* the uproar of the Roman stock market is deliberately juxtaposed with the African sequences of the women in their apartment, all quiet voices and natural textures in black and white. Antonioni's films everywhere demonstrate basic contrasts that generate, and modulate, meaning.

Return now to the opening titles. They provide, as I suggested, an

107

image, an "overture" of transience, which is then refined and amplified by the next sequence—the dawn scene of the "ragging" students in their open vehicle. To a European eye the scene is rich in information. Everywhere in Europe matriculating freshmen, usually at the end of March, celebrate Rag-week, *la festa delle matricole.* Dressed in costumes akin to those of the commedia dell'arte, they run about the streets performing improvised games and tricks, cadging money for charity. Both custom and costumes are medieval in origin; and Antonioni emphasizes the survivals from the past by pointedly showing us other living survivals: black nuns passing, scarlet-coated Guards foot stamping in front of Saint James Palace. Why? Because the past survives in the lives of those who, like the mod world, would consciously discount it, even while it *lives them,* an unacknowledged presence—or compensatory agent—in their ordinary behavior.

Past and present stand in an odd but revealing parallel tension that is kept constantly before the viewer. The antique shop, for instance, is a simple device for suggesting the obsolescence of the human past—all styles and arts jumbled together, primitives jostling baroque, elbowing early modern, itself already passé, Roman heads framed by romantic landscapes, the whole "hoard" protected by a sullen old man holding off the young vandals eager to appropriate it. They *want* it; like Thomas, they *"must* have it." This pull of the past is a thematic constant in the director's work, for the past, though obsolete in one sense, continues to exert a deep underground pull on the present; the relics of old ways, old customs, are still potently, though almost invisibly, at work. "Thomas," Antonioni observed, "has chosen to take part in the revolution which has affected English life, customs, and morality, at least among the young—the young artists, trend-setters, advertising executives . . . who have been inspired by the Pop movement. He leads a life as regulated as a ceremony although he claims to know no other law but anarchy."[1] As regulated as a ceremony; the words are carefully chosen. The thematic point, I suggest, is this: those who think themselves most liberated from the past or the primitive, from nature and animal rhythms—the subtle but powerful operation *in them* of leaf and beast living on in them, their own unsuperseded phylogeny—are in fact the least liberated. It is precisely these people on whom nature and the past exert their compensatory power most fully. The suppressed element in them rises in unsuspected ways to reclaim them. They become "sleepwalkers," zombies even, "living" according to a style and rhythm of which they are mostly unaware and would indignantly disown. Those who keep in touch with this suppressed reality, who come gradually to discover their affinity with it, are the waking ones, the incipient *individuals* of Antonioni's oeuvre, emerging from the faceless crowd of anonymous sleepers. I think, for instance, of Vittoria in *Eclipse,* with her fossil flower; or of Valentina and Lidia in *La notte,* with their talismanic trees; or of Giuliana in *Red Desert,* with her animistic Sardinian seascape.

108

The others, the unindividuated sleepwalkers, constantly reveal, in their compensatory behavior—expressed as a kind of automatism, collectively reinforced—the effect upon them of this suppressed reality. The land developers of *Zabriskie Point*, for instance, respond unconsciously to a reality—the desert world, the frontier, the wilderness—that they exploit and that in turn secretly claims them. For their exploitation is based upon the power, both real and symbolic, of the desert and its appeal—whether as "suppressed reality" or the "frontier myth" or the past—to the inhabitants of California's urban jungles. The point isn't primitivism or a return to nature. What matters is *balance*, equilibrium. "I have never felt salvation in nature," remarked Antonioni; "I love cities above all."[2] But again and again the films report the conversation of binaries—the city contrasted with country; or with what Italians call *la periferia*; or the contrasts of center city against outer city or residential park.

It is, for instance, no accident that the antique shop and the park are physically contiguous; their proximity is thematic. The appeal of the antique shop to Thomas is similar to the pull of the park. Both represent—as past or as nature—the appeal of a reality suppressed by the city, which thinks itself free of both nature and the past. Thomas wants the antique shop because he wants props for his studio, but also for his own living quarters. The mod world is moving closer and closer to the antique shop; this means that the neighborhood will suddenly become fashionable, or, as Thomas puts it, with a quite thematic violence, "go like a bomb." Antiques, and even old junk, are valuable because, in a time of drastic change, they represent lost stability, the permanence of the past. They have potency, cachet, talismanic properties, like a piece of petrified wood or a fossil flower or fish, persisting in a world whose momentum of change is so rapid that the object Thomas *must* have, a twenty-year-old World War II propeller, has become an antique. The power of such "stilled" objects can be inferred from Thomas' studio, with its modish mixture of past and present, rustic and modern, straight lines and curves.

Thomas' studio is an eclectic living space, really an extended studio filled with talismanic objects: quartz crystals, a Louis Quinze inscription on the wall beside a professional painting in the style of a child's finger-painting; a photograph of a black caravan moving across a cream expanse, transformed by its passage into a desert; below it a bench flanked by two rococo grisette Madonnas. Downstairs, other emblematic devices: the cigar-store Turk, the desk where the Oriental secretary sits; and, by the stairs, constantly in view as Thomas enters, or works, or leaves, the mutually reinforcing images of parachutist and frogman. The dark exposed wooden beams, rigid horizontals, and acute angles are softened by contrasting textures and colors: a lavender rug, soft blue-white florescent light over the print of the desert caravan, the plum-colored velour of the couch, and the blue "sky" of the alcove from which Thomas summons down the sleeping "birds"—or as we Americans would say, "chicks."

109

Through its decor and principles of arrangement, Thomas' studio is designed to represent the world outside the studio—the exterior "mix" of different ages, dress, cultures, generation, and style. The Faustian buildings we see everywhere under construction—untopped high-rises, the unfinished housing project on the hilltop—are an architectural representation of violent social changes, analogs for human nature in metamorphosis. Thomas himself, as image maker, fashions—also, in part, enacts—the party-colored life of "bomb culture" London. A chameleon man in a chameleon world: ephemeral as fashions that flaunt their delight in change; that celebrate the vivacity of color and sheen; that find ecstasy in the buoyant manipulation of reality; and that worship a noisy, restless exhilaration.

But at the same time the other reality is marginally there. The green trees of Thomas' courtyard, swaying in the breeze, signal their presence when Thomas telephones Ron. The frame is equally divided: on one side, blank white wall; on the other, windowed nature with its visual echo of the park and the park's proximity to *us*, even in midcity. It is *there*, in the quartz crystals; the childlike painting; in the ubiquity of the past in the antique shop and studio; and in Thomas' affectionate relation to this past (as when he fondly pats the stone lace cap of the rococo Madonna, the gesture ironically stressed by his remarks about his failed marriage). The stone girlfriend persists, loyal; flesh-and-blood relationships are fleeting. A persistent visual theme, this: the constant juxtaposition of transient life and the hard, flesh-encasing stone, steel, brick, and glass (as in the initial sequence of the ragging students in their vehicle, circling and gesticulating noisily, set against the concrete and steel facade of the new buildings). We see this other reality, and hear it too: in Thomas' wistful way of talking about "peace" or the "stillness" in the park; in those rare moments when he relaxes, as at Patricia's house, and closes his eyes. Often the effect is synesthetic, visual image supporting the aural, the *sight* of leaves *rustling* in the wind. The essential colors of this other world are dull, unsaturated—matte green, dun, olive, stone color, ocher—its unpretentiousness, drabness, even humility pointedly contrasted with mod London, with its bravado of the man-made moment—the polychrome *Now*.

But the contrast is never total. Each reality is present in its opposite. The park could never become wholly paradisal. Repeatedly, we see apartments perched on the hill in the background above the park. When Thomas initially enters the park, our first sight is of a plump attendant stolidly spearing litter. She's posted there to prevent us from feeling romantic sentiments about idyllic nature. When Thomas returns to the park at night to find the body, his way is lit by the neon sign—advertising an airline, I take it—by whose pallid light he sees the white face of the corpse. But equally the park is a subdued presence in the city; we see that in the treed courtyard outside Thomas' studio, or in the image of a stunted tree planted in the sidewalk of the red-brick desert near the flophouse. Even in the clown white

of the ragging students' faces we may detect the neon pallor of the murdered man's face. Subdued or retiring, this "other" world is never wholly
absent. It is *there*—a reality *we* come to see, as Thomas gradually discovers it.
Persistently, it makes itself felt and, wherever most strenuously repressed,
reasserts itself through unconscious compensatory behavior in those who
ignore or deny its claims. The peace of the park conceals the murderer's
pointed pistol in Thomas' blow-up; and always beneath the bustling gaiety
of mod London lies—as glimpsed briefly in the crude black-and-white
placards of the peace marchers—the suppressed violence of atomic explosion, the Blow-up.

Pointed polarities everywhere. On one hand the carnival world of the
colored city, with its youthful maskers and raucous machines, its assurance;
on the other, fading red brick, the *unpainted* world of the flophouse, with its
derelicts and human outcasts, the silent suffering that the jaunty city of the
affluent young has pushed to the fringes of the social frame. The drab,
sepia-colored brick buildings are audibly confirmed by the low muttering
and silence—a silence stressed by the passing of the overhead train. The
sidewalk sapling that struggles there amid the hostile brick world speaks of
desperation, not lifelessness. Later, when Thomas shows Ron the photographs from the flophouse, we suddenly *see* the inner side, the suffering
suppressed by the city—and also a source of its latent violence. And what
we see is emphatically informed by the *context*, the black-and-white photos
of the flophouse displayed against a glass of wine, napkins, plates of food.

Why, we might ask, does Thomas visit the flophouse and want to
include its photographs in his new book? Because the affluent mod world in
which he makes his living demands as *art* what it cannot tolerate as reality.
The book of black-and-white documentary stills that Thomas is preparing is
a luxury product designed for fashionable West End coffee tables; designed
to be bought by those leisurely sleepwalkers whose lives, drugged with
appearance and manipulated by Faustian magicians like Thomas, require
every so often a dose of discreetly administered reality. The crowd of
stoned sophisticates needs art, culture: "In the room the women come and
go / Talking of Michelangelo."[3] The sleepwalker now and then needs to
waken; the addict needs to know he needs his fix. A major theme in Antonioni's next film, *Zabriskie Point*, is the organized stimulation of desire, manu-
factured Eros—a stimulation to which the stimulators are themselves extremely vulnerable. Their commercial skill is their ability to market their
own addictions, and thereby multiply the addicts. Advertisers and developers—in Antonioni's work these are the supreme "pushers." Still later, in
The Passenger, Antonioni deals explicitly with the suppressed violence that
afflicts the world, but above all the outwardly ordered West, and its source
in the sleepwalker's exploitation of his hunger for raw reality, for real
feelings; for the cause he does not have and which he must therefore borrow
from others, as a living man might borrow a dead man's identity. And in

the mod London of *Blow-up*, pain is packaged for painless consumption. Suffering is distanced; violence, vicarious. Even Thomas' plan for his "serious book—dozens of black-and-white documentary photos of violence and suffering, rounded off by an upbeat sequence of "love in the park"—is a commerical recipe. The book will impose a predictable formula upon a world that has been preperceived. Thomas' initial sense of what is happening in the park also imposes upon reality a routinely coded perception, but the reality in the park finally refuses to submit to the viewer's perception of it.

I want to stress the point. The chief strategy of the film is to bring Thomas—and us—to the point at which the suppressed reality discloses *itself*. Of *Blow-up* Antonioni remarked: "I want to re-create reality in an abstract form. I'm really questioning the nature of reality. This is an essential point to remember about the visual aspects of the film, since one of its chief themes is 'to see or not to see properly the true value of things.'"[4] When one is no longer concerned with fitting reality to his needs and routine perceptions, the world—which is *there*, prior to all seeming and seeing as well as all deconstruction—opens up around him as he opens his eyes. Thomas "wakens" from sleep—to use the metaphoric language of the film—and for the first time actually sees what is there. By so doing he sees himself as he is: a very small part of a reality which is prior to him and us, and larger. He is no longer an "outside" figure, blown up as it were, out of all proportion to nature, but rather "reduced," "scaled down" to his true human proportions. And when this happens, he may cease to be sleepwalker or automaton; he will be freed from his own technology, his unreal codes and his "objective" illusions. The film is *not*, I believe, about the relation of illusion to reality but rather of suppressed reality to apparent reality; of natural to man-made; of background to foreground; of black-and-white to chroma.

We first encounter Thomas in a flophouse world few of us ever see. He is there on his own business, as masked actor, an exploiter even. But he's also there, we *come* to see, because he has an obscure affinity for this drab world. In his own world of chromatic illusion he's obviously at ease, both participant and observer. But *something*, we see, is troubling Thomas. He's restless, agitated; he wants something else: "There are other things I want on the reel." Like everyone in the film, like almost everyone in Antonioni's films, he wants to "escape." To fly, to exchange identities, to run away. The girl in the antique store, playing Hawaiian music, tells Thomas, "I'd like to try something different. Get off somewhere." Thomas, peering out of the restaurant window, says to Ron, "I'm going off London this week. . . . It doesn't do anything for me. . . . I wish I had tons of money. Then I'd be free." The antique store woman wants to escape to Nepal or Morocco, from musty antiques to the real article, to *primitive* things. But Nepal, as Thomas says, is "all antiques." There is no escape. Verushka, the model, on her way to Paris finds Paris in London. Thomas is temperamentally restless, his movements

112

abrupt, impulsive. But he's also restless in his *chosen* role, no longer quite "at home" with himself or his profession. We see the emerging Thomas, as we must, against the profile of the old Thomas. Returning to his studio from the flophouse, he returns to a world defined by old habits, by professional power and technical skill become reflex.

Thomas is a Faustian magician. In the initial scenes in the studio, he manipulates reality like a powerful wizard among obedient servants. He enters the studio proper; we see him outsize—a giant among pygmies—defined by contrast with his model who is hunched in the bottom left of the frame and thus reduced by the filter in which she's reflected. His working manner is brusque, overbearing, rude. His hands move restlessly over the technical equipment which in fact governs his chosen mode of seeing: tapes, phonograph, car radio, intercom, strobes, lights, enlargers. But above all the camera, which he uses like a prosthetic extension of himself. With the model, Verushka, he uses the camera like a tool, to stimulate and also simulate sexual passion. His studio includes a living area in which there is no personal or private space. Except for the bedroom (of which we catch only one glimpse), the layout shows that the profession is synonymous with the man. His staccato gestures are those of a "workaholic": "I don't have a moment even to have my appendix out," he says, flicking on a tape, then "walking" a florin across his knuckles. He takes a sip of wine, a swallow of beer. In his car, he drives brusquely and jerkily.

But these behavior patterns are periodically interrupted by new ones, marked by inward discontent, a profound fatigue expressed as a yearning for peace and the desire to escape the confines of his professional life. We see his face in revealing repose as Patricia runs her fingers tenderly through his hair. He's tired of London, "fed up with those bitches." Sex is not what interests him; cloyed or in search of escape, he wants "something else," "other things."

Following that impulse, wholly his own, free of any professional interest, he enters the park. Quite of his own volition, he is suddenly in another world, suddenly *free*, not unlike Locke in *The Passenger*. In the antique shop he anticipates himself. Asked what sort of paintings he wants, he speaks his own unknowing desire: "Landscapes." In the park he acts out this wish, physically entering the landscape world he vaguely thinks of. What he feels is *release, freedom* expressed as play.

Thomas chases the pigeons with his camera, then focuses on *one*—*one* bird in *free flight* (that obsessive theme in Antonioni's work)—soaring over the apartment cresting the hill, and then he bounds up the steps like a schoolboy released from school. The release is in marked contrast to his jerky movements earlier, and revealingly "out of character" with the professional photographer. (Also, I suspect, with Hemming's own personal style. One can almost hear the director's instructions to the actor.) His desires are projected now, not on the "birds" in the studio loft but on the real thing, the

birds trilling on the hillside. In the studio he had shouted "Wake up!" to his models. Then, intuiting their fatigue from his own, he tells them to "shut their eyes" and makes his exit, leaving them imprisoned in their filter frames and mod costumes, swaying like sleepwalkers to the music on the tape. He has *decided* to leave, to *get out*. Like so many Antonioni characters, Thomas must escape or die. In the background of that decision, clarifying and reinforcing it, we hear the 'Lovin' Spoonful' playing John Sebastian's song:

Did you ever have to fin'lly decide
And say yes to one and let the other one ride?
There's so many changes
And tears you must hide.
Did you ever have to fin'lly decide?

Did you ever have to make up your mind
And pick up on one and leave the other behind?
It's not often easy,
And not often kind.
Did you ever have to make up your mind?[5]

Moving to this "theme" song of his own, he suddenly makes up his mind to visit Patricia. The decision may be subliminal, but it's a decision gathering in that dramatic instant before it becomes *conscious* decision. We watch a man trying to wake from the coma of habitual behavior, out of the stupor of routine perception and collectively unexamined life. Again and again Thomas acts out metaphors of sleeping and waking. The sleepwalker wakes to find himself in a world he has never really known. Thomas, we need to remember, has spent the entire previous night awake in the underground world of the flophouse. When he returns to the studio, some of the flophouse world returns with him. He removes his tattered jacket and, still dressed in his flophouse shirt and trousers, presumably more attractive to the model for being so, he "makes love" with his camera. When he orders the "birds" to "wake up" ("I can't see your eyeballs any more. They're just slits. Go on, close your eyes"), he speaks with that part of himself that is struggling to waken, struggling to *stay awake, to become*. Later, after lunching with Ron, he returns to his studio and finds the street deathly quiet: not a soul, not a sound. So he presses the horn, as though wanting to shatter the oppressive silence, to waken sleepers or the dead, himself included. So, in *La notte*, the young Valentina says she is not intelligent, but *sveglia* (alert, awake). When we first glimpse her, she is shown reading Broch's *Sleepwalkers*; later, we see her gratuitously waken a dozing guest at her father's party. Her function, like Thomas', is to waken herself and others—the somnambulists—to what cannot be seen, except with waking eyes.

Thomas is persistently depicted as a transient, a passenger, moving,

however gropingly, toward an unknown destination. We see him tentatively advancing, retreating, then advancing again, constantly in passage. A transitional man, his passage is measured by his movement between the binaries that constitute his world, that is, between the brilliant mod chromatics and Carnaby Street decor of his studio, on the one hand, and, on the other, the unobtrusively quiet world of the park with its matte green field. He is not wholly at home in either, and his uncertainty is depicted in the stylized manner with which Antonioni reveals life decisions or "turnings." Advancing, he's serious, even anxious. Vanessa, the woman in the park, interests him from the outset, not simply because she is beautiful, but because she is *passionate,* awake; he sees a seriousness in her and in Patricia wholly absent in the "birds" and the teenyboppers. As his behavior shows, it's not sex that he wants, but something else—rapport, a serious *simpatia* which includes but is not synonymous with sex; a reciprocal rhythm of feeling and understanding once called "love." In his relation to Vanessa and to Patricia—revealed by nuances of voice and gesture—Thomas is clearly attracted to something he can't quite name; but something more serious than the labile relations of "swinging" London. His erotic feelings veer, in fact, toward the same suppressed reality that lures him, first, to the flophouse, then to the antique shop, and finally to the park. He is disturbed by feelings new to him; but feelings that claim him, demanding to be recognized. "This is a generation," remarked Antonioni of *Blow-up,* "that has approached a certain individual freedom . . . and freedom from feelings, too. . . . I don't know whether they can love the way we loved."[6] Thomas breaks with his own generation and moves toward an individuation mediated by his chance encounter with serious passion and death.

But *is* the encounter chance? Consider Thomas' first entrance into the park. Here is the critical first step toward his final discovery. He had gone to the antique shop in search of photographic props, studio *objets.* When asked what sort of picture he is looking for he says *the first thing that pops into his mind:* "Landscapes." The answer, being unpremeditated, is revealing. He uncovers a dun-colored mountain landscape. Antiques and landscape fuse; both are part of that "other" world sought by Thomas, that secret reality repressed in his glamorous workaday world and the carnival city.

He leaves. Standing in the street, he takes shots of the shop. Then, from inside the park, *we* look out at Thomas. In the foreground the trunks of four trees, leaves swaying gently; beyond, the path funneling toward the street where he stands, camera dangling. He *looks* into the park. We *see and hear* the rustling of the leaves; then birdsong, inviting: come in. And the man who went to the antique store and blurted out "Landscapes" is literally *drawn* into the landscape of the park, following an impulse which is no part of his programmed day. Of his own choice, he freely consents to the pull of the park, following his eyes—not his camera—where they lead him, entering slowly, even gravely, into the world opening out before him. A world of

115

natural greens, silence, rustling feelings. The place is obviously new to him and strangely appealing, islanded—but not removed—within the city. He enters a new world. But the trespass is intermittent. He advances, then retreats. At the top of the steps, he stops, concealed by a flowering branch; his big eyes dilate and narrow, like a range finder, fixing the coordinates. Then the raised camera and the "shooting" begins.

Everywhere the film insists upon Thomas' ambivalence. He is variously the professional and the child, but the professional is himself a child in the world which is finally disclosed in the park—love linked to violence, murder, transience, death. This discovery of death, always intensely personal, individuates, separating the discoverer from those who have not had his experience. The discovery is precarious because it is lonely. The temptation to renounce the experience is strong. And the struggle to cleave to his perceptions is threatened by the effort of the world he has left—the carnival collective—to coerce him back within the fold, to make him conform to its optics, luring him with protective warmth, anonymity, color. His only defense against that appeal is the reality of what he has seen—that dead body in the grass, mouldering it seems, in the grainy desolation of the last blow-up. The catalyst of individuality is this discovery of death. There is almost no Antonioni film which does not contain two recurrent features. First, a death or suicide, real or attempted—or a deathlike disappearance, like Anna's in *L'avventura*. Second, an individuation—like Giuliana's in *Red Desert* or Claudia's in *L'avventura*—by which the protagonist is isolated from others and confronts the relative solitude which is his or her fate.

Thomas' individuation follows the same pattern. Restless for something he can't express but vaguely identifies with "flight," he slowly, gropingly, detaches himself from the others, guided only by feelings and perceptions. The world opens up before his camera, revealing to his needy eyes what he could not have seen until his preinterpretation of reality had been deposed by events. His encounter with this new world separates him from others. Their somnambulism is purposive, designed to repress awareness of another reality. To repress it because living with "open eyes"—in the presence of death and transience—is painful. Except for rare moments of transcendence called "love," or "happiness," solitude is inescapable. The alternative is death-in-life, somnambulism, the collective narcosis of the anonymous crowd. In an uprooted world human feelings become as mobile as the people in it. Mobile because all the old institutions, founded on stable affections, rooted ties, grounded reality, have failed—church, family, and *paese*—have *disintegrated*, leaving only Eros to take their place. Eros must bear the burden of all the failed institutions; and this is more than Eros can do. People huddle together, but the huddling doesn't help. Hence the pervasive malaise of Eros in Antonioni's films, crippled by the huge burden imposed upon it. Hence, too, the culture of "swinging" London, founded on impermanence and mobility, mass societal anonymity, a compulsive and collective gaiety beneath the shadow of the Bomb, the Great Blow-up. In this London Antonioni presents the image of "culture" as something possessed of an undeniable geniality and even bravado, achieved by collective repression of whatever reality would trouble the general make-believe, the group game. The medieval Dance of Death prostrated itself before Death as before a god; it *reveled* in death. The contemporary dance of death—the collective Game which is one of the central metaphors of the film—denies death by compulsive celebration of life. Thomas' individuation is informed by the collective background of the Game.

Individuation is the aim of the beautifully functional narrative of Thomas' discovery of the murder. In the final blow-up, visible even in the grainy print, the gun discloses itself. *Here*, under the superficial peace of the park, is the secret violence. On first viewing *we*, the viewers, are involved in Thomas' detective discovery—blow-up to blow-up, back and forth, adding, correcting. We don't perhaps immediately notice that a great deal more is going on, that Antonioni has focused his attention on Thomas, who is being *discovered* in the act of *discovering*. Repeatedly the camera takes us *behind* the two large prints hanging on the wire, showing Thomas with a glass of wine or magnifying glass, studying the photos. We witness him *through* them, just as we see him, by the way he arranges the blow-ups, repeating his own shooting of the sequence in order to *read* the meaning. The world and the viewer interpret and define each other; we *read* Thomas as he *reads* what he has shot. In some sense his shots "read" him—as we are "read" by Sophocles or Shakespeare. It is not simply a case of detective discovery but of the detective detected, defined. The point is crucial.

Thomas, the film insists, is himself implicated—at least vicariously—in the murder he discovers. While blowing up the negatives, he rehearses the shooting of the scene, and this rehearsal forcefully recalls, by reenacting, the actual shooting. We first see Thomas stalking his quarry. He peers from behind the leaves of a flowering shrub, then crouches and creeps forward, taking cover behind a tree. The field widens to disclose a second tree on the left of the frame. Thomas, too conspicuous in his white pants, crouches down like a hunter, then scurries to the cover of the second trunk. There he "shoots," runs furtively to the picket fence, vaults over, and starts shooting from the bushes. The sequence is purposely protracted. The camera makes its point by *"holding"*; and the analogy between Thomas stalking his prey and the murderer stalking his victim cannot be coincidental. In the next-to-last blow-up we see the same picket fence, the same bushes, the metallic glint of the revolver barrel just visible, exactly corresponding to the earlier shot of Thomas squatting behind the fence and squinting through the leaves, while the shutter clicks. One "shoots" a camera, one "shoots" a gun.[7] Whatever else Antonioni may be saying, he wants his viewer to *see* that the potential violence concealed by carnival London—a violence made glancingly visible by the peace marchers, whose ineffectuality is silent witness to

117

the unspeakable power of the blow-up their posters protest—is also *in* the park, *in* Thomas, *in* the others, surfacing in little things, like the violence of Thomas' driving. The violence may be latent, but it's *there*, biding its time—as potential, as looming catastrophe.

Thomas returns to his studio to find the photographs and negatives gone; there he is visited by Patricia. The scene between the two is one of the film's most brilliant, conveying with extreme economy Thomas' vicarious implication in the murder that he has discovered. Gesture and facial expression in the scenes between Thomas and Patricia make unmistakably clear the nature of their relationship. It is not simply sexual desire—for Thomas has moved beyond desire—but desire amplified by understanding: incipient love, conscious of itself in both. They communicate mostly by looks and gestures, with few words. When Thomas, in the preceding scene, watches Patricia and Bill making love, the only significant communication—an appealing, desperate look at the instant of Bill's orgasm—occurs between Patricia and Thomas. When she enters the studio shortly afterward, her needs and Thomas' intersect so intricately and simply that there can be no real doubt of the scene's essential purpose. The murder which Thomas has uncovered is a latent possibility in the relationship between Thomas, Patricia, and Bill. It is a violence that Eros always can create—but especially in times when Eros has become an *all*. Thomas shows her the only piece of evidence remaining, the barely visible corpse decomposing into the grass, and Patricia says: "It looks like one of Bill's paintings." The film script continues:

THOMAS: Yes.
The mention of Bill's name seems to compel them to consider the strange situation they are in. PATRICIA *puts down the photograph. She wanders about a bit, deep in thought, then again she turns to* THOMAS.
PATRICIA: Will you help me?
Close-up of THOMAS *seen over* PATRICIA'S *shoulder. She seems distraught.*
PATRICIA: I don't know what to do.
Resume on PATRICIA. THOMAS *draws near her. He watches her, perhaps for the first time trying to fathom what it might be that is disturbing her.*
THOMAS: What is it? Huh?
A pause. PATRICIA *moves away.*
Resume on THOMAS, *with* PATRICIA *standing a little away from him. She moves away, glancing at the fragment of photographic paper.*
PATRICIA: I wonder why they shot him . . .
She turns toward him.
Close-up of THOMAS. *He leans back, looking at her.*
Close-up of PATRICIA. *She lowers her eyes.*
Resume on the two of them. THOMAS *puts the torn corner of the photograph on the cabinet behind him.*

THOMAS: I didn't ask.

Close-up of PATRICIA. *Camera follows her as she starts to go out, then stops again under the ostrich plumes as if to say somethng. But she just smiles at him and walks down the stairs.*

THOMAS *stands there lost in thought as the sound of* PATRICIA'S *footsteps recedes.*[8]

The camera exploration of the two during this elliptical but elo-quent exchange reveals the answer to Patricia's "I wonder why they shot him . . ."; and it also links Thomas' discovery of the murder to his own personal life. The linking is all the tighter because the scene with Patricia follows so closely upon Thomas' discovery of the murder. His first unthink-ing reaction is to share his discovery with the person closest to him. This leads him to Patricia's and Bill's. Then, after Patricia leaves, he tries, unsuc-cessfully, to telephone Ron.

What we *see* taking place between Thomas and Patricia is incipient love, a passion which contains, by implication, the capacity for violence, even the capacity to kill. Thomas is at least vicariously involved and, if *we* understand how it is with him, then we are vicariously involved as well.

"It looks like one of Bill's paintings," says Patricia of the sole surviving blow-up—the grainy outline of the face and upper part of a man's body; it seems to be literally dissolving into the earth. The analogy between Thomas' blow-up and Bill's painting is intruded here because it is essential to the finale, and also because it is only now, in the aftermath of Thomas' discovery, that the earlier conversation with Bill makes its crucial point. Bill, we recall, refused to give or sell Thomas his five-year-old painting. Why? Because his work is Bill's mode of self-discovery, of *becoming*. As he says, "They don't mean anything when I do them . . . just a mess. Afterwards I find something to hang onto . . . like that . . . like . . . like . . . that leg. . . . And then it sorts itself out. It adds up. It's like finding a clue in a detective story." The parallel is pat, perhaps too pat. But what we *see* in Bill's latest painting (glanced at once again in the later scene at his house) is an abstract work of soft, grainy, pastel points, with no discernible pattern, where nothng has yet "sorted itself out." For Thomas the sole surviving photograph is one which, in the absence of the cumulative suspense of shots leading up to it, is meaningful only to himself; to other people it would provide neither evidence nor clue. When Patricia asks him why he doesn't go to the police, he points to the surviving blow-up, saying "That's the body," as if to say, "Who would believe me?"

But that blow-up is *his*—Thomas'—picture. It is the picture that defines *him*, as it also defines, by making visible at last, the violence and death concealed in the park, and that also reveals to us, if not to him, his participa-tion in that reality.

But the image involves more than death; it is also transience itself. The corpse appears to be *dissolving* into the leaves and grass. When at dawn

119

Thomas goes to the park the second time, he finds the body vanished; of that human figure lying on the grass, wax white in the neon light, nothing remains but the almost invisible impress of a human form on the grass. The man has *dissolved*. The shot of the grass is immediately followed by Thomas' upward look toward the rustling sound overhead, then a lingering shot of a leafy branch, waving in the dawn breeze. Thomas looks down again, at the ground where the body lay; nothing there but grass. Then a medium shot of Thomas, looking about as though wondering where the body could be; around him bushes and leaves quiver in the wind, answering. The meaning, the image, could not be more plain, evoking as it does all the old great texts of human transience.

As in Homer:

As is the generation of leaves, so is that of humanity. The wind scatters the leaves on the ground, but the live timber burgeons with leaves again in the season of spring returning. So one generation of men will grow while another generation dies. . . .[9]

Or the Psalms:

As for man, his days are as grass; as a flower of the field, so he flourisheth. For the wind passeth over it, and it is gone; and the place thereof shall know it no more.[10]

Or, perhaps most pertinent of all, in Leopardi:

. . . E come il vento
odo stormir tra queste piante, io quello
infinito silenzio a questa voce
vo comparando: e mi sovvien l'eterno,
e le morte stagioni, e la presente
e viva, e il suon di lei. . . .

(. . . And when I hear
The wind come blustering among the trees,
I set that voice against this infinite silence:
And then I call to mind Eternity,
The ages that are dead, and the living present
And all the noise of it. . . .)[11]

The bright chromatics fade into the graininess from which they sprang. The graininess guarantees the reality of what we see—the abstract documentary fact conceded beneath the colored representation. This is what Thomas' decoded text and the world "out there"—the reality which is prior to him and his text but which includes both—have together revealed.

For him, too, the photograph, like Bill's painting, points to a muddle, a mystery in which no pattern is at the time perceptible; but now the meaning emerges in the grainy uncertainty of experience.

Death *emerges;* and from that moment Thomas is a changed man. His pace as he returns to the studio from the park is solemn, slow; the old restlessness is gone; the face is serious, even sad. In the exquisite coda to the film, Thomas' new, and therefore precarious, consciousness of transience and mortality is juxtaposed with the players at their Game. Here, the whole film converges. The ragging students with their harlequin costumes, squealing Landrover, and dead-white masks—by now we should know them. They are the murmuring pot smokers and raucous drinkers at the party in the fashionable house in Chelsea; they are the party-colored zombies of the rock session at Ricky-Tick's listening to the Yardbirds doing "You ain't gonna see no more my kind," and then struggling furiously for possession of the broken guitar stem. They are the sleepy, mod-garbed models in Thomas' studio swaying to a pop tune, and they are also, I think, the two teenyboppers. Typically, Antonioni enjambs the climactic stages of Thomas' photographic detective work with the sudden irruption of the two teenyboppers. The scene is crucial to the tempo, but also to the meaning. "The sequence is neither erotic nor vulgar," Antonioni said. "It's fresh, light, and—I hope—funny. . . . I needed this scene in the film."[12] Rhythmically and structurally the scene again juxtaposes the contrast stated in the opening credits of *Blow-Up*.

Before the teenyboppers' entrance, Thomas' mood is intensely serious. In contrast, the teenyboppers recall the unconscious merriment of the carnival city and the Games of the ragging students. The point, I believe, is *gaiety*, a kind of puissant grace, not frivolity. If the Game is viewed as mere illusion and superficiality, it loses its point as a contemporary "dance of death" under the shadow of the bomb. As the filmmaker said:

> The young people among whom my film is situated are all aimless, without any drive but to reach that aimless freedom. . . . They must suffer, I guess, but I'm sure they suffer for reasons very different from ours . . . never romantic. . . . Maybe it is also a legitimate way to get nearer a happier condition of life. Who can tell?[13]

Antonioni is, of course, more articulate with images than with words, but his words suggest that, although he does not wholly share the mood of his carnival maskers, he grants their games a kind of dignity, tangible as animal gaiety and pathos. The literary viewer should be wary of letting his preference for the moral and tragic over the comic, for the depths rather than the surface, confuse the point. *Blow-up* is *not*, I believe, a Pirandellian meditation on appearance and reality. It is an account of the experienced world *being* experienced precisely as it appears to those who continue to

experience it and to adapt or evolve accordingly. What one once took for solid reality is painfully superseded; it was never an illusion, but an aspect of a reality-that-changes, that discloses itself to eyes prepared to accept disclosure. "I've always wanted," said Antonioni, "to make . . . a mechanism not of facts, but of moments that recount the hidden tensions of those facts, as blossoms reveal the fact of a tree."[14] "The director's problem is that of embracing a reality that ripens and consumes itself, this reaching a point and then advancing, as fresh perception."[15]

So in *Blow-up* reality ripens, at least for Thomas, a typical Antonioni protagonist in the process of becoming an individual. From his viewpoint that world which he once shared with the mod collective can be said to be a shared illusion; he sees what the collective is organized not to see. But this does not mean that their world is an appearance and his a reality. They are linked by process, by becoming; the blossom can no more disavow the bud than *now* can disavow *then*. Thomas is a man changing—moving away from the collective style of his own "bomb-culture" generation represented by Thomas, Patricia, Bill, Vanessa, Ron, the young woman in the antique store—moving away from and then toward a perspective that is individual and, in the large sense, moral and tragic, perhaps even obsolescent. Like almost all of Antonioni's protagonists—Mark in *Zabriskie Point*, Locke in *The Passenger*, Giuliana in *Red Desert*, Lidia in *La notte*—Thomas *becomes* a "loner"; the experience of solitude and death has individuated him. He is also the observer, and as such, is carefully contrasted with the others, who are participants. When he asks the stoned Ron to go with him to the park, Ron replies, "I'm not a photographer," to which Thomas emphatically replies, "I *am.*" In the coda we see him watching the improvised game of mock tennis, but watching it apart, *alone*, at the corner of the court, while the others are grouped *together* along the fence at the other end. The accurate observer is denied the privilege of playing the game, or of playing without a certain detachment. In part, Thomas is alienated from the Game by his discovery of the murder; but his professional role, if taken seriously, imposes upon him another optics, a different perspective, which isolates and individuates.

In the scene with the teenyboppers these two perspectives are starkly juxtaposed, partially in and through Antonioni's use of color. Before the arrival of the teenyboppers, Thomas develops his negatives with mounting excitement and seriousness. His mood is matched by a significant chromatic shift. As fashion photographer he works in *color*, but in the flophouse and the blow-ups of the murder he is the "documentary" photographer, working in black and white. More and more, after he develops the negatives, black and white gradually displaces the brilliant chromatics of his world. Slowly but surely, the Carnaby Street colors are abandoned for the matte colors of nature—olive green, dun, sepia, navy blue—which belong to that suppressed reality, now emerging in its own right, in its "true colors."

The film's action, compressed within a single day, unfolds in natural

chromatic sequence; we move from sepias and the gray dawn light of the flophouse, through the morning (studio, antique store, and park) to lunch with Ron; then through the afternoon (scenes with Vanessa and the tee-nyboppers; blowing up the negatives) and the evening (the park, the rock session, the Chelsea party); and then the half-light of the dawn scene in the park, and the coda at the tennis court. Thomas is shown moving *professionally* from sepias to brilliant color and finally to black and white. This chromatic progress is indicated by his various changes of clothes. In the flophouse he wears dingy beige trousers, a ragged black jacket over a deep purple shirt. When he "shoots" the first model, Verushka, he prepares for it chromatically by removing the jacket; in purple shirt, he sinks erotically into the black-purple world of the backdrop chosen for the shots; the session "consum-mated," he drops down, sated, into the gray-lavender couch. Then we see him shaving and dressing: sky blue checked shirt, white trousers. When he leaves for the antique store, he wears a jacket, dark navy or black according to the light. In the park at night, when he goes to verify the reality revealed in his black-and-white blow-ups, he is a figure wholly defined, except for his hair, by black and white.

Humanly and professionally, he literally advances into a *darker* world, into his own documentary. In terms of Thomas' customary chromatics, it is a new dimension—a black-and-white world in which color is, as a matter of principle, suppressed. The documentary photographer—like the painter who etches or draws, renouncing the sensuous distraction of color in order to stress form and line—works in the medium appropriate to what he has to say. And so Thomas indicates his choice by dress as well as by selection of decor and environment. According to the director's guiding principle, peo-ple tend to express their internal world by situating themselves in an exter-nal world—a place, an arrangement of furniture, a geography—which con-forms to, and therefore reveals, their interior "landscape." Just as Thomas reveals himself by entering the park, so he discloses himself by his choice of color and clothing. And the growth in his own certainty, his sense of "finding himself," is conveyed by the gradual *convergence* of behavior, dress, time, professional purpose, and sense of identity. That gradual convergence corresponds to his own developing sense of identity, new self still forming, inchoate and uncertain; and the integration achieved in turn explains how he gradually acquires the strength to resist the temptations to which he is subjected.

The teenyboppers are distraction and temptation. But the point of the diversion is to make us see, through violent contrast, how matters stand with Thomas, not only his seriousness of purpose but also its precarious-ness, its liability to distraction. Tonally, the contrast is obvious. Thomas, tensely involved in what he is discovering, answers the bell, expecting the caller will be Vanessa. The teenyboppers' giggling girlish exuberance—their busy stripes, a flurry of fluorescent panty hose—is contrasted with

Thomas' seriousness, mirrored now by the studio, hung everywhere with huge black-and-white blow-ups, framed by white wall and black girders or beams. The contrast is made and then, revealingly, dissolved, as we see Thomas lured out of his new seriousness back into the Game—acted out by the teenyboppers and Thomas on the warm sea-violet "bed" of the crackling backdrop of no-seam paper. In an earlier scene the model, Verushka, poses against the black-purple backdrop paper, as does Vanessa; so here, too, Thomas "sinks" into that spectrum of lavender-violet-purple which, lightened or darkened according to the occasion, is designed to suggest immersion in the erotic, in "oceanic feeling."

The whole sequence of sexual rough-and-tumble on the violet paper is meant to convey the sense of animal high spirits and childish gaiety. Nothing is salacious or offensive about it; the dominant note is childish play, animal hilarity. For the first time in the film we see Thomas *laugh*, really laugh, like a child. The naked teenyboppers turn into mermaids frolicking on a crackling violet sea; then the twosome turns into a threesome (as in the "paradisal" sequence of copulating couples and trios in the Death Valley sequence of *Zabriskie Point*). The whole scene is intentionally amoral, not immoral: there is no moral consequence to a tumble in the waves between two teenage Nereids and a would-be frogman. The sequence simply *happens*; and it happens without aiming at, and without winning, a meaning. It aims, in fact, at registering a kind of innocence possible only to those who have renounced the habit of needing (or making) a meaning; who, like the animals, simply *are*. The two nymphs, like the carnival world generally, ask no question of existence and expect no answer. They dance, play, or make love, unconsciously and compulsively, swaying to the beat, *with* it; never, like Thomas when he advises Vanessa to move as he does, "against the beat," thereby savoring not only his consciousness of the beat but also his ability to resist it. He can move with it; more important, he can move *against* it.

That these contrasts and countercontrasts are the essential purpose of the teenybopper scene is confirmed, I believe, by the final shot in the sequence. Thomas is seated on the paper, the two girls are putting on his shoes. But his eyes are riveted on *something* beyond him, his face taut and serious. Then he rises, takes the magnifying glass, and moves forward to examine a detail in the blow-up hanging on the wall. He has suddenly intuited the crime, the murder toward which his backward reconstruction has been pointing. The sequence with the teenyboppers turns out, in retrospect, to be an interlude, a distraction in which he has apparently lost himself. But all the while the question, the problem raised by the photographs, has been, as it were, germinating. Brusquely, he leaves the two girls. And, as he stands there inspecting the blow-up with his magnifying glass, the frame is divided equally between the black-and-white photograph and the primary colors of the sophisticated, childlike painting on the wall. In

one superb summative image we are given a "recap" of the teenybopper sequence—the childlike, colored world in which Thomas once lived, and to which he momentarily reverted, only to move back firmly toward the "other" world, that unknown black-and-white dimension that indicates a different order of reality. The Game is reenacted: first with the two young women; again in the rock session and the struggle for the guitar stem; once again when Thomas succumbs to Ron's beckoning at the Cheslea party; and finally at the tennis game. Each reenactment reveals Thomas' regression under temptation, but also his insistent advances, his movement away from the colored Game to his encounter with black and white—with solitude and death. Thomas is *ripening*, changing.

Look now at the coda—the mimic tennis match, with its schematic but metaphorically dramatic confrontation. Here the whole film converges.

We see Thomas, from behind. His camera dangling, he descends from the upper park: a glimpse of the vehicle roaring by below. Then the camera moves back and forth, from different angles, until Thomas and the vehicle intersect near the tennis court. There the players, holding imaginary rackets, are volleying an imaginary ball. The man misses a return, slams down his racket, his gesture recalling that of the frustrated guitarist at Ricky-Tick's. In the background we see a number of students grouped along the fence. Thomas, as though to separate himself from them, walks to the far end of the court. He stands there, alone, camera dangling, outside, looking in. Hold on Thomas. Then a long shot of the players. Then, again, the Ragweek students clustered along the fence, eyes swiveling, intensely absorbed by the game. The camera proceeds to explore the relation between the players, the watching students, and Thomas, picking out the details of a whole. More and more purposively the players strive to engage Thomas' perception, to coerce his participation. The man slams wildly, the "ball" hits the fence, the watchers recoiling as it "hits," while Thomas watches. A sad, sympathetic smile, expressive of his amused detachment, passes over his face. His eyes move to and fro, watching the resumed game. The players continue their efforts to involve him: *he*, not yet claimed by their "game," is their real audience.

A medium shot of Thomas from behind, watching. Then a shot of the whole court, a dark mulberry color. The woman feigns missing a return, turns toward the fence to retrieve the "ball." She shrugs at Thomas, as if to say *c'est la vie!* Then a medium shot of Thomas, from behind the young woman. Diffidently, he acknowledges her gesture. His detachment is explicit in the next shot: Thomas, standing alone at the corner of the court, apparently is no longer looking. The game is resumed. Then a shot of the watchers *as a group*, then Thomas standing alone at the corner, isolated. Hold on the group. Now a long shot from behind Thomas—his perspective—of the woman and man volleying. Thomas watches with mild interest. The male player hits a high ball that arches over the fence, followed by the

camera to its stopping place in the grass. The girl runs up and imploringly asks Thomas to shag the ball. At precisely this point the students make their supreme effort to draw him into the "game," to involve him. As audience, he is crucial to the meaning, the *reality* of their illusion, their performance; alone and isolated, he threatens the collective make-believe. But, because he is alone, he is also vulnerable, and, as a result, he is lured to comply. Loping after the invisible ball, Thomas hefts and returns it.

We have seen him succumb to the lure of the Group and its Games before: with the teenyboppers in his studio; in the frantic struggle over the broken guitar stem at Ricky-Tick's; and at the Chelsea pot party. Now, in the coda, all of these earlier efforts by the Players to draw Thomas into their Game are recapitulated, but this time there is a discreet advance in his individuation. Here, if he succumbs it is only briefly, perhaps because he is stronger, more loyal to his perceptions and experience, by virtue of having been so overwhelmingly tested and tempted.

The lure of the Game is extremely powerful, its pull indicated not only by Thomas' susceptibility to it but by the intrusion now onto the sound track of the *sound* of the nonexistent ball hitting the gut of the nonexistent rackets. We hear the power of the illusion that has tempted him, once again, to succumb to the Game. The sound grows louder, more insistent. A close-up of Thomas' face: a very faint smile, sad and gentle. The eyes continue to follow the volleying of the nonexistent but persistent ball. Then the whole face saddens, the smile disappears, and slowly, very slowly, the eyes look down. Down at the grass, the ground from which, in the opening credits, the film arose, like an aperture opening in the earth, and to which it returns in the park scene earlier. His eyes look down, down at the reality which is now his, and which, like the ultimate blow-up—that grainy, coarse moldering into the humus—*defines* him and claims him. Then the final shot, confirming the discreet change in the photographer's status: Thomas, a tiny figure, in black and white, seen from high overhead, in human scale at last—a small, transient form against the sea of environing green. He stoops to pick up his camera—a changed man, a changed photographer—his last action before dissolving, like the murdered man's body in the park, into the grass beneath him. Below, in black, the legend—THE END—appears on the green field. Above it, *BLOW-UP* then fade.

Zabriskie Point

The decision of Daria—on her way to meet Rod, the Sunny Dunes developer—to detour and see Jimmy Patterson and his kids is characteristically ellipical, so elliptical, in fact, that I have heard intelligent critics complain that Antonioni could at least have gotten his geography straight before doing an American film. Yet Daria's decision to *turn* is clearly there, stated in a few glancingly allusive but sufficient frames. From overhead we see the looping cement arteries of the freeways reaching purposively into the desert: out from L.A. to Riverside, then past San Jacinto and down into true desert, with Palm Springs, then the Imperial Valley, and beyond them, Arizona. We see Daria stop at the stop sign, reach for a map, trace out a road, and then turn north, off the freeway, which means off the beaten path, striking out on her own—as she does so often—against the imposed and arbitrary routing. The casual spontaneity is revealing; it tells us something about how Daria lives, swaying with her impulses and feelings, in unison, just as we see her later, in one of the most lovely scenes of the film, after she learns on the car radio of Mark's death, swaying like a keening Indian, her back to the camera, facing her green talismanic world, those desert shrubs, mesquite and jacaranda, that are also swaying softly in the wind. This is her life and rhythm, of course, as flower child, smoker of grass and bearer of seeds, the role confirmed by the pothead escape song we hear playing on her car radio:

127

ANTONIONI

Brother Mary . . . Trust in Harry
He don't care what the people say
He's getting everything together
Telling everybody gotta get away
Leaving in the morning at the break of dawn
Carrying a pocket of seeds . . .[1]

But as a flower child she is also clearly linked to many of Antonioni's protagonists: to Vittoria in *Eclipse*, with her fossil flower and affinity for leaves, made clear in the scene where she caresses the photos of a baobab tree and of the Zambezi Falls; to Giuliana in *Red Desert* with her blues and earth greens (*celeste e verde*, the original title of the film); to Thomas in *Blow-up*, who is lured by a kind of secret purposiveness in the green peace and moving leaves of the park; or even to Lidia in *La notte*, moving toward the green of the suburbs (her own past), where we see her leaning against a tree, listening to the life beneath the bark and the sap rising from the rhizome, deep in the ground. The personal life rhythms of the individual, his or her pace, the sense of an affinity with a larger, prior life, even an openness toward a suppressed reality—all these things are declared, elliptically, but with revealing persistence, by Antonioni. Elliptically because in some sense these manifestations are not so much unconscious as preconscious, tied together by a subvocal affinity revealed in gesture and movement and expressive silence. The character declares what he is by what he does, not what he says. NO WORDS says the motto on the painted airplane. Character *is* destiny, but the destiny reveals itself as destiny by being subvocal and silently purposive. Observe Daria on her detour, or follow any Antonioni character on one of those walks, or trips, or journeys, and then watch the passage itself—the style of movement, the revelation of self in the choice of destination, in swervings and pauses in his pace and tempo of feeling, tensed or relaxed, in the affinity for textures and landscapes; observe an Antonioni character take his walks and you have, in completely cinematic terms, the revelation of his nature and destiny.

So it is with Daria. We see her pause and then swerve; a silent decision to make a detour from the route to Phoenix. She herself is dressed in green; a matte green, earth green; a turquoise bracelet and rings; a Navaho turquoise necklace, and a red-green Sioux bead belt. These articles are her declaration—both youth-cultural and personal—that she is temperamentally Indian, that it is not the city but the desert Southwest, its life, that is her psychical habitat. She is not, I think, shown as a stereotyped flower child, with sympathy or hostility, but simply as a phenomenon in whom a common cultural style finds congenial individual expression. She is now, as she swerves, doing precisely what her instincts tell her to do—to escape the city, to go into the desert. But she doesn't really *want* to go to Phoenix (or rather, Carefree, a development–resort about thirty miles north of Phoe-

128

nix), and this is why she swerves. The whole point is in the turning; she turns at the *turning point*, and her action expresses both positive and negative volition. She desires the desert, for which Jimmy Patterson and his kids provides the pretext (even flower children need pretext, especially those who work for outfits like the Sunny Dunes Corporation). She wants to escape L.A. and to defer her arrival in Phoenix, that Arizona colony of L.A. and of the Faustian developers of Sunny Dunes.

Antonioni has said that what he hoped to achieve with his characters in *Zabriskie Point* was a sense of "rich interior life," and the dictum has puzzled his critics. Yet I think it is precisely this kind of complex and elliptical interior life implied by gesture, nuance, and action that he had in mind. This may be, at least in part, why the script is so monosyllabic and often banal; and why the faces of the two main actors are so disturbingly deadpan, lacking in that physiognomic richness and delicacy so apparent in the earlier films, especially those done with Monica Vitti, who was to Antonioni what Liv Ullman was to Ingmar Bergman, or a Stradivarius was to Paganini, that is, an instrument of astonishing expressive virtuosity. (Monica Vitti may not be, by ordinary standards, a great actress; but Antonioni's vision required not a great actress or one with conventional good looks but a certain kind of face capable of expressing, in extremely subtle and mostly subvocal richness, what the director's vision required: a physiognomy which, in its affinity with leaf and light, in its ability to suggest the awakened life of all the senses in harmonious ensemble, could suggest the power of a buried life and a suppressed reality.) In the case of *Zabriskie Point*, it is at any rate worth asking whether Antonioni, a specialist in physiognomy, did not intend Mark's face to be as impassive as it is, so lacking in expressive subtlety, with such deadness of effect. Thomas in *Blow-up* has a face which, except for the eyes, seems undeveloped, as though the overdevelopment of the outsized eyes had stunted the body and the face. Jack Nicholson in *The Passenger* seems to have been selected precisely because his blandness and inexpressive deadness of feature suggest so convincingly the look of a man in desperate need of an identity, the archetypal hollow man, who lives, vampirelike, on a borrowed life.

As for the script of *Zabriskie Point*, it is often clumsy and wooden; but the very banality, I suggest, is at least partly intentional. In the first place, the banality is realistic; youth culture of the sixties was not renowned for its distinction of language and style; second, the effect of the banality is to emphasize the technique of ellipsis (NO WORDS), to drive inarticulate motivation inward and express it as action. This means, of course, asking more of both director and audience as well as placing great weight on the visual images and the emotional chromatics created by the film. If we ask—as we must—why Mark returns to L.A., we will not find it in the script. The script tells us only that he has made a conscious decision; the motivation is in the

sequence of visual images and the intricately developed intersection of the different worlds of Daria and Mark.

An example. When Mark arrives at the airport, we watch a small corporate jet taxi up. The executives, assured and confident, like Rod,[2] disembark, and the camera holds on the black hole of the roaring pod, as though the deafening sound were the sound of power itself, a controlled but potentially lethal violence. Then we see Mark, his face lowering and impassive, sullenly inexpressive. Behind him we see, surely not put there by inadvertence, the blazing red strip along the nose and wing of a plane. Behind this red in *Zabriskie Point* stands a whole series of earlier, inflected reds—red fans turning overhead while a siren wails, the police cars with their blazing red blinkers, the blood on the sidewalk, the bloody banner lifted aloft. The common denominator of these reds is violence. And it is this red we now see as the chromatic inflection of Mark's look—a sullenness reddened to hatred, the hatred expressed not by the face, which is impassive, but by the red background. It is at this point, I suggest, that Mark decides to steal a plane; why should he be denied what these executives possess? Hatred motivates the theft; hatred as remembered violence, remembered red. So we see decisions forming as in real life they *are* formed. A feeling is defined by a context, given urgency by it.

Mark's trip to the airport begins as we see him running away from the campus, while all around and behind him a band of greenery, green leaves. The green is shelter and safety, the green is life. Then the green leaves are metamorphosed into a green light which gradually defines itself as the antiglare glass of a bus that Mark has taken. He hides, head lowered, in the cool comfort of that green light. He rides the bus to the end of the line, the honky-tonk strip near the airport. He hasn't gone to the airport on purpose. Overhead, the huge sign FLY UNITED. LET'S GET AWAY FROM IT ALL makes its imperative suggestion, and we see him suddenly walk, with a clearly purposive stride, toward the airport. But not, I think, with the idea of stealing a plane. Not yet. The theft of the plane is, like the decision to take flight—he doesn't know how, he has no money—impulsive. Executive privilege, remembered reds, the image of raw power—these precipitate, in this fundamentally middle-class dropout radical, the decision to "borrow" a plane.

But advance just a little further into this chromatic motivation. We see Mark standing beside a row of small private planes, then an overhead long shot, which shows the different colors of the ranked planes. Passing by a handsome black-and-white plane, Mark stops to examine a pink plane called Lily. Why the pink plane? The answer is given us later, as we watch the intersection of Mark and Daria in the desert. Her car is a sun-faded lavender, once purple. Why? Because it fits without incongruity into the ocher, then pink and lavender of the desert; because she—unconsciously, that is, chromatically—fits into the world into which she *consciously* detours.

Mark's plane is pink for the same reason—it matches all those rosy pinks of the desert. We can say, if we like, that the director has himself chosen the colors because they suit his chromatic and thematic purpose. But he *shows* us Mark choosing the pink plane and in this way tells us something of Mark's state of mind, his desire to escape the city whose colors are blazing, aniline primaries. His initial escape is by choice of color, a color that declares, by anticipation, his desire to get off the ground and lose himself in the desert over which, with a kind of random but secret purposiveness, we see him flying. There his course intersects with the lavender car, which Daria borrows for her trip to Phoenix, but then suits to her deeper inner purpose. Once arrived at Zabriskie Point, we see them insert themselves ever deeper into the environing reality of that lavender-pink world, following it down into the dust-colored ochers and whites at the bottom of Death Valley. Only there are they secure from the hot, noisy chromatics of the city.

Just as park and center city constantly intersect in *Blow-up*, so too in *Zabriskie Point* do we see the desert reach into the city (the synthetic adobe of Rod's office, the token cactus), and, correspondingly, the city extend out into the desert (the road, the railroad, the loping verticals of the telephone wires, also the long bulldozed Faustian construction following alongside the road and then suddenly giving out). Even at the overlook of Zabriskie Point the city arrives. We see it in the glaring reds of the two toilets, in the bright blue of the nomadic camper, and again in the police car. It is against the violent background of one of those red toilets that Mark cocks his pistol and aims it at the cop. And it is his experience of the desert, with Daria, indeed his entry into Daria's world, that precipitates his decision to return to L.A. That decision is rendered entirely in visual and chromatic terms. We see Mark, defined almost wholly by the red wall against which he leans, as if he were all of one violent element. Then the camera shows us Daria, framed by the desert—earth and sky behind her; then Daria advancing, with sympathy and concern, into *his* frame of red; and then his partial entry into her world; then the emptying of the pistol and the couple moving off, away from the reds, into the frame of earth and sky. In *Eclipse*, similarly, Antonioni shows us the troubled relation of two lovers who live in different but briefly intersecting worlds. In that film the young man, Piero, says, looking at the unfamiliar meadow around him, "I feel like I am in a foreign country," and the woman, Vittoria, replies, "Odd, that's exactly the way I feel when I'm with you." In both films, polar geographies intersect, in brief transcendence, then separate. But the effect lasts, as we see Mark gentled by his contact with Daria, and then Daria, radicalized by Mark's death, returning to his world with the reds and oranges of the house she has, in hatred, exploded. But whereas in *Eclipse* the intersection of personal geographies is defined as much by words as by image, in *Zabriskie Point* the technique is wholly visual.

Return now to Daria, whom I left at the stop sign, about to detour

131

northeast into the desert. She has, we can see, no sense of time; there is no wristwatch on the arm we see when her finger follows the road on the map (as there is on Rod's hand at the wheel of his car). She lives in almost complete disregard for time; this indifference is personal and instinctive, however, not an external or elective lifestyle. Hence the telephone conversation between Rod and the boy whose car Daria has taken. *He* is stereotypical youth culture, systematically turning straight culture upside down, saying "Good-bye!" instead of the expected "Hello!"

Whatever else this film may be, it is not a sentimental advocacy of youth culture, any more than it is a radical or revolutionary film, or a hostile caricature of a vulgar America. As phenomenon, as mass movement, Antonioni gives both radicalism and hippie culture serious attention; the attention is clinical and also critical. But it is not dismissive; youth culture may have been a transient movement, but the movement is revealing. And Antonioni accords it the serious attention one gives to any phenomenon that expresses crisis or strain in the culture at large. If I am right, that crisis in American—and indeed Western—culture is represented here as the crisis of individualism in an emerging world culture or mass society, that is, in a society of institutions. The attitude of the director is, I insist, clinical and serious; *Zabriskie Point* is neither a sentimental jeremiad against technology or mass society nor an essay in the advocacy of alternative culture, like Charles Reich's *Greening of America*. Antonioni's attitude toward technology has always been ambivalent. Vittoria in *Eclipse* affectionately pats the nose of the small plane that takes her to Verona; she sits on the veranda of the small airport café, clearly at home in a world which still possesses a human scale, where the city seems to be a natural extension of plain and mountains, still in real rapport with the country world from which it sprang. The toy robot in *Red Desert* is in itself not frightening; what makes it frightening is the automatism—the android quality—of the irresponsible engineers and businessmen, the somnambulists, who created it. Here in *Zabriskie Point* we find the same ambivalence and the same realism. Our future culture contains no other possibility than mass society, that is, enormous aggregates of groups and organizations defined by bureaucratic modes of behavior. Frighteningly incapable of intelligent human control, these institutions seem literally autonomous, turning their putative managers into servants of their own social technologies. No less than mass organization, technology is our almost certain future; the problem is to ensure that the machines are made to the measure of man rather than the other way around. The crucial element, as always in human society, is control; but the very power of the technology and the complexity of the mass organizations make effective control and human scale more imperative, and also more unlikely.

Put it historically. Individuals now live by a creed of obsolescent individualism in a world whose mass and scale have dwarfed those who created that world in the first place. The individual is literally threatened

132

with his own demise, at least in those forms—aggressive, Faustian, willful, macho, exploitative—in which his individualism has, since the Renaissance, been expressed. At the present moment, the Faustian boom world of the late sixties, with its proliferating city, its self-exciting economy and mystique of exponential growth, seems less threatening, perhaps. But we should not confuse a lull with the end of the storm. The powers that have been gathering force since the Industrial Revolution, when technology and capitalism were bonded together in the most revolutionary event in human history, have not diminished but are merely less visible. And the cogency of Antonioni's analysis of our general, recurrent cultural crisis has not been rendered obsolete by the eclipse of the radicalism and youth culture of the sixties.

This film, I am saying, is no dated "period piece" (like *Easy Rider*, the film that MGM wanted it to compete with) but an exceptionally clear-sighted and concentrated account of a great crisis of modern culture. It is in large part because the individual is threatened with extinction by the manipulative and exploitative power of his own machines, managed by no controlling human hand—those machines for whose measure, he, man the measure, has increasingly been fitted—that political movements, subcultures, religious cults, erotic disorder, come into existence, all of them desperate and mostly unavailing attempts to impose human constraints and control of the autonomous machinery of an increasingly monstrous culture. With impressive clarity Antonioni shows us the failure of these movements along with the *reasons* for their failure—above all the fact that they are aggregates of individuals who cannot, precisely because they are individuals, bond themselves together long enough to accomplish a common purpose, which in any case they do not share. Worse, the potential leaders of these groups are precisely the most individualized, therefore the most distrusted by their natural followers; for, like *Zabriskie Point*'s Mark, they refuse to sink personal identity in organization and discipline, that is, to deny their own individuality by merging with the crowd from which they emerged. The mystique of the middle-class individual in the middle-class society, which above all honors the heroic individual as its founder, is strong. And in Mark, with eloquent ellipsis, Antonioni shows us how the mystique operates, how it translates itself into the ethics of individual action, all summed up in Mark's *acte gratuit*—his silent decision to return to L.A. and to take the risks to which his nature and history condemn him.

It is crucial to be precise at this point, to avoid seeing Mark's death as so futile that it is not seen as *revealingly*, generally futile; or alternatively, to suppose, out of our own mystique of individualism, that it represents a saving heroic assertion. Neither is true. I believe that Mark courageously decides to put his individualistic values to the test by returning to the city that professes to honor individual worth and to value life but which consistently—or rather, *in*-consistently, absentmindedly—dishonors it. The

133

test fails, and we are meant to conclude that the individualism that created the ethos in the first place is obsolete. Mark, too, is obsolete, like so many of the people in the film: the old-timer in the desert saloon; the derelict kids; the old prizefighter; in fact, all the loners. This conclusion does not mean, I think, that Antonioni sees the modern world as one in which individuals cannot exist, but rather that the old individualism, as a meaningful response to the great change in human life, is moribund or dead.

It is *that* knowledge which links together frustrated or angry individuals, like the student radical group at the beginning. Which links them, but does not *bind* them. For, composed as they are of individuals, they are politically impotent, incapable of real revolution. Experience, background, diversity of purpose, all divide them. It is this division, not unity, that the opening sequence reveals. One by one the camera picks out individual faces in a kind of visual demography of individualism. Angry and bitter blacks, well-meaning but ineffectual and innocent white liberals, a sprinkling of intellectuals, an Oriental or Chicano face—and Mark. The colors are a fantasy of oranges and reddish yellows, a kind of borderline violence and anger, that we will see transformed into the blazing yellows and oranges and firestorm reds of the exploding house at the end of the film. The sound track is a democratic cacophony, everyone talking at once, to small purpose; dying away in jokes and frustration. The camera tells a story of earnest ineffectiveness and the absence of galvanizing general purpose; even the blacks, who provide a kind of cadre united by oppression, are in the end drowned out by the discord of individuals (that revealing joke about *whose* car? *Whose* private property?). One student appeals to Lenin, Mao, Castro; but where is this group's Mao? And, so far as the whites are concerned, what is the bonding element but guilt? In the camera's clinical examination, we *see* the implicit futility of this meeting, and therefore understand Mark's contemptuous departure. For it is at just this point that Mark rises, bourgeois individualist that he is to make his individualistic assertion that he is *bored* with all these words, willing to die but not of boredom—and leaves. A marginal man, a dropout, he now leaves the meeting, on his way to dropping out of the Movement too, alienated even from the alienated.

And at this point the film cuts to another marginal loner, Daria, in the synthetic world of the Sunny Dunes corporate offices, trying to recover the book she left on the roof because she didn't want to eat in the cafeteria with the others—an action that renders her suspect to the security guard for whom, as for the police, individuality is subversive, a clear violation of the rules of the institiution, of the mass organization that he is paid to protect. The point is not, I think, to show the guard's *personal* hostility—though that is there—but rather the way in which this hostility derives from his service to an institiutional *ethos*. It is the mass—in this case the corporation—not its agents and servants, that declares the individual subversive. And if one turns to the putative leaders of the mass, like Rod, one finds only another bland

and decent face, no less controlled by the institution over which he presides than those like the security guard who also serves, but for menial wages.

By means of this crosscutting between the radicals and the Sunny Dunes corporate offices, the two worlds of the student radicals and corporate Faustians come into reciprocal definition. Apparently contrasted, the resemblances are the red paint. If the students are an ill-defined aggregate, the Faustians are well organized, with a hierarchical structure which leaves nobody in doubt about who has power—the power we see descending via the elevator from the top of the Mobil Building to the bottom, and sealed by the guard's studied servility toward Rod. Here is authority: Rod is the top man in this Faustian world. Later, at the level of the sky, his equal, we see Rod's head framed by the buildings he has built. Behind him is the American flag, and the green trees on the roof of the old Los Angeles Municipal Building; in this image we *see* the link between financial power and L.A., and via the flag, outward toward Phoenix and the nation. We see Rod enter the building, an impressive vertical; and we are meant, I think, to feel its vertical thrust, its scale and assault on the sky. Then, from roof level, we see Rod's easy, even affable, domination of the world below, his eye scanning the horizon for fresh worlds to conquer, even as the TV screens show us a helicopter scanning the desert for likely Sunny Dunes lots. The Faustian surveys the world he exploits from *above*; the Faustian looks down on the earth from a privileged, even godlike, overview. This is why we have so many shots of what might be called overview positions, so many Faustian command posts or Olympian aeries—the shots of the control towers at the airport; the overflying helicopters of developers and police; Rod's office; even the outlook at Zabriskie Point; and, most impressive of all, the developer's house[3] north of Phoenix, which surveys the desert below like a fort and, for all the talk about "fitting buildings to the environment," visible to the naked eye from miles away.

The camera shows us Rod's godlike status by a kind of fawning. Meekly, it accepts his domination and crawls under the desk, from where it peers up at him, groveling at foot level, the camera eye traveling up his body—as if it were one of those presidential abominations on Mount Rushmore, as though Rod were an American pharaoh. As for the world, the Jove-like Rod touches it fastidiously with instruments only (very much like the early Thomas of *Blow-up*, using his camera like a tool on the willingly prostrate model): TV and telephone; dials of weather and temperature and humidity; the clocks turning round and round on the TV. He speaks to his secretary through his intercom, and Antonioni shows us the diverse human reality—the secretary enclosed in a tiny closetlike space, the plastic divider pushing her almost out of the frame, while Rod scans the ample blue world behind him with his fingertips. It is an impressive sequence. Significantly, there is nothing demonological about it. Rod's manner is suave, affable, pleasant; Antonioni's point is that arrogance is so assured it has no need to

135

disable the irritability of more dubious power. It is directly godlike, completely poised, radiating confidence and ease. For Rod there are no contingencies against which he could possibly need a reserve of $30 million; for the developer there are no acts of God. For this man who creates lakes in the desert, who moves mountains and creates whole cities, there is only a world of rough material to be endlessly shaped according to his own divine Plan—a plan whose only purpose is to stimulate the need for more creations, a second- or third-stage genesis.

"Think?" he says in astonishment to Daria, when she tells him she wants to meditate; and his exclamation tells us that his confidence is born of suboptimal certainty. ("Suboptimal" is a splendid term in the jargon of engineering, which means to be efficient in the production of a possibly undesirable output.) Rod's world is the wholly suboptimal world of the developer who can create only according to a self-perpetuating and unthinking plan. Sunny Dunes is based upon desire for goods, above all; of the justice and compassion of the Ideal City we do not hear a word. The content of Rod's vision is, of course, made visible by the Sunny Dunes ads, with their plastic people and their stimulation of desire. A plan is good only when it excites a craving to possess what one does not have and presumably may not need. The message is consumption; synthetic individuality (buy a Sunny Dunes lot and become an instant frontiersman); a merchandised appliance paradise. Plastic products for a plastic world. Yet Rod himself has no desire to plasticize the world. This is the problem with the latter-day Faust; he is a decent fellow doing his own suboptimal thing, tending the massive autonomous machinery of a System whose only purpose is infinite proliferation. Once, Rod would have been the pioneering industrialist, the rugged entrepreneur; arrogant and exploitative, the slumlord god of a sweatshop world. But today he is only a decent, faceless manager, the human shape of a system that in fact rules him even in his aerie. As the black woman says in the opening scene, "The enemy is invisible. Things happen."

Things, in fact, are what happens, and we *see* them happening. Earlier I termed this economy "self-exciting," and it is Antonioni's point that even the managers are subject to the excitements they manage: addicted pushers of their own drugs. Everywhere, in fact, this world spews out its message of desire and consumption, as in the Sunny Dunes ad. In one scene we see a burly hard hat telling the storekeeper to put lots of mayonnaise on his sandwich ("I ain't on no diet, Mac"), and then, as Mark leaves, we see where the source of this desire for mayonnaise comes from—a huge sign for sandwich spread dwarfing the store. Daria's car radio blares a song about eating, and we see Daria obediently reach for an apple and start eating (just as in *Blow-up* we see the model, lying on the floor in *post coitum triste*, rise like an automaton at the ringing of a telephone in the distance). Rod's car passes under the American Airlines ad, with its image of a wristwatch on an arm, and its message: "Fly. Save time." And pat to this "signal," we see Rod

passively look at his watch, obedient to the imperative, and then, his jaw muscles clenched, he leans forward in his seat and steps on the gas. It is *things* that happen. There is no human control. Hence the bland, decent, torpid, mindless, innocent vacuousness of so many of these faces; they are not required to think, merely to consume. In this society, thought is subversive (hence the general anti-intellectualism, the fear of books among cops and guards). Hence, too, the general obesity, the result of that same imperative to consume. At Zabriskie Point the paunchy tourist with the blue camper, the fat wife, the ice cream–sucking kid imprisoned in glass, all are simply the expression of what this nomadic, restless world culture (for it is not merely American, as any intelligent Italian or German or Frenchman knows) does to human beings, shaping them as they once shaped it. Medieval man thought the world's wheel was controlled by Fortune, goddess Contingency. Renaissance man, like Marlowe's Tamburlaine, thought he, not Fortune, turned the wheel. In the modern world the wheel controls the pilot, spinning where it wills, permitting the helmsman only the illusion of a firm hand on the rudder.

And the ramifications? The infinite stimulation of infinite desire is a fatally divisive act, indeed a revolutionary one. The System spews out objects freighted with the only value there is, all other values being meaningless. Everything is charged with *desire*. It was at Watts, Antonioni declared, that he first learned that a refrigerator was a revolutionary object, being loaded with desire (like the guitar stem in *Blow-up*). Other objects of desire are clothes, cars, desert homes, food, consumer goods; hence Daria's explicit explosion of a refrigerator, a TV set, a clothing rack. She obliterates the desire-charged objects whose pursuit has divided the world, poisoned the atmoshpere (note the image of Mark, dejected, standing in traffic before a smog-inspection station), and desacralized the earth. It is this perspective, I think, that reveals most clearly the nonrevolutionary meaning of this film and subtly but effectively undermines the dignity and value of any political revolution that aims not at revaluing the world and making the machine responsive to truly human control but simply at ensuring a more equitable distribution of these desire-freighted goods. Finally, we see that the revolutionaries have accepted not only the values created by the system but even its methods. Revolution becomes a zero-sum game, in which all roles are bureaucratized. Mark's roommate fills out a mass-arrest form that the police have prepared in order to save time. Riot is processed like Spam, and prospective rioters oblige—in order to save time. Arraignments are thereby abbreviated, as a convenience to both lawbreakers and police; when one is dealing with great numbers, with a mass, the forms are bureaucratized. Mark is personnaly affronted by the policeman who tells him that his roommate's arraignment may take "five minutes or five hours." But the cop is telling the plain bureaucratic truth; arraignments can be speeded up if the arraigned man has filled out the appropriate form in advance.

That this is Antonioni's point—the depiction of a society bureau-cratized in order to deal with sheer numbers—is made clear in the simplest cinematic way. The booking scene at the police station, for instance, is introduced by a jump cut to the face of a secretary; the camera then pans across filing cabinets to a police typist at work. Numbers constantly spill out of radios and tapes in a vivid auditory demography of a mass society. Concomitant anonymity is everywhere, and the atrophy of the surname is so marked in these late films that the critic is constantly forced to use the actor's name because the character impersonated is so anonymous—we speak of Daria, or Rod, or Mark, or the Girl. The director's stress is on massed or syndicated action everywhere, contrasted with the plight of the forlorn and obsolescent individual. On the campus, for instance, the confrontation begins with a close-up of a gas mask—anonymity helmeted—followed by a medium shot of rows of creased trouser legs, then a long shot of the ranked and gas-masked riot police. There are no individuals here.

As for the relationship between the police and the rioters, it is dialectical, and the film insists upon our observing this fact. Polarization requires mass arrests and calculated violence. The purpose, as one student says, is to force the cops to perceive every student as a potential enemy. The polarization succeeds, and the violence at the police station (including the denial of *habeas corpus*, that quintessential individualistic writ) tells us that the strategy is successful. Mark's death is one effect of the dialectic. Some critics have said that Antonioni's film is flawed by a rhetoric of cops, a police demonology. This may, in part, be true; the police are very brutal. But the director, it seems to me, carefully distinguishes between the police when off duty and relaxed, as individuals (helmets off, laughing, chatting—or, most individual of all, in dying), and the police when on duty, helmeted and gas-masked, they dissolve into their group life and the individual disappears. It is this dialectic that provides everywhere the central dynamic—the way in which mass action threatens and obliterates all individual definition of value, whether in protesters or police. Each side, polarizing and polarized, becomes what it is perceived to be: inhuman, monstrous, *other*. As Mark returns in the plane from the desert, the airport is seen as peaceful, even gentle: a low murmur of human voices. Then everything is galvanized by the sighting of Mark's plane, and the police disappear behind dark glasses, which in turn fade into the blinking red eyes of the police cars. Instruments everywhere, as the noise gathers, and the human faces disappear into uniformed anonymity. Then the instruments take over: control tower, walkie-talkies, idling motors speeding up, sirens, helicopters—and then a gunshot and silence again, the sirens cycling down and fading before the human fact of death.

Finally, we should note what I have already hinted at—that Faustian men are far removed from the slightest moderating influence of environing nature. *Blow-up* closes with the photographer's discovery of his own human

eyes, and also of human transience, revealed to him in the park where he goes back to find the body gone. Nothing remains but the grass, and overhead the wind moving in the leaves, those leaves that, like men in Homer's great figure,[4] perish and return, generation after generation.

In *Eclipse*, simililarly, one of the ways in which Vittoria keeps her human balance is by holding to the perspective of prehistoric time contained in her fossil flower[5]—a flower to which she is linked but by a perspective so vast that she has no temptation, like her lover, to thrust men center stage and exalt mere present-mindedness. At least since *Il grido*, Antonioni's most persistent, perhaps his deepest, artistic purpose has been to create stories that tell, in terms of individuals and cultures, of this suppressed and most forgotten reality of our origin and the penalty—in accomplished inhumanity—for forgetting what we are, where we come from, where we go. For the Faustians of *Zabriskie Point*, success has completely broken the relationship that once, as pioneers and immigrants, the old individualists had with physical nature. Nature was once partner, or enemy, or friend, but it was *there*, the dominant fact of life, something that sustained them, or destroyed them. Today it has eerily vanished behind institutional systems. The result is that, as the earth has steadily receded beneath man, becoming simply *object* to his *subject*, he himself has become both less human and less individual. This is why the Sunny Dunes ads invite the frustrated city dweller, threatened in his individual and generic humanity, to become a pioneer again, to "bag a mountain lion" or to go quail hunting. The purpose is not so much parody as contrasting pathos—the intense *individual* appeal, marketed for mass consumption, of a vanished role, a lost quest, that can now be bought from those syndicated individualists we see in their corporate aeries, scanning the marketable earth.

Long, long ago, I left Daria just turning onto the road northeast into the desert. She is detouring toward herself, toward the landscape of her own psyche, and therefore away from the city. She moves in time, as well as in space, for this is a journey that will take her from modern L.A. to the bottom of Death Valley, 5 to 10 million years into the past. Everything confirms the director's intention to make total the contest of city and desert. From the thing-cluttered, noise-shattering world of L.A. (the roar of jets, the sign montage of corporate power and injunctions to consume) we move by degrees to absolute desert—a world that to a city eye like Mark's looks dead, but to Daria, a flower child, the same desert looks peaceful. The camera opens up to show us huge expanses not because they are beautiful but because they are empty of inhabitants. When we see the human beings in their environment, they appear in human proportion—tiny figures against huge landscapes of calm, enfolding space and time, or they are heard making human noises, shouting like children, in the surrounding silence. They play, too, like kids. Indeed, the whole journey from L.A., for both Mark and Daria, is filled with feelings of relief and then of childish

gaiety, culminating in the violently erotic and technological courtship of car and airplane, with its images of free flight. (Recall in *Blow-up* the frisky, bounding leaps with which Thomas first enters the park, leaving the city behind, chasing squirrels and pigeons with his camera, like any kid, free from school.) With each step down the road, Mark and Daria leave more and more of the city behind; as they walk around Zabriskie Point they take no property; indeed, they deliberately leave it all in the car—driver's license, credit cards, birth certificate—everything except a joint. They divest themselves utterly, and their journey down is a true regression into time, a passage down toward the buried fossils. This is not romantic primitivism on Antonioni's part. For any organism, as Freud tells us, the paradisal impulse is the hunger, when confronted by the terrors of being and becoming, for a prior stage of existence. Ontogeny recapitulates phylogeny—forward, or in reverse. Here we see it in reverse, a reversion which is contextually an effort to recover psychic balance by fleeing to the polar opposite of what is felt to be humanly, vitally, toxic. The aim of Daria and Mark's Zabriskie Point journey is to bring back the missing dimension, the lost or forgotten sentiments, the reality suppressed by the Faustian city.

That missing reality is essentially the earth life—the million-year-old life which *humans* share with plant and animal; and the lost sentiment is Eros, which the absolute city suppresses or sublimates, thereby redirecting it, by the dialectic I have described, into violence. Eros then becomes organized and syndicated aggression, that is, Thanatos, a force lethal to life. Eros and Thanatos, of course, are terms taken from *Civilization and Its Discontents*, Freud's classic diagnosis of the great governing malaise of modern culture. The presence of Freud's work is everywhere visible, as even a brief glance will demonstrate.

In this film, *Zabriskie Point*, Antonioni's only departures from realism are in Daria's two marijuana-induced dreams, each of which, in violation of Antonioni's usual practice, is accompanied by musical commentary—quite as if the director, by violating his own practice, were telling us that these scenes took place in some surreal, hallucinogenic or symbolic dimension. As indeed they do. But even here, I imagine, Antonioni is being loyal to the *real* power of pot, according to its users, to enhance and heighten reality, to "expand the mind." The only analogy to this scene in Antonioni's work, I believe, is Giuliana's paradisal fantasy in the *Red Desert*, which is introduced, less realistically, as a sudden eruption, during a moment of weak conscious control, of the contents of the unconscious. In *Zabriskie Point*, for a brief moment, we *see* what is in Daria's mind; she herself, as a kind of *clairvoyant*, gives us access to the public meaning of the symbols that, throughout the film, have been struggling to emerge, to make their epiphany. Daria's "visions" *reveal* what we, imprisoned in our routine, or unexpanded, world, would otherwise be unable to see, or incapable of seeing with such *apocalyptic clarity*. The visions are obviously structural, functional opposites, stand-

ing in clearly defined relationship to each other. Each vision multiplies reality exponentially (just as the Faustians constantly dream of exponential growth, an infinitely expanding population, boundless desires). And each of Daria's dreams, as opposite, informs the other with the help of its contextual source—the desert, in one case, and, in the other, the developer's house, also in the desert. The desert vision is of pure Eros, the unindividuated world (hence the trios and couples whirling, rolling on the ground, constantly combining, like so many Chimeras or hippocampi, into mythical and chaotic beasts); the human beings *become* animals, as well as the earth and each other, uniting with *everything* as far as the eye can see. The sequence closes with the whole screen going sand-colored, dust, a single matte sheet of continuous, unindividuated being. Man, alienated first from nature, then from other men, finally from himself, now fuses again with the ground from which he came, all estrangement overcome, in seamless unity with nature.

The opposed pendant dream of the exploding house is the expression of naked aggression, hatred, violence, against a house perceived as lethal. If we duly note that Daria, the flower child, has been radicalized—by her experiences at the developer's house, as well as by the news of Mark's death—into aggression at last, we should also note that the polarization of the world goes far beyond anything dreamed of by radicals. We should also note that what precipitates her flight from the house is the recognition scene between herself and the Indian maid at the foot of the stairs. A look, the beginning of a smile, *human* recognition, passes between them, and the maid disappears; imprisoned in glass, up the stairs. And at this point Daria suddenly recognizes herself as also imprisoned like the maid, indigenous but a prisoner in her own country, the desert. The flower child sees the house for what it is, the desert outpost of another invasion, even more lethal than the last—and she runs for dear life.

Then as Daria stops her car and looks back at the house, the camera looks back with her, returns to the house, choosing its details, carefully lingering, setting the explosives with scrupulous attentive hatred under the arrogant, Faustian house perched on the boulder, all these perverse desire-filled objects, and the endlessly talking, planning, decent developers, standing like gods, lovers, or children with a toy earth, standing over the landscape (again, the camera, under the table, groveling, looking *up* at the Faustian faces). Guns, violence mounted and framed, behind the developers. Back with Daria, a shot shows the desert quivering in the late light, a dusk breeze stirring the leaves of the plants, *her* plants, quiet, peaceful. And then the explosions, red and orange, picking up all the implicit violence of the film's beginning, and all the violent reds, the blood colors scattered everywhere by the explosion. Over and over again, with compulsive intensity the black smoke billows up into the mushroom cloud over the firestorm through which Daria vents her hatred, multiplied, a million times, onto the planners,

141

seen now as the enemy, a dehumanized, diabolized *they!* Then, with a kind of aesthetic relish, the director explodes objects—refrigerator, bookcase, swimming-pool chairs and tables, TV, clothes racks—explodes them into "thingy" abstractions. This, too, is chaos, but it is, unlike the chaos of the couples in Daria's earlier desert dream, a chaos of discretely *separated* things, an atomized world, not the organic world of the young woman's earlier vision. This chaos is pointillist—atomized points of light (like Bill's painting in *Blow-up*), and the slow motion with which the objects explode, while the sound track roars and screams, tell us that this is a gravityless world, that there is no more "up" or "down" because the earth itself is gone. The last object to be exploded is, appropriately, a bookcase filled with books. It bursts outward, like a Jackson Pollock painting, unfolding in whites, browns, and reddish blacks, with terrible intensity. "Knowledge is power"—this is the central Faustian text, hence the violence and beauty of this final image, with its memory of Marlowe's Faustus saying, "I'll burn my books," just before he disintegrates into elements and into the shattered limbs that the scholars discover the next morning. These final frames of *Zabriskie Point* are exquisitely beautiful, their images of disintegration as magnificent as the end of the world will probably be. Then the legend—THE END—and the screen goes black, black space, while the frightening music continues, and then stops.[6]

Let me set here some relevant passages from Freud's *Civilization and Its Discontents:*

Men are . . . creatures among whose instinctual endowments is to be reckoned a powerful share of aggressiveness. As a result, their neighbour is for them not only a potential helper or sexual object, but also someone who tempts them to satisfy their aggressiveness on him. . . .

This aggressive instinct is the derivative and the main representative of the death instinct which we have found alongside of Eros, and which shares world-dominion with it. And now, I think, the meaning of the evolution of civilization is no longer obscure to us. It must present the struggle between Eros and Death, between the instinct of life and the instinct of destruction, as it works itself out in the human species. . . .

It may be that in this respect precisely the present time deserves a special interest. Men have gained control over the forces of nature to such an extent that with their help they would have no difficulty in exterminating one another to the last man. They know this, and hence comes a large part of their current unrest, their unhappiness and their mood of anxiety.[7]

Clearly, Freud's text is central to *Zabriskie Point.* Civilization requires "aim-inhibitors" for sexuality and aggressiveness. In *Zabriskie Point*, by means of Daria's "mind-expanding" pot, these aim-inhibitors are removed in order that we may see aggressiveness and sexuality unmasked, naked. There Anto-

nioni, like Freud, leaves us. No prophecy, no consolation. Simply an image of the apocalypse biding its time, latently waiting.

There is much more, for films like this—in their ideas as well as in their aesthetics—are richly inflected. Structurally, for instance, we should note the extremely schematic treatment of the narratives of Mark and Daria, and their overlapping, mutually correcting meanings. Mark's painted airplane, especially its mottoes, deserves a long excursus—as does his decision to return—but the gist should be tolerably clear. It is, I suppose, a symbol—perhaps too much so; with too many meanings. Certainly the cops shoot at it in part *because* it is outlandish, a "monster" bird rearing and flopping around on the runway; it is *symbolically* threatening. Why? Because it obviously comes from a past in themselves, the disguised wilderness that they have only learned to shoot at, to destroy, not to recognize as theirs, not to live with (like the prospective Sunny Dunes residents, tempted with dreams of bagging a mountain lion). The face of our own unrecognized aggressiveness is not easy to look at, so we transfer it to nature, wild animals, or others—and once transferred label it "wild" with kindness or hatred, and put it in a zoo, or on a reservation, and there, in one way or another kill it, kill that part of ourselves which it is.

As he pilots his "monster" bird back to L.A., Mark's message to the Faustian city is meant in part to be humbling: long before we learned to fly, pterodactyls did it. The plane is also a reminder to the divided city of Thanatos about the unity from which all life was born, and of the proper role of Eros, which is to bind men together, not divide them by charging objects with murderous desire. Mark's plane also suggests the immense perspective of the human past, a phylogeny which is kin to the scales of fish and saurian, and to the sheath of green-brushed leaves we see toward the rear of the plane, enclosing the cockpit with a sheltering tracery of green. The flying beast has a mouth, too, with a playfully defiant tongue stuck out, like the protruding tongue of one of the Chaikin dancers in the desert; but the plane offers no words because it is a subvocal message from Eros, from the IT of HE-SHE-IT, and therefore polymorphically contains both sexes, with the breasts and testicles of our unindividuated, chaotic nature. And the "monster" bird is, I suppose, threatening, too, for it is above all the image or symbol of the reality suppressed by the Faustian city. One can call it the "unconscious" surfacing, but this seems to me a mistake, for the simple reason that the idea of the unconscious is an abstraction. It no longer connotes our underground, dream-surfacing terrors but buffers them with a veil of Faustian words. The director's purpose is to restore the cloud of images and symbols from which the unconscious was abstracted, to quicken them into fresh life, by renewing our sense of the fossil surviving in us, the swaying leaf, the long, slow ascent from sea and swamp to the primate and primitive so vivid in human blood and history. This, at least, seems to be the director's intent—the epiphany in monstrous but playful form of the sup-

143

pressed reality, so threatening to the Faustian city that it has, like all wild things, to be hunted and shot.

Long, long ago, I left Daria turning north and east into the desert, and I had in mind the principle that the part should bear the weight of, but also inform, the pattern of the whole. Look back now to the scene. Contextually, it provides an interim world, a halfway house between absolute city and zero desert, a place where those two symbolic geographies intersect. Daria, I suggested, was traveling back, regressively, into time, into her own indigenous country of green desert plants, carrying "grass" and, probably, seed. She arrives at Alistar, an old frontier town "a place of Arizona history." There, in a small building surmounted by one of citified country's agribusiness steers (automated meat), she finds the café where she calls Rod. There are two customers, both old-timers, each in his own way frozen in the past. One sits there listening to the Tennessee Waltz, oblivious to everything but the music and his dream; he is, as Daria's attempt to question him reveals, utterly alone. The other is the toothless wreck of a former prizefighter, an old time-humbled macho individualist, discarded by the society as useless, still another of the casualties that litter the landscape. He too is alone; it is a place of old people, used up and discarded; of junk and dead dreams.

Around the café spreads the desert, filled with the refuse of the city, derelict cars, trash, rubbish. This wasteland is filled with kids, themselves derelicts from the deathly city. Everywhere one has the sense of an *interim* world, half desert, half city. Across the middle of the screen in gaunt verticals march the telephone poles that connect Rod in his Faustian world with the desert and Daria. The desert spills into town as eroticism; as early as *L'avventura*, Antonioni was talking about the "diseased Eros of our time," showing it constantly, in epiphany after epiphany, as a force that devalues, by its own intensity and beauty, everything else. "Love makes an emptiness all around," says Valentina in *La notte*. In *L'avventura* the Sicilian unemployed stand, backs to the wall, ogling Monica Vitti—an image repeated in juvenile form here in *Zabriskie Point* as a ten-year-old boy looks Daria over with a cool professional eye. When the other institutions of culture fail, the erotic relationship takes their place—a fact which places an unbearable strain upon Eros, making it sick. So, too, here. Boredom and isolation create and bond this community of old and young derelicts—but city and desert alike impose their claims. From the city comes violence—the dialectic again— symbolized by the shattered plate-glass window in the café, echoing, deliberately, the shattered door seen earlier at the campus library, with the tear gas pouring out. Inside the café the old-timers, except for the café owner, are soundproofed against violence, locked in their private worlds. Across the generation gap the only communication is shattering glass. The old men are alone, alienated from each other. The kids, like the city world, are syndicated, united; all in a pack they assail Daria, tearing at her panties in a

strangely violent erotic play. Then, the panties taken, they fall to fighting over the spoils, as Daria, frightened, runs.

Aggression and Eros—this is the whole meaning of the town and the sequence—the intersection of Antonioni's two controlling terms, city and desert/Thanatos and Eros, as Daria leaves the little desert town and heads on to her encounter with Mark in the desert, with its strange mingling of technological violence and erotic play, and then on to the naked, unimpeded Eros, Freecome Valley, which is also, as an absolute form, a kind of Death. It is in the intolerable tension of those two terms, Eros and Thanatos, that Daria and Mark live their lives—a tension that can be avoided only by becoming infantile god in the Faustian city or animal in the zero desert. It is a hard choice; but, as Antonioni seems to suggest, the hardest choice of all is staying with the tension, remaining human.

The Passenger

If the doors of perception were cleansed
every thing would appear to man as it is: Infinite.
    For man has closed himself up, till he sees
all things thro' narrow chinks of his cavern.
                —William Blake, *The Marriage of Heaven and Hell*, plate 14

"This is a film," Antonioni commented, "about someone who is following his destiny, a man watching reality as reported, in the same way that I was watching him"—this to the interviewer—"in the same way that you are pursuing me. You could go back and find another camera watching me and another one watching the other camera. It's surrealistic, isn't it?"[1]

The surrealistic quality is, of course, deliberate, sustained with fastidious technical control throughout, in narrative, theme, dialogue, composition. Realities fold into one another; disparate geographies suddenly intersect, revealing the emergent "character" as the personal continuity, even the consciousness, linking these otherwise disconnected landscapes. People fade, disappear, or melt into each other, then reemerge, come into focus. Past and present overlap, as in the flashback via the tape voice-over in the opening scenes in the desert hotel, or in the flashback crosscutting

146

between Locke's London house and the wedding in the rococo church in Munich.

The shaping is schematic; the effect often ironic. Locke, following a white horse-drawn bridal cab—which might be a funeral cab—the wrong way down a one-way street, enters a cemetery to come upon a wedding, which in turn intersects with the death (fallen petals, burning boughs) of his own London marriage. The past lives the characters, the future keeps opening into the past. The destiny Locke is following is another man's, yet he can make it his own only because he is finally *not* the other man but himself—a new man emerging from the old. But his destiny lies *through* that borrowed identity. *Lui, c'est moi.*

Locke must lose himself before finally coming on a self that is, however inchoate and brief, finally *his*. Locke is a self dissolving, then forming. The others, it is suggested, are also partly interchangeable identities. "Are you still looking for Locke?" Rachel's lover asks her. In the dim corridors of Gaudí's neo-Gothic Palacio Güell, the Girl, disappearing, says: "People disappear every day." "Yes," Locke replies, "every time they leave the room." On the filmviewer Rachel and Knight watch the shots of an African witch doctor, filmed by Locke, who turns the tables on his interviewer by reversing the camera, turning it on Locke. Whereupon Locke makes the witch doctor's (and the director's) point by abruptly moving from between the curtains, *off* the frame, literally dissolving from view. Knight at the filmviewer, telling Rachel of *his* vain search for Locke in Barcelona, scores the point, saying: "He disappeared."

Or the same events are reported by different media, different observers, for different audiences. The camera itself makes autonomous assertions, from the point of view of no identifiable observer, as though to declare the presence of an unseen watcher, a camera eye/"I"—that sees what those it observes do not and so provides us with another perspective. It is this unknown observer that shows us Locke in medium shot by his sand-buried vehicle, then on his knees in frustration, and finally, as though to give that medium shot the wide-angled perspective of the desert, follows the direction toward which Locke kneels, panning on and on over the salmon pink desert. The same camera follows the black insects crawling up the light cord in Locke's bedroom, or the picture hanging over the bed in the Hotel de la Gloria. Nothing is quite what it seems to be; nothing is ever *all* it might be. The director gives us the process of Becoming itself: an iridescent, intermittent reality that defines itself by dissolving and then reforming, acquiring shape, texture, and solidity, according to a complex cinematic poetry of the unfolding world of the "given." Closely observed, with growing detachment, the sensuous solidities of routinely coded vision dissolve to reveal themselves in new and unsuspected ways, as though we had never seen them before. We see the object, but as through a looking glass: existing according to a different logic, in a surreal dimension. Beneath

the hatched outlines, as the perspective changes, detaching itself from the clichés of narrative and character, the real object begins to emerge. In the individual and idiosyncratic we begin to glimpse the generic; the infinite in the finite. The aim is that of any classically ambitious art—the disclosure of the full reality of things by fusion of "foreground" and "background," "here" and "there," time and the timeless. We see "with parted eyes, / When everything seems double." Past and present fuse; place and space coalesce into an all-inclusive "space"; the limited individual reveals the species' passion for transcendence; the bounds between life and death, body and soul, dissolve before us.

The source of this scrupulous doubling by the dislocated eye lies not in Antonioni's penchant for surrealism or Pirandellian "metaphysics" but in his own lifelong meditation on transcendence. Not transcendence in the philosophical sense but rather as the ego's passage beyond the limits of the self, its merging with, or dying into, the larger world, the "other" that lies beyond the ego.

In *The Passenger*, above all in the miraculous final "take," the director's persistent effort to give *visual* expression to the idea of transcendence culminates. But with a striking difference from the earlier films—a difference defined by the prodigious technical skills brought to bear upon its visual articulation.[2] Here, for the first time in Antonioni's oeuvre, the theme of transcendence takes on an overt, though typically understated, religious dimension. The point is crucial though it will doubtless be resisted by those viewers who have, quite properly, stressed the essentially secular outlook of the earlier films. But with *The Passenger* the religious theme is, however tentative, tangibly, powerfully present; the film will inevitably be underread or misread if the viewer imposes his own expectations or fails to confront the *fact* of the visual text. The religious theme is, in point of fact, an emerging theme of his work, as the director has himself stated. Four years after *The Passenger*, Antonioni began work on a film entitled *Patire o morire* (*Suffer or Die*); production was canceled at the last moment for financial reasons. The film would have been a transcendental story, or, as Antonioni said, one which would "fundamentally express the groping of the protagonist toward God—a protagonist who does not believe in God but is moving in that direction."[3] We should not, of course, confuse the director with his protagonist; *The Passenger* is the work of a firmly secular director characteristically curious about all human behavior, and above all the passion for transcendence, whether its expression is religious, quasi-religious, erotic, or technological.

The transcendence expressed by the earlier films is patently secular, and, for the most part, negative in its aspect as a metaphor or symptom of contemporary malaise, above all that of Eros. Insofar as it is positive, it produces that sense of tragic loneliness (sometimes mistakenly called "alienation") felt by the individual who refuses to surrender his fragile, emerging

148

"self" to the warm oblivion of Eros or to the embrace of the collective "One." But whether secular or religious, negative or positive, the idea is rooted in what might be called "the pathos of the self"—that pathos that hungers to escape the limits of the body and "burns a hole in our being without ever attaining its goal: true otherness."[4] An example would be *La notte*, where it is expressed by the desperate yearning of the party "sleepwalkers" to escape, through compulsive eroticism, the pain of individuality. The shimmering blank void of the black swimming pool lures them toward it, *into* it, just as the bubble of Roberto's car, sliding slowly through the rain, its occupants oblivious of everything else, sealed in each other, expresses its brief, doomed bliss. And in *Blow-up* it is the collective effort of the Carnaby Street crowd of "swinging London" to make Thomas forget what he has seen in the park—that individuating discovery of death; in *Eclipse*, the struggle of Vittoria's "imprisoned feelings" to escape the bars of their cell. Without exception every film repeatedly reports this yearning for transcendence, for escape from the pervasive solipsism of the modern self, estranged from all forms of traditional community, and to that degree its hunger for otherness intensified and exacerbated.

But there is another form of transcendence, which is a crucial theme in almost every film. If men transcend themseves by "dying into" others, a larger identity that promises to annul the pathos of self, there is also a Faustian form of transcendence—the yearning to sprout wings, or fins, to transcend mortality by *technological escape* into another world, even beyond this world; to experience the divinity of technical power. In the photographer's studio in *Blow-up* are two centrally placed photographs of a parachutist and a frogman—men changing, adapting, transcending themselves. The amateur rocketeers in *La notte* express the exhilaration of reaching out "for the moon"; in *Eclipse* it is the relief of escape as the plane lifts off from the troubled ground of Rome, making for Verona. But nowhere is it more perfectly portrayed than in *The Passenger* itself, in the image of Locke, liberated, he supposes, from the prison of his old self, leaning out of the cage of the cable car moving over the deep blue of Barcelona harbor, waggling his wings like a gull. The same idea of technological power as quasi-divine release from the earth underlies the film's concerns with cars and the theme of escape from "reality" symbolized by these prosthetic machines whose breakdowns at key points in the film trigger Locke's essential "decisions." Relentlessly, the director chops away at Locke's machines, his cameras and tape recorders, even his dark glasses, leaving him at last alone with himself to meet his death.

Technological escape is, in turn, linked to Antonioni's primitivist themes. Painfully conscious of his weakness and sterility, "civilized" Western man tries to revive himself by returning to his origins, to the primitive or past creature in himself, even the animal. Hence the African sequence in *Eclipse*; the girl in *La notte* embracing the flanks of a stone satyr; the obsession

149

with aphrodisiacs in *Red Desert*; the pterodactyl–airplane in *Zabriskie Point*; the nostalgia for the sea and the past in *L'avventura*. In *The Passenger* Locke's very presence in Africa—his personal need to make contact with the rebels fighting in the desert—tells us indirectly, as does the witch doctor directly, more about Locke than about the elusive rebels, for his desire to reach the rebels reveals his hunger for a vitality he does not himself possess. But Locke's *means* of making contact—that blue vehicle with its invasive roar in the desert silence; the tape recorder and camera; the media protocol of "factual" questions that prohibit meaningful response—these are the instruments of the transcendental Faustian. We know him by his instruments and by his reliance upon them. Locke is like Thomas in *Blow-up*; only when he abandons, or is abandoned by, his prosthetic devices is he capable of a different way of viewing and a different kind of transcendence. Hence the pointed failure of the Faustian devices at both the beginning and the end of the film—the image of the stalled vehicle repeated in the useless rented car with its punctured oil pan. When the Faustian equipment fails, Locke has an unmediated encounter with a very different reality—one from which every shred of social and cultural privilege has been stripped away. Just as Thomas in *Blow-up* learns at last to see, to use his human eyes, so Locke can confront death as a contemporary "unaccommodated man." You can learn most about a man, the film suggests, by looking at his luggage, not his personal history; so the film chops away at Locke's luggage, leaving him finally nothing but himself, the traveler divested of everything, and finally, even his passenger. In the final scene he is nothing but that self which, because he feared it didn't exist, made it possible for him to usurp another man's identity, which he then feels compelled to live, even at the risk of death, and so dies into himself.

Compelled to live, that is, all the way, "for better or worse." So, at first, it seems: for "better" with the money that liberates him in the cable car over the blue Barcelona water; for "worse" as he moves down his road, back toward Africa, to his fateful erotic encounters with the mysteriously coded ladies—Daisy, Marina, Lucy—of Robertson's appointment book. He watches his borrowed identity unfold and then, at the film's end, by active possession, become his own. Clearly, there has to be a self before it can be transcended. But the transcendence depends upon its being *seen*, upon our involvement in this unfolding destiny which is vicariously the viewer's also. We see different events, as through different cameras at different angles, all watching each other. First, a man living on borrowed papers—an existential Mattia Pascal[5]—becomes himself; then the same man, fulfilling the identity he has borrowed, transcends himself. *Lui, c'est moi:* we *see* it.

Here in *The Passenger*, for the first time, the director confronts the religious matrix of his various transcendental themes. In earlier films religion is merely a significant absence—for example, shots of empty churches whose emptiness is offered as a tacit, at times ironic, gloss upon the rituals

of Eros that have replaced institutional religion. Eros is ill because it must perform the tasks of all the dead or dying institutions of traditional culture—family, *paese*, and religion. This is more than Eros can do, a fact that deforms it into a compulsive neurosis. Emptied of its original religious and metaphysical source—escape from the self and its selfishness into a larger community, a higher fulfillment—its energies are diverted into mere serial eroticism, the desperate attempt to drown "one-self" in another's being, in the narcosis of pleasure, irresponsibility, oblivion. Being metaphysical or religious in origin, this Eros cannot be satisfied by surrogates. Locke wants to die as "Locke," to become Robertson; but gunrunning isn't enough; there is a subliminal spiritual purpose behind gunrunning—a mission, a "vocation," even.

This metaphysical quest cannot be evaded in dealing with a body of work like Antonioni's, whose master theme is "the fantasy of freedom," the radical need of the imprisoned self to escape its prison, to move beyond the "frame" that confines it, to *become* whatever in it is struggling to emerge. The classical text for this theme is the famous passage in Plato's *Symposium* where Aristophanes explains why lovers crave each other so desperately. Men were originally, he says, united creatures, bisexual wholes; then, because of our arrogance, we were divided, like the halves of a tally:

> And so, when . . . any lover is fortunate enough to meet his other half, they are both so intoxicated with affection, friendship and love; so intoxicated that they cannot let each other out of sight for a single instant. . . . The fact is that both their souls are longing for a *something else* [*ti allo*]—a something to which they can neither of them give a name, and of which they can only give an inkling in cryptic sayings and prophetic riddles.[6]

Ti allo. Something else—an X, some condition to which neither lover can give a name. It is discontented Eros craving this *ti allo* that Locke's search for a new self, a *vita nuova*, reveals, and that achieves such astonishing visual expression in the final sequence. Where the poetry is, there one finds the poet. Whether *The Passenger* is ultimately a religious film is not the real question; but Locke's "passion" must be understood in terms no less spiritual than those imposed by the script and the visuals. That "passion" is visually expressed in the film's last seven minutes as a literal passage of the soul or psyche through the bars of its cell, shown in language of such intense, wordless, kinetic purity that it is impossible to suppose that the director is merely aesthetically involved. The whole film seems, in fact, to have been made for this finale, for this visualization, vision even, of what Dante called *trasumanar*—the process whereby the human transcends itself and which, as Dante himself declared, is quite beyond the power of words to express:

151

ANTONIONI

> Trasumanar significar per verba
> non si poria; però, l'essemplo basti
> a cui esperïenza grazia serba.[7]

> (That *passing beyond humanity* may not be put into words;
> therefore, let the example suffice
> anyone for whom grace reserves that experience.)

In images but also in the narrative of a journey as an unfolding destiny, the film, shows Locke to be, in some unconsciously groping way, a transcendental man. In the life he borrows from Robertson, he discovers the secular residue of what would once have been a religious vocation. The point will no doubt be vigorously resisted; yet the religious nature of Locke's odyssey is suggested with an insistence that, for the usually elliptical Antonioni, propounds thematic urgency. This is not to say that *The Passenger* is an overtly religious film or that the director has renounced his earlier secular viewpoint. For whatever reason, the attentive viewer is required to come to terms with an account of human destiny that is both contemporary and secular, but also in some clear sense spiritual. It would be critically mistaken to insist on the primacy of either of these two accounts; the religious must not be reduced to the secular, nor the secular treated as though it were a mere gloss on the "deeper" spiritual account. At stake is the continuity of the transcendental impulse in *both* accounts; the way in which foreground and background, apparently discontinuous, intersect at a deeper level, and finally dissolve into each other.

At least twice the script alludes to the difficulty of shaking old habits—habits that persist beneath all efforts to adopt a new identity, to remake oneself. Smoking is an example, at the most trivial level. At a deeper level, the whole world of genetic and cultural inheritance, including the human disposition to violence and aggression. As the old man in the Umbraculo says to Locke: "Other people look at children and they imagine a new world. . . . But me . . . me, when I watch them, I just see the same old tragedies about to begin all over again. . . . They can't escape from us." The children are biologically *bound*. In the genes they inherit, the whole human past shapes them, *lives* them. The world of the foreground—*now*, the present and contemporary—has the appeal of boundless freedom, even infinity, about it. But the body that hungers for that freedom is a finite thing, limited by its past, by constraints of nature and culture, by its specific and generic habits, by its instincts. But also by its cultural conditioning—the social habits created by physical environment and habitat—the world of objects and products, of buildings, roads, language, gardens, billboards, customs, even articles of personal use, everything that is "luggage." Locke's deepest desire is to dissolve; he does so by doing away with everything that has hitherto defined him—all those objects, relations, and habits that com-

152

pose the artifact called "Locke." Inwardly he feels hollow, filled with an emptiness like the desert to which he feels drawn, emptiness to emptiness. There in the desert he dissolves, becomes Robertson. Stripped of the accidental, he can discover the necessary and essential—the life stirring like the breath of wind moving through the dead Robertson's room there in the expectant void of the desert. Locke is a dissolving man disappearing into the desert horizon; like Antonioni's characters generally, he declares his psychic reality by inserting himself into the apposite geography, a landscape and an emptiness like his own. He reveals his interior state by his journey. Destiny is destination. A man moves toward what he is becoming, as Locke moves persistently, even while wavering and retreating, toward the desert, just as Aldo in *Il grido* moves toward the great waste expanse of the Po Delta whose receding horizon expresses the *ti allo* concealed in his obsessive love for Irma. The journey is thus potentially dramatic, not narrative, expressing both what the disappearing traveler now is, but also the man he is becoming—the man "appearing." The "passenger" (Ital. *passagero*, a wayfarer, a transient-in-passage) declares his immediate psychic state by the landscape he seeks, but also by the fact that *something* is changing: he is drawn to a place which is himself but also "other" and more than himself—the tally of his own incomplete nature. The emptiness in him is pregnant with new life.

Locke in the desert of Chad is a man in transit, defined by a borrowed mission that partly expresses himself. He is a man in crisis, trapped in a dying marriage and a professional "success" that prevent him from changing or growing. The professional but also personal mission of this caged man is an encounter with unknown and elusive rebels struggling for freedom against what oppresses them. This mission, Locke believes, will give him, as a professional observer, a firsthand relation to reality. The rebels in this sense *are* Locke, what he wants to be—a man struggling for freedom. To Robertson he says that it is men, not landscapes, that interest him, but his actions belie his words. Locke's vehicle roars into the frame—the desert we see before and after the transient intruder, so sharply contrasted with the image of the majestic Bedouin floating silently by on his camel, at home in the desert—and, there where the road gives out, digs in. Then we see Locke enraged and frustrated—frustration in every gesture, the whole impasse of his life declared as he throws up his arms and shouts, "I don't care!" Then a medium shot, and we see him sink to his knees, arms stretched out before him, forehead touching the ground and body extended *away* from the vehicle toward the desert stretching on into the infinity lying beyond the frame. It is this reaching out that is now revealed—Locke reaching out toward the desert, and then the desert reaching out beyond itself, as the camera pans slowly, steadily, right. But it is in fact helplessness and resignation, even despair—the "death wish," one might say, of the "old" Locke—expressed by a ritualized gesture, and unmistakable salaam.[8] Slowly, trem-

blingly, following Locke's extended arms, the camera pans on and on over the infinity of apricot-colored dunes, forcing the viewer to see and feel this wide-angled immensity as a vast *otherness*. Later, back in Locke's hotel bedroom, the camera makes the same point in a tiny detail: an image of black beetles or termites crawling slowly up the electric cord on the wide expanse of whitewashed wall. As the wall diminishes the beetles, so the desert's infinity dwarfs the human being prostrate before it, in human scale, expressing for us, if not for him, a sense of his finitude and insignificance, even humiliation. His Faustian machine bogged down, Locke is suddenly humanly humbled, helpless, though perhaps not yet fully aware of the fact or of the meaning of his own gesture.

Later on, toward the close of the film Locke will half-consciously recognize his limitations and significance. His rented car broken down, he sits on the curb; behind him a white wall broken by a green-blinded window. We see him grope in the street, pick something up, place it against the white wall and squash it: a cochineal bug (no flower), a tiny red bloodstain on the white desert of the wall. The abrupt violence with which Locke squashes the insect shows that he *sees*, resents, but also tentatively accepts his own analogous fate, his transience and insignificance, even the extinction irritably enacted by his own hand. All this without a word. But it is this nonverbal acceptance, this acquiescing "decision," that gives the suggestion of a latent sacrifice; of Locke as a knowing, even willing (or perhaps will-less) sacrificial victim. His life may be irritably given, but it is, for the moment, given. Obedient to his unfolding fate—for his acceptance of it means that it is *his*, not Robertson's—Locke freely chooses to risk his life, even to sacrifice himself. Later, outside his window on the bullring oval of the plaza of Osuna, we hear, among other sounds, a muted bullring trumpet saluting the death of the sacrificial victim.

The film is so constructed as to reveal, step by step—now advancing, hesitating, or retreating—Locke's groping aspiration to make or, more precisely, to let the "new Locke" supersede, the "old Locke," caged in his coded world. Everything converges in the last shot. Like the exploding house in *Zabriskie Point*, or the fablelike coda of *Red Desert*, or the great montage of *Eclipse*, the final shot of *The Passenger* is an epiphany that binds the various themes in a single comprehensive kinetic image, itself a wholly new statement of those themes at a higher level. Viewed from the finale, the film's structure is immediately apparent. A formal prologue states the main themes in their visual and chromatic terms: internal and external geographies, the narrative "quest," dissolving identity, the desert (like Eliot's in *The Waste Land*) as the condition of a spiritual death and rebirth. The narrative proper—Locke's discovery of himself in Robertson's identity—ends with the breakdown of the rented car, corresponding to the stalled vehicle with which the narrative begins. As so often in Antonioni, that narrative is essentially internal. The external world with its landscapes and stopovers,

the events of its story line, express the psychological stages of Locke's journey as the making of an identity, an identity, according to the director's effort to create here and elsewhere, a visual poetics of destiny. Beneath the intricately detailed *poetry* of the narrative, Locke's secular pilgrimage gathers momentum as it moves slowly toward its destination—that destiny revealed in the transcendence of the finale. Guided by no conventionally accepted sense of "vocation," Locke vacillates, feeling his way according to the nudgings of genetic memory and purpose, the voice of some hidden but insistent daimon. That voice is hard to hear, overwhelmed as it is by the coded noises and roles of the public world. Hence Locke's constant progression but equally persistent regression as he struggles to heed religious feelings that have no normalized place in a secular age. Hence, too, the director's efforts to avoid overtly conscious striving; the dissolving Locke simply doesn't know, at least until the close, where he is going. Words don't matter; what counts is the visuals, which express the inarticulateness of gathering consciousness. Locke dissolves, dying as Locke in order to come upon a prior, deeper "self"—that tougher self, "Who," in Eliot's words, "never talks, who cannot argue."9

Only by dissolving can Locke discover this new self and appear at last in his own right—only to disappear again but at a higher level. Robertson in this sense is Locke's alter ego. If Locke *initially* feels the exhilaration of a new identity, of *being* Robertson, he later comes, first by necessity and then by some velleity of choice, to accept the responsibility imposed by that new identity. Through responsible possession of his own emerging fate, shadow Locke finally become true Locke—no longer Robertson but the person potentially present, buried beneath the old Locke and Robertson's borrowed persona. "I never knew him" says Rachel when the police ask her to identify Locke's body; and she is right. The Girl, asked if she knows him, answers, "Yes"; and she too is right. The new Locke has emerged from the old.

That emergence of the "new" from the "old" is made explicit in two crucial scenes, both of which were—inexplicably, infuriatingly—excised by MGM editors from the American print. (European viewers can see the integral version, as the director shot it.) In the first of these scenes, Locke, newly returned from Africa, enters his house in Lansdowne Crescent. Upstairs he finds, pinned to the door, a note from his wife to her lover. In the study, as he removes money and papers from the desk drawer, we see a book on the desk—Alberto Moravia's *What Tribe Do You Belong To?*—which Locke had presumably been reading in preparation for his African trip. But the unanswered question echoing in that title is clearly addressed to Locke as a man. What tribe does *he* belong to? The tribe of mindlessly opining or "objectively" reporting media role-players, or that of free autonomous individual human beings? The second, and much more important, of the excised sequences comes near the end of the film, just after the visit to Plaza de la

Iglesia. Locke and the Girl enter a beautifully green, almost paradisal, lemon grove. Lying on the lush grass, looking up at the green leaves overhead, Locke talks of giving up his effort to keep Robertson's appointments. "The old me," he says, pointedly rising, "is getting hungry." Disgusted by his rejection of Robertson's itinerary, the Girl leaves the frame; as she leaves, the frame divides. On one side is the Girl, walking up the dry bed of a sand-colored arroyo; on the other, the "old" Locke, sheltered in the green of the lemon trees. He leaps after her, out of the grove and into the arroyo. Overtaking her, he persuades her to continue on his journey toward the desert landscape to which the "new" Locke is now committed.

His attenuated sense of identity makes it initially possible for Locke to melt easily into Robertson. But even in this negative form, however faintly at first, his hunger for transcendence can be discerned. It is this yearning that draws him toward the desert, itself defined as a waiting, breathing expectancy; it is the desert, or *something* in the desert, if only a void waiting to be filled, that triggers his adoption of Robertson's identity. When he finds Robertson, facedown on the bed, the clothes on the wall rustle ever so slightly. But the rustling is apparent only because the camera shows us Locke leaving the frame; in the abandoned vacancy, which his departure forces the viewer to inspect, the clothes on the wall begin to stir. *Something* is there—a barely perceptible breath. What? Locke goes to the window, opens the shutter, looks out. At what? Desert immensity, and now on the sound track the sound of a flute; then, in the foreground, a herd of goats scattering, defining the expanse of desert reaching to the horizon, and revealing the source of the flute—a goatherd. Locke returns to the room, looks up: a fan slowly revolving—time passing. The camera pans down the electric cord, and suddenly there is Locke in Robertson's shirt, transformed to Robertson. Clearly Locke goes to the window and looks out because he intuitively links the stirring of the clothes on the wall with a breath of air coming from the desert world outside the shuttered window. The room is a cell, *locking* him (the wordplay is persistent) into the stale air of his old self, cutting him off from whatever it is that lies—a living, breathing presence—beyond the confines of cell and frame. Only later does the slowly revolving fan reveal itself as the "cause" that lures Locke to the window.

In one masterly summary the director gives us a wordless visual account of Locke's first decisive transformation and its personal motives (the sense of imprisonment, of being trapped in old habits and encoded clichés), and the metaphysical quality of his decision to move "off the frame" by disappearing into the desert, that destination now gathering direction within him. In his conversation with Robertson, Locke declares that he prefers people to landscapes; this is the "old" Locke speaking. The emerging Locke, whose motives we see gestating in this shot, unconsciously shares the attitude expressed by Robertson in the later flashback glossing this scene: "The desert is beautiful. . . . It's the immobility—a kind of waiting,

an eternal suspension." The language is reminiscent of Pavese: the notion of a place, usually a clearing, in which the absent god lives on; a living suspension. As the narrator of Pavese's *Dialogues with Leucò* says of the wild country around him: "What else could those people have looked for in a place like this, if not an encounter with the gods?" and the response is, "But in every abandoned place, an emptiness, an expectation remains."[10]

But the most telling visual statement of Locke's emerging "vocation" is the secular sacrament performed with the agents of the Chadian rebels in front of the high altar of the rococo church in Munich. Locke reaches this church by a kind of self-revealing serendipity, aimlessly following a bridal coach. Passing through a graveyard embowered in leaves and flowers, he enters the church, as the old secular Locke would presumably have done, through a side door. He is, knowingly or unknowingly, retracing his past, above all his own dead marriage. But that past and its memories are cultural as well as personal. He stands quietly in the church, by his chosen position excluded from the wedding ceremony by an iron grille. The wedding itself is intricately crosscut with scenes of Locke's London home and marriage, past and present combining as though simultaneous or taking place in some timeless present. The ceremony over, Locke, presumably immersed in memories, sits in a pew, meditating. There he is interrupted by the Chadian agents. The contractual "sacrament," enacted before the altar, compels the viewer to see the ritual exchange of money as somehow related to the altar, as an ironic sacrament of its own. Repeatedly the camera picks up the gleaming gold of the altar cross and the gilded frames of the Stations of the Cross flanking the altarpiece. After the exchange of money, the camera pans slowly *down* the whole altar, revealing a formal Gloria, the *ascent* of a saint in ecstasy, surrounded by clouds and angels, all enclosed in the intricate scrollwork, the leaf-and-shell-forms of Bavarian rococo. Then, as though to make clear the context of this Gloria, the director shows us the whole church—a continuous tissue of sculptured and painted architecture. It is at *this* point that Locke opens the envelope the Chadians gave him and says in quiet astonishment, "Christ." Then, as though suddenly aware of his surroundings, he exclaims, in embarrassed apology: "Christ."[11]

Locke is semiconsciously participating in a shadow sacrament. From this point on his progess is portrayed as a groping passage through the Stations of the Cross, a religious "mission" implicit in his later conscious "decision" to complete Robertson's itinerary. If his mission never becomes overtly religious, it nonetheless tangibly informs the rest of the film, making the viewer aware of an older ghostly meaning surviving in the secular gloria of the finale, which corresponds to the formal Gloria in the Munich church. The Girl has her own personal reasons—she believes in Locke, she loves him—for urging him to keep Robertson's appointment in Osuna: "He believed in something. That's what you wanted, isn't it?" But her personal reasons are wholly compatible with the secular gloria of the finale, which

corresponds to the quasi-sacramental analogy. The "something" in which Robertson, and later Locke, believed, is Antonioni's equivalent of Plato's *ti allo*, the transcendent object of that hunger for meaning and a redeeming purpose which Locke cannot renounce. Antonioni's purposes may be to offer a covertly religious account of human aspiration, or at least of Locke's behavior here; but more probably the purpose is to suggest the persistence of the passion for transcendence in an age when creeds no longer enlist that passion. It survives not as formal religious behavior like the traditional saint's ecstasy but as the impulse that once found adequate expression in that ecstasy and persists even now as existential or cultural "vocation." The one habit men cannot, without ceasing to be men, "kick" is the habit of meaning; they can no more rid themselves of that habit than they can "kick" the habit of evolving, adapting. Divest a man of everything; let him arrive at his destination without "luggage," either religious or physical, and he will inevitably display the quality that makes him human—above all, his passion for transcending himself, for evolving. The book Locke was evidently reading when Robertson died, the book he picks up on leaving his room, and which we see among his possessions when they are opened by Rachel is entitled *The Soul of the Ape*.[12]

Prehistoric man evolved as man when his arboreal ape ancestors descended from the trees and adapted themselves to the vast treeless savannas of central Africa. Caged and sheltered by their green Edenic habitat, the prehuman forest apes had no need to evolve. But when the Miocene forest shrank in the great Pleistocene drought, these forest apes suddenly had to adapt or die. It was the adaptive, evolving ape who left his native trees and made himself human in the empty grasslands of the central African plateau and the South African veldt. It is this tale of adaptation—how the ape acquired a human "soul," that is, a new consciousness of himself—that Locke has been reading. Beneath the narrative of the evolving Locke there is a running analogy with the evolution of the species. Locke's emerging persona is, in fact, a complex of three discrete but cohering strands—personal, religious, and anthropological. Their common denominator is change. Personally, Locke is a man in crisis, at a point of "passage," in midlife and career frustration; a man changing. Religiously, he is the secular pilgrim passing through the upward stations of *his* cross, toward a new vocation and an unknown fate. Anthropologically, he is emerging and "ascending" man, leaving the shelter of his treed life, at once paradise and prison, for the exposure of open country and the dangers of the void. The anthropological metaphor is more glancingly stated than the religious, but is no less urgent and pervasive. Its first overt articulation is that book—*The Soul of the Ape*—which we see lying in Locke's suitcase. There is, of course, no literary allusion intended here. We are not expected to be familiar with the book; the title serves simply as a visual introduction to the images which will sustain the governing idea. The *idea of a transcendental ape*—not easily

conveyed visually—is the immediate point (just as later, in the final minutes it will be the idea of the *soul* or psyche itself). In the sequence at Barcelona, for instance, we see Knight pursuing Locke. Locke disappears behind a group of birdcages stacked on the sidewalk; the last shot is of a caged monkey being lifted across the frame and disappearing in the same direction as Locke. The metaphor is more actively present in the studied portrayal of Europe (London, Munich, and Barcelona) as an arboreal habitat that Locke leaves for the treeless expanse of Africa or African Spain where, by transcendence or mutation, he at last becomes himself.

The film everywhere presents an elaborate image of modern Europe as a green bower—a bower constantly contrasted with Locke's ascetic desert geography. Hence the severely inflected polarities, so typical of Antonioni: Europe and Africa; city and country; present and past; man-made colors contrasted with quieter earth colors. In human terms, it is predictably the woman—the Girl, played by Maria Schneider—who, as "a finer filter of reality," embodies the sense of the world-as-arbor. When we first see the Girl—Schneider's pleasantly simian features nicely adjusted to the arbor imagery of her habitat—she is sitting in the court of the Bloomsbury Centre, reading. She leans back, her head framed by the green leaves of the plants behind her, and the motif is stressed by the floral tracery of her blouse. Visually, she is in "her element." But she is also adaptable. Like Vittoria in *Eclipse*, she has the natural knack of mobility, *balance*; unlike the maladaptive Locke, she constantly corrects for excessive light or shade, for too many trees or too much open space. If boskiness is her natural element, she is also visibly at home in open country, as in the large open court of the Centre, where she can still touch the leaves. When she and Locke veer off the road in the desert broom and mesquite of southern Spain, she looks at the huge expanse of scorched mountains and blue sky and says simply, "It's beautiful." In one of the film's most striking shots, the Girl is contrasted and then paired with Locke as his *natural* complement. She asks him, "What are you running away from?" Locke replies, "Turn your back to the front seat." We see her standing in the car, looking back, her arms outspread among the branches and leaves of the trees overhead, at home now in her element as he was at home in free flight over the deep blue water of Barcelona harbor. Then we see her from the front of the car, and the road and the trees, but above all the trees, converging and disappearing behind the car—the silent visual answer to Locke's question. Her world is Nature; the attenuating vital and emotional energies of Locke (superbly portrayed by Nicholson's low-key, deadpan manner) stand for that extinction of animal spirits, the death wish of the body required by the Spirit.

For Locke is literally running toward the desert and his own death, homing toward the parched, almost African world of southern Spain. He moves *away* from the leaves, leaving the green, bowered world behind him. In one of the more violent cuts in the film, through the blazing gasoline

159

crackle of *green* leaves burning (no autumn leaves, these), we glimpse the figure of Locke. He has deliberately pruned away every green leaf and bough he can reach, arousing protests from his neighbor and, more important, from Rachel, who comes rushing out in her nightgown, shouting, "Are you *crazy?*" He is symbolically destroying the protective screen of his English arbor; the leaves are burned with a violent glee that reveals his detestation of the green cage in which he perceives himself as imprisoned. Hence the almost obsessive boskiness of Locke's house in Lansdowne Crescent, with its hedge of encircling green and blossoming flowers, placed so carefully beside the steps where he mounts, and the glimpse of greenery into which he disappears. The excessive vegetation of Lansdowne Crescent is then repeated in the florid rococo Munich church with its bridal flowers and leafy scrolls and fernlike iron grille. Depending on where one stands, these bowered worlds are variously paradise—the security of the protecting leafiness against the glaring light of an intolerable reality—or prison, where the feelings are penned in and change is impossible. The Munich wedding itself suggests a stifling vernal imprisonment: the green gemütlichkeit of German and Western middle-class life, designed to screen out reality, to protect its inhabitants from the spectacle of change and immensity that might otherwise open up around them. Even death—those prettified gravestones with their floral carvings and symbols of easy resurrection—is adapted to the uses of snuggery, the sense of the world as man's natural nest.

In sum, what the director gives us is an image of the modern world self-protectively still embowered in the Ptolemaic universe, still in the grip of its old heady Renaissance illusion of Central Man and Central Man's self-centered certainties. The idea is not a new one for Antonioni, who persistently employs cosmological perspective in his films. In the famous Cannes interview after *L'avventura*, he remarked that modern man "no longer possesses the exuberant confidence of Renaissance man who, unlike us, inhabited a Ptolemaic universe." Modern man lives scientifically and technologically in the present, but morally in the past, burdened by the "baggage of old habits. . . . Man, who has today no fear of the scientific unknown, is afraid of the moral unknown."[13] In *The Passenger* the Ptolemaic universe is depicted as a huge bower, excluding the reality that lies "beyond the frame"—the new, exploding, isotopically receding, perhaps infinite post-Copernican universe, with its incalculable violence, its incomprehensible event horizons. Toward that unknown world beyond the Western frame, toward the blinding white light of a new reality, Locke is drawn—a man in adaptation, a man evolving—out of his cozy green shelter.

Europe in this perspective is metaphorically both bower and birdcage—continent of birdcage-cities represented in miniature by the birdcages stacked on the sidewalk of Barcelona, itself a beautiful birdcage-city. But these paradisal cages can never quite exclude the threatening reality outside. The desert keeps intruding: that desert violence that sud-

denly erupts at a sidewalk café in Barcelona, masked by playing fountains; or the secret violence contained in the "black hole" of the locker in the Munich airport—a violence which Europe exports to Africa as marketable Faustian technology, and which returns to Europe as political violence and terrorism. In Munich Antonioni juxtaposes two incongruous architectures—the functional modern geometry of the Munich airport, its blazing primary chromatics contrasted with the green pretense of the rococo church on the dead suburban street. In London, too, Lansdowne Crescent—the fashionable, mindless pretense of English middle-class life—is contrasted with the square of the Bloomsbury Centre, all birdcage cubicles and concrete, where Locke first sees the Girl, reading no doubt a book on architecture. She has presumably been drawn there by the architect's (unsuccessful) effort to create an apartment complex that is not, like Lansdowne Crescent, a regression into the past, nor, at the opposite extreme, a purely functional and geometrically dead modernity. In both complexes the purpose is contrast and incongruity: an architectural commentary designed to elucidate the tension between past and present, natural and man-made, organic and functional. In Barcelona the commentary is also architectural, both glancing and comprehensive. Thus the two Gaudí buildings shown generalize the image first presented by the Umbraculo: latticed light; a slatted roof curving upward like the top of an ornate birdcage, but a birdcage open to the world, where Locke waits for his mysterious appointment. There, for the first time in his career, Locke really interviews an old man—without camera, without recorder—who begins his life story, with its vista of time and space, "Once a long ways from here . . ."

That birdcage image is more strongly emphasized in the first Gaudí building, the Palacio Güell. That this structure is a cage—superbly habitable no doubt, but still a cage—is indicated by the birdcage hanging over the head of the appropriately drowsing custodian. The interior is dark, "good for hiding in," the Girl observes, and we see what she means. At the top of the domed room starlike holes admit a Ptolemaic illumination. The camera pans down the wall, where the slotted lateral windows admit "a dim religious light." On every side, with each shift of camera angle, a richly embowered texture: vine leaves, tendrils of stone and wood; ornamental brickwork; lacy designs of Moorish inspiration. But most noteworthy is the neo-Gothic quality of the ensemble—the religious gloom; the sense of the medieval past in those dark enclosing textures, in the organ and paintings, and in the dozing custodian. An image of a drowsing world, almost a dead one. It is the sense of claustrophobic enclosure that triggers Locke's departure for another Gaudí building, one more suited to his psychic needs. We are not told why he leaves; the motivation is stated elliptically by the fact of departure and the stark contrast between the two buildings. Just as Locke keeps moving steadily toward the desert, so in Barcelona he moves from building to building in the self-defining mode of Antonioni's characters,

who constantly tend to insert themselves in an external world that matches and thereby reveals their internal reality. In Gaudí's famous Casa Milà, where Locke and the Girl now go, the sense of the architectural birdcage abruptly vanishes. It is open space, not enclosing interiors and cubicles, that Locke wants, and, when we first see him and the Girl in Casa Milà, they are already on the roof, somehow at home in that fantasy landscape whose monochrome tiles and sculpted abstractions recall the expanse of the desert, its wind-eroded shapes, even its termitaries. Compare, for instance, Gaudí's fantastically sculpted chimneys and ventilators with the photographs of the desert—odd buttes, stony outcroppings—hanging over the reception desk of Locke's hotel in Chad, and the affinity is apparent; indeed, it is generally held that Gaudí's structures were inspired by the landscape of Chad during the architect's visits to Africa. Even in the monochrome tiles Antonioni subtly evokes the desert; those same triangles of tile, white or ocher like those glimpsed earlier on the reception desk of the Chad hotel.

But unlike the Bloomsbury Centre in London, Casa Milà is an attempt, in an apartment complex, to relocate man *in* nature. Not man *over* nature, center stage, as in the Ptolemaic conception, but a great architect's attempt to restore the balance between organic and functional, public and personal, free space and privacy. Hence the shot of the whole facade of Casa Milà—a lingering shot, permitting us to recognize the serpentine movement of the chamfered floor slabs, and the intricate iron scrollwork, like tendrils of seaweed seemingly woven about the cavelike openings of balconies and windows. Man and god; light and dark; natural forms merging with functional purpose; curve and line, creating the sense of privacy and peace; a world designed to permit shelter and security—the bower feelings—but also open to the larger world, the "other" world of nature and society. Everywhere the design insists upon forms derived from desert and sea, and all that they imply of vistas of time and space. Foreground and background in formal balance; the transient confronted by the permanent in a way that does not mock the transient or deny permanence by prettifying it or screening it out. The building is one of Gaudí's most striking secular designs; but there is evidence that the structure was originally to have been surmounted by a colossal statue of the Virgin, who would thus preside over the foreground wilderness of sculptured abstractions that house ventilators and chimneys. Here, combining desert abstractions with the clotheslines of everyday life (emphasized in the film by a domestic argument taking place on a balcony below), Gaudí intended to place the divinity to whom the whole building was to be dedicated and in whose absence we see an image of the desert as glimpsed by Robertson: beautiful, immobile, waiting.

As Locke and the Girl move southward down the Costa del Sol, the desert and sea loom larger. The trees thin out, the parched horizon opens up. We don't see the sea, but we hear its movement, always louder. But the more the landscape opens out, the more compulsive become the human

efforts to contrive a screen against it. At a sidewalk café, Locke and the Girl are seated at a table. An iron grille separates *them* from *us*; interwoven with the straight bars of the grillwork are beautiful volutes of iron, crescents, tendrils. One tendril curls down around Locke's head from the right; another loops the Girl's head on the left, holding them briefly bonded in the tension of line and curve. Behind Locke, stacked cases of empty bottles, their emptiness reflecting his.[14] Beyond them a man sits staring at the white light pouring in at the fringe of the frame; on the sound track, the sea beating on the shore. Their privacy, the image suggests, is relative to the world lying beyond them; it looks *outward* toward what it excludes—us, the seated man. The seated man also looks outward toward the world beyond the frame—toward the white light and the sound of the sea. In earlier films the problem of Eros is rooted in the compulsive privacy with which the lovers seal themselves off; Eros blots out the environing world in the obsessive intimacy of the "close-up." Here, on the contrary, Eros is depicted as healthy; its necessary inwardness is, like the privacy of Casa Milà, intensified through its relation to a larger environing world. The world beyond the frame is *seen*, heeded.

Locke and the Girl press on. The next sequence is set in a compulsively overdone Moorish restaurant, all flowers and filigree, where the police locate Locke's rented car. The pretty coziness of the restaurant stands in direct intentional contrast to the bleakness of the world it attempts to exclude. From behind still another grille we see Locke and the Girl embowered in almost aggressive floweriness. Locke gazes out toward the blue of the sea in the distance; we hear its beating on the shore as he gazes. But is he perhaps looking at the attractive woman in the red bathing suit in the foreground? When the Girl asks him what he's thinking about, he smiles and says, "Nothing." And we know he has been looking at the sea, at that expectant blue nothingness. The restaurant, with its obsessively decorative embowering, is architecturally designed to occlude the sea, just as on the street side it purposively screens out the man-made desert of the tourist strip, jangling and intrusive. When Locke and the Girl go outside to meet the policeman, the restaurant's exterior is revealed for the first time: fake Moorish crenellations, a long row of thickly intergrown arborvitae planted as a screen. Against what? Against what we next see and what there is no artistic need to reveal unless the purpose is to indicate just what that cozy arbor of the restaurant excludes: the coastal highway, a broad band of ugly cement, parched yellow mountains to the left, streetlights overhead, a clutter of dreary apartment buildings, two motorcycles roaring away. The dirt and ugliness, in short, of the "real" world expressed verbally in Locke's parable of the blind man at the close.

Steadily south. The sound of the sea grows louder. When Locke reaches Plaza de la Iglesia, the camera shows part of the buildings before he and the Girl enter the frame. Our attention is being directed to the site and

the architecture: functional modern buildings, geometric and soulless, apparently abandoned, grass prinking up between the cement slabs, the church itself nothing but a godbox. Of trees and shrubbery hardly a sign; only the glaring sun, a white light beating down on white buildings; one or two people. In the siesta stillness can be heard, just off the frame, as it were, the sound of the sea. "No one here," says Locke to the Girl (echoing Claudia's unanswered "Anyone here?" [non c'è nessuno] in the uninhabited development town of L'avventura).

The sea remains out of sight. The director is saving that image—the sea as visible nothingness or otherness, an infinite blue void associated with death—for the final sequence. We *hear* it, an absent presence coming ominously closer, as the surf sound increases. Linked to that sound is the indelible image of a rebel Chadian being executed by government soldiers (according to Antonioni, an actual, not a simulated, execution). Shocking but also strangely, even beautifully, moving, the killing is as disturbing to Rachel and Knight watching it on the filmviewer as it must have been to Locke (and the director) when it was filmed. The condemned man, in a pinkish shirt, hands bound across his chest, stands before a group of stacked barrels, striped light blue at top and bottom; in the middle a band of pink matching the condemned man's shirt and the desert. The execution is pointedly set on the shore, the blue of Lake Chad beyond it. A shot of the firing squad; then, immediately after, a shot of an expanse of blue water and surf, nothing else. The shots ring out, the victim sags and shudders under the impact of the bullets, then convulsively lifts his bound hands—a wing motion, the trembling flutter of escape—and then a shot of the sea. Blue water, nothing else. The sequence of execution and blue water—foreground and background constantly related—declares the connection between death and the blue void of sea and sky. An execution, a death, violence, light pink and blue, pink desert, blue sea, the sound of the surf—images of death and transcendence, of death *as* transcendence. An image, too, of a sacrifice—the prisoner's bound hands lifting, as though in prayer—a passion. And the sound linked to this kinesthetic cluster is heard now in the distant beating of the surf which we hear later, linked again to a shot of sea and sky, in the coda at Osuna.

A related point. It is the emphasis upon transcendence—on Locke's desire to supersede himself, to become his own internal void at a redeeming level—that makes the love story here so simple and natural. Because his real aspirations lie elsewhere, "beyond," Locke is not tempted—like Sandro or Anna in L'avventura, or the sleepwalkers in La notte, or Aldo in Il grido—to make of Eros a consuming all. Moved by other purposes, something beyond sex, Locke and the Girl are not subject to the obsessive eroticism of the "human zoo." Locke and the Girl *like* each other. They are lovers and, by conventional standards, strangers—though the banality of the conversation between them is offset by the deeper *visual* intimacy, far deeper than the old

bond between Locke and Rachel (or between Rachel and her coarse lover). We discern their intimacy visually, by means of the grilles and enclosures looping and linking them, excluding us. We see them in their hotel room from outside: two small figures on a balcony, their intimacy intensified by the dwarfing expanse of the wall. Only once, presumably to resolve doubts, the narrative camera intervenes to show them at a tactfully discreet distance down the corridor, lying on a bed, comfortably naked, side by side. Because they accept transience—the passing moment and what it brings—they have no designs on eternity, no need of that compulsive Eros that else-where in Antonioni's work obliterates the background and feeds compul-sively on its dread of what has been excluded. Their love is fragile, casual, provisional, affectionate, natural, uncaged. They recognize each other as transients, as peregrine; as much at home in reality, both foreground and background, as it is possible to be. Their paradise is a provisional bower, daily built to suit the needs of the site, the time, and themselves. They hear the sea, they see the sky. If Locke emerges as something more than a passenger on Robertson's identity, it is in large part because of what has happened between him and the Girl. Not because love makes the world less ugly, but because it makes the void habitable and the ugliness en-durable. As Robertson observes, men *do* love—with manifest dignity, as that Bedouin passing by on his camel so expressively shows us—in the desert.

In the final shot, as I said, everything converges. It is quite impossible to do this sequence, as brilliant artistically as it is technically, critical justice. Stripped of all his luggage, shielded from the blinding white light only by his green-tinted glasses—all that's left him of the green scrim of his Europen past—Locke checks into the modest Hotel de la Gloria. The Girl has preceded him. As though blind already, or acting out the blindness of his own fable, he asks her, now physically half removed from him (they share adjoining rooms), what she can see from the window. Framed in the glass of the wardrobe, she tells him: details of ordinary life. "And dust. It's very dusty." His eyes are shut as she sits down, touching his face, and caressing his closed eyes as though to screen them from the savage light outside. Locke tells her his parable of the blind man who recovered his sight. At first elated, like Locke in the fresh elation of Robertson's identity and the dis-avowal of his own, he was gradually overwhelmed by the ugliness around him, then locked himself into the darkness. Three years later he killed himself. Locke's story is clearly about himself, but also about the embow-ered world he has left behind. In that world, too, the curtains are drawn against the naked white light of an intolerable reality. Its denizens are those who have, by long habit, blinded themselves, instinctively screening out the light, accustoming themselves to "living" in darkness. Unlike the Girl, her-self a native of that world, *they* never leave it, fearing everything that would suddenly be revealed—the dirt, the ugliness, the boredom—if they left the

organized pretense of their boxes. Humankind, as Antonioni's favorite poet wrote, "cannot bear very much reality."

Blindness and sight. One need not be a classicist to see here at least a casual resemblance to that Oedipus who, when he had eyes, could not see; and came to see, like Tiresias, only when his blindness made it possible to see with visionary eyes. And there are the Tiresias-like figures of the film's two old men—the old man with the cane in the Umbraculo, who reminds Locke of the recurrently enacted human tragedy; also the old man with the dog in the plaza at Osuna, watching the recurrent tragedy. Or the figure of the blind man guided by a girl who acts as his eyes. And the whole controlling metaphorical structure of sight and blindness in both the Greek play and the film.

However that may be, it is clearly optics and perception that Antonioni has in mind throughout, but above all at the close, just before the final encounter with death. "Now at last I see things with a certain lucidity," said the dying Tommaso in La notte; sedated with morphine, only when dying does he at last see with waking vision what, as a sleepwalker drugged with work and career, he could not. Again, in Blow-up, the photographer at the film's close at last sees with human eyes that reality to which his optics and professionalized routine perception have blinded him—a breakthrough that occurs only after his encounter in the park with death and transience. So with Locke here.

At dusk the sky reddens; the sun is setting. Locke tells the Girl to leave. We see her dress blowing in the gentle breeze, like the clothes on the wall in Robertson's room: something is stirring, something outside, out there, moving in the air. As she leaves, Locke opens the windows onto the plaza, repeating his own action in Robertson's room after discovering the dead body. We look out at the plaza: a man passing. Then we are shown Locke, the bed, the small picture hanging over the bed. The camera pans up the picture: water, a stream, vegetation, trees rising on the left, a hill or cliff, and at the top a building—a monastery it seems—and then, higher still, clouds and sky. An ascent from stream and trees to buildings, and then the bare hill; beyond the hill, blue sky. Locke takes a cigarette and lies down on the bed, eyes open, looking out the window. On the bed lie his discarded dark glasses. Off now, off for good. In the adjoining room the Girl, seated on a chair, huddles into herself. All we can see now is Locke's feet and legs and trunk lying right side up on the bed. Then feet and legs turn over, the body face down, in the same position as Robertson's dead body on the salmon pink blanket of the bed where Locke found him.

Then, from outside, the slow, patient detailing of the life of the plaza. An old man, appearing with something—what?—from a door. The learner-driver car. The Girl looking back apprehensively at the barred window. The plaza itself, with its looping Moorish wall and, through an open arch, an ogive of blue, the blue sky beyond the walled enclosure. Then the boy in

the red shirt—the old violence beginning all over ("They can't get away from us")—as the murderers' Citroen drives up. The two men moving toward the camera; a girl running. Time is narrated in discrete, apparently unconnected events. Only the vantage point seems fixed, unchanging, the camera behind the barred window looking steadily, taking in everything that unfolds before it. Slowly we become aware that even this fixed point is also moving, the eye slowly advancing while the right- and left-hand sides of the frame shrink, and then there is nothing but the bars and the world beyond it, and the spaces between the bars gradually widening. But at this point a motorcycle sputters, then the dull *pom* of a pistol (or is it a motor backfiring?) followed by a trumpet phrase—a bullring fanfare—in the distance, and a car driving off. And now the camera begins its long, slow glide toward freedom, floating out, ever so gently rocking, like a disembodied thing, toward the unimpeded world of the plaza. Only two bars remain in the window; a siren sounds, and, with something like a shudder, the camera—the eye, the "I," or it, whatever "it" might be that acts like this, the psyche, the soul, could it be?—squeezes through the bars. There it hesitates briefly, as though looking for a way out—what way? where?—loops in a long double curve around the plaza, feeling out this new enclosure, the larger social space of the plaza. But now we see that the plaza itself is only a larger cell, a new cage with its own barrier encircling it—that Moorish wall through which, as once through the bars of Locke's room, we glimpse the larger world beyond in the ogive of blue sky, the aperture of the wall. And now, above the wall, that larger space defines itself as a horizontal band of blue sky. The camera, a disembodied, floating X, still groping, but more purposively now, suddenly reaches the end of the wall—where sea and sky open out toward infinity and final freedom. A blue world now suddenly revealed—no bars, no impediment—in which all the blues of sea and sky in the film converge in an image of absolute transcendence. Then, finally completing its circle, the camera comes to rest on the immediate foreground, on Rachel's car, and the small bulk of the Hotel de la Gloria profiled against a blue-white sky.

Now, from outside, excluded by the grilled window from which it has just escaped, the camera looks into the room, disclosing Locke's body. But the body is no longer in the same position in which we last saw it, face downward on the bed, back turned to the light. Now feet and legs lie right side up. The body is *faceup*, as it must have been when Locke faced his murderer, looking his own death in the face. It is astonishingly elliptical, but an ellipsis wholly characteristic of a director who fastidiously disdains traditional narrative realism, insistently demanding that the visuals, not the script, carry the essentials of the story. As in poetry, whose meaning often lies in the density of the unspoken thing, so here the crucial fact of Locke's possession of his own identity is wholly contained in a single visual sequence. In all of Antonioni's work, there is no more extreme ellipsis than

this. To fulfill Robertson's fate, Locke has only to die. This he can do as we see him preparing to do, turning over on his stomach like the blind man in his own parable, passively waiting for death. Up to this point, Locke's fate is parallel to, superimposed upon, Robertson's. Until now the narrative question has been: Will Locke have the courage to fulfill the identity he has usurped? He is a passenger on Robertson's passport, as the Girl is a passenger on Locke's destiny, "along for the ride." Locke became a passenger in part because he was sick of being an observer. Robertson and Locke both die as strangers and transients in another country to which they come as nomads. They both die, like strangers, in rented rooms. Locke, in short, fulfills Robertson's destiny, keeps Robertson's appointments. But, much more important, he also dies *his own*—Locke's own—death. In dying, he comes upon himself, becomes himself. In Antonioni's ellipsis—the turning over, face upward, to the light, confronting death—lies the essential, self-defining individaul act: a decision to face death, life, reality with seeing eyes, unshielded, without spectacles, just as in a parallel death and passion the Chadian victim faces the firing squad. This body in the bed is not that of "Robertson" played by an actor simulating him in life and death; nor is it any longer the body of Locke, the old Locke, as Rachel and the Girl make clear in their identification of it.

I spoke of a "passion." However secular or elliptical, Locke's death is also a passion—lowercase, to be sure—and part of a lowercase secular gloria. That passion and gloria mark the attainment of an unfolding destiny. Locke's fate is one in which his own self-awareness and emergent "decision" are implied. He chooses to risk death and thereby freely participates in his own unfolding fate. At the outset it was *something* in Locke— that generic human quest for *ti allo*, for meaning and a redeeming purpose—that drew him to the desert. There is in Locke, we come to see, an interior void. He *is* the desert to which he is drawn. But the film steadily inflects the idea of the desert. Like death in Bakhtin's famous phrase, the desert is pregnant. This void world, image by image, is refined as a void in which there is a mysterious tremor, a strange expectancy. A *living* void: we think the air is dead, but the clothes on the wall begin to stir; the black dots in the foreground reveal themselves as running goats; the silence seems absolute until broken by the sound of an insect buzzing. And, scene by scene, image by image, Locke's emptiness is shown to be *like* this desert. His hollowness begins to stir as, one by one, the collection of useless habits that once defined him, and the defenses he still carries with him, fall away. His silence increases; the prepared script of past life and professional "viewpoint" are discarded for a kind of rudimentary and daily improvised "action." He is the hollow man who, precisely because he is hollow, is capable of being filled, of becoming more than himself; whose emptiness is the condition of his transcendence. Negative transcendence, as in Eliot's poem:

. . . In order to arrive there,
To arrive where you are, to get from where you are not,
You must go by a way wherein there is no ecstasy.
. . .

In order to possess what you do not possess
You must go by the way of dispossession.
In order to arrive at what you are not
You must go through the way in which you are not.[15]

Again it is the hollow man who, because he is hollow, can reveal the generic beneath the individual, the genotype that precedes the phenotype. Locke reveals, as his individual habits and old identity dissolve, the generic human hunger for transcendence and meaning. *We* are Locke. Hence the informing parallel with the pilgrim or saint, whose assumption is a literal elevation *out of* and *beyond* himself in a ecstasy which means not joy but loss of self, passage into a larger life. Hence also the parallel with evolving Pleistocene man, who dies as the forest creature he used to be in order to adapt to the dangerous void in which a changing environment, a changed world, require him—and us—to live. For that void is ours, the viewer's; now that our world has changed, we too must strip away the habits that bind us to the Eden we have lost. We must adapt or die, even when adaptation means dying out of oneself, dying into change.

This *trasumanar—transhumanization*—is the meaning of the final shot. We see first the "soul" separating from the body, body and soul "riving," just as the camera "awareness" squeezes with a final shudder through the bars of its cell, out into the larger world of others, the great social "arena" of the plaza—another form of the void that lures Locke from the beginning: the world of the collective life, participation in the endlessly repeated human tragedy, acceptance of life and death. And, finally, a third transcendence as "it" gropes its way along the wall of the plaza, seeking the blue it can see through the wall and above it, and finally breaks through into the freedom of blue sea, blue sky.

Down below the lights at dusk come on, and over the door of the Hotel de la Gloria the stained-glass panel lights up—red, green, blue—in sign of a secular glory attained. The lights burn more brightly now, the rightly modest image of the building outlined against the sky; from within, a din of voices—men, women, children. An affirming image of the ordinary world at its ancient business of figuring, and transfiguring, itself. A real, an ordinary world. Profiled against a larger evening sky of darkening milky blue, the doorway grows slowly, gradually luminous. But the light is immanent radiating from within, not without. And this ordinary white light generates a small panel of warm colors glowing above the door, as a kind of supervening chromatic gloria, white becoming color just as the ordinary generates the extraordinary, or as body, by virtue of some evolving aspira-

tion, out of its own discontent, its feeling of being void and incomplete, creates a spirit of its own, a soul.

The gloria born of this conviction of inward discontent—the feeling of incompleteness, of a needy inner void that produces the hunger for *ti allo*— is nowhere better expressed than by Leopardi, in many ways so like Antonioni, above all in his anguish of solitude and his obsession with transience and mortality, and his lifetime preoccupation with that metaphysical tedium that Italians call *noia*:

Noia is in some sense the most sublime of human emotions. Not that I believe the examination of this emotion yields the consequences which many philosophers have sought to derive from it. And yet there is certainly our inability to be satisfied by any earthly thing or even by the entire world. . . . To imagine the infinite number of worlds and the infinite universe and feel that our minds and desires would still be greater than such a universe; *always to accuse things of insufficiency and nothingness, and to suffer the want and the void: this seems to me the best proof of the grandeur and nobility of human nature.*[16]

Il grido (The Cry). 1956. A worker at a sugar refinery in northern Italy, Aldo (Steve Cochran), is told by his mistress, Irma (Alida Valli), that she is leaving him. Furious and ashamed, he leaves town, taking his daughter, Rosina, and wanders about the Po River Delta. After stopping briefly at the home of an old love, Elvia (Betsy Blair), he moves on and takes up with Virginia (Dorian Gray), who has her own service station. Aldo stays to help her run the station and, when it becomes necessary, to place Virginia's father in an old-folk's home. Unable to care for his daughter, Aldo sends her back to Irma and then leaves Virginia, finding a new relationship with Andreina (Lynn Shaw), but she betrays him and he heads back to his original home, Goriano. When Aldo arrives he finds that the town and the surrounding fields are about to be destroyed in order to make way for a new airport. Seeing Irma in a new home with her baby, he then returns to the sugar refinery where he worked, climbing to the top of a tower from which he falls to his death.

L'avventura. 1960. Anna (Lea Massari), her close friend Claudia (Monica Vitti), and Anna's lover, Sandro (Gabriele Ferzetti), join Patrizia, Raimondo, Corrado, and Giulia for a yacht cruise among the Aeolian islands,

but Anna suddenly disappears. Searching for her first on one of the islands, they continue on the Sicilian mainland, with Claudia and Sandro going in separate directions. At the Montaltos' villa, Claudia rejoins the people from the yacht, as well as the princess who owns the villa and her grandson, Goffredo, a young painter. In Messina, Sandro bribes a local journalist to print the story about Anna having been seen by a druggist in Troina, which leads Claudia to show up there. Now Sandro and Claudia together pursue every rumor that might lead them to Anna, and, in the process, fall in love. In the little town of Noto where they stop, Sandro, an architect who has made a handsome living in recent years by making estimates for buildings, is taken with the baroque architecture, and Claudia is ecstatic over the feelings she has for Sandro. They leave Noto for a hotel in Taormina, where they again meet Patrizia and her husband Ettore, the developer for whom Sandro has been making estimates. Much to her shock and dismay, Claudia discovers Sandro in a sexual liaison with a young woman, Gloria Perkins (Dorothy De Poliolo).

La notte (The Night). 1961. Giovanni Pontano (Marcello Mastroianni) and his wife Lidia (Jeanne Moreau) visit Tommaso (Bernhard Wicki), a dying friend, in the hospital and then attend a cocktail party to honor Giovanni's latest book. Lidia leaves and walks about Milan, eventually reaching the outskirts where she and Giovanni used to meet as young lovers. He joins her briefly, and later that evening they go out, first to a nightclub where they watch an acrobatic striptease, and then on to an all-night party at the house of a wealthy industrialist, Signor Gherardini (Vincenzo Corbella), who is trying to entice the writer to work for him. Giovanni is attracted to the industrialist's daughter Valentina (Monica Vitti), and Lidia is pursued by one of the guests, Roberto (Giorgio Negro). In a call to the hospital, Lidia learns that Tommaso has died. As dawn breaks over the Gherardini estate, Giovanni and Lidia walk out onto an adjacent golf course, where she reads to him a passionate love letter. He doesn't recognize the writing at first, but Lidia reveals that it is in fact a letter that he wrote to her. Giovanni tries to force himself upon her in a sandpit.

Eclipse (*L'eclisse*). 1962. After a long night of talk in his apartment, Vittoria (Monica Vitti) ends her affair with Riccardo (Francisco Rabal) and walks to her own apartment in the EUR section of Rome. To find her mother, Vittoria goes to the Borsa, or stock market, in the center of town. There she meets a stockbroker, Piero (Alain Delon), and afterward spends time with a friend, Anita, at the apartment of another friend, Marta, who was born and raised in Kenya. They dress in native costume, and Vittoria dances. The next day she and Anita fly in a small plane to Verona. After a stock market crash, Piero goes to find Vittoria; as he stands outside her apartment a drunk steals his car, and, as they discover the next day, drives the vehicle into a nearby pond and drowns. Piero and Vittoria begin an

affair, meeting in the old apartment of his parents and in his offices. At the end of one of these visits, they promise to meet that evening and every evening thereafter at a street corner where they have met before, but the film ends with a study of that site, and they do not show up.

Red Desert (*Deserto rosso*). 1964. In the industrial city of Ravenna, a strike is in force at one of the local factories as Giuliana (Monica Vitti) and her son, Valerio, walk by. Corrado Zeller (Richard Harris), who has come to town to find workmen for a project in Patagonia, South America, begins to pursue Giuliana, and she accompanies him as he looks for these workers. They talk extensively, and it becomes clear that Giuliana is trying to recover from a nervous breakdown. At her home Giuliana feels estranged from her husband, Ugo (Carlo Chionetti), and her young son, who pretends that he cannot walk. At his request she tells him the story about a young girl who lives an idyllic life alone on an island (Sardinia), playing on the beach and totally at one with her natural surroundings. When Giuliana discovers that Valerio is faking his inability to walk, she runs to Corrado's hotel room, where they make love. At dockside, Giuliana meets a Turkish sailor and tries to explain to him what she feels, but neither person speaks the other's language. The film ends with Valerio and Giuliana walking again in front of several factories as she tells him that the birds have learned to fly around the poisonous fumes that pour out of the smokestacks.

Blow-up. 1966. Thomas (David Hemmings), a photographer in London, spends the night in a flophouse to obtain some images, then returns to his home, which is also his studio, for a session with various fashion models. Leaving them, he briefly visits the adjacent apartment of some friends, the painter Bill (John Castle) and his lover, Patricia (Sarah Miles). Returning to his quarters to retrieve the flophouse photographs, Thomas is about to leave when he is accosted by two young women—teenyboppers—who try to get him to take pictures of them. He refuses and then drives to an antique shop, hoping to buy its contents, but the owner is away. The old man in the shop is not particularly helpful, and Thomas goes into a nearby park where he takes photographs, first shooting some birds and then a couple he spies upon. The woman, Jane (Vanessa Redgrave), realizing that Thomas is taking photographs, tries unsuccessfully to take away his camera. Thomas returns to the antique shop and buys a propeller from the owner, then meets his editor, Ron, at a restaurant and shows him the photographs he took in the flophouse. When Thomas arrives home, Jane accosts him, demanding the photographs. They go inside and are about to make love when the propeller is delivered. Pretending to give Jane the photographs, Thomas waits until she leaves and then blows up the images he took of her in the park, only to discover what appears to be the shadowy figure of a gunman in the bushes. Calling to tell Ron that he has prevented a murder, Thomas is interrupted by the arrival of the two teenyboppers. They take off each

other's clothes, as well as those of Thomas, and all three frolic about until he is struck with a new thought about the photographs and dismisses the young women. As he blows up the images even more, Thomas thinks he discovers a body, but to be sure he goes to the park and there finds the corpse of the man seen earlier with Jane. Returning to Bill and Patricia's apartment, the photographer discovers them making love, and when he returns to his own apartment, Thomas finds that it has been ransacked. All the negatives and prints have been taken except one, which is indecipherable out of context. Driving to find Ron, Thomas thinks he sees Jane and follows her into a rock studio where a broken guitar is thrown his way and he runs out, throwing the instrument away. At a party, Thomas tries to get Ron to go with him to the park but he, like everyone else, is stupefied from smoking marijuana. Going alone to the park in the morning, Thomas finds that the body has disappeared, and, leaving, he comes upon a group of mummers, whom he saw at the beginning of the film, now playing an imaginary tennis game. When the illusory ball accidentally is knocked out of the court, they persuade Thomas to retrieve it and throw it back. After he reaches down to pick up his camera, Thomas slowly disappears and only the grass of the park is visible.

Zabriskie Point. 1970. In Los Angeles, California, some students are meeting to plan a strike against a university. Fed up with all the talk, one of them, Mark (Mark Frechette) leaves, while, in another part of town a young woman, Daria (Daria Halprin), is seen trying to retrieve a book at the place where she works, the Sunny Dunes Development Corporation. She is helped by one of the company's officers, Lee Allen (Rod Taylor). When the university strike occurs, police are called in and one of them is killed. Present with a gun, Mark is suspected, so he steals a plane and flies toward the desert. Daria is already there, driving to meet Lee. Stopping off in a small town to find a friend, she is accosted by a group of young boys and flees. After Mark buzzes her car several times, the plane runs out of gas and he is forced to land. Daria gives him a ride to get gas, and at Zabriskie Point they make love in the desert, an experience that is replicated dozens of times in a fantasy of other seminude couples cavorting in the sand. Mark and Daria return to the plane, painted to look like a prehistoric bird, and he flies back to the city while Daria goes on to the house where Lee is staying and holding a business meeting. Just before she arrives at the house, Daria hears that Mark was shot and killed when he landed at the airport. She looks around at the elaborate house where she is meeting Lee and then leaves; when she stops to look back she imagines that the house and all its contents explode.

The Passenger (Professione: Reporter). 1975. The journalist Locke (Jack Nicholson) is in Africa trying to make contact with a rebel movement, but he is unsuccessful. Disgusted with his career, himself, and a bad marriage,

Locke seizes an opportunity when Robertson, his neighbor at the hotel, dies. Altering the passports, he exchanges identities with Robertson and returns briefly to London before wandering about Europe—discovering in Munich that Robertson was selling arms to the same rebels Locke was trying to find in Africa. After taking money from them, Locke, following Robertson's own itinerary, goes to Barcelona, where he meets the Girl (Maria Schneider). They leave the city together, pursued by his producer friend, Martin Knight (Ian Hendry), and by representatives of the African country's legitimate government, who want to stop Locke from running guns. Rachel (Jenny Runacre), Locke's wife, opening the luggage returned to her, discovers the altered passport and goes herself to Europe in search of Robertson, where she is followed by the same representatives of the legitimate government. As they move through southern Spain, Locke and the Girl evade everyone until their car breaks down; he sends her away, planning to keep one last appointment of Robertson's at the Hotel de la Gloria. The Girl is waiting for him and, while she walks outside the hotel, Locke is shot in his room by one of the representatives of the African government. As the Girl returns to his room, Locke's wife arrives, and the two women enter the room where Locke now lies dead on his bed.

Notes

Introduction

1. Rhodes Scholar, Rockefeller and Guggenheim Fellow, recipient of numerous honorary degrees and prizes, including the *Prix de Rome*, Arrowsmith enjoyed a reputation based not only on his esteemed translations of Euripides, Petronius, Aristophanes, Pavese, and Montale but also upon his work as an editor, teacher, and founder of several important journals, including *Arion*, *Hudson Review*, and *The Chimera*. His literary essays on Greek drama and on writers such as T. S. Eliot are well known and highly regarded, as are his essays on education, the most famous of which is "The Shame of the Graduate Schools" (*Harper's Magazine*, March 1966).

2. From Arrowsmith's original lecture on *L'avventura*. Uncited Arrowsmith quotes in my introduction come from the present book.

3. Quoted by Gideon Bachmann in his "Antonioni after China: Art versus Science," *Film Quarterly* 28.4 (Summer 1975): 27.

4. Michelangelo Antonioni, "Let's Talk about *Zabriskie Point*," *Esquire* 74.2 (August 1970): 146.

5. See note 4 in the chapter on *L'avventura*.

6. From Arrowsmith's original lecture on *L'avventura*.

7. Antonioni, "Let's Talk about *Zabriskie Point*," 146.

8. Quoted by Gideon Bachmann in his "A Love of Today: An Interview with Michelangelo Antonioni," *Film Quarterly* 36.4 (Summer 1983): 4.

177

9. From page 27 of an unpublished Arrowsmith manuscript, dated October 3, 1990, entitled "The Responsibility of the Film Critic," which was originally delivered as the American Film Institute's Patricia Wise Lecture.

Il grido

1. Arrowsmith's translation; it seems to be based in part upon a passage from this version of the script: Michelangelo Antonioni, *Il grido,* ed. Elio Bartolini (Bologna: Cappelli editore, 1957), 131–32. [*Ed.*]

2. In one of his original lectures Arrowsmith indicated that he used this term in the "Spenglerian sense: the will to power over objects, founded upon intellectual knowledge, and generally contemptuous of both nature and the past." [*Ed.*]

3. As quoted by Melton S. Davis in his "Most Controversial Director," *New York Times Magazine* (November 15, 1964), 110. [*Ed.*]

4. Arrowsmith's translation of a section from Cesare Pavese's "Mal di mestiere," in the latter's *Feria d'agosto* (Torino: Giulio Einaudi editore, 1959), 235–36. [*Ed.*]

L'avventura

1. From a statement made by Antonioni at the press conference given for the opening of *L'avventura* at the 1960 Cannes Film Festival and widely reprinted in whole or part, e.g., in *L'avventura,* ed. Seymour Chatman and Guido Fink (New Brunswick, N.J.: Rutgers University Press, 1989), 177–79. [*Ed.*]

2. F. Scott Fitzgerald, *Tender Is the Night* (New York: Charles Scribner's Sons, 1933), 201. [*Ed.*]

3. See the title of Andrew Sarris' article, "Antoniennui à la mode," *Village Voice* (February 11, 1965), 14, 16, which is reprinted in his *Confessions of a Cultist* (New York: Simon and Schuster, 1970), 189–93. [*Ed.*]

4. The transcript of this discussion was published as *"La malattia dei sentimenti: Colloquio con Michelangelo Antonioni,"* Bianco e nero 22.2–3 (February–March 1961): 69–95. This particular quote can be found on page 54 in an English-language version of the discussion, "A Talk with Michelangelo Antonioni on His Work," *Film Culture* 24 (Spring 1962): 45–61; and on pages 215–16 of the same article as reprinted in *Film Makers on Film Making,* ed. Harry M. Geduld (Bloomington: Indiana Univ. Press, 1967), 197–223. During the discussion at the Centro Sperimentale, Antonioni read the Cannes statement cited in note 1 [*Ed.*]

5. A portion of the Pavese poem "Words from Confinement," in his *Hard Labor,* trans. William Arrowsmith (New York: Viking Press, 1976), 84. [*Ed.*]

6. From the Cannes statement as published several places, e.g., Chatman and Fink, *L'avventura,* 177–78. [*Ed.*]

7. Arrowsmith uses Vanessa, and sometimes Jane, to refer to the character of Jane, played by Vanessa Redgrave, in *Blow-up.* For the sake of consistency, I have everywhere, except in the appendix, referred to her as Vanessa, acknowledging the difficulty that Arrowsmith himself points out (see note 2 in the chapter on *Zabriskie Point*) about character names in the later Antonioni films. [*Ed.*]

8. Cf. *La nuit* (Paris: Buchet/Chastel, 1961), 74 and 76, where Valentina's statements are very similar. Although the meaning is substantially the same, her

remarks are somewhat longer and slightly different in the U.S. version of the *La notte* film: "I think love places certain limitations on a person. It fools us; it creates an emptiness around us," and, a few moments later, she adds, "Each time I tried to . . . [*groping for words*] communicate with someone, love disappeared [Mi sembra che l'amore debba limitare una persona. Qualcosa di sbagliato, che fa il vuoto attorno. . . . Tutte le volte che ho cercato di . . . (cerca la parola) di communicare con qualcuno, l'amore è andato via]." [*Ed.*]

9. From "Gerontion," in T. S. Eliot, *The Complete Poems and Plays, 1909–1950* (New York: Harcourt, Brace, 1952), 23. [*Ed.*]

10. Siegfried Giedion, *Space, Time and Architecture: The Growth of a New Tradition* (Cambridge, Mass.: Harvard Univ. Press, 1982), 71. [*Ed.*]

11. José Ortega y Gassett, *The Revolt of the Masses*, authorized translation (New York: W. W. Norton, 1957), 78. [*Ed.*]

La notte

1. T. S. Eliot, "The Waste Land," in *The Complete Poems and Plays, 1909–1950* (New York: Harcourt, Brace, 1952), 39. [*Ed.*]

2. From *"Il passero solitario,"* Canto XI of the *Canti*, in Giacomo Leopardi, *Opere*, vol. 1, ed. Sergio Solmi (Milan: Riccardo Ricciardi editore, 1966), 56. In his original manuscript Arrowsmith had provided his own English translation, but some of his handwriting was illegible; rather than misquote him I have provided another, given in *Giacomo Leopardi: Selected Prose and Poetry*, ed. and trans. Iris Origo and John Heath-Stubbs (New York: New American Library, 1967), 239. [*Ed.*]

After the Leopardi quote Arrowsmith had added the following parenthetical comment: "I introduce these lines without apology. It would be monstrous to suggest that Antonioni's works, especially the films of his Italian years, do not suffer a real loss by being uprooted for export, torn away from a context in which their most glancingly effective meanings depend upon a still living poetic culture. Is there any educated Italian who does not have both Dante and Leopardi in his ears and bloodstream? I doubt it." [*Ed.*]

3. The same point is made, I think, in the weed-grown cement paving of the Plaza de la Iglesia in *The Passenger*; the green world is already announcing its conquest of these briefly intrusive buildings, just as in the *Iliad* the poet deliberately gives us a glimpse of the great wall the Greeks have built as it will someday be when the sea has dealt with it—nothing left but the sand, like a child's castle, leveled by the waves.

4. Arrowsmith's frequent references to this fossil may seem out of keeping with what is seen in *Eclipse*, since there is only a glimpse of a fossil that Vittoria attempts to hang on her apartment wall, but no doubt he was aware of the entire sequence involving Vittoria and the fossil, as scripted for the Museum of Natural History in Verona; most of it was cut from the released film. The original scene is described in *L'eclisse*, a film by Michelangelo Antonioni, ed. John Francis Lane (Bologna: Cappelli editore, 1962), 62–63. [*Ed.*]

5. Here Antonioni glances with knowing irony at the actual penchant of Italian industrialists for acquiring intellectuals—a deliberate imitation of those Renaissance princes and *condottieri* who commissioned poets and humanists to immortalize their works in supposedly "deathless" verse or prose.

6. See note 8 of the chapter on *L'avventura*. [*Ed.*]

7. Tears are also the subject of a similar scene in *Zabriskie Point* when Daria moistens her face and dress in the water spilling from the rock at the developer's Arizona house.

8. José Ortega y Gassett, *The Revolt of the Masses*, authorized translation (New York: W. W. Norton, 1957), 156–57. [*Ed.*]

9. *Encyclopedia of Modern Architecture* (New York: Harry N. Abrams, 1964), 208. [*Ed.*]

10. As, for instance, Antonioni's use of the desert in *Zabriskie Point*.

11. Arrowsmith noted here that this last scene provides a "glimpse of the same natural intensity into which the *Blow-up* photographer dissolves, as well as the great salmon-pink desert in which Locke's vehicle grinds to a helpless halt." [*Ed.*]

Eclipse

1. Cattle, or oxen, pen. The Rome stock exchange, or Borsa, was built in part on the site of an ancient cattle market. [*Ed.*]

2. This modern section of Rome, the area around Riccardo's apartment, as well as Vittoria's, was once the site of Mussolini's ill-fated exposition, which was to have opened in 1942. Hence the letters EUR, which stand for Esposizione Universale Roma. [*Ed.*]

3. Think of Locke in *The Passenger*, over the blue water at Barcelona, in the first exhilaration of a new identity, freed from the prison of his past and self, his rapture expressed by his waggling of his arms as though they were wings, and the miraculous intensity of the blues beneath him, fixed in that godlike moment before he begins to learn the burdens and barriers, the limitations, of his adopted role. Or, in *Red Desert*, think of Giuliana's Sardinian escape, all intense chromatic fantasy, into the pink lagoon of the unconscious, away from her imprisonment in the poisoned marshes of quotidian Ravenna.

4. T. S. Eliot, "The Waste Land," in *The Complete Poems and Plays, 1909–1950* (New York: Harcourt, Brace, 1952), 49. [*Ed.*]

5. The kind of transcendence that so unites two people they become one. In *L'avventura* Claudia says to Sandro in the hotel room at Noto, "When you leave me, it will be as though you'd lost a leg [*zoppicherai*]."

6. ". . . non sono una donna sola . . . per quanto . . . a volte . . . è come . . . separata . . . no, non da mio marito, i corpi . . . sono . . . separati." A portion of the speech that Giuliana makes to the foreign sailor in the next to the last scene of the film. [*Ed.*]

7. See note 4 in the chapter on *La notte*. [*Ed.*]

8. Here, too, in this cloud is the vaporized form of the pool in which the drunk drowns earlier in the film, as though he could not drink enough, as though he wanted to become that sheet of unindividuated being shimmering in the nightlife. "How beautiful the pool looks in the darkness," says Berenice in *La notte*, who thereby tells us something about herself, but also Anna in *L'avventura* and Giuliana in *Red Desert*.

9. Oswald Spengler, *The Decline of the West*, vol. 2, trans. Charles Francis Atkinson (New York: Alfred A. Knopf, 1957), 97–98. [*Ed.*]

10. Ibid., 94.

The epigraph to this chapter is my own translation. Arrowsmith had cited the original French text from an interview conducted by Michèle Manceaux, published in *L'Express* (Paris, January 16, 1964), as quoted in *Il deserto rosso de Michelangelo Antonioni*, ed. Carlo di Carlo (Bologna: Cappelli editore, 1978), 24. The interview was translated, in part, into English as "In the *Red Desert*," *Sight and Sound*, 33.3 (Summer 1964): 118–19. [*Ed.*]

1. See Antonioni's pertinent comments in "A Talk with Michelangelo Antonioni on His Work," *Film Culture* 24 (Spring 1962): 54: "Lucretius, who was certainly one of the greatest poets who ever lived, once said, 'Nothing appears as it should in a world where nothing is certain. The only thing certain is the existence of a secret violence that makes everything uncertain.' Think about this for a moment. What Lucretius said of his time is still a disturbing reality, for it seems to me that this uncertainty is very much part of our own time. But this is unquestionably a philosophical matter. Now you really don't expect me to resolve such problems or propose any solutions? Inasmuch as I am the product of a middle-class society, and am preoccupied with making middle-class dramas, I am not equipped to do so. The middle class doesn't give me the means with which to resolve any middle-class problems. That's why I confine myself to pointing out existing problems without proposing any solutions. I think it is equally [as] important to point out the problems as it is to propose solutions." For other English reprints of this original text, see note 4 in the chapter on *L'avventura*. [*Ed.*]

2. Antonioni's remarks on the causes and nature of Giuliana's neurosis make quite clear that the sense in which "reality" is portrayed as a pollution goes far beyond ecological sentiment; indeed, it extends directly to that unconscious and apparently uncontrollable hubris which is the chronic infirmity of our Faustian world: "I want to underline the fact that it isn't the milieu that gives birth to the breakdown: it only makes it show. One may think that outside of this milieu, there is no breakdown. But that's not true. Our life, even if we don't take account of it, is dominated by 'industry.' And 'industry' shouldn't be understood to mean factories only, but also and above all, products. These products are everywhere, they enter our homes, made of plastics and other materials unknown barely a few years ago; they overtake us wherever we may be. With the help of advertising, which considers our psychology and our subconscious more and more carefully, they obsess us. I can say this: by situating the story of *Red Desert* in the world of factories, I have gone back to the source of that sort of crisis which, like a torrential river, swells a thousand tributaries, divides into a thousand branches in order, finally, to submerge everything and spread everywhere." From "An Interview with Michelangelo Antonioni by Jean-Luc Godard," *Cahiers du cinéma*, No. 160 (November 1964): 12–16; Arrowsmith's translation; another English version of this interview appears in Andrew Sarris, *Interviews with Film Directors* (Indianapolis, Ind.: Bobbs-Merrill, 1967), 3–11, and in *Cahiers du cinéma in English*, No. 1 (January 1966): 19–30, where a slightly different version of this quote appears on page 23. [*Ed.*]

3. Consider, for instance, Aldo in *Il grido*: a man whose entire world is destroyed when his common-law marriage breaks up and he is expelled from the enclosing comfort of his *paese*, out of the "magic circle" of familiar faces and things, into the increasingly desolate and boundless landscape of the lower Po, whose

yearly floods, sweeping everything before them, stand as an image of a world-in-change in which Aldo, having lost a crucial part of himself, can no longer keep his "psychic balance." His situation is mirrored by that of his daughter Rosina (just as the little boy's "paralysis" in *Red Desert* mirrors and informs Giuliana's neurosis), who stands at her father's side, looking longingly from the street into the comforting enclosure of a schoolyard. In *L'avventura* the intensity of love fuses the two lovers into a single being, an erotic *participation mystique* so total that Claudia can say to Sandro: "When you go out without me, it will be like losing a leg; you'll be lame." In *La notte* Valentina—alert to the dangers of the "red desert"—refuses her lover by saying, "Love's a bit of a fraud. It makes an emptiness all around you." The idea is visually expressed in the magnificent sequence of the magic bubble of the car containing Lidia and Roberto moving, sealed away from the world, through the rain; finally, it is confirmed by the love letter that Lidia reads to Giovanni, and that culminates in the evocation of that night "which I felt would never end, but would go on forever; that you were not only mine, but even more, *a part of me* . . ." Finally, in *Zabriskie Point* the erotic intensity hitherto expressed as metaphor or fantasy surfaces in film *action*, as lovemaking in the *desert* which the lovemaking, by its intensity, creates.

4. Ultimately, of course, the reasons for this are personal, a matter of artistic vision. But we should not ignore the great *visual* potential of paradisal imagery. Bergman, for instance, returns as obsessively as Antonioni to imagery and evocations of "earthly paradise" (wild strawberries; shots of the midnight sun and Swedish island summers). *Summer Interlude* depends almost wholly upon our perception that the ballerina is unable to develop and grow because she has been paralyzed by a remembrance of paradise lost; the protagonist of *Monika* remains a vulgarly erotic child because she cannot accept her expulsion from her summer Eden. The same imagery persists through the exquisite comedy of *Smiles of a Summer Night* to *Wild Strawberries* and *Virgin Spring*. In the "trilogy" we recognize it by its absence, articulated as "God's silence." Finally it appears, this time blended with apocalyptic imagery and themes (compare Antonioni's blend of "erotic desert" and nuclear apocalypse in *Zabriskie Point*), in *Shame* and *Passion of Anna*.

5. A paraphrase of a passage in Sapir's remarkable essay, "Culture, Genuine and Spurious," in *Selected Writings of Edward Sapir in Language, Culture, and Personality*, ed. David G. Mandelbaum (Berkeley: Univ. of California Press, 1968), 308–31.

6. Cf. Lucien Lévy-Bruhl, *Primitive Mentality* (London: George Allen and Unwin, 1923); and also *The "Soul" of the Primitive* (London: George Allen and Unwin, 1928).

7. An echo of Antonioni's remarks in the famous Cannes statement at the exhibition of *L'avventura*: "To be critically aware . . . is not enough or serves no purpose. And here we witness the crumbling of a myth, which proclaims it is enough for us to know, to be critically conscious of ourselves, to analyze ourselves in all our complexities. . . . The fact of the matter is that such an examination is not enough. It is only a preliminary step."

8. *Civilization and Its Discontents*, trans. James Strachey (New York: W. W. Norton, 1962), 55.

9. See note 3 of the chapter on *Il grido*. [*Ed.*]

10. C. G. Jung, *Civilization in Transition*, vol. 10 of the *Collected Works*, trans. R. F. C. Hull, 2d ed. (Princeton, N.J.: Princeton Univ. Press, 1970), 277.

11. In the Italian, *ingranare*. The point has been obscured by insensitive subtit-ling; thus the technological metaphor used here by Ugo to describe his wife's illness is blandly ignored (even though Ugo visibly searches for the right phrase—that is, the director, as it were, italicized Ugo's language). Gone, too, is Ugo's reference to some of his workers as *ottimi elementi* ("splendid elements"), as though they were so many transistors—a use of language wholly in accord with the scene that shows us anxious workers stacked in rows for export like bottles. Perhaps the worst failure, however, occurs in the first scene, when the sound track reproaches the "scab": "Romeo Salviati . . . tu sei uno che lavora per dare mangiare ai tuoi figli" (literally: "Romeo Salviati . . . you're a man who works to give *food [eating]* to your children." It is the word *mangiare* ("to eat") that provides the *klang*-association that sends Giuliana in pursuit of the young workman eating his roll. The subtitler, by ren-dering *mangiare* as "support," manages to strip the scene of its motivating cue.

12. "My intention . . . was to express the beauty of this world where even the factories can be very beautiful. . . . The line, the curves of the factories and their chimneys are perhaps much more beautiful than a line of trees, of which the eye has already seen too much. It is a rich world, lively, useful. For my part, I say that the sort of neurosis one sees in *Red Desert* is entirely a question of adaptability. There are some people who adapt themselves and others who have not been able to do so, for they are too tied to the structures or rhythms of life which are now obsolete. This is the case with Giuliana. . . . If I had chosen a normally adaptable woman, there would have been no drama." From "An interview with Michelangelo Antonioni by Jean-Luc Godard"; Arrowsmith's translation; this quote appears in another English translation on pages 20 and 23 of *Cahiers du cinéma in English*, No. 1 (January 1966), and on page 4 of Sarris, *Interviews with Film Directors*. [*Ed.*]

13. Ibid. Arrowsmith's translation; another English translation of this quote appears on page 7 of Sarris, *Interviews with Film Directors*, and on page 26 of *Cahiers du cinéma in English*, No. 1 (January 1966). [*Ed.*]

14. Cf., for instance, J. P. Sartre: "Absolute responsibility is not resignation; it is simply the logical requirement of the consequences of our freedom. What hap-pens to me happens through me, and I can neither affect myself with it nor revolt against it nor resign myself to it. Moreover, everything which happens to me is *mine*. . . . The most terrible situations of war, the worst tortures do not create a non-human state of things; there is no non-human situation. It is only through fear, flight, and recourse to magical types of conduct that I shall decide on the non-human. . . . Thus there are no *accidents* in a life. . . . The one who realizes in anguish his condition as *being* thrown into a responsibility which extends to his very abandonment has no longer either remorse or regret or excuse; he is no longer anything but a freedom which perfectly reveals itself and whose being resides in this very revelation. But . . . most of the time we flee anguish in bad faith." *Existentialism and Human Emotions* (New York: Philosophical Library, 1957), 53ff.

15. "I think it is important at this time," said Antonioni a few years before *Red Desert*, "for cinema to turn towards this internal form of film-making, towards ways of expression that are absolutely free, as free as those of literature, as free as those of painting which has reached abstraction. Perhaps one day cinema will also achieve the heights of abstraction; perhaps cinema will even construct poetry, a cinematic poem in rhyme. Today this may seem absolutely unthinkable, and yet little by little, perhaps even the public will come to accept this kind of cinema." From "A Talk with

Michelangelo Antonioni on His Work," *Film Culture* 24 (Spring 1962): 47–48. Reprinted in *Film Makers on Film Making*, ed. Harry Geduld (Bloomington: Indiana Univ. Press, 1967), 195–223, where this quote appears on page 203. [*Ed.*]

16. Jung, *Civilization in Transition*, vol. 10, pp. 169–70ff. Despite the numerous citations of Jung and my persistent use of Jungian terms, I must insist that I have no intention of suggesting that *Red Desert* is a Jungian account of neurosis. There seems to me not the slightest doubt that Antonioni has been much influenced by Jung; but there is also a clear debt to Freud (and to the existentialists; to Spengler; to Gaston Bachelard; perhaps to the phenomenologists; to Leopardi, F. Scott Fitzgerald, Musil, Joyce, Rilke). Antonioni is a widely read director (as even the most cursory survey of his interviews and statements demonstrates), but he is as eclectic as most European intellectuals. All that one can say of *Red Desert* is that the account of neurosis is not sufficiently clinical to indicate any particular school of therapy; besides, its intentions are more metaphysical and cultural than they are clinical (which is perhaps why Jung, with his broad humanistic interests, above all in the phenomena of consciousness, seems more pertinent than Freud; though Freud's theory of regression as the organism's effort, by reverting to a prior existential state, to avoid the pain of change, is wholly appropriate here). But only damage is done by interpreting Antonioni as anything but an artist, visibly influenced by the major thinkers of the age. To paraphrase Italo Svevo, artists have a habit of playing with ideas without really being in a position to expound them. They falsify them, but they also humanize them.

17. Cf., for instance, Jung's account in "Anima and Animus," *Two Essays on Analytical Psychology*, vol. 7 of the *Collected Works*, Trans. R. F. C. Hull, 2d rev. ed., (Princeton, N.J.: Princeton Univ. Press, 1966), pp. 188, 206. "Woman," he observes, "with her very dissimilar psychology, is and always has been a source of information about things for which a man has no eyes. She can be his inspiration; her intuitive capacity, often superior to man's, can give him timely warning, and her feeling, always directed toward the personal, can show him ways which his own less personally accented feeling would never have discovered. . . . An inferior consciousness cannot *eo ipso* be ascribed to women: it is merely different from masculine consciousness. But, just as a woman is often clearly conscious of things which a man is still groping for in the dark, so there are naturally fields of experience in a man which, for woman, are still wrapped in the shadows of non-differentiation. . . . The wide fields of commerce, politics, technology, and science, the whole realm of the applied masculine mind, she relegates to the penumbra of consciousness; while, on the other hand, she develops a minute consciousness of personal relationships, the infinite nuances of which usually escape the man entirely." But, for a quite different account, see Freud's essay "On Narcissism: An Introduction," in volume 14 of the *Standard Edition of the Complete Psychological Works* (London: Hogarth Press, 1974), 89: "The importance of this [narcissistic] type of woman for the erotic life of mankind is to be rated very high. Such women have the greatest fascination for men, not only for aesthetic reasons, . . . but also because of a combination of interesting psychological factors."

18. Examples of this identity—or rather affinity—between woman and the life of plants are innumerable. One thinks immediately of: Vittoria, walking with Piero, caressing a branch; of her fossil plant; the constant framing of her against trees, among vegetable and fibrous textures; the shot of a tree, shuddering in the dawn

breeze, at which Claudia looks, in the coda of *L'avventura*; Lidia in *La notte* leaning fondly against a tree; and Valentina, later, reading on a tape recorder: "Put your ear against the trunk of a tree and if you wait long enough, you'll hear a sound. Maybe it comes from inside us, but I like to think it's the tree." Or Giuliana's affinity for vegetation greens, and her fantasy's integration of the girl with the plants, rocks, and life of her island. So too in *Blow-up*, it is the green silence and mystery of the park that so attract the restless Thomas, that provide him with the psychic peace that also attracts him to Patricia, the character played by Sarah Miles.

The metaphor of the "rhizome" is Jung's. In the introduction to his autobiography Jung writes "Life has always seemed to me like a plant that lives on its rhizome. Its true life is invisible, hidden in the rhizome. The part that appears above ground lasts only a single summer. Then it withers away—an ephemeral apparition. When we think of the unending growth and decay of life and civilizations, we cannot escape the impression of absolute nullity. Yet I have never lost a sense of something that lives and endures underneath the eternal flux. What we see is the blossom, which passes. The rhizome remains." *Memories, Dreams, Reflections*, ed. Richard Winston and Clara Winston (New York: Pantheon Books, 1961), 4.

19. Jung, "Stages of Life," in *The Structure and Dynamics of the Psyche*, vol. 8 of the *Collected Works*, trans. R. F. C. Hull, 2d ed. (Princeton, N.J.: Princeton Univ. Press, 1966), p. 393. [*Ed.*]

Blow-up

1. "Antonioni—English Style," in *Blow-up*, a film by Michelangelo Antonioni (New York: Simon and Schuster, 1971), 15. The complete essay appeared in the January 1967 issue of *Cahiers du cinéma*. [*Ed.*]

2. Nadine Liber, "Michelangelo Antonioni Talks about His Work," in *Blow-up*, 19. The complete interview appeared in the January 1967 issue of *Life*. [*Ed.*]

3. T. S. Eliot, "The Love Song of J. Alfred Prufrock," in *The Complete Poems and Plays, 1909–1950* (New York: Harcourt Brace, 1952), 4. [*Ed.*]

4. Quoted in "Antonioni—English Style," in *Blow-up*, 14. [*Ed.*]

5. From the John Sebastian song, "Did You Ever Have to Make Up Your Mind?" recorded by the Lovin' Spoonful and heard on their album *Do You Believe in Magic?* (1965). The quote contains some of the words in the song, but they are not what we hear in the background of the U.S. version of the film; the part of the song that we can hear is: "Did you ever have to make up your mind? Say yes to one and leave the other behind? It's not often easy, and not often kind. Did you ever have to make up your mind? Sometimes you really dig a girl and you get distracted by her older sister. Then in walks her father and takes you . . ." The complete lyrics can be found in the *History of Rock: Mid 60s* (Milwaukee, Wis.: Hal Leonard Publishing, 1991), 138–40. [*Ed.*]

6. Liber, "Michelangelo Antonioni Talks about His Work," 18. [*Ed.*]

7. When Thomas photographs the model in his studio, the film script reads: "He goes closer to her, clutching the camera to his chest like a machine gun, taking one shot after another."

8. From *Blow-up*, 102–3. [*Ed.*]

9. *The Iliad*, Book VI, lines 146–50. [*Ed.*]

10. *Psalms* 103: 15–16. [*Ed.*]

11. From the poem *"L'infinito,"* Canto XII of the *Canti,* in Giacomo Leopardi, *Opere,* vol. 1, ed. Sergio Solmi (Milan: Riccardo Ricciardi editore, 1966), 58. In his original manuscript Arrowsmith had provided his own English translation, but some of his handwriting was illegible; rather than misquote his translation, I have provided another, given in *Giacomo Leopardi: Selected Prose and Poetry,* ed. and trans. Iris Origo and John Heath-Stubbs (New York: New American Library, 1967), 205. [*Ed.*]

12. Quoted in "Antonioni—English Style," 16. [*Ed.*]

13. Liber, "Michelangelo Antonioni Talks about His Work," 18. [*Ed.*]

14. Michelangelo Antonioni, "Toward the Frontier," in his *That Bowling Alley on the Tiber,* trans. Wm. Arrowsmith (New York: Oxford University Press, 1986), 103. [*Ed.*]

15. I think that this is Arrowsmith's translation of a statement by Michelangelo Antonioni in "Il 'fatto' e l'immagine," *Cinema nuovo* 12.164 (July–August 1963): 249, which was translated as "The Event and the Image," *Sight and Sound* 33.1 (Winter 1963): 14. But Antonioni said something similar several times, e.g., in the introduction to his *Screenplays* (New York: Orion Press, 1963), viii. [*Ed.*]

Zabriskie Point

1. Performed by the Kaleidoscope. The complete song can be heard on the MGM record *Zabriskie Point* (SE-4668ST), which contains much of the music from the film. [*Ed.*]

2. Arrowsmith refers to the Rod Taylor character as Rod throughout his text, presumably because Mark and Daria share screen names with their offscreen real names, but in Rod's case the character's name in the film is actually Lee Allen. Later in this chapter Arrowsmith acknowledges the problem of character names for the critic of Antonioni's later films "because the character impersonated is so anonymous." [*Ed.*]

3. Actually the Hovgaard House in Carefree, Arizona, and formally called "Boulder Reign."

4. See note 9 in the chapter on *Blow-up.* [*Ed.*]

5. See note 4 in the chapter on *La notte.* [*Ed.*]

6. Arrowsmith describes the ending as Antonioni intended it, ignoring the material (the Roy Orbison song heard as Daria drives away) that, against Antonioni's wishes, was tacked on by the producers, MGM, for the released version of the film. Later the false ending seems to have been removed; it is not on the videocassette available in the United States, for instance. [*Ed.*]

7. Sigmund Freud, *Civilization and Its Discontents,* trans. James Strachey (New York: W. W. Norton, 1962), 58–59, 69, 92. [*Ed.*]

The Passenger

1. In an interview by Renée Epstein, "Antonioni Speaks—and Listens," *Film Comment* 11.4 (July–August 1975): 7.

2. See Antonioni's own account of the filming of the concluding seven-

minute shot in "Michelangelo Antonioni Discusses 'The Passenger,'" *Filmmakers Newsletter* 8.9 (July 1975): 25.

3. See "Antonioni Returns in a Film Reflecting a Religioso Turn" in *Variety* (October 4, 1978), 6. The title *Patire o morire* is the motto of the Carmelite Order founded by Saint Theresa. Antonioni's narrative nucleus for the script of this uncomplicated film is "Quel corpo di fango" (The Body of Filth) in the director's collection entitled *Quel Bowling sul Tevere* (Turin: Giulio Einaudi editore, 1983); translated into English by Arrowsmith as *That Bowling Alley on the Tiber* (New York: Oxford University Press, 1986) [*Ed.*]. Production on the film was actually begun in 1979; the cast included Francesco De Sapio, Giancarlo Giannini, Mick Jagger, Amy Irving, and Romolo Valli. The film was abandoned for financial reasons.

4. Roger Shattuck, *Marcel Proust* (New York: Viking Press, 1974), 102ff.

5. The disappearing "hero" of Pirandello's novel *Il fu Mattia Pascal* (The Late Mattia Pascal), who takes advantage, unsuccessfully, of his own reported death to make a new life for himself.

6. Plato, *Symposium*. The translation seems to be Arrowsmith's; cf. the "Symposium, or the Drinking Party," in *The Collected Dialogues of Plato*, trans. Michael Joyce, ed. Edith Hamilton and Huntington Cairns (Princeton, N.J.: Princeton Univ. Press, 1961), 545. [*Ed.*]

7. *Paradiso* 1:70–72.

8. Only the perceptive Penelope Gilliatt has noticed the religious nature of Locke's gesture and posture—in "a position like a Muslim praying." See her article, "About Reprieve," in *The New Yorker* (April 14, 1975), 112ff.

9. Edward's words in *The Cocktail Party*, Act I, Scene 2, found in T. S. Eliot, *The Complete Poems and Plays, 1909–1950* (New York: Harcourt, Brace, 1952), 326. [*Ed.*]

10. Cesare Pavese, "The Gods," in *Dialogues with Leucò*, trans. Wm. Arrowsmith and D. S. Carne-Ross (Ann Arbor: Univ. of Michigan Press, 1965), 165. [*Ed.*]

11. Arrowsmith has Locke saying "Christ" here, which is true in some versions, but in the U.S. print Locke says "Sorry." One script has him saying "Shit." [*Ed.*]

12. By Eugène Marais; reprinted in 1969 with an introduction by Robert Ardrey (New York: Atheneum). Marais was a South African zoologist, the author of *My Friends the Baboons*, *The Soul of the Ape*, and *The Soul of the White Ant* (a study of South African termitaries, plagiarized by the Nobel laureate Maurice Maeterlink).

13. Arrowsmith's translation of a portion of the Cannes statement, *Bianco e nero* 22.2–3 (February–March 1961): 69–95. See the English translation in *L'avventura*, ed. Seymour Chatman and Guido Fink (New Brunswick, N.J.: Rutgers Univ. Press, 1989), 177–79. [*Ed.*]

14. For the same visual idea-image, compare the scene in *Red Desert* in which Corrado discusses his Argentinean expedition with the workers he hopes to recruit. The empty blue demijohns—designed for oil or wine—are an image of those workers over whose faces the camera pans, suggestive of their condition: human beings stacked for export but also men anxious, empty, drained, their own internal void corresponding to the unknown world to which they are being expelled.

15. From the "East Coker" section of "The Four Quartets," in T. S. Eliot, *The Complete Poems and Plays, 1909–1950* (New York: Harcourt, Brace, 1952), 127. [*Ed.*]

16. Giacomo Leopardi, *Pensieri*, 68. Roughly the same idea is expressed in Eliot's famous dictum: "We mean all sorts of things, I know, by Beauty. But the

essential advantage for a poet is not to have a beautiful world with which to deal: it is to be able to see beneath both beauty and ugliness; to see the boredom, and the horror, and the glory."

The italics are Arrowsmith's, as is, I presume, the *Pensieri* translation. Cf. Giacomo Leopardi, *Pensieri*, trans. W. S. Di Piero (Baton Rouge: Louisiana State University Press, 1981), 112–13, which, as a bilingual edition, also contains the original Italian of the *Pensieri*. [*Ed.*]

Further Reading

The amount of literature on Antonioni is quite large, but the works on this selected list contain extensive listings of other sources, such as articles, interviews, and screenplays, as well as filmographies, credits, and film synopses.

Chatman, Seymour. *Antonioni, or, the Surface of the World.* Berkeley: Univ. of California Press, 1985.

Cuccu, Lorenzo. *La visione come problema: forme e svolgimento del cinema di Antonioni.* Rome: Bulzoni editore, 1973.

Di Carlo, Carlo, ed. *Michelangelo Antonioni.* Rome: Edizioni di Bianco e Nero, 1964.

Fink, Guido, et al. *Michelangelo Antonioni: Identificazione di un autore.* A cura del Comune di Ferrara, Ufficio Cinema. Parma: Pratiche Editrice, 1983.

Leprohon, Pierre. *Michelangelo Antonioni: An Introduction.* New York: Simon and Schuster, 1963.

Mancini, Michele, and Giuseppe Perrella. *Michelangelo Antonioni: Architetture della visione.* 2 vols. Rome: Coneditor Consorzio Coop, 1986.

Perry, Ted, and René Prieto. *Michelangelo Antonioni: A Guide to References and Resources.* Boston: G. K. Hall, 1986.

Rifkin, Edwin Lee. *Antonioni's Visual Language.* Ann Arbor, Mich.: UMI Research Press, 1982.

Rohdie, Sam. *Antonioni.* London: British Film Institute, 1990.

Tinazzi, Giorgio. *Michelangelo Antonioni.* Florence: La nuova Italia, 1974.

Index

Adaptation: difficulties of, 13, 15–16, 28–29, 47, 52, 93, 183n.12; need for, 54, 61, 92, 169; and story of prehistoric man and Locke, 158, 160. *See also* Change
Adorno, Theodor, 49
Le amiche, 20, 22
L'amore in città, 20
Antoniennui, 34, 48
Antonioni, Michelangelo: appraisal of 4, 6, 12–13, 23, 46–48, 49–50, 87; artistic vision of, 9, 12; complexity and density of expression in films of, 9–11, 23, 47–48; demands on audience, 85–86; moral dimension of, 12–13, 33–34, 50; narrative form in films of, 34, 54; subject matter and themes in films of, 12–13, 47, 49–50; work as an oeuvre, 18, 47, 49–50
Architecture, 14, 34, 44, 63, 80, 109, 161–62, 164
Aristophanes, 151

Automatism, 43, 55, 109. *See also* Compensatory behavior; Individual: crisis of; Responsibility: disowning of; Somnambulism
L'avventura, vii, 5–7, 9, 14–18, 20, 22–23, 26, 31–49, 53, 55, 57–58, 61, 70, 72–74, 80, 91–92, 96, 116, 144, 150, 164, 171, 178n.1, 180nn.8, 5, 182nn.3, 7, 185n.18

Bachelard, Gaston, 184n.16
Background, 9, 11–12, 41, 53–54, 57, 71, 112. *See also* Architecture; Immensity; Landscape; Nature
Bad faith. *See* Responsibility: disowning of
Balance, 69–70, 75–78, 139, 162; difficulty in maintaining and loss of, 28–29, 70–72, 86, 95–96, 104; need for, 47, 55, 60–61, 64, 72, 74, 104, 109, 140. *See also* Polarities
Bakhtin, Mikhail, 168

191

INDEX